NATIONAL PARKS

EXCLUDING NATIONAL HISTORICAL PARKS, MONUMENTS, BATTLEFIELDS, ETC.

OUR NATIONAL PARK POLICY

A CRITICAL HISTORY

Decorative sketches by Kate Lord

Our

National Park Policy

A CRITICAL HISTORY

by John Ise

PUBLISHED FOR RESOURCES FOR THE FUTURE, INC.

BY THE JOHNS HOPKINS PRESS, BALTIMORE

RESOURCES FOR THE FUTURE, INC., WASHINGTON, D. C.

Resources for the Future is a nonprofit corporation for research and education in the development, conservation, and use of natural resources. It was established in 1952 with the co-operation of The Ford Foundation and its activities since then have been financed by grants from that Foundation. Part of the work of Resources for the Future is carried out by its resident staff, part supported by grants to universities and other nonprofit organizations. Unless otherwise stated, interpretations and conclusions in RFF publications are those of the authors; the organization takes responsibility for the selection of significant subjects for study, the competence of the researchers, and their freedom of inquiry.

This book is one of RFF's studies in land use and management, which are directed by Marion Clawson. The author, John Ise, is Professor Emeritus, the University of Kansas. The study was made under a Resources for the Future grant to the University of Kansas.

STAFF EDITORS, Henry Jarrett and Vera W. Dodds

TO MY SON JOHN, JR., AND TO THE

MEMORY OF MY SON CHARLES,

BOTH LOVERS OF THE NATIONAL PARKS

Foreword

This history and analysis of our national park policy completes a series of natural resource policy studies begun by Professor Ise more than forty years ago. His *United States Forest Policy,* published in 1920, still stands as a classic example of federal policy analysis, and his *United States Oil Policy,* a pioneering work in this field published in 1926, is still widely read.

When, four years ago, Professor Ise approached Resources for the Future with a proposal for assistance in completing a comprehensive study of the history of policy for national parks, we saw in this an opportunity to carry a step further the work on land use and management in which we are engaged. Knowing Professor Ise as a scholar, historian, and active lover of the parks, we were sure that the result would be a study of lasting stature. Much of the research had, in fact, already been done through years of extracurricular work which included first-hand knowledge of the areas he was examining. This book amply fulfills our expectations. Coming at a time when park values are being re-examined in the light of vastly increased use, it is unique in presenting the views of a man who was devoted to studying the parks even before the National Park Service was established.

Of the ten land-use studies Resources for the Future has itself had published or has contributed toward over the past four years, several have dealt with some aspects of the problems Professor Ise examines in his book. In *The Federal Lands—Their Use and Management* the management of the national parks, in common with other federal lands, was analyzed. In *Statistics for Recreation* and *A User-Resource Recreation Planning Method,* the focus was on the recreational use of the parks as well as other recreational areas; the same is true to a degree of *Land for the Future.* None of them, however, has looked at the national parks as a national entity the evolution of which is as significant an aspect of United States land policy as any other part of our history.

History is, of course, one with the future—a fact which Professor Ise makes very clear throughout his writing. If we are to plan wisely for a more crowded America, it is important to understand how the parks achieved their present status and what they promise for future generations.

Marion Clawson
April 12, 1960

Preface

Perhaps the title of this book is misleading; it may suggest that the book covers all kinds of national park areas—scenic, archeological, historical, military, and recreational. Because of limitation on time and energy, however, I have been obliged to limit the project mainly to the scenic and archeological parks and monuments, although I have considered historical and recreational areas at some points. I have also been tempted to give some attention to forest and grazing lands, and to the general problems of conservation, for the national parks and monuments are related to other federal, and even state, areas in various ways. For instance, many of the national monuments adjoin or are surrounded by federal grazing lands, and any abuse of these lands may affect the monuments adversely. Conservation, of all kinds of resources, is really one problem, not a dozen separable problems.

In my work, I have had assistance from various organizations and individuals, and to them I extend acknowledgment and thanks. Resources for the Future provided a grant for two years, which enabled me to devote all my time to research. Dr. Marion Clawson of that organization also read the manuscript, caught many errors, and offered excellent suggestions on various points. Mr. Horace Albright, former Director of the Park Service, took time from his crowded schedule to read the manuscript, and from his wide knowledge gave me many valuable suggestions. I am deeply indebted to him. Mr. Philip Raup, a graduate student at the University of Kansas twenty years ago, did a thorough and competent job checking the government records for the earlier period. The library here at the university has extended every possible assistance and courtesy, particularly Mr. George Caldwell and Mrs. Phyllis Grumm of the document room. It is hard to express fully my indebtedness to them. Mrs. Grumm kindly searched out and brought me numberless reports and documents, saving me many days of time. Professor E. Raymond Hall, of the University of Kansas and a member of the Advisory Board on National Parks, Historic Sites, Buildings and Monuments, not only turned over his records to me, but read the chapter on wildlife carefully, correcting errors, and making many pertinent suggestions.

The Park Service has helped me in many ways. In particular, I should mention the assistance of Edmund B. Rogers, Special Assistant to the Director of the National Park Service, in the field office at Denver, Colorado. Mr. Rogers read the entire manuscript and, from his vast knowledge of bills, laws, reports, and other historical data, helped me to correct many errors of omission and commission. In acknowledging the Service's assistance, I wish to make it very clear that neither the Park Service nor Resources for the Future is in any way responsible for the views or opinions expressed in this book. All conclusions on matters of policy are my own.

While teaching recently at Trinity University, San Antonio, Texas, I have had the very kind and generous assistance of Dr. Eunice Kitchell, who in every possible way helped me to conserve the time and energies I needed to work on this book. My debt to her is very heavy. Freeman Tilden visited me and in a few hours gave me valuable perspectives on various national park problems.

My wife read most of the chapters for English construction and even typed several chapters for me.

Special acknowledgment should be tendered to Alfred A. Knopf, publisher, for his kind permission to quote a number of passages from *Steve Mather of the National Parks,* by Robert Shankland.

John Ise, Professor Emeritus
University of Kansas
March 18, 1960

Contents

Introduction

The United States has not been a very progressive country in land policies, but we have originated two land policies of world-wide significance, the national park policy and the Tennessee Valley Authority policy. Our national park policy has not only attracted the attention of leaders throughout the world but has been copied or adapted in various ways by a number of foreign countries.

We have in the United States in 1960 an extensive national park system comprising 180 areas covering nearly 23 million acres, and several other areas, under the jurisdiction of the National Park Service. How these areas are classified is shown in the table on page 2.

The national parks are mainly scenic, but a few represent other values such as wildlife, volcanic, archeological, or hot springs.

As we shall see from the record in this book, we have this great system of national parks, monuments, and other areas not as a result of a public demand but because a few farsighted, unselfish, and idealistic men and women foresaw the national need and got the areas established and protected in one way or another, fighting public inertia and selfish commercial interests at every step. The present volume is largely the story of that long struggle. This story is much like that of the national forests, which were similarly estab-

1

*Summary of Areas Administered by the National Park Service,
January 1, 1960*

Type of area	Number	Federal land (acres)	Lands within exterior boundaries not federally owned (acres)	Total lands within exterior boundaries (acres)
National Parks	29	13,205,071.01	250,307.45	13,455,378.46
National Historical Parks	7	31,841.66	5,359.87	37,201.53
National Monuments	83	8,984,449.45	145,087.79	9,129,537.24
National Military Parks	12	26,324.71	2,383.57	28,708.28
National Memorial Park	1	68,708.36	1,665.94	70,374.30
National Battlefield Parks	3	5,318.07	2,170.03	7,488.10
National Battlefield Sites	5	188.63	547.35	735.98
National Historic Sites	12	1,491.40	2.12	1,493.52
National Memorials	13	4,447.96	152.00	4,599.96
National Cemeteries	10	215.10	5.00	220.10
National Seashore Recreational Area	1	24,705.23	3,794.77	28,500.00
National Parkways	3	91,429.72	21,458.44	112,888.16
National Capital Parks1	1	39,503.53	1,444.00	40,947.53
Total, National Park System	180	22,483,694.83	434,378.33	22,918,073.16
Other Areas				
National Recreation Areas	3	2,013,768.00	54,900.00	2,068,668.00
Grand Total	183	24,497,462.83	489,278.33	24,986,741.16

1 Includes Catoctin Mountain Park, Chesapeake and Ohio Canal, Prince William Forest Park, Baltimore-Washington Parkway, Suitland Parkway among the 780 units administered.

lished and preserved as a result of the persistent efforts of a handful of wise and farsighted men, Theodore Roosevelt and Gifford Pinchot prominent among them.

In Congress a number of men have worked hard for the parks, from Pomeroy, Clagett and Vest down to Lacey, Cramton, Nye, Norbeck, Kendrick, Leavitt, Kent, Smoot, Barbour, Gearhart, Taylor, Humphrey, Morse, Neuberger, Douglas, Saylor, and others. Their achievements are in the record as traced in this book. Most of the Presidents have been interested in the national parks, some more than others. Herbert Hoover merits special mention here, but Franklin Roosevelt probably did more for the parks than any other President. Without his active support it is possible that one or two of the parks—Olympic or Kings Canyon, perhaps one or two others—might not have been established. Franklin Roosevelt was not only favorable to the parks; he worked hard for them. The various Secretaries of the Interior, from Carl Schurz down to Fred Seaton, with a few exceptions, were interested in the creation and protection of the parks, and some of them worked diligently at it. Harold Ickes was one of the most indomitable in his support.

There have been no half-timers among the Directors of the Park Service; all have worked indefatigably for the parks, have fought off selfish commercial interests in a running battle in which there were only lulls, never final and decisive victories. The Directors have differed in their conception of wise park policy; some have favored more development, more recreation, less rigorous wilderness preservation than others, have had less exacting standards for admission to the park system and for protection of the parks; but all have defended park principles according to their lights. Of all the park Directors, probably Drury came nearest to the purist attitude, but he was not religious in his adherence to that general view.

Most of the park superintendents have been dedicated men, as indeed have been most of the rangers; and it might not be amiss to include the wives of superintendents and rangers, who have often had to be contented with modest or even primitive accommodations and multifarious tasks, with no allowance for overtime.

A number of civilians devoted their energies, individually and through more than a hundred conservation organizations, to the promotion and protection of the national parks: such men as John Muir, who spent his life exploring and preaching national parks to all who would listen or read; Will Steel, who devoted much of his life to the promotion and development of Crater Lake; George B. Dorr, who with John D. Rockefeller, Jr., and a few others, gave us Acadia; William Kent and wife, who gave us the only coast redwood area in the national park system; and hundreds of others who worked and gave unselfishly to the cause of nature protection. Thousands were enrolled here, yet they were only a very small proportion of the population. The princely gifts and consistent interest and support of John D. Rockefeller, Jr., merit special mention, for without them the national park system would lack some of the finest areas and features that it has. Rockefeller never thought of his vast fortune as something for him to enjoy or as the means to secure great power, but as a means of serving the most people best, in the highest and most enduring way possible, not only in the national parks but in scenic areas of all kinds, and in the preservation of historic sites of national importance. His total benefactions for parks of all kinds were probably near $75 million although some gifts were doubtless never known to the public, for Rockefeller was a modest man.[1]

That these men have made a great contribution to American life and culture will no longer be questioned. The 62.8 million visits of 1959 attest the public appreciation of the parks and other areas in the park system; and there can be little doubt that, if incomes continue to rise and more leisure is available to the people, the parks will be needed and appreciated more and more.

Perhaps no one has stated the justification of the parks better than Bernard DeVoto: "First of all, silence. In any park, 3 minutes walk will permit you to be alone in the primeval, and this single fact is enough to justify the entire National Park System. Moreover, you will enjoy the intimacy of nature as your forefathers knew it. . . . Our civilization excludes steadily increasing numbers of Americans from first-hand knowledge of nature—streams, plants, forests, animals, birds, even the effects of storm—and yet their need of it can never be extinguished. . . .

"The National parks preserve not only the organic relationships of nature; they also preserve the extremes of natural spectacle and natural beauty. . . . If the simple experience of uncontaminated nature is inestimably good, so is such an equally simple experience as glimpsing the processes of creation in what the Colorado River and the wind and rain have done at the Grand Canyon—or how a glacier has gutted a peak, how a mountain range has slipped and folded along a fault line, how in the aeons of time the fundamental earth has been erected and then redistributed grain by grain."[2]

Secretary of the Interior Ray Lyman Wilbur saw that future generations would rate the parks high:

"One hundred years from now, as people look back on our use of this continent, we shall not be praised for our reckless use of its oil, nor the weakening of our watershed values through overgrazing, nor the loss of our forests; we shall be heartily damned for all

[1] See *A Contribution to the Heritage of Every American: The Conservation Activities of John D. Rockefeller, Jr.,* by Nancy Newhall. This beautiful book was published in 1957 by Alfred A. Knopf, himself a devoted and influential friend of the parks.

[2] *Report, Secretary of the Interior, 1947,* 340, 341.

these things. But we may take comfort in the knowledge that we shall certainly be thanked for the national parks."[3]

This appears clearly if we consider the results that would have followed a policy of grant or sale of our scenic lands to private interests. These areas would have been taken up by individuals and corporations and would largely have been developed as tourist centers or as home sites. In such tourist centers hotels would have been built, as on Mackinac Island, around Bar Harbor, and in many scenic areas of the East, perhaps very expensive hotels, with swimming pools, golf links, tennis courts, and dance halls, where only the rich could afford to stay. One or a few hotel interests might possibly have monopolized such splendid scenic areas as Acadia, Yosemite Valley, the Grand Canyon of the Yellowstone, Zion and Bryce Canyon and Glacier. Probably little attention would have been given to protection of natural features, there would have been no free campgrounds, no visitor centers, no guide or interpretive service, perhaps no wildlife. Single wealthy individuals or a very few might conceivably have got control of small areas such as Crater Lake, Zion, Bryce Canyon, Jenny Lake, and Carlsbad Caverns. Private monopoly of such unique scenic wonders would be repugnant to all sense of justice and propriety. Many of our ancient cliff dwellings and pueblos would have been destroyed. Something like all this is what we avoided when we established the national park system, which thus stands as one of the finest and most democratic of American institutions.

Are the parks safe for the future? Some recent developments— the defeat of the nearly successful rape of Dinosaur, for instance— have indicated that the parks have strong public support, and should be reasonably secure, at least for the immediate future. The need for recreational areas and facilities has been increasing very rapidly in recent years, because of the rapid growth of population, the rise in real incomes, the increase in leisure time, and the increasing mobility of Americans; and it seems likely that these factors will bring further demand for recreation. The park areas will be more and more needed.[4]

There are other factors, however, that may work against some of the parks. As long as we have plenty of land and of the products

3 *Report, Secretary of the Interior, 1931*, 36.

4 Marion Clawson, *Statistics on Outdoor Recreation* (Washington: Resources for the Future, 1959), 12.

of land, we can hold the park areas out of commercial use without appreciable deprivation, but if the present birth rate in the United States is maintained and the population reaches 200 million or 250 million, or perhaps even more, the demand for lumber, for water for irrigation, power and municipal use, and the demand for more grazing land may possibly bring commercial invasion of such parks as Olympic, Yellowstone, Yosemite, Everglades, Great Smoky Mountains, Isle Royale, Kings Canyon, and Glacier. If the time should come when acquisitive businessmen find themselves backed by many people who really need the park resources, they may possibly prove an irresistible political force. The dismantling would presumably be slow, bit by bit, and not all at once.

Here is the reason why park lovers oppose every effort at commercial invasion of the parks. Drury has expressed this well: "No resources should be consumed or features destroyed through lumbering, grazing, mining, hunting, water-control developments or other industrial uses.

"This is a cardinal point, which park agencies and executives have learned must be adhered to as closely as possible. Nearly always there is arrayed against it the mutiple use philosophy of public resource management which holds that scenic and recreational resources may be used for numerous other purposes without sacrificing the scenic and recreational values; that selective logging will save timber from decay and waste and will leave a forest that will be 'just as good' for park purposes; that grazing by livestock will reduce the fire hazard and make a more attractive park; that the damming of streams and lakes for irrigation and power will make them more useful for recreation, will do little harm, and will bring great economic benefits. This is an attractive philosophy to the utilitarians, but it misses the point, so far as the purposes of national park areas are concerned. The simple fact is that the natural forest is more satisfying, more inspiring, than the cutover forest; the virgin mountain meadow with its clean streams, wild flowers and native wildlife is more pleasing and interesting than the cow pasture; the natural streams and lakes with their normal seasonal variations are more satisfying to people for recreation than the fluctuating reservoir with its unsightly shoreline of dead vegetation or the stream that has for all practical purposes been dried up by diversion structures.

"If we are going to succeed in preserving the greatness of the national parks, they must be held inviolate. They represent the last stand of primitive America. If we are going to whittle away at them we should recognize, at the very beginning, that all such whittlings are cumulative and that the end result will be mediocrity. Greatness will be gone."[5]

It may be, however, as Marion Clawson has suggested, that the greatest danger to the parks is not commercial exploitation, but deterioration of the parks from overuse by the swarming hordes of vacationists. We need not indulge in prediction here, for a serious condition is upon us now, today, and it is likely to grow worse. Old Faithful area is a town, laid out in blocks of nearly identical cabins, with a mile or more of parked cars and drivers of other cars seeking parking places, and hundreds of people hurrying over to see Old Faithful in eruption; Yosemite Valley may almost be called an overcrowded slum. Zion, once, before too many tourists had found it, a lovely place to spend a few days, is cluttered up with closely spaced cabins, campgrounds crowded, and lines of cars sputtering up and down the canyon road. In many of the parks are the same problems: crowds of people and lines of cars, and in places insufficiency even of parking space, and the clear probability that the situation will get worse. Mission 66 promises some amelioration, but by the time it is in full operation the crowds of people will have increased—to 80 million by 1966!

In most park areas the main scenic wonders can be seen in spite of the crowds. Some of the pools and geysers of Yellowstone have suffered from vandalism, and are not as easy of access as they once were, but visitors can see such wonders as Old Faithful, Mount Rainier, Grand Canyon, the Grand Tetons, the walls of Zion, and General Sherman Tree; but the atmosphere of many park concession areas is somewhat that of a Fourth of July celebration, without firecrackers.

From another point of view, however, it might be argued that all this shows that the national parks are doing magnificently—serving more and more people; but just what or how much do these visitors get from a visit to the parks? Some gain a great deal, enjoy the scenery, perhaps learn something; others come because they enjoy pumping the accelerator and going somewhere, and the parks are

5 *National Parks Magazine*, No. 97, April-June 1949, 28.

a place to go, getting little good from their visits but looking forward to telling their friends that they have seen the wonders, like the woman the writer overheard at the rim of Grand Canyon: "Hell of a ditch! Let's go and get something to eat." Between these extremes are all grades of people, in proportions which vary with the attitudes of observers, aesthetes tending to a rather condescending view of their cultural capacities, some, including many park men, viewing them more respectfully. At any rate, here they are, 62 million strong, having what they must think is a good time, perhaps unmindful of the crowds. Many people do not mind crowds very much.[6]

The price measure of their appreciation is of little use here because these visitors pay only a small part of the expense of maintaining the parks. Presumably they get a satisfaction at least equal to the entrance fee—now about one-seventeenth of the cost of administering the park system. If the government provided free moving pictures and the people swarmed to the movies we would not conclude that they obtained a great total satisfaction from the movies; and to get a more accurate appraisal of tourist enjoyment of the parks we would have to raise the admission fees to the point where they would pay the full cost of tourist visits—so that the visitors could be said to be getting *their* money's worth and not the *government's* money's worth.

The aesthete can have his peace and quiet if he wants them enough to walk away from the crowded areas, but the great scenery is usually at the congested areas, and he probably does not want to walk. He is in a quandary, here and elsewhere. He wants good roads, and he wants quiet, and these are seldom found together anywhere in the United States; wherever there are roads there are crowds and cars and carbon monoxide and turmoil. The tourists of forty years ago found more peace and quiet in the parks partly because roads were poor, in and outside the parks—which might suggest that a possible remedy for congestion would be a return to the poor roads of forty years ago. If in addition to that we should return to the entrance fees of 1916, congestion might not be a serious problem.

What we shall apparently have, then, is a system of national parks which, at the main points of interest, will not offer much of primeval quiet and serenity to the lover of nature, but will be over-

6 For a defense of the tourist, see *National Parks Magazine*, June 1959, 5.

run with millions of people. In some respects the parks will more and more take on the characteristics of recreation areas without objectionable recreation activities, resorts without offensive resort amusements. All this will not be the result of any mismanagement by the Park Service, it will be merely one aspect of the transformation wrought in America by various factors, including our population explosion and the ubiquitous automobile, which are turning our fair land into a madhouse.

PART ONE

The

Early Parks

1872-1916

CHAPTER I

Yellowstone Park

Hot Springs National Reservation was the first "national reservation" to be set aside, in 1832, but it was not a "park" in the strict sense of the word. It was not scenically important, and was reserved to the government because of the hot springs which were thought to be valuable in the treatment of certain ailments. The wonders of Yosemite Valley were given Congressional attention in 1864, as we shall see, not by reservation as a national park but by cession to the state of California to be used as a sort of state park. Yellowstone was really the first national park to be created, in 1872, although some do claim that distinction for Yosemite.[1]

Yellowstone Park is largely a high plateau, with valleys and mountains, and with somewhat lower areas along the north, west, and southwest boundaries. Much of the park is above 7,000 feet high—Yellowstone Lake is 7,731 feet high—and the continental divide passes through the park. No other large area in the United States has so high an elevation except parts of Colorado and the high Sierra region of California; and this, with its location pretty far north, makes it cool in its short summers and very cold in winter. With its hundreds of geysers, pools of hot water, lakes, clear

[1] *Sierra Club Bulletin,* March 1948, 47. *National Parks Magazine,* May 1959, 2; August 1959, 16.

rivers and waterfalls, particularly the Lower Falls of the Yellowstone, and the beautifully colored Grand Canyon of the Yellowstone, it is one of the most scenic and interesting areas in the world.

EXPLORATION   There are many stories as to who discovered the Yellowstone Park region, but at any rate it was discovered early in the nineteenth century.[2] During the next sixty years a number of men, mostly hunters and trappers, including the famous hunter and scout, James Bridger, reported seeing much of the Yellowstone area, including the geysers; but their stories sounded fantastic to most listeners and did not stir widespread interest. In 1859-60 Brigadier General W. F. Reynolds led an exploration expedition into the Yellowstone region, and wrote a report describing many of the wonders, illustrated with a map of the country; but the report was not published until 1868.[3]

The next exploring expedition into the area was the Folsom-Cook expedition of 1869, but Folsom had great difficulty getting his report published because his descriptions sounded fantastic. This was indeed the trouble with all early stories and reports—they were not believed! It appears, however, that this expedition had something to do with the later Washburn-Langford-Doane expedition, and that Folsom actually discussed with Washburn the possibility of establishing a park here. In 1870 an exploration party of nineteen men was organized by several influential Montana citizens: Nathaniel P. Langford; Samuel T. Hauser, president of the First National Bank of Helena; Cornelius Hedges, a leading lawyer; Truman C. Everts, United States Assessor for Montana; Walter

2 On the early history of the Yellowstone, and on the later story of the park down to 1915, see Hiram M. Chittenden, *Yellowstone National Park, Historical and Descriptive,* 1915 (rev. ed., Cincinnati: Stewart and Kidd Co., 1917). Chittenden was engineer in charge of road building in the park in early years, and a man of broad interests, perhaps the best authority on the early history of the park. Louis C. Cramton, *Early History of Yellowstone Park and Its Relation to National Park Policies* (Washington: U. S. Government Printing Office, 1932) traces the early history of the park and the Congressional history down to 1897. Cramton, able representative from Michigan and for some years chairman of the subcommittee on appropriations of the House Public Lands Committee, probably knew as much about the early parks as anyone in Congress. See also *American Forests,* Aug. 1929, 457; July 1931, 387; *Magazine of American History,* June 1934, 497.

3 Sen. Ex. Doc. 77, 40 Cong. 2 Sess.

YELLOWSTONE NATIONAL PARK

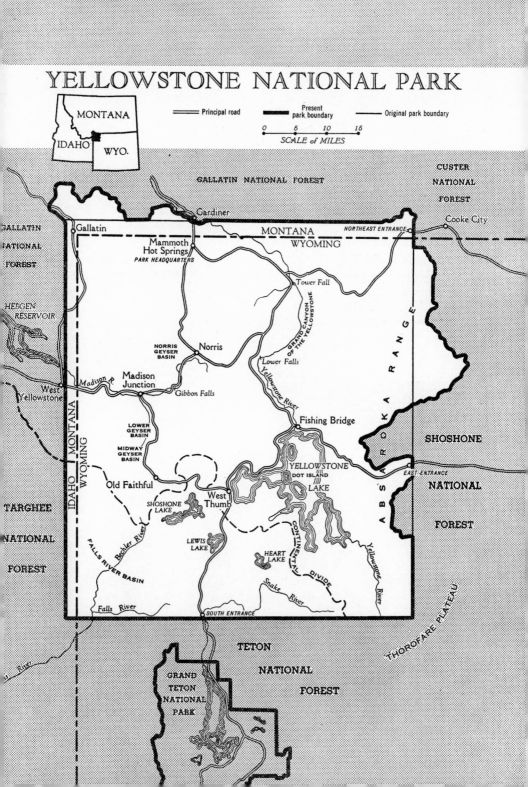

Principal road — Present park boundary — Original park boundary

SCALE of MILES
0   5   10   15

MONTANA
IDAHO   WYO.

CUSTER NATIONAL FOREST

GALLATIN NATIONAL FOREST

Gardiner

Gallatin

MONTANA
WYOMING

NORTHEAST ENTRANCE

Cooke City

GALLATIN NATIONAL FOREST

Mammoth Hot Springs
PARK HEADQUARTERS

Tower Fall

HEBGEN RESERVOIR

NORRIS GEYSER BASIN

Norris

GRAND CANYON OF THE YELLOWSTONE

Lower Falls

A B S A R O K A   R A N G E

Madison R.

West Yellowstone

Madison Junction

Gibbon Falls

Yellowstone River

Fishing Bridge

SHOSHONE

LOWER GEYSER BASIN

MIDWAY GEYSER BASIN

YELLOWSTONE LAKE
DOT ISLAND

EAST ENTRANCE

NATIONAL

TARGHEE

Old Faithful

West Thumb

SHOSHONE LAKE

CONTINENTAL

FOREST

NATIONAL

FOREST

Bechler River

LEWIS LAKE

HEART LAKE

DIVIDE

Yellowstone River

FALLS RIVER BASIN

Falls River

Snake River

SOUTH ENTRANCE

THOROFARE PLATEAU

River

TETON

NATIONAL

GRAND TETON NATIONAL PARK

FOREST

IDAHO MONTANA
WYOMING

Trumbull, son of Senator Trumbull; Warren C. Gillette; and General H. D. Washburn. These men were important enough to induce the War Department to detail a second lieutenant, Gustavus Doane, and a sergeant and four privates to escort the party, and to pay the expenses. A military escort was needed because the Crow, Blackfeet, Nez Perces and Bannock Indians were intermittently on the warpath. A number of explorers had been killed by the Indians.

In spite of all hazards these men completed their survey, Langford (later known as "National Park Langford") and Doane taking notes as they went along. A report written by Doane was given considerable publicity in newspapers and magazines, and Langford gave lectures in the East. Doane summarized his impressions of the region as follows: "As a country for sightseers, it is without parallel; as a field for scientific research, it promises great results; in the branches of geology, mineralogy, botany, zoology, and ornithology, it is probably the greatest laboratory that nature furnishes on the surface of the globe."[4]

While they were in camp one night discussing the wonders that they had seen, the question was raised as to what should be done with the land of wonders, and Hedges suggested that it should be set aside as a park for all the people forever. Langford agreed, and both set about persuading the rest of the party that they should try to get it reserved as a park—a momentous and historic decision.

THE YELLOWSTONE PARK ACT   In 1871 Professor F. V. Hayden, United States Geologist, with a fairly large party of scientists and with the photographer William H. Jackson and two painters, Henry Elliott and Thomas Moran, spent the summer making a survey of the "sources of the Missouri and Yellowstone rivers," and on his return published a detailed geological and descriptive report, which was published as a government document.[5] No longer were descriptions of Yellowstone received with incredulity and derision. The Washburn-Langford-Doane- and Hayden reports carried convincing weight, and aroused some public interest in Yellowstone. Hayden, like Langford and Hedges, wanted the area made a national park, and the three soon found others who backed them up. Several of the men spent time in Washington lobbying, enlisting

4 Sen. Ex. Doc. 51, 41 Cong. 3 Sess.
5 Sen. Ex. Doc. 66, 42 Cong. 2 Sess.

the support of newspapers and magazines, and persuading Senator
Pomeroy of Kansas and Delegate Clagett of Montana to introduce
a bill for the creation of Yellowstone Park. This bill was introduced
on December 18, 1871, in both houses. The Pomeroy Bill passed
first. The bill passed the House on February 27, 1872, by a vote of
115 to 65, 60 not voting.

There was some debate in the Senate. Senator Edmunds of Vermont, one of the earliest conservationists in Congress, spoke in favor
of the bill, but Senator Cole of California voiced opposition in a
speech which was fairly typical of the land-looting spirit of the
time:

> I have grave doubts about the propriety of passing this bill.
> The natural curiosities there cannot be interfered with by any-
> thing that man can do. The geysers will remain, no matter where
> the ownership of the land may be, and I do not know why settlers
> should be excluded from a tract of land forty miles square, as I
> understand this to be, in the Rocky Mountains or any other
> place. I cannot see how the natural curiosities can be interfered
> with if settlers are allowed to appropriate them. I suppose there
> is very little timber on this tract of land, certainly no more than
> is necessary for the use and convenience of persons going upon it.
> I do not see the reason or propriety of setting apart a large tract
> of land of that kind in the Territories of the United States for
> a public park. There is abundance of public park ground in the
> Rocky Mountains that will never be occupied. It is all one great
> park, and never can be anything else; large portions of it at all
> events. There are some places, perhaps this is one, where persons
> can and would go and settle and improve and cultivate the
> grounds, if there be ground fit for cultivation.[6]

Edmunds suggested that the land in the area was not adapted to
cultivation, and Trumbull of Illinois spoke for the bill in the language of statesmanship:

> I think our experience with the wonderful natural curiosity,
> if I may so call it, in the Senator's own state (California), should
> admonish us of the propriety of passing such a bill as this. There
> is the wonderful Yosemite Valley, which one or two persons are
> now claiming by virtue of a preemption. Here is a region of
> country away up in the Rocky Mountains, where there are the
> most wonderful geysers on the face of the earth; a country that
> is not likely ever to be inhabited for the purposes of agriculture;
> but it is possible that some person may go there and plant him-

6 *Congressional Globe*, Jan. 30, 1872, 697.

self right across the only path that leads to these wonders, and charge every man that passes along between the gorges of these mountains a fee of a dollar or five dollars. He may place an obstruction there, and toll may be gathered from every person who goes to see these wonders of creation.

. . . I think it is a very proper bill to pass, and now is the time to enact it. We did set apart the region of the country on which the mammoth trees grow in California, and the Yosemite Valley also we have undertaken to reserve, but there is a dispute about it. Now, before there is any dispute as to this wonderful country, I hope we shall except it from the general disposition of the public lands, and reserve it to the Government. At some future time, if we desire to do so, we can repeal this law if it is in anybody's way; but now I think it a very appropriate bill to pass.[7]

The vote was largely on political lines, with the Republicans favoring the bill and most of the Democrats opposing. It was promptly signed by President Grant on March 1, 1872.[8]

It was not long before there arose dispute as to who deserved credit for the creation of Yellowstone Park, Hedges, Langford, Folsom, Hayden, Pomeroy, and Clagett each coming in for mention. All these men, and others, helped in this historic legislation. It was not realized at the time that Yellowstone was to be merely the first of what were to be, in 1960, 183 park areas of various kinds.

The reservation of this large tract of over 2 million acres of land—larger than a couple of the smallest eastern states—with its wealth of timber, game, grass, water power, and possible minerals barred from all private use, was so dramatic a departure from the general public land policy of Congress that it seems almost a miracle. This was the period when any bill for getting rid of public lands was likely to get the support of Congress, the era of land-stealing, timber-stealing, exploitation and spoliation, when only a few idealists gave thought to the interests of the people as a whole, particularly the future interests. The establishment of Yellowstone was, of course, due partly to the efforts of a few of these idealists, several of them men of influence. Reservation was possible because most private interests were not looking so far west at this early date, for there were no railroads within hundreds of miles of Yellowstone. Lumbermen had moved into the Lake States and were too busy slashing the pine forests there to reach out for timber lands in

7 *Ibid.*, 697.
8 S. 392, H. R. 464, 42 Cong. 2 Sess. Stat. 17, 32.

this inaccessible region; the hunters and trappers were here, but were not an important political force; the cattlemen, who have been in recent years so powerful an influence against some conservation legislation, were not yet invading the Far West in large numbers; the water-power interests that have been among the most serious threats to a few later national parks were not interested here. With Indians still a lurking danger, the "poor settlers" had not ventured into this region in great numbers and were not calling for Congressional consideration.

It would probably have been better in some ways if the establishment of the park could have been delayed ten or fifteen years. Its establishment and the advertising of its wonders no doubt increased the number of people who went there on one mission or another and committed vandalism, since there was no protection for several years; but ten years or so later there would have been so many commercial and vested interests in the area that perhaps the park could not have been established at all.

The reservation policy had been applied to certain resources, however, since early in our history. In colonial history some timber had been reserved for use in His Majesty's ships, and later in a few cases, timber reservations had been set up in the South. Early in our national history copper deposits in Michigan had been reserved to the government.

PROVISIONS OF YELLOWSTONE ACT   Since the act establishing the park set the pattern for later national parks, it will be pertinent to note its provisions carefully.

After defining the boundaries, the act provided that the park area "is hereby reserved and withdrawn from settlement, occupancy, or sale under the laws of the United States, and dedicated and set apart as a public park or pleasuring-ground for the benefit and enjoyment of the people; and all persons who shall locate or settle upon or occupy the same, or any part thereof, except as hereinafter provided, shall be considered trespassers and removed therefrom." Jurisdiction was given to the Secretary of the Interior, who was directed to publish rules and regulations; and "Such regulations shall provide for the preservation, from injury or spoliation, of all timber, mineral deposits, natural curiosities, or wonders within said park, and their retention in their natural condition.

. . . The Secretary may in his discretion, grant leases for building purposes for terms not exceeding ten years, of small parcels of ground, at such places in said park as shall require the erection of buildings for the accommodation of visitors; all the proceeds of such leases, and all other revenues that shall be derived from any source connected with said park, to be expended under his direction in the management of the same, and the construction of roads and bridle paths therein. He shall provide against the wanton destruction of the fish and game found within said park, and against their capture or destruction for the purposes of merchandise or profit. He shall also cause all persons trespassing upon the same after the passage of this act to be removed therefrom, and generally shall be authorized to take all such measures as shall be necessary or proper to fully carry out the objects and purposes of this act."[9]

Under the provisions of this act, the Secretary of the Interior, Carl Schurz, published rules in 1877 prohibiting hunting, trapping, or fishing in the park, except for recreation or to supply food for visitors or actual residents, and prohibiting sales of fish or game taken in the park to anyone outside the parks; prohibiting cutting of timber without permission, removal or breaking of natural deposits, or setting of unnecessary fires, or leaving fires burning. No person was allowed to reside permanently in the park, and those living there at the time were to vacate within thirty days after being served notice.

With the park created and the rules laid down, everything looked fairly good, on paper; but unfortunately the law and regulations were not self-enforcing. It is difficult today, when millions of people have visited Yellowstone Park, to realize how isolated and inaccessible it was in the early seventies, and how few people knew anything about it or cared what happened in the far away mountain wilderness. As late as 1878 Superintendent P. W. Norris described the two routes to the park as follows: (1) "The northern route from Bismarck (North Dakota) is still the natural one, by steamboat up the Missouri, 400 miles; the Yellowstone 360, to the mouth of the Big Horn, and probably some 60 further that of Clarks Fork; and by coach 160 miles to Bozeman, the main town and outfitting point of those regions. Thence it is by coach 72 miles to the Mammoth Hot Springs, within the Park—from Bismarck, distance 1,050; time ascending, 12 or 14 days; descending, much less; ex-

9 Stat. 17, 32.

penses about $100." (2) "The southern route is by the Union Pacific Railroad from Omaha to Ogden, near Salt Lake, 1,033 miles; Utah Northern to Port Neuf Cañon, near Snake River, 150 miles; coach via Pleasant Valley and Virginia City, 380 miles to Bozeman, and 72 miles to the Park, or an aggregate of 1,635 miles; time 10 days, expenses $200."[10]

DIFFICULTIES OF ADMINISTRATION   As a fitting recognition of his work in exploration, Nathaniel P. Langford was appointed Superintendent of the park, without salary and without any appropriations for five years. He faced an imposing array of difficulties and impossibilities, aside from the difficulty of living on his private income. It was assumed at the time the park was established that it would be self-supporting, that concessioners would pay as rents enough to provide for administration and protection, and that there would be no need for Congressional appropriations. Hayden had given assurances on this point to get the park established, and Langford also believed the park would be self-supporting, although he thought that an appropriation would be necessary at first to mark the boundaries and protect the game and natural formations which were being destroyed by visitors. Langford, like Congress, had the theory that only private enterprise could do things efficiently, and suggested that it might be well to lease the important points of interest to concessioners, who would be authorized to protect them, and grant leases for toll roads, which would be self-supporting. Travel in the park was for several years by pack train only.

The fact that the boundaries of the park were not marked, were not even known on the ground—for there had been no survey with markers—created great difficulty. There were a few mining prospectors, particularly along the north side of the park, and often they could not determine whether they were trespassing on park limits or not, if they cared. There were also men along the borders who wanted to file claims with the purpose of providing tourist accommodations just outside the park limits, but who could not tell where the limits were. Hunters and trappers also were ignorant of the boundaries, but most of them did not care. With no rangers to bother them, they continuously slaughtered the buffalo, elk, deer, bighorn sheep, antelope, beaver, and other wildlife.

10 *Report, Secretary of the Interior, 1878,* 995.

The Yellowstone Act was not well drawn for the protection of wildlife; this had been pointed out in the Senate debates. The Pomeroy Bill had merely forbidden the killing of wildlife "for gain or profit," and Senator Anthony of Rhode Island had suggested that the words "for gain or profit" be struck out, to prevent all killing in the park: "We do not want sportsmen going over there with their guns." Senator Tipton of Nebraska expressed the same view: "There should be a prohibition against their destruction for any purpose, for if the door is opened I fear there will ultimately be an entire destruction of all the game in that park." It was widely believed, however, that the visiting campers would have to depend on the fish and game for their sustenance, and Pomeroy thought the Secretary of the Interior would prevent unreasonable destruction of fish and game through regulation.[11]

Not only were the boundaries undefined, but Langford himself for several years, knew little about the park, except for a few main points of interest. With no salary and no funds, Langford was unable to do much for the park, and was very unhappy because he was frequently criticized for the conditions over which he had no control. Whether he resigned or left his position otherwise, he was succeeded, on April 18, 1877, by an energetic and indefatigable man from Michigan, P. W. Norris, who promptly made a tour of the park to see just what was there and get some idea as to possible routes for roads. He discovered wonders that had been unknown, narrowly escaping death in a fall from his horse and suffering great hardships otherwise. For several years he spent some time exploring, and his accounts indicate that these explorations were nothing for weaklings. On a trip over the Geyser road to Gibbon Falls, for instance: "Having effected one crossing of this stream by swimming the swollen, ice-cold waters, and in the same manner having made five crossings (within a distance of six miles) of the waters of the Madison in its cañon, we reached the open valley below. The members of the party were unanimously of the opinion that this Cañon route was dangerous, if not indeed impassable, during a large part of each year."[12]

The boundaries, in fact, had been badly drawn in establishing the park. Little was known about the Yellowstone terrain and the park had been set up as a perfectly rectangular area, almost square,

11 *Congressional Globe*, Jan. 30, 1872, 697.
12 *Report, Secretary of the Interior, 1880*, 574.

with no regard to natural topography; boundaries ran up and down
mountain ranges, across rivers and valleys, with no regard for the
problems of administration and protection.

INDIAN TROUBLES   It was often said that the Indians had
a superstitious fear of the geysers, pools, and cataracts, and did not
venture into the park often, but Indians were a real danger in the
early years. There were several tribes in the neighborhood—the
Bannocks, Crows, Shoshones, Blackfeet, and Nez Perces—and several
parties of hunters, trappers, and explorers were molested, a few
men were killed, and horses and equipment were sometimes taken.
In 1870 the Bannocks invaded the park from the west. In 1877 there
was a great deal of trouble, particularly with the Nez Perces. Unfortunately the park region, like the rest of the United States, belonged to the Indians, although the areas belonging to the different
tribes were fixed only within vague limits. As usual in our treatment of the Indians, whenever the whites wanted a given area the
government would "negotiate" a "treaty" with the Indians the general purport of which was "Get the hell out of here!" The result of
one of these treaties was that the Nez Perce Indians, who had long
been friendly and peaceable under the leadership of Chief Joseph,
one of the greatest military leaders in American history, killed a
few tourists and others, burned the Henderson Ranch, north of the
park, Baronett's bridge and a few buildings, and stole horses and
equipment. Government troops pursued them for 1,500 miles and
finally defeated them, but with heavy losses on both sides.

The next year the building of roads and facilities at Mammoth
Hot Springs was delayed by the threat of a Bannock raid, but Superintendent Norris organized a party of well-armed men and managed to build three miles of road up the Mammoth Hot Springs
terraces and through the pass to West Gardiner Valley. A party of
men near Henry's Lake lost animals and all their goods to Indian
raiders. Fearful of a raid on the park headquarters, Norris sent official and other valuables to Bottler's, twenty-five miles north of
the park. But General Miles was not far away, and he defeated the
Indians and drove them out of the park. In 1880 the government
made a treaty with the Indians, which was faithfully observed, and
there was no more trouble.

It appears that in the early years most tourists carried guns for protection and for hunting. The report of Superintendent Norris in 1880 indicates this: "While the Park remained a haunt of hostile savages, and was without roads, hotel, or other conveniences of civilization, tourists necessarily went fully armed for self protection as well as to secure food; but with the disappearance of the necessity for carrying heavy long-range rifles, their use should be discontinued."[13] The carrying of firearms was forbidden in 1894, after the passage of the Lacey Act for the protection of Yellowstone wildlife.

WILDLIFE   It is impossible to tell how abundant game animals were in early Yellowstone. From some of the early reports of the Secretary of the Interior, it would appear that there was an abundance of wildlife of many kinds, including geese, swans, and other waterfowl. "Yellowstone Kelly" wrote of the swans and pelicans on the lake, of the abundance of fish and of elk, and of "vast herds" of buffalo, in 1878 and 1879.[14] In 1877 Superintendent Norris reported that the game had been so decimated in most of the park as to be hardly worth protecting, although there was still some in the eastern part of the park. In 1880, however, Norris reported an abundance of bison, moose, elk, deer, antelope and bighorns, bear and wolverines, but that the animals were being slaughtered in vast numbers, especially antelope, elk, and beaver. He estimated that there were some 600 bison in three herds in the park, and an abundance of swans, pelicans, geese, and brants, and also some ducks, sage hens, pheasants, sandhill cranes, and grouse. He complained of the vast number of skunks, and said that he and his men had to kill "hundreds" around the Mammoth headquarters before they could sleep at night. Perhaps there may be a measure of exaggeration here, and some question as to the possibility of sleeping with so many dead skunks lying around.

On the other hand, William Rush, a distinguished authority, has stated that game animals were scarce in the park in the seventies and early eighties.[15] In 1891 the Secretary reported that there were no fish in some streams, and that some of the fish in Yellowstone

13 *Report, Secretary of the Interior, 1880,* 596.
14 *"Yellowstone Kelly": The Memoirs of Luther S. Kelly* (New Haven: Yale University Press, 1926) , Chap. XIII.
15 *American Forests and Forest Life,* Feb. 1929, 93.

Lake were infected with worms, as a result of which some bears became infected with intestinal worms and developed bad disposi-
tions. Whatever the number of animals at the beginning, there was
a great slaughter from early years. The Superintendent reported
seeing, in the spring of 1875, some 2,000 hides of elk, nearly as many
each of bighorn sheep, deer, and antelope, and scores if not hundreds of moose and bison. These estimates seem greatly exaggerated,
however, and should be taken with ample reservations. Fish were
taken by every effective means, some by use of explosives. Sportsmen
were trying hard to live up to the great American tradition: "Here
is something useful, let's waste it; here is something alive, let's kill
it." Many elk were killed merely for their hides or tongues, or even
for their teeth—the emblems of the Benevolent and Protective Order of Elks; sometimes in winter they were tracked down in snowshoes, and tomahawked.

Alarmed by the decimation of some animals, Secretary Carl
Schurz prohibited all killing of game in 1880, but he had little
money with which to enforce his edict. Yellowstone was naturally a
great game country, and the park administration tried hard to protect the wildlife; almost every report of the Superintendent discussed wildlife conditions at great length. But it was impossible to
afford much protection. When, two years after Yellowstone was
established, Langford and Secretary Delano attempted to get a law
enacted to provide marking of boundaries, punishment for poaching and vandalism, and $100,000 for roads and facilities, Congress
made no response. Entirely without funds, and with no rangers to
patrol the park, Langford tried appealing to the public in nearby
towns, publicizing the laws governing hunting, but the poachers
insisted that everyone was hunting in the park, and therefore no
one could be blamed for doing it. There was really no legal procedure that could be used in punishing poachers anyhow. The law
forbade poaching, but even if there had been rangers or guards, the
only penalty was ejection from the park, and of course the poachers
could come back the next day. There were no courts within 150
miles before whom they could be tried, even if there had been a
penalty, and there were practically no roads in the park. In despera-
tion the Superintendent once confiscated the firearms and outfits
of poachers, but the Attorney General ruled that this was illegal,
and ordered the property returned to the poachers. This was in
1886, fourteen years after the park was established.

In response to repeated requests for better protection, Congress, in 1883, authorized the Secretary of War to send troops to guard the park, and three years later Secretary Lamar called for them.[16] Yet in 1891, with soldiers guarding the park, Acting Superintendent George S. Anderson reported a great deal of poaching. Confiscation of property—all that could be done under the law—meant little when buffalo heads could be sold in Bozeman for $400 to $1,000. Two years later Anderson seemed to believe that game animals were still fairly plentiful, but by 1901 the Acting Superintendent reported the buffalo in the park to number not over twenty-five— the only wild buffalo in the country except a few in Lost Park, Colorado—and the deer and antelope and swans to be headed for decimation or extinction.

Not all the killing was done by poachers. The law setting up the park merely prohibited the "wanton" destruction of fish and game, and "their capture or destruction for the purposes of merchandise or profit"; and the rules of the Secretary of the Interior permitted hunting "for recreation, or to supply food for visitors or actual residents." Any time that a tourist felt that he needed a bit of recreation he might go out and shoot a few elk or deer. As late as 1880 Superintendent Norris himself reported his indulgence in this sport: "Elk, deer, and other game being driven by storms into the sheltered glens and valleys, we were enabled to secure an abundant winter's supply of fresh meat, and also fine hides of the bear, wolf, and wolverine. Although severe and dangerous, hunting in the Park was excellent sport, and the only recreation I enjoyed during the season."[17] Some of the park employees, political appointees, often of no character or loyalty to their jobs, killed game for sport or profit. At the time, it seemed to be thought that the visitors could live on the native game, but the hunters who furnished meat to the hotels and camps grossly abused this privilege and the Secretary tried to abolish it altogether. Even after this the hunters furnished some meat to the hotels, in violation of the order. There were game hogs in early Yellowstone as everywhere. One writer tells of a man and wife catching more than five hundred fish in two days, as late as 1900.[18]

16 Stat. 22, 626, 627.
17 *Report, Secretary of the Interior, 1880*, 576.
18 *The Nation*, Sept. 27, 1900, 248.

Park policy was in the making and some of Superintendent Norris's ideas on wildlife seem weird today. He had an idea that hunting and the sale of the meat of wildlife could be made to yield a profit, and that it might be a good idea to domesticate some of the animals!

In 1890 Secretary Noble suggested that there should be an enclosure where some of the animals could be kept and be seen by tourists. Five years later a corral was built near Mammoth Hot Springs with $3,000 from the Smithsonian Institution, but it was found difficult to get the animals to stay in, and they did not thrive, so it was given up in 1897. In 1902, as a result of President Theodore Roosevelt's recommendation, Congress included in the appropriation for Yellowstone the sum of $15,000 for the purchase of buffalo and feed for them and for building a fence around a suitable enclosure. For some years various superintendents had been suggesting that there should be some kind of enclosure where the animals could be kept for the edification of visitors. Each year for many years there was an appropriation for the salary of the "buffalo keeper" and feed for the buffalo.[19]

At least as early as 1897 the Superintendent embarked on another wildlife policy which was later to be criticized by some—the establishment of bear-feeding stations near the hotels where tourists could see garbage fed to the bears. They were a great attraction to tourists, who could see black and grizzly bears at close range, and without doubt contributed to the popularity of the park and to the number of visitors.

VANDALISM   Vandalism of all kinds was rampant in the early years, and indeed for many years after the park was established. In 1877 Superintendent Norris reported: "Millions of specimens have been obtained by the grossest vandalism, many of the inimitable scalloped cones and turbaned borders of geysers, salzas, and springs, specimens of centuries of nature's matchless handiwork, demolished for mere fragments which, as such, were not worth—and often not carried away. Careless use of fire has also destroyed vast groves of timber . . ."[20]

19 Stat. 32, 574.
20 *Report, Secretary of the Interior, 1877,* 842.

One of the favorite pastimes of some of the visitors was poking limbs of trees into the geysers and pools. In 1886 Acting Superintendent Harris reported that not one of the notable geyser formations had escaped mutilation or defacement in some form. The Superintendent had not enough men to guard the formations, and in 1897 Acting Superintendent Young considered a wild scheme for erecting a bulletin board for the vandals, with the heading "All fools and idiots required to register here only." Doubtless it would have done no good. Referring to the violations of park rules, Young quoted Muir's dictum: "The smallest reserve, and the first ever heard of, was in the Garden of Eden, and though its boundaries were drawn by the Lord, and embraced only one tree, yet the rules were violated by the only two settlers that were permitted on suffrage [*sic*] to live in it."21

With no funds, there could be no road-building, although the Superintendent in exploring the park tried to locate routes for the roads when they could be built. At first all travel was by pack train, and very much of an adventure. The Superintendent built the roads and bridges from 1878 to 1882, but in 1883 road-building was turned over to the Corps of Engineers—Army Engineers—who did that work until 1916. From 1883 to 1885 the Department of the Interior was entrusted with the administration and protection of the park while the Army Engineers built the roads and improvements. From 1886 to 1918 the Army troops furnished protection, and from 1887 to 1901 the Army had entire charge, under supervision of the Secretary of the Interior; but from 1902 to 1917 the Department of the Interior was again voted some money for administration and for help in protection, although the Army troops provided most of the protection, and the Army Engineers built the roads. From 1917 on the Park Service, in the Department of the Interior, had charge of everything. At various times the Army Engineers have had charge of road-building and improvements in Mount Rainier and Crater Lake, but not in the other parks.

Forest fires were a persistent plague of the park authorities. Poachers sometimes set fires to drive the game in certain directions; teamsters were sometimes careless with their campfires and set forest fires, as did campers and others. In the early years campers were allowed to camp anywhere not less than 100 feet from a traveled

21 *Report, Secretary of the Interior, 1896,* 743.

road—lest they frighten the stage horses—and were difficult to supervise. At least as early as 1890 Secretary Noble pointed out the
need of established camp grounds, and in 1892 a few were opened
and $1,000 was spent in policing them; in 1894 a system of registry
of campers and directors of camping parties was established, which
helped to reduce violations of regulations. Yet in the 1896 season
more than a hundred smouldering fires were extinguished by
troopers, many of them left by campers. The troopers had to maintain a constant patrol to put out fires.

It was impossible to punish severely even more serious offenses.
Several times in the early years stages were held up by highwaymen.
In 1889 robbers held up and robbed the tourists in a coach, but
after turning the robbers over to Montana authorities, the park
officers found they could impose only the penalty for larceny.

It appears from some of the early reports that the guides hanging
around the park were among the worst citizens. Superintendent
Norris describes some of these in 1880: "While the leading men of
intelligence of all classes and stations in life in these regions, as
elsewhere, have mainly been the warm and reliable friends of the
National Park, of all efforts for improvements therein, and of the
persons most active in making them, there have ever been among
the many honest and reliable guides and mountain-ramblers within
and adjacent to the Park a few of a widely opposite disposition.
The latter usually divide their time between acting as guides, and
pillaging, plundering game, valuable natural specimens, and often
the outfit of those employing them, their ill-gotten gains being
squandered in the vilest haunts of the neighboring towns, while
they there lie in wait to entrap fresh tourists. These men, usually
having neither ability, principle, nor habits suited to honorable
employment, prefer to continue on in the lawless manner mentioned. Hence, like the ignorant, selfish, short-sighted, and often
short-lived opponents of improvement elsewhere, they have constantly proved the greatest enemies of the Park and its visitors.
They have been active, unscrupulous opponents of its exploration,
and blatant slanderers, personally and in the press when available,
of those earnestly and honestly engaged in the improvement of
this region. It is this small but despicable class of prowlers who, in
addition to kindling devastating fires, slaughtering game, despoiling geyser-cones and other interesting formations, have, by extor-

tion demands, robbed tourists, and who, to prevent the latter from following plain roads and trails, and from ascertaining routes and names of objects visited, have destroyed the boards designating the same."22

The report of Captain Moses Harris, Acting Superintendent, in 1889, paints a similar picture: "Rules and regulations were ignored, while outlaws and vagabonds from the surrounding region made the national pleasure ground a place of refuge. The hotels were frequented by gamblers and adventurers, who preyed upon the unwary tourists, while forest fires, originating mysteriously in remote and inaccessible places, raged unchecked."23

Horace Albright, later Superintendent of Yellowstone, and E. T. Scoyen, now Associate Director of the National Parks Service, both believe that these reports exaggerate the number of crooks in early years. Scoyen suggests that some of the teamsters and drivers were a rather tough lot.

CONGRESSIONAL APPROPRIATIONS   At long last, in June 1878, Congress appropriated $20,000 for the protection, preservation and improvement of Yellowstone Park, and the next year granted $10,000. Referring to one of the smaller appropriations, Superintendent Norris reported: "This cautious and prudent Congress at its first session, with a flattering unanimity, made an appropriation of $10,000 for the protection and improvement of the park."24 With these modest appropriations Superintendent Norris built about sixty miles of rough but passable road, from Mammoth Hot Springs to the Upper Geyser Basin via the Norris Geyser Basin. Now tourists could go from Mammoth Hot Springs to Upper Geyser Basin (Old Faithful), by wagon, but beyond that they had to use saddle and pack horses. Norris also hired a "gamekeeper," Harry Yount, who spent the winter of 1880-81 trying to keep poachers out of the park; but Yount saw that one man could not do the job and urged the formation of a ranger force—from which he was sometimes called the "father of the ranger service." Somewhat later the Superintendent built "snowshoe cabins" at various points,

22 *Report, Secretary of the Interior, 1880,* 584.
23 *Report, Secretary of the Interior, 1889,* 134.
24 *Report, Secretary of the Interior, 1878,* 994.

where supplies could be kept and where the rangers could stop at night. These cabins facilitated the work of protection, but occasionally poachers or bear would break in and steal the provisions.

Having once provided funds, Congress got the habit, and voted modest amounts until, in 1883, it raised the appropriations to $40,000, raised the Superintendent's salary from $1,000 to $2,000, and provided for him ten assistants at $900 each, all of whom were required to live continuously in the park. In the first years the Superintendent could not live in the park in winter for various reasons, one of which was that he had no quarters there. After the assistants were authorized there were no quarters for them, but Acting Superintendent Conger built modest quarters for them at his own expense and was reimbursed seven years later. (The reimbursement was for $169.37.) The 1883 appropriation was mostly for roads, which were to be built under supervision of an engineer from the War Department. Thus was inaugurated the policy, which persisted until about 1917, of turning road-building over to the Army Engineers. Many of the roads in Yellowstone were built under the supervision of H. M. Chittenden, and they were of course built well. Yellowstone roads were better than those of other national parks.

As roads were built and improved, traffic increased rapidly, and transportation became a rather impressive business. In 1897 the following vehicles and horses were being used:

> 2 six-horse coaches and spring wagons,
> 83 four-horse coaches and spring wagons,
> 53 two-horse surreys and spring wagons,
> 22 four-horse vehicles in temporary employ,
> 78 two-horse vehicles in temporary employ,
> 282 regular team horses,
> 412 employed team horses and extra teams for baggage.

With hundreds of horses around, stabled near the hotels, it was inevitable that there should be a great deal of unpleasant litter and flies. As late as 1907 Secretary Garfield reported that the hotels were good but around the barns and stables there were masses of manure, rubbish, waste material and dump from the hotels, as there were also around the permanent camps. The "horse and buggy days" lacked a few points in sanitation.

WYOMING LENDS A HAND   Poaching and vandalism continued, with a modest sprinkling of highway robberies, even after small grants were made by Congress for protection. From one to ten men could not police the park, even if the boundaries had been marked and there had been a law for the punishment of offenses. The failure of Congress to provide any real protection in the early years led Secretary Teller, in May 1883, to write the Governor of Wyoming, asking for help in arresting and punishing poachers and trespassers; and the next year the Wyoming legislature passed a law authorizing the appointment of justices of the peace and constables, to be located in the most frequented points in the park, with authority to arrest and try offenders, and appropriating $8,000 for expenses. This arrangement was infected with various vices at the very start. The Justice of the Peace employed was a former woodchopper who got his compensation from fees, but the assistants who made the arrests got half of the fines. So was the profit motive hitched to public service, but the profit incentive proved too potent, too many arrests were made, and when an assistant arrested Representative Payson of Illinois who was visiting the park—the man who later introduced the bill setting up Yosemite Park—and the Justice fined him $50.00, there was trouble at once. The idea of Wyoming Territory controlling federal lands was fantastic anyhow, clearly illegal, and was soon recognized to be so; and in March 1886 the Wyoming law was repealed.

Referring to the short Wyoming administration, Chittenden says: "The common verdict, as gathered from official reports and other sources, is that the body of police, styled assistant superintendents, were not only inefficient, but positively corrupt. They were, for the most part, creatures of political favoritism, and were totally unused to the service required of them. Commissioned as guardians of the rarest natural wonders on the globe, they not infrequently made merchandise of the treasures which they were appointed to preserve. Under their surveillance, vandalism was practically unchecked; and the slaughter of game was carried on for private profit almost in sight of the superintendent's quarters."[25]

The effect of the withdrawal of the Wyoming guardians was, however, to advertise the fact that the park was entirely without

[25] Chittenden, *op. cit.* (1915 ed.) , 114. *Report, Secretary of the Interior, 1889,* 133 ff.

protection, and conditions became even worse than they had been
before.

TOURIST FACILITIES   In the act setting aside Yellowstone,
private enterprise was relied on to furnish visitors facilities. The
government, the park management, might of course have provided
these services, but that would have been practically impossible.
Congress for several years would not even vote funds for management and protection of the park. There was no suggestion that the
government might provide the facilities; that would have been
dangerous "paternalism." Only private business could do such
things well. As the government functioned at the time, with cum-
bersome inefficiency, often with heartbreaking delays, and even
occasionally with stupidity and graft and corruption, it could not
have provided the facilities. At any rate the act creating the park
provided for private concessions, regulated by the Secretary of the
Interior, the concessions to run for not more than ten years with
no definite assurance of renewal at the end of that time, although
there was always the possibility that if the concessioner gave good
service he would get a renewal. There was no certainty of this, however. The park management was riddled with politics at times, and
there were examples of competent and conscientious concessioners
displaced by political hacks, perhaps on orders from Wyoming or
Montana politicians.

Leasing provisions were not wise. Businessmen naturally did not
grab at the privilege of building hotels and cabins for a prospect
of ten years' business: camps and transportation facilities—horses
and stages—did not represent so much fixed capital, and were a
more attractive investment, since they could be later taken out of
the park if necessary. From the very first there were adventurous
men who offered riding-horse and pack-train accommodations for
trips into the park, and as soon as roads were built stages were
brought in. In 1878 saddle and pack animals were offered at Mammoth Hot Springs at $1.00 a day, with guide $2.00 a day; and in
1880 stage lines carried visitors as far as the Upper Geyser Basin
(Old Faithful). The camping companies presented a serious problem for years. Some of them were dishonest and unscrupulous, ensnared the tourists outside the park and exploited them on the trip;
but for years the Superintendent could do little about it. Not until

1894 did he establish a registry of campers and require a license for carrying on this business, and so shut out irresponsible characters. The next year twelve licenses were issued.

The earliest facilities were built before the park was established, on land to which the owners had no right or title. Among these were the McCartney "hotel" at Mammoth Hot Springs, built in 1871; a small McGuirk building in the same place, also built in 1871, the Marshall "hotel" at Lower Geyser Basin, reported to have cost $1,000, and the Baronett Bridge, across the Yellowstone River in the north part of the park, below the falls, built about the same time, the only bridge across the river and needed by park authorities, although it was unsafe and badly located. To cross the river, rangers and others had to go far out of the way to the north. Baronett charged rather heavy tolls for crossing, and the Superintendent did not like tolls in the park. McCartney was allowed to continue operating his hotel, and in 1878 was appointed Assistant Superintendent. Langford and, later, Norris tried to get Congress to provide funds to compensate these men for their improvements, and bills were introduced from time to time for the next twenty-seven years before a law was passed in 1899 making a small grant for this purpose.[26] Three years later Congress voted $7,780.44 to repay Wyoming for her ill-starred effort to protect the park in 1884.[27]

Hotels were slow to appear. McCartney had not only a primitive hotel but also a bathhouse in which he used the hot water from the Mammoth Hot Springs. Norris did not regard the McCartney hotel very favorably, for in 1880 he reported that there was not a hotel in the park. Several years later McCartney turned his building into a saloon, to the distress of the Superintendent who tried to oust him from the park; but he seemed to have political support from somewhere and refused to move.

In the early days the park was really much like any pioneer settlement of the time, as appears from the description of buildings in the Reports of the Secretary of the Interior:

"An earth-roofed, loop-holed cabin, 16 by 20 feet in diameter."

"A log house upon the point just above the Forks of the Yellowstone, built by C. J. Baronette in the spring of 1871."

26 Stat. 30, 918.
27 Stat. 32, 236.

"Earth-roofed log house in the ravine flanking the Mammoth Hot Springs, built by J. C. McCartney and Henry Hor in the summer of 1871."

"An earth-roofed log house, and also a cabin bath-house, built by M. McGuirk in 1871-72, near Mammoth Hot Springs."

"Earth-roofed cabin at Toppin's Point, near the foot of Yellowstone Lake, built by Captain Toppin in 1875."

"Fine shingle-roof block-house of hewn timber, with a balcony and three wings, and surmounted by a gun-turret . . . built by the Superintendent of the Park for use as headquarters in the summer of 1879."

"Earth-roofed cabin in a small grove upon the bank of the Fire Hole River."

"Block-house, barn, blacksmith shop, and bath-house at the Mammoth Hot Springs."

"Earth-roofed log house and barn, for the Riverside mail-station . . ."

"Fine-shingle roofed mail-station and hotel, with barn and out-buildings . . ."

"Rude earth-roofed cabin and barn at the Norris Fork mail-station."

"Earth-roofed cabin for gamekeeper . . ."

No concessions were granted for several years. In spite of the ten-year limitation on leases there were applicants, but Langford said that he did not know them well enough to grant any leases. In 1877 his successor Norris reported that there were no improvements in the park except some of those described above. The only tourist accommodations were at Mammoth Hot Springs. When Secretary Teller came in 1882, however, he began making a few leases of an informal sort, one of them for the operation of a steamboat on Yellowstone Lake. There had been a boat on Yellowstone Lake as early as 1871, and another was built in 1875. In 1880 Superintendent Harris used a boat built by Billy Hoffer in exploring the lake. One of these boats was named the "Susie," after the daughter of Senator Dawes of Massachusetts, who had played an important role in the creation of Yellowstone. Not much was reported for some years about the boat trips, but in 1889 Secretary Noble gave a lease for a gasoline launch, and in 1891 there was a small steamer on the lake, carrying 125 passengers. In 1896 the Yellowstone Lake Boat Company trips were reported to be very popular, although there were complaints that the fares were excessive—$3.00 for the eighteen-mile trip from West Thumb to the Lake Hotel, stopping at Dot Island where the company had fenced in a few bison, elk, and mountain sheep. The next year 2,589 took the regular trip, and many others made trips in excursion parties. In 1905, 7,362 tourists took the regular trip, but there were increasing complaints about the charges and about the conditions under which the animals on Dot Island were kept; and in 1908 the company was ousted, to be succeeded by a man named Hoffer.

THE HOBART-DOUGLAS-HATCH LEASE   A more important and controversial lease was that made by Assistant Secretary Joslyn, in the absence of Secretary Teller, to Carrol Hobart and Henry Douglas, two adventurers from Dakota later joined by a man named Hatch, to build hotels and telegraph lines in the park, and buy stages. In August 1883 a splendid 200-room hotel costing $100,000 was reported as opened at Mammoth Hot Springs; but the truth was that it was not completed until several years later, after the Hobart-Douglas-Hatch combination had fallen into bankruptcy.

The Hobart-Douglas-Hatch "lease" presently began to smell in Congress, and Senator Vest of Missouri, the able and valiant friend of Yellowstone during these years, introduced a resolution in the Senate on December 7, 1882, calling on Secretary Teller to report to Congress the contracts or leases that had been made in Yellowstone, which was agreed to. Teller reported the terms of the Hobart-Douglas-Hatch lease as follows: A total of ten acres leased, in seven parcels of from one to two acres at different points, no parcel to be less than one-fourth mile from any geyser or the Falls, the lessee to pay $2.00 a year rent for each parcel, and not to sublease any parcel. At the end of the lease, the lessee was to surrender the land to the Secretary and be paid the assessed value of the buildings if Congress approved; or, presumably the lease might be renewed, but this was not stated. Lessees must do no mining or cutting of timber except by permission, must not kill game or commit vandalism, their employees must wear uniforms, rates must be approved by the Secretary; and no member of Congress could have any interest in the lease.[28]

28 H. Ex. Doc. 139, 48 Cong. 1 Sess.

There was little that could be criticized in this lease, as it was thus reported, unless it was the leasing of seven parcels to the same lessee—a provision implying a possible monopoly by one lessee of all the points of interest; but Teller had favored monopoly in the park, and was right in doing so, although he had not stated whether he meant monopoly of each given point or monopoly of all points. The concessions should have been regarded as a natural monopoly, and many years later were so recognized. The trouble was that the lease or agreement either was not what Teller reported or that the lessees violated its provisions grossly. The truth was that Hobart, Douglas, and Hatch, incorporated in New Jersey as the Yellowstone Park Improvement Company, with a capitalization reported at $800,000 or $2,000,000, with thirty-two directors, nearly all eastern men, apparently through the help of William Windom of Minnesota, President Garfield's Secretary of the Treasury, had got a sort of informal lease or agreement from Assistant Secretary Joslyn while Teller was absent and in opposition to the recommendation of Superintendent Conger. Under this lease the Alger boys of the Yellowstone Park Improvement Company appropriated seven "small parcels" of about a square mile each, covering all the important geyser basins, Mammoth Hot Springs, the Canyon, and Falls, and began chopping trees with which to build their hotel. It was said that they also had a contract to get 20,000 pounds of meat to feed the workers on the hotel, to be secured from the Yellowstone wildlife.

When these terms became public they aroused public and Congressional indignation. These adventurers were clearly bent on securing monopoly control of the important points in the park and of park business. They thought they had a plan to make some money in Yellowstone.[29]

Senator Vest and Representative Deuster of Wisconsin introduced a bill to have the leases cancelled and to provide better protection, and when the appropriation bill came up in February 1883, Representative McCook of New York offered an amendment abolishing all leases already made, prohibiting the making of any more until Congress had established better rules, and authorizing the Secretary

29 Chittenden, *op. cit.* (1915 ed.), 111, 112. Robert Shankland, *Steve Mather of the National Parks* (New York: Alfred A. Knopf, 1951), 114 ff; *Congressional Record*, Feb. 26, 1883, 3268-70; Dec. 7, 1882, 71; Dec. 12, 1882, 193; Jan. 5, 1883, 870; Feb. 23, 1883, 3193-95; Feb. 26, 1883, 3268 ff.

of War to send troops to guard the park.[30] The discussions of these various proposals showed how nebulous were the ideas of most men in Congress as to the proper park policy. Congress had assumed that the park should be self-supporting, and the lease looked like a logical way to achieve this end. When, in the first years, it appeared that there was no hope of getting appropriations for protection, Langford had suggested the possibility of handing over the protection of the geysers and other wonders to concessioners. There was yet no admission fee, and the rents amounted to very little, so if these promoters fenced in the natural wonders and charged admission, they might have made the park self-supporting or even profitable. Congress had the prevailing theory that private enterprise was preferable to government operation, and if only private enterprise could operate the hotels efficiently it could also protect the geysers more efficiently. Yet the lease was generally condemned. Congress had not thought through the problem of park administration.

LEASE PROVISIONS IN CONGRESS   On many points there were wide differences of opinion. As to size of parcels of land leased, some favored eighty acres, some forty, some twenty; and Senators Benjamin Harrison of Indiana—later President—and Vest thought ten acres was enough. After considerable discussion a motion to reduce to ten acres carried 21 to 16—no quorum. Conger of Michigan argued that the concessioners would need considerable tracts of land behind the hotels for grazing of cattle and horses—the concessioners were largely self-sufficient and would need cows for milk, and horses or mules for transportation. Hale of Maine was opposed to a strict rule on the size of parcels, thought they would have to trust the Secretary on such matters. Plumb of Kansas suggested that ten acres could be taken in such form as to block the public from the wonders as well as eighty acres, and was opposed to hotels in the park anyhow—thought the visitors should "rough it."

Ingalls of Kansas, more an orator and poet than statesman, thought the park should be surveyed and sold: "It is getting to be a good deal of an incubus, and it is very rapidly assuming troublesome and elephantine proportions. . . . I do not understand myself

[30] S. 2317, H. R. 7439, S. Rept. 911, 47 Cong. 2 Sess. *Congressional Record,* Feb. 23, 1883, 3193-94; Mar. 1, 1883, 3482-88.

what the necessity is for the Government entering into the show business in the Yellowstone National Park." Ingalls favored "leaving it to private enterprise, which is the surest guarantee for proper protection for such objects of care as the great natural curiosities in that region."[31] Vest thought this proposal irrelevant at the time: "Mr. President, the great curse of this age and of the American people is its materialistic tendencies. Money, money, 'l'argent, l'argent,' is the cry everywhere, until our people are held up already to the world as noted for nothing except the acquisition of money at the expense of all aesthetic taste and of all love of nature and its great mysteries and wonders."[32]

There was some dispute on other points: on the distance required for hotels from the natural wonders and on the proposal to allow the Army to take over; but on March 3 the appropriation bill was approved with most of the provisions that Vest wanted.[33] The park was granted $40,000 which was to cover $2,000 for the salary of the Superintendent and $900 for each of ten assistants, who must reside continuously in the park—formerly they had been there only in summer—the rest of the money to be spent for roads and bridges, under the direction of an engineer from the War Department. The Secretary might lease up to ten acres in each tract, for ten years, but the leases must not cover the wonders and must be one-fourth mile from them, and no concessioner was to have more than ten acres. Leases already granted were declared invalid and no new lease was to grant any "exclusive privilege." Thus competition was to rule. The Secretary of War, on request of the Secretary of the Interior, was authorized and directed to make a detail of troops to protect the park.

The leasing provisions of the 1883 amendment to the appropriation act were unwise in several respects: the term for leases was left at ten years, which was too short; each concessioner was restricted to ten acres, which might not be enough; no concessioner could have any "exclusive privilege"—no more Hobart-Douglas-Hatch leases—and all facilities must be built at least one-fourth of a mile from any natural wonder, which was too far. Such provisions were not calculated to attract concessioners, but in spite of them the Northern Pacific, which reached Cinnabar in 1883, soon entered

31 *Congressional Record*, Mar. 1, 1883, 3488.
32 *Ibid.*, 3488.
33 Stat. 22, 626.

the concession business, fired by a desire to build up its park passenger traffic. The railroad was in a different position from that of ordinary business concerns; it could operate concessions at cost, or even less for a while if in that way it could build up its park passenger traffic, and it wanted the services in the park to be good and reasonable in price.

A bill to change the leasing provisions was introduced by Representative Hayes of Iowa in January 1894, and passed with little discussion; it was signed by President Cleveland on August 3, 1894.[34] This law unfortunately left the term of leases at ten years, but it allowed a concessioner a total of twenty acres, ten acres in any one tract which, as in the law of 1883, must not include any geysers or other "objects of curiosity or interest" or exclude the public from free and convenient access to them; and the hotels might be built within one-eighth of a mile of the geysers and wonders. The leases were not to "convey, either expressly or by implication, any exclusive privilege within the park. . . ." So Congress still clung to the theory of competition, although the Northern Pacific had something approaching monopoly control of some services. An ambiguous provision of the act added that it was not to be construed as mandatory upon the Secretary, whose authority under the act was "to be exercised in his sound discretion."[35]

In 1906 the leasing law was amended to allow the Secretary to lease to any person or corporation separate tracts up to ten, of 20 acres each—a total of 200 acres. This began to look like a recognition of monopoly. Concessioners were also authorized to execute mortgages on their properties and rights.[36] The next year 20-year leases were authorized.[37]

"WYLIE WAY"   In the early eighties a notable development in tourist service was inaugurated with the entry of W. W. Wylie into the business. At first he took tourists around in ten-day tours, using portable tents; later he established permanent tent camps, with lodges for meals, an inexpensive and simple service. The Superintendent did not like "Wylie Way," thought it was a return

34 H. R. 5293, 53 Cong. 2 Sess.
35 Stat. 28, 222.
36 Stat. 34, 207.
37 Stat. 34, 1219.

to old objectionable business methods, but it proved very popular and Wylie thrived. In 1906, however, he sold out to A. W. Miles and left the park, and Miles continued the business under the name of Wylie Permanent Camping Company until 1917. Wylie appeared at Zion Park in 1917 and operated there and at Grand Canyon for several years.[38] The service was somewhat unique. The tents were chilly on mornings when ice froze in the washpans, but at seven o'clock an attendant came to the cabins, unlocked the doors, made a wood fire in the little stoves and set kettles of water on for washing. A half hour later the occupants would arise in a warm room and wash in hot water. Wylie sensed the fact that good food contributed heavily to contentment, and in his lodges the meals were superb—probably better than in the hotels. By 1913 Miles was operating 128 vehicles and carrying more than half of the tourists.

In 1894 D. A. Curry and wife, of Ogden, Utah, began a transportation business from Ogden to the park; but on advice of the Union Pacific Curry refused to pay a license fee, and was soon obliged to seek other fields of enterprise. There were many complaints, of unfulfilled promises, unnecessary delays, insufficient food and bad cooking, but they persisted for several years, then moved to Yosemite Park and started a camp business somewhat like Wylie's, which prospered in spite of some hostility on the part of the park management. As a result of better lease terms a total of $1 million was reported invested in Yellowstone by concessioners by 1910, and two years later total receipts were $1 million. About 1914 a concession was granted Henry J. Brothers for the operation of a bathhouse, using the hot geyser waters.

THE TELLER ADMINISTRATION   The Hobart-Douglas-Hatch lease was not the only lapse of the Teller-Joslyn regime, which was inefficient and in some of its operations even worse. The next Secretary of the Interior, L. Q. C. Lamar, under President Cleveland, was highly critical of the conditions he found when he took over in 1885. He reported that he found government stock worn out and almost useless, discipline in the ranger force bad, and that game had been shot with impunity and sold to the hotels without interference, while as to the leases: "Under none of these leases have the persons

38 The writer toured Yellowstone in the summer of 1917 on what was advertised as "Wylie Way" and enjoyed it thoroughly.

to whom they were made fully complied with the terms of their respective leases either as to location or erection and completion of the buildings contemplated."[39]

Teller's administration as Secretary of the Interior was generally not on a high plane, he was often friendly with the looters and exploiters. President Cleveland's administration was on a high level of integrity in every department, including the Department of the Interior.

Superintendent Conger was a conscientious man, but unequal to the task of administration; perhaps the ablest man would have been helpless under the political conditions prevailing at the time. In July 1884 he resigned and was succeeded by a political hack named Robert Carpenter, a devotee of private enterprise, who tried to wreck the park. In co-operation with the Yellowstone Park Improvement Company, he went to Washington to lobby for a bill to throw open parts of the park to private ownership. Confident of success, some of this crew even filed claims on the tracts to be disposed of; but the bill failed and Carpenter was removed from office. Following him, a man named Wear was appointed, but he served only a little more than a year.

On February 17, 1883, Senator Vest tried to push through a resolution for the appointment of a special committee of five to study the needs of the park, to ask the Secretary to take no further action on the Hobart-Douglas-Hatch lease, and asking him also to call on the military authorities for troops to protect the park. From the debates it appeared that General Sheridan, who was roaming this area in the early 1880's, was much interested in the protection of the park, and that he was even favorable to an extension of its boundaries, but talk of this brought protests from adjoining ranchmen, miners, and others. The Committee on Territories, at the suggestion of General Sheridan, had introduced a bill to enlarge the park, but it was conceded that it had no chance of passage. Vest read a letter from Secretary Teller stating that no definite lease had been given to the Hobart-Douglas-Hatch outfit, but that if Congress did not pass any legislation he expected to make the lease, and that he had issued an order forbidding the cutting of trees and killing of game. Apparently Teller thought the lease was wise and proper. After some discussion, in which nearly everyone agreed that gross vandalism was being perpetrated in Yellowstone but only

39 *Report, Secretary of the Interior, 1885*, 72 ff.

Vest and a few others cared to do anything about it, the Vest resolution was dropped from consideration. To no avail were also
several later efforts of Vest to secure the protection of Yellowstone.[40]

RAILROAD INTERFERENCE   This unfortunate situation led
Senator Vest to try another plan in late 1883. In December he introduced a bill which was considered in the Senate the next March.
This bill eliminated the narrow strips of park land in Montana and
Idaho, and extended the south boundary about nine miles southward and the east boundary thirty miles farther east; it made the
park a part of Gallatin County, Montana, for administration of
justice—Montana, not Wyoming, because of accessibility—and provided penalties for offenses and an appropriation for a Superintendent at $2,000 a year and for fifteen assistants at $900 a year,
with power to make arrests. It provided for road-building by the
Army Engineers and authorized leases for hotels, the proceeds of
which were to be available for improvements. After some debate the
bill passed the Senate, but in the House Committee on Territories
amendments were made to cut out a section on the north for a railroad, and in the conference committee the bill was lost.[41]

There was still no law providing penalties for offenses although
Yellowstone was getting $40,000 a year, $11,000 of it for salaries of
the Superintendent and ten assistants; and Vest tried repeatedly
to get jurisdiction and penalties and get the boundaries fixed, aided
in the Senate by Senators Logan (soon to be Republican candidate
for Vice President), Harrison (later President, the man who introduced the first bills to establish Grand Canyon Park), Conger of
Michigan, Garland of Arkansas, Call of Florida, and Voorhees of
Indiana. The "Vest Bill" passed the Senate three times, the last
time by unanimous vote; but in the House it was always amended
to grant a right of way to the Cinnabar and Clark's Fork Railroad
Company across the northeast corner of the park, or to cut out a
part of the park for commercial development of some kind, and this
defeated the bill. The railroad was wanted by mining interests
around Cooke City, northeast of the park, although the mining
amounted to very little, and the railroad would never have been
worth its cost, if worth anything.

40 *Congressional Record*, 47 Cong. 2 Sess., 2835 ff., 3214, 3268 ff.
41 S. 221, 48 Cong. 1 Sess.

The pertinacity and power of the railroad promoters is difficult to understand. It was said that one of the big railroad companies was behind it, presumably the Northern Pacific, but the Northern Pacific stated that it had no interest in it. A few Western men plumped for it, but on the other hand the railroad amendment was always offered in the House Committee on Public Lands and was used to defeat every effort to provide better protection *in the House,* where the eastern states were most strongly represented. Bills for better protection passed the Senate several times. In 1884, however, a Senate committee, in approving one of the rights-of-way bills, did express a fairly common American view: "The committee have not felt justified in permitting a mere pleasure ground, of however great interest, to be a barrier to the development of important and material interests of the country."[42]

The spoilsmen not only sabotaged Vest's efforts; they brought up bills year after year for railroad construction or for chopping off parts of the park, or for power dams or an electric railroad through the park. In September 1893 Senator Shoup of Idaho and Representative Doolittle of Washington tried to get a bill through to build an electric railroad through the park, damming two waterfalls for power needed for operation, but neither bill came near passage.[43] An electric railroad through the park did not seem as bad at the time as it would today. With poor roads and only horse-drawn stages for transportation, an electric line might have seemed rather luxurious to the tourists, although something of a desecration. Today it would seem so completely unnecessary as to be unthinkable.

OTHER ATTEMPTS AT SABOTAGE   In the nineties the park barely missed vandalism of a different sort. In May 1890 a man named May asked for and was granted a lease to build an elevator at the side of the Lower Falls of the Yellowstone to enable visitors to go down to the foot of the falls. By October, Secretary Noble had changed his mind and notified May that the elevator would be an eyesore and must not be built. Three years later May asked for a reissue of the lease, and two different government investigators

42 S. 2436, 49 Cong. 2 Sess. S. 283, 50 Cong. 1 Sess. 491, S. 1275, 51 Cong. 1 Sess. S. 428, 52 Cong. 1 Sess. S. 43, 53 Cong. 1 Sess. S. Ex. Rept. 239, 48 Cong. 1 Sess.
43 S. 884, H. R. 59, 53 Cong. 1 Sess.

reported favorably on it. Secretary Francis was apparently on the point of approving the project when Congress heard of it and ordered an investigation, as a result of which the enterprise was abandoned.[44]

Looking back on the history of these years and the attempts to loot the park, one can hardly understand how Yellowstone escaped grave mutilation or even abolition. Some of the spoilsmen's bills came perilously near to passage. Much of the credit for the defeat of these schemes should go to Senator Vest, who assumed the leadership in every fight against them. Without a Senator Vest during these years we might well be without Yellowstone Park today. He was a great orator (his speech in praise of a dog is a classic) and a man of statesmanlike breadth and vision. At one time in 1892 he became discouraged and was on the point of conceding defeat, but other friends of the park rallied to him and defeated a mutilation bill fathered by Senator Warren of Wyoming and supported by Platt of Connecticut and Teller of Colorado. This Senator Orville Platt was the man after whom Platt National Park in Oklahoma was later named. Teller's support of the Warren Bill lends support to the criticisms of his administration as Secretary of the Interior a few years earlier. Behind Vest were not only some of the men mentioned above but others, conspicuously Representatives McRae of Arkansas and Lacey of Iowa, both devoted leaders in forest and park conservation and in good government and administration.[45]

TROOPS IN THE PARK   The scandals of the Teller-Joslyn-Conger-Carpenter era had brought the park to such low repute that in 1886 Congress declined to appropriate money for its administration, and Secretary Lamar was obliged to call on the Secretary of War for the troops authorized in 1883. On August 20, 1886, Captain Moses Harris moved into office as Acting Superintendent and the era of Army control was inaugurated—to last thirty years. It was a fortunate arrangement, under the circumstances. The task was one of protection mainly, and that the troop cavalry could perform excellently, or at least as well as possible without judicial machinery and legal penalties. Captain Harris was an energetic and conscientious officer, who revised the regulations and enforced them with

44 S. Doc. 151, 54 Cong. 2 Sess.
45 S. 2373, 52 Cong. 1 Sess.

vigor as far as he could. John Muir was often impressed with the excellence of the army administration as he saw it in Yosemite. Not long after Captain Harris took over he wrote, "In pleasing contrast to the noisy, ever changing management, or mismanagement, of blustering, blundering, plundering, money-making vote-sellers who receive their places from boss politicians as purchased goods, the soldiers do their duty so quietly that the traveler is scarcely aware of their presence."[46]

WILDLIFE PROTECTION   Up to 1894 all mutilation and spoliation bills had been defeated, and after 1886 the troops had done as good a job in protection as could be expected. A law for the protection of wildlife was secured as a result of an episode of March 1894. A notorious poacher, Ed Howell, was caught by a park scout in the Pelican Valley skinning a buffalo he had killed, four other dead buffalo lay near, and there were heads and hides of six others in his camp. He was evidently going to clean out the herd. Emerson Hough, a writer sent out to the park by George Bird Grinnell, the fighting conservationist editor of *Forest and Stream,* was in the park at the time, and he wrote up the incident in *Forest and Stream.* The public had a sentimental interest in the buffalo, now that he was about exterminated, and Hough's story stirred up such public indignation that Congress had to forget about mining railroads and park mutilations long enough to pass a law for the protection of the wildlife. Albright gave Grinnell most of the credit for this law.[47] The law needed was provided for in a bill introduced by Representative Lacey of Iowa, one of the most energetic of the conservationists in Congress, in March 1894, which passed both houses promptly and was signed by President Cleveland on May 7, 1894.[48]

The "Act to Protect the Birds and Animals in Yellowstone National Park" set the park up as a part of the United States judicial district of Wyoming, and the laws of Wyoming were to govern except where laws of the United States were applicable; but a com-

46 *The National Parks: Sketches from the Atlantic Monthly* (Boston and New York: Houghton Mifflin and Co., 1901) , 70.

47 Robert Shankland, *op. cit.,* 45. Chittenden, *op. cit.,* 119, 120. *Yosemite Nature Notes,* Dec. 1931, 25.

48 H. R. 6442, 53 Cong. 2 Sess. Stat. 28, 73.

plete schedule of punishments was provided for various offenses. All hunting or killing, except when necessary to protect human life or protect from injury, was prohibited; fishing was restricted to hook and line, and only at seasons and times and in such manner as directed by the Secretary. The Secretary was directed to publish rules and regulations for protection of the park. Possession of the dead bodies of animals or birds was to be prima facie evidence of guilt, and the transportation of carcasses of animals, birds, or fish was declared a misdemeanor. Violation of any rule of the Secretary was punishable by a fine of not more than $1,000 or imprisonment for not exceeding two years, or both; all guns, traps, horses, etc. used by poachers were to be forfeited to the government. To enforce these laws and regulations a commissioner was provided for, with power to arrest and punish; and any officer of the government was also authorized to arrest without process anyone caught in the act of violating a law or regulation. The commissioner was allowed the fees collected and a salary of $1,000. To complete the enforcement provisions, $5,000 was given to erect a jail. The penalties imposed by this law were too severe, so severe as to take certain offenses out of the jurisdiction of the commissioner, and in 1916 they were reduced to $500 or six months imprisonment or both.[49]

Twenty-two years after the establishment of the park, its protection was thus finally provided for, and as a further aid Acting Superintendent Anderson established a system of registry for camping parties—there was still no admission fee to keep records of those who entered. Not all problems were solved, of course. Campers continued to set fires occasionally, and a few poachers operated along the boundaries. The states of Wyoming and Montana cooperated reasonably well in game protection, but Idaho was indifferent to poaching. Along the boundaries, which had not yet been well marked, some of the poachers evaded punishment by claiming that the skins and carcasses in their possession had been taken outside the park. In 1895 Acting Superintendent Anderson organized three parties to operate against buffalo poachers who were operating in the Henrys Lake area and elsewhere. They found the carcasses of ten buffalo and encountered a party of poachers, who escaped. In Butte, Montana, they found a man who was offering buffalo scalps for sale and prosecuted him, but could not prove that the buffalo were killed in the park. In that year, however, the Su-

49 Stat. 39, 238.

perintendent reported twelve convictions under the 1894 law. The next year, 1896, the Army Engineers began marking the boundaries, which helped in protection.

Poachers were not the only threat to the wildlife; predators took a considerable toll—coyotes, wolves, bobcats, and mountain lions. The park, with its growing population of elk, deer, and antelope, was a banquet hall for predators, and of course the better the wild-life was protected from poachers the better for the predators. At least as early as 1889 Secretary Noble suggested that predators should be checked, and in 1893 a pack of hounds and a hunter were brought in to hunt down mountain lions. In 1896 Secretary Francis ordered a campaign for the reduction of coyotes, which were numerous in the park. Thus was begun the program of predator reduction which was pushed for many years, with 100 or more coyotes killed every year—270 in 1912—by guns, traps and poison. Wolves and mountain lions were first to be brought under control, and some years later wolves were exterminated and mountain lions all but eliminated. Predator reduction was later recognized as an unwise policy.

One obstacle to the protection of the wildlife in the early years was the hostility of some of the ranchers along the boundaries of the park, who had trouble protecting their grazing lands and their haystacks from the animals that wandered out of the park limits. As the number of tourists increased, however, more of the people around the park found summer employment in the park, and this tended to bring a more favorable attitude.

As early as 1891 some animals were live-trapped and sent to zoos in various parts of the country; and this business grew, although it was not certain that it was legal. In January 1923 an amendment to the appropriation act authorized the Secretary to give surplus elk, buffalo, bear, beaver, and predatory animals to zoos and parks, and to sell or otherwise dispose of surplus buffalo.[50]

The main problems of park administration just preceding the establishment of the National Park Service in 1916 were those of getting more money for roads and facilities, fighting off irrigation dams, cleaning out incompetent political concessioners, and of securing an extension of the park boundaries to lower land for winter forage for the wildlife. This extension was urged by the various Secretaries of the Interior and Superintendents almost from the

50 Stat. 42, 1214.

very first, but without effect. In 1905, however, in response to a fear
that the antelope and mountain sheep in the park might be headed
for extinction, the state of Wyoming established a game reserve
twenty-five miles wide along the south boundary of the park, and
a few years later Montana set aside a strip along the north line.

THE FOREST RESERVE ACT   The Forest Reserve Act of 1891
and the establishment by President Harrison, in March 1891, of
a "public forest reservation," east and south of the park—later included in the Shoshone and Teton National Forests—did not help
much in wildlife protection because hunting was permitted in the
forest reserves; and neither the Forest Reserve Act nor the establishment of the reservation afforded any immediate protection for
timber, because the lands set aside as forest reserves were given no
protection until 1897, and very little for years after that. They did,
however, keep out settlers and some kinds of land claimants, and
this was to prove a very important contribution to the cause of
conservation.[51]

The Forest Reserve Act was perhaps the most important measure
in the history of conservation, and is worth quoting. The act, only
a few lines added to an omnibus land law revision in conference
committee, read as follows:

> That the President of the United States may, from time to
> time, set apart and reserve, in any State or Territory having pub-
> lic land bearing forests, in any part of the public lands wholly or
> in part covered with timber or undergrowth, whether of com-
> mercial value or not, as public reservations, and the President
> shall, by public proclamation, declare the establishment of such
> reservations and the limits thereof.[52]

Under this act President Harrison and later Presidents Cleveland,
McKinley, and Theodore Roosevelt set aside about 175 million
acres of forest lands, which were later given reasonable protection.
Roosevelt set aside about 148 million acres. In this way not only
was the future lumber supply of the country conserved but, perhaps
even more important, the watersheds of western streams were protected along with scenic and recreational values in the forest areas.

51 Stat. 26, Proclamation, 23.
52 Stat. 26, 1103.

The forest reserves—now national forests—today serve as many visitors as the national parks.

FOLLOWING YELLOWSTONE   Between 1872 and 1890, when three California parks—Yosemite, Sequoia, and General Grant— were established, a period of eighteen years, Yellowstone was the only national park except Mackinac Island National Park, which by some chance was set aside in 1875, excluding the Fort itself, for the "health, comfort, pleasure, benefit, and enjoyment of the people"—a rather broader and more inclusive purpose than that behind the establishment of Yellowstone. The minerals and natural wonders of Mackinac were to be protected as well as the game and fish, and administration and protection were entrusted to the Secretary of War: the park was a sort of combination of national park and military park. It was apparently known in Congress that California had abused the land in Yosemite Valley since it had been granted to the state, so a suggestion that Mackinac be placed under the control of the state of Michigan was turned down, and the act prohibited any settlement in the park. Curiously enough, Senator Holman objected to the creation of the park because of the expense incurred in the establishment of Yellowstone. Congress had not yet spent a penny on Yellowstone.[53]

Notwithstanding the care with which Mackinac National Park was set up, it was not well protected; many leases were made, and it was largely denuded of timber. The Island itself became a rich man's summer resort, and in July 1887 the Grand Hotel (1,300 beds) was opened with a dinner for 1,000 society members, including the Vanderbilts, Astors, Bushes, Palmers and Fields, and Mark Twain.[54] In 1895 an amendment to the sundry civil act authorized the Secretary of War to turn the park over to the state of Michigan for a state park, but for no other purpose.[55]

Between 1872 and 1890 there were efforts, in and out of Congress, to establish other parks, state and national, worthy and unworthy. Senator Benjamin Harrison tried several times to get Grand Canyon

53 S. 28, 43 Cong. 2 Sess., introduced by Senator Ferry of Michigan. Stat. 18, 517.
54 Hans Huth, *Nature and the American* (Berkeley and Los Angeles: University of California Press, 1957), 146.
55 Stat. 28, 946.

established; Senator Miller and Representative Converse made efforts to get a big national park in the Sierra to protect the giant sequoias; Colorado men tried to get state park status for the Royal Arch—probably Royal Gorge—Garden of the Gods, and Pagosa Springs. Springs were attractive to many Congressmen at the time, for some reason. Oregon men tried several times to get Crater Lake as a state park.

These attempts to get grants of land for state parks followed a precedent set in 1850 when the Swamp Land Act was passed turning swamp lands over to the states, under the theory but not the requirement that the states would drain them. This policy was to be followed to some extent in regard to other kinds of lands for many years. The idea that the federal government should keep the public domain, or any part of it, for the benefit of *all the people* was not yet widely entertained, notwithstanding the creation of Yellowstone, and would not gain general acceptance for many years. There was a fairly widespread notion that federal lands in any given state should at least be handled in accordance with the wishes of that state, if not given to the state.

The states wanted these state parks because they had no conception of the expense that would be involved in administering them, believed that they would be self-supporting or even assets to the states. When in later years they saw that national parks and state parks could not be self-supporting they turned to a demand that scenic areas be set up as national parks, so that the federal government would pay the expenses.

None of these state and national park proposals received Congressional approval, except for the three national parks established in California in 1890—Sequoia, Yosemite, and General Grant. To these we now turn.

CHAPTER II

Yosemite Park

The discussion of Yosemite National Park is somewhat confusing because there were two parts of what is now Yosemite: the Valley, which was ceded to the state of California in 1864, and the high Sierra country surrounding the Valley, which was set aside as "reserved forest lands" in 1890, a doughnut-shaped park, to which the Central Valley was added in 1906.

EARLY HISTORY   The Valley of *Yosemite*—Indian for "great full-grown grizzly bear," but called *Ahwahnee*, "deep grassy valley in the heart of the sky mountain," by the Ahwahneechee tribe of Indians who lived there—was seen by the Joseph Walker party in 1833. It was doubtless also seen by some miners in the gold rush in 1849, but little was known of it until 1851, when a battalion of men under James Savage invaded the Valley to punish the Yosemite Indians who, after suffering many acts of cruelty and injustice at the hands of miners, had retaliated by burning three trading posts and killing several men. As in Yellowstone, the land belonged to the Indians, and the whites proceeded to drive them out, killing many of them in the process. When the Indians were gone, miners and settlers began to trickle into the Valley. In 1855 James M. Hutchings organized the first party of sightseers to enter the Valley; in 1856 the Mariposa trail was completed; the next year Galen Clark settled on the South Fork of the Merced at Clark's Station (now Wawona); and in 1857 a man named Cunningham built the "Lower Hotel." Two years later James C. Lamon located a homestead claim at the head of the Valley, built a log cabin and planted an orchard; and in 1860 an "enterprising citizen" tried to organize a grand lottery scheme to raffle titles to the land in the Valley, but the scheme failed. By some miracle no clear land titles were secured in the Valley before 1864, when the federal government turned it over to the state and so eliminated all chance of filing claims.[1]

Up to about this time, most people in the East knew nothing of Yosemite, or, indeed, of much of the West except that there was gold in California; their idea of grand scenery was Mammoth Cave ("the largest cave in the world"), Niagara Falls, Natural Bridge, and the Adirondack Mountains. In 1859, however, Horace Greeley visited Yosemite Valley, which he pronounced "the most unique and majestic of nature's marvels," and the next year and in early 1861 the *Boston Evening Transcript* published eight articles by Thomas Starr King which aroused a great deal of interest. A number of photographs were taken during these years, and Albert Bierstadt, the famous painter, made a visit to the Valley in 1863 and painted a picture of it which Easterners found impressive. In 1863 the great landscape architect, Frederick Law Olmsted, visited the Valley and was soon busy with plans for making it a public park for all the people.[2]

YOSEMITE STATE PARK   In 1864 Congress turned Yosemite Valley over to the state of California, not the entire park as we know it, but only Yo-Semite Valley—the "Cleft" or "Gorge"—and

[1] Carl P. Russel, *One Hundred Years in Yosemite* (Yosemite: Yosemite Natural History Association, 1957). Ralph S. Kuykendall, *Early History of Yosemite Valley, California* (Washington: U. S. Government Printing Office, 1919). Virginia and Ansel Adams, *Illustrated Guide to Yosemite Valley* (Stanford: Stanford University Press, 1952). *Yosemite Guide Book* (Geological Survey of California, 1870), Ch. I. Roderick Peattie, *The Sierra Nevada: The Range of Light* (New York: Vanguard Press, 1947), 60 ff., 342 ff. Hans Huth, *Nature and the American* (Berkeley and Los Angeles: University of California Press, 1957), 143, 147, 149, 150, 155. *Sierra Club Bulletin*, Mar. 1948, 46 ff.

[2] Huth, *op. cit.*, 148 ff.

YOSEMITE NATIONAL PARK

NEV.

CALIF.

====== Principal road   ▬▬ Present park boundary

——— Original grant to state of California   ——— Boundary of Yosemite Forest Reserve of 1890

0   5   10

SCALE of MILES

TOIYABE

NATIONAL

FOREST

FOREST

NATIONAL

INYO

NATIONAL

FOREST

MONO LAKE

Eleanor Creek

LAKE ELEANOR

HETCH HETCHY RESERVOIR

GRAND CANYON OF THE TUOLUMNE

TIOGA PASS ENTRANCE

TUOLUMNE MEADOWS

TENAYA LAKE

BIG OAK FLAT ENTRANCE

TIOGA ROAD SUMMER ONLY

BIG OAK FLAT ROAD

Yosemite Village
PARK HEADQUARTERS

NORTH DOME
7,531

EL CAPITAN
7,564

VALLEY

HALF DOME
8,852

Merced River

YOSEMITE

El Portal

Merced River

M I N A R E T S

DEVILS POSTPILE NATIONAL MONUMENT

Wawona

MARIPOSA GROVE

SIERRA   NATIONAL   FOREST

the Mariposa Big Tree Grove. The California representative of
the Central American Steamship Transit Company of New York
suggested to Senator John Conness of California that the Valley
should be given to California, and Conness got the transfer through
Congress, with a bill prepared by the Commissioner of the Land
Office, with the assistance, it is said, of Olmsted.[3] Josiah Dwight
Whitney, head of the State Geological Survey, and others of the Survey helped in the project. Under the provisions of the bill the state
was required to hold the lands for public use, resort and recreation,
inalienable for all time, but leases might be granted for not over
ten years. The park was to be managed by the governor of the state
and eight commissioners, who should serve without compensation.
The boundaries were indicated only vaguely, to be determined exactly later.

This bill passed Congress with almost no comment. In the House
one of the Congressmen asked about the size of the Mariposa Big
Tree area, and was told "about a mile," whatever that meant. It was
conceded that there was in the bill no clause providing for protection, but Senator Conness of California explained that "certain
gentlemen in California, gentlemen of fortune, of taste, and of re-
finement" had suggested the bill to him, and he promised: "The
State will take good care of these big trees; the object of this bill is
to prevent their being cut down or destroyed." No need for written
provisions in dealing with gentlemen of fortune, taste and refine-
ment! One man, Senator Foster of Connecticut, did make a pertinent remark: "It struck me as being a rather singular grant, unprecedented so far as my recollection goes." This was not altogether
correct, however, for grants to the states were not uncommon, although not of park lands.

Like most land grants to the states, the Yosemite Valley and
Mariposa Grove grant was not a brilliant piece of statecraft, although it may have been fortunate that the Valley was turned over
to California rather than retained by the federal government. The
state did not dare to alienate the land, so it was safe from land
claims; if the federal government had kept it as public domain, the
Valley land might soon have been taken up by homesteaders, pre-
emptors and claimants under various land laws, and its final use
as a national park would have been all but impossible. If it had

[3] S. 203, 38 Cong. 1 Sess. *Congressional Record,* Mar. 28, 1864, 1310; May 17.
1864, 2300. Stat. 13, 325.

been established as a national park under federal control, that
might have been better; but the federal record on Yellowstone was
not brilliant or reassuring, and Yellowstone was established eight
years later. Congress had no conception of a national park as we
think of it today.

California accepted the grant in 1866 and Governor Low appointed commissioners to manage it, with Olmsted as chairman and
including J. D. Whitney, State Geologist, along with some political
appointees—a reputable commission, although unfortunately Olmsted soon resigned and went back to New York where he was to
plan Central Park. The commission met only twice a year and appointed a venerable pioneer, the discoverer of Mariposa Grove,
Galen Clark, as manager at a salary of $500 a year. Clark was con-
scientious, but lacked the training needed to administer a park, and
he had little money to work with, although California voted $2,000
to start the park off in style.

Like the federal government later in Yellowstone, the state of
California had the notion that the park would be self-supporting
and would need little money. The state did, however, survey the
Valley and the Mariposa Grove and establish boundaries, and even
more important, the commissioners invited the settlers in the Valley to vacate their holdings. This was a wise decree, for it meant
that the Park Service later did not have to contend with the irritating problem of private holdings in the Valley; but it was drastic
and seemed even unjust to at least two of the land claimants. J. M.
Hutchings, an educated man, a lover of nature and a journalist,
had bought a little hotel and the land claim adjoining it only a
few months before the Valley was turned over to California, and
had done much to advertise the Valley, but the land was unsurveyed
public domain and therefore not open to homesteading. James C.
Lamon was really living on his claim, as required by the Homestead
Act; but he had no right to homestead unsurveyed land and his
claim was therefore not valid.

There were a few other settlers, none of whom had acquired
patents. The commissioners were inclined to treat these claimants
with all possible consideration, and offered Hutchings and Lamon
leases for ten years at a nominal rent, but the claimants refused the
offer, believing that they could bring enough influence to bear on
the legislature to get better terms, perhaps even titles. The legislature tried to do better, passed a bill giving each of them 160 acres

of land and asking Congress to confirm the grants. It was said that because of a clerical oversight this bill did not really pass the legislature, but a bill to confirm it was brought up in Congress and passed the House, but not the Senate. Hutchings and the other claimants refused to surrender their property, however, and fought the commissioners' orders all the way up to the United States Supreme Court, where the decision was against them. They lost their property, but the commissioners apparently gave Hutchings a lease, for he was operating a sort of hotel for some years afterward; and the state legislature later granted him $24,000 compensation, Lamon $12,000, and two other hotel proprietors $13,000 and $6,000.[4]

Without adequate funds, Clark could not do a good job of management. One difficulty was that, like Yellowstone at first, the Valley was highly inaccessible. The Central Pacific Railroad reached Stockton in 1869, about 110 miles from the park, but the Valley was bounded by high, steep walls. For the first ten years the only way to get in was by horseback or muleback, over steep, rough, and even dangerous trails. In the middle seventies several toll roads were built into the canyon, but they were also steep, rough, often dusty and dangerous. Easy access did not come until the advent of a railroad in 1907.

YOSEMITE NATIONAL PARK   Mackinac Island National Park, in Michigan, was established in 1875, only three years after Yellowstone, but it never amounted to much, and the next national parks created came fifteen years later, in 1890, when Sequoia, Yosemite, and General Grant were established. There had been some publicity about the giant sequoias and the shameful cutting of those venerable trees; and on September 25, 1890, this led to the establishment of Sequoia as a "public park or pleasure ground" to save the Giant Forest of sequoias.[5] A few days later, on October 1, 1890, another act was passed, establishing Yosemite and General Grant as "reserved forest lands," and adding to Sequoia; but the names "Sequoia," "Yosemite," and "General Grant" do not appear in either act; they were given later by Secretary Noble.[6] Congress thought of the new areas as forest reservations, although the Forest Reserve

4 Russel, *op. cit.*, 149-151. *Yosemite Guide Book*, cited above, 20, 21.
5 Stat. 26, 478.
6 Stat. 26, 650.

Act was not passed until the next year—and that act just *happened* to slip through both houses. Obviously, too, Congress was still thinking of parks as self-supporting, for revenues from leases—authorized for not more than ten years—were to be used in management and in building roads and trails. And in the Yosemite and General Grant Act there was a provision: "Nothing in this act shall authorize rules or contracts touching the protection and improvement of said reservations, beyond the sums that may be received by the Secretary of the Interior under the foregoing provisions, or authorize any charge against the treasury of the United States." In other words: "Don't look to us for money." Congress lived up to this handsomely by granting no money for any of them until eight years later.

Although Yosemite was established a few days after Sequoia, it will be well to consider Yosemite first, since we have been discussing the Yosemite Valley, later to be added to the Yosemite Park which surrounded it. The establishment of Yosemite Park was largely due to the persistent efforts of John Muir. Muir came to the Sierra in 1868, and soon began writing descriptions of the mountains there which were published in various journals, particularly in *Century Magazine*. With the help of Robert Underwood Johnson, editor of *Century Magazine,* Muir carried on a tireless campaign to make a national park of the high Sierra surrounding the Valley.[7]

In Congress there was little interest in Muir's project for some time. In December 1879, in the 46th Congress, Representative Converse of Ohio introduced a bill "To authorize the President to reserve from sale or other disposition certain timber lands in the State of California," which passed the House with no debate.[8] In the next Congress Converse brought up the same bill, which made no progress.[9] In the same Congress, in December 1881, Senator Miller of California introduced two bills, one "To provide for enlargement of the Yosemite Valley and the Mariposa Big Tree Grove Grants," and one "To provide for setting apart a certain tract of land in the State of California as a public park."[10] Three years later Miller again tried to get an enlargement of Yosemite Valley and Mari-

7 Robert Shankland, *Steve Mather of the National Parks* (New York: Alfred A. Knopf, 1951), 45-47. *American Forests,* April 1958, 32.

8 H. R. 2914, 46 Cong. 2 Sess.

9 H. R. 1272, 47 Cong. 2 Sess.

10 S. 363, S. 463, 47 Cong. 2 Sess.

posa Grove grants, and in 1886 Representative Louttit tried the same thing without success.[11] There was, however, a slowly awakening interest in the giant sequoia trees, which were being bought or stolen by lumbermen and speculators and in many cases destroyed; but there were powerful interests, particularly lumbermen, miners, sheepmen and cattlemen, and hunters, who wanted no restriction of their operations.

In March 1890 Representative Vandever of California introduced a bill "To establish the Yosemite National Park in California," and on September 30, 1890, Representative Payson of Illinois reported a substitute bill from the Committee on Public Lands with the title changed, for some reason, to read "To set apart a certain tract of land in the State of California as a forest reservation." In presenting the substitute, Payson described the scenery of the area—including that of the Valley, which was not involved—and pleaded well for its preservation: "The preservation by the Government in all its original beauty of a region like this seems to the committee to be a duty to the present and to future generations. The rapid increase of population and the resulting destruction of natural objects make it incumbent on the Government in so far as may be to preserve the wonders and beauties of our country from injury and destruction, in order that they may afford pleasure as well as instruction to the people." The area of the park as proposed was reported at about 2,096,640 acres, almost the size of Yellowstone, and the area of claims and patents was estimated at 134,400 acres, which proved to be too high.[12] The substitute bill (H. R. 12187) passed the House with no debate, and was taken over to the Senate and reported favorably that same day by Senator Plumb of Kansas, who said it had been recommended by all the California delegation, by the Governor and the Department of the Interior. Hale of Maine said the park should have been set aside long ago, and there was no opposition to the passage of the bill.[13]. It was signed by President Harrison the next day, October 1.[14]

This bill—the substitute bill—was thus introduced and passed both houses in one day; something of a record. How could this have

11 S. 2454, 48 Cong. 2 Sess. H. R. 5568, 49 Cong. 1 Sess.

12 H. R. 8350, H. R. 12187, 51 Cong. 1 Sess. *Congressional Record*, Sept. 30. 1890, 10751, 10752.

13 *Congressional Record*, Sept. 30, 1890, 10740.

14 Stat. 26, 650.

happened? The park was soon to be the object of denunciations and complaints, of petitions for abolition, of bills to reduce or abolish; yet there was no objection to its establishment. Were the mining and lumbering and grazing interests and the sportsmen asleep? It is difficult to understand, but perhaps the speed with which the bill proceeded to passage prevented the commercial interests from mustering their forces. Also it is likely that men in Congress confused the new park with the Valley, which was widely known for its magnificence. The committee reports could easily have led to such confusion. Perhaps the establishment of Sequoia Park a few days before may have helped to build support for Yosemite.

THE YOSEMITE ACT   Under this act about two million acres of the high Sierra country surrounding the Valley, including the Merced and Tuolomne groves of giant sequoias, were set aside "as a forest reservation" or as "reserved forest lands," under control of the Secretary of the Interior. As in the Yellowstone Act from which much of this act was copied, the Secretary was to make and publish rules and regulations providing "for the preservation from injury of all timber, mineral deposits, natural curiosities, or wonders . . . and their retention in their natural condition"; but he might grant leases of not more than five acres for ten years and use the revenues for management and building of roads and paths. As in the case of Yellowstone, it was assumed that the park would be self-supporting. As in the Yellowstone Act, too, the Secretary was to "provide against the wanton destruction of the fish and game found within said reservation, and against their capture or destruction, for the purposes of merchandise or profit"; but, again as in Yellowstone, the only penalty for trespassing was ejection from the park.

The establishing act created a rather peculiar situation—a national park surrounding a neglected and abused state park—and this situation persisted for sixteen years, until 1906.

INADEQUATE PROTECTION   Most of the wildlife on both the state and the national park had been destroyed, much of the grass overgrazed ruinously, wild flowers cropped to the point of destruction, some of the timber cut and some burned over.[15] The park had been established but, as in Yellowstone, no appropriation was made

15 *Report, Secretary of the Interior, 1891,* CXXXIX ff.

for administration and protection; none was to be made until 1898 ($8,000). More fortunate than Yellowstone at first, Yosemite was given a measure of protection from the beginning by a detail of cavalry from the War Department, with Captain A. E. Wood as Acting Superintendent. This use of troops was probably illegal, but it worked just as well as if it had been legal. Secretary John W. Noble expressed some rather natural sentiments in his second annual report in 1891: "It is peculiar and inexplicable that Congress imposes upon the Department of the Interior the custody and management of the several national parks, but makes no appropriations for the purpose, and even omits to enact any penalties for violations of the rules or regulations required to be formulated by the Secretary."[16]

Captain Wood did his best to protect the park, but with the facilities at hand, his best could not be very good. With no penalty for trespassing but ejection from the park, sheep herders and poachers and mining prospectors and others were not much afraid of being caught, and if ejected they were likely to be back again the next day.

"HOOFED LOCUSTS" The highlands of the Sierra had been for some years the grazing grounds of the "hoofed locusts," as John Muir called the sheep, and these timid animals were the curse of the mountains. They grazed in masses, trampled the nests of quail and grouse, destroyed the eggs or crushed the young before they were able to fly; they sometimes separated the does from their fawns. In the fall as the herders left the high grounds they set fires to burn over the forests in their rear so the sunshine the next spring could sooner melt the snows and provide early grass forage. The sheepherders even had spies in the park, who reported the movements of the troops, using signal fires at night.

The 1899 report of Acting Superintendent Caine gives a rather graphic story of the fires started by sheepherders: "During the early part of September there were three or four large fires in the district west of the Yosemite Valley. Twenty troopers were kept constantly at work for a period of two weeks, and all of these fires were gotten under control. But no sooner had the last one been put out than another started less than a mile away. This one was extinguished, when a third one started in a place most favorable to the wind. In

16 *Ibid.*

a short time the flames were in the tops of the fir trees, and with a
heavy wind were soon beyond all control. Being satisfied that this
fire had been started by a herder, I divided the fire squad into several small detachments and started them to scour that side of the
park for herders, leaving the fire to burn itself out. At the same time
I sent out other squads from the home camp, covering nearly the
entire park simultaneously with a patrol that was moving in all
directions. The result of this raid was the capture of some twenty-
four herders, the scattering of thousands of sheep, and the ending of
forest fires." But Caine could impose no further penalties, or at any
rate believed that he could not.[17]

The character of the high Sierra range was such that few sheep
or none should have been grazed there. In this region there are
heavy snows in the winter, but in summer very little or no rain; and
toward the end of the summer the soil becomes so dry that grazing
is very destructive of the grass cover. On such land sheep are pe-
culiarly destructive because of their sharp hooves, and because with
their protruding teeth they bite the grass down to the very roots or
even pull the roots out. John Muir's love of nature never extended
to sheep. He often expressed his intense dislike for them—as he saw
them in the Sierra; and he knew their habits for he had been a
sheepherder for a time when he first came to the Sierra.

The park administration seemed to believe that there was no law
under which offenses could be punished; and this was true for most
offenses. But the setting of fires should have been punishable under
an act of 1888, an act codifying, revising, and amending the penal
laws of the United States. In that law Congress provided a fine of
$500 or imprisonment for not more than one year, or both, for cut-
ting or wantonly injuring any tree on any land reserved by the
United States, which should apparently have applied to the national parks, although the law was designed mostly for the protection of the public domain and Indian lands.[18] This act was repeated
and amended in 1909 and 1910, extending further protection to
Indian lands. None of these laws, however, provided any judicial
system for the parks.[19]

There was also a law passed in 1905 authorizing employees of a
park administration or of the Forest Service to make arrests for vio-

17 *Report, Secretary of the Interior, 1899*, 1060.
18 Stat. 25, 166.
19 Stat. 35, 1098; 36, 857.

lation of laws and regulations committed in the presence of the employees. Where there was no commissioner before whom offenders could be tried this was of limited value, but it should have been of some use. It was never referred to in complaints about the lack of proper laws and penalties.[20]

For several years Secretary Noble and his successor, Hoke Smith, complained of the depredations of trespassing sheepherders, mostly foreigners. Some of them were allowed to cross the park to get to other lands—forest reserves, where they were allowed to graze, or privately owned lands, and they often left a trail of desolation behind them. There were no quarters for the army patrols in the park so they were obliged to spend the winter outside, and it was the custom of some of the trespassers to come in with their sheep before the patrols returned, or after they left in the fall. In the spring of 1896 when the patrols came back they found 7,000 sheep grazing, in violation of law.

With no penalty but ejection from the park, the guarding troopers tried various means of making trespassing unprofitable. They tried scattering the flocks, and so putting the herder to the trouble of finding and uniting them again; then they tried ejecting the sheep on one side of the park and the herders on the opposite side, thus forcing them to walk many miles to get back to their sheep; finally they tried ejecting the sheep on one side of the park, the wagons and outfits on another, and the herders on still another, as far away as possible. This did no doubt discourage trespassing. Every report of the Secretary for years called for legal procedure and adequate penalties, but Congress was busy with more important matters.

There was some trespassing by cattlemen too, but cattlemen were not a serious nuisance because there were not so many of them and because cattle were not so destructive of the grass and lands. Many of the cattle were owned by private landholders in the park, who generally, but not always, observed park regulations. Mining prospectors were occasionally caught operating illegally, but they were not a serious cause of trouble. Some of them had got titles to valuable land fraudulently, claiming mineral deposits where there were none, and some were guilty of cutting timber from public lands; but they were less destructive than the sheep men.

20 See S. 6578, S. 7123, H. R. 16060, 57 Cong. 2 Sess. H. R. 7296, 58 Cong. 2 Sess. Stat. 33, 700.

At the beginning of the Spanish-American War the park suffered severely from sheep and cattle grazing. The troops came in early in the spring of 1898 but were soon obliged to go to war, leaving the park with almost no protection. Grazing was excellent in the park, which had been fairly well protected, and was poor outside the park limits, and when the troops left swarms of sheep and cattle were brought in. The Acting Superintendent called on California forest agents for help and tried desperately to keep the tide of animals out, but for a while without success. Near the end of the season the grass was so closely clipped that the horses used on patrols could scarcely subsist. It was a hard year for some of the sheep men, a year of severe drought in which some sheep died of starvation. In that year, however, Congress finally made a small appropriation for protection, and the Acting Superintendent was able to hire two assistants, who drove 189,500 sheep, 300 horses, and 1,000 cattle out of the park, and put out several fires that had been started. Later in the season of 1898, the Secretary of War detailed a company of Utah volunteer cavalry to take over the patrol duties and they were able to help in protection, although there was still no law setting penalties for trespassing.

POACHING IN THE PARK   There was trespassing by hunters, too, although there was not much game in the park at first. Hunters had had free range of the Sierra before the park was established, and many found it difficult to content themselves with such game as could be found outside. Some game was killed by market hunters and trappers who came into the park in the fall after the troops had left, or in early spring, before the troops came back. Indians from Nevada sometimes came over late in the fall and killed deer. Many hunters did not need to enter the park, for they could kill the game as it came down from the high park area seeking forage on lower land in the late fall and winter—the same situation as prevailed in Yellowstone. It appears that many of the campers and tourists were also "sportsmen," for a surprising number of them carried firearms. Acting Superintendent Benson, in 1905, commented on the "spectacle of five to seven men arriving on the first day of the 'open' season, each with a rifle and perhaps a shot gun" for protection against the savage beasts that roamed the park. Fishing was usually permitted and the state of California established a fish hatchery outside the park to maintain the supply, but occasional fishermen were caught shooting the fish or fishing with explosives.

Toward the middle of the decade of the nineties the park administration got poaching under some measure of control and game began to increase. Yet, ten years later some hunters came in during the winter when there were only two rangers on guard, and shot game, particularly in the Valley, where deer and other game tended to come because it was lower and warmer than the rest of the park. The Valley was something of a death trap in winter. Occasionally hunters would try to get permits to carry arms, perhaps write ahead asking for them, hoping they might get them without being obliged to sign the regulations. In 1896 a rule was adopted requiring all guns brought into the park to be sealed at the entrance. In 1896 more than 200 stands of arms were taken from persons entering the park by the two main roads; but some people with guns of course sneaked into the park without discovery.

As in all the early parks, campers did a great deal of damage. They sometimes caused forest fires by leaving their camp fires burning, killed nesting ducks, grouse and quail, and usually left a litter of tin cans, bottles, newspapers, and other debris at their camps.

Every year for several years the Secretary of the Interior and the Acting Superintendent of the park called for a law providing adequate legal procedure and penalties for violation of park rules, for appropriations for improvements, and for the elimination of private holdings in the park, but Congress vouchsafed no response. Congress seemed to believe that the United States cavalry should be able to protect the park without any laws or expense to the government. In 1897 the Acting Superintendent, Captain Alex Rodgers, complained: "Yosemite National Park has now been in existence for nearly seven years. During this time the officers and enlisted men on duty here have done much hard work to carry out the purpose of the act of Congress creating the park. No money has been appropriated for its maintenance; no penalty has been imposed for violation of the law and of the regulations prescribed under the law. In order to carry out the intent of the act, money must be expended and violators of the law must be punished. This park should be put upon the same footing as the Yellowstone National Park."[21]

21 *Report, Secretary of the Interior, 1897,* 812.

Congress did finally provide a little money for protection: $8,000 in 1898, $4,000 for roads in 1899, $4,000 for improvement in 1900. In 1900, ten years after the park was established, a law was passed authorizing the Secretary of War to send troops to protect Yosemite, Sequoia, and General Grant—authorizing what had been done for ten years. As Secretary Hoke Smith suggested in 1893, there was serious doubt whether the Secretary of War acted legally in detailing troops in 1890. The law of 1883 under which troops were authorized for Yellowstone applied to that park only, and no authorization had been made for the California parks.[22]

In 1901 Congress found time to pass a Right-of-Way Act, which was destined to do irreparable damage to the park, an act authorizing rights of way across the California parks for electrical plants, poles and lines for electrical power, telephone and telegraph, canals, pipes and flumes—well, for about any purpose whatever; but such rights of way might be revoked by the Secretary at any time. Congress could not do much to protect its parks, but was ready to promote the more practical, material, mundane business interests of California.[23]

SPOLIATION IN FOREST RESERVES   During these years the President was setting aside forested public lands as "forest reserves" —later, after 1907, called "national forests"—under the Forest Reserve Act of 1891, several of them adjoining the new California parks. These forest reserves accomplished one good purpose: they shut out some future land claims—under the Homestead and Preemption acts, for instance—although it was still possible to get public forest land through mining claims. On the new forest reserves there was no protection whatever until 1897, and not very much for years afterward, with the result that roving sheep and cattle almost ruined some of the land. On one occasion fishermen on an adjoining forest reserve found they could not stay because their horses could find no forage and were starving.

During the early years of the California parks John Muir often wrote of the protection afforded by the troops in the parks—even without a judicial system—as compared with the total lack of protection and the melancholy devastation in the forest reserves. Muir

22 Stat. 31, 618.
23 Stat. 31, 790.

always loved the Sierra more than any other mountains and thought the Sierra Forest Reserve very beautiful but terribly in need of protection. In 1898 he wrote: "In the fog of tariff, silver, and annexation politics it is left wholly unguarded though the management of the adjacent national parks by a few soldiers shows how well and how easily it can be preserved. In the meantime, lumbermen are allowed to spoil it at their will, and sheep in uncountable ravenous hordes to trample it and devour every green leaf within reach; while the shepherds, like destroying angels, set innumerable fires, which burn not only the undergrowth of seedlings on which the permanence of the forest depends, but countless thousands of venerable giants."[24] The Commissioner of the Land Office asked for troops to protect them, but the Secretary of War decided that he could not send them without authorization of Congress. [25]

The troops did a generally excellent job, considering that there was no judicial system in the park and no commissioners before whom offenders could be tried. It was necessary to take poachers, trespassers, and other offenders out of the park, over rough roads or trails to the nearest court. As we have seen, laws were passed in 1888, 1905, 1909, and 1910, which should have been useful in protection but were seldom or never referred to by park officers. These laws provided penalties. In the act of 1916, setting up the Park Service, these penalty provisions were repeated, along with a vague reference to the protection of the wildlife.[26]

Four years later, on June 2, 1920, in accepting jurisdiction over Yosemite, Congress adopted the usual regulations and penalties for protection, and provided for a commissioner for Yosemite and another for Sequoia and General Grant. Thirty years after the park was established, it had the judicial machinery and legal penalties for protection![27]

PRIVATE LANDS IN THE PARK   One of the most serious problems faced by the park administration was that of patented lands in the park. Secretary Hoke Smith estimated in 1893 that there were about 65,000 acres in homestead, pre-emption and timber claims,

24 *Atlantic Monthly*, Jan. 1898, 27.
25 *Report, Secretary of the Interior, 1893*, LX ff.
26 Stat. 39, 535.
27 Stat. 41, 731.

most of which had been taken under one or another of the land laws, and perhaps 300 or more mining claims. In 1898 the House Committee on Public Lands reckoned the privately owned lands at 53,931 acres. Whatever the total, the private owners were a nuisance in many ways, even if they tried to observe park rules. There had been no accurate surveys and many did not know exactly the metes and bounds of their holdings, and at times trespassed on park lands unwittingly. Since the boundaries were not known precisely the lands could not be fenced. Many had to take their livestock out of the park in late fall, and in driving them out and back in the spring did more or less damage in crossing park land. Many of the private land holdings belonged to absentee owners who took little interest in their holdings, but hoped for speculative gain in value; and when the patrols wanted to consult them they had much difficulty finding out where they lived.

Many private owners were not scrupulous, however, in observing the park regulations or in confining their activities to their own property. One cattleman, for instance, with title to only 160 acres, claimed the right to use a township, and for some time drove off campers who ventured to camp on the land to which he had no title. Owners of another 300-acre tract were reported in 1905 to be in the habit of pasturing on 45,000 acres. Acting Superintendent Benson refused them permission to drive in until their 300 acres had been surveyed and the metes and bounds pointed out, which they refused to have done, since their land was almost worthless and would not have maintained five head of stock.[28] Another man, owner or lessee of 640 acres, turned 500 cattle loose in the forest reserve adjoining, and the cattle immediately wandered over to their old feeding ground in the park. The troopers impounded them at Wawona. A great many of the private lands were mining claims initiated before the park was established.

Congress usually showed a deep sympathy for the "poor settlers" who had initiated claims in the national parks and forests, or perhaps had only squatted on public land, and had not got patents. There were some of this gentry in Yosemite, in fact much of the entire Valley of some 1,100 acres was claimed by men who had no titles, and these settlers, in the Valley and outside, were the object of solicitude from the very time of the establishment of the park,

28 *Report, Secretary of the Interior, 1905,* 693 ff.

because they had votes, and also because it was always proper and decorous for a senator or representative to sympathize with the misfortunes of his constituents. In 1894 Senator Kyle and Representative Bowers and Senator Pettigrew of South Dakota tried to get a bill through to authorize the Secretary to "ascertain damages to persons in Yosemite and Sequoia prior to October 1, 1890," but the bill was not reported.[29]

In the next Congress Bowers' bill, for the relief of owners and claimants in the California forest reserves as well as parks, was reported favorably by the House Committee on Public Lands, which had turned hostile to the park administration, but it made no further progress. In the committee report there were the typical western criticisms of federal reservations, and assertions that the soldiers were killing more game than the sportsmen had killed before the park was created—which was probably an exaggeration, although soldiers did sometimes kill game. So serious, in fact, did this practice become that the Acting Superintendent was finally obliged to limit the number of cartridges allotted to the soldiers and require them to account for any that had been fired.[30]

Senator Pettigrew of South Dakota was out of his own territory here, but he was at this time engaged in a pertinacious attack on the forest reserves that President Cleveland had set aside, an attack which came within an ace of success in abolishing them. He was not generally hostile to the forest reserves, but the miners in the Black Hills were engaged in some extensive timber cutting and Pettigrew was afraid there might be interference with this business.[31] Most of the claims had been patented, however, and these patented lands presented a different problem. Various schemes were suggested to rid the park of these private holdings. One proposal was that they be purchased, but there was no money for this and little hope of getting any.

Another proposal was to extend to the park the "lieu-scrip" provisions already applicable to the forest reserves. In 1897 Congress had passed the iniquitous Forest Lieu Act, which provided that where an unperfected claim or patent was included in a forest re-

29 S. 1502, S. 1521, H. R. 5747, 53 Cong. 2 Sess.

30 S. Ex. Doc. 49, 52 Cong. 1 Sess. S. 106, S. 1074, H. R. 7256, H. Rept. 1814, 54 Cong. 1 Sess.

31 See the author's, *United States Forest Policy* (New Haven: Yale University Press, 1920), 115, 116, 132, 133, 139, 140, 173, 180, 185.

serve the owner of it might relinquish the tract and select another tract of land on the public domain outside the reserve; and this act was the source of many kinds of fraud and abuse for years. Some men filed land claims with no purpose but that of surrendering their claims and selecting land elsewhere; some owners stripped their land of timber and then surrendered it. It was a trade in which the government was sure to lose. It is true that the government did sometimes trade lands on the public domain for private lands in the parks, but it did so after some higgling and bargaining and under no compulsion to make the trades; and even so, the government doubtless was short-changed in most of the trades. It had only one advantage—it would wait longer than some of the land owners. The "scrip" issued under the Forest Lieu Act became a common object of sale and was bought up at a profit by land speculators and others. To apply this law to Yosemite would have been very unfortunate but there were several attempts to do this.[32] Early in 1898, Representative De Vries of California introduced a bill to cut out the land valuable for timber, which was reported, but fortunately no further action was taken.[33]

Obviously there was another way to get rid of some of the privately owned lands—cut out of the parks the areas where most of them were—and this was what was done. In 1894 Representative Caminetti of California introduced a bill which would have authorized the President and the Secretary of the Interior, after due investigation, to make such cuts in the boundaries as seemed wise. Superintendent Wood had favored excisions on the grounds that most of the land privately claimed was not of great interest or importance as park land or as watershed, and that there were natural boundaries which would serve better; and the Public Lands Committee agreed, but the bill did not proceed to a vote.[34] Four years later Representative De Vries of California brought up a bill— introduced three times in the same session for some reason—which was reported but not voted on.[35] In the next Congress, in 1900, he again introduced a similar bill three times, to restore all timber in

[32] Stat. 30, 36. H. R. 11841, H. Rept. 1700, 56 Cong. 1 Sess. H. R. 14511, H. Rept. 2165, 57 Cong. 1 Sess. See the author's *United States Forest Policy*, 139, 140, 176-90, 292, 331.

[33] H. R. 5859, H. Rept. 1547, 55 Cong. 2 Sess.

[34] H. R. 7872, H. Rept. 1485, 53 Cong. 3 Sess.

[35] H. R. 5857, H. R. 5858, H. R. 5859, 55 Cong. 2 Sess.

Yosemite, Sequoia, and General Grant to the public domain, which was not reported.[36]

Four years later, Senator Perkins and Representative Gillett of California brought in bills to transfer certain lands from Yosemite to the Sierra Forest Reserve. The Forest Lieu Act still applied to the forest reserves, and if these lands had been transferred they would have become subject to lieu-scrip selections, which the Secretary did not want; so Secretary Hitchcock reported adversely on the Gillett bill and helped the House Committee to work out a new bill,[37] which exempted the lands from forest lieu provisions.[38] The bill did not pass, but the sundry civil appropriation act of April 28, 1904, granted $3,000 for an examination to ascertain "what portions of said park are not necessary for park purposes but can be returned to the public domain," and also to determine the location and cost of a new road into the Valley.[39]

In June 1904 Secretary Hitchcock commissioned the well-known engineer, Hiram M. Chittenden, and two others to make the investigation, and on August 31, 1904, the commission made its report. It estimated that there were $4 million worth of private lands in the park, including many mining claims and timber holdings, largely between the Merced and Tuolumne rivers. The largest body of timber surrounded the Merced and Tuolumne groves of sequoias, which were on public lands. The private lands had been sold mostly to fraudulent claimants for $2.50 an acre, but were worth up to $30.00 per acre. These the commission thought should be got by exchange or purchase, but the appropriation suggested for this, $100,000, was painfully inadequate. The mining claims farther east should be added to the Sierra Forest Reserve, where the miners could continue their operations under government control. The commission also recommended that the Right-of-Way Act of 1901, which had been pushed through Congress by Representative De Vries, be repealed. It was thought that with the excision of so much land it would not be needed. The Secretary had refused to grant any rights of way in Yosemite under this act, on the ground that it was inconsistent with the terms of the act setting up the park, and some of the California "developers" were indignant about

36 H. R. 78, H. R. 79, H. R. 80, 56 Cong. 1 Sess.
37 H. R. 15191.
38 S. 5567, H. R. 9310, 58 Cong. 2 Sess.
39 Stat. 33, 487.

this. Finally the Chittenden Commission recommended a new road
up Merced Canyon, but was opposed to the purchase of the old toll
roads at any but nominal prices.[40]

So distinguished a man as Chittenden commanded respect, but
when Gillett embodied his recommendations in a bill it did not
pass, at first. In the next session, however, Gillett was up with substantially the same bill, revising the boundaries as recommended
by the Chittenden Commission, excluding 542 square miles and
adding 113 square miles, providing for payments for rights of way
under the act of 1901 on the land shifted to the forest reserve, the
receipts to be used in improving the park, and denying patent-
holders the use of forest lieu-scrip provisions. Finally the bill authorized the President to change the boundaries of the forest reserve,
to take in the lands transferred, as authorized under the Forest
Reserve Act of 1891. The bill, approved by Secretary Hitchcock,
passed both houses with no opposition and was signed by President
Roosevelt on February 7, 1905.[41]

At the time, the elimination of these private lands caused little
outcry, except from the Sierra Club, which was fighting every assault
on the national parks; but it presently appeared that very fine scenic
areas had been lopped off—the Devils Postpile, Red Meadows,
Rainbow Falls, and the Minarets. Devils Postpile, symmetrical
columns 60 feet high, fitting closely together, was set aside as a
national monument in 1911, to include also Rainbow Falls. The
Minarets are still in a national forest, and difficult of access. The
minerals which were offered as an excuse for the elimination never
amounted to anything.

The next year, in the act accepting the recession of Yosemite
Valley, the boundaries were changed again on the south and west
by adding 54 square miles and subtracting 13 square miles.[42] These
acts of 1905 and 1906 cut out about all the lands lower than 5,000
feet and put them into the Sierra Forest Reserve, where mining,
hunting, and trapping could be carried on without interference,
and the result was a slaughter of game animals. As in Yellowstone,
the animals, grown tame in the park, went down lower in late fall
and were killed by hundreds. Much of the effort of the troopers

40 S. Doc. 34, 58 Cong. 3 Sess. *Report, Secretary of the Interior, 1905,* 170.
41 H. R. 17345, 58 Cong. 3 Sess. Stat. 33, 702.
42 Stat. 34, 831.

to build up the wildlife in the park was rendered fruitless.[43] Yet some of the California statesmen, Representatives Needham, Raker, and Barbour, continued their efforts to make further cuts in the park, or to transfer the parks to the Department of Agriculture. Raker tried to get lands on the north and west boundaries transferred to the Stanislaus National Forest. None of these bills was reported.[44]

THE VALLEY STATE PARK   For sixteen years, from 1890 to 1906, Yosemite was a mountain national park surrounding a badly managed state park in the Valley. It is pertinent now to turn back to the story of the state park and its final recession to the federal government.

The Valley was neglected or abused, badly managed from the first. Galen Clark did the best he could, but he had little or no money for administration for some years, and was under the orders of the commissioners who knew less about park management than he did, and were often guided by political considerations and by their desire to get maximum revenue from the park to meet the costs of administration. California had evidently believed she was getting an asset out of the grant, but only by skimping on the park and abusing the scenic features was able to avoid a heavy deficit. The commissioners turned the Valley into a farm, allowed some of the land to be cultivated or fenced for pasturage, permitted the cutting of trees, dammed Mirror Lake for irrigation, with little regard for the tourists or the preservation of the scenic values of the Valley. As Robert Underwood Johnson, editor of the *Century Magazine,* said: "It is too evidently true that the artistic instinct—if it has ever existed in connection with the management of the Valley—has been sacrificed to the commercial, and the conservation of natural beauty has been outweighed too frequently by the supposed necessity of providing mules, horses, and horned cattle with pasturage and hay at the least possible cost to the owners of those beasts."[45] Johnson battered persistently at the park administration,

[43] *Report, Secretary of the Interior, 1906,* 191.
[44] H. R. 7017, 59 Cong. 1 Sess. H. R. 568, 60 Cong. 1 Sess. H. R. 21954, H. R. 24802, H. R. 25001, H. R. 25821, 62 Cong. 2 Sess. H. R. 6421, 68 Cong. 1 Sess.
[45] *Century Magazine,* Jan. 1890, 474.

interviewed tourists in the Valley and published their reports, even took a hundred pictures of the facilities to show how poor they were.

In the middle eighties the state commissioners improved the administration of the Valley, even got the state to appropriate $40,000 for a new hotel—the Stoneman Hotel, "strangely commonplace and repellent," of cheap construction and unsafe, with a pigsty in the rear which added little to its dignity. There was much complaint about the hotels anyhow, complaints of poor service and high rates, and for these the commissioners were blamed, to some extent unjustly. Hotels in the Valley were built and operated at high cost. The lumber used in building was hewed and sawed by hand, for there was no lumber mill in the Valley, and most furnishings were made in the same way or carried in on horseback or muleback, as were some of the supplies needed. The number of failures among the hotel operators does not suggest a bonanza in the business. Much of the time the hotel accommodations were inadequate and of primitive type. In at least one of them the rooms were separated by muslin sheets hung on wires.

In 1903 the state commissioners were obliged to order the transportation companies to take no more tourists into the Valley. But the commissioners were not mainly responsible for the shortage of accommodations. Not only were costs high, but the commissioners were authorized to issue permits for only ten years, not long enough to justify investment in substantial facilities. Like the federal government, the state commissioners were committed to the principle of private operation of concessions but did not dare offer long enough leases to attract private businessmen.

When Yosemite Park was created, surrounding the Valley, there were additional difficulties and complications in administration, and friction between the state and the federal government—in game protection for instance, where the state laws differed from those of the national park. Still more important, the Valley, low enough to be habitable in winter, was the natural center for administration of the entire region, and its use would have simplified the problems of administration and protection.

Complaints and criticisms increased. Robert Underwood Johnson continued his attacks on the administration and insisted that the Valley should be receded to the federal government.[46] In 1891,

46 *Century Magazine*, Jan. 1890, 474; Sept. 1890, 656; Nov. 1891, 154; Jan. 1893, 472; Apr. 1893, 951. See also *The Nation*, Feb. 6, 1890, 106.

twenty-seven years after the grant was made, Secretary Noble made an investigation of the state administration and reported that "there has been very great destruction of the timber there; some of which has been used for buildings, fences and fuel; some removed simply to clear the lands for cultivation, and a great deal laid waste through carelessness and wantonness; that more than half of the valley has been fenced with *barbed-wire* fencing and cultivated with grass and grain; that these inclosures have confined travel to narrow limits between the fences and the slope of the mountains, and have left but little room for paths for pedestrians up this valley; that a great many rare plants which were new to botany have been destroyed, if not exterminated, by plowing and pasturing the valley; that the management has fallen into the hands of a monopoly, and no competition seems to be permitted in hotel accommodations, transportation facilities, nor in furnishing provender for the animals of tourists; the main road up the middle of the valley has been closed; and that the uninclosed portion of the valley is pastured by the stock of the stable and transportation men, almost to the exclusion of the animals of the tourists or visitors; that these acts of spoliation and trespass have been permitted for a number of years, and seem to have become a part of the settled policy of the management."[47]

Secretary Noble stated that the reports of the California commissioners from 1885 to 1888 had recommended the cultivation and seeding of 1,000 acres of the floor of the Valley from wall to wall with useful grasses "for the augmentation of the revenue of the State." Noble did not believe that it had been the purpose of Congress to have the state of California turn the park into a farm or stock ranch. There was even some hog raising in the Valley.[48]

A special agent of the General Land Office declared in 1892: "Speculation, traffic, and gain are the dominating features of the management. . . . In my opinion the State of California should be asked to relinquish this trust." To the same effect was the recommendation of the Secretary of the Interior.[49] He reported that although the guardian, Galen Clark, was apparently doing his best to protect the park, the hotel charges were high, for primitive accommodations, the charges for stabling or hiring vehicles or saddle

[47] *Report, Secretary of the Interior, 1891*, CXLII.
[48] On the condition of the Valley under state jurisdiction see *Garden and Forest*, Feb. 1892, 74.
[49] *Report, Secretary of the Interior, 1892*, CXXXIII ff.

animals were "beyond all reason," and as a result the park was "inaccessible except to persons of ample time and means," although some 2,000 tourists visited the park that year, about half of them from foreign countries. He laid the blame for this largely on the Southern Pacific Railroad Company, which apparently controlled the Yosemite Stage and Transportation Company, and tried to monopolize transportation into and within the park.[50]

The state was often blamed for this situation, but in 1906 it was reported that the state had spent $495,000 on the park. The truth was that the task of administration was beyond the resources of the state, which was still sparsely populated and was finding the park a considerable financial burden.

RECESSION OF THE VALLEY   As early as 1895, John Muir urged recession of the Valley to the federal government, and the Sierra Club and other civic organizations early saw the logic of such a policy. When President Theodore Roosevelt made a pack trip into the region with Muir, in 1903, Muir persuaded him to use his influence to get the Valley back. Governor Pardee favored recession, as did many other citizens of California, for the administration of the park—even poor administration—was expensive. Some people contrasted conditions in the Valley with the much better conditions in Yellowstone under federal control; and Congress evinced an unwillingness to vote appropriations for the national park as long as the badly managed state park lay within its borders. On the other hand, there were Californians who as a matter of state pride, wanted to keep the Valley, and it was said that certain members of the California legislature had acquired rights in the area which would lapse if the federal government took it over; but whether this was true the writer cannot say. At any rate, on March 3, 1905, the legislature gave the Valley back to the federal government.[51]

It was now necessary that Congress accept the recession, and this turned out to be a rather complicated problem. Senator Perkins of California introduced a Senate resolution providing for acceptance of recession, along with an appropriation of $20,000 for administration, which passed the Senate with little discussion; but in the House the recession section was stricken out, leaving the title unchanged,

50 *Ibid.*, CXXXIV.
51 *Report, Secretary of the Interior, 1905*, 172 ff.

and retaining the $20,000 appropriation. The title suggested that the recession was accepted, but there was nothing in the bill but an appropriation. Was the recession accepted? The Comptroller of the Treasury said yes, but a few of the California commissioners said no. The resolution was approved by the President on March 3, 1905, the same day that the Governor of California signed the law ceding the Valley.[52] Since there was uncertainty as to the status of the Valley, the Secretary did not spend any of the money granted.

A number of other men brought in bills to make the recession unquestionably valid. Gillett of California introduced a House joint resolution in the next Congress which passed both houses with only a bit of objection in the Senate, objection because the resolution did not provide for the punishment of crimes. As signed by President Roosevelt, on June 11, 1906, the resolution accepted recession, changing the boundary of the park slightly.[53] State authorities were not prepared to leave the Valley at once, insisting that the considerable amount of state property there should be paid for, but an informal agreement was reached as to payment, the price to be determined later, and on August 1 the state of California moved out. Soon afterward the superintendent of the park moved many of the administrative offices and activities down into the Valley.

By 1906 Yosemite Park had been consolidated, and reduced twice, to a point where game would have to go down to lower lands in winter and be shot. California sportsmen had secured so much, and for several years afterward the Secretary of the Interior reported game decreasing. The park was getting a little money every year, and a few employees received salaries. In 1908 the supervisor received $1,200 a year, and rangers as much as $1,000. The Yosemite Valley Railroad, running from Merced up Merced River Canyon to a point within sixteen miles of the Valley camp, was completed in 1907, and the next year 8,850 tourists entered the park.

It should be said here that all early figures as to the number of tourists entering the parks are subject to a wide margin of error, for no admission fee was charged and therefore no accurate count was kept. Furthermore, the figures as to "tourists" or "visitors" refer to the number who entered, with no allowance for duplication—for the fact that some visitors came more than once. For this reason the

52 S. Res. 115, 58 Cong. 3 Sess. Stat. 33, 1286.
53 H. J. Res. 118, 59 Cong. 1 Sess. Stat. 34, 831. *Report, Secretary of the Interior, 1905,* 172.

number of "visitors" was always less than the number of "visits." In
recent years figures are generally given in terms of "visits" rather
than "visitors."

CONTINUING DIFFICULTIES   There were many flies in the
honey, many perplexing problems to be solved. The Valley was still
something of a jungle, although there had been cleaning up and the
fences had been removed. The roads were still very poor, the Tioga
Road practically impassable. In summer the dust made travel very
disagreeable and there were no funds for sprinkling. There was only
one hotel in the Valley, a very primitive hostelry. There were still
20,000 acres of private holdings in the park; lumbermen were slashing the timber on the mountain sides outside the park and coming
closer, threatening a tract of magnificent sugar pines along the Wawona Road. Lack of proper sanitation was a constant complaint.
Campers were obliged to get drinking water from the Merced River.
There was still need for better legal provisions for punishing violators of regulations, for the nearest United States Commissioners
were a hundred miles away. The troops had done as well as could
have been expected, but they usually served only one season, not
long enough to get familiar with the park and its problems, even if
they had been temperamentally fitted for such a task. A trained force
of rangers was needed. Finally, and worst of all, the city of San
Francisco was reaching out for the Hetch Hetchy Valley, one of the
most magnificent parts of the park. The park administration had
plenty to worry about.

TOLL ROADS   Toll roads were completed into the Valley in
1874 and 1875. In 1859 the Coulterville and Yosemite Turnpike
Company had been set up, and somewhat later got a ten-year lease
from the commissioners to build a road down to the floor. The lease
was drawn to give the company exclusive rights on the north side
of the Valley, but soon afterward the Big Oak Flat and Yosemite
Turnpike Company applied for a lease, also on the north side, and
the commissioners refused to violate their agreement with the Coulterville company; but the legislature passed an act granting this second lease. The turnpike business was apparently regarded as highly
profitable, for within eleven years from the time of the grant to California three roads were completed into the Valley: the Coulterville

Road (1874), the Big Oak Flat Road (1874), and the Wawona Road —from the south— (1875). These roads were steep, even dangerously steep, rough, often very dusty. The tolls were from 2 to 3½ cents a mile, and the fare on the stages was 15 cents a mile.

The Tioga Road, leading from Tioga Pass westward, was built by the Great Sierra Mining Company in 1883 at a cost of $64,000. At one time there were 350 mining locations in the Tioga District, and the road was built to enable the company to haul its machinery in and later its ore out. The company spent $300,000 at Tioga, but in 1884 disaster struck and all work was dropped. It has been said that the mine was later "salted" and stocks sold to the public. At any rate, no ore was ever hauled out and the road was never maintained. There were a number of other roads in the area, some of them connecting with trails that led into the Valley or to points near.

These toll roads were the object of constant complaint by tourists and by the park administration, and of repeated efforts to get Congress to appropriate money for their purchase. The park administration was opposed to tolls in a national park, and there could be no hope of early termination of the road franchises, which for three of the main roads did not expire until 1920, 1921, and 1934—apparently granted by the Secretary under the Right-of-Way Act of 1901, for the state commissioners were not authorized to grant leases for more than ten years. In 1885, 1886, and 1887 the California legislature had appropriated money to buy the part of the roads that lay in the Valley, and make them free to the public; but the sections outside the Valley remained in private hands, and when Congress set up the park around the Valley, these toll roads were maligned by tourists and by the park management.

In 1892 Congress granted Mariposa County a right of way for a wagon road across a part of the park from Mariposa to the Valley, thus providing for a southwestern entrance to the park, but the federal government was not to be liable for expenses of upkeep of the road.[54] A little later Secretary Noble directed a committee of three army officers to examine the toll roads and see what should be done about them, and the committee recommended that they be bought.[55] Senator White and Representative Johnson made several efforts to get an appropriation for purchase, but without success.[56] In the same

54 H. R. 5439, H. R. 6792, 52 Cong. 1 Sess. Stat. 27, 235.
55 S. Rept. 863, 54 Cong. 1 Sess.
56 S. 1371, S. 2708, H. R. 1693, H. R. 7712, H. Doc. 261, 54 Cong. 1 Sess.

session of Congress the Senate Committee on Forest Reservations introduced a similar bill, which was reported favorably, with an estimate of $200,000 as the probable cost of the roads. This bill passed the Senate, but in the House Committee on Public Lands there was opposition to immediate purchase and an amendment was substituted, favored by Secretary Francis, calling for an appraisal of the roads on the basis of net income for the preceding five years. As amended the bill made no further progress.[57]

In the next Congress, in 1897, Representatives Castle and De Vries tried to get surveys for new roads. The De Vries bill called for surveys of a new road from the Valley to Mono Lake, apparently duplicating the Tioga Road, which was now impassable.[58] The California delegation was active in efforts to free the toll roads during these years, and the California legislature petitioned Congress to buy them. Most of the tourists visiting the park were from California, so California wanted the tolls eliminated; and there were no local commercial interests opposed. Bills introduced to benefit the park were likely to be favored by the California delegation and by men from other western states, and sometimes passed the Senate, where western states were disproportionately represented; in the House they were most likely to be opposed by eastern men, who represented the states that would have to pay most of the costs and would get little of the benefits of park improvement. Bills for the benefit of local commercial interests, on the other hand, however injurious to the park, had the approval of most California and some other western men, and often fared well in the Senate and less well in the House. Congress apparently still believed that the parks should be largely self-supporting and was slow to vote money for them. In the next session of Congress, in 1898, Senator Perkins and Representative De Vries made several attempts to get money to buy the roads or do something about roads in the park, but to no avail.[59]

The toll roads had been studied and surveyed and investigated for several years, by the Secretary and others, and enough was known about them, but in the 55th Congress Perkins brought up a bill appropriating $3,000 for another investigation, which passed the Sen-

57 S. 3064, S. Rept. 863, H. Rept. 2973, 54 Cong. 2 Sess.
58 H. R. 3496, 55 Cong. 1 Sess., H. R. 8350, 55 Cong. 2 Sess.
59 S. 2819, H. R. 5012, H. R. 7872, 55 Cong. 2 Sess.

ate but was defeated in the House because it appropriated $3,000 and because it would have taken the time of army officers who were needed in the Spanish-American War.[60] Perkins then offered an amendment to the next appropriation bill providing for an investigation, and this passed on March 3, 1899. The commission, composed of two army officers and a man from the California Highway Commission, made its report on February 8, 1900, giving details as to the costs, receipts, and expenditures of the roads, and recommending that they be purchased and that other new ones be built.[61] It was an excellent report but it brought no action by Congress. In the same session of Congress, on May 9, 1900, Senator Bard offered an amendment to the sundry civil appropriation bill, to appropriate $50,000 for construction of a wagon road, $50,000 to buy the toll roads, and $31,300 to protect Sequoia Park; but of course such extravagance had no appeal in Congress.[62]

In the next session of Congress Senator Bard and Representative Metcalf brought up bills to "make free the toll roads in Yosemite," and the Metcalf bill was reported favorably by the House Committee on Public Lands with some emphatic arguments for its passage: "It is . . . unseemly and improper for the United States to invite its own people, as well as the people of the whole world, to visit this Yosemite National Park to witness its grand scenery, and then allow them to be charged toll for viewing these great natural wonders." The Committee made some calculations showing that Yosemite had been treated unfairly, that the park had been given only $16,000 while Yellowstone had received $968,872, and Chickamauga and Chattanooga and Gettysburg—national military parks—had been granted $1,293,-000 and $425,920, respectively. The Committee was of the opinion that a state that had created such vast wealth (in gold) merited better treatment.[63] Congress, however, did nothing about this injustice.

In the next Congress, in 1902, Bard and Metcalf were up again with toll road bills, which got no attention.[64] Two years later Representative Needham threw into the hopper a bill to build a wagon road that would serve as an all-winter route into the Valley, which

60 S. 3675, 55 Cong. 2 Sess.
61 S. Doc. 155, 56 Cong. 1 Sess.
62 *Congressional Record*, May 9, 1900, 5309.
63 S. 5430, H. R. 12552, H. Rept. 2989, 56 Cong. 2 Sess.
64 S. 4428, H. R. 4582, 57 Cong. 1 Sess.

was reported favorably but that was all.[65] Two or three years later Representative Raker took up the torch and tried unsuccessfully to do something about the roads, particularly Tioga.[66]

In 1896 various California men worked to get a right of way for the Yosemite Valley and Merced Railway to run from Merced up the Merced Canyon to El Portal, near the entrance to the park. None of these efforts was successful, but it was presently found possible to get a right of way under the Right-of-Way Act of 1901, without an act of Congress. A permit was issued to the Yosemite Valley Railroad Company in September, 1905, and the railroad was completed in 1907, to change the toll road and stage business drastically. Long stage rides were no longer necessary, and this business dropped, although the lines continued to operate, with reduced schedules except for the Big Tree routes. The railroad brought a great increase in the number of park visitors, and big fleets of stages were needed to meet the trains at El Portal. The purchase of the toll roads was no longer a very important question. Stephen T. Mather, the first Director of the National Park Service, with a few friends, bought the Tioga Road in 1915, and the Big Oak Flat Road and the Wawona Road were acquired in 1917. The railroad, however, soon faced rising competition from automobiles, lost heavily in a great flood in Merced Canyon in 1937, and in 1945 folded up.[67]

CONCESSIONS   Like Yellowstone, Yosemite had a long history of concession troubles. Those connected with the roads have been considered. As in Yellowstone, the first accommodations were provided informally by men who squatted on the land and built simple or even primitive accommodations. In 1855 the town of Mariposa conceived a plan for damming the Valley for a water supply, and the first house was built the next year by the company interested in this project. The first hotel, the Lower Hotel, built of planks split from pine logs, was started that year on a site opposite Yosemite Falls. This hotel was torn down in 1869 and replaced by "Black's." In 1859 the Upper Hotel was started, and completed two years later, but it never prospered and in 1864 was bought by Hutchings for a song or two and operated by him for several years under a lease from

65 H. R. 10140, 58 Cong. 2 Sess.
66 H. R. 26878, 62 Cong. 3 Sess. H. R. 125, H. R. 126, 63 Cong. 1 Sess.
67 *Report, Secretary of the Interior, 1906*, 195. Russel, *op. cit.*, 68-70.

the commissioners. John Muir worked for Hutchings sometimes in these early years—until he would get enough money to go exploring. Hutchings added three other buildings, but in 1872 the state extinguished all private claims in the Valley and bought his property for $24,000. Coulter and Murphy operated the hotel for several years and in 1876 built the Sentinel Hotel. Galen Clark settled in the Valley in 1857 and built a cabin where visitors were entertained, but he was not a success as a businessman, and in 1870 turned part ownership of his property over to a partner. Black's and Leidig's followed, and in 1872 the "swanky" Cosmopolitan was built, with billiard hall, bathing rooms, barber shop, and saloon where "brandy-cocktails, gin-slings, barber's poles, eye openers, mint julep, Samson with the hair on, corpse-revivers, rattlesnakes, and other potent combinations" were served. All the splendid furnishings of this hotel were brought in twenty miles on muleback. In 1869-70 Albert Snow completed a horse trail from the Valley to the flat between Vernal and Nevada Falls, and built La Casa Nevada chalet at the latter point; occasionally hotel owners built trails and perhaps conducted parties to various points.

By 1878 the number of campers had grown to a point where camp grounds were needed, and the commissioners set aside a part of the old Lamon claim for a camp ground and granted a man named Harris the right to administer it. Apparently there was no charge for camping, but Harris sold feed for the animals and rented stable facilities and equipment of various kinds. Here was the forerunner of the public camp grounds and housekeeping camps, which came twenty years later. In 1884 John Degnan established a bakery under a lease from the commissioners, which operated for many years, later adding a restaurant; and in 1887 the pretentious four-story Stoneman House was completed by California State, at a cost of $40,000, to accommodate 150 guests. There were often insufficient accommodations in the Valley, and the state wanted to encourage tourists.

The Acting Superintendents sometimes had trouble with the concessioners, as in Yellowstone. The concessioners sometimes built fences around areas near the hotels to keep tourists' horses out and for other purposes; and the Acting Superintendent worked for several years to get unauthorized fences torn down. Gabriel Souvelewski, a noted character in early Yosemite history, and later Acting Superintendent at times, in winter, was in charge of the troops that achieved this.

In 1899 D. A. Curry and wife, who had once operated in Yellowstone, came to Yosemite and soon established a business which prospered and has continued to the present. Their first venture was seven tents and a woman cook and a few college students who got their summer expenses for working around the camp. The Currys provided popular campfire entertainment, including a revival of the "firefall," which had been started by a James McCauley in 1871 or '72, but later discontinued. This "firefall" consisted in setting fire to a pile of bark and wood at Glacier Point at night and pushing the burning embers over the cliff, to fall slowly to the Valley floor—a rather impressive sight, but not strictly consonant with national park principles. The camp business proved so successful that competitors invaded the field, but the Currys outlasted them all, joining one of them (the Yosemite National Park Company, successor of the Desmond Park Service Company) in 1925, to establish the Yosemite Park and Curry Company, with a practical monopoly of most tourist facilities, which it still has.[68]

At first there were complaints that the state commissioners were too niggardly in granting leases, but they presently loosened up and gave out leases freely. When the Valley was returned to the federal government in 1906, Secretary Hitchcock found twenty-seven concessions in force, which he thought was too many. He found great inequalities in rents charged, indicating favoritism. One residence paid $20.00 rent, another $1.00, one photo shop paid $20.00 rent and two others $250 each. He extended the leases for a year but evened up a few of the worst inequalities.[69]

From this time until the National Park Service was established in 1916 there were too many concessioners, although the number had been reduced to nineteen in 1908. Reliance was on competition. When Mather came in, however, he tried to substitute a system of regulated monopoly, and by 1925 he achieved it.

Ten-year leases were too short. Year after year the Secretary pointed this out and asked that the period be extended, but it was not until 1913 that *one* twenty-year lease was authorized. On June 23 of that year an appropriation act was signed by President Wilson applying the Yellowstone lease provisions to Yosemite—not over ten tracts of not over twenty acres each to any concessioner, for up to twenty years, but the bill authorized the Secretary to grant only *a*

68 Russel, *op. cit.*, Chap VIII. Shankland, *op. cit.*, 130-33.
69 *Report, Secretary of the Interior, 1906*, 201.

lease for "*a* substantial hotel and buildings in connection there-with."[70] This limitation proved not very important, however, be-cause the next year Congress authorized leases up to twenty years. Representative Raker introduced a bill providing for this, early in 1914, which passed with just enough debate to show how little some congressmen knew about park problems. Twenty-year leases were really needed, but Representative Madden of Illinois was firmly op-posed to the bill, particularly to a provision allowing concessioners to mortgage their property, and no explanations could make him budge: "I have read the report and all connected with it, and I do not believe the Government of the United States ought to authorize anybody to make mortgages or to authorize the Department of the Interior to accept mortgages or to authorize such conditions as the bill provides for in any way, so I insist on my objection." His objec-tion sent the bill back to the calendar, but the next time it came up he was apparently absent and it passed with no further opposition.[71] In an effort to make concessions attractive the act provided that in case a lease was not renewed at termination the Secretary might ar-range for payment to the concessioner by his successor of the ap-praised value of his property. In 1916 the National Park Act pro-vided for twenty-year leases in all the national parks.

THE PRIVATE LANDS AFTER 1905   The drastic amputations to which Yosemite was subjected in 1905 did not eliminate all pri-vate holdings in the park, and there were efforts later to get these lands in some way, particularly those on which the giant sugar pines grew—sometimes to a diameter of seven or eight feet. Some of these the lumbermen were preparing to cut.

Even before the 1905 slash there were efforts to provide for ex-changes, by Senator Bard and Representative Daniels of California and by the great conservationist Lacey of Iowa, but to no effect. In 1911 Senator Perkins of California brought up a bill authorizing the exchange of privately owned timberlands in the park for timber-lands of equal value outside the park, or of timberlands along the roads in the park for timber elsewhere in the park. As amended in the House Committee on Public Lands, and passed, the act of April 9, 1912, provided that in order to eliminate private holdings and pre-

70 Stat. 38, 49.
71 H. R. 1694, 63 Cong. 1 and 2 Sess. *Congressional Record*, 8789. Stat. 38, 554.

serve the natural timber along the roads in scenic parts of the park, on both patented and park lands, the Secretary might exchange for private timber lands in the park decayed or matured timber of equal value in other parts of the park where the cutting would not affect scenic beauty. He might also exchange for only the timber on patented lands along the roads, timber of equal value elsewhere in the park, the Secretary to arrange the exchanges at his discretion. Finally, the Secretary was authorized to sell matured or dead or down timber as he might deem "necessary or advisable for the protection or improvement of the park," but the proceeds must be covered into the Treasury, therefore he could not use them after all for "protection or improvement." The law was badly conceived and poorly written, but was of some use.[72]

Two years later Senator Works and Representative Raker tried to improve the 1912 act by including national forests in its provisions, authorizing the Secretaries of the Interior and Agriculture to secure private holdings in the park by exchanging timber or timber and lands in the park or in the Sierra and Stanislaus National Forests. There were about 640 acres of very fine privately owned timber along the Wawona Road that Secretary Lane and the Superintendent wanted, because the owner was threatening to log them; and the bill authorized the Secretaries to exchange for them any "lands of the United States," even if outside the park. The government had tried to buy the land, but the Yosemite Lumber Company had wanted too high a price; proposals for exchange of timber in other parts of the park were also refused, so this bill was introduced and passed on April 16, 1914.[73] The acts of 1912 and 1914 were used in making some other exchanges, but not much of the private land in the park was secured in this way. There were areas of giant sugar pines that were acquired later but largely by purchase.[74]

A month later, in 1914, Congress authorized the Secretary of the Interior, on recommendation of the Secretary of Agriculture, to exchange government-owned lands in the Sierra National Forest for privately owned timber lands of equal value in the Sierra Forest and in the park. The act specified the lands that might be acquired in

72 S. 5718, 62 Cong. 2 Sess. Stat. 37, 80.
73 S. 4943, 63 Cong. 2 Sess. Stat. 38, 345.
74 S. 4943, H. R. 12533, 63 Cong. 2 Sess. Stat. 38, 345. It was the Works bill, S. 4943, that passed.

this way.[75] Two years later, in 1916, the Secretary was generously authorized to accept donations of lands or rights of way in the park.

HETCH HETCHY DAM   In 1913 Yosemite suffered the worst disaster ever to come to any national park, in the loss of Hetch Hetchy Valley to the city of San Francisco—the "Rape of Hetch Hetchy" or the "Hetch Hetchy Steal," as it is often called by conservationists. Hetch Hetchy, on the Tuolumne River, is one of the noblest canyons in America, much like Yosemite Valley, and according to some park men quite equal to Yosemite; but it was wrenched from park control and turned over to San Francisco for a city water and power reservoir, paradoxically, by men most of whom were leaders in conservation.

The Hetch Hetchy Valley had for some years been eyed covetously by San Francisco, as well as by power companies. The city bought a considerable area of land in the valley, variously reported in the debates at from 780 to 1,960 acres. The city was growing rapidly, and was looking about for an adequate future water supply and for hydroelectric power—coal was far away and expensive. The city even considered the possibility of going as far as Lake Tahoe. As early as 1876 an engineer, George Mendell, made for the city a report on all possible sources of water supply, enumerating fourteen that could be used. In 1882 Hetch Hetchy had been considered as a reservoir site, and there were two studies by the United States Geological Survey in years following. In 1900 the city made a study of the cost of developing a reservoir here, as did several electrical companies, but no report was published. Later Secretary Hitchcock criticized them for thus surveying a national park without permission.

The Right-of-Way Act of 1901 has been referred to, but must be considered more fully here, for it had much to do with the rape of Hetch Hetchy. The bill was introduced on May 29, 1900, by Representative De Vries of Stockton, about sixty miles east of San Francisco, referred to the Public Lands Committee, and reported back the very next day. Up for passage six days later, it was questioned by Representatives Payne of New York and Lacey of Iowa, stalwart conservationists, but passed the House, and months later, piloted by

75 Stat. 38, 376.

Senator Perkins of California, passed the Senate with no difficulty
and was promptly signed by President McKinley on February 15,
1901.[76] The act was in most respects perfectly tailored for looters of
the parks, for it authorized the Secretary to grant rights of way
through government reservations of all kinds, Indian reservations,
and the California parks, for practically any sort of business that
might want a right of way, including "the supplying of water for
domestic, public, or any other beneficial uses," provided the right of
way was not "incompatible with the public interest." Whether
De Vries had Hetch Hetchy in mind when he wrote this provision, it
is impossible to say, but it seems likely, for San Francisco was already
reaching for the valley, he lived not far from San Francisco, and
this provision was as nicely designed for the use of the city as if the
city council had written it. There was one fly in the honey, however
—the rights of way were revocable by the Secretary or his successor at
any time.

Mayor James D. Phelan, a wealthy nabob of San Francisco, kicked
off in 1901, by hiring an engineering firm, at his own expense, to
make surveys and draw preliminary plans for dams on Hetch Hetchy
and Lake Eleanor, and to file claims in Phelan's name. This was done
with the least possible publicity. Secretary Hitchcock had some convictions, and pointed out that the act establishing Yosemite, in directing preservation of "natural curiosities, or wonders" in "their
natural condition," precluded the granting of any such permit, and
he denied the application. Meantime three water power companies
filed on Lake Eleanor and Hetch Hetchy. Hitchcock's decision looked
like the final answer to the scheme, but Franklin K. Lane, City Attorney of San Francisco, later Secretary of the Interior, a leader in
promoting the enterprise, appealed to President Roosevelt, and
pushed the scheme as hard as he could. More potent, perhaps, than
anyone else, Gifford Pinchot, the great leader in the conservation
movement, joined in the enterprise and pledged all the assistance in
his power in wrecking Hetch Hetchy.

This is hard to understand. It is true that as chief of the Forest
Service Pinchot had always insisted that conservation meant *use*
rather than *reservation* from use. As a trained forester he would naturally have taken this attitude, and as a fairly shrewd politician he

[76] H. R. 11973, 56 Cong. 1 Sess. Stat. 31, 790. See also H. R. 6076, and H. R.
10225 of the same Congress.

could see that it was the only attitude he could possibly take to save the national forests from being dismantled. Yet it does seem strange that Pinchot, a man of broad culture, should have had apparently no interest in the parks or in the preservation of great scenery, that he should not have seen that great scenery enjoyed by millions of tourists is being *used* as truly as forests cut for lumber, and used without depletion of the resource. He had seen the giant sequoias and was shocked by the wanton destruction of them, but had made no effort, as far as the writer knows, to secure their absolute protection. His name never appears in connection with the promotion of national parks. In the Conference of Governors in May, 1908, devoted to conservation, the program, drawn up by Pinchot, gave only a little time to George Kunz, president of the American Scenic and Historic Preservation Society, for a talk on scenic values. The chairman of the conference arbitrarily asked J. Horace McFarland, president of the American Civic Association and influential leader in the early park movement, to give an address, but it was not on the program. Pinchot seemed to think that conservation of scenery was not important. In his autobiography[77] there is no reference to national parks or to any of the prominent figures in the national park movement—Lane, Payne, Works, Wilbur, Ickes, Mather, Albright, or Cammerer—although he had at least fought some of these men at times. He had great influence with Roosevelt, but Roosevelt played no active part in pushing Phelan's plan.

Perhaps Pinchot's European training in forestry had something to do with his lack of interest in national parks. In most European countries there were no national parks, and national forests served the purposes of both forests and parks fairly satisfactorily. Perhaps even more important than this, in explanation of Pinchot's attitude, is the fact that the dam to be built by the city was to represent "public power," which Pinchot had been pushing for years. By his own initiative and persistence he had saved most of the power sites in the national forests from private appropriation, and with President Theodore Roosevelt's backing and later the backing of President Wilson, had done much for the cause of public power.

With Hitchcock adamant against the permit, Phelan and his associates could only wait until a new Secretary assumed office and hope he would be more amiable. On March 4, 1907, he came—James R.

77 *Breaking New Ground* (New York: Harcourt Brace and Co., 1947).

Garfield, son of the former President, a man of uncertain conservation principles, although much interested in national forests—and soon showed that he was their man. He went to a meeting in San Francisco in July 1907, and the next year, on May 11, 1908, he reinstated the Phelan application and granted the permit, stipulating, however, that Lake Eleanor should be dammed first and Hetch Hetchy reserved for later development if necessary. This was favorable but not final, for under the act of 1901 such permits were revocable by any succeeding Secretary; and the promoters promptly turned to Congress.

Several of the California delegation proceeded to pour Senate and House resolutions into Congress to make the permits legal and permanent.[78] One bill tried to make this easier by proposing an exchange for Hetch Hetchy of certain lands owned by San Francisco outside the park, "not improperly known as Hog Ranch." On one of the resolutions there were hearings in 1908-9, and many park conservationists and conservation organizations voiced their opposition. There was of course the fighting Sierra Club, with letters from John Muir and others. Muir trumpeted his opposition with characteristic eloquence: "These temple destroyers, devotees of ravaging commercialism, seem to have a perfect contempt for nature, and, instead of lifting their eyes to the God of the Mountains, lift them to the almighty dollar. Dam Hetch Hetchy! As well dam for water tanks the people's cathedrals and churches; for no holier temple has ever been consecrated by the heart of man."[79] The park was defended by other men and organizations: Robert Underwood Johnson of *Century Magazine,* J. Horace McFarland, Frederick Law Olmsted, and by representatives of the American Civic Association, the American Forestry Association, the American Scenic and Historic Society, the Appalachian Club, and others. The printed minutes of the hearings covered 150 pages of protests. The result was that the resolutions failed.

Lined up with the park conservationists, by a peculiar turn of fortune, were the private utility interests, particularly the Pacific Gas and Electric Company, which had hoped to develop the power here. It was an odd fight: the park lovers and the private utilities—

78 H. J. Res. 184, 60 Cong. 1 Sess. S. R. 123, H. J. Res. 223, 60 Cong. 2 Sess. S. J. Res. 4, H. J. Res. 26, 28, 61 Cong. 1 Sess.
79 Peattie, *op. cit.,* 35.

which had so often tried to loot the parks—against the public power advocates and the city of San Francisco. The public power issue was given little attention, however, in the debates; it was behind-the-screen manipulation.[80]

In 1909 Richard Ballinger came in as Secretary under President Taft. He visited Hetch Hetchy in person, and had a study made by the Geological Survey which showed that Lake Eleanor and Cherry Creek, in Stanislaus National Forest, were sufficient for the needs of the city; whereupon, in February 1910, he issued a citation to the mayor and supervisors of the city and county of San Francisco to show cause why the Hetch Hetchy Valley and reservoir should not be eliminated from the permit, which had provided that Lake Eleanor should be utilized first—the city had not done enough work on the dam to establish any use right in the site. Hearings were held, at which the city asked for more time, really to delay until a new Secretary would take office. Unfortunately Ballinger asked the Secretary of War to detail a board of engineers to study the problem—unfortunately, because this board was destined to provide the spoilers with ammunition for their enterprise.

In 1911 Ballinger was succeeded by Walter Fisher, another man stubbornly devoted to park preservation, and Fisher promptly refused to proceed with the permit, on the ground that he had no authority to do so. This again left the city uncertain as to its rights, and suggested that its only recourse was Congress. Senator Perkins promptly introduced three bills, Representative Raker introduced four, and Representative Mondell of Wyoming brought in a bill, to authorize the Hetch Hetchy Dam.

In Congress several factors favored the spoilers and the public power advocates. The Army Engineers made a report in favor of the dam, of course, for Army Engineers care little for scenic values and always enjoy building dams. Their estimate was that the Hetch Hetchy project would be 20 million dollars cheaper than any other available project, and would develop more power. (The city was after power as much as water.) Perhaps more important, President Wilson, in 1913, appointed Franklin K. Lane as Secretary of the Interior, and Lane, as City Attorney of San Francisco, had committed himself to the Hetch Hetchy project. Lane's national park principles

---

[80] On the public power issue in this fight see Judson King, *The Conservation Fight* (Washington: Public Affairs Press, 1959), Chap. V.

were wobbly anyhow. In the fight on Hetch Hetchy he did all he could for the spoilers, and as Secretary he was able to tip the balance in their favor.[81]

Secretary Ballinger should receive a little attention at this point. His name was for some years under a cloud because of an altercation with Pinchot in 1910—the famous "Ballinger-Pinchot Controversy." In that case, a man named Cunningham and associates had staked out thirty-three coal claims in Alaska, in the interest of the Guggenheims, who were seeking to get control of as much of Alaska as possible. Several land agents had reported unfavorably on the claims, even that they were "fraudulent"; but Ballinger, first as Commissioner of the Land Office and later as Secretary of the Interior, had tried to issue patents, against the protests of several land agents, Gifford Pinchot, and others. There were charges and countercharges in one of the most heated controversies in years; President Taft, Attorney General Wickersham, the Forest Service and other government agencies were dragged into the melee and political noses were bloodied; but the real issue was whether the Alaska lands should be sold or leased. Ballinger favored sale, and Pinchot and his friends favored government ownership and leasing of the coal deposits. The upshot of the fight was that Taft dismissed Pinchot from his post as Chief of the Forest Service and Ballinger resigned under a cloud. His policy on the Alaska coal claims was not that of a conservationist but on the national parks his record was exemplary.[82]

Years later, in January 1940, Ickes happened to read Henry E. Pringle's *Life and Times of William Howard Taft*,[83] which advanced the conclusion that a grave injustice had been done Ballinger in the publicity regarding the Ballinger-Pinchot affair, and that Pinchot and the land agent Glavis had really "framed" Ballinger. Ickes was convinced by the evidence presented in Pringle's book, and soon afterward he made an investigation of the case, coming up

81 See the author's *United States Oil Policy* (New Haven: Yale University Press, 1926), 334-37. Shankland, *op. cit.*, 202-4, 211-13.

82 See the author's *United States Forest Policy*, 201-5, 295, and *United States Oil Policy*, 313. David Cushman Coyle, *Conservation* (New Brunswick: Rutgers University Press, 1957), 73 ff., has a very interesting discussion of the controversy; and Gifford Pinchot's *Breaking New Ground* has a complete discussion of the Ballinger-Pinchot controversy. See also Rose M. Stahl, *The Ballinger-Pinchot Controversy* (Northampton: Smith College Department of History, 1926).

83 *Life and Times of William Howard Taft* (New York and Toronto: Farrar and Rhinehart, 1939).

with the conclusion that Ballinger was entirely innocent of any mal-
feasance. Perhaps Ickes' conclusion was colored by his many tussles
with Pinchot and his dislike of him (later changed).[84]

In Congress there were long debates, particularly on the bill introduced by Representative Raker of California in August 1913.[85]
The Raker Bill was reported with unanimous approval by the House
Committee on Public Lands, and with the approval of all the California delegation but one—Senator Works—and of many high government officials: Secretary Lane, Secretary David F. Houston of the
Department of Agriculture, George Otis Smith of the Geological
Survey, F. H. Newell of the Reclamation Commission, Chief For-
ester Henry S. Graves, Gifford Pinchot, former Chief Forester, and
of course of the Army Engineers. The bill was a long, thirteen-page
affair, "verbose, prolix, diffuse, and conflicting," as described by
Representative Mondell of Wyoming. In it the city and county of
San Francisco was to get Hetch Hetchy, Lake Eleanor and Cherry
Valley, with the right to construct flumes, etc., through Yosemite
Park, Stanislaus National Forest and public lands, for a municipal
water supply and for hydroelectric power production. There was to
be some sort of division of the water and power with other cities in
the Bay area, but the process of division was not clearly specified;
and there was also to be a division with the irrigators of the San
Joaquin Valley, but this was also nebulously described. In the bill
the city agreed to build a road around the lake reservoir and various
trails, and to pay $15,000 rent for ten years, $20,000 for the next ten
years and $30,000 a year thereafter.

Ferris of Oklahoma, as chairman of the House Public Lands Committee, pushed the bill with vigor. He asserted that San Francisco
was suffering from a water famine, that one-third of the city was
without water connection, and that the city could not get water from
any other source at a price it could afford. "I contend," he said, "and
I believe this committee [of the whole House] will conclude that
there can be no higher form of conservation than to use flood waters
for drinking, bathing, and other domestic purposes rather than to
let them flow idly, unsubdued and unattended into the sea."[86] Fer-

---

84 "Not Guilty: R. A. Ballinger, An American Dreyfus," *Saturday Evening
Post*, May 25, 1940, 9. *Secret Diary of Harold L. Ickes* (New York: Simon and
Schuster, 1955), Vol. II, 131, 237, 238; Vol. III, 111, 118.

85 H. R. 7207, 63 Cong. 1 Sess.

86 *Congressional Record*, 63 Cong. 1 Sess., 3895.

ris was fairly respectful of the conservationists who were working against the bill, but thought they were mere theorists: "These patriotic earnest men believe it is a crime to clip a twig, turn over a rock or in any way interfere with Nature's task. I should be grieved if I thought practicability should completely drive out of me my love of nature in its crude form, but when it comes to weighing the highest conservation, on the one hand, of water for domestic use against the preservation of a rocky, craggy canyon, allowing 200,000 gallons of water daily to run idly to the sea, doing no one any good, there is nothing that will appeal to a thoughtful brain of a commonsense, practical man."[87]

Representative Martin Dies of Texas was somewhat less respectful of conservationists: "I am not for reservations and parks. I would have the great timber and mineral and coal resources of this country opened to the people, and I only want to say, Mr. Chairman, that your Pinchots and your conservationists generally are theorists who are not, in my humble judgment, making a propaganda in the interest of the American people. Let California have it, and let Alaska open her coal mines. God Almighty has located the resources of this country in such a form as that His children will not use them in disproportion, and your Pinchots will not be able to controvert and circumvent the laws of God Almighty." Applause and cries of "Vote, Vote."[88]

Several men argued that the dam and reservoir would really improve the valley scenically, particularly since San Francisco would build a road to the dam, around the lake and from there north to Tioga Road, and trails up to Tiltill Valley. "You will have one of the scenic roads of the world built to this valley," declared Raker, "and instead of having barren cliffs on either side you will have boulevards around this lake, so that the people may see the wonders of Hetch Hetchy Valley."[89] Probably Raker believed what he was saying, but his prophecy as to the roads that would be built proved wildly in error.

One of the few voices raised in favor of the preservation of the park was that of Representative Steenerson of Minnesota. He ridiculed the argument that San Francisco faced an emergency, for there were other sources that could be used but would not produce so

87 *Ibid.*, 3895.
88 *Ibid.*, 4004.
89 *Ibid.*, 3902.

much power. "As I have already remarked," said Steenerson, "this is not a local question. The people of the whole United States are interested in it. . . . If the entire New York delegation should come here unanimously demanding that Niagara Falls be destroyed for the purpose of creating power, would we from the other portions of the United States stand here indifferent? Could we recognize the claim that nobody except the State of New York is interested? . . . Of course, you understand that in a dry time when water is needed the reservoir will probably be empty, as all reservoirs are at those times, and you will have in place of the beautiful floor of the Hetch Hetchy Valley, as described by Mr. Muir, a dirty, muddy pond with the water drained off to supply San Francisco, and probably some dead fish and frogs in it. Will that be beautiful? And then there will be perhaps large generating works, with rolling wheels and buzzing machinery and transmission wires with a devilish, hissing noise echoing and reechoing sounds strange and cacophonous. That is what you will offer us in place of the temple of the gods that has been made ready for our admiration. . . . I am opposed to the eternal drawing upon the Federal Government resources and of the people to make cities more attractive at the expense of the country. . . . It is said this park is hard of access; that only a few hundred people reach it every year; that more will reach it when you have destroyed it."[90]

There was not a great deal of debate about the preservation of the park, however; most of the discussion was concerned with the rights of the San Joaquin irrigators to water, and with the cost of other sources of supply. It appeared that the irrigationists had been opposed to the bill and had sent a delegation to Washington to work against it, but the San Francisco men had patched up a compromise with them which was said to be satisfactory to the irrigators' delegation, but not to the farmers at home. There was a little evidence of opposition from Los Angeles, and more than half of the Sierra Club in San Francisco were said to be opposed; but the San Francisco machine was tightly organized and, with the public power advocates, voted down every important amendment; finally the bill got through the House by a vote of 183 to 43, 194 not voting.

In the Senate there were long debates, with Senator Myers of Montana pushing the bill, against the conservationists who "would rather have the babes of the community suffering anguish and per-

90 *Ibid.*, 3973, 3974.

ishing for want of sufficient water than destroy something that they may go once in many years and gaze upon in order to satisfy their aesthetic and exquisite taste for natural beauty."[91] Senator Works, the only opposing member of the California delegation, argued that San Francisco could easily get water from at least four other sources, that several provisions of the bill were illegal, in direct contradiction with the laws of California governing water, and that the bill did not protect the irrigators of the San Joaquin Valley adequately. Hetch Hetchy would provide much more water than San Francisco needed at the time, and the city was supposed to divide with the irrigation farmers, but Smoot pointed out that if any of the farmers filed for surplus water, the city, looking ahead to a larger population, would fight against such an application, and there could be many lawsuits.

There were fairly potent forces against the bill in the Senate: many conservationists and conservation organizations, including such men as former Secretaries John W. Noble and E. A. Hitchcock, the Pacific Gas and Electric Company, and other private utilities. The press was said to be generally opposed, and Senator Pittman of Nevada presented an editorial from the *Boston Advertiser* which did not waste words in amenities: "It is a steal, pure and simple. San Francisco wants additional water and is too stingy to pay a proper price for it. No more malodorous job than the plot of the San Francisco politicians has been exhibited in Congress for a great many years."[92] Smoot said he believed he had received five thousand letters opposing the bill, but Smoot opposed public power.

Most of the Senators, however, were little interested in the protection of Hetch Hetchy from spoliation, and the bill finally passed the Senate 43 to 25, and was signed by President Wilson on December 19, 1913.[93] It was a disheartening defeat to the park lovers, and especially to John Muir, who died the next year. Today, when Yosemite Valley is jammed with visitors and thousands are turned away because there is no room for them, the loss of Hetch Hetchy can be recognized as a real calamity to the park system.

San Francisco proceeded to build, but with the beginning of the war in 1914 the project proved a big task. By 1925 the Hetch Hetchy

91 *Congressional Record,* Dec. 1, 1913, 17.
92 *Congressional Record,* Nov. 6, 1913, 5863.
93 Stat. 38, 242.

Dam was finished, but ten years later the project was not entirely completed.

With the Valley in her pocket, the city lost all interest in living up to its commitments under the granting act. Contrary to that act, the city tried to keep the public out of the Valley, did not build the roads and trails required by the act, and sold excess power to a private corporation for resale. Representative Cramton, in charge of the appropriation bill in December 1930, complained of these violations, and as a result the city allowed the public to visit the Valley and finally built a stub of a road, but not what was required by the act.

The sale of Hetch Hetchy electricity to a private company was forbidden by the Raker Act, but San Francisco for years sold the electricity to the Pacific Gas and Electric Company, which resold to the people and business firms in the city, presumably at a profit, although the company claimed it was doing this merely as a public service. In 1935 Secretary Ickes began to investigate this violation, and finally brought suit against the city, which was fought all the way to the Supreme Court, where the decision was against the city. This was in 1941, twenty-eight years after the grant. The citizens were then asked to adopt a plan for acquiring a distributing system to sell the electricity in the city and to municipalities and irrigation districts—which was permissible, but apparently the city officials presented the matter to the people in such a way as to induce them to vote it down. The city next tried to get a bill through Congress amending the granting act to allow it to sell the current to private companies, but Ickes was Secretary at the time, not Lane, and he moved against the bill and it was defeated. In the meantime Hetch Hetchy was for several years a rather hot issue. In 1938 President Roosevelt while in California did not go to Hetch Hetchy Dam. Mayor Rossi of the city had hoped to get Roosevelt to dedicate the dam, and so repudiate Ickes, who had so stubbornly insisted that the city live up to its commitments. Roosevelt was a friend of public power but he was also a lover of the parks.

Finally, in 1942, Ickes persuaded the government to build an aluminum reduction plant at Riverbank, and the current was sold to the plant.[94] In 1944 the aluminum plant was closed and the city again sold power to the Pacific Gas and Electric. That company is

94 *Congressional Record*, Dec. 8, 1930, 349. *Report, Secretary of the Interior, 1918*, 120; 1941, 83; 1942, XII.

still selling some of the Hetch Hetchy power under very complicated agreements which need not be described here. Since the agreements were approved by Ickes it may be assumed that the interests of the people of San Francisco are fairly well protected. The valley is still accessible to the public, but the road does not run around the reservoir as promised but only barely to it, and few visitors go to see it.[95]

In 1914 the troops left Yosemite and a ranger force was substituted; Mark Daniels, as landscape engineer, outlined a plan to give a concession to a large operator who was to build a large hotel on the floor of Yosemite Valley, a smaller one at Glacier Point, and fifteen mountain inns in the high Sierra in the park; and good hotels had been built in the Valley and at Glacier Point. A museum had been built; insect pest control had been established by an entomologist from the Bureau of Entomology; an information bureau had been set up; automobiles were admitted in 1913 and 1914, and the number of visitors was increasing rapidly, most of them from California. In 1916 Congress gave $150,000 to build a hydroelectric plant. Yet many things were needed. There were still extensive patented lands in the park, and some owners were planning to subdivide and build resorts; there were only a few miles of macademized road, but surveys were being made for a new El Portal road. Sanitary conditions were bad; sewage was being dumped into the Merced River; and the swarms of flies and mosquitoes in the Valley were a nuisance and a health hazard.

95 National Parks Magazine, Jan.-Mar. 1956, 43. Century Magazine, Aug. 1908, 632; Jan. 1909, 464. Independent, May 14, 1908, 1079; Jan. 14, 1909, 111; Aug. 18, 1910, 375; Oct. 13, 1910, 831; July 28, 1910, 201. The Nation, Jan. 7, 1909, 15. Outlook, Jan. 30, 1909, 234, 252. World's Work, April 1909, 11441. American Forests, Dec. 1934, 567, article by Yard.

CHAPTER III

Sequoia and General Grant Parks

The origin of the name *Sequoia* is not definitely known, but it has been stated that the Austrian botanist, Stephen Endlicher, who studied the sequoias in early years, named the tree after the great Cherokee Indian, Sequoyah, who invented the Cherokee alphabet more than a century ago. Sequoya, or Sequoyah, was one of the most remarkable men in the annals of America. Born about 1773, the son of a Cherokee woman and a man named George or Nathaniel Gist, he fought against the British in the War of 1812, finished his alphabet by about 1822, and planned alphabets for other Indian tribes but never finished them. He moved to San Fernando, Tamalpais, Mexico, where there were some Cherokee Indians, and was reported to have died in 1843.[1]

EARLY HISTORY   It is not certain what white men first saw the giant sequoias, or when, but there is evidence that the Joseph R. Walker exploration party saw either the Merced or the Tuolumne Grove in 1833. In 1852 the North Calaveras Grove was dis-

[1] *American Forests,* May 1959, 31, 46-48.

covered by a hunter, and soon afterward two enterprising vandals stripped the bark off one of the giants and shipped it to eastern cities for exhibition. In 1854 they took it to Sydenham, England, for exhibition at the Crystal Palace there; but the people thought it was bogus, could not believe that the bark came from a single tree, and the men had to close their exhibit. The exhibit in eastern cities did, however, arouse protests against the butchery of the giant sequoias, from such men as James Russell Lowell and Oliver Wendell Holmes.[2] Before many years passed other men saw the giant sequoias, and by 1870 most of the larger groves were known; but reports on their size were commonly regarded as grossly exaggerated and did not arouse as much interest as they should have. The Giant Forest of what was later Sequoia Park, covering about thirty-two separate groves, was discovered by Hale Tharp in 1858, who used one of the hollow logs as a home.[3]

SPECIES OF REDWOOD   There are two related species of the sequoias or redwoods and there has been confusion in the naming of them. Both are members of the *Sequoia* family, both are redwoods. The larger species, which grows in scattered groves in the Sierra at an altitude of 4,000 to 8,000 feet, usually mixed with other species, has been called *Sequoia gigantea* (giant sequoia), or big tree, or Sierra redwood. The smaller species, which grows from San Francisco north to southern Oregon, apparently dependent on the fogs that roll in from the Pacific Ocean, has been called *Sequoia sempervirens,* or merely redwood, or coast redwood. The name "redwood" is not good, for the giant sequoias are also redwoods; but the term "coast redwood" does distinguish this tree from the larger species of giant sequoia or Sierra redwood. The California State Park Commission and the State Forester suggest that the two species be named the Sierra redwood and the coast redwood, which would make the correct distinction. Nevertheless, since the national park is called Sequoia, and since the larger species has long been called sequoia or giant sequoia, that name will be used here, and

2 Hans Huth, *Nature and the American* (Berkeley and Los Angeles: University of California Press, 1957) , 142, 143.

3 Walter Fry and John R. White, *Big Trees* (Stanford: Stanford University Press, 1938) , 10-15.

SEQUOIA AND KINGS CANYON NATIONAL PARKS

NEV.

CALIF.

Principal road   Present park boundary

Boundary of Sequoia and General Grant Parks of 1890

0   5   10

SCALE of MILES

SIERRA

NATIONAL

FOREST

EVOLUTION VALLEY

INYO

KINGS CANYON

SIMPSON MEADOW

King River

Middle Fork Kings

NATIONAL PARK

South Fork Kings River

NATIONAL

TEMPLE VALLEY

Kings River

KINGS RIVER CANYON

CEDAR GROVE

ZUMWALT MEADOWS

FOREST

SEQUOIA

BIG MEADOW

Roaring River

GENERAL GRANT GROVE

NATIONAL

GIANT FOREST

MT. WHITNEY 14,495

SEQUOIA NATIONAL PARK

Ash Mountain PARK HEADQUARTERS

Atwell Mill

MINERAL KING

Kern River

Kaweah River

FOREST

the smaller species will be called the coast redwood, even though they are both members of *Sequoia,* and both are redwoods.[4]

The giant sequoias reach a diameter of 33 feet, or even 40 feet if measured near to the ground, and a height of nearly 300 feet. Fry and White claim to have measured fallen trees that were up to 347 feet high. They report a hollow log, the "Father of the 'Forest' " in Calaveras North Grove which in its prime was probably about 400 feet high and 110 feet around the base.[5] These trees are doubtless the largest living things on earth. The largest are more than 3,000 years old, perhaps as old as 4,000 years, which may possibly make them also about the oldest living things on earth; but it is impossible to be positive about the age of great trees. A writer in *American Forests* has asserted that there is a Sierra juniper in Stanislaus National Forest which is over 42 feet in circumference and at least 6,000 years old.[6] More recently a naturalist has come up with the conclusion that the Methuselah Tree, in the Sierra, a Bristlecone pine, lives to the age of 4,600 years or more.[7]

The sequoias belong to an ancient family, dating back to the Cretaceous period which ended about 60 million years ago. From fossil remains it was believed until recently that this species of sequoias once flourished over much of the northern hemisphere during the Miocene epoch; but the discovery in China in 1944 of the dawn-redwood, *Metasequoia,* a closely related but deciduous genus, indicated that it was this tree rather than the sequoia itself which was found in fossils in many regions, particularly in arctic regions. Some of the petrified forests of Yellowstone were sequoias, but those of Petrified Forest National Monument were not. Quite aside from their majestic size and great age, the sequoias are amazing trees. Their beautiful bark, of a reddish brown color, in some cases as much as two feet thick, is almost impervious to fire or insects—some giants have withstood as many as a hundred fires. Their wood is marvelously durable; fallen trees that have lain on the ground for perhaps a century have been found to be still largely sound wood.

4 See a report by the State Park Commission and the State Forester to the California State Legislature on "The Status of *Sequoia Gigantea* in the Sierra Nevada," 1952.

5 Fry and White, *op. cit.,* 49.

6 Apr. 1943, 146.

7 *National Geographic Magazine,* Mar. 1958, 355 ff.

The other species of sequoia, the coast redwoods, reach an age of only about 2,200 years and grow to a diameter of only some seventeen feet—about half that of the sequoias—but are taller, reaching a height of 364 feet, perhaps the tallest trees in the world, although the Australian mountain ash trees are sometimes said to grow taller. To some observers the coast redwoods are quite as impressive as the giant sequoias, because of their extraordinary straightness and height and because they grow in such dense groves; but none has ever been covered in a national park (although Muir Woods National Monument contains a virgin stand), because they are easily accessible to lumbermen, and because they make supremely excellent lumber, and conservationists have never been able to fight off the lumbermen. As John Muir once said: ". . . as lumber the coast redwoods were too good to live." In this they differ from the giant sequoias, which yield a brittle wood, not very good as lumber. Under the coast redwood groves, there is usually a lush growth of ferns.

DESTRUCTION OF THE SEQUOIAS   The more accessible of the giant sequoias were scarcely found before they were appropriated by speculators and lumbermen, in most cases fraudulently, under the Homestead Act, Swamp Land Act, or other land laws; and within a few years the lumbermen were busy with their saws and axes and with dynamite, destroying these ancient and irreplaceable monuments—irreplaceable in any period of time that can easily be comprehended. Logging began as early as 1862 and reached its peak from 1880 to 1910, when many groves were cut. Nearly all would have been cut but for the fact that some groves were inaccessible and the trees difficult to lumber because of their great size. It is said that it took twenty-three days to fell one of the first giants.

Writing in 1890, John Muir described this widespread destruction: "Fifteen years ago (1875) I found five mills located on or near the lower margin of the main sequoia belt, all of which were cutting big tree lumber. Most of the Fresno group are doomed to feed the large mills established near them, and a company with ample means is about ready for work on the magnificent forests of King's River. In these mill operations waste far exceeds use. For after the young, manageable trees have been cut, blasted, and sawed, the woods are fired to clear the ground of limbs and refuse, and of course the seedlings and saplings, and many of the unmanageable

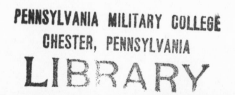

giants, are destroyed, leaving but little more than black, charred monuments."[8] Dr. Gustav Eisen reported to the California Academy of Science in August 1890 on the "appalling and terrible" destruction that had been going on: "The reckless waste of timber must be seen to be understood; it is hardly possible to believe that intelligent beings could be guilty of such recklessness and purposeless destruction."

Purposeless it was, really, for the giant trees were largely wasted in lumbering, and the wood was so brittle as to be unsatisfactory for most purposes. The trees were so large that they could not be cut down with any saws then used, and when they were finally blasted and haggled to a point where they would fall, they often splintered in falling, and then there were no saws large enough to cut them into lumber economically. So they were largely wasted, in some cases felled and left on the ground, perhaps burned to make room for logs more easily managed.[9] The unmanageable size of the trees was the main reason more of them were not destroyed—there was too little profit in their destruction.[10]

Muir thought that sheep did more damage than the lumbermen. In a book published in 1894 he described the devastation wrought by sheep: "These mill ravages, however, are small as compared with the comprehensive destruction caused by 'sheepmen.' Incredible numbers of sheep are driven to the mountain pastures every summer, and their course is ever marked by desolation. Every wild garden is trodden down, the shrubs are stripped of leaves as if devoured by locusts, and the woods are burned. Running fires are set everywhere, with a view to clearing the ground of prostrate trunks, to facilitate the movements of the flocks and improve the pastures. The entire forest belt is thus swept and devastated from one extremity of the range to the other, and with the exception of the resinous *Pinus contorta,* Sequoia suffers most of all. Indians burn off the underbrush in certain localities to facilitate deer hunting; mountaineers and lumbermen carelessly allow their campfires to burn; but the fires of the sheepmen, or 'muttoneers' form more than

8 *Century Magazine,* Aug. 1890, 40, 483.

9 Dr. Eisen reported the destruction of one tree 41⅓ feet in diameter, eight feet larger than any now standing, with 6,126 rings. Most authorities do not believe there were ever trees as large and old as this, so it may have been an exaggeration.

10 See *The Giant Sequoias of California,* by Lawrence F. Cook, of the National Park Service, 1942. *Report, Secretary of the Interior, 1890,* CXXIII ff.

ninety per cent of all destructive fires that range the Sierra forests. It appears, therefore, that notwithstanding our forest king might live on gloriously in Nature's keeping, it is rapidly vanishing before the fire and steel of man; and unless protective measures be speedily invented and applied, in a few decades, at the farthest, all that will be left of Sequoia gigantea will be a few hacked and scarred monuments.[11] In the Dead Grove, the ten giants growing were felled and never taken out of the forest; the Fresno Grove was partly cut over in 1888-90, just before the park was established; the Big Stump Grove was all cut over from 1880 to 1890, hence the name, leaving the Adams Stump, once perhaps the largest of all giant sequoias.

Others agreed with Muir as to the desolating effects of sheep grazing in the Sierra. In 1892 Secretary Noble reported that 500,000 sheep had been grazing in the Kern and King's river valleys, and that the creation of the park had crowded them onto the land outside. "These immense herds have devoured almost everything in the way of vegetation, leaving in places only a thin growth of trees and a few weeds, without any grass."[12]

PROTESTS AGAINST DESTRUCTION   Conservationists protested against the stupid destruction of these irreplaceable wonders, John Muir of course playing a leading role. In 1879 Secretary of the Interior Carl Schurz voiced deep indignation at the wanton destruction going on: "The waste and destruction of the redwood (Sequoia sempervirens) and 'big trees' (Sequoia gigantea) of California have been and continue to be so great as to cause apprehension that these species of trees, the noblest and oldest in the world, will entirely disappear unless some measures be soon taken to preserve at least a portion of them. I am informed that in the more inaccessible sections of the coast range in the northern and on the west side of the Sierra Nevada Mountains in the southern section of California, some forests of these trees still remain, that may and should be preserved, either wholly or least in part."[13] Schurz pointed out that men of science both here and abroad were interested in these trees,

11 John Muir, The Mountains of California (New York: The Century Press, 1911) , 199, 200.
12 Report, Secretary of the Interior, 1892, CXXXII.
13 Report, Secretary of the Interior, 1879, 29.

and urged the President to withdraw some of them from sale. In his report for 1881, Secretary Kirkwood urged Congress to authorize the President to withdraw both the coast redwoods and the big trees from all appropriation lest they all be destroyed.[14] The California Academy of Sciences and the National Academy of Sciences took an energetic interest in the preservation of the trees, both coast redwoods and giant sequoias, and the editor of *Forest and Stream* played a heroic role in publicizing the vandalism going on, and the need for protection.

As we have seen, Representative Converse of Ohio and Senator Miller of California introduced several bills to set aside large areas of the western slope of the Sierra, which would have saved most of the giant sequoias. The lumbermen, cattle and sheep men, and other commercial interests easily defeated these proposals. Perhaps influenced by his aggressively conservationist Commissioner of the Land Office, William Sparks—who served in his first administration—President Cleveland did withdraw the Sierra Forest Reserve in 1893, which included some of the giant sequoia groves; but Congress provided no protection for several years.

SAVING SOME OF THE SEQUOIAS   Something was finally done. One of the motives for turning Yosemite Valley and the Mariposa Grove over to the state of California was to insure protection of the Mariposa Grove. In 1873 the California state legislature passed a law declaring it a misdemeanor to cut or strip of its bark or destroy by fire any tree over 16 feet in diameter, but the law was largely ignored in early cutting. The law is still on the statute books, and is said to be reasonably well observed in recent years, although there is some doubt as to its constitutionality.

The establishment of the Sequoia and General Grant national parks was largely due to the efforts of four local men: Colonel George Stewart, publisher and editor of the Visalia *Delta*—later known as "Father of the Sequoia National Park"; Frank Walker of the same newspaper; Tipton Lindsey, former Receiver of the Visalia Land Office; and John Tuohy, a sheepman; Stewart doing most of the work. Visalia, founded in 1852, the county seat of Tulare County, was only about fifty miles west of what is now General Grant Grove, and the lumbermen were setting up sawmills near with the purpose

14 *Report, Secretary of the Interior, 1881*, XXXIX.

of slaughtering the trees. As early as 1879 Stewart's *Delta* began a campaign to set aside General Grant as a park. The first move was to get the land reserved from entry, for entrymen were trying to get titles to these forests; and here Lindsey played his important role. As Receiver of the Land Office at Visalia, he asked J. D. Hyde, Register of the Land Office—fortunately in favor of the project—to ask the Surveyor General at San Francisco to suspend entries on the four sections believed to cover the big trees. The Surveyor General did this in the nick of time, for lumbermen were making pertinacious efforts to get titles to the land with its giant sequoias. Whenever an entryman filed a claim, Stewart and his men sent protests to the Land Office in Washington. They also enlisted the support of Senator John Miller, who introduced the bill for a large Sierra park in 1881, and of several men in Tulare County, who joined in the project to create a park.[15]

Stewart went to Honolulu about 1880, and when he got back in 1883 he soon found himself in a real battle for preservation of the sequoias. In 1885 three men tried to get possession of the Giant Forest by having men from the Bay region file for them, but Stewart and his men detected the fraud in their applications and Hyde secured the suspension of their claims, saving the Giant Forest just in time. The Kaweah Colony, which later destroyed many trees in Sequoia Park, claimed an interest in these suspended locations. Later in 1885 Secretary Lamar suspended entries on eighteen townships, covering practically all the sequoias in Fresno and Tulare counties. Still later Secretary Noble revoked the suspension, and some forty men promptly left Visalia and other valley towns for the mountains to file claims; but Stewart and his men wired a protest and petition with many signatures to Washington, and Noble backed off from his revocation, but too late to prevent some men from getting titles.

In 1889, at a meeting of Tulare County citizens a resolution was adopted in favor of creating a forest reserve, but soon afterward the promoters turned to the idea of a national park, and got General Vandever to introduce a park bill. They really wanted a big park such as Senator Miller had proposed, but decided on one of modest proportions because they knew the larger one could never get Congressional approval. There were too many commercial interests opposed.[16]

15 S. 363, S. 463, 47 Cong. 1 Sess.
16 See Fry and White, *op. cit.*, 22-29.

The Vandever Bill was introduced on July 28, 1890, reported favorably by Payson of Illinois, and with Secretary Noble's approval passed the House without debate; in the Senate it was presented by Senator Plumb of Kansas and passed with no discussion, and was signed by President Harrison on September 25, 1890.[17] Thus a few men, led by Colonel Stewart, succeeded in making one of the most important contributions in the history of conservation—the saving of some of the ancient and mighty sequoias in the Giant Forest and other groves. But for Stewart and his men this forest might not have been saved, might have passed into private hands to be destroyed like the Converse Basin Forest. A few other parks were established largely through the efforts of one man or a few men—Yellowstone and Crater Lake, for instance, and several others as we shall see; but in no other case did the very survival of the scenic wonder so clearly depend on the patriotic efforts of the men. Yellowstone would likely have been preserved in some way even if the Washburn-Langford-Doane party and Hayden had not proposed the park in 1870, perhaps with the wonders injured and the boundaries haggled; the Giant Forest in Sequoia might no longer exist if Stewart and his men had not worked so hard and persistently for their preservation.

Sequoia Park was established a few days before Yosemite, as a "public park" "to preserve at least some" of the giant sequoias; but in the Yosemite Act of October 1 more land was added to Sequoia, and General Grant was established as "reserved forest lands," a small area covering one of the most important groves and including one of the very largest trees, the General Grant. General Grant was established largely through the persuasive influence of D. K. Zumwalt of Visalia, who was in Washington when the Yosemite Act was being considered. Zumwalt Meadows, in the present King's Canyon National Park, was named in honor of him. Both Sequoia and General Grant included areas of privately owned giant sequoias which were not acquired by the government for many years.[18] Neither Sequoia nor General Grant was named in either act; the names were later given by Secretary Noble. Sequoia Park was fittingly named after the sequoia tree. General Grant was not contiguous with Sequoia, between them was the Redwood Canyon or Redwood Mountain Grove of sequoias, privately owned and partly logged, which

17 H. R. 11570, 51 Cong. 1 Sess. Stat. 26, 478.
18 Stat. 26, 478, 650.

should have been reserved and bought. Secretary Hoke Smith urged
Congress to do this in 1893, but to no avail.[19]

THE SEQUOIA ACT   Sequoia and General Grant were "tree
parks," set aside to protect the giant sequoias and nothing else, covering no noteworthy scenery; and they were generally administered
together. Soon after the parks were established agitation was begun
to expand Sequoia to the north and to the east, to take in Mount
Whitney and a part of the Sierra and so add scenic lands; and *thirty-
six years afterwards* this was achieved.

The establishing act was much like that of Yellowstone and of
Yosemite. The Secretary was to adopt regulations for protection, but
no penalty except ejection was provided for trespassing. He was to
provide against "the wanton destruction of the fish and game," and
against their capture or destruction "for purposes of merchandise or
profit," as in Yellowstone and Yosemite; but no judicial machinery
was set up and no penalties set. Congress had learned little in the
eighteen years since Yellowstone was established. As in Yosemite,
the Secretary might lease to concessioners for ten years small parcels
of land of not above five acres wherever needed, and the revenues
could be used in the management of the park and in building roads
and trails.[20] This provision was of no advantage at first because there
were no concessions in the park, or in General Grant Park. As in
Yosemite, and Yellowstone for some years, Congress made no appropriations for protection, so the army took over, although for some
ten years there was no legal authority for this, and there was no
permanent camp for the soldiers.

SEQUOIAS OUTSIDE THE PARKS   The establishment of Sequoia, Yosemite, and General Grant parks did not provide protection for all the giant sequoias, for there were privately owned groves
in the parks and outside; and these the lumbermen continued to
hack and slash in a regime of criminal vandalism that has seldom
been approached in its callous disregard of the public interest. The
Atwell Grove was entirely cut over, the Dillonwood Grove was
partly logged, the Redwood Canyon Grove and the East Fork Grove

19 *Report, Secretary of the Interior, 1893,* LXVII.
20 Stat. 26, 478.

were partly cut over. Worst of all, the Converse Basin Grove, once perhaps as great as the Giant Forest, covering 6,000 acres of splendid giant sequoias, was blasted, sawed and hacked and then burned over, converted to a melancholy desolation. "Scores and scores of trunks remained on the ground, of which not one fifth of what was commercially valuable had been used. . . . Probably not one half of the trees destroyed, of all species, ever reached the mill to be converted into lumber; quite possibly not one-third."[21] One big tree, the Boole Tree, was left. Perhaps the foreman, Frank Boole, had a twinge of conscience when he came to this last tree of the great wasted forest. The Converse Basin was gutted about 1900 or a little later. There have been various estimates as to the percentage of the original giant sequoias that were cut. Fry and White estimated it at 75 per cent; others have put it at 50 per cent; and in 1952 the California State Park Commission and State Forester estimated that 21 per cent had been cut prior to 1910, and 13 per cent in recent years, largely since 1943.

There were strong protests against this devastation. Late in 1890 Secretary Noble declared, referring to the sequoias: "Their destruction is useless, wasteful, lamentable. At the mills, millions of feet of lumber are decaying on the ground. Trees 30 and 40 feet in diameter have been cut for curiosity's sake. The stump of the greatest of all, the Centennial Tree should be covered with metal roofing; in this way it may be preserved one thousand years."[22] The next year Noble called for the addition of other groves to Sequoia.[23] Acting Superintendent Dorst even saw the significance of timber preservation in watershed protection for the irrigation farmers below. In 1892 the editor of *Garden and Forest* warned against the efforts of the sheepmen and lumbermen to despoil the parks.[24] The next year Secretary Hoke Smith urged the enlargement of Sequoia to protect more groves, and repeated this in 1894. In 1896 Secretary David Francis urged the addition of other giant sequoia groves that were being cut. In 1899 Acting Superintendent Clark described the situation in Sequoia and General Grant as follows: "The titles of lands in the two parks, generally taken from the State as 'swamp land' should be extinguished. There are sixteen different owners, but their

21 Fry and White, *op. cit.*, 20.
22 *Report, Secretary of the Interior, 1890,* CXXIII.
23 *Report, Secretary of the Interior, 1891,* CXLIV.
24 *Garden and Forest,* Aug. 27, 1892, 193.

combined tracts, by the county records of March 1, 1899, only aggregate 5,440 acres, and there is but little value attached to the land since the country surrounding the meadows is strictly guarded by the Government, thus making the grants of private land too small for profitable grazing, and of no great value for the cutting of timber. The Atwell sawmill has again started, and is fast denuding that vicinity of a most beautiful grove of sequoias. The property is leased for three years yet, and the rent is a certain percentage of the lumber cut, really setting a premium on the death of the big trees; and for what purpose? Only to make shingles, posts and flume boards! The estate should be acquired by the government at once and thus save this most beautiful sequoia grove. There are seven groves in all within the park boundaries, but this is the only one to which a title was ever completely proved."[25]

As to General Grant, Clark reported: "Trees of Giant Forest are better preserved than those of General Grant. The 'General Grant' itself has been badly burned and scarred. For a hundred feet up the trunk, can be seen sticks and arrows shot into the bark years ago and bearing the names of enthusiastic admirers who visited the region before the present rules were enforced."[26]

In 1901 Secretary Hitchcock reported that many pieces of bark had been cut from the General Grant Tree—a common form of vandalism—and urged better appropriations for protection. Nearly every report of the Secretary from 1890 on urged better protection and the enlargement of Sequoia to protect more of the giants.

EFFORTS TO SAVE THE SEQUOIAS   President Theodore Roosevelt early showed a deep interest in the preservation of both the giant sequoias and the coast redwoods. In a speech at Stanford University on May 12, 1903, he made a strong plea for this: "Yesterday I saw for the first time a grove of your great trees, a grove which it has taken the ages several thousand years to build up; and I feel most emphatically that we should not turn into shingles a tree which was old when the first Egyptian conqueror penetrated to the valley of the Euphrates, which it has taken so many thousands of years to build up, and which can be put to better use. That, you may say,

25 Report, Secretary of the Interior, 1899, 510, 511.
26 Ibid., 512.

is not looking at the matter from the practical standpoint. There is nothing more practical in the end than the preservation of beauty, than the preservation of anything that appeals to the higher emotions of mankind.

"The forests of this state stand alone in the world. There are none others like them anywhere. There are no other trees anywhere like the giant Sequoias; nowhere else is there a more beautiful forest than that which clothes the western slope of the Sierra. . . .

"I appeal to you . . . to protect these mighty trees, these wonderful monuments of beauty. I appeal to you to protect them for the sake of their beauty, but I also make the appeal just as strongly on economic grounds."[27]

As late as 1903 Acting Superintendent Charles Young reported: "In the Atwell Mill country [private claims within the park] where these big trees grew close to the county road, the owners have cut them by the wholesale and put the lumber upon the market, so that where once there was a fine forest of these magnificent giants there now is but devastation and ruin in the shape of stumps and sawdust piles on either side of the high road. . . . The owners of these lands are only detained from cutting the timber, including the giant forest trees, by the want of public or private roads leading to a market for it, the General Government having forbidden them the use of its road for this purpose."[28]

There were no passable roads in either Sequoia or General Grant Park, and no money for about ten years with which to build roads. The General Grant Park was almost entirely inaccessible. Not until 1900, ten years after the park was established, did Congress appropriate anything for protection and improvement of the park—$10,000 for that year. Not until 1903 was a road completed to the Giant Forest of Sequoia. The absence of roads meant that few tourists could come in, and that there was great difficulty in getting to any fires that were started; but on the other hand it delayed the cutting of privately owned timber in the park, because there was no way to get some of the lumber out. There was occasional trespass by sheep and cattle men, but much of the complaint of livestock trespass concerned the Sequoia Forest Reserve which enfolded Sequoia and General Grant Parks on three sides. From the forest

27 *Bulletin*, Save-the-Redwoods League, Fall and Winter, 1958.
28 *Report, Secretary of the Interior, 1903*, 548, 549.

reserve the livestock sometimes invaded the parks. Under the Forest Reserve Act of 1891, President Cleveland had set aside this forest reserve in 1893, but for several years Congress had made no provision for protecting it, and it was infested with vast flocks of sheep which wrought indescribable damage to the grass and the soil—in some cases irreparable damage. Acting Superintendent of Sequoia, George Gale, made the pertinent comment in 1896: "Thus these lands present the curious anomaly of parks with guards, but no law to punish, and a forest reserve land under practically the same conditions as the parks, with ample law to punish, but no guards to enforce."29 During the Spanish-American War, when the troops were sent to war, these parks, like Yosemite, suffered greatly from trespassing sheep; at least 200,000 were reported as roaming the parks in 1899.30 The Sierra Forest Reserve covered several sequoia groves, which were fortunately protected from land claimants but not from vandals.

WILDLIFE IN THE PARKS   Poaching was not a serious evil during the summer season while the troops were on guard, but as in Yosemite, when the troops left in the fall—there being no quarters for them in the parks—hunters came in at will. During the Spanish-American War poachers had free range of the parks and decimated the game. In 1899 Secretary Hitchcock reported game less abundant and some rarer species extinct, elk and mountain sheep gone, deer still common but decreasing. During these years the California Grizzly was becoming steadily scarcer and more infrequently seen, but it did not become extinct until some time during the 1920's.

In 1902 Miller and Lux, owners of a large ranch in Kern County, offered to give the government 100 elk that they had been protecting on their land. Congress appropriated $1,000 for the cost of transportation, and the Secretary of the Interior set aside an elk reserve in Sequoia for them. Several were injured and died in shipment, but the rest were reported to be doing well and increasing. Perhaps influenced by stories of the buffalo in Yellowstone Park, Acting Superintendent C. C. Smith, reporting in 1908, wanted Congress to appropriate $10,000 for a herd for Sequoia. In his con-

29 *Report, Secretary of the Interior, 1896,* 746.
30 *Report, Secretary of the Interior, 1899,* 507, 508.

cern for game he suggested that mountain lions, wildcats, wolves and coyotes, and even wolverines, porcupines, skunks, hawks, and rattlesnakes should be killed wherever seen. Years later, in 1938, thirty-eight wild turkeys from the California Board of Fish and Game Commissioners were turned loose in Sequoia.

PROTECTION OF THE PARKS   For some years Sequoia and General Grant were little troubled with tourists, so tourist offenses were not very common; yet tourists did occasionally start fires, and some found happiness and fulfillment in chopping the bark off the giant sequoias to carry away as souvenirs; and of course they commonly left untidy camp sites. A few came in with guns, to hunt with or to defend themselves against wild beasts. In these parks, as in Yellowstone and Yosemite, protection from livestock herders, poachers, and vandals was difficult because there were no adequate legal provisions for punishing offenders. Almost every year the Secretary repeated his petition that Congress enact an effective law, but without effect. Finally, in 1902, the Acting Superintendent, Captain Frank A. Barton, secured a commission as deputy state fish and game commissioner from the State Board of California, to serve without pay, and this gave him authority equal to that of a sheriff, with power to arrest anyone violating state laws in the parks and turn him over to civil authorities. The 1908 report of the Secretary of the Interior stated that all the park rangers were made game wardens of the state with power to bring offenders to justice; but there was still no judicial machinery for the parks, no commissioners before whom offenders could be tried, and no schedule of penalties.

There was yet another difficulty in protecting these parks. As in the other early parks, the boundaries were not well marked until about 1903, when a fence was built around the General Grant Grove and the General Sherman Tree. Recognizable markers were not established around Sequoia until 1910. One of the most serious problems was that of private claims in the parks, although the total of these holdings was small compared with that of Yosemite—3,716 acres in Sequoia and 160 acres in General Grant. Unfortunately, many of the giant sequoias were in private claims, and some were being cut.

PRIVATE LANDS IN THE PARKS   Not all the private claims
were valid. Secretary Hitchcock reported in 1901 that some of them
were filed under the law applying to "swamp and overflowed land"
(in the high Sierra!). Some were homestead entries, mostly fraudulent, because no one could make a farm home in this region. If the
claims had not passed to patent when the park was created, park
authorities could chase the claimants off, but where a claim, however fraudulent, had passed to patent, the government could get the
land back only by purchase or exchange. Since these private holdings were surrounded by national park land, the Superintendent
was sometimes able to prevent cutting, as we have seen, by refusing
to allow the lumbermen to use the government roads to haul out
lumber.

While the Secretary of the Interior and the Acting Superintendent
of the park were trying to fight off fraudulent claimants and save
as many giant sequoias as possible for the public, several senators
and representatives were striving to make sure that the "poor settlers" were not treated unjustly by their brutal and tyrannical government. A number of bills were introduced in Congress calling
for investigation of the "damages to persons in Sequoia and Yosemite
prior to October 1, 1890"—prior to the establishment of the park.[31]

The most notorious case of "damage to settlers" was that of the
Kaweah Co-operative Commonwealth Colony, a utopian com-
munist group who filed claims on a grove of giant sequoias nine
miles from the Giant Forest of Sequoia and began cutting the trees.
There is conflicting evidence as to the true nature of their operations, but there is much reason to believe that the settlers were being
"used" for "dummy" claims, which were later to be turned over to
a lumber company. The company paid their expenses for filing the
claims, most of which were filed in the names of men who did not
live near the forest. The head of the colony was apparently working
for the lumber company, and when the settlers discovered the frauds
that were being perpetrated they ousted him and moved outside the
park, with strong encouragement from the park authorities. They
had been cutting the giant trees on land to which they had no title,
but they set up a cry about the unjust treatment they had received,
and asked for $100,000 compensation for the road they had built.

31 S. 1502, S. 1521, H. R. 5747, 53 Cong. 2 Sess. S. 106, S. 1074, H. R. 7256, 54
Cong. 1 Sess.

If this is the true story of this colony it is a story that could be told over and over again in the record of California lumber companies.[32]

It was estimated as late as 1909 that more than half of the giant sequoias were in private hands, and the private hands were those of lumbermen, some of them grasping saws and axes; and almost every Secretary of the Interior from 1893 on called for the government to get title to them. Conservation societies and organizations worked tirelessly to get this done. Where the claims had not been patented this was done, as in the case of the Kaweah; where the claims had been patented the government could either buy them or try to trade other public lands of "equal value" for them. Outright purchase of sequoia groves, by far the best way to get them, was seldom considered in Congress, but late in the year 1899 a critical situation arose with respect to two groves in Calaveras County, north of Yosemite Park, among the first discovered and in some respects the finest of all. The groves had been owned by one J. L. Sperry of Oakland, who held them for years hoping that the government would buy them for a reasonable price; but age and poor health compelled Sperry to sell, for $100,000, to a man named Robert Whiteside, who planned to cut the trees. If they were to be saved something must be done immediately. Various individuals and organizations joined in a chorus of protests against the planned destruction of the trees and in a vigorous demand that the government should save them. President David Starr Jordan of Stanford University wrote letters; the Sierra Club, the San Joaquin Valley Commercial Association, the San Diego Chamber of Commerce, and other men and organizations demanded that the trees be saved. But Whiteside refused to negotiate a sale. Secretary Hitchcock then directed a temporary withdrawal of all vacant land in the vicinity of the two groves, and called on Congress for a law to permit the use of eminent domain to pry the lands out of Whiteside's hands, and wrote a bill to accomplish this.

For once Congress moved with dispatch. Representative De Vries of California introduced a joint resolution on February 12, 1900, and Perkins presented a Senate resolution a week later, authorizing the Secretary to "procure a bond" on the lands and report to Con-

32 S. Res. 150, S. Rept. 1248, 52 Cong. 2 Sess. S. Doc. 48, 55 Cong. 2 Sess. For examples of land frauds, see the author's *United States Forest Policy* (New Haven: Yale University Press, 1920) , 74-77, 224-26.

114 THE EARLY PARKS: 1872-1916

gress. The De Vries resolution passed both houses with little discussion and was signed by President McKinley on March 8, 1900.[33] The next step was to get money to buy the groves; and late in 1903 Representative Gillett and Senator Perkins of California introduced bills to provide up to $200,000 for this. Both bills were reported favorably, even with urgent recommendation that they pass, but Congress was in no mood to squander public money on trees.[34] In the same session an amendment was offered to the appropriation bill, granting $200,000 for purchase, but it likewise failed. Also futile were efforts of Senator Bard and Representatives Daniels of California and Lacey of Iowa to acquire private lands in Sequoia and General Grant by exchange.[35]

Efforts to save the Calaveras groves persisted. It seemed clear that Congress would not appropriate money to buy the groves, and in 1907 Perkins introduced two bills to set them up as the Calaveras Big Tree National Forest, getting the land by trading land or timber outside.[36] The discussions in Congress were rather depressing, for in the face of the threat of losing these irreplaceable monuments most of the statesmen were mainly interested in protecting the public treasury from any possible levies. Representative Underwood feared that the bill might call for an appropriation and wanted an amendment to prevent this; Sherley of Kentucky feared that the government might be mulcted in trades, and objected to consideration of the bill. The constitutionality of the proposal was questioned, although lands had been bought for military parks. Pertinaciously lobbying for the bill, at her own expense, was a San Francisco woman, Mrs. Lovell White, representing the California Club; and the passage of the bill has been attributed largely to her efforts. At any rate the bill passed both houses and was signed by President Taft on February 18, 1909.[37]

The Perkins Act, "to create Calaveras Big Tree National Forest," authorized the Secretary of Agriculture to secure the sequoias in one or both of two ways—the act states *three* ways but only two are evi-

[33] H. J. Res. 170, S. Res. 90, H. Doc. 626, 56 Cong. 1 Sess. Stat. 31, 711. *Report, Secretary of the Interior, 1900,* CLXXXVIII.
[34] H. R. 3581, S. 2223, 58 Cong. 2 Sess.
[35] S. 3376, H. R. 12302, H. R. 9321, 58 Cong. 2 Sess.
[36] S. 8117, 59 Cong. 2 Sess. S. 1574, 60 Cong. 1 Sess.
[37] S. 1574, 60 Cong. 1 Sess. Stat. 35, 626. *World's Work,* June 1909, 11697.

dent— (1) through lieu selections of equal area and equal value, and (2) by giving the right to cut from national forest land an equal amount of lumber. The first method was badly outlined because it would have been difficult to find a lieu selection which was of both equal area and equal value. There was no uncertainty in a final provision, however, that there should be no charge against the United States Treasury.

What happened under the Perkins Act is a rather tangled story, but at any rate the Calaveras North Grove was not acquired under the act. On April 13, 1928, Congress passed an act providing for the transfer to California, upon application by the Governor and approval by federal officials, of 1,200 acres of national forest lands in the area, *between* the North and South groves, provided that the state, within six years, had acquired either the North or South Calaveras Groves, or both.[38] California acquired the North Grove, along with some fine sugar pines, in 1931 with money contributed through the Save-the-Redwoods League ($100,000) and the Calaveras Grove Association ($37,500), the State Park Commission matching these sums. Years later, in 1954, as a result of a long fight by Horace Albright, Newton Drury, Frederick Law Olmsted, the Save-the-Redwoods League and other organizations, and a gift of $1 million by John D. Rockefeller, Jr., the South Grove was acquired by the California State Park Commission. By 1955 the Forest Service managed to use the Perkins Act to acquire some fine giant sugar pines between the two sequoia groves.[39]

Exchange of lands was urged as a means of getting other giant sequoias, by extending the Forest Lieu Act of 1897 to the national parks. Owners of these trees were of course likely to demand a highly advantageous trade, but even at extravagant terms of exchange the sequoias should have been preserved. In 1902 Secretary Hitchcock urged that the Forest Lieu Act be extended to the national parks and a bill was introduced to provide this, but fortunately passed only the House. The timber exchange acts of 1912 and 1914 applied only to Yosemite, but in 1916 the Secretary was

38 Stat. 45, 428.
39 The author is indebted to Frederick A. Meyer, State Park Forester of the California Division of Beaches and Parks, for his kindness in searching out the information on the Calaveras groves, and to George S. James and D. J. Lewis, of the United States Forest Service, California Region.

authorized to accept donations of private lands, and $50,000 was granted to buy an important private grove threatened by cutting. This amount proved insufficient, and the National Geographic Society contributed the additional $20,000 needed.[40]

A number of giant sequoia groves were preserved from private exploitation in the years following the establishment of the Park Service. In 1938 the Park Service acquired the Redwood Canyon Grove at a cost of $655,750 and added it to the new Kings Canyon National Park two years later. A study completed in 1952 showed the following distribution of ownership of giant sequoia lands:

Public ownership:	Acres	Per Cent
National Park Service	14,570	41
U. S. Forest Service	13,315	38
State of California	2,512	7
Other public agencies	840	2
Total public land	31,237	88
Private ownership	4,370	12
Grand total	35,607	100

Of the virgin stands of giant sequoias the Park Service had a somewhat larger percentage, 57, and private owners less, 8 per cent. The Bureau of Indian Affairs had one grove, the Bureau of Land Management part of one grove. Of the lands belonging to California, the California Division of Forestry had four groves, acquired in 1946 at a cost of $550,000; the California Division of Beaches and Parks had the Big Tree State Park (and was later, 1954, to add South Calaveras Grove to it) ; the University of California had one grove, donated in 1915; Tulare County had a part of one grove. Thus California did its part nobly in saving the giant sequoias, and is hoping to add two or three more groves to the state park system. No giant sequoia groves should be privately owned, although in a very few cases private owners are preserving their trees. All such lands should be acquired by the Park Service or the Forest Service or by California for its park system. In very recent years, since 1945, more than half of the privately owned sequoia lands have been logged, in a continuation of the disgraceful regime of vandalism which began in the early sixties.[41]

40 Stat. 39, 308.

41 Report of the California State Park Commission, 1952, as cited above.

In 1926 Superintendent White erected a sign before one of the giant sequoias with an eloquent appeal:

Friends: This is one of the oldest and largest living things on earth. This tree was in lusty growth when Christ walked in Palestine; when Moses gave the ten commandments to the Hebrews, it was a sturdy young tree, a few hundred years old; when the cohorts of the Assyrians descended on Greece, and when Cheops built his pyramid, it was already thrusting a slender spire of tender green into California's blue sky.

Treat this tree with the reverence it should inspire. Do not deface nature's largest and oldest living monument by carving your name, by removing the smallest particle of bark or by trampling down the natural protective covering over the roots. What one person might be permitted to do with insignificant damage to the tree must not be done by the many thousands. We ask your cooperation in preserving this grand old man in his patriarchal perfection for the admiration of your children and your children's children.

John R. White, Superintendent[42]

For twenty years conservationists called for action to save the sequoia groves, and California senators and congressmen introduced a number of bills to buy or to exchange, or perhaps to save the trees by transferring the parks to the Department of Agriculture, or to the general domain—where they could be cut promptly.[43] Representative Fordney of Michigan evinced some interest in extending the Forest Lieu Act of 1897 to these sequoia groves. Fordney was a Michigan lumberman who, when the Michigan forests were about gone, invested in California timber. Perhaps he saw in the Forest Lieu Act a chance to make good trades of some kind.[44]

There were four interesting caves in Sequoia. Secretary Hitchcock reported in 1901 that the Clough Cave had been so vandalized as to be hardly worth saving, but the Palmer Cave was unimpaired. Two other caves were discovered in 1906, Paradise and Marble; but there was insufficient ranger force to protect them and they were closed for years. In 1918 another cave was discovered and explored.

---

[42] *National Parks Bulletin,* No. 48, Feb. 1926.

[43] See H. R. 7017, 59 Cong. 1 Sess; and H. R. 568, 60 Cong. 1 Sess.; by Needham of California.

[44] H. R. 6523, 57 Cong. 1 Sess.

When Stephen Mather took over under the National Park Act of 1916, Sequoia had more than 5,000 visits, more than 4,000 of which were from California, and General Grant had even more, also mostly from California. There were some tent accommodations, but not enough; a poor road had been built to both parks and automobiles were coming in, bringing in some revenue which, added to a $15,550 annual appropriation, enabled the Superintendent to hire a few rangers who served in addition to the troops. In 1911 Secretary Fisher had begun to call for the removal of the troops. Wildlife was being fairly well protected and predators were being killed, and so most "wanted" wild animals were increasing. There was still no judicial machinery or code of penalties for punishment of offenders; these were not to come until 1920, when jurisdiction was accepted.[45]

This brings the story of the California parks down to and beyond the time when Congress passed the act setting up the National Park Service in 1916. By that time ten other national parks had been established: Mount Rainier (1899), Crater Lake (1902), Wind Cave (1903), Sullys Hill (1904), Mesa Verde and Platt (1906), Glacier (1910), Rocky Mountain (1915), and Hawaii and Lassen Volcanic (1916); and the National Park Service assumed general jurisdiction over all the parks in April 1917.

45 Stat. 41, 737.

CHAPTER IV

Mount Rainier Park

Until recently Mount Rainier, elevation 14,410 feet, was rated by fairly common consent the greatest mountain in the United States. Now that Alaska and Hawaii are among the states of the Union, it is dwarfed by the immensity of several Alaskan peaks, including Mount McKinley, which at 20,320 feet is the highest mountain in North America. In the older states four other mountains are higher—Mount Whitney (14,495), in the California Sierra, Mount Elbert (14,431), Mount Harvard (14,420), and Mount Massive (14,418), in the Colorado Rockies; but none of these mountains is so impressive as Mount Rainier, high above the surrounding terrain, symmetrical and ethereal; none has so many glaciers—twenty-six of them covering 40 square miles of the high mountain slopes. The mountain, like many of the isolated mountains of the Cascades, from Mount Baker in northern Washington to Lassen Peak in northern California, is of volcanic origin and steam still issues from vents in the crater. The park is notable mostly for the great mountain and its glaciers, but there are remarkable trees in the park, including giant Western red cedars eleven feet in diameter, and wildflowers that are scarcely equaled anywhere else.

119

EARLY HISTORY   Among the first white men to see "the Mountain" was Captain George Vancouver, a British officer, who saw it in 1792 and named it in honor of his friend Admiral Peter Rainier. While he was at it, Vancouver proceeded to name Puget Sound after a lieutenant, and Mount Hood and Mount Baker after British Lords of the Admiralty, although there had been Spanish settlements in the region before he came.[1] During the next century the mountain was of interest mainly to mountain climbers, two of whom finally reached its summit in 1870.[2]

In 1893 President Cleveland set aside the Pacific Forest Reserve covering the mountain and surrounding region, and in the same year a movement was inaugurated by the National Geographic Society, the American Association for the Advancement of Science, the Geographic Society of America, the Sierra Club, and the Appalachian Mountain Club, to get national park status for Mount Rainier; and Senator Squire and Representative Doolittle of Washington were asked to introduce park bills. These bills provided for setting aside lands of the Pacific Forest Reserve as "Washington National Park."[3] In February 1895 the faculty of the University of Washington adopted a memorial to Congress calling for the establishment of Mount Rainier National Park, "in the interests of science and the public welfare."[4] The following year Squire and Doolittle tried again for a Washington National Park. The Doolittle bill passed both houses, but in the House Committee on Public Lands, the stronghold of the railroad interests, an amendment was tacked on giving a right of way and other extravagant privileges to the Northern Pacific, and these brought strong objection from Senator Vest of Missouri and from President Cleveland, who pocketvetoed the bill.[5] It is significant of the attitude of Congress that Doolittle was obliged to promise not to ask for any appropriation for the park. About this time John Muir urged the establishment of Mount Rainier National Park.

1 *Review of Reviews*, Feb. 1894, 163.
2 See *Outing*, July 1901, 386, for the story of early mountain climbing, and *American Forests and Forest Life*, Aug. 1929, 464.
3 S. 1250, S. 2204, H. R. 4989, S. Misc. Doc. 247, 53 Cong. 2 Sess.
4 S. Misc. Doc. 95, 53 Cong. 3 Sess. *American Forests*, April 1949, 14 ff.
5 S. 164. H. R. 327, H. R. 4058, 54 Cong. 1 Sess.

MOUNT RAINIER NATIONAL PARK

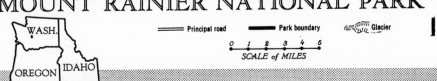

WASH.

OREGON | IDAHO

——— Principal road ▬▬▬ Park boundary 🏔 Glacier

0   1   2   3   4   5
SCALE of MILES

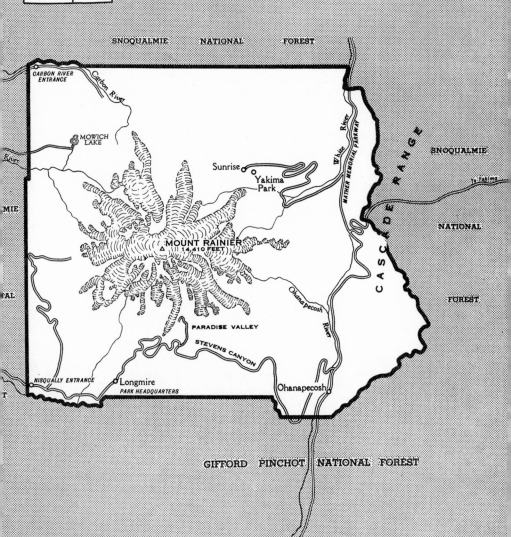

SNOQUALMIE NATIONAL FOREST

CARBON RIVER ENTRANCE

Carbon River

MOWICH LAKE

River

MIE

Sunrise

Yakima Park

White River

MATHER MEMORIAL PARKWAY

SNOQUALMIE

To Yakima

MOUNT RAINIER
△ (14,410 FEET)

NATIONAL

C A S C A D E   R A N G E

Ohanapecosh

FOREST

TAL

PARADISE VALLEY

STEVENS CANYON

River

NISQUALLY ENTRANCE

Longmire
PARK HEADQUARTERS

T

Ohanapecosh

GIFFORD PINCHOT NATIONAL FOREST

To Portland

THE PARK ESTABLISHED   In the next Congress, the 55th, Mount Rainier Park bills were introduced by Senator Wilson and by Representatives Jones and Lewis.[6] The Wilson Bill, with the usual objectionable privileges for the Northern Pacific, but with the name changed from Washington to Mount Rainier, passed both houses and was signed by President McKinley on March 2, 1899.[7] The early establishment of Mount Rainier was possible because there was not much in the area to attract commercial interests. It was very inaccessible, much of the area was bare rocks, and there were no valuable minerals, although it was to take some hundreds of prospectors several years to be convinced of this. Most of the region was too high to be valuable for grazing, or to grow the best grade of trees, and the terrain was so rough as to make any commercial use difficult and expensive. Hunting was good in most of the surrounding country; it was a natural park and not much else. The fact that the Northern Pacific had a large area of rocks in the proposed park which it wanted to trade for good land elsewhere put financial power behind the movement for a park.

THE MOUNT RAINIER ACT   The Mount Rainier Park Act included somewhat the same provisions as the Yellowstone, Yosemite, and Sequoia acts, some of them in identical words. The park was to be under the control of the Secretary of the Interior, who should make regulations for the protection of "all timber, mineral deposits, natural curiosities or wonders within said park." He might grant leases to concessioners and rights of way to any railroad through the adjoining Pacific Forest Reserve and into the park. As in Yellowstone and the California parks, he was to "provide against the wanton destruction of the fish and game found within said park, and against their capture or destruction for the purposes of merchandise or profit." Trespassers were to be ejected, but no penalty was provided. Then followed a provision allowing the Northern Pacific Railroad Company to relinquish any of its lands in the park, or in the Pacific Forest Reserve, that had been granted by the government, surveyed or unsurveyed, and select "lieu lands,"

6 S. 349, H. R. 5024, H. R. 9146.

7 S. 2552, 55 Cong. 2 Sess. Stat. 30, 993. Robert Shankland, *Steve Mather of the National Parks* (New York: Alfred A. Knopf, 1951) , 76, 77.

surveyed or unsurveyed, in any state into or through which the railroad ran. This was outrageously generous, in allowing the selection of *unsurveyed* lands, in any state into or through which the railroad ran. Secretary Hitchcock interpreted this to permit the selection of land *anywhere* in those states. The railroad had only a few miles of road in Oregon, but it was allowed to select lands in the rich timber regions of western Oregon in lieu of snow-covered mountainsides and comparatively worthless mountain lands in the park and forest reserve. It was once stated in Congress that the railroad relinquished 450,000 acres of land within three days after the Mount Rainier act was signed. Many people wanted the park established for perfectly good reasons, but this provision of the act suggests that it was drawn under careful supervision of agents of the Northern Pacific—one of whom was apparently Senator Wilson.[8] A second evil provision of the Mount Rainier act permitted prospecting and mining in the park, and a third provision which was at least questionable extended the Forest Lieu Act of 1897 to the park. This provision was of no importance in Mount Rainier Park, however, because there were only about eighteen acres of private holdings in the park in the beginning, aside from the railroad lands.

EARLY DIFFICULTIES IN ADMINISTRATION   The park had been set aside, but for several years nothing was changed. As in Yellowstone and the California parks, the boundaries were not marked, there was no judicial machinery or schedule of penalties for offenses and no passable roads, miners and mining prospectors had free range of the park; and for seven years there was no money for administration, even for the Superintendent's salary. Three years after the park was established the Secretary persuaded the Forest Supervisor of the State of Washington to take charge, without salary; but with no ranger force the Supervisor could do little.[9] In 1902 Senator Foster of Washington introduced a bill to authorize the Secretary of the Interior to ask the Secretary of War to send troops, as in the earlier parks, which was reported favorably, but

8 See the author's *United States Forest Policy* (New Haven: Yale University Press, 1920) , 184, 185.

9 This is the statement of the Secretary of the Interior, but it has been stated that from 1899 to 1910 Supervisor Grenville Allen, of the Rainier Forest Reserve, served as Acting Superintendent. (*American Forests*, April 1949, 14.)

did not pass. Several years later Senator Piles tried this again with the same result.[10]

The first Congressional recognition of the new park was in money for roads, which were indeed needed for there were no passable roads in the park—$10,000 in 1903 to the Secretary of War for survey and construction, $30,000 the next year, and $50,000 in 1906. The road was built by the widely known builder of national park roads, Major H. M. Chittenden. On the rough, mountainous terrain of the park, road-building was expensive but by 1910 a barely passable road was built as far as Paradise Valley.

WILDLIFE IN THE PARK   For several years the Secretary issued no regulations since there was no means of enforcing them, and hunters, miners and prospectors, and the Cowlitz Indians from the neighboring reservation had free run of the park. At Fairfax, a coal-mining village five miles from the west boundary, some men kept hounds to hunt down the deer and help hunters from Tacoma, Seattle, and elsewhere. Campers often brought in rifles with no purpose but to hunt, and many of the "mining prospectors" were really hunters. Even when money for protection became available not much could be done for the wildlife because of the topography of the park. Like Yellowstone and the California parks, Mount Rainier covered mostly high mountain terrain, which was good range for wildlife in the summer but quite too severe in winter. Snowfall at Paradise Valley, and even at Longmire Springs, is extremely heavy, of generally *wet* snow and few animals can live under such conditions; so they drifted downward out of the park where they were shot by hunters. Already in 1899 the Commissioner of the Land Office, Binger Hermann, and also Bailey Willis of the Geological Survey urged the extension of the park to include lower lands for winter grazing; and this demand was repeated year after year but to no effect. In 1907 Secretary Garfield suggested that the government establish a game refuge in part of the adjoining forest reserve, but Congress paid no attention to the suggestion. The state of Washington for some years prohibited hunting in the fall, but the prohibition was doubtless violated a great deal.

Wildlife suffered not only from hunters and prospectors and campers but of course from predators. In 1905 Secretary Hitchcock

10 S. 270, 57 Cong. 1 Sess. S. 4654, 61 Cong. 2 Sess.

reported that beavers and otters had been exterminated and that mountain goats were diminishing and might be approaching extinction. He suggested that it might be well to try to kill the cougars, and three years later reported four killed. Wolves, bears, wildcats, wolverines, and fishers were also destructive of game, and, except for the bears, these predators were gradually reduced, finally almost to extinction.

The Washington senators and representatives made repeated efforts to get appropriations for roads and administration and, as noted, got some money for roads in 1903 and 1904. In 1906 the prodigal sum of $2,500 was granted for protection and improvement, rising to $5,400 in 1911. In response to the first appropriation Secretary Hitchcock drew up regulations, but there was still no judicial system for the park and no penalties had been provided, except under the general law of 1905 applying to all national parks, which authorized park rangers to arrest law violators.[11]

MINING IN THE PARK   The provision allowing prospecting and mining caused more trouble than anything else. The provision should never have been in the bill, but of course the western men always had an obsession about mining which has done serious damage to other parks, as well as Mount Rainier—Yosemite, for instance. There were no valuable minerals in Mount Rainier, yet an army of prospectors moved in every June with guns and saws and axes, filed claims, cut timber to build shacks, did a few days of nominal assessment work, hunted and fished, and went back to their regular jobs. In 1903 Secretary Hitchcock issued regulations forbidding prospectors or miners to cut any timber or injure any mineral deposits or natural curiosities outside the boundaries of their claims, but of course without any ranger force, he could not enforce the regulations. In 1904 Secretary Hitchcock reported 73 prospectors in the park; in 1905, 90 prospectors; and in 1907, Secretary Garfield reported 165 mining claims located during the year. Doubtless a few represented bona fide hopes of finding a new Homestake, but most of these claims were filed by men who enjoyed the summer in Rainier or hoped to establish rights that would some day be valuable, perhaps for summer homes. One claim was so located as to include trees 10 feet in diameter and larger. In 1914 Secretary

11 Stat. 33, 700.

Lane reported that there had been no ore shipments from any mine, although operations, mostly building of tunnels, had been in progress for twenty years. Every Secretary of the Interior from 1899 on protested against prospecting and mining in the park, and finally, in 1908, a provision was inserted in the sundry civil appropriation bill prohibiting the filing of mining claims; but the Secretary was wrestling with the problem of claims already filed for several years afterward.[12]

TOURIST FACILITIES   Tourists, at first mostly campers, did not come in large enough numbers to do very great damage. At the time the park was set aside there was a wagon road leading in as far as Longmire Springs, just inside the park limits. In 1902 there were two hotels and a tent hotel with eight tents at Paradise Valley operated by a man named John Reece (rate $2.00 a day or $10.00 a week), and one at Longmire Springs owned by James Longmire, who had got title to his land with springs through a mineral claim. By 1906 both hotels had been enlarged to accommodate some thirty guests, and several boarding houses had been set up outside the boundaries. In that year there were 1,786 visits and the accommodations were inadequate. At first Secretary Hitchcock made no leases to concessioners because there were no regulations for the government of the park, but in 1902 he made a lease for transportation, and by 1908 several leases had been made. In making leases Secretary Garfield depended largely on competition to keep the quality of service up.[13]

By about 1908, automobiles were honking to get into the park and Secretary Garfield worked out regulations governing their use. With a written permit from the Superintendent, they were allowed on the government road to a point beyond Longmire Springs, but only between 9 and 11 A.M. and 3:30 and 5:30 P.M. and must be kept ahead of stages. When teams of horses approached they must take a position on the outer edge of the roadway, regardless of the direction in which they were going, being careful to leave sufficient room on the inside for the passage of teams; they must stop when teams approached and remain at rest until the teams had passed or until teamsters were satisfied that their horses were safe. Speed

12 Stat. 35, 365.
13 *Report, Secretary of the Interior, 1908*, 467 ff.

was limited to six miles per hour except on straight stretches where approaching teams would be visible, when, if no teams were in sight, they might increase speed. At or near every bend in the road they must sound their horns. Teams, in short, had the right of way, and autos must allow them safe passage even if that called for backing or handling otherwise.[14] The park was not opened fully to automobiles until 1915.

THREATS OF COMMERCIALIZATION   Early in the history of the park there were schemes for "developing" it, commercializing it, making it attractive to tourists. One scheme proposed, even before the park was established, was to build a tramway or cog road from Paradise Valley to the summit of the mountain, part of the way through tunnels. Another scheme was to build a monument on top to make it the highest or next-highest mountain. In 1908 Secretary Garfield was asked for a lease for the business of quarrying ice from the glaciers on Rainier, to be hauled to Tacoma and Seattle. This would have been first-class ice, but Garfield denied the application.

CESSION OF JURISDICTION   Parks which had merely been set aside were under a sort of joint jurisdiction of the state and the park administration, and to give the federal government, through the park administration, complete jurisdiction it was necessary for the state to cede jurisdiction and Congress to accept it. On March 16, 1901, the Legislature and the Governor of the state of Washington ceded jurisdiction of Mount Rainier Park, but since no money had been appropriated for administration and protection, Secretary Hitchcock did not move to have the cession accepted. Fifteen years later Congress finally passed a bill accepting the cession.[15] Like the California acts ceding jurisdiction over Sequoia, General Grant, and Yosemite, the Washington act ceding jurisdiction reserved to the state the right to tax persons, corporations, franchises, and property, and to collect license fees for fishing in the park. In accepting jurisdiction of Mount Rainier in 1916, Congress finally provided regulations and judicial procedure for their enforcement and penalties for violations.

14 *Ibid.*, 477.
15 S. 3928, by Jones of Washington, 64 Cong. 1 Sess. Stat. 39, 243.

"RAINIER" OR "TACOMA"? A few years after the park was created some people in Washington began to argue that the great mountain should be called Mount Tacoma rather than Mount Rainier, because Tacoma was what the Indians called it—Indian for "The Mountain that was God." There was indeed some sense in their argument and not much logic in naming it after a man, Rainier, who never saw it and, as an English officer, had presumably been fighting against the American colonists a few years before. The Northern Pacific had tried to get the name changed as early as 1883. In 1917 the state legislature adopted a joint memorial petitioning the United States Geographic Board to change the name to Tacoma, but the Geographic Board denied the petition. In 1924 several men in Congress introduced joint resolutions to change the name to Tacoma, or Lincoln, approved by the Governor and by the mayors of Seattle and Tacoma; but none passed, although one passed the Senate.[16] On June 16, 1930, Senator Dill presented in Congress an article by A. H. Denman tracing the history of the names of the mountain and proving that Tacoma—spelled in various ways—was the Indian name, and that Admiral Rainier never even saw the mountain. Mount Rainier was on the maps and in most of the literature, however, and in spite of all agitation, Mount Rainier it remained.[17]

By 1916, when the National Park Service was established, Mount Rainier Park was being fairly well administered and protected. Mining had been prohibited, a good automobile road had been extended to Paradise Valley, appropriations were $30,000, there were several rangers on duty, two of whom remained in the park all winter, predators were being killed and wildlife was increasing, boundaries were established, a judicial system had been set up and penalties provided. The main needs of the park were more roads and better roads, a good hotel—to come in 1917—and more campgrounds, and extensions of the boundaries into lower lands. The Park Service was to be busy with these projects for a number of years.

16 S. J. Res. 64, S. J. Res. 86, H. J. Res. 145, H. J. Res. 192, 68 Cong. 1 Sess.
17 *Congressional Record*, 76 Cong. 2 Sess., p. 10872. See also an article by B. Browne, *Mentor*, July 15, 1918, 1.

CHAPTER V

Crater Lake Park

Crater Lake National Park was set aside three years after Mount Rainier. Just as Mount Rainier is the mightiest mountain in the United States outside of Alaska, Crater Lake might be thought of as the most beautiful lake in the world, for no other lake could be so beautiful. Other lakes have more beautiful surrounding rims or shores—Lake Louise in Banff National Park, Canada, and Jenny Lake in Grand Teton National Park, Wyoming, for instance—but in its lovely, clear, unbelievably blue water Crater Lake stands alone. It lies in the crater of a great extinct volcano, formed by a mighty explosion which blew off the top of Mount Mazama, and gets its deep blue color from its great depth—nearly 2,000 feet. The water in the lake comes altogether from rain and from the 50 feet, or even up to 70 feet, of snow that falls in the crater every year, for no river flows into the lake or out of it. The amount of water from rain and from melting snow is greater than the evaporation, which indicates that there is some sort of subterranean leakage, for the level of the lake remains constant. There were no fish in the lake until 1888, when William Gladstone Steel brought some rainbow trout up from Medford. It has been said that Steel carried about two dozen small fish in a pail, walking the distance in three days, stopping at springs on the way to change the

128

water, and at night burying the bucket at the edge of a stream in such a way that the water could flow in and out, but the fish could not escape. He reached the lake with half his fish alive. For years he worked on the problem of finding the right food for them, for there was no other life in the lake.[1]

EARLY HISTORY   The lake was of course known to the Indians, who were said to have some sort of superstition about it, but it was perhaps first known to white men in 1853. The first authentic account of it came from John Westey Hillman, a young prospector who saw it while leading a party in search of a rumored "Lost Cabin Mine," and named it Deep Blue Lake. Hillman's discovery was apparently forgotten in the excitement of gold discoveries and Indian wars, but in October 1862 another party of prospectors, led by Chauncey Nye, saw the lake and, thinking they had made a discovery, named it Blue Lake. Three years later two soldiers from Fort Klamath discovered it again and named it Lake Majestic. In 1869 visitors from Jacksonville saw it and named it Crater Lake.

WILLIAM GLADSTONE STEEL MAKES HIS DEBUT   Few people visited the lake for years, but in August 1885 Judge William Gladstone Steel saw it and conceived a new purpose in life. Perhaps because he came from Kansas, where water was often deficient and lakes a rare feature of the landscape, Steel was vastly impressed, as almost everyone is at seeing Crater Lake for the first time. There is a story to the effect that when a school boy he had heard of the discovery of the lake and had vowed that he would some day go to see it, but he was in Oregon nine years before he was able to do this. When he stood on the rim and saw the unearthly, unbelievable blue of the lake, lovelier than he ever could have pictured it, he resolved that he would make it a national park; and he devoted the rest of his life to this great purpose, and to the care of the park after it was established. When the government failed to provide adequate funds for protection, Steel stated his life course well, at the 1911 national parks conference: "Aside from the United States

[1] Henry Ottridge Reik, *A Tour of America's National Parks* (New York: E. P. Dutton and Co., 1920) , 112, 113.

government itself, every penny that was ever spent in the creation of Crater Lake National Park came out of my pocket, and besides that, it required many years of hard labor that was freely given. When that was accomplished, I felt that my long labor was finished, and was so green, so simple-minded, that I thought that the United States government would go ahead and develop the proposition. In this, I found that I was mistaken, so I had to go to work again. All the money I have is in the park, and if I had more, it would go there too. This is my life's work, and I propose to see it through."[2]

After seeing the lake, Steel and a few friends sent a petition to President Cleveland asking that it be made a national park. Cleveland could not set up national parks, but five months later he issued an executive order withdrawing ten townships, including Crater Lake, from settlement. Steel devoted the rest of his life to the cause of making the lake known to the people and getting it set aside as a national park, and served as its second superintendent and later as park commissioner until his death.[3]

CONGRESSIONAL INTEREST   There was some Congressional interest in Crater Lake as early as 1886, when Senator Dolph and Representative Hermann introduced identical bills to set the lake aside as a public park.[4] The bills were not reported, but two years later Dolph came up with two bills to set Crater Lake up as a *state* park, perhaps influenced by the precedent of Yosemite Valley. The grant must be accepted by the state within three years, and no timber was to be cut in the park. One of the bills passed the Senate, but moved no further.[5] Undeterred, Dolph brought up another bill two years later, which also passed the Senate; and two years later, in 1892, he and Hermann again brought up state park bills along with a bill to provide for a wagon road to the lake. In discussing Dolph's state park bill the only question raised in Congress concerned the extent to which money received from leases in the park would be used for building roads. Dolph promised that the money

2 Robert Shankland, *Steve Mather of the National Parks* (New York: Alfred Knopf, 1951), 141, 142.
3 *Ibid.*, 74, 75.
4 S. 1111, H. R. 5075, 49 Cong. 1 Sess.
5 S. 16, S. 1817, 50 Cong. 1 Sess.

CRATER LAKE NATIONAL PARK

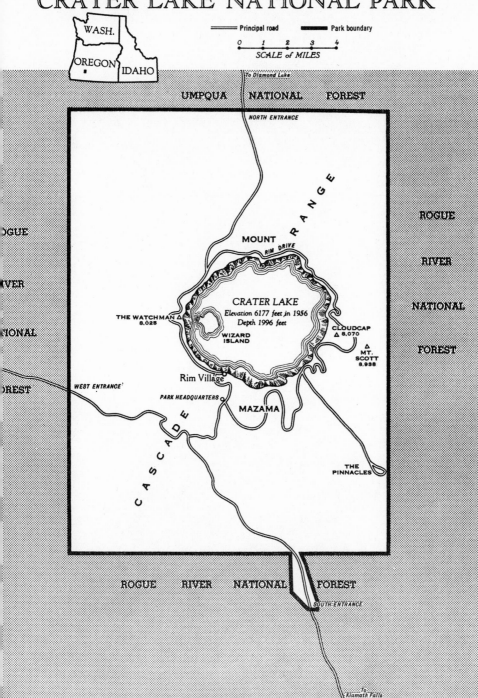

WASH.

OREGON IDAHO

═══ Principal road   ▬▬▬ Park boundary

0   1   2   3   4
SCALE of MILES

To Diamond Lake

UMPQUA   NATIONAL   FOREST

NORTH ENTRANCE

MOUNT

RANGE

RIM DRIVE

ROGUE

RIVER

NATIONAL

FOREST

CRATER LAKE
*Elevation 6177 feet in 1956
Depth 1996 feet*

THE WATCHMAN △
8.025

WIZARD
ISLAND

CLOUDCAP
△ 8.070

△
MT.
SCOTT
8.938

Rim Village

WEST ENTRANCE

PARK HEADQUARTERS

MAZAMA

CASCADE

THE
PINNACLES

ROGUE   RIVER   NATIONAL   FOREST

SOUTH ENTRANCE

To
Klamath Falls

would be used for roads to make the park accessible, and the bill passed the Senate.[6] From the zeal of Dolph and Hermann in pushing for a state park, and from the apparent assumption that the revenues would amount to enough to build considerable stretches of roads, it was evident that few in Congress realized how small would be the revenues and how much the operation of the park and the building of roads would cost. The notion was still widely held that the parks would eventually be self-supporting.

In the next Congress Dolph was up again with bills for a state park and for road-building, and the state park bill again passed the Senate.[7] Soon the state legislature became interested, and petitioned Congress for a guardian for the "Crater Lake Reserve"—there was vandalism and poaching going on; and in 1897 Representative Tongue of Oregon introduced a bill for a national park, supported by many scientists and others. The bill was favorably reported by the House Committee on Public Lands but did not come to a vote.[8] In the next Congress Senator McBride tried for a national park but failed; Tongue tried again, but achieved only the unanimous approval of the Public Lands Committee.[9] In the next Congress Senator Mitchell and Representative Tongue, prodded by Steel, brought up bills, and this time Tongue struck water. His bill allowed mining in the park, and McRae of Arkansas objected to that, and suggested that perhaps too many parks were being created; but there was not much discussion. A section of the bill provided for Army control; there was some objection to that, and it was eliminated in the House Committee. As amended, the bill passed without much debate and was signed by President Roosevelt on May 22, 1902.[10]

The establishment of Crater Lake Park was possible, with relative ease, because it was a small area, highly inaccessible and therefore not much wanted by lumbermen or other commercial interests; and of course the lake was so marvelously beautiful that all observers reported on it in superlatives. Then, too, there was Will Steel, working indefatigably to keep the Oregon senators and representatives on the job of promotion.

6 S. 67, 51 Cong. 1 Sess. S. 625, S. 2888, H. R. 3966, 52 Cong. 1 Sess.
7 S. 69, S. 72, 53 Cong. 1 Sess.
8 H. R. 7200, 55 Cong. 2 Sess.
9 S. 3938, H. R. 2976, 56 Cong. 1 Sess.
10 S. 5261, H. R. 4393, 57 Cong. 1 Sess. Stat. 32, 202.

THE CRATER LAKE ACT　　Like the Mount Rainier Act, the Crater Lake Act authorized mining, but in one respect it was an advance over earlier park establishment acts—it not only authorized the Secretary to establish rules and regulations but prescribed penalties for their violation. Unfortunately, however, it provided no judicial system, no commissioner before whom offenders could be tried, and this was a fairly serious omission because the nearest towns to which offenders could be taken were seventy or eighty miles away, and there were no roads into the park.

FINANCIAL DIFFICULTIES　　A few weeks after the park was established a miracle transpired. Congress voted $2,000 for protection and improvement, as a result of which W. F. Arant of Klamath Falls was appointed Superintendent at $900 a year, and a beginning was made in road building. By 1905 a barely passable road was completed to the crater. Superintendent Arant lived in a tent in the park—at Camp Arant, five miles from the lake—until 1905 when a home and office building were built at Camp Arant, but no shelter for horses. In winter he moved down to Klamath Falls. The buildings in the park fared ill in the heavy snowfall of Crater Lake; they "tended to collapse" in the winter of 1908-9, and had to be rebuilt with heavier timbers, steeper roofs, and better workmanship.

Two years after the park was established there were 1,500 visitors —campers, for there was no hotel until 1914. The campers camped where they pleased and made some trouble, cut boughs from the trees, carved names, set fires, carried guns sometimes and presumably shot game when they could; one ranger (until as late as 1912) could not do much to keep them in order. The park was inadequately protected for years. When the ranger left the park on September 30, poachers and vandals could roam about freely on snowshoes, sometimes doing serious damage. In the winter of 1911-12 vandals broke into a building used as a hotel and used and destroyed supplies and furnishings. When another ranger was added, it was still impossible to protect the park well because one man was needed to issue licenses and register the visitors.

The problem of financing the park would have been a little more manageable if the Superintendent could have kept the receipts from leases and permits, to use in protection and administration but, since the act did not so stipulate, receipts had to be covered into the Treasury. Oregon Senators Bourne and Chamberlain and Representative Hawley tried again and again to get this requirement changed—as in Yellowstone.[11] In 1916 concession receipts were covered into the Treasury in Crater Lake, Mesa Verde, Rocky Mountain, Hawaii and Lassen Volcanics; in the other parks they were used for improvement. In spite of the marvelous beauty of the Lake, appropriations remained at $3,000 nearly every year until 1912. In 1912 the Army Engineers were granted $50,000 for road-building, and other fairly generous appropriations brought some passable roads by 1916.

The provisions authorizing mining did not make much trouble after all, for Secretary Hitchcock construed the mining section to mean that only such mining "as would not interfere with the general purposes of the park" should be permitted, and drew up regulations to that effect, as a result of which there were almost no mining entries.[12]

WILDLIFE   Wildlife did not fare well in the park, partly because there was little ranger protection, partly because, like the other parks, Crater Lake was high, with heavy snowfall; and all the animals, except the bear, went down to lower altitudes outside the park in winter and, being tame, were easily shot there. In 1908 and every year thereafter the Secretary called for an extension of the park into lower territory or for the creation of game preserves adjoining the park on the north and west, but no extension was to come until 1932 when a very small addition was granted to improve the approach to the park. As in the other parks, predator control was soon urged. In 1911 Secretary Fisher indicated that he was in favor of exterminating panthers, bobcats, wolves, and coyotes, but did not say that he was trying to do that. When Mather came in as Director of all the parks he adopted a general policy of predator control.

CONCESSION AND OTHER TROUBLES   For several years there were no concessions in the park, but on May 1, 1907, Secretary Garfield awarded Will Steel a license to operate camping and transpor-

11 S. 8282, 61 Cong. 2 Sess. S. 1174, 62 Cong. 1 Sess. H. R. 26187, 62 Cong. 2 Sess. S. 2223, H. R. 4812, 63 Cong. 1 Sess. H. R. 4666, 64 Cong. 1 Sess.
12 *Report, Secretary of the Interior, 1904,* 434.

tation accommodations and maintain a gasoline launch and row-boats on the Lake. Steel's company, the Crater Lake Company, was accorded a renewal of its license in 1909, and in 1912 the license was surrendered and a new twenty-year lease was granted, covering ho-tels as well as other services. This looked like monopoly in conces-sions, which was wise where there was not much business, but in 1912 Secretary Fisher gave the Klamath Development Company a permit to operate six automobiles for tourists. In 1909 two camps were opened, Camp Crater on the rim and Camp Arant down by the Superintendent's headquarters, five miles below the rim. The Crater Lake Lodge, on the rim, was not opened until 1915, by which time it was greatly needed because in that year there were 11,371 visits, 8,869 of which were from Oregon. Steel was deeply devoted to the park and did all he could for it, but he was not a good businessman and never had enough capital to develop or oper-ate his concessions well. He served as Superintendent of the park after Arant left—1913 to 1916—while still interested in concessions, which was somewhat irregular. Concession troubles were rather chronic in Crater Lake until Mather took over in 1916, and for some time afterward. In 1914 Steel suggested that the government should acquire and lease all hotels and improvements in the parks—a wise suggestion but bound to be ignored.

Private lands were never a very serious problem in Crater Lake, yet there were fourteen land entries at the time the park was set up, eight of which were patented, two approved, and four unapproved bona fide claims. There was danger that summer homes might be built on these holdings, and year after year the Secretary urged that they be bought, but for many years without results.

Cession of jurisdiction over Crater Lake National Park to the United States Government was not accomplished until fourteen years after the park was established. In 1916 Representative Sinnot of Oregon introduced a bill to accept exclusive jurisdiction, and this passed and was signed by the President on August 21, 1916. The bill, as usual with such acceptance bills, included careful regu-lations for the government of the park, and provided for a Commis-sioner at $1,500 a year to preside at court proceedings, who must live in the park—a rather severe requirement, for once snowed in only a vigorous man could get out in winter, on snowshoes. This act was amended in 1935, to eliminate the provision requiring the

Superintendent to live in the park all winter.[13] Steel was appointed Commissioner, in recognition of his great services to the park.[14]

With the acceptance of jurisdiction and with somewhat more generous appropriations, better administration was possible. Yet much remained to be done. The concessions were not well managed, the trail down to the lake was almost impassable, a road was needed around the lake but was being planned; all roads were very dusty much of the summer although there was some sprinkling; private lands should be bought; extensions of the park area were needed into lower lands and northward to take in beautiful Diamond Lake and Mount Thielsen. Some of these things were to come in the years ahead, but unfortunately not the Diamond Lake extension.

13 Stat. 49, 422.
14 H. R. 14868, 64 Cong. 1 Sess. Stat. 39, 521.

CHAPTER VI

Three Inferior National Parks:

Wind Cave, Sullys Hill, and Platt

There were in 1902 six national parks of superlative magnificence; but between 1902 and 1906 three new parks were set aside—Wind Cave, Sullys Hill, and Platt—which did not measure up to this high standard. There was as yet no Congressional policy governing the establishment of national parks, no Park Service to screen park proposals; and these parks just happened to be established.

WIND CAVE   Wind Cave was no doubt known to the Sioux Indians long ago, but it is commonly believed that the first white man to see it was a Black Hills settler named Bingham who, when hunting deer in 1881, heard a strange whistling sound and found it came from a small hole in the ground, the entrance to the cave. At times the air blew into this hole and at other times blew out, according to the barometric pressure outside—hence Wind Cave.

Wind Cave got little attention until 1898, when two geologists made an examination and pronounced it splendid. In 1900 the Commissioner of the Land Office reported that he had heard very enthusiastic reports about the Cave, but since there were some unperfected entries near he did not recommend it as a national park. On June 11 and June 13, 1902, however, Senator Gamble of South Dakota and staunch conservationist Representative Lacey of Iowa introduced bills to set aside Wind Cave as a national park. Apparently Lacey had been misled by some of the glowing reports on the cave, for he described the proposed park as "substantially what the Yellowstone would be if the geysers should die"—a very considerable exaggeration. In Congress there was discussion of the private claims in the area, and some objection to a provision permitting private owners to exchange their holdings for other land on the public domain; but there was not much debate in either house, and Gamble's bill passed and was signed by President Roosevelt on January 9, 1903. As in the case of Yellowstone, the first bill offered to create the Wind Cave Park passed and became law, partly, no doubt, because few men in Congress knew anything about Wind Cave, or about national park principles.[1]

The establishing act set up a park of 900 acres under the Secretary of the Interior, who was directed to prescribe rules and regulations; and penalties were fixed for their violation. The Secretary might use receipts from rentals and leases for administering the park, but no judicial system was set up for the trial of offenses. A strange provision authorized him to lease the cave or parcels of land above it for tourist accommodations. There were ten private entries in the park, four of which were cancelled and one suspended, leaving five valid; the owners were permitted to surrender their land and select other lands on the public domain, but they were slow to make exchanges. Some of the South Dakota school lands were included in the park and the Secretary set for himself the task of trying to trade outside lands for these school lands. Nothing was said in the act about wildlife, for there was little wildlife except prairie dogs.

Congress appropriated $2,500 for management and improvement within two months after the park was established. Forest Supervisor Seth Bullock was directed to assume charge of the park, in collaboration with William Rankin of Deadwood, Superintendent, who apparently owned land in the park—a somewhat irregular arrangement. Rankin must have found his salary of $900 inadequate, for he gave his wife a permit to serve meals to tourists at 50 cents a meal, although he made no leases for several years. There was no

1 S. 6138, H. R. 15086, 57 Cong. 1 Sess. Stat. 32, 765.

need or demand for concessions. Not much was done for the park
for years. A water supply was needed, but this was provided in 1906.
In dry seasons, however, the supply proved inadequate, and in 1911
more was secured by adding to the park lands adjoining on which
there were springs. The cave needed a lighting system, and still
needed it in 1915, although the Superintendent was at that time
experimenting with storage batteries, to avoid the necessity of running wires through the cave.

Although Congress had passed the first Wind Cave bill that was
presented, it soon turned sour on the new park, and whenever appropriations were up there was likely to be some merriment and
satire at the expense of the South Dakota delegation. Appropriations for the park ran at $2,500 every year but one until 1918. In
1912, however, an effort was made to add interest to the park by
establishing a game preserve in it, with a few bison and elk and,
later, antelope and deer, and prairie dogs, which did not need to
be introduced. Congress appropriated $26,000 for the game pre-
serve, the Secretary of Agriculture built a fence around it, added
lands to get more water, built sheds and buildings, and the American Bison Society presented the bison. The enclosure was near the
road so visitors could see the animals, and the animals proved as
attractive as the cave.[2] In 1931 the park was extended by adding a
part of Harney National Forest,[3] and in 1935, in the act amending
the Migratory Bird Law, Wind Cave National Game Preserve was
abolished and all property in it was transferred to Wind Cave National Park.[4]

Some people regard Wind Cave highly, worthy of national park
status. The geologists appear to have thought it was rather splendid
when they studied it in 1898. In 1915 Mark Daniels, General Supervisor and Landscape Engineer of the National Parks reported on
it: "As a curious wonder, I doubt if there is anything in the country which equals the Wind Cave in this park, which contains over
90 miles of explored passages, which are hung with stalactites and
sparkling crystals." Daniels had a somewhat exaggerated notion as
to the extent of the cave.[5] Freeman Tilden, who knows a vast
amount about the national parks, writes of it with modest approval.

2 Stat. 37, 293.
3 Stat. 46, 1518.
4 Stat. 49, 383.
5 *Report, Secretary of the Interior, 1915*, 857.

On the other hand, Secretary Ballinger, in 1910, declared it should not be a national park, and in 1916 R. B. Marshall did not include it in his list of "national parks of the first order." One reason why some of the early observers overrated Wind Cave was that they had only Mammoth Cave, the great cave of the time, as a standard for comparison; Wind Cave does not compare unfavorably with Mammoth. Had the truly magnificent Carlsbad Caverns been known at the time, Wind Cave would have seemed less impressive.

Wind Cave does contain a great deal of what is termed *boxwork* and *frostwork* formations on the walls, and the animals in the game reserve can be seen more easily than those in most other places. It has the advantage of location near a number of other interesting sights. The Black Hills are well forested and modestly impressive. Jewel Cave National Monument, a small but attractive cave is very near, as is the Mount Rushmore National Memorial, where the faces of Washington, Jefferson, Lincoln, and Theodore Roosevelt are chiseled in the mountain in giant size. Within a short distance are the Devils Tower and Badlands national monuments. Not far away, at Lead, a quaint and historic mining town, is the Homestake Mine, the most productive gold mine in the country and often claimed to be the oldest—dating from 1875—and Deadwood, where for those who like cemeteries is the one in which Deadwood Dick, Wild Bill Hickock, Preacher Smith, and Calamity Jane are buried.[6]

Whether such interesting surroundings justify national park status for Wind Cave may be questioned. The unique boxwork designs on its walls suggest that it belongs in the class of national monuments, many of which have some peculiar archeological, geological, or botanical feature, rather than scenic splendor.

SULLYS HILL   The most unworthy national park ever created, if it was created, was the Sullys Hill Park. It was never understood clearly whether it was intended to be a *national* park but it was sometimes referred to and classified as such. It became a park through a fluke. On April 27, 1904, Congress passed a bill amending an agreement with the Indians of the Devils Lake Reservation in North Dakota, and adding a proviso that the President might

6 Freeman Tilden, *The National Parks* (New York: Alfred A. Knopf, 1955), 219 ff. Dorr Yeager, *Your Western National Parks* (New York: Dodd, Mead and Co., 1947), 28-31.

reserve a tract embracing Sullys Hill in a "park" of about 960 acres; and under this provision, the President proclaimed Sullys Hill Park on June 2, 1904, on the shore of Devils Lake. From the name "Sullys Hill Park" it does not appear that the President intended to create a national park. Congress did not create a *national* park here, the President's proclamation did not set up a national park, and the area lacked every attribute of a national park, yet for some reason, perhaps because it was *not* a state park, it was often listed among the national parks, and even later recognized by Congress as such. It was reported that the area included a number of prehistoric mounds where skeletons and copper and ivory trinkets were found, but such reports were gross exaggerations; it was said to contain valuable minerals, but a Congressional appropriation of $5,000 to find these minerals revealed none of value.[7] Aside from this, Congress appropriated nothing until 1914, when $5,000 was granted to provide for a game preserve in the park, to build sheds, corrals and headquarters, etc.[8] In 1931 the "Sullys Hill National Park," as Congress named it, was definitely changed to a national game preserve and transferred to the Department of Agriculture.[9]

PLATT   The springs—some thirty-two of them—near Sulphur, Oklahoma, were bought by the federal government from the Choctaw and Chickasaw Indians in 1902, and jurisdiction over them given to the Secretary of the Interior as a sort of informal reservation. Two years later 78 acres were added to the original 640 acres, and when Oklahoma was admitted to the Union in 1906 the Sulphur Springs Reservation was retained by the federal government.[10] Early in 1906 Representative Sperry and Senator Brandegee of Connecticut presented identical resolutions directing that the Sulphur Springs Reservation be named the "Platt National Park" in honor of Senator Orville Platt of Connecticut, who had been prominent in Indian affairs and had died a short time before.[11] No one raised any questions, and the resolution passed both houses without debate, and was signed by President Roosevelt on June 29, 1906, about

7 Stat. 38, 92.
8 Stat. 38, 434.
9 Stat. 46, 1509.
10 Stat. 32, 655; 33, 220; 34, 267.
11 H. J. Res. 181, S. Res. 69, 59 Cong. 1 Sess.

two weeks after Congress provided for the admission of Oklahoma to the Union.[12]

The new park was not highly regarded by the Department of the Interior. In 1910 Secretary Ballinger left it out of his list of worthy parks and insisted that it should be ceded to Oklahoma, but Oklahoma did not want it. Unfortunately the park had persistent sewer trouble. The springs were located below the town of Sulphur, which had an inadequate sewer system, and the town's sewage tended to overflow the medicinal springs—surely an unfortunate condition. Year after year there were demands for money from Congress to rebuild the Sulphur sewer system; and in 1909 $16,000 was appropriated for this purpose, and $17,500 in 1912, Sulphur to pay half the cost.

The Oklahoma politicians were zealous in their efforts to get money for the park, in addition to the money for the sewer. Senators and representatives from Oklahoma were constantly calling for money for improvement, for a fish hatchery, for a home for disabled veterans in the park, for a railroad, and trolley and telegraph and telephone lines through the park. One Oklahoma representative wanted $30,000 to build roads, causeways, bridges, dams, retaining walls, toilets, repair buildings, purchase tools, and otherwise improve and beautify the park.[13] The legislature of Oklahoma adopted a memorial asking that part of the town of Sulphur be included in the park. These requests did not get a warm reception in Congress. Often when the appropriation for Platt came up there was a great deal of sarcasm and merriment. When one of the appropriation items came up Representative Smith of Iowa said that the park was good for two things: to take care of the five men employed there, and to act as a sewage receptacle for the town of Sulphur; and he recommended that Platt, and also Wind Cave, be given to the states or returned to the Indians. On another occasion Representative Mann of Illinois was moved to wonder how so much money could be spent on a 900-acre plot where there was nothing.[14] In later years there was criticism of the political administration of the park.

Oklahoma senators and representatives defended their park with gusto. They pronounced the scenery splendid, extolled the health-

12 Stat. 34, 837.
13 H. R. 11774, 66 Cong. 2 Sess.
14 *Congressional Record*, 61 Cong. 1 Sess., 3370.

giving and invigorating waters of the springs, and above all pointed to the numbers of visitors—more than were registered at some of the worthy parks. These visitors were largely local, however—people who came occasionally to fish, swim, dance, and dine. Platt would have made a rather attractive city or local park, but not national park.

Congress did not vote extravagant sums for the park, aside from the sewer appropriations—from $5,000 to $10,000 for some years. After the Park Service was established the Service tried to add some interest by introducing a few deer and elk from Yellowstone and bison from the Wichita Mountains National Game Reserve; and a state veterans' hospital was built just outside the park. Years later, Representative Cramton of Michigan, valiant defender of park standards, tried to get Platt abolished or reduced to the status of national monument, but without success.[15]

This discussion of the three questionable or unworthy parks does not, it should be stated, represent the view of men in the Park Service, who voice no criticism and as a matter of fact generously defend all the units of their park domain. These parks show clearly the need there was at the time for the Park Service. Without the Park Service we should no doubt have many more doubtful or inferior parks.

[15] H. R. 8283, H. R. 8284, 71 Cong. 2 Sess.

CHAPTER VII

The Antiquities Act:
The National Monuments

The story of the archeological ruins of the Southwest is a rather depressing story of gross vandalism for many years, somewhat like the vandalism of the giant sequoias; a story of pertinacious but, for several years, futile efforts on the part of a few devoted people and organizations to secure protection, and of final success in saving some of what was left of the ruins and of the priceless archeological objects in them. The events leading up to passage of the Antiquities Act, which enabled the setting aside of special areas as national monuments, also paved the way for establishing Mesa Verde as a national park.

EARLY HISTORY   Most of these archeological ruins—cliff dwellings and pueblos, thousands of them—are in the Southwest, mostly in Arizona, New Mexico, Utah, and Colorado. Some of them were of course seen early by the Spaniards. Father Kino was said to have seen the Casa Grande ruin, in the Gila River Valley of Arizona, as early as 1694, and the Spanish Franciscan missionary and explorer, Escalante, saw and reported on large and conspicuous ruins in 1775—a year before the Declaration of Independence. The

143

Spaniards massacred Navajos in Cañon del Muerto of what is now Canyon de Chelly National Monument in 1805, and very likely knew of the ruins earlier than this. Beginning in 1859, various men visited and explored parts of the Mesa Verde area.

The last inhabitants of these ruins had lived in them for a span of nearly thirteen centuries, but had left suddenly—as history goes— between 1276 and 1300, apparently driven out by a twenty-four-year drought which began in 1276. They abandoned their dwellings in good condition, just as they had been for centuries. Fortunately, the other Indians were not vandals of the cliff dwellings. While the cliff dwellers and pueblo dwellers lived in their homes they were subject to frequent forays by warlike and predatory tribes—this may well have been the reason why they built their homes in the almost inaccessible cliffs—but when they were gone their vacant dwellings were of no interest to the marauding Navajos and Apaches and other tribes. The Spaniards who came later saw no promise of gold in these abandoned apartments and did little damage to them.

But cliff dwellings and pueblos were not the only objects of interest in the Southwest and elsewhere. There were the Petrified Forests in Arizona, living forests of giant cacti, old Spanish missions, natural bridges, caves, gorgeous pink cliffs and canyons, and some important historic sites and buildings dating back only two or three centuries—a great variety of objects of historic, scenic, and scientific importance.

WHOLESALE VANDALISM   When the people from the eastern states began to move into the Southwest, a depressing story unfolds, a story of devastating vandalism. As early as May 9, 1882, Senator Hoar of Massachusetts presented a petition of the New England Historic Genealogical Society, praying that Congress take steps to stop the looting of archeological ruins in the Southwest. Senator Hoar was favorable to the petition, as was also Senator Plumb of Kansas; but Plumb thought it would be quite too costly to guard all the ruins, and that the best plan would be for the conservation associations to go out and loot the ruins first.[1]

Dr. Jesse Nusbaum, for years Superintendent of Mesa Verde Park and perhaps the greatest authority on the archeological ruins, de-

[1] *Congressional Record*, 47 Cong. 1 Sess., 3777.

scribed conditions in the early years as follows: "The heyday, during the 1890's, of wholesale commercial looting of archaeological sites in the Southwest by 'pot hunters' to meet increasing market demands for artifacts and comprehensive collections caused prodigious damaging, destruction and loss of archeological sites and values, since these pot hunters sporadically searched ruin sites solely for maximum salable loot by the most expeditious methods of unscientific excavation."[2]

Elsewhere Nusbaum reported: "This deplorable and destructive looting, which started in the Western States in the mid-1880's, reached its maximum heyday expansion about the turn of the century. In 1904, two years prior to enactment of the Antiquities Act, and on the bases of very critical reports, the Commissioner of Public Lands [General Land Office] instructed Agent Holsinger, of the bureau's Phoenix, Arizona, office, to investigate and terminate, if possible, further excavation in the Chaco Canyon region of New Mexico by the Hyde Exploring Expedition, then concentrating its activities on excavation of the great and classic Pueblo Bonito ruin within the expedition leader's unperfected homestead. The Holsinger investigation terminated forthwith not only further excavations at Pueblo Bonito but the sub-Expedition's digs and lootings of sites since 1893 in the Four-Corners Region of Colorado, Utah, Arizona and New Mexico. Further, Pueblo Bonito and the land about it was withdrawn from the Richard Wetherill unperfected homestead. These factors and ensuing liquidation of this dominant and widely incorporated expedition served as a forthright warning to others to desist."[3]

In his report in 1909, Superintendent Hans Randolph describes the vandalism at Cliff Palace—not included in Mesa Verde Park until 1913: "Probably no cliff dwelling in the Southwest has been more thoroughly dug over in search of pottery and other objects for commercial purposes than Cliff Palace. Parties of 'curio seekers' camped on the ruin for several winters, and it is reported that many hundred specimens therefrom have been carried down the mesa and sold to private individuals. Some of these objects are now in museums, but many are forever lost to science. In order to secure

2 From a letter to the author, Feb. 11, 12, 1959.
3 From letter of Dr. Jesse Nusbaum to Floyd E. Dotson, Department of the Interior, Mar. 7, 1956.

this valuable archeological material, walls were broken down with giant powder often simply to let light into the darker rooms; floors were invariably opened and buried kivas mutilated. To facilitate this work and get rid of the dust, great openings were broken through the five walls which form the front of the ruin. Beams were used for firewood to so great an extent that not a single roof now remains. This work of destruction, added to that resulting from erosion due to rain, left Cliff Palace in a sad condition."4

Dr. Nusbaum, in a letter to the author, gives an account of the manner in which this quotation was salvaged which is perhaps significant of the carelessness with which Mesa Verde was administered at first—perhaps partly because of insufficient funds: "Among historical records found in the wood and coal box at the Superintendent's office at Mancos in 1921 [when Nusbaum became Superintendent] were most of the Park Office records dating from Supt. Randolph's appointment in 1907—including 5 volumes of wet-press carbon copies of long-hand inked, and later typed correspondence and records—500 pages per volume. Supt. Rickner had discarded these prior to my arrival as his successor. Among loose papers were copies of the Annual Reports of the Superintendent to the Secretary of the Interior, later to the Director of the N.P.S. Dr. Edgar L. Hewett [one of the early and most tireless workers for conservation of archeological ruins] rough-drafted the reports that Supt. Randolph submitted—and among these, in Hewett's handwriting, was the report you quote on vandalism in Cliff Palace."5

This vandalism was carried on for years, but it was not until the end of the nineteenth century that much attention was given to it, and not until twenty years later that much was done about protecting these ancient apartments—when Dr. Nusbaum became Superintendent of Mesa Verde Park. Fortunately, some of the cliff dwellings were hidden away in canyons so seldom visited that they were not found until some protection could be given. They were often almost inaccessible except by ladder or toe and handholds cut into the rock formations, some of them built in cliffs of scenic magnificence. The pueblos were usually on flat land, easily accessible, and they suffered more from vandals and also, of course, from the elements. Many were mere heaps of rubble and dirt, which had to be excavated to bring out the outlines of the original apartments.

4 *Report, Secretary of the Interior, 1909,* 486.
5 Nusbaum, *op. cit.*

INTEREST IN PROTECTION   There was some interest in protection fairly early. In March 1889, on an appropriation bill, Congress appropriated $2,000 for the protection of Casa Grande ruin and authorized the President to reserve the land on which it stood, and for years afterward appropriated small amounts for protection.[6] By executive order of June 22, 1892, President Harrison reserved the ruin.[7]

Near the end of the nineteenth century there was an upsurge of protest against the vandalism, and of interest in protection, by heads and staff members of many scientific and educational institutions and organizations: Smithsonian Institution, especially the Bureau of American Ethnology of that institution, the Archeological Institute of America, and the Colorado Cliff Dwellers Association, the latter established and promoted by a tireless worker for archeological conservation, particularly of the ruins in the Mesa Verde area, Mrs. Gilbert McClurg. The Secretary of the Interior, Ethan Allen Hitchcock, was interested, as were also the Commissioners of the General Land Office, Binger Hermann (1897-1902) and W. A. Richards (1903-1906). Commissioner Richards took a particularly active interest in the protection of the ruins. Much concerned too were the Geological Survey and Office of Indian Affairs. At first the various organizations worked separately but later joined forces to present a united front. The secretary of the Smithsonian Institution designated Dr. Edgar L. Hewett, at the time ethnological assistant in the Bureau of American Ethnology, to serve at Washington as secretary to the representatives of the institutions and organizations that were working for protection of the ruins. From that time on Hewett worked closely with the interested government departments and offices, and with Representative John F. Lacey of Iowa, chairman of the House Public Lands Committee.

JOHN F. LACEY, STAUNCH CONSERVATIONIST   Representative John F. Lacey of Iowa, so prominent here, was one of the towering figures in the conservation movement, interested in conservation of various resources. As we have seen, it was he who introduced the bill for the protection of Yellowstone wildlife in 1894, and secured the law of 1900 for the protection of wildlife generally. In the field

6 Stat. 25, 961.
7 Exec. Order 28A.

of antiquities he was working indefatigably all the time for the protection of the archeological ruins, including those in the Bandelier
area. In forest conservation he was always ready to do battle for the
protection of the forest reserves and for wise use of the public domain. When the western land looters tried to secure the revocation
of President Cleveland's forest reserve proclamations of February
22, 1897, it was Lacey who headed them off and saved the reserves.
In 1900 he tried, unsuccessfully, to get a law to permit forest rangers to arrest vandals engaged in violation of regulations, and tried
also to secure a law authorizing a charge for grazing privileges on
the forest reserves. In 1904 the western men were pushing a bill to
open, without discrimination, agricultural lands in the forest reserves to settlement; it was Lacey who checked this and reserved
control of the land elimination to the Secretary. In 1905 he tried,
without success, to repeal the iniquitous Timber and Stone Act.
Without Lacey's pervasive and persistent influence, the history of
conservation in the United States would be very different, and our
situation today would be worse, perhaps very much worse.[8]

SOME PROTECTION AFFORDED   In 1904 Hewett reported
that he had been able to get custodians only for Casa Grande, Walnut Canyon and Cañon del Muerto, but Commissioner Richards
did all he could. He got several important ruins withdrawn from
settlement: Pajarito (the area around and including Bandelier),
Jemez Cliff Dwellers' region, El Morro or Inscription Rock, Mesa
Verde and Montezuma Castle; but could do little for their protection. However, he sent out a letter asking forest supervisors to have
their rangers protect as well as possible the ruins on forest reserves;
he and Secretary Hitchcock posted notices at or near all important
ruins, forbidding trespass. Even without a specific law, the General
Land Office could punish vandals for trespass—if it had anyone
around to arrest them. Richards also tried to get the Indian Service
to help protect ruins in Canyon de Chelly, and he tried to enlist
the help of superintendents of Indian Schools, agents, and farmers.
So Richards, with the help of Hewett, worked out a policy which,
as he expressed it, "mobilizes, so to speak, a force of forest supervisors, rangers, special agents, Indian school superintendents and

8 See the author's *United States Forest Policy* (New Haven: Yale University
Press, 1920) , 129-131, 162, 163, 172.

teachers, Indian agents and police, and even enlists the Indians themselves, a particularly sagacious step, in the protection of these ruins. . . ."9 Yet the protection was grossly inadequate.

ARCHEOLOGICAL PROTECTION IN CONGRESS   There was thus a great deal of interest in preserving archeological ruins before 1900, but the Antiquities Act was not passed until 1906. One reason it took so long was that it was difficult to get all interested parties to agree on the provisions that should go into the act. On February 5, 1900, Representative Dolliver of Iowa introduced a bill for the preservation of archeological ruins and objects which would have authorized the President, or the Secretary of the Interior or the Commissioner of the General Land Office, under his direction, to set aside "as a public park or reservation, in the same manner and form as now provided by law and regulation for forestry reservations, any prehistoric or primitive works, monuments, cliff dwellings, cave dwellings, cemeteries, graves, mounds, forts, or any other work of prehistoric or primitive man, and also any natural formation of scientific or scenic values or interest, or natural wonder or curiosity on the public domain," with a suitable acreage of surrounding land. Whether Dolliver's bill was introduced at the request of the Smithsonian Institution or perhaps of John F. Lacey—also from Iowa—is not clear, but at any rate it was broadly generous in covering other than archeological values.10 Dolliver was a progressive, and a friend and supporter of Theodore Roosevelt.

The next day Representative Shafroth of Colorado introduced a bill which simply provided that any destruction, injury, or carrying away of any ruin or antiquity should be punished by fine and imprisonment.11 About a month later Shafroth introduced another bill under which the Geological Survey was to make surveys in the four states where the archeological ruins were and report to the Secretary those worthy of reservation. The Secretary might then set these aside, with not to exceed 320 acres of land, and turn them over to the custody of the Bureau of American Ethnology of the Smithsonian Institution.12 This bill was obviously defective in at

9 *Science*, n.s. Vol. XX, No. 517, Nov. 25, 1904.
10 H. R. 8066, 56 Cong., 1 Sess.
11 H. R. 8195, 56 Cong., 1 Sess.
12 H. R. 2245, 56 Cong. 1 Sess.

least two respects: the Geological Survey was not the most competent agency to determine the value of ruins, and the Smithsonian
Institution was not well equipped to administer them.

The Dolliver and Shafroth bills were referred to the House Public Lands Committee and, on March 9, 1900, Lacey, the chairman of
that committee, turned the bills over to the Secretary of the Interior
for his report on them. The Secretary in turn asked the Commissioner of the General Land Office, Binger Hermann, to report on
them. Hermann, while approving of the general purpose of the
bills, and agreeing that the archeological reservations should be set
aside by Executive proclamation like the forest reservations—rather
than by Congress, because Congress could not act with enough expedition—found none of the bills satisfactory. The first Shafroth
bill was too meager in its provisions, the Dolliver bill had some unnecessary provisions, and the second Shafroth bill was defective in
providing for surveys by the Geological Survey and custody by the
Smithsonian Institution. Hermann therefore prepared a substitute
bill which was introduced by Lacey on April 26, 1900.[13]

The substitute bill authorized the President to reserve tracts of
public land "which for their scenic beauty, natural wonders or
curiosities, ancient ruins or relics, or other objects of scientific or
historic interest, or springs of medicinal or other properties it is
desirable to protect and utilize in the interest of the public." Thus
the bill was broad in its authorization. The reservations were to be
called "national parks" and the Secretary was to protect them and
was authorized to permit examinations by qualified scientific and
educational institutions. He might also grant concessions for the
entertainment of visitors. Severe penalties were provided for violations of the regulations for protection.

Although Lacey introduced the substitute bill, he wrote Secretary Hitchcock that the Public Lands Committee did not favor the
provision authorizing the Department of the Interior to create
national parks and thought the areas reserved should be restricted
to 320 acres. Secretary Hitchcock replied that the bill did not authorize the Department of the Interior to set aside national parks,
but rather the President, and he thought 320 acres might not be
enough. This was on April 24, 1900.

In the meantime, a Public Lands Committee bill had been introduced by Shafroth on April 5, 1900, and reported by the committee,

13 N. R. 11021; 56 Cong. 1.

which restricted the areas set aside to 320 acres, in the two states Colorado and Utah, and the territories of New Mexico and Arizona; but no further action was taken. Four other bills were reported but got no further.[14] In the next session Delegate Perea of New Mexico brought in a reservation bill which got no attention.[15]

In 1902 Lacey made a trip to New Mexico, and with Edgar L. Hewett visited some of the ruins and came away with a firm determination to get some protection for them, a determination which President Roosevelt shared. Roosevelt leaned heavily on Lacey in pursuing his conservation policy.[16]

For several years thereafter little was done about antiquities, although the Commissioner of the General Land Office persistently, in every report, called for legislation. Finally, on March 4, 1904, Lacey presented again the amended Committee Bill (similar to H. R. 10451 above).[17] A month before this, Senator Cullom of Illinois introduced a bill which authorized the reservation of archeological ruins only—not scenic lands etc.; and Commissioner Richards objected to this limitation, and also to a section providing a sort of joint custody by the Secretary of the Interior and the Smithsonian Institution.[18] He urged the introduction again of the Committee Bill (H. R. 13478). Governor Alexander O. Brodie of the territory of Arizona wrote a letter to the Secretary of Agriculture strongly recommending federal supervision of the ruins in Arizona and the establishment of a small reserve around each one. At this time there was some interest in the establishment of reserves to protect Montezuma Castle and Mesa Verde, which tended to fan the interest in the preservation of all antiquities.

A number of bills were introduced about this time, in the 58th Congress, by Representative Hitt of Illinois.[19] Delegate Rodey of New Mexico,[20] Representative Rodenberg of Illinois,[21] and Senator Lodge of Massachusetts.[22] The Rodenberg-Lodge bill was referred to the Committee on Public Lands, and hearings were held

14 H. R. 10451, 56 Cong. 1 Sess.
15 H. R. 14227, 56 Cong. 2 Sess.
16 *Art and Archeology*, Aug. 1920, 3.
17 H. R. 13478, 58 Cong. 2 Sess.
18 S. 4127, 58 Cong. 2 Sess.
19 H. R. 12447.
20 H. R. 12141.
21 H. R. 13349.
22 S. 5603.

before a subcommittee of that committee, on April 22, 1904, at
which a number of educational and scientific institutions and Commissioner William A. Jones of the Office of Indian Affairs testified.
The consensus of those testifying was that the Rodenberg-Lodge
bill was the best yet offered, and the bill passed the Senate but proceeded no further.

There was continuing interest in protection. In September 1904
Professor Hewett submitted a report on the continuing vandalism
which did not mince words: "It is well known that during recent
years an extensive traffic has arisen in relics from these ruins. In
securing these, buildings, mounds, etc., have been destroyed. These
relics are priceless when secured by proper scientific methods and of
comparatively little value when scattered about either in museums
or private collections without accompanying records. No scientific
man is true to the highest ideals of science who does not protest
against this outrageous traffic, and it will be a lasting reproach upon
our government if it does not use its power to restrain it."

THE LACEY ACT   By 1905 there had been ample debate and
discussion of the various bills and of the best provisions of an antiquities bill, and on January 9, 1906, Lacey introduced a new bill,
drafted in the office of Commissioner Richards with the co-operation
of Lacey and Dr. Hewett, which was reported with minor amendments and referred to the Committee of the Whole House.[23] Lacey
asked Senator Patterson of Colorado to introduce an identical bill
in the Senate,[24] which was reported on favorably by Commissioner
Richards, reported unanimously for passage by the Senate Committee on Public Lands, passed immediately, on the next day was referred to the House Public Lands Committee, reported to the House
and passed on June 5, 1906, and was approved by President Roosevelt on June 8, 1906. Thus it was the Patterson Bill that became
law, but the Antiquities Act is called the Lacey Act, because Lacey
was the moving spirit behind it.[25] There was little debate, and the
only objection was voiced by Senator Stephens of Texas who feared
that it would tie up large areas of land. It was reported in the hearings that Senator Teller would oppose any bill that did not establish

23 H. R. 11016, 59 Cong. 1 Sess.
24 S. 4698.
25 Stat. 34, 225.

a maximum limit of 640 acres for any reservation, but that limit was not in the act that passed.

The Act for the Preservation of Antiquities, the Lacey Act, started with a penalty—not more than $500 fine or ninety days' imprisonment for destroying, excavating, or injuring any historic or prehistoric ruin or monument or any object of antiquity situated on lands controlled by the United States. Thus the law applied to most of the ruins, for many of the ruins were located on the public domain, or forest reserves, or on Indian reservations over which the United States had some control. The President was authorized to set aside by proclamation historic spots, landmarks, structures etc. on government lands, or if on land privately claimed the Secretary of the Interior was authorized to accept gifts of such lands. Permits for the examination of ruins, for excavation and the gathering of objects of antiquity might be granted by the Secretary having jurisdiction over the land—Interior for public lands, Agriculture for forest reserves, and War for lands controlled by the War Department—to qualified persons, for the benefit of reputable museums, universities, colleges and scientific or educational institutions; and the Secretary of the proper department was instructed to publish rules and regulations.

FOSSILS AND OTHER OBJECTS OF SCIENTIFIC INTEREST   The act obviously referred principally to archeological ruins, to the ancient cliff dwellings and pueblos, although "historic" as well as prehistoric ruins were included, and "other objects of scientific interest." This was a fortunate inclusion. Within a year or two Secretary Fisher of the Department of the Interior submitted to the Secretary of the Smithsonian Institution an application for a permit to collect fossil remains of great vertebrates on an Indian reservation, for his recommendation, saying that he was uncertain whether the Antiquities Act covered fossils. Secretary Wolcott replied that whether intended or not, he thought fossil collecting should be handled under the act because of the extensive laboratory work and expense involved in preparing and mounting specimens for exhibition. Thereafter paleontological permits were required for fossil collecting on federal lands, whether animal or plant.

This did not settle the question to the satisfaction of some paleontologists, who objected to the requirement that they get permits for collecting fossils. The Antiquities Act had forbidden collection of archeological or "scientific" objects on any land controlled by the United States, without permit, and for years some paleontologists collected fossils and other objects on the public lands without permits. Dr. J. LeRoy Kay, for instance, at one time head field explorer, geology and paleontology, and later curator of vertebrate paleontology, of Carnegie Museum of Pittsburgh, and others, for years roamed the western states collecting fossils and also archeological objects, without permits. Dr. Nusbaum filed charges against him. Such violations were fairly common up to very recent years. The Society of Vertebrate Paleontology has tried to get the Antiquities Act or the regulations relating to it amended to release its members from permit requirements.

NATIONAL PARKS AND NATIONAL MONUMENTS   The word "monument" presently applied to reservations under the act was not well chosen, for a great variety of objects were reserved. Battlefields, forts, mountains, canyons, cliffs, glaciers, sand dunes, islands, caves, deserts, trees, cacti, birthplaces of famous men, church missions and homesteads: most of these cannot appropriately be called "monuments." Perhaps "national reservations" would be a better word, although "national monuments" has been used so long that its meaning is not too obscure to those familiar with the subject. Perhaps we are merely inventing a new meaning for the word "monument."

Yet there has been some misunderstanding of the word, particularly as to the distinction between national "monument" and national "park." Superintendent of National Parks R. B. Marshall said in 1917 that the principal difference between a monument and a park is that a national monument is merely made safe from encroachment by private interests and enterprise, while a national park is in process of development by roads and trails and hotels to make it a convenient resort for the people to visit and enjoy.[26] This has some truth in it, but it is not altogether correct; some national monuments, as for instance the Petrified Forest, are "developed" in somewhat the same way as national parks, and some national parks, as for instance Isle Royale and Kings Canyon, have few or no roads or hotels within park limits.

26 Report, Secretary of the Interior, 1916, 753, 754.

Frank Bond, chief clerk of the General Land Office, speaking at the First National Park Conference in September 1911, had pronounced parks and monuments "as alike as two peas in a pod"; and Horace Albright, later Director of the National Park Service, agreed that they were "practically identical" but that the monuments were usually smaller. This comes near the truth. Nearly all the national parks are areas of outstanding grandeur or of outstanding merit in some other respect; national monuments are areas which are not sufficiently outstanding to justify park status, yet have some scenic or other value which calls for government protection and control. Also, the term "national monument" includes an extraordinary diversity of values. Frank Waugh once correctly said: "A National Monument is a piece of land containing from 1 to 1,000,000 acres, either flat or rough, timbered or bare. . . . But the most clearly outstanding character of the National Monument is its complete inconsistency."[27] In the manner of their establishment, national parks are set up by Congress, and national monuments by Congress or by Presidential proclamation.[28]

Several of the national parks were first proclaimed as national monuments, and here appears one of the most valuable uses of the Antiquities Act. In several cases where a given area was recognized as outstandingly magnificent the President has proclaimed it a national monument, and so protected it and forestalled further private land claims until Congress, almost always dilatory in such matters, could make it a national park. Of course the President is likely to be guided by the advice of someone familiar with park matters—the Secretary of the Interior, the Secretary of Agriculture, the Commissioner of the Land Office, or even more particularly, someone in national park management. National monuments set up on the public domain, which was controlled by the Secretary of the Interior, remained under his control; those set up in forest reserves, which were under control of the Secretary of Agriculture, remained under his control until 1933; and two monuments set up on lands belonging to the War Department remained under the control of the Secretary of War until 1933.

27 *Outlook*, Sept. 28, 1921, 130.
28 *Report, Secretary of the Interior, 1917*, 784 ff. *National Parks Magazine*, July-Sept. 1956, 99.

NATIONAL MONUMENTS ESTABLISHED   Secretary Hitchcock
of the Department of the Interior, Secretary James Wilson of the
Department of Agriculture, and Secretary William Taft of the War
Department drew up a careful schedule of regulations, and President Theodore Roosevelt promptly made use of the new Antiquities
Act and set aside a number of national monuments within two
years. *Devils Tower* in eastern Wyoming was the first, on September
24, 1906, a great fluted, almost perpendicular shaft of volcanic
basalt pushing 865 feet above the surrounding terrain; on December 8, 1906, he proclaimed three—*Petrified Forest* and *Montezuma
Castle* in Arizona, and *El Morro* or Inscription Rock in New Mexico.
The Petrified Forest had attracted a great deal of attention for
years because of the gross vandalism, and there had been many
efforts in Congress to establish it as a national park. Lacey was particularly interested in the preservation of the petrified wood; he
knew that it was being hauled away by the wagonload, that vandals
were even blowing up the trees to get at the most beautiful mineral
formations; but his efforts were unavailing. In response to a House
memorial of the legislature of Arizona in February 1895, Commissioner of the Land Office Binger Hermann had made temporary
withdrawal of the area from all entry in 1896 and 1899, but of
course this afforded no protection from vandalism. Administration
of this monument was difficult at first because the Santa Fe Railroad owned half of the land, in alternate sections. The government
was later able to make exchanges for the railroad lands. The
Painted Desert was added to the monument in 1932.[29]

Montezuma Castle is an impressive five-story cliff palace, one of
the best preserved, high up in the face of a cliff. To it was added
Montezuma Well in 1947, a peculiar well or deep pool high up on
the hillside. El Morro is a high cliff, "Inscription Rock," on which
are carved prehistoric petroglyphs and hundreds of inscriptions of
early Spanish explorers and early American emigrants and settlers.
Among them is the inscription of Don Juan de Onate, made in
1605—fifteen years before the Pilgrims landed at Plymouth Rock.

President Roosevelt's next monument was *Chaco Canyon* in
northwestern New Mexico on March 11, 1907, including the ruins
of the Pueblo Bonito, the "beautiful village," which at one time

29 H. R. 10368, 54 Cong. 2 Sess., H. R. 1113, 55 Cong. 1 Sess.; H. R. 9634, 56
Cong. 1 Sess.; H. R. 8326, 57 Cong. 1 Sess.; H. R. 2529, 58 Cong. 1 Sess.; H. R.
8966, 59 Cong. 1 Sess. *Report, Secretary of the Interior, 1900*, 396.

had 800 rooms—one of the largest apartment houses in the world at one time, of the finest masonry construction found in any pueblo. Soon afterward he set aside *Lassen Peak* in northern California, a volcano erroneously believed to be dead, and *Cinder Cone,* a perfectly formed volcanic cone nearby, both to be included later in Lassen Volcanic National Park. Late in 1907 came *Gila Cliff Dwellings* in a canyon of the Gila River in southwestern New Mexico; and *Tonto,* pueblo cliff dwellings in Arizona.

Some of these proclamations did not prohibit forestry or other uses, but no destruction was permitted, and the monument use was declared the dominant use.

Early in 1908 Roosevelt proclaimed the *Muir Woods* National Monument near San Francisco, the only area covering California redwoods in the national park system. These giant redwoods had been saved from the lumbermen by former Congressman William Kent and his wife, who offered the grove to the government, asking that it be named not after themselves but after the famous naturalist John Muir. Mr. and Mrs. Kent made several additional gifts later. Two days after Muir Woods came *Grand Canyon,* later to become a national park; a few days later *Pinnacles* in California, a small area of rough canyons, spires and domes hundreds of feet high; then *Jewel Cave,* a small cave coated with dogtooth spar in the Black Hills; and the *Natural Bridges* in southeastern Utah, which covers several natural bridges, the largest 220 feet high, in magnificent red rock surroundings. (In February 1916 President Wilson was obliged to proclaim this monument again because the first survey had been incorrect.) A month later, on May 11, 1908, the *Lewis and Clark Cavern* in Montana was proclaimed; a few months later, the *Tumacacori Mission* in Arizona, one of the chains of missions built by the Jesuit Fathers about two hundred to three hundred years ago, badly abused by vandals but partly restored. The United States Government believed it had title to the land on which the mission stood, but private owners later proved their title good, and then gave the land to the government. In December 1908 *Wheeler* National Monument was proclaimed—like Pinnacles, an area of weird canyons and spires—near Creede, Colorado. Here the ill-fated expedition of John C. Fremont had met disaster in 1848. This monument was later abandoned.

President Taft continued the good work, setting aside *Mount Olympus* National Monument on the Olympic Peninsula in Wash-

ington in March 1909, an area of majestic mountains and some of
the densest forest growth in the world. A few weeks later he set
aside the *Navajo* National Monument in Arizona, covering three of
the largest and most spectacular cave villages in the Southwest—
Betatakin, Keet Seel, and Inscription House—built in great caves in
mighty cliffs which in themselves are scenic attractions. Luckily
these cliff dwellings were discovered late—in 1893 and 1909—and
were subject to little vandalism. In 1912 the monument was reduced
in area to three separate plots, one for each village.[30] In September
1909 Taft proclaimed *Shoshone Cavern* in Wyoming, beautiful but
for years inaccessible to visitors and finally, in 1954, turned over to
the city of Cody for a public park, with the provision that if Cody
failed to care for it, it should revert to the United States. Taft also
enlarged the Natural Bridges Monument to take in ruins nearby.
On July 12, 1909, he set aside the *Oregon Caves,* a series of subterranean rooms, some very large. In November 1909 he proclaimed
the *Gran Quivira,* the ruin of another early Franciscan mission in
New Mexico, begun in 1629, and enlarged the *Casa Grande Ruin*
Reservation near Florence, Arizona, an ancient clay watchtower
four stories high, built about 1350. This area was first established as
a sort of national park in 1889, but the land described in the
creating act for some reason did not cover the ruin, and President
Taft's proclamation brought it in. In March 1910 the President invaded more recent history by proclaiming the *Sitka* National Monument, covering the site of the "Battle of Alaska" between the Rus-
sians and the Alaskan Indians from 1802 to 1804, and including
some totem poles that had deteriorated badly and needed protection. In May 1910 *Rainbow Bridge* was set aside in southern Utah,
near the Arizona line, the largest natural bridge in this country or
perhaps in the world, 309 feet high, with a span of 278 feet—large
enough to cover the Capitol Building at Washington—a pink-rock
bridge in gorgeous, magnificent surroundings of pink and red rocks,
cliffs and canyons, quite worthy of national park status. Rainbow
Bridge had been discovered the previous year. On June 23, 1910,
he set aside the *Big Hole Battlefield,* the scene of an important
battle along the route of the famous retreat of the great Chief
Joseph and his Nez Perce Indians in 1877. About this time several
monuments were reduced in size—Petrified Forest, Navajo, and

30 *National Parks Bulletin,* No. 54, Nov. 1927.

Mount Olympus. Most of the national monuments were located in little-known regions, perhaps unsurveyed, and it was inevitable that some corrections in size and boundaries would be found necessary.

President Taft rested from his labors for nearly a year, then in May 1911 issued a second proclamation covering an addition to Lewis and Clark Cavern in Montana. Part of the land in this monument was owned by the Northern Pacific Railroad, which generously donated its land to the government for use as long as the monument was maintained. A few days later, at the request of Edward Taylor, Representative from Colorado, he proclaimed *Colorado* National Monument in western Colorado, near Grand Junction, an impressive nature-sculptured red rock mountain; and in July the *Devils Postpile,* in the Sierra, which commercial interests had managed to have eliminated from Yosemite Park in 1905, was proclaimed a national monument. While it was under control of the Forest Service, an application had been filed for permission to blast the basaltic columns into the San Joaquin River to dam it for mining operations, but this was denied by the District Forest Service Engineer; and to make it safe from spoliation Taft had made it a national monument, still under control of the Forest Service. In the proclamation he was obliged to state that the forest uses of the land should not be impaired.

President Woodrow Wilson was as much interested as his predecessors in parks and monuments, and set aside several monuments between 1913 and 1919. In October 1913 he proclaimed the *Cabrillo* National Monument, honoring the discoverer of California, on Point Loma, near San Diego; and in January 1914 proclaimed *Papago Saguaro* in Arizona, to protect the giant cacti, yucca palm, and other characteristic desert flora and some prehistoric pictographs. The Saguaro is one of the most remarkable desert plants, growing to a height of more than fifty feet, and achieving a weight of ten tons, the older plants with limbs growing straight up. The great cacti were and still are subject to two grave hazards, a bacterium that kills many of the older plants, and a failure to reproduce in new growth, apparently because of man's disturbance of the natural conditions in the desert area. There was, and still is, doubt as to the survival of the species when the present stands are gone—which would not be very soon, however, because the Saguaro are estimated to live as long as two hundred years.

In October 1915 President Wilson set aside the *Dinosaur* National Monument in northwestern Colorado, a small area covering dinosaur footprints and bones, which had been withdrawn previously for its possible coal and phosphate deposits. A few weeks later he proclaimed *Walnut Canyon* in Arizona, with many cliff dwellings already badly despoiled by vandals.

Some years after the Antiquities Act was passed some of the western men saw that the reservation of some of these areas was a threat to the economic "development" of their states, and turned sour on the reservation policy. Many bills were introduced to amend the act, some of them to abolish the President's power to set aside national monuments; but the attempts always failed.

INADEQUATE PROTECTION   The proclamation of these national monuments protected those on the public domain—controlled by the Department of the Interior—from further private land claims; those in the Forest Reserves were not subject to land claims. Otherwise the monuments were afforded little protection because Congress did not vote any money for protection until 1916, ten years after the Antiquities Act was passed, and then only $3,500 for the protection of some thirty widely scattered national monuments—about $120 each—and not much more for another ten years. It is true that it was a violation of law to despoil the monuments, but most vandals cared little about that when there were no rangers around.[31]

More than protection was needed. Many of the archeological monuments needed a great deal of excavation work. Many ruins were covered, some completely covered, with earth and rubble that had drifted over them for centuries, and only by patient excavation could their outlines be brought to light. For such ruins as Chaco Canyon this was a monumental job. Some of the ruins were in need of repairs, with foundations settling, walls cracked, and adobe or clay mortar between the rocks disintegrating. Repair work was a delicate task, for the idea followed was to preserve the original character of the ruin as far as possible—using earthen or soil cement, for instance, rather than modern cement. Repair, not restoration,

31 A grant of $2,000 was made in 1889 to protect and repair the Casa Grande Ruin Reservation, sometimes called a national park but later made a national monument.

was the purpose, prevention of further disintegration rather than any attempt to rebuild the ruins to their original condition. "It is better to preserve than to repair; better to repair than to restore; and better to restore than reconstruct."

Fortunately the government found ways to secure a small measure of protection without funds. Representatives of the departments having jurisdiction over the monuments were sometimes able to designate employees in the vicinity as temporary custodians. This was of course unsatisfactory, for these men had other jobs that required most of their time, but it was better than no protection at all. For examination, excavation, and repair work the Secretaries of the Interior and of Agriculture depended on scientific organizations, museums, and universities. Soon after the Antiquities Act was passed, uniform regulations governing this work were issued, and in 1907 the Secretary of the Interior reported eighteen applications for permission to make examinations, to excavate and gather antiquities, eight of which were granted. A number of scientific societies engaged in this work: the Archeological Institute of America, the Smithsonian Institution, the Peabody Museum of Harvard, the School of American Research, the Royal Ontario Museum of Toronto, the Bureau of American Ethnology, the American Museum of Natural History, and a number of universities. These agencies of course carried away the antiquities that they found, but they did to some extent protect the monuments where they were working. Perhaps some of the antiquities serve a more important use in great museums in the cities than they would at the monuments, even if there were museums on the grounds in which to keep them. A few foreign scientists worked in the monuments. A German scientist was allowed to take 500 pounds of petrified wood from the Petrified Forest.

This brings us down to 1916, the time of the establishment of the National Park Service. The national monuments created thereafter will be discussed in connection with the creation of national parks.

It should be noted at this point that national parks and monuments were not the only kind of reservations being established during these years. In the early nineties Congress inaugurated a policy of establishing national military parks, battlefield sites, historic sites and memorials: Chicamauga and Chattanooga National Military Park and Antietam Battlefield Site in 1890, Shiloh National

Military Park in 1894, Gettysburg National Military Park in 1895, and many others in the years following. There are now in the national park system sixty-three national historical parks, national military parks, national memorial parks (only one), national battlefield parks, national battlefield sites, national historic sites, national memorials, and national cemeteries; these, however, are not the subject of the present book. In addition, about thirty-two of the national monuments are historical in character.

CHAPTER VIII

Mesa Verde Park

☆ Let us turn now to our only cliff-dwelling national park, Mesa Verde, established a few weeks after the Antiquities Act was passed.

EARLY HISTORY   The Mesa Verde National Park covers the greatest area of archeological ruins in the southwest. It is a mesa 2,000 feet above the surrounding country, green with piñon and juniper trees, slashed across by deep canyons of scenic magnificence, in which hundreds of cliff ruins—three hundred to four hundred— stand in as many caves. The mesa was inhabited from about 1 A.D. to about 1300 by successive Indian cultures which archeologists have been studying with great interest. Major Macomb and a party of explorers ascended the north escarpment of the mesa in 1859, and in 1876 a geologist, J. S. Newberry, made a report on Macomb's expedition. In his report he named the mesa Mesa Verde—"green table." It had previously been known as Fortified Hills or Fortification Hills, and was not named Mesa Verde by early Spanish explorers, as has often been stated. A United States Geological Survey

163

164

party saw Mancos Canyon in 1874, and W. H. Jackson, the famous pioneer photographer, did much to make the ruins known to the public. In 1888 Cliff Palace and other ruins were visited by R. Wetherill and C. Mason, cowboys, and later explorers and commercial exploiters and vandals of southwestern ruins. Wetherill later filed a homestead claim covering much of Pueblo Bonito but failed to get title. In 1892 Baron Nordenskjöld led the first organized archeological expedition into the area. Prospectors had been wandering through parts of it since the middle sixties.

CONGRESSIONAL INTEREST IN PROTECTION   There was some interest in the protection and preservation of the ruins at least as early as 1891, when the legislature of Colorado memorialized Congress for the establishment of a national park on a part of the Ute Indian Reservation.[1] Several similar petitions were presented in the next few years. There were efforts in Congress to set aside Mesa Verde, at first under the name Colorado Cliff Dwellings National Park, and later with the name Mesa Verde. On February 22, 1901, Representative Shafroth of Colorado introduced a bill to create Colorado Cliff Dwellings National Park, but it was not reported.[2] Later in the year he tried again, without success.[3] About the same time, Representative Bell ventured a bill, and Representative Patterson presented an amendment to the appropriation bill to provide $500 to purchase Mesa Verde from the Ute Indians, but failed. It was in 1901 that the Colorado Cliff Dwelling Association was authorized by Congress to lease for ten years from the Wiminuchi Band of Ute Indians some of the deeded land on which most of the ruins were located, to protect the ruins; but the lease was never made. Mrs. Gilbert McClurg, who organized and promoted the Association, worked diligently for several years on the project but failed to get the signatures of all the members of the tribal Council. This was not to come until 1913.[4]

Late in the year 1903, Shafroth tried again, unsuccessfully, and Representative Hogg of Colorado brought in a bill which was reported favorably by the Public Lands Committee, with the sugges-

1 Congressional Record, Feb. 18, 1891, 2832.
2 H. R. 14262, 56 Cong. 2 Sess.
3 H. R. 6270, 57 Cong. 1 Sess.
4 Stat. 31, 1162.

MESA VERDE NATIONAL PARK

UTAH | COLO.

ARIZ. | N.M.

═══ Principal road ▬▬▬ Park boundary

0   1   2   3
SCALE of MILES

Mancos

Cortez

PARK ENTRANCE

MONTEZUMA VALLEY

Mancos River

MANCOS VALLEY

TUNNEL

FAR VIEW GROUP

SODA CANYON

PROSECUTION CANYON

PRATER CANYON

MORFIELD CANYON

LONG CANYON

SPRUCE CANYON

CEDAR TREE. TOWER RUINS

SPRUCE TREE HOUSE. PARK HEADQUARTERS

ROCK CANYON

SOUTHERN UTE INDIAN RESERVATION

SOUTHERN UTE INDIAN RESERVATION

SQUARE TOWER HOUSE

SUN TEMPLE
CLIFF PALACE
BALCONY HOUSE

Mancos River MANCOS CANYON

tion that the name be changed to Mesa Verde and that a like area known as Pajarito—at present known as Bandelier National Monument and vicinity—be reserved in New Mexico.[5]

In December 1905 Representative Hogg introduced a Mesa Verde bill, and a month later Senator Patterson brought up one in the House. The Patterson bill was amended in the Senate to permit mining in the park except in areas one-half mile or less on each side of the ruins, but the Hogg bill permitted no mining, and it was the one which passed both houses with no debate and was signed by President Roosevelt on June 29, 1906. The fact that it passed without debate indicates the strong appeal of conservation of the cliff dwellings.[6]

The Mesa Park bill, as it was passed, authorized the Secretary of the Interior to establish rules and regulations for the protection of the ruins in the park and within five miles outside of its boundaries, and prescribed a fine of $1,000 or a year of imprisonment, or both, for anyone who should "remove, disturb, destroy, or molest" any ruin or anything in a ruin. As in the Antiquities Act, the Secretary was authorized to permit examinations, excavations, and gathering of objects by persons duly qualified, but only for the benefit of reputable museums, universities, colleges, or other recognized scientific or educational institutions, with a view to increasing the knowledge of such objects and aiding the general advancement of archeological science. Nothing was said about the protection of wildlife, although there were some wild animals in the park.

LATER AMENDMENTS   It seemed to be thought that there would be no need for tourist accommodations, for there was no authorization of leases and permits; but within the next few years Representative Haggot and Senator Guggenheim of Colorado tried to get amendments through Congress authorizing leases for tourist accommodations and also for mining coal.[7] Senator Teller of Colorado, former Secretary of the Interior, tried to get a mining permit for a man named Todd of Cortez.[8] This bill failed, but Todd later opened up a coal mine on Ute deeded land just west of the

5 H. R. 6784, 58 Cong. 2 Sess.; H. R. 15968, 58 Cong. 3 Sess.

6 S. 3245, H. R. 5998, 59 Cong. 1 Sess Stat. 32, 765.

7 H. R. 19861, 60 Cong. 1 Sess. S. 1751, 61 Cong. 1 Sess.

8 S. 6818, 60 Cong. 1 Sess.

park boundary, near the top of the north Mesa Verde escarpment. In the debates on the Guggenheim bill, leases for mining coal came up for discussion. With the provision authorizing coal mining there was a provision that royalties should be used for park improvement, to make the idea more palatable to conservationists; but in the House this section was stricken out. In the House there was some objection to mining anyhow, but Representative Mondell of Wyoming explained that the only coal reserves for the general area were in the park, and argued that a mine or two not too near the ruins would not hurt the park. The people of Montezuma County had to have coal shipped in from Hesperus or Durango and then haul it ten to twenty miles from the railroad. Later, mines were developed at Mancos. The committee finally amended the bill to allow mining for use in Montezuma County only. The bill passed both houses, but when it came up to President Taft he vetoed it because it did not give the revenues to the park for improvement— because it lacked the provision that the House had stricken out.

In the next session of Congress Senator Guggenheim again offered a bill to authorize concession leases and permit mining, the revenues to go to the park for improvement and not into the United States Treasury. This bill passed the Senate without discussion, but got no further.[9] Other efforts to permit mining and to make park revenues available for improvement likewise failed,[10] until June 25, 1910, when an amendment to the urgent deficiency act authorized the Secretary to grant concession and mining leases, but the revenues had to be turned into the United States Treasury.[11] Because of the rather isolated location of the park and the lack of roads, few tourists came in the early years—250 in 1910, and 502 in 1914. Although nothing was said about grazing in the establishing act or in the 1910 amendment, the Secretary for a few years allowed some cattle grazing in the park. In 1921, 1,320 head of cattle were allowed to graze for five months of the year, but in 1922 Superintendent Nusbaum, one of the outstanding figures in the history of Mesa Verde and other southwestern parks and monuments, required a 20 per cent reduction each year, and in 1927 all grazing was ended.

9 S. 8108, 61 Cong. 2 Sess.
10 S. 6818, 60 Cong. 1 Sess. H. R. 21303, 63 Cong. 3 Sess. H. R. 4817, 64 Cong. 1 Sess. H. R. 1697, 65 Cong. 1 Sess.
11 Stat. 36, 796.

ADMINISTRATIVE DEVELOPMENTS   Mesa Verde revenues had to be turned in to the Treasury, and in the following years Representative Taylor of Colorado, a consistent friend of the park and of conservation generally, made several attempts to allow these revenues to be used in improvement of the park, but without success. There was a suggestion from the Secretary that his jurisdiction over the five-mile strip around the park be abandoned, and in 1913 this was allowed, but on only three sides, because of faulty drawing of the bill.[12]

Unfortunately the park, as set up, did not cover some of the most valuable of the ruins, including Cliff Palace, which were on Ute deeded lands. The Colorado Cliff Dwelling Association had failed even to get a lease on some of this land, but continued to work for the preservation of it. In the winter of 1906 the Secretary of the Interior called for an archeological survey of the Mesa Verde area to determine what great cliff dwellings and ruins situated on Ute Indian deeded lands should be embraced in a Mesa Verde national park, the proposed boundaries and the acreage involved, the survey to be made by the Smithsonian Institution. The Smithsonian named Dr. Edgar Hewett, Dr. A. V. Kidder, and Dr. Jesse Nusbaum, just beginning a distinguished career in archeology, and others. This survey was made in the summer of 1907; but the Utes steadily refused to trade until 1913, when they finally agreed to trade the lands for a much larger acreage of their own selection. Congress authorized the exchange.[13] Nusbaum worked for Hewett in and near Mesa Verde in the summer of 1908, then in 1909 began work in the newly founded School of American Archeology and Museum of New Mexico at Santa Fe.

Congress was more prompt than usual in providing funds for the new park. With no money the first year, the Secretary was obliged to appoint as Acting Superintendent, William Leonard, Superintendent of the Ute Indian Training and Industrial School, without salary; but in 1907, $7,500 was appropriated, and each year thereafter at least as much was voted. In 1907 a regular Superintendent was appointed, Major Hans Randolph, but for several years there was no building in the park for headquarters, which were maintained at Mancos until 1921. When Jesse Nusbaum was appointed Superin-

12 Stat. 38, 82.
13 Idem.

tendent in June 1921, he promptly moved into a tent at the park headquarters with his family, who were the first white people to live year around in the park. The next spring he moved into a new Superintendent's residence which he had built.

The one ranger employed in 1907 was not able to guard all the ruins, and the next year two more were employed, but no rangers stayed in the park in winter until 1922. Fortunately for the ruins, there was no road into the park, and the only way to get up the mesa was by horseback, the carriage road ending at the foot of the mesa. In 1913 the Knife Edge Road was completed up the 2,000-foot face of the mesa, a road so steep that some cars could not get up, and so narrow that cars could not pass on it and drivers wishing to go up or down had to telephone to the Superintendent's office at Mancos before starting. It was a really scenic road, but frightening to timid drivers, even dangerous, and there was much complaint about it until a less spectacular entrance road was begun in 1918.

The water supply of the park was soon seen to be inadequate, so a dam was built at the head of Spruce Tree Canyon and several cisterns were dug, which proved satisfactory for several years. Years later a 4,109-foot deep well was dug outside the park, but this proved inadequate and finally a 26-mile gravity flow pipeline was built to the La Plata Mountains to meet the greatly increasing demand for water.

Preservation of the ruins for highest public use and enjoyment was the main object in creating the park. Under the provision permitting approved excavations, the Secretary authorized Dr. J. Walter Fewkes of the Smithsonian Institution to work in the park. Dr. Fewkes began work in 1908 and finished excavating and repairing Cliff Palace, the largest of the cliff dwellings, two years later. This "apartment" had over two hundred rooms and probably sheltered about four hundred people. This was of course only a beginning, in a park where there are some four hundred ruins, but Dr. Fewkes worked at his task for years, and in 1915 and 1916 uncovered the Sun Temple and Far-View House—the latter a pueblo ruin so located that from it one has a magnificent view of the scenery in four states. Even today, however, only a few examples of the ruins have been excavated for interpretive use. In 1928 Congress passed a law authorizing the secretary of the Smithsonian Institution to co-operate with any state, with educational or scientific organizations, for archeological research in the ruins, and appropriated $20,000 for the work throughout the country.[14]

"Excavation and repair" were permitted, and when ruins have been excavated, repair and stabilization are often necessary, for with the passage of centuries of time, and through vandalism, some of the structures have been weakened, and are in need of preservation measures. National Park officers distinguish between "repair" and "restoration," stabilization being the work required for such bracing up as to make the ruins safe from further deterioration, while restoration would represent an effort to build them back to their original condition. There has been a little of the latter where it has seemed wise, but it is contrary to the general rule governing such archeological treasures.

In digging out the rubble over and around ancient walls, many pottery objects, baskets, artifacts, and even mummified bodies were found, and here an important question arose: Where should they be kept? There was no safe place in or near the park, and yet these relics really belonged there. In 1908 Secretary Garfield requested funds to construct a museum, but there was no building of any kind in the park until several years later. In 1917 Secretary Lane announced a hope that some day a school of archeology might be established in the park, and the Superintendent asked for funds to convert a two-room ranger house opposite Spruce Tree House to museum purposes, so that artifacts, etc. collected in the park could be exhibited. According to some reports this was done the following year, but if some of the rangers, as reported, were selling artifacts at the time it is difficult to see how it could have been much of a museum, at any rate before the time of Nusbaum. Albright does not believe there was any real museum in Mesa Verde at this time.

Superintendent Randolph seemed interested in the protection of the ruins, but there is evidence that the ruins would have fared better if his successor Rickner had never seen the park, for he was apparently himself a spoiler of the ruins. His son-in-law, appointed ranger, vandalized the ruins and sold artifacts that he found. By 1921, however, some relics had been sent to the Smithsonian Institution. Perhaps this was the safest place for them, accessible to the greatest number of interested visitors, and when other ruins were

14 Stat. 45, 413. See *Archeological Excavations in Mesa Verde National Park, Colorado*, published by the National Park Service, 1954.

excavated more artifacts were found for the Mesa Verde museum.

The state of Colorado was for some reason in ill humor about her parks, Mesa Verde and Rocky Mountain, for several years, and did not cede jurisdiction over Mesa Verde until 1927, reserving the right to tax. Cession was accepted the next year.[15]

Some problems that loomed large in other parks were not serious here. There were only about 400 acres of patented land in the park, 480 acres of unpatented entries and 2,080 acres of state school lands. In 1914 the Superintendent reported 720 acres of patented land. Superintendent Nusbaum exchanged grazing rights for 80 acres of this, and later asked Representative Taylor, chairman of the House Subcommittee on Appropriations, to request $5,000 for the purchase of the much-desired Prater and Norfield lands totaling 480 acres— a "good buy," as it appears now. The state school lands were secured by exchange of other federal lands. Today there is only one 40-acre tract of patented land in the park, along the Mancos River, far from public view.

The park boundaries were changed several times, without any great debate or uproar such as always accompanied proposals for changes in the boundaries of some of the other parks. Wildlife was not important, although there were some mule deer and smaller animals, and plenty of predatory animals. The Ute Indians sometimes came into the park to shoot the deer.

Lacey and other men in Congress tried a number of times to set up the Bandelier area as a national park, but were not successful. Bandelier was proclaimed a national monument in 1916.

15 Stat. 45, 458.

CHAPTER IX

Glacier Park

Glacier Park might be so named because it is glacial in origin, the result of the action of mighty glaciers which scoured out the valleys, leaving the precipitous mountain walls that characterize the park, or because it still has many glaciers. It is one of the most beautiful of our mountain parks. Although the mountains are not nearly as high as the high mountains of Colorado or the High Sierra—in the ratio of 10,000 to 14,000 feet—they appear quite as impressive because they rise from a lower base and because they are so steep and rugged and somewhat colored; and the several lakes are as lovely as can be found in the United States, excepting Crater Lake.

EARLY HISTORY   The Glacier Park region was visited by white men fairly early in our history—perhaps by Lewis and Clark in 1804, and surely as early as 1810 when several men crossed Marias Pass. In 1846 Hugh Monroe is said to have visited and named St. Mary Lake; in 1853 A. W. Tinkham, an engineer, came in from the west, and the next year James Doty, traveling with a railroad survey

171

party, entered the park area from the east. In 1882 Professor Raphael Pumpelly tried to cross Cut Bank Pass, but found the snow too deep, but the next year he crossed the pass and discovered what was later named Pumpelly Glacier. With him was W. A. Stiles, for years editor of Professor Sargent's *Garden and Forest,* and W. R. Logan, long in the service of the Indian Bureau, and later first superintendent of Glacier Park. Logan Pass is named after him. Pumpelly and Stiles were vastly impressed with the scenery here.

In 1885 George Bird Grinnell, explorer, scientist, conservationist, and friend of the Indians, went to the Glacier country on a hunting trip, and went again in several later years, exploring as well as hunting. He discovered Grinnell and Blackfoot glaciers and gave names to many of the features of the area. More important, about 1891 he conceived the idea of a national park here, and in the *Century Magazine* of September 1901 he proposed such a "reservation." In 1897, at the insistence of Professor Charles S. Sargent and others, the area had been made a forest reserve. Grinnell was much concerned about forest fires, often set by Indian hunters, and about the conservation of the glaciers and watersheds.

The part of the park east of the continental divide was originally included in the Blackfeet Indian Reservation, but at various times the Indians made "agreements" to part with more and more of their lands. About 1885 a prospector discovered what he thought were signs of gold and silver in what was still Blackfeet land, and soon, in spite of government and Indian police, prospectors swarmed over the area, hopefully digging holes in the mountainsides. Finding no minerals they presently departed. In the early nineties a little copper ore was found and there was another invasion by prospectors seeking copper, gold, silver, and even oil. The prospectors had a notion that ore veins extended to the east side of the divide, but that was owned by the Indians. The result was that there was agitation for the purchase of this land.

The Secretary of the Interior appointed a commission to treat with the Indians, with Grinnell a member at the request of the Indians; and a purchase of the east slope was arranged for $1.5 million. There was active prospecting for a while but little copper and gold and silver, and the miners drifted away. Then fishermen found that the lakes abounded in fish. The result of these invasions by prospectors and fishermen and by a few explorers, particularly

GLACIER NATIONAL PARK

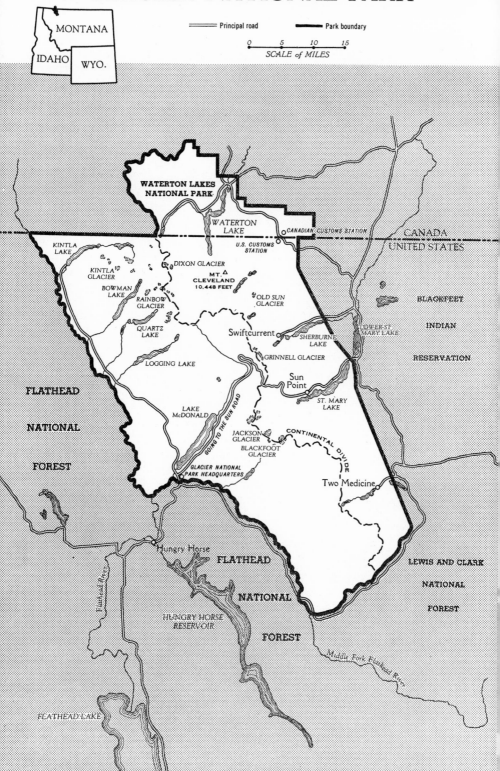

Principal road   Park boundary

0   5   10   15
SCALE of MILES

MONTANA

IDAHO   WYO.

WATERTON LAKES
NATIONAL PARK

WATERTON
LAKE

CANADIAN CUSTOMS STATION

CANADA
UNITED STATES

U.S. CUSTOMS
STATION

KINTLA
LAKE

DIXON GLACIER

MT.
CLEVELAND
10,448 FEET

BLACKFEET

KINTLA
GLACIER

OLD SUN
GLACIER

INDIAN

BOWMAN
LAKE

RAINBOW
GLACIER

LOWER ST.
MARY LAKE

RESERVATION

QUARTZ
LAKE

Swiftcurrent

SHERBURNE
LAKE

LOGGING LAKE

GRINNELL GLACIER

Sun
Point

FLATHEAD

ST. MARY
LAKE

LAKE
McDONALD

NATIONAL

JACKSON
GLACIER

CONTINENTAL DIVIDE

BLACKFOOT
GLACIER

FOREST

GLACIER NATIONAL
PARK HEADQUARTERS

GOING TO THE SUN ROAD

Two Medicine

Hungry Horse

FLATHEAD

LEWIS AND CLARK

NATIONAL

NATIONAL

HUNGRY HORSE
RESERVOIR

FOREST

FOREST

Middle Fork Flathead River

Flathead River

FLATHEAD LAKE

Grinnell, was that something was learned of the beauty of the scenery and presently published to the country.[1]

NATIONAL PARK PROMOTION IN CONGRESS When the mining excitement died down, Grinnell decided that it was a good time to push his national park proposal. Various conservation organizations, including the Sierra Club, supported him, as presently did L. W. Hill, of the Great Northern Railroad, who saw the possibility of increased passenger traffic if the park were created, since the railroad provided the only railway access to it.[2]

Several factors favored the establishment of a national park here, aside from the unique beauty of the scenery. The prospectors had proved that probably there were no minerals of enough value to attract the cupidity of mining interests; there was not much grazing land that livestock men would covet; although there was good timber, much of it was rather inaccessible, and some of the timber was too small to be of high value; and finally, much of the land belonged to the Indians, and nearly all the rest already belonged to the government, in national forests. Furthermore, by the early years of the twentieth century, tourist traffic to Yellowstone and the other national parks had grown to such a point as to provide a great deal of business and keep a lot of "money in circulation" in the areas adjacent to the parks; and even commercially minded people were beginning to see that national parks are "good business," great assets to the surrounding regions.

There was some concern about the Glacier Park region as early as 1884, when Senator Edmonds of Vermont, one of the early conservationists, proposed the establishment of a forest reservation "on the headwaters of the Missouri River and the headwaters of Clark's Park of the Columbia River." Edmonds was concerned about watershed protection, and his bill passed the Senate in spite of the opposition of Ingalls of Kansas—who had also favored abolition of Yellowstone Park.[3]

1 Marius Campbell, *The Glacier National Park: A Popular Guide to Its Geology and Scenery* (Washington: U. S. Government Printing Office, 1914) , 5. For a rather complete early history of the region see Madison Grant, *Early History of Glacier National Park, Montana*, National Park Service, 1919.

2 See *American Forests and Forest Life*, Aug. 1929, 489 ff.

3 S. 1824, 48 Cong. 1 Sess.

Grinnell, with the backing of Hill, approached Senator Tom Carter and Representative Pray of Montana, and persuaded some of his friends to do so too, and as a result Carter introduced two bills in 1908—"To establish the Glacier National Park, west of the summit of the Rocky Mountains and south of the international boundary line in Montana." As this bill passed the Senate it placed the "park," of about a million acres, under control of the Secretary of Agriculture rather than the Secretary of the Interior, left it open to power development and the building of railroads; and an amendment was offered in the House opening it up to irrigation dams. There were already summer homes in the area. In this form it was not really a national park bill at all; with control vested in the Secretary of Agriculture, it was, rather, a national forest bill. In the national forests power and irrigation developments, and also mining, hunting, grazing, and summer homes were allowed, which is the reason why western business interests often preferred national forest administration. There was much changing and amending in the two houses, shifting control to the Secretary of the Interior and eliminating some of the worst provisions of the bill, but introducing others, including a section permitting the leasing of summer homes in the park; but the bill did not pass.[4]

In the next Congress Carter again offered a Glacier Park bill somewhat like the first, which was debated for a short time. Senator Bacon of Georgia objected to the cost that would be involved and suggested that the park be given to Montana to maintain, but Senator Penrose of Pennsylvania pointed out the international aspects of the park—Canada had already set aside lands across the border and he thought Glacier would be an appropriate part of a sort of international park, which should be under federal control. There was some discussion of railroad "indemnity selections" which might be made by the railroad if it lost land in the park, and the conclusion was reached that the railroad should not make indemnity selections. Even so, there were plenty of bugs in the bill as it passed the Senate. Some of the western men, who have disproportionate power in the Senate, did not want a real national park but they liked the name.

In the House, where there were relatively more eastern men, several amendments were adopted: (1) striking out the provision al-

4 S. 2032, S. 5648, 60 Cong. 1 and 2 Sess.

lowing railroad rights of way in the park, (2) striking out the section permitting reclamation projects, and (3) striking out the provision forbidding railroad indemnity selections in the park. In the conference committee the House finally backed off from its amendments, and a bad Glacier Park bill passed, and was signed by President Taft, on May 11, 1910.[5]

THE GLACIER PARK ACT   The bill as finally passed included the following provisions:

1. Rights of way were authorized for steam or electric railways. This was contrary to general park principles. Yellowstone Park, it will be remembered, had fought stubbornly against all railroad intrusion, partly because locomotives were likely to set forest fires and partly because railroads are an incongruous element in a park.

2. The Reclamation Service was allowed to enter and use the streams for power and irrigation projects. This again had been fought by the park administration in Yellowstone and elsewhere.

3. No indemnity selections for lands included in the park were allowed for railroads or other corporations. This was good.

4. The Secretary of the Interior was authorized to lease up to ten acres to any person or corporation for as long as twenty years for facilities to accommodate visitors. This was better than the provision for ten-year leases in some earlier parks because it offered more security to concessioners.

5. The Secretary was authorized to give twenty-year leases to those who had built summer homes or to those who might want to build summer homes. This was a violation of national park principles.

6. The Secretary was authorized to sell dead and down timber. The park administration has usually opposed the sale of timber, indeed of *anything*. No judicial system was set up and no penalties for offenses were specified.

Glacier Park was not really a national park, in the proper sense of the word, but a sort of hybrid national forest with a few park features, and it was at first administered as such. In his report in October 1911 Superintendent W. R. Logan announced that he had placed an order for a sawmill and shingle machine to saw up dead

5 S. 2777, 61 Cong. 1 Sess. Stat. 36, 354.

and down and insect-infested timber, and even mature timber, to use in buildings and to *sell*. "In a short time it is believed that lumber will rank first among the sources of revenue," he declared, obviously thinking he was supervising a national forest and not a national park. It was not uncommon for the park superintendents to permit concessioners to use park timber to build needed buildings, under strict regulations, but not to make a business of selling. The Glacier Park sawmill was a feature of the park landscape for many years. The writer remembers a large pile of sawdust near Glacier Hotel in 1917. According to Mr. Scoyen of the Park Service, whose recollection would be open to little question, there was a sawmill in operation on Lake McDonald on the west side of the divide, cutting lumber for a new hotel as late as 1925; Mather blew it up because the Great Northern persistently failed to remove it.[6]

DIFFICULTIES OF ADMINISTRATION   Even if the park law had been properly drawn there would have been many difficult problems for the park management. In the first place, there was no definite statute placing law enforcement in the park administration, providing rules and regulations and penalties for their violation. Some of the Montana citizens threatened to hunt in the park if the federal government did not take over. There was another difficulty in the early years of the park; and even in the early years of Mather's administration—too much politics! Such shrewd politicians as Senators Tom Carter, Tom Walsh, and others had too much power in the administration of the park. Mather had one of his roughest fights in cleaning political appointees out of Glacier, and Yellowstone too.

Jurisdiction was needed for protection of the park, and the state of Montana ceded it promptly in February 1911; and bills, modeled after the one accepting jurisdiction over Yellowstone, were presented by Senators Carter and Myers, and by Representatives Pray and Evans, all of Montana. In these acceptance bills a Commissioner was usually provided for, to try cases and impose penalties, but when Senator Myers introduced a bill in the 62nd Con-

6 Shankland places the sawmill on Lake "McDermott," the early name for Lake McDonald. (*Steve Mather of the National Parks* [New York: Alfred A. Knopf, 1951], 209.)

gress, in 1911, there was objection to this because the Commissioner was authorized to try cases without a jury.[7] In the 63rd Congress, Myers tried for acceptance, and after some debate, mainly on the constitutionality of the Commissioner's function of trying cases without a jury, the Myers bill passed the Senate. It passed the House without debate, and was approved by President Wilson on August 22, 1914.[8] This was unusual dispatch for Congress. In some cases the parks had to wait as long as ten years, or even longer, before jurisdiction was accepted and Commissioners were appointed. The new law required the Commissioner to live in the park, but unfortunately there was no house there for him to live in.

With jurisdiction established, there were still some difficulties in administering the park. In the first place there was no suitable administrative headquarters for several years, but when Mather came in he bought a site with his own money, near Belton. This was not entirely satisfactory, however, for most of the tourist activity was on the east side of the divide, and the headquarters should have been there, near St. Mary Lake.

Glacier Park was in one respect particularly difficult to administer; as far as use was concerned, it was really two parks, one on each side of the continental divide, of mountains so steep that it was difficult even to cross on foot until 1918 when the Logan Pass Trail was completed. Automobile tourists who visited the east side could get to the west side only by loading their cars on the Great Northern and going around to the west entrance by rail. A road across this precipitous divide was needed but it presented a tremendous undertaking. There was an appropriation of $195,000 partly for it in 1921, but it was not begun until 1925. It followed a trail, part of which had been marked out by Steven Mather himself. Year after year the road wound its way up and around the mountain cliffs and through tunnels here and there, past peaks and glaciers. On July 15, 1933, dedication ceremonies were held at Logan Pass to celebrate the completion of what some travellers have pronounced the most magnificently beautiful high road in the United States, or perhaps in the world.

Glacier Park lies across the boundary from Waterton Lakes Park

---

7 S. 7318, 62 Cong. 2 and 3 Sess. See also S. 10894, H. R. 32948, 61 Cong. 3 Sess. H. R. 1679, 62 Cong. 1 Sess.

8 S. 654, 63 Cong. 1 Sess. Stat. 38, 699.

in Canada, and on May 2, 1932, Congress decreed that it should become a part of an international park known as the Waterton-Glacier International Peace Park.[9]

WILDLIFE IN THE PARK   There were deer, elk, black and grizzly bears, a few moose, bighorn sheep, and Rocky Mountain goats—rather peculiar to this region—the usual complement of coyotes and mountain lions, a few wolves; but the wild animals had been seriously depleted before the park was established, and in the severe winter of 1911-12 many of the elk and deer starved. As in the other parks, the wildlife that the park management wanted to preserve suffered from predators and poachers and from the lack of winter forage on lower lands. In accordance with the prevailing theory of wildlife management, the Superintendent adopted a policy of trapping and poisoning coyotes and hunting down the mountain lions with hounds. Such activities were discontinued in 1934. With fairly generous appropriations from the first, the Superintendent was able to prevent extensive poaching, yet there was some by the whites and by the Blackfeet Indians.

Much of the loss of wildlife was, however, not due to poachers but to killing outside the park limits. Like Yellowstone, Crater Lake, Rainier, and Yosemite, Glacier included mostly high land, good for summer range for animals but too severe in winter; and when the animals went outside to the lower lands around and particularly east of the park in the late fall, they fell to waiting hunters. The park should have included some of the lower land on the east side for winter range, but this land was not included because it was wanted for mining—although it proved to have no minerals of value, and it belonged to the Blackfeet Indians. The Secretaries and Park Superintendent made repeated recommendations that the park be extended to the east, and there were efforts to do this, but always without success.

There were fewer reports of fires than in some other parks, but some of the fires were widely destructive. A fire in 1910, before the park was established, burned over thousands of acres, and a later fire burned nearly all summer and enrolled more than three thousand fire fighters before it was extinguished.

9 Stat. 47, 145.

ROADS AND TRAILS   Roads and trails presented a serious problem. Fortunately, Congress from the start was unaccountably generous. Whereas the first appropriation for Yellowstone came six years after the park was established, for Sequoia ten years, for General Grant ten years, for Rainier four years—and mere monetary dribbles even then—Glacier Park received $15,000 the year that it was established, $69,200 the second year, and by 1916 was granted $110,000. In 1911 Congress authorized the Secretary to use proceeds from leases or other sources in the management and improvement of the park.[10] With such revenues some very satisfactory trails were built, and by 1917 a satisfactory road was completed along the east side of the park penetrating to two or three of the lakes, the Great Northern helping.

CONCESSION TROUBLES   Glacier had her full share of concession troubles, although in hotel concessions for tourist accommodations the park was fortunate. The Great Northern had a fine hotel on private lands at Glacier Park near the east end of the park, from which stages took tourists into the park. In 1911 this hotel reported 3,227 guests—more than half of the 6,257 tourists who entered that year. The railroad financed hotels and chalets of architectural beauty and did a splendid job in caring for the tourists. In 1927 the railroad built the Prince of Wales Hotel in Waterton Park, across the border in Canada. There were a great many other concessions, particularly for saddle and pack horses, needed because in the early years of the park the roads were so few and so poor that travel was largely by horseback. Glacier was largely a "trail park" for years, with 1,600 horses in the park at one time.

Summer home concessions were a vexatious problem. The establishing act provided for such concessions, contrary to national park principles, and in 1912 there were seventeen residence concessions. At first the Superintendent followed the policy of renewing these concessions when they expired, but in 1918 Secretary Lane announced an end to the policy of leasing for summer homes, although leases already made would not be canceled.[11] The summer home privileges were not abolished by law until 1931.[12]

10 Stat. 36, 1421.
11 *Report, Secretary of the Interior, 1918*, 110 ff.
12 Stat. 46, 1043.

PRIVATE AND STATE LAND HOLDINGS   Privately owned lands in the park presented a more serious problem than the summer home permits. At the time the park was established there were in it 8,864 acres of patented lands and 7,803 acres of unperfected bona fide claims; and some of these presented irritating problems for many years. Some fine timber lands were owned by lumber companies, in one or two cases adjacent to park roads, and the lumber companies threatened to log them. There was particular anxiety about some fine cedars around Lake McDonald. In 1914 Senator Walsh introduced a bill, approved by Secretary Lane, to permit the Secretary to exchange for these lands other lands in the park more remote from roads or, with the consent of the Secretary of Agriculture, timber in any national forest in Montana.

In the debates on this bill the question was raised whether any railroad owned lands in the park, and there was some discussion of the frauds that had characterized "Lieu selections" by private owners in national forests and parks. Yet Walsh's bill passed the Senate.[13] In the next Congress Walsh again presented a bill, again approved by Secretary Lane, and it passed both houses with little discussion and was signed by President Wilson on March 3, 1917. The Secretary of Agriculture approved the bill but, jealous of his own demesne, did not believe that all private lands in Glacier should be traded for national forest land or timber. Six years later an act was passed authorizing the Secretary to trade for private lands in the park lands on the public domain anywhere in Montana.[14]

There were a number of private buildings used for summer homes on beautiful Lake McDonald, on the west side of the divide, two of them owned by Montana senators, Walsh and Wheeler. Walsh was for some years a virulent and indefatigable enemy of the park administration, although not of the park itself as long as he was allowed to have the deciding voice in its administration.[15]

The state of Montana owned some lands in the park, and it was not until 1948 that Representative D'Ewart of Montana got a bill passed providing for federal acquisition of some of these state lands. In some other cases, where national parks were established, states .

13 S. 5433, 63 Cong. 2 Sess.
14 S. 778, 64 Cong. 1 Sess. Stat. 39, 1122; 42, 1324.
15 See Robert Shankland, *op. cit.*, for an illuminating story of Walsh and his long fight with the National Park Service.

were required to cede state lands free of cost, but here the Secretary was authorized to buy them for such consideration as he thought advisable.[16]

In Glacier Park, as in some other parks, particularly Yosemite, the settlers who got caught without final patents in the establishment of the new park enjoyed the sympathetic interest of the senators and representatives of the state. There were eight entrymen who had filed homestead claims in the park but for some reason had not secured patents, possibly because they had no intention of making homes there but were trying to get title to valuable timber lands or sites for summer homes. Homestead entrymen were obliged to live on their claims for several years, and little of the land in Glacier Park was fitted for homesteads. At any rate, Senator Myers of Montana took an interest in their sufferings and introduced two bills to exclude their claims from the effect of the act creating the park and giving them more time to perfect their claims and get title. One of the bills passed both houses with very little debate and was signed by President Wilson on July 3, 1916.[17] This law did not necessarily mean that the entrymen would get title. If their claims were bona fide and if they were able to live on their claims the required number of years—for homestead entries five years—they could get title, but otherwise they might not be able to perfect their claims, which would revert to the government.

The provision allowing the construction of railroads in the park was never used, but the Great Northern, which served as the south border of the park, wanted permission to change its right of way, and Senator Myers tried to get this permission but without success.[18] In 1917, however, Senator Walsh got a bill through Congress providing for the sale to the Glacier Park Hotel Company, owned by the Great Northern, of five acres of land across the Flathead River near the western gateway but outside the park, for a new hotel. The Great Northern needed the land and generally it served the park well.[19]

The provision authorizing dams in the park spoiled beautiful Sherburne Lake. The impounded waters killed trees along the shores, and the irrigation company was slow in cleaning out the

16 H. R. 4980, 80 Cong. 2 Sess. Stat. 62, 80.
17 S. 4320, 63 Cong. 3 Sess. S. 1741, 64 Cong. 1 Sess. Stat. 39, 342.
18 S. 3897, 63 Cong. 2 Sess.
19 S. 784, 64 Cong. 2 Sess. Stat. 39, 994.

dead trees. Finally it did this, using Civilian Conservation Corps labor, but of course the lake is somewhat unsightly late in the season when the water is low.

In Glacier Park, although the bill creating the National Park Service in 1916 had opened all the parks but Yellowstone to grazing, at the discretion of the Secretary of the Interior, there was little trouble with grazing interests until the beginning of the First World War.

PART TWO

The National
Park Service

1916-1959

CHAPTER X

The Mather Administration

1917-1928

THE PARK SERVICE ESTABLISHED:

ROCKY MOUNTAIN PARK AND HAWAII PARK

🔆 LACK OF A CENTRAL PARK BUREAU OR SERVICE   We turn now
to the movement to establish a general office or bureau to manage
all the parks, those already established and those that were to follow, in a unified plan. Up to 1916 each park was officially a separate
unit, administratively unrelated to the others. Although the parks
were under the Secretary of the Interior, who gave some unity to
the administration, he had a dozen other jobs and could not give
a great deal of time to park management. As J. Horace McFarland,
of the American Civic Association, one of the staunchest friends of
the parks in the early years, described the situation: "Nowhere in
official Washington can an inquirer find an office of the national
parks or a single desk devoted solely to their management. By passing around through three Departments, and consulting clerks who
have taken on the extra work of doing what they can for the nation's
playgrounds, it is possible to come at a little information."[1] Furthermore, some of the national monuments were in the Department of
Agriculture, and two were in the War Department along with the
military national parks.

[1] Robert Shankland, *Steve Mather of the National Parks* (New York: Alfred
A. Knopf, 1951), 53.

As Shankland describes the situation: "The concessioners operated under widely variant regulations from park to park. The division of authority among the parks, and even inside a single park, came close to chaos. In Yellowstone all improvements and their appropriations were managed by an officer of the Army Corps of Engineers, who answered to neither the Interior Department nor the park superintendent; the Superintendent was himself an army officer, appointed by the Secretary of War; and 'exclusive control' rested with the Secretary of the Interior. Crater Lake and Mount Rainier, like Yellowstone, used Army engineers for road-building and improvements, but in those two parks the superintendent was a civilian, appointed by the Secretary of the Interior. On the other hand, Yosemite, Sequoia, and General Grant had Army Superintendents but no Army engineers."[2]

Probably the worst trouble with this lack of central control was that, as Buck said: "Without responsible direction, the establishment of parks and the efforts to secure appropriations for them in several instances deteriorated into a scramble for federal appropriations."[3] Some locality with an area of very modest scenic values, or perhaps nothing of value at all, with an eye to Congressional appropriations and profitable tourist traffic, might steam up a campaign to have it made a national park, and if it had an influential delegation in Congress might succeed in it. There was no over-all administrative authority to check on the quality of national park proposals. So we got such parks as Mackinac, Platt, and Sullys Hill.

The establishment of these inferior parks was really a rather serious matter. It was responsible for some of the starving of the worthy parks, for whatever money was wasted on them could of course not be used on the better parks; and also they offered some justification for the unwillingness of Congress to appropriate more for the park system. Appropriations for them smacked too much of the pork barrel. Some of the Secretaries of the Department of the Interior, and the Park Service when it was established, would have been glad to get rid of most of them, or all of them, and did finally get Mackinac shifted to the state of Michigan and Sullys Hill turned into a game preserve; but when, in 1910, an effort was made to turn Platt over to the state of Oklahoma, the Oklahoma delegation arose

2 *Ibid.*, 104.

3 Paul Herman Buck, *The Evolution of the National Park System of the United States* (Washington: U. S. Government Printing Office, 1946), 40.

as one man in opposition, frankly admitting that the park was a means of getting their share of federal appropriations.[4] Platt is unworthy of park status, but it seems likely that it will retain park status for the indefinite future. The status of Wind Cave is somewhat more doubtful, but it should probably not be a national park. The Park Service has said nothing about it, no doubt because to do so would antagonize the South Dakota delegation in Congress. With a national park in their state, they have been rather generally favorable to national parks.

Some co-ordination was secured in various ways from about 1911 on. For several years W. B. Acker, a conservation-minded attorney in the Department of the Interior, worked part-time for the parks, with modest clerical assistance; but it was more than a part-time job. When in 1913 Franklin K. Lane became Secretary of the Interior under President Wilson, spurred by McFarland he brought Adolph C. Miller to Washington as Assistant to the Secretary, with the parks and several bureaus under his wing; and Miller brought in Horace M. Albright, destined to play a lead part in park affairs for many years. Miller was a very able man and was soon promoted to the Federal Reserve Board. While in the Department he was assisted by Robert B. Marshall, borrowed from the United States Geological Survey, and given the title of Superintendent of National Parks on December 10, 1915. Some co-ordination was secured even before this by the appointment of Mark Daniels, in June 1914, as general superintendent and landscape engineer for all the national parks, with office in San Francisco. The urgent deficiency bill of February 28, 1916, authorized the transfer of this office to Washington.[5] Daniels had been commissioned as landscape engineer in Yosemite to prepare a comprehensive general plan for the Valley, and his new job was largely that of drawing landscape plans for the parks. On July 1, 1916, Congress passed a law authorizing the Secretary to use some of his appropriation to employ a Superintendent of National Parks with up to four assistants.[6] The Secretary tried to get a measure of co-ordination in other ways. Walter Fisher, Secretary under President Taft, called the first National Park Conference in 1911, and it became an almost annual affair. It was attended by various national parks officers, and representatives of the Depart-

4 *Ibid.*
5 *Report, Secretary of the Interior, 1916,* 752, 753.
6 Stat. 39, 309.

ments of the Interior, Agriculture, and War, of the railroads, and some of the concessioners, who discussed various problems of park administration. Secretary Lane set up a central purchasing agency on April 1, 1915, to buy supplies for several of the western parks.[7]

During these years there were insistent voices calling for a national parks office or bureau. Perhaps the first was that of Representative Lacey of Iowa, an early friend of the parks and forests, and one of the ablest men in Congress, who introduced a bill on April 26, 1900, "to establish and administer national parks."[8] Representative Stevens of Minnesota introduced two bills in 1902, "to provide for a national park commission."[9] W. B. Acker urged the creation of the bureau in 1905, and the Sierra Club, always active and vocal in park matters, soon took up the cry and in 1910 appointed a promotion committee. In 1911 and 1912 national park conferences recommended the project, as did R. B. Marshall, chief geographer of the Geological Survey, Frederick Law Olmsted, noted landscape architect, Frank Bond, chief clerk of the General Land Office, and other conservationists.

Secretary Ballinger urged the establishment of the new service in his 1910 report, and asked J. Horace McFarland to confer with him on the preparation of a bill to accomplish this. McFarland promptly called on Frederick Law Olmsted, Jr., perhaps the leading authority in the country on park planning. McFarland and Olmsted had worked together on the problems presented by Niagara Falls, and in the struggle to save Hetch Hetchy; and they had similar views on park problems. Olmsted thought that Ballinger's draft of the bill was defective in stating nothing about the future development of the parks and in failing to define their purpose, and suggested the insertion of a passage which clearly prohibited the use of the parks in any way that would be detrimental to the natural scenery or objects of interest, or would prevent their being conserved "unimpaired" for future generations. Ballinger accepted the amendment.[10]

The Forest Service was said to be opposed to the bill. Chief

7 *Report, Secretary of the Interior, 1914*, 83 ff.

8 H. R. 11021, 56 Cong. 1 Sess.

9 H. R. 12092, H. R. 13326, 57 Cong. 1 Sess.

10 Hans Huth, *Nature and the American* (Berkeley and Los Angeles: University of California Press, 1957), 190, 191.

forester Graves, successor to Pinchot, seems to have had a notion that the national parks might be combined with the national forests in some way, under control of the Forest Service. Graves said that in the national forests he had always distinguished between areas that needed special protection, such as Grand Canyon, and other areas that could properly be used for commercial purposes. Some, but not all, of the national park values could have been provided by properly managed national forests, as they are in some European countries where there are very few national parks; and it is possible that a measure of the hostility that foresters have sometimes shown toward the national parks was due to the European origin of American forestry principles.

Ballinger's successor, Walter Fisher, repeated the recommendation for a park bill in 1911, as did Secretary Lane in 1913. Behind these men and doing much of the work to create the service was J. Horace McFarland. He persuaded President Taft to speak at the American Civic Association's annual convention in 1911, and Taft made an effective appeal for the service:

> Now we have in the United States a great many natural wonders, and in that lazy way we have in our government of first taking up one thing and then another, we have set aside a number of national parks, of forest reservations covering what ought to be national parks, and what are called "national monuments." We have said to ourselves, "Those cannot get away. We have surrounded them by a law which makes them necessarily government property forever, and we will wait in our own good time to make them useful as parks to the people. Since the Interior Department is the 'lumber room' of the government, into which we put everything that we don't know how to classify, and don't know what to do with, we will just put them under the Secretary of the Interior." That is the condition of the national parks today.[11]

CONGRESSIONAL INTEREST IN A CO-ORDINATING SERVICE On February 2, 1912, President Taft sent a special message to the Congress urging the establishment of a Bureau of National Parks, but there was no immediate response. Within the next two or three

[11] Shankland, *op. cit.*, 51 ff. See also article by Robert Sterling Yard, *American Forests and Forest Life*, Aug. 1929, 462 ff.

years, however, a number of bills were introduced by Senator Smoot of Utah, Representative Davidson of Wisconsin, and Representatives Kent and Raker of California, in the 62nd, 63rd, and 64th Congresses.[12] Raker's efforts might have seemed worthy of success, but unfortunately he was not liked by James R. Mann, House minority leader, so the conservationists working for the bill decided to get William Kent, a friend of Mann's and an ardent conservationist, to introduce a fresh bill in the 64th Congress, said to have been drawn up with the assistance of Frederick Law Olmsted.[13] It was Kent's bill that was considered, passed the House without much debate, but somewhat amended. The Director's salary was reduced from $5,000 to $4,500, the Secretary of the Interior was given the authority to grant grazing privileges, and some national monuments were left with the Department of Agriculture, although by virtue of a previous bill the President could by proclamation turn them over to the Department of the Interior.

In the Senate the bill was championed by Senator Smoot and passed with an amendment striking out the provisions allowing grazing. So a conference committee was necessary, and it was a very difficult matter to get the committee together, for the end of the session was near. The conference committee was finally rounded up, however, and agreed to let the grazing provision remain, except for Yellowstone. So amended, the bill passed both houses and was signed by President Wilson on August 25, 1916.[14] In the House committee report on the bill it was suggested that although the Secretary of Agriculture did not actually agree to the transfer to the Park Service of the national monuments which were under the Department of Agriculture, he recognized that a time would come when the transfer would be made. The House Committee on Public Lands agreed that the transfer should be made immediately or very soon.[15] At the time, Horace McFarland was insisting that three departments handling national parks and monuments was an obvious absurdity.

12 S. 3463, H. R. 16090, H. R. 18716, H. R. 22474, H. R. 22995, 62 Cong. 2 Sess. S. 826, H. R. 104, 63 Cong. 1 Sess. S. 38, H. R. 434, H. R. 8661, H. R. 8668, H. R. 15437, H. R. 15522, 64 Cong. 1 Sess.

13 Shankland, op. cit., 53.

14 H. R. 15522; 64 Cong. 1 Sess. Stat. 39, 535. For an interesting and detailed account of the trip of this bill through Congress, see Shankland, op. cit., 100 ff.

15 H. R. 700, 64 Cong. 1 Sess.

NATIONAL MONUMENTS IN THE DEPARTMENT OF AGRICULTURE
There were good reasons why some of the national monuments were left with the Department of Agriculture. When national monuments were established they were left under the jurisdiction which controlled at the time—if in a national forest they were left with the Forest Service, in the Department of Agriculture; if on the public domain, they were left with the Department of the Interior, which controlled the public domain (the public lands owned by the federal government but not set aside in any kind of federal reservation). There was economy in this as long as little or no money was appropriated for their protection. Monuments within national forests could be protected a bit, if not very well, by the Forest Service which was guarding the surrounding land; protected better than if they had been put under the jurisdiction of the Department of the Interior which had no control of the surrounding areas and little or no funds for protection before 1916. In that year, for the protection of the twenty-one national monuments administered by the Department of the Interior, Congress finally appropriated $3,500—$166 each, enough to hire a guardian for a month or two if he could build his own living quarters. There was little increase until 1924, when $20,750 was appropriated, but even this was painfully inadequate. So it was perhaps fortunate that until 1933 some of the monuments were administered by the Department of Agriculture.

THE NATIONAL PARKS ACT   The National Parks Act as passed provided for establishment of the National Park Service, with a Director at $4,500, one Assistant Director at $2,500, one Chief Clerk at $2,000, one draftsman at $1,800, one messenger at $600, and as many other employees as could be hired for a total of $19,500—not princely salaries nor munificent support, thanks to Representative Lenroot of Wisconsin, no friend of the parks. In stating the purpose of the Park Service the act stated: "The service thus established shall promote and regulate the use of Federal areas known as national parks, monuments and reservations hereinafter specified by such means and measures as conform to the fundamental purpose of said parks, monuments and reservations, which purpose is to conserve the scenery and the natural and historic objects and the wild life therein, and to provide for the enjoyment of the same in such manner and by such means as will leave them unimpaired for the enjoyment of future generations." The Secretary was directed to make and publish such rules and regulations as he thought necessary, and violations of these regulations were to be punished as provided in the penal act of 1909, as amended by the Act of 1910.[16] He was also authorized to sell or dispose of timber where the cutting was necessary "to control the attacks of insects or diseases or otherwise conserve the scenery or the natural or historic objects," and might provide for the destruction of such animals and plant life as was detrimental to the use of the parks. He was authorized to grant concessions for twenty years for tourist accommodations and leases for grazing livestock in all the parks except Yellowstone when in his judgment grazing was not detrimental to the primary purpose of the parks—the western livestock men had to be made happy.[17]

For the first thirty-five years after the creation of Yellowstone, leases for hotels and camps had been limited to ten years. The acts establishing Yosemite, Sequoia, and General Grant also fixed a ten-year limit. This was a serious handicap in attracting concessioners, not a long enough lease to justify the construction of substantial buildings and facilities. In the acts establishing Mount Rainier, Crater Lake, Wind Cave, Sullys Hill, and Mesa Verde nothing was said about the terms of leases. The term was extended to twenty years for Yellowstone in 1907, and for Yosemite in 1914; so Sequoia and General Grant were the only parks where the ten-year limitation was in effect in 1916. Yet it was well that the National Parks Act made the term of leases uniform for all parks.

The National Parks Act made no effective provision for the protection of wildlife beyond the statement that the purpose of the act was to conserve the scenery and the natural and historic objects "and the wildlife therein" and to authorize the Secretary to destroy such animals as were detrimental to the use of the parks. We have already noted that when Yellowstone was established the Secretary was required merely "to provide against the wanton destruction of the fish and game found within said park, and against their capture or destruction for the purposes of merchandise or profit" and this

16 Stat. 36, 857.
17 Stat. 39, 535.

had afforded little protection; but in 1894 effective protection had been provided for Yellowstone under the Lacey Act. For some of the other parks already established, however, the ineffective Yellowstone Act provision had been repeated in the establishing acts, or game and birds had been mentioned or perhaps had not even been mentioned and nothing further had been provided. This was true of Yosemite, Sequoia, General Grant, Crater Lake, Platt, Wind Cave, Mesa Verde, Rocky Mountain, Hawaii, and Lassen Volcanic. Jurisdiction had been accepted for Rainier and Glacier, and the acceptance acts had covered careful regulations for the protection of wildlife; but for the other parks mentioned legal protection was grossly inadequate.

STEVEN MATHER AS DIRECTOR   No money was granted in the act, so Robert B. Marshall acted as head for a short time until the Service could be organized. In April 1917 funds were appropriated and Secretary Lane named Steven T. Mather Director—he had been Assistant to the Secretary, since January 21, 1915, as director in charge of the parks—and Horace M. Albright Assistant. Here was a team of devoted spirits, destined to be close friends as long as Mather lived.[18]

Mather was a man of prodigious and explosive energy, a tireless worker, a born promoter, "a practical idealist of the live-wire type," with a generous devotion to his job which is reminiscent of some of America's greatest—Washington, Thomas Paine, and Gifford Pinchot. He had been a lover of the outdoors, a mountain climber, a member of the American Civic Association and of the Sierra Club since 1904, and had made a fortune in borax before Lane called him to Washington. Handsome, of winning personality, he commanded respect and admiration and was able to win many friends for the parks. "He was pictured, written up, dined and feted. His appearances were applauded and his words were treasured and quoted. His journeys criss-crossing the country were blazed with newspaper headlines and punctuated with interviews."[19] In his years in the Park Service he gave much of his fortune to the promotion of the parks, and gave of his energies so prodigally that his

18 Stat. 40, 151.
19 Yard, *op. cit.*, 463.

health broke several times and he died in 1930 at the age of sixty-three, after only twelve years as Director.[20]

His great achievements—and our park system would be much poorer without him if indeed we had a park system at all—were essentially the work of a rich man. His wealth gave him not only prestige and the power to do some things with his own money when Congress would not provide funds, but it gave him a position of independence. He would take a strong stand when he wanted to, without worrying about his job. Of course he had help, the help of such able men as Albright and Cammerer, but they were his men, men that he had picked out and trained. Mather's administration lasted, in a sense, for years after he died.

PRINCIPLES OF PARK MANAGEMENT   In a letter to Mather on May 13, 1918, Secretary Lane outlined the administrative policy that should govern the parks.

"First, that the national parks must be maintained in absolutely unimpaired form for the use of future generations as well as those of our own time; second, that they are set aside for the use, observation, health, and pleasure of the people; and third, that the national interest must dictate all decisions affecting public or private enterprise in the parks."

In all parks but Yellowstone grazing by cattle but not by sheep might be permitted in areas not frequented by visitors.

There should be no leasing for summer homes.

There should be no cutting of trees except for buildings and where it would not hurt the forests or landscape.

Roads must harmonize with the landscape.

The Department and Service should urge cession of exclusive jurisdiction in all parks where it had not been granted.

Private holdings should be eliminated.

All outdoor sports, including winter sports, should be encouraged.

Educational as well as recreational use of the parks should be encouraged.

Low-priced camps should be maintained, and high-class hotels.

[20] Shankland's *Steve Mather of the National Parks*, cited frequently throughout this book, is the story of his life and achievements, ably and very interestingly written.

Concessioners should be protected against competition if they were giving good service; and they should yield a revenue to the government, but the development of the revenues should not impose a burden on visitors.

Auto fees should be reduced as motor travel increased.

The Service should use the Railroad Administration to advertise the parks and should co-operate with chambers of commerce, tourist bureaus and auto-highway associations to advertise travel to the parks.

The Service should keep informed as to municipal, county, and state parks and co-operate with them.

The Service should co-operate with the Canadian park service.

In studying new park projects, the Service should seek to find "scenery of supreme and distinctive quality or some natural features so extraordinary or unique as to be of national interest and importance."

The national park system as now constituted "should not be lowered in standard, dignity, and prestige by the inclusion of areas which express in less than the highest terms the particular class or kind of exhibit which they represent."

Parks need not be large.

The Service should study existing parks with the idea of improving them by adding adjacent areas; for instance adding to Sequoia and adding the Tetons to Yellowstone, and should co-operate with the Forest Service in planning for this.[21]

Lane's letter—doubtless written in co-operation with Mather, or more likely written by Mather—was a statesmanlike presentation of the principles that should govern park administration; but to put some of them into operation was a task of no mean proportions.

MATHER PROMOTES THE PARKS   Mather had not assumed the office of Director before he suffered a nervous breakdown in January 1917 as a result of overwork, an irritating quarrel with Senator Walsh over a Yellowstone concession in which one of Walsh's friends was interested, and as a result of some trouble with Robert Marshall, whom he was obliged to ease out of the Service. Mather was unable to do much work for some eighteen months, and

21 *Report, Secretary of the Interior, 1918*, 110.

Albright assumed the task of organizing the new Service, but Mather came back in late 1918 with his usual energy and proceeded to "promote" the parks in every way possible. He courted senators and representatives and government dignitaries, writers—Herbert Quick, Enos Mills, and Emerson Hough, for instance—and newspaper owners and reporters. He made friends of painters of national park scenes and exhibited their paintings. At the 1917 National Parks Conference he arranged a loan exhibition of forty-five paintings of national park scenes by various painters, including Thomas Moran, Albert Bierstadt, and Thomas Hill. He persuaded western railroad officials to help in advertising the parks and in some cases to provide accommodations in the parks—this some of them had already done for some years. Unable to see that most visitors to the parks would soon be coming in automobiles, the railroads were interested in developing the park tourist traffic. In 1915 the Santa Fe and Union Pacific spent half a million for national park exhibits, and the next year seventeen railroads spent $43,000 helping to finance the first edition of 275,000 copies of the *National Parks Portfolio,* a beautiful booklet of pictures of the national parks prepared by Robert Sterling Yard in 1916. Mather himself contributed part of the cost of the Portfolio. A second edition was sold by the Superintendent of Documents. Yard also got up a booklet, *Glimpses of our National Parks,* 117,000 copies of which were sent out free. Free distribution presently was found to run afoul of an 1895 statute limiting free copies of government books to 1,000 copies, but in 1923 Congress provided money for printing the book. The Park Service also encouraged the making of pictures, including motion pictures, in the parks, and lent them out to various organizations.

In his promotional work Mather was assisted by the press, by the General Federation of Women's Clubs, by tourist and commercial organizations in the West, by the travel bureaus of the express companies, by the National Parks Highway Association, the National Park-to-Park Highway Association which was organized in 1916, and by the Far Western Travellers' Association.[22] Mather asked Yard to help in the job of promotion, apparently helping him financially in some way, but in 1918 Congress forbade the payment

[22] *Report, Secretary of the Interior, 1917,* 791 ff.; 1918, 815 ff. *Report, Director of Park Service, 1920,* 38 ff. Shankland, *op. cit.*

for government work by private funds, and in 1919 Yard helped to set up the National Parks Association, which promoted and defended the parks—sometimes too stridently. During the First World War, Europe was off-limits to tourists and the Park Service drummed for the national parks as a substitute for the castles and cathedrals of Europe, the sort of travel that would "keep the money at home," whereas, as Daniels had argued, little of the money spent in Europe returns to the United States. This was bad economics, but no worse than the average citizen uses and was therefore good promotion.

One of Mather's favorite methods of promotion was to take influential men, senators, representatives, newspapermen, writers, and others who might help promote the parks on trips through some of the parks. If the trips proved pleasant the guests would enjoy them and were likely to be favorably inclined to the natural wonders thereafter; if because of bad roads or other inadequacies of the parks they encountered hardships, they might well want the parks to be better financed. In the summer of 1920 some of the members of the House Committee on Appropriations visited a number of the national parks on a trip arranged by the Park Service and the Reclamation Bureau; western cities paid the cost of the trip, the concessioners provided free accommodations in the parks, officials of the railroads accompanied them on their respective lines, and Park Service officials acted as guides. Only one of the eleven members of the committee had ever seen the parks, which no doubt explains in part the common indifference of Congress to national park problems. This trip was apparently a success, for the next year appropriations began to climb.[23]

The railroads did more than finance publicity. They offered special summer rates to the parks, including several parks in a trip, by different railroads. The Bureau of Service, National Parks and Monuments, set up by the United States Railroad Administration in June 1918 while the railroads were run by the government, also co-operated with the Park Service in informing the public about the parks. The railroads did more than this. The Santa Fe had provided visitor accommodations at the south rim of Grand Canyon in the El Tovar Hotel as early as 1904, the Great Northern had provided about the first good accommodations in Yellowstone, the Great Northern provided excellent tourist facilities in Glacier, as

[23] *Report, Secretary of the Interior, 1920,* 17.

did still later the Union Pacific in Zion, Bryce Canyon, and the north rim of the Grand Canyon. The railroads have contributed greatly to the national parks through much of their history.

Mather was wise in advertising and promoting the parks, for the more tourists there were the greater would be the support for Congressional appropriations, and the stronger the defense against commercial invasion; but he had some promotional ideas that would not now be approved by park experts, in the light of later developments. In November 1916, referring to Yellowstone, he wrote: "Golf links, tennis courts, swimming pools, and other equipment for outdoor pastime and exercise should be provided by concessions, and the park should be extensively advertised as a place to spend the summer instead of five or six days of hurried sight-seeing under constant pressure to keep moving. . . . There is no national park better suited by nature for spending leisurely vacations."[24] At the time, this was not bad, perhaps, but it involves a confusion of two functions of parks which should have been and later were distinguished—the function of preserving the natural wonders and making them accessible to the public, and the function of mere recreation, which is appropriate not to national parks but to state, municipal and county parks and private recreational agencies. A criticism often aimed at Yosemite was that it was devoted too largely to recreational activities, mere amusements, while the scenic wonders were too little considered.

Mather was breaking new ground. There were no national parks in the world, except in Canada, whose experiences could serve as guides, and Mather and his men had to lay out their plans from scratch. His general program, as he conceived it from the first and as it developed in the first few years, called for a vigorous promotion and advertising drive to get the public and Congress acquainted with the parks, with serious educational or interpretive work in the parks to get visitors to understand what they saw. This called for trained men, naturalist lectures, museums and libraries; better development of the parks; better roads, hotels and other accommodations; better water supplies, sanitation, and supervision. And to get all this he needed better appropriations from Congress. Although the troops in four of the older parks had done a splendid job in protecting the parks, he wanted a trained ranger staff of his own

24 *Progress in the Development of the National Parks* (Washington: U. S. Government Printing Office, 1916), 10.

for the parks. The concession system was not satisfactory in several of the parks, and he saw that it must be overhauled. He saw that there were other areas in the country that should be reserved as national parks and monuments, and that several existing parks should be expanded; and he soon came to see that a system of state parks would supplement the national parks excellently and provide for some of the recreational needs of the people. The privately owned lands in the national parks were always a serious and persistent problem, and he hoped he might be able to acquire them. The parks had to be protected from exploiting commercial interests and, finally, wildlife problems were always critical in one way or another, and Mather was to be wrestling with them as long as he lived.

EDUCATIONAL AND INTERPRETIVE ACTIVITY   From the first Mather and his men saw that an important function of the parks would be interpretive work to help the visitors to understand the wonders of the parks, through nature study trips, information services, lectures, motion pictures, photographs, lantern slides, signs and markers, libraries and museums. "Following these early activities, the Secretary of the Interior appointed a committee to make a thorough study of educational possibilities in the national parks, the expenses of the survey to be met by a donation from the Laura Spelman Rockefeller Memorial Fund. This group, consisting of John C. Merriam, Herman C. Bumpus, Harold C. Bryant, Vernon Kellog, and Frank R. Oastler, went into the field and produced a preliminary report full of practical suggestions for 'promoting the educational and inspirational aspects of the parks.' "[25]

Soon afterward the Educational Advisory Board of the National Park Service was set up, which conducted field investigations in the parks and monuments and served in an advisory capacity. The various national parks are superb places to study geologic history and geologic forces at work, natural history, animals and birds and trees and flowers, because here all these are in fairly natural condition, little disturbed by man's destructive and disruptive activities. In 1916 Yard was put in charge of the Educational Section in the Park

[25] Freeman Tilden, *Interpreting our Heritage* (Chapel Hill: University of North Carolina Press, 1957), 34. *National Parks Magazine*, No. 91. Oct.-Dec., 1947.

Service, but the work failed to catch on and Yard turned to the organization of the National Parks Association in 1918. Charles D. Walcott was the first president of the Association, Yard was executive secretary, and at the first meeting in May 1919 its objective was announced: "To defend the National Parks and Monuments fearlessly against assaults of private interests and aggressive commercialism." Yard and his associates were fearless indeed, but sometimes he was lacking in tact and judgment and at times his relations with Mather were a bit strained.[26]

Nevertheless the educational work developed in many ways. Trained naturalists gave campfire lectures to visiting tourists. Universities began to take students to the parks, the University of California leading, in Yosemite.

In the summer of 1918 Mather learned of some nature-study work being carried on at Lake Tahoe under the patronage of Mr. and Mrs. C. M. Goethe of Sacramento, who were paying the salaries of two California professors, Dr. Harold C. Bryant and Dr. Loye H. Miller, to do the work of building and marking trails and developing nature studies. When Mather saw what was being done he wanted to transfer the operations to Yosemite, and managed this in the season of 1920. Bryant and Miller not only gave campfire lectures and conducted nature study trips in Yosemite, but gave lectures in the Midwest and East. The Yosemite program was under the administrative leadership of Ansel F. Hall, the first Yosemite naturalist. The University of California had sponsored lectures on geology, botany, and folklore in Yosemite in 1919. In 1921 several parks put on a similar program. By 1927, there were few of the parks that did not have at least a part-time naturalist. Publications of various kinds were printed and circulated, and much later, as we shall see, the Service hired trained research men to study the various problems encountered in the parks.[27] When Secretary Work came to office in 1923 interpretive work was pushed with much energy, for Work was much interested in it.

MUSEUMS   One of the obvious ways of doing educational and interpretive work is through the use of museums, and Mather and Albright wanted museums. As we have seen, a sort of museum

26 *National Parks Bulletin* No. 68, July, 1940, 5.
27 Shankland, *op. cit.*, 258, 259. *School and Society*, July 31, 1926, 132.

was completed in Mesa Verde in 1918 and expanded in the next few years, largely with money given by Rockefeller and by Mrs. Stella Leviston of San Francisco. Some people who had taken curiosities from the park gave them back to the museum. About 1919 the Park Service was building museums in Yellowstone and Casa Grande. Ansel Hall, of Yosemite, was an industrious collector, and beginning in 1919, assembled various collectors' items—Indian arrowheads, baskets, flowers, stuffed animals and the various things that make a museum—built his own showcases, and raised several thousand dollars toward the cost of a museum building. Chauncey Hamlin, president of the American Association of Museums, learned of his efforts and helped him to raise funds, even to get the Laura Spelman Rockefeller Memorial to give $70,500 for a new museum building in Yosemite. Another gift of $5,000 was made by the Memorial to cover the expenses of investigating the possibility of developing museums in other parks. In 1927 the Memorial also gave $10,000 toward a museum at Grand Canyon, and the Hawaii Volcano Research Association donated an observatory and branch museum at Kilauea. In 1930 a museum was completed at Grand Canyon, and exhibits were placed at Yavapai. About this time the Indian museum at Acadia was deeded to the government. The Laura Spelman Rockefeller Memorial gave $118,000 for museums in Yellowstone, which were artistically designed and built. During the years of the Great Depression CCC labor was used to build a number of museums in the parks, and today there are more than a hundred, many of them in historical parks.[28]

But something must be said as to the essence of the educational work of the Park Service. For some years the word "education" was used, and the work was "educational" in the sense of imparting information, enlarging the knowledge of visitors through pamphlets, lectures and in various other ways. Later—no date can be set—the Service turned more and more to the word and the concept of "interpretation," which Freeman Tilden has defined as "an educational activity which aims to reveal meanings and relationships through the use of original objects, by firsthand experience, and by illustrative media, rather than simply to communicate factual information." It is "the revelation of a larger truth that lies behind any statement of fact"; its chief aim "is not instruction, but provocation," and it

28 For a very interesting discussion of educational activities and the development of museums, see Shankland, *op. cit.*, 258-62.

"should aim to present a whole rather than a part, and must address itself to the whole man rather than any phase. . . . Information, as such, is not interpretation, interpretation is revelation based upon information. But they are entirely different things. However, all interpretation includes information."

In other words, the interpretive work of the Park Service was more and more designed not altogether to give the visitors more information about the parks, although that was involved, but to enable them to understand and appreciate what they saw. Unfortunately there are not many interpreters of Freeman Tilden's stature.[29]

IMPROVING PARK FACILITIES   Improvement of the park facilities was a pressing need. The parks needed about everything, and the automobile tourists were beginning to crowd into the parks by the thousand. Automobiles had been admitted to Mount Rainier in 1908, General Grant in 1910, Crater Lake in 1911, Glacier in 1912, Yosemite and Sequoia in 1913, Mesa Verde in 1914, and Yellowstone in 1915. Some of the tourists who had used the horse-drawn coaches thought that the introduction of gasoline-driven vehicles involved a loss of the old-time flavor of romance, but of course there was also an absence of the old-time litter and flies that the horses brought. At any rate, as Mather could foresee, the machine had its way, and it made good roads essential.

Only two of the parks, Yosemite and Yellowstone, had more than a few miles of roads, and those of Yosemite were execrable, not nearly as good as the state highways. Those of Yellowstone, built by the Army Engineers, were much the best, yet they were narrow, with steep grades which washed badly in rains and in dry weather were sometimes shockingly dusty although there had been some sprinkling of the roads for several years. As early as 1919 Mather was trying to get the roads in a few of the parks paved, but this was not to be achieved for a number of years. One trouble with all the roads was that it was Congressional practice to vote money in irregular driblets which meant that the Service—or the Army Engineers, who built the roads in several of the parks—could build only piecemeal stretches, without any general comprehensive plan. It meant poor and in the long run really expensive road-construction. Millions were needed

29 See Tilden, *op. cit.*, particularly Chap. I.

for roads, and Mather did not get very substantial increases for several years.

In Yellowstone there was another difficulty. On the Grand Loup Road the stage horses were unaccustomed to automobiles, and it was necessary to operate the horse-drawn stages on schedules that prevented the horses and the automobiles from meeting anywhere in the park. This caused some inconvenience, and Mather met it by motorizing the transportation lines in 1917.

Some automobile entrants complained about the entrance fees, which were really fairly high, but Mather needed the revenues badly. In 1917, however, with increasing numbers of automobiles entering, he thought it wise to reduce some of the entrance fees. The fee had been $10.00 for Yellowstone, $8.00 for Yosemite, and $6.00 for Rainier. These were reduced to $7.50, $5.00, and $2.50, respectively. In 1926 motor fees were again reduced in several national parks: in Yellowstone to $3.00, in Yosemite to $2.00, in Mount Rainier to $1.00, in Glacier and Crater Lake from $2.50 to $1.00, in Sequoia from $2.50 to $1.00. Whether these reductions were wise or not is a question which will be deferred to a later chapter.[30]

Hotel and lodge accommodations varied widely in the different parks at the time Mather came. Yellowstone had several good hotels, a bathhouse at Old Faithful which used water from the springs for hot baths, adequate camp grounds, and better roads than any other park, if not really very good. There were three gateways to the park —north, west, and east, the Cody entrance having been recently completed; and the south entrance was being planned. From the reports of the time it appears that some of the automobile camps were auto "shelter camps," apparently with some sort of shelter for the automobiles. Yosemite had several new lodges and camps, and was getting new hotels at Glacier Point and in the Valley. Because of the wretched condition of the roads the accommodations were usually adequate although not good. Glacier Park, thanks to the Glacier Park Hotel Company, operated by the Great Northern Railroad Company, had excellent hotels and chalets, artistically designed to fit the surroundings, and several tepee camps. But there was much complaint of shortage of horses, and the Park Service needed administrative headquarters. At Mount Rainier there were only two camps and two or three primitive hotels, but the concessioner was building a

[30] *National Parks Bulletin* No. 49, Mar. 1926. See Chap. XXIX.

hotel camp in Paradise Valley. There was only one road, following Nisqually River to Paradise Valley.

Crater Lake's accommodations were poor, inadequate, and badly managed, and there was a need for a water system, a small electric plant, and passable roads. Lack of water in the Crater Lake Lodge caused much inconvenience in the summer of 1916. Sequoia, General Grant, and Mesa Verde lacked roads, hotels, lodges, water and sewer systems, and adequate administration buildings. In Rocky Mountain Park, which had more visitors than any other large scenic park, the accommodations were so inadequate that stage lines were sometimes obliged to refuse transportation because there were no accommodations in the park. Roads were poor, but the state of Colorado was building the Fall River and Milner Pass road across the divide.[31]

Sanitary facilities in some parks were primitive and there were no systematic sanitary arrangements in any park, no real sewer system in Yosemite, Sequoia, General Grant, Crater Lake, or Mesa Verde. "Room and path" was conventional. In Yosemite flies and mosquitoes were a nuisance, and several of the parks where many horses were kept were infested with flies. Mather got a sanitation expert, Harry B. Hommon, from the Public Health Service, to "do such things as locating sources of pure water, prescribing means of keeping it pure, testing milk, designing water systems, designing and laying out sewer systems, selecting sites for garbage disposal units, discouraging mosquitoes, and training park personnel in the use of sanitation equipment."[32] Hommon was an efficient man, and within the next ten or twelve years was able to get decided improvement. In 1923 Yellowstone got $25,000 for a sewer system at the lake, and there were appropriations for sewer systems in one or more parks nearly every year for several years.

From the very first, Mather saw that the roads and buildings must be well and artistically planned if they were not to desecrate the natural surroundings, and the Park Service always devoted a great deal of attention to planning. More money was needed. World War I was being fought when Mather assumed office, and Congress was busy with war matters even before the United States joined in the war; yet in 1916 $150,000 was granted for an electric plant in Yosem-

31 Mather, *op. cit.*
32 Shankland, *op. cit.*, 253.

ite, and the next year, when we entered the conflict, $235,000 was appropriated for that park.

Mather, and Congress too, evinced considerable interest in Hot Springs, and Congress voted $190,000 for that park, and $334,000 for Yellowstone in 1918. About 1919 Congress began to loosen up, and a few years later the parks began to fare reasonably well. In 1921, $100,000 was granted for the "road over the mountain" in Glacier—the Going-to-the-Sun Road across the divide, one of the most scenic roads in the world; and considerable sums were appropriated for this road for several years. In 1924, in addition to fairly generous appropriations largely for roads and physical improvements in some of the parks—including $100,000 to build a trail down into Grand Canyon or to buy the Bright Angel toll trail—Congress appropriated $2.5 million a year for three years for road construction.[33] This appropriation was the fruit of a determined effort by Senator Smoot of Utah and Representative Sinnott of Oregon. It was becoming rather obvious that with automobiles swarming into the parks better roads were needed, but Sinnott's bill was debated at some length in the House. Some of the eastern representatives thought the East was paying a disproportionate share of the cost of the park roads, but the bill passed the House, and passed the Senate without discussion.[34]

GROWING CONGRESSIONAL INTEREST   In some other ways Congress began to show a somewhat more generous spirit. In the severe winter of 1919-20 about 15,000 elk in Yellowstone were reported to have starved—Albright believes it was only about 6,000—and in the 1920 deficiency appropriation Congress voted $35,026 for fire fighting and feeding the elk, then added $8,000 for more hay. The Park Service at this time was killing game predators—mountain lions and wolves and coyotes—and the elk and deer became too numerous. After dry summers and in severe winters there was heavy loss of these animals. In an effort to meet this situation in the 1923 appropriation bill Congress authorized the Secretary to sell surplus Yellowstone bison and give surplus elk, bear, beaver, and predatory animals to zoos or other institutions.[35] In 1921 a separate item of $25,000 was

33 Stat. 43, 90.
34 S. 959, H. R. 3682, 68 Cong. 1 Sess. S. 782, 69 Cong. 1 Sess.
35 Stat. 42, 1214.

granted for fighting fires, but the Secretary was required to make a detailed report to Congress on every fire. A foolish provision was added in 1922 that none of the money was to be used for any precautionary fire protection or patrol work. Fire lookouts were not authorized until 1931. In 1922 Congress gave the Park Service more freedom in its expenditure of funds by making 10 per cent of the total appropriation interchangeable. Unusual catastrophes, floods and fires, sometimes called for heavy expenditures, and in the 1924 appropriation Congress gave $20,000 for such emergencies, a regular appropriation thereafter, gradually growing. In 1927 the Secretary was authorized to add $60,000 to this item from the rest of the appropriations. In the 1923 appropriation, a small amount was granted for printing *Glimpses of Our National Parks*. Some of the national parks have considerable areas of forests, and forest insects were a constant menace, which Congress finally recognized in 1926, in a $20,000 grant for fighting insects.

Touring in the national parks was apparently a slightly hazardous business, for in July 1928 Congress passed an act "to facilitate and simplify the work of the National Park Service," authorizing the Secretary to aid and assist visitors in emergencies, and sell them food or supplies sufficient "to enable them to reach safely a point where such food or supplies can be purchased." The Secretary was also authorized to provide medical services for employees located in isolated places, and in case of death remove bodies of deceased employees to the nearest place for shipment or for burial.[36]

If all the parks had been permitted to use their revenues for improvement, they would have fared better. In 1916 Secretary Lane pointed out that this was not permitted in Crater Lake, Mesa Verde, Rocky Mountain, Hawaii, and Lassen, and suggested that all parks should be treated alike. He and other Secretaries, and of course Mather and Albright, would have liked to see all parks permitted to use their revenues; but the response of Congress was a provision in the sundry civil bill of June 12, 1917, requiring revenues from *all* the parks except Hot Springs to be covered into the United States Treasury after July 1, 1918.[37] There was reason for this, for the needs of the different parks did not always correlate with their revenues. It was generally good administration, anyhow, or would have been if Congress had shown more interest in the parks and more intelligence in dealing with them. At any rate, it showed the usual concern of

36 Stat. 44, 900.
37 Stat. 40, 152.

that body over its powers and prerogatives, a concern which was also shown in other ways.

For instance, in 1912 Congress had established a limit of $1,000 for any administration building in any national park, except by authorization of Congress. This was entirely too low to permit the construction of dignified buildings appropriate to surroundings of grandeur, and various Secretaries pointed this out; Mather finally, on July 1, 1918, got the limit raised to $1,500. The $1,500 limitation remained until February 13, 1940, when it was raised to $3,000 as a result of persistent efforts on the part of Senator Adams of Colorado and Representative De Rouen of Louisiana, and despite stubborn resistance by Representatives Taber of New York, Wolcott of Michigan, and Rich of Pennsylvania.[38] In somewhat the same picayune spirit Congress had imposed a limit of $600 on the yearly cost of maintaining a car in Crater Lake, and a few years later took pains to specify that waterproof footwear might be listed as park equipment![39] Somewhat more latitude would have made park management easier and more efficient. It is true that in the Park Service, as elsewhere, an occasional rascal would allow his acquisitive instincts to prevail over his loyalty to his job—a Superintendent of Glacier Park once did this—but generally the Park Service officials maintained a high standard of efficiency and integrity.

In 1923 the Park Service was allowed to buy supplies and services up to $50.00 worth in the open market "in the manner common among businessmen," and in 1927 the amount was raised to $100.[40] In 1926, the Secretary was authorized to "contract for medical attention and service for employees and to make necessary pay-roll deductions," and in 1930 he was allowed to maintain central warehouses in the parks and monuments for supplies and materials.[41]

In the appropriation for 1925, a new policy was established in appropriating $1.5 million, part of this however representing unused appropriations made in 1924, and authorizing the Secretary to make further contracts obligating the government for a million additional. This gave the Secretary more freedom, enabled him to look further ahead, and was the policy generally followed in later years;

38 S. 2056, H. R. 6350, 75 Cong. 1 Sess. S. 2624, H. R. 6657, 76 Cong. 1 Sess. Stat. 37, 460; 40, 679; 54, 36.

39 Stat. 45, 238.

40 Stat. 42, 1215; 44, 936.

41 Stat. 44, 491; 46, 219.

but in later years a part of each appropriation was used to pay the obligations incurred the year before. In 1931, for instance, $5 million was voted, but $2.5 million of this was to be used to pay obligations incurred in 1930.

NEED FOR A RANGER FORCE   Mather and the Park Service wanted their own ranger force instead of United States troops. Yosemite, Sequoia, and General Grant had been protected by cavalry troops from the beginning, and Yellowstone had been obliged to call upon the Army for protection against trespassers in 1886, as authorized by a law passed three years earlier.[42] By Mather's time the functions of these protectors had changed so that soldiers were not well suited to perform them. Protection from poachers and vandals—that they had provided excellently, although it was sometimes said that a few troopers would do a little poaching themselves occasionally; but there was no longer much poaching. The rangers' job had more to do with guiding tourists and explaining the various natural phenomena of the parks, and this called for men of very different training. The Army Acting Superintendents were capable, conscientious men, but they were trained soldiers, not foresters or conservators of animal life, or easy hosts to swarms of tourists; and, like the soldiers, they were likely to be moved out just when they were beginning to learn something about the job. Also, army business methods are usually lavish, with much red tape.[43] Furthermore, the Secretary of War wanted to pull out, pointing out that the Army in fifteen years had spent $1 million in Yellowstone, and now with the onset of the war had other duties for the troops. The troops had been withdrawn from the California parks in 1914, and in 1916 they were withdrawn from Yellowstone by arrangement between the War and Interior Departments, and the Park Service organized a civilian ranger force; but Congress thought the War Department should remain and gave the Park Service no money, so Secretary Lane had to recall the cavalry. Lane was able to show Congress the need for a civilian force, however, and an appropriation was made for it, and in the summer of 1918 the Park Service organized a ranger force of one chief, four assistant chiefs, and twenty-five rangers.[44]

[42] Stat. 22, 627.
[43] *The Survey*, Feb. 1, 1926, 542.
[44] *Report, Secretary of the Interior, 1918,* 842 ff. H. Doc. 1502, 63 Cong. 3 Sess.

The Army Engineers continued to build the roads in some of the parks, but in 1924 the Secretary of the Interior was authorized to construct roads in national parks and monuments, using some material given by the War Department, through the Secretary of Agriculture.[45]

CONCESSION PROBLEMS   The problem of concessions and concessioners engaged Mather's attention from the first. (In the early years of the parks the term "concessionaire" was used; later the term "concessioner" was usually employed.) The service offered by most concessioners in Yellowstone was perhaps as good as should have been expected, yet not as good as it should have been. There were some political hacks and fly-by-night adventurers even there, and in a few of the other parks there were no facilities at all, and no men anxious to provide the facilities under the conditions prevailing.

Unfortunately the general theory for some years had been that competition should be depended on to keep the prices down and the quality of services up; which meant that there were so many concessioners in Yellowstone and Yosemite that few of them could make a reasonable return on investment even while rendering poor service. Not many careful businessmen cared to get into that kind of a business morass, where at best they could make only a modest return and at worst stood a fair chance of losing their investment; and one result of this was that too many of the men seeking concessions were reckless adventurers, often with inadequate capital.

It was a rather hazardous business in many ways. Returns in most parks had to be earned in the three summer months—most of it in two months, July and August—and in parks near centers of populations, Yosemite and Mount Rainier, for instance, a disproportionate amount of the revenues had to be taken in on week ends; whereas interest, depreciation and obsolescence ran against buildings and equipment for twelve months. There was a considerable risk of loss in the winter when buildings were left largely unguarded, risk of burglary, vandalism by men and bears, fire, and storms—as for instance the caving in of the hotel roof in Crater Lake under a heavy snow. Some supplies had to be hauled long distances from railroad points outside the parks. In building the lodge at the North Rim of the Grand Canyon some of the supplies had to be hauled 200 miles,

45 Stat. 43, 90.

over execrable roads. Government policies were somewhat unpredictable, and, as many concessioners were to see when the United States entered World War I, a war can reduce tourist travel to a point where only well-financed men can stand the strain.

On the other hand, the concessioners did have some advantages as compared with businessmen in cities. Their buildings, where used only in the summer, did not have to be as well built as buildings in the cities, and the tents of the permanent camps were inexpensive. They paid no rent for land used, although the concession fee charged may be thought of as including an element of rent, and they often hired college students for modest wages, students who wanted a summer "vacation" in pleasant surroundings, but who were probably not as efficient as trained employees.

At the time Mather came to Washington in 1915 there were in Yellowstone a chain of five hotels and two lunch stations, owned by the Yellowstone Park Hotel Company and operated by Harry W. Child, president of the company. There were two stage lines, one run by Child from the north entrance, one run by F. Jay Haynes from the west entrance, and another run by Tex Holm from Cody to Lake Junction but not around the park. Holm had to put up his passengers from Cody at his Holm Lodge on the first night and at a camp on Sylvan Lake on the second night, for the trip required three days. There were three permanent camp systems (camps with semipermanent tents, often boarded up two or three feet high and canvas above), one run "Wylie Way," one by Shaw and Powell, and one by the Old Faithful Camp Company, each with five camps, two lunch stations, and transportation to the camps from the northern and western entrances; and there were several traveling camps. To support so many concessioners, rates had to be higher or service poorer than necessary.[46]

There were other evils too. Competing transportation companies meeting trains offered a potpourri of barkers' appeals that was embarrassing to tourists and not consonant with the dignity of a national park, or sometimes with the service that the tourist got when he had been ensnared. There was often little co-operation between the hotels and the transportation companies, which was detrimental to both and to the tourists as well. The multiplicity of concessioners, furthermore, called for more land space, buildings, more managers, more labor—it involved all the wastes of competition, in a business

46 Shankland, *op. cit.*, 120.

that was a natural monopoly. Hotels and transportation companies should have been operated by a single agency. Whenever the services got into anything approaching monopoly there were likely to be tirades in Congress, yet it was under such circumstances that the service was best—for instance in Glacier Park when the Great Northern controlled, and in Yellowstone when the Northern Pacific had much of the business.

As fast as he could, Mather reduced the number of concessioners, but he promptly ran into political difficulties with Senators Walsh and Myers and Representative Stout, who had friends operating concessions in Yellowstone. Walsh had a theory that anyone who wanted to operate any sort of concession in Yellowstone Park should be allowed to do so, at any rate if he was a friend of Walsh, and he had a fairly loud voice in the concession business of Yellowstone. But Mather wanted to get the concession business in such shape that he could attract good men, and he stood firm. In 1917 he reported that he had granted a concession to a single transportation company, a single hotel company, and that the two camping companies had combined and dropped their transportation business. By 1924 he had the concession business pretty well monopolized, except for the general stores and a few minor concessions.

In 1928 Mather got an act from Congress authorizing the Secretary to grant leases without advertising and without competitive bids. No leases were to be assigned without permission of the Secretary, but the Secretary was authorized to permit concessioners to mortgage their property for the purpose of installing, enlarging, or improving plant and equipment.[47]

Mather did not have any one theory as to the charges to be exacted of concessioners, whether a fixed sum or one that varied with net profits or gross income or something else: it varied with the kind of business and with other considerations. He favored some kind of profit-sharing plan, allowing the concessioner 6 per cent on his investment, and dividing the profit above this between the concessioner and the government in some ratio; but he did not use this plan altogether because he did not have the trained accountants to supervise it.

A great need in Mather's time was better living quarters for employees, many of whom had to live in tents or skimpy temporary quarters or wherever they could find a hook to hang their clothes on.

47 Stat. 45, 235.

Mather personally built a $25,000 rangers' club house at Yosemite in 1920, but employee housing was always substandard, down to the present time.

ROCKY MOUNTAIN PARK   Mather had great ambitions for more parks and for additions to some of those already established. Rocky Mountain National Park, covering the Longs Peak region in Colorado, one of the highest mountain areas in the United States, was added only a few days after Mather came to serve the parks. The area was seen by Colonel Stephen H. Long and his official exploring party in 1820, and the great mountain was later named after him. Joel Estes visited the area in 1859 or 1860 and settled there, to have Estes Park named after him in later years. In 1872 an Irish nobleman, the Earl of Dunraven, crossed the divide on a hunting expedition and, seeing the lovely meadows at the foot of the high mountain range, decided to build a great estate and game preserve. He bought up a great many claims in and around Estes Park but never rounded out his great estate, for Colorado people had the area thrown open to settlement and homesteaders and others filed on some of the land. In the eighties there was a mining boom and prospectors and others came into the area and filed claims, but the mining business never thrived and most of the claims were abandoned.[48]

From 1908 or 1909 a few tourists and summer home seekers began to come into the region, among them the Rocky Mountain naturalist Enos Mills—the "John Muir of the Rockies." Mills built a cabin at the foot of Longs Peak, explored the area and decided it should be a national park. The summer home owners organized an association to protect the area, but the task was beyond their resources and they joined Mills in his crusade for a national park. Mills wrote articles for a number of publications, including *Saturday Evening Post,* and was able to stir up wide interest in the project, particularly since the citizens of Colorado wanted the advertisement of a national park here and saw that its establishment would relieve them of some financial burdens. By this time it was generally known that national parks brought tourists and increasing business to the adjacent areas. The Colorado legislature adopted memorials to Congress calling for the establishment of the new park, but the Forest Service was opposed.[49]

48 *Outing,* May, 1911, 202. *Nature Magazine,* May, 1932, 305.
49 See Shankland, *op. cit.,* 79; and *Review of Reviews,* July 1913, 51.

Secretary of the Interior Walter Fisher was interested in the new park project and delegated Robert B. Marshall, chief geographer of the United States Geological Survey, to make a personal examination of the region, and Marshall's report was definitely favorable.

Early in 1913 Senator Thomas and Representative Rucker of Colorado introduced bills to establish the Rocky Mountain National Park, but they were not reported out of committee.[50] In the first session of the next Congress, in 1914, Senator Thomas and Representative Taylor brought in bills which were not reported.[51] In the next session Thomas brought up two bills and Taylor introduced one, and one of the Thomas bills was reported and passed the Senate.[52] This bill, S. 6309, provided for the exchange of individually or municipally owned lands in the park area for lands outside but not in national forests or reservations, with the consent of the Secretary of the Interior, or for lands in national forests with the consent also of the Secretary of Agriculture. This provision was injected to meet the opposition of private land owners. The park area included a great many private holdings. In the House the bill was reported favorably, with amendments, and debated at some length. Those favoring the bill stressed the high altitude of the area—the lowest point was 7,500 feet, and there were fourteen peaks exceeding 13,000 feet elevation, more than could be found almost anywhere else in the country—and they pointed out that this park was nearer, more accessible to the people of the mid-continent area than any others. On the other hand some senators and representatives argued that the cost of maintaining our park system was excessive, and that the parks should be supported by the states rather than by the national government. Senator Smoot, generally a supporter of parks, proposed that the bureau of national parks, which was under consideration, should first be created so that a general view of the park system could be taken before any new parks were established.

In spite of opposition, but with a proviso that appropriations for the park should not exceed $10,000 a year, the bill passed and was signed by President Wilson on January 26, 1915.[53]

The establishing act was not a perfect national park law. In addition to the sections guaranteeing existing entries, permitting leases

50 S. 8403, H. R. 28649, 62 Cong. 3 Sess.
51 S. 530, H. R. 1634, 63 Cong. 1 Sess.
52 S. 6007, S. 6309, H. R. 17614.
53 Stat. 38, 798 (S. 6309 was the bill that passed).

of not more than twenty acres for twenty years for hotels and cabins —these provisions were customary—the act provided "that the United States Reclamation Service . . . may enter upon and utilize for flowage or other purposes any area within said park which may be necessary for the development and maintenance of a government reclamation project." This was to cause trouble later. Whenever consistent with the primary purposes of the park, the Right-of-Way Act of 1901 was made applicable for irrigation and other purposes; and as in Glacier Park, the Secretary was authorized to grant rights of way for steam, electric, or similar transportation.

Ten thousand dollars a year was of course inadequate. Secretary Lane appointed three rangers at $900 a year, and this took $2,700, leaving little of the first $3,000 appropriation for other expenses. The next appropriation was $8,000, the next $10,000. Supporters of the park promptly set to work to get the $10,000 limitation removed. With the support of Secretary Lane, Senator Shafroth offered a bill in 1916 to remove the $10,000 limitation, and Representative Timberlake brought up a bill for an appropriation for the park.[54] The Shafroth bill passed the Senate in the next session.

On April 10, 1917, in the 65th Congress, Shafroth and Timberlake were up with bills again, and the Shafroth bill was reported favorably and passed the Senate, although Senator Smoot of Utah reminded the Senate that the park would not have been established in the first place without this limitation. Timberlake's House bill was objected to by Representative Stafford of Wisconsin who insisted that Rocky Mountain was essentially a state park, and his objection stopped consideration of the bill.[55] In the next session of Congress, however, the bill passed with little debate.[56]

Before the Timberlake bill finally passed, Senator Shafroth tried a different tack. He introduced a weird bill providing that the federal government should grant to any state having a national park an area of public lands equal to the park area which the state might sell at not less than $2.50 per acre, the proceeds to go to improving the park. He conceded that his proposal was designed primarily to raise money for Rocky Mountain park but was made general to broaden support for it. Senator Walsh objected because the bill would take 3,000 sections of land in Montana from the reclamation fund, others

54 S. 6854, H. R. 10122, 64 Cong. 1 Sess.
55 S. 1555, H. R. 171, 65 Cong. 1 and 2 Sess.
56 Stat. 40, 1270.

objected because it would reduce irrigation funds or deprive homesteaders of lands for homesteading. A fear was voiced that the bill
would be used by speculators to profit from the sale of the lands. The
bill did not proceed to a vote.[57]

Scarcely had the park been established when efforts were made to
enlarge it. Some of the peaks south of Longs Peak had been eliminated from the original blueprint by mining interests, and Mather
wanted these included—covering Mount Arapahoe and Arapahoe
Glacier, the largest glacier in Colorado, and other peaks—along with
the Never Summer Range northwest of the park, and the Mount
Evans area west of Denver, perhaps as a disconnected annex to the
park. Colorado had men in Congress who were willing to work for
these additions. In 1916, in the 64th Congress, Representative Timberlake introduced a bill to add Gem Lake, Twin Sisters Peak, and
Deer Mountain—a total area of about 25,000 acres—and this bill was
debated at some length. Representative Sherley of Kentucky pointed
out that the park was near Denver and of use mainly to Colorado
residents, and argued that it should be supported by Denver or the
state of Colorado. He hinted that this situation prevailed with respect to other parks too, that the states were glad to load onto the
federal government the financial burden of supporting national
parks that were of more use to them than to others. In this argument
he was joined by a number of other representatives, but the bill was
reported favorably by the committee in the House and passed, passed
the Senate without debate, and was signed by President Wilson on
February 14, 1917.[58]

In 1924 there was a small excision. The farmers living east of the
divide needed water for irrigation, and wanted to dam the Cache
La Poudre River on the northern edge of the park; and the Secretary
of the Interior had no right to authorize it, so they proposed to have
354 acres of land transferred from the park to the Colorado National
Forest in which dams were allowed. Representative Timberlake offered bills for the transfer, approved by the Secretaries of the Interior
and Agriculture, and one of them passed both houses with no debate.[59]

57 S. 4472, 65 Cong. 2 Sess.
58 H. R. 10124, 64 Cong. 1 Sess. Stat. 39, 916.
59 H. R. 13385, 67 Cong. 4 Sess. H. R. 2713, 68 Cong. 1 Sess. Stat. 43, 252.
Shankland, *op. cit.*, 177.

Two years later the boundaries were revised inward again, on the north and east sides, by identical bills introduced by Senator Phipps and Representative Timberlake "To eliminate certain privately owned lands from the Rocky Mountain National Park and to transfer certain other lands from the Rocky Mountain National Park to the Colorado National Forest, Colorado." The purpose of the bill was to eliminate some of the extensive private holdings along the east boundary, and to authorize the Secretary to permit the use of a small acreage along the north border needed in connection with a small reservoir—the Arbuckle Number 2 Reservoir. The bill passed both houses and was signed by President Coolidge on June 9, 1926.[60]

On June 21, 1930, Congress authorized the President to add certain specified lands in the Estes Park and Grand Lake areas, including Grand Lake itself; and soon afterward President Hoover proclaimed an addition, and in 1932 another.[61] In 1936 President Roosevelt proclaimed a further addition, but the Park Service had plans for making Grand Lake Village into a typical frontier village of log cabins before it should be taken into the park, and was never able to get this done, so Grand Lake remains outside the park. The village is a fairly typical resort town, not badly described as a "mess."[62]

In June 1939 Senator Ashurst of Arizona brought up a resolution authorizing the Committee on Public Lands to make a thorough investigation of all questions relating to the proposed enlargement of Rocky Mountain, and about the same time Senator Hatch of New Mexico and Representative De Rouen introduced bills to add the Arapahoe region, but were unable to get the attention of Congress.[63]

The Never Summer Range was finally added, but the southward extension and Mount Evans area were never included. Probably it was well that the Mount Evans region was not included, for it would have been largely for the use of Denver people, and its scenery was similar to that of Rocky Mountain Park.

The state of Colorado co-operated modestly in the improvement and protection of the park. In 1920 the state completed the Fall

---

[60] S. 3176, H. R. 9390, 69 Cong. 1 Sess. Stat. 44, 712.

[61] Stat. 46, 791, 3029; 47, 2498.

[62] Stat. 49, 3501.

[63] S. Res. 147, S. 2651, H. R. 6655, 76 Cong. 1 Sess. S. Res. 3121, 76 Cong. 3 Sess.

River Road over the divide at a cost of $162,000. It was not a road
for timid drivers. Some of the turns near the summit were so sharp
that drivers could not go around without stopping, backing, and
starting on again; and some did not enjoy backing toward a 3,000-
foot cliff. The Fall River Road offered real adventure. There was a
question as to who owned the road since the state had built it and
had not yet ceded jurisdiction over the park. It was not until 1932
that the Park Service completed a fine road over the pass, four miles
of it above 12,000 feet high. Colorado established a state game reserve east of the park in 1919 to help in game preservation. The elk
were about exterminated when the park was established, but the
state got a small herd from Yellowstone and soon had a fair elk
population.

Wildlife never played as important a part as in Yellowstone. The
Bighorn sheep were the most characteristic animal, but when the
park was established there were a few deer and elk, bear, beaver and
the usual complement of coyotes and mountain lions. Birds were
reported as scarce. Within a few years most wildlife was much more
abundant, although protection was somewhat difficult for years
because the federal government did not have jurisdiction. The state
of Colorado considered ceding in January 1926, but there was opposition in the legislature at the time and the matter was dropped.
When Mather tried to get an exclusive transportation franchise set
up, he found himself stymied because the state had not ceded jurisdiction. The case was carried to the Supreme Court, where the decision was against the Park Service.[64] The House Appropriations Committee announced that there would be no more appropriations for
roads until jurisdiction was established, and the state later ceded it;
Congress accepted it in 1929 and President Coolidge approved on
March 2, 1929—fourteen years after the park was established.[65]

For several years the park administration was handicapped by lack
of suitable headquarters, and in 1922 the Estes Park Women's Club
offered to donate a site in Estes Park Village for this purpose if the
government would build the building before December 31, 1923.
Senator Nicholson and Representative Timberlake introduced bills
for acceptance and Timberlake's bill passed both houses with little
comment and was signed by President Harding on September 18,
1922. A building site in Estes Park Village was not an extravagant

64 *Congressional Record*, Jan. 11, 1926, 1850 ff.
65 H. R. 17101, 70 Cong. 1 Sess. Stat. 45, 1536.

contribution, but it showed a friendly spirit, and besides, the building brought business to the village.[66]

Tourist use of the park was extensive from the start. When the summer heat came to the Middle West, many people went to the cool mountains, which for some meant Rocky Mountain National Park, it being the nearest. In 1920 Secretary Payne reported 115,588 car passengers, 87,542 of whom were from Colorado. In 1919 Director Mather reported hotels crowded and more camp grounds needed. Most of the land suitable for camp grounds was privately owned, and in 1924 he bought three tracts with the park appropriations; but for some years private owners monopolized the best camp sites.

HAWAII PARK   In 1916 two more national parks were added, Hawaii and Lassen Volcanic. Hawaii, covering the two active volcanoes, Kilauea and Mauna Loa, on the island of Hawaii, the latter 13,680 feet high, and the 10,000-foot Haleakala on Maui Island, apparently about extinct. It was a magnificent addition to the park system. Albright is said to have rated it about the finest of the national parks.

The establishment of Hawaii National Park was urged as early as 1903, and in 1906 Lorrin A. Thurston, a Honolulu publisher, began a campaign which was to bring the park to realization ten years later. He was aided by Governor Frear of Hawaii, by the territorial legislature, and by many others in Hawaii, and he had the encouragement of Theodore Roosevelt, John Muir, Lane, and others in the United States. An American scientist, Thomas Jaggar, with other men set up the Hawaiian Volcano Research Association in 1912, with a small observatory on Mount Kilauea, and this association worked persistently for the park. Thurston, Jaggar, Governor Frear and others worked out park bills and sent them to Delegate Kalanianaole at Washington, who tried to get them through Congress, assisted by Lane, the Park Service men and many others.[67]

As early as January 1911, Kalanianaole introduced a bill in the House to establish a park in Hawaii, with a resolution of the Hawaiian legislature suggesting a reduction to 38,275 acres in the proposed park in order to reduce opposition to the bill. The pro-

66 S. 2583, H. R. 8675, 67 Cong. 1 Sess. Stat. 42, 847.
67 See Nash Castro, *The Land of Pele: A Historical Sketch of Hawaii National Park* (Hilo, Hawaii: Hilo Tribune Herald, Ltd., 1953).

posal was for a park covering the active crater of Kilauea and volcanic formations, excluding timber and grazing lands. The bill was not reported from committee.[68] In the next Congress Kalanianaole brought up his bill again, but again it failed of a committee report.

In 1915 a delegation of 124 Congressmen visited Hawaii and Thurston and Jaggar sold them the park idea without difficulty. Soon afterward Kalanianaole came up again with a bill to create a bigger park to cover the active volcano Kilauea and the occasionally active Mauna Loa, both on the island of Hawaii, and a right of way between them, and also the extinct volcano Haleakala on the island of Maui. This bill had the usual provisions—no interference with valid claims, leases to concessioners of land up to twenty acres for twenty years—but there was to be no appropriation for improvement or maintenance until the United States got such perpetual easements and rights of way as were needed to make the park accessible, and no appropriation for more than $10,000 annually without express authorization by law. It passed the House without any objection, even from Mann of Illinois, the Cerberus who commonly guarded the Treasury against too many parks. In the Senate, the limit on appropriations was struck out, although Overman of Texas thought no appropriation would be needed and Lane of Oregon thought "it should not cost anything to run a volcano." The Senate finally receded from its amendment striking out the $10,000 limitation, and the bill was passed and signed by President Wilson on August 1, 1916.[69] The act did not require that all private lands should be bought by the Hawaiian government but only as much as was necessary to provide access to points of interest.

The park was created subject to the Right-of-Way Act of 1901, which permitted rights of way for irrigation and other purposes, and also for steam, electric, and other transportation. In the next Congress Senators Saulsbury of Delaware and Kalanianaole brought in bills to authorize the Governor of Hawaii to acquire privately owned lands in the park, but neither passed and in the next Congress Kalanianaole tried again, this time successfully, on February 27, 1920. There were two large estates, the Bishop estate and the Parker estate, the former situated around Kilauea Crater, a part of

68 H. R. 32316, 61 Cong. 3 Sess.
69 H. R. 11612, 62 Cong. 1 Sess. H. R. 1995, 63 Cong. 1 Sess. H. R. 9525, S. 722, H. R. 68, 64 Cong. 1 Sess. Stat. 39, 432.

which the manager was planning to subdivide and sell for summer homes. There were also some private lands on Mauna Loa and Haleakala.[70]

Under the provisions of this law the Governor proceeded with dispatch and vigor, and got much of the private land by 1922, by purchase, donation, and by exchanging territorial public domain for it. Some of the land needed was already owned by the territory as public domain and this could be turned over directly to the federal government. For some reason the park was dedicated on July 9, 1921 and the Park Service arranged for administration, although much of the land was not accepted by the Secretary until September 27, 1922. Perhaps the reason was that there was need for prompt action. Vandals were breaking off the stalactites in the lava caves on Kilauea and pulling up the beautiful silver-sword plants (found nowhere else in the world) in the crater of Haleakala. Congress appropriated only $750 in 1918 and in 1919, and $1,000 in 1920, just for the expenses incident to securing the donations of land, so the Park Service could do practically nothing for protection. Even the $10,000 granted in 1921 and for several years thereafter was not enough to provide much protection.[71]

The Park Service had scarcely taken over Hawaii before it appeared that, as in many cases, the park did not cover all that should have been included; that Kau Lava Flow in the Kau Desert, about 43,000 acres, should be added. This lava flow was still active, could be seen moving, and it was believed that the area might once have been inhabited and that under it there might be important archeological data. The Governor set the area aside, and late in 1921 Representative Curry of California brought up a bill to add this area to the park, which passed both houses without debate and was signed by President Harding on May 1, 1922.[72]

The next step in the development of Hawaii Park was to get the $10,000 limitation on appropriations wiped out. This was reminiscent of the temperance pledges often signed in the old days of campaigns against the demon rum; and it was maintained about as long. The park needed roads. There were 41,150 visitors in 1923,

70 S. 5323, H. R. 13699, 65 Cong. 2 Sess. H. R. 3654, 66 Cong. 1 Sess. Stat. 41, 452. *Report, Secretary of the Interior, 1918*, 125, 879 ff; 1919, 149, 1019. *Report, Director, Park Service, 1920*, 151.

71 See *Report, Secretary of the Interior, 1916-20.*

72 H. R. 8690, 67 Cong. 1 Sess. Stat. 42, 503.

and the roads ranged from poor to execrable. Congress was considering a bill setting up a three-year program for roads in the parks, with $260,000 to be allotted to Hawaii parks, and this could not be spent until the limitation was repealed. In 1924 Representative Newton of Missouri introduced a bill to accomplish this, which passed both houses without debate and was approved by President Coolidge on June 5, 1924.[73]

The Park Service proceeded with work on the roads and on a camp at Kilauea. There were difficulties enough: heavy volcanic activity from Kilauea in 1927, which seemed to make it a somewhat dangerous place for there were only three rangers for the entire park; some vandalism still, and some injury to vegetation from wild goats, wild pigs, and burros, which had become a nuisance; and the federal government still did not have exclusive jurisdiction. In 1927 and 1928 the boundaries were further considerably enlarged, the act of 1928 adding a particularly beautiful shoreline and one of the few unspoiled native villages.[74] In January 1930 Delegate Houston of Hawaii introduced a bill to provide for exclusive jurisdiction by the United States, and it passed both houses with little discussion and was signed by President Hoover on April 19, 1930.[75]

[73] H. R. 4985, 68 Cong. 1 Sess. Stat. 43, 390.
[74] Stat. 44, 1087; 45, 424.
[75] H. R. 9183, 71 Cong. 2 Sess. Stat. 46, 227.

CHAPTER XI

The Mather Administration

1917-1928

LASSEN VOLCANIC PARK, MOUNT MCKINLEY

PARK, GRAND CANYON PARK, ACADIA PARK,

AND ZION PARK

LASSEN VOLCANIC PARK   Lassen Volcanic National Park was added on August 9, 1916. Mount Lassen, in northern California, the only active volcano in continental United States, had been studied by J. S. Diller of the United States Geological Survey for more than thirty years. It was known at least as early as 1865, but only to a few local residents. It was covered into a national forest, and on May 6, 1907, President Theodore Roosevelt set aside as national monuments Cinder Cone, elevation 6,913 feet, and Lassen Peak, elevation 10,453 feet, both active more than a half century before but apparently dead or dormant.[1]

Only a few years later, in 1911, Representative Raker of California, who was taking an active part in getting the Park Service established, developed a great interest in the promotion of Cinder Cone and Lassen Peak to the status of national park—under the name Peter Lassen National Park, after a Danish pioneer in California by that name. In the 62nd, 63rd, and 64th Congresses he worked for the new park, alone, for no one else in Congress seemed interested, although he had the support of chambers of commerce

[1] Stat. 35, 2131, 2132.

of nearby towns and even of San Francisco, of several women's clubs, geologists, and other individuals. Presently nature came to help him, with a series of volcanic explosions from Lassen Peak, beginning in May 1914 and increasing in intensity until May 19, 1915. Snow—thirty-five to forty-five feet deep—was melted, and torrents of water and mud tore eighteen miles down the mountainside, pushing great and small boulders along and leveling large trees over a wide area. There would have been some loss of life but for heroic warning of inhabitants of exposed areas. Such spectacular eruptions were reported widely and no doubt made people volcano-conscious and well disposed toward Raker's bills.[2] So when Raker brought up a bill on December 6, 1915, it passed with little discussion and no opposition.[3]

It was not a real national park bill, but was designed to give the name "national park" to an area which, like Glacier, was a sort of hybrid cross between a national park and national forest. It did not affect existing claims and patents—a customary provision; it allowed grants of rights of way for steam, electric, and automobile roads; it opened the park to reclamation projects; directed the Secretary of the Interior to publish regulations, "such regulations being primarily aimed at the freest use of said park for recreation purposes by the public"; and authorized the Secretary to grant leases of ten acres for twenty years for public accommodations or one acre for twenty years for summer homes. The Secretary was authorized to sell dead and down timber and permit grazing. Apparently the bill was designed to permit hunting for, like the Yellowstone establishing act, it instructed the Secretary merely to "provide against the wanton destruction of the fish and game found within said park and against their capture or destruction for purposes of merchandise or profit." If it had allowed mining and the sale of timber other than dead and down, it would have provided for just what was there before the monument was established—a typical national forest. Appropriations were limited to $10,000 annually—the same temper-

2 *American Forests*, Nov. 1941, 518. *Travel*, Sept. 1934, 28. *Review of Reviews*, April 1915, 487. *Science*, May 26, 1916, 727. *Scientific Monthly*, Jan. 1935, 21.

3 H. R. 348, 64 Cong. 1 Sess. Among earlier Raker bills were H. R. 19557, H. R. 22352, 62 Cong. 2 Sess.; H. R. 52, 63 Cong. 1 Sess.; H. R. 21533, 63 Cong. 3 Sess.

ance pledge found in Rocky Mountain and Hawaii bills. This was changed in committee to $5,000 and, so amended, the bill passed both houses.[4]

This hybrid act was not acceptable to Mather, to Secretary Lane, or to Secretary Houston of the Department of Agriculture, who thought the Forest Service was doing an acceptable job in protecting the volcanoes. Mather, who was away, wired Lane urging him to advise President Wilson to veto it, but Lane disliked to offend Raker, who had been generally friendly to the parks and let the President sign it. When Mather saw the new park he was glad that Lane had not followed his advice. There was a good chance that the worst provisions could be changed later, as indeed they were, in 1931.[5]

The new "park" was more a national forest than park, and for all purposes remained a national forest for several years. No money was voted for administration until 1920, so the Forest Service continued to administer it. The 1920 appropriation of $2,500 was not enough to do much, so the Park Service was obliged to co-operate with the Forest Service in protection. Appropriations never rose above $3,000 until 1925, nine years after the park was established. Since Congress would not vote real money for protection, a movement was started by people in northern California, some of them cattle and sheep men, to abolish the park and restore the land to the national forest; but this did not attract wide support. In 1923, at the request of the Lassen Volcanic National Park Association, the legislature of California voted $8,000 to be used with the $3,000 appropriated by Congress for a road and development program. Secretary Work and Mather were dragging their feet in road building for there were some private holdings in the park, and of course roads would enhance the value of these holdings. They hoped to get the private lands before going too heavily into road construction.

In the meantime, in the 64th, 65th, 66th, 67th, and 68th Congresses Raker worked industriously "for the protection and improvement of the park" in a spate of some eight bills, but with no success. So he turned to the job of getting the $5,000 limitation on

4 A score or more of bills were introduced to establish Lassen Volcanic Park, mostly by Raker. It will be unnecessary to cite them all.

5 Robert Shankland, *Steve Mather of the National Parks* (New York: Alfred A. Knopf, 1951), 170, 171.

appropriations removed. His bill to accomplish this passed Congress in spite of strenuous objection from Representative Mann of Illinois, who insisted that the park bill would not have passed without this limitation. The repeal bill was signed by President Harding on April 29, 1922.[6]

For a few years Lassen Volcanic got little attention in Congress. Appropriations gradually increased to a modest $25,300 in 1929, and the park was cared for in some fashion. In late 1928 and 1929, however, it appeared that a few things ought to be done. There were some state-owned lands in the park, and Senator Shortridge and Representatives Lea and Englebright of California moved to get these exchanged for "unreserved, non-minerals, vacant lands" owned by the federal government somewhere in California; and Englebright's bill to effect this exchange passed Congress without debate and was signed by President Coolidge on May 21, 1928.[7] The next year thirty-nine square miles of volcanic area were added, and the park was exempted from the Water Power Act.[8]

There were also lands in the park owned by private individuals, some of which were in scenic parts of the park, and Englebright offered a bill in the House to permit the Secretary of the Interior to exchange for these lands other lands in the park that were of less scenic importance, or to trade timber elsewhere. Land owned by lumber companies was usually wanted almost altogether for its standing timber and a trade of timber for land might sometimes be made. This bill passed with little opposition, and was signed by President Hoover on March 1, 1929.[9]

The next year the President was authorized, on joint recommendation of the Secretaries of the Interior and of Agriculture, to add several sections of land to the park; and in January 1931 the provision in the establishing act allowing the Secretary to issue permits for summer homes and rights of way for railways or roads was abolished. The Secretary might, however, at his discretion, renew summer home permits formerly granted.[10]

6 H. R. 5588, 67 Cong. 1 Sess. Stat. 42, 503.

7 S. 3920, H. R. 10278, 69 Cong. 1 Sess. S. 1270, H. R. 11405, 70 Cong. 1 Sess. Stat. 45, 644.

8 Stat. 45, 1081.

9 H. R. 11406, 70 Cong. 2 Sess. Stat. 45, 1443.

10 Stat. 46, 853, 1043.

MOUNT MCKINLEY PARK   Mount McKinley National Park, next to Yellowstone the largest of the national parks (although exceeded in size by Katmai and Glacier national monuments), was added on February 26, 1917, to protect from extinction the Dall or white Alaska mountain sheep, caribou, Alaska moose, grizzly bear, and other animals which were the prey of hunters, and incidentally to protect Mount McKinley, snow covered, magnificently aloof among its mountain neighbors. This great mountain, 20,320 feet high, is much the highest mountain in the United States, perhaps the highest mountain in the world from its base, for unlike such mountains as Everest and our own Whitney, Elbert, Harvard, and Massive, it rises from a rather low surrounding terrain—2,500 to 3,000 feet elevation. The area had been highly inaccessible. It could be reached from the seacoast by pack train, dogsled, or small boat— a hard trip—or could be reached from the north by a longer and somewhat less arduous journey; yet of course some sportsmen are always willing to undergo such hardships for the joy of killing something. The government railroad, authorized in 1914,[11] was being built near, and there was a reasonable fear that the railroad would bring in an army of hunters.[12]

Mount McKinley had been described as early as 1897 by W. A. Dickey, who estimated its height at 20,000 feet. Soon afterward various surveys were made, and in 1913 Archdeacon Hudson Stuck, Harry Karstens and native companions climbed the peak. Dr. Frederick Cook claimed to have done this earlier, but his story was usually regarded as a hoax.[13]

The idea of making a park originated with the Boone and Crockett Club, of New York, originally founded by Theodore Roosevelt and others as a hunting club, but later turned to conservation and, with the Campfire Club of America, an organization devoted to the saving of wildlife. Charles Sheldon, of the Boone and Crockett Club, spent some time in Washington working for the park, aided and abetted of course by Mather when Mather came to the Park Service.[14]

11 Stat. 38, 305.
12 *Scribners,* Oct. 1917, 399.
13 *National Geographic Magazine,* Jan. 1917, 69. *National Parks Magazine,* No. 96, Jan.-Mar. 1949, 20.
14 Shankland, *op. cit.,* 171.

Efforts in Congress date only from 1916, when bills were introduced by Senator Pittman of Nevada and Wickersham, Delegate from Alaska. Pittman's bill provided for a park twenty-five miles square, to be open to irrigation enterprises under the law of February 15, 1901, and to mining. There was to be no hunting except to protect human or other animal life or to provide necessary food for prospectors; and violations of the provisions of the act or of the Secretary's regulations should be punished by a $500 fine and/or six months' imprisonment. The usual provision permitted leases of twenty acres for twenty years to concessioners. In the Senate the section providing punishment for violations was eliminated, and as thus amended the bill passed without opposition. In the House two other amendments were adopted, limiting appropriations to $10,000 annually, and covering revenues from leases into the Treasury. The Senate concurred in the amendments and the bill passed without objection; it was signed by President Wilson on February 26, 1917.[15]

The reasons advanced for the creation of the park were (1) stimulation of travel to Alaska, (2) preservation of the natural scenery, and (3) protection of the wildlife. Probably the last was the most important and accounted for the lack of serious opposition to the bill.

The act as passed had several bugs in it. The park was left subject to the 1901 act allowing rights of way for irrigation and other purposes; mining was permitted, and prospectors and miners were allowed to kill game for food. The last provision was to be grossly abused.

Following its usual procedure, Congress apparently assumed that the new park would be protected by God, at no expense. After the bill had passed Senator Pittman submitted an amendment to the sundry civil appropriation act granting $10,000 for the park, but nothing came of it. So there was no money for several years, and the Park Service could not assume the administration of it, but was obliged to turn the job of protection of the wildlife over to the Governor of Alaska, who had very modest funds for such a task and could do little. The game laws of Alaska were not well suited to this task, the game wardens were often inefficient or worse, the population generally hostile, and Governor Riggs was not enthusi-

15 S. 5716, H. R. 14775, 64 Cong. 1 Sess. Stat. 39, 938.

astic about the new status of the area but thought the laws of Alaska should be applied.

In 1919 Mather reported that the Park Service would not open the park soon, but would try to protect the wildlife, and the next year reported, "No appropriations have been made, no control of the park has been established, and it has no protection aside from the incidental attention it has received from the ridiculously small gamewarden force of the Territory of Alaska." Charles Sheldon appeared before the appropriations committee that year and pleaded for protection of the game. The next year $8,000 was granted, to maintain, protect and improve 2,650 square miles of wilderness, pay the salary of the Superintendent and assistants, the upkeep of a dog team, and the cost of erecting needed buildings, building trails and protecting the sheep and caribou; and the Park Service assumed control, appointed a Superintendent and arranged for a survey of the boundaries.[16]

As long as little or nothing was appropriated, the $10,000 limitation on appropriations made no difference, but efforts were soon made to eliminate the provision.

Surveying boundaries of the park, Mather just naturally decided that they should be extended, that the park should include a large area to the east; and he got Delegate Sutherland to bring up a bill to add 445 square miles of mountainous land that surveyors of the United States Geological Survey had reported as a natural breeding ground for mountain sheep and caribou, yet unsuited to agriculture. The bill was pounced upon by a few representatives of mining interests, but they were quieted by the assurance that mining was permitted in the park. Even Mann of Illinois favored the bill because it would forestall private claims which were such a nuisance in many of the parks. In the Senate, King of Utah leaped to the protection of the miners, but he too was assured that the park was open to mining and withdrew his objections; the bill passed and was signed by President Harding on January 30, 1922.[17]

The Park Service now had a good big park and a little money for administration and protection. In 1920 Mather reported that there was little poaching, but that the mining prospectors were killing many animals for themselves and for their dogs and that many did not observe the rules. It may be assumed that some of the "hardy

16 *Report, Secretary of the Interior, 1920,* 65; 1921, 129.
17 H. R. 6262, 67 Cong. 1 Sess. Stat. 42, 359.

prospectors" were after game and not minerals. The Service secured the co-operation of the Alaska Road Commission in developing roads and trails, and of the Land Office in making surveys; but the roads were slow coming. By 1923 the railroad was opened and afforded access to the park, but there were no roads or trails across. A local homesteader outside the park was building a log roadhouse for local travel, and he also applied to the Park Service for a lease to build six shelter tents in the park with stoves and beds but no food. A *Brooklyn Daily Eagle* party of seventy held dedicatory exercises at the gate on July 9, 1923.

The appropriation maximum of $10,000 was inadequate to protect so large an area, and the hunting privilege accorded prospectors and miners was being abused, as Mather reported year after year; and in March 1924 Delegate Sutherland was induced to bring up a bill to remove the $10,000 limit and the miners' hunting privilege, but it was not reported. In January 1927 Senator Willis of Ohio introduced a similar bill which passed the Senate, in spite of some objection from Senator King of Utah, who thought it was a bill to establish a new national park, and that Congress had "gone perfectly mad in the establishment of these parks throughout the United States."[18]

In the next Congress Senator Willis was up with his bill again, but failed to get results.[19] In the same session, however, Representative Curry of California brought in a bill which passed Congress with little debate, and was approved by President Coolidge on May 21, 1928.[20] Four years later the boundary of the park was again changed.[21] In 1931 the Secretary was authorized to prescribe regulations for mining and require registration of all prospectors and miners who entered the park.[22]

Tourist accommodations were nicely adjusted to the need for them—almost no one there, and no place to stay. Sixty-two visitors were reported in 1924, and that year a camp was established on the Savage River with accommodations for twenty-four visitors, but the hotel was not finished until 1939. The accommodations were apparently inadequate or unsatisfactory or both, and in 1940 Congress

18 H. R. 8020, 68 Cong. 1 Sess. S. 5006, 69 Cong. 2 Sess.
19 S. 1711, 70 Cong. 1 Sess.
20 H. R. 8126, 70 Cong. 1 Sess. Stat. 45, 622.
21 H. R. 6485, 72 Cong. 1 Sess. Stat. 47, 68.
22 Stat. 46, 1043.

authorized the President to buy the property of the Mount McKinley Tourist and Transportation Company and provide needed facilities, appropriating $30,000 for this purpose.[23] President Roosevelt did not act immediately, and in 1941 an appropriation of $30,-000 was again considered in Congress.[24] In 1946, $200,000 was provided, and for several years thereafter the appropriation for the Alaska Railroad included something for facilities in the park—in addition to the regular appropriation for the Park Service.[25]

Two years after Mount McKinley, three more parks were added: Grand Canyon and Lafayette (later Acadia) on February 26, 1919, and Zion on November 19, 1919—all three formerly national monuments.

GRAND CANYON PARK   Grand Canyon is remarkable mainly as our most spectacular scenic wonder, but it has less important attractions, such as a few cliff dwellings, and here and there footprints of prehistoric reptiles and animals. John Muir described Grand Canyon well in the late nineties: "No matter how far you have wandered hitherto, or how many famous gorges and valleys you have seen, this one, the Grand Canyon of the Colorado, will seem as novel to you, as unearthly in the color and grandeur and quantity of its architecture, as if you had found it after death, on some other star; so incomparably lovely and grand and supreme is it above all the other canyons in our fire-moulded, earthquake-shaken, rain-washed, wave-washed, river and glacier sculptured world."[26]

The canyon was seen by a trapper, James Pattie, some time before 1831, and by other trappers and traders in the following years, but they thought it a rather terrible place or unworthy of mention. In 1858 Lieutenant Ives explored a part of the canyon, and was greatly impressed; but very little was known in the East about the great canyon until Major J. W. Powell, a one-armed veteran of the Civil War and a geologist, made his famous trip down the river in

[23] Stat. 54, 80.

[24] *Congressional Record,* 77 Cong. 1 Sess., 4071, 4072.

[25] Stat. 60, 383.

[26] John Muir, *Our National Parks, Sketches from the Atlantic Monthly,* (Boston & New York: Houghton Mifflin and Co., 1901) , 35.

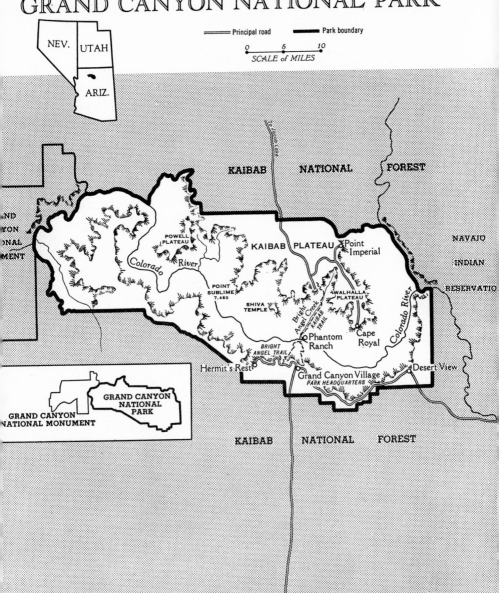

GRAND CANYON NATIONAL PARK

Principal road   Park boundary

0   5   10
SCALE of MILES

NEV. UTAH

ARIZ.

To Jacob Lake

KAIBAB   NATIONAL   FOREST

POWELL PLATEAU

KAIBAB   PLATEAU

Point Imperial

NAVAJO

INDIAN

RESERVATION

Colorado River

POINT SUBLIME 7,460

SHIVA TEMPLE

WALHALLA PLATEAU

Bright Angel Creek

KAIBAB TRAIL

Cape Royal

Colorado River

Phantom Ranch

BRIGHT ANGEL TRAIL

Hermit's Rest

Grand Canyon Village
PARK HEADQUARTERS

Desert View

GRAND CANYON NATIONAL MONUMENT

GRAND CANYON NATIONAL PARK

KAIBAB   NATIONAL   FOREST

GRAND CANYON NATIONAL MONUMENT

To Flagstaff

1869, with nine men in four boats, and published a description of the river and canyon. This aroused interest, but there was not much travel to the canyon until 1901, when the Santa Fe Railroad built a spur from Williams to the South Rim, and in 1904 built the famous El Tovar Hotel.[27]

The area has had a checkered career: set aside as a national forest in 1893;[28] creation of game reserve authorized in 1906;[29] game preserve established covering part of it later in 1906;[30] proclaimed a national monument by President Roosevelt in 1908, under the jurisdiction of the Department of Agriculture, to keep out further mining claims;[31] and established as a national park on February 26, 1919.[32] In addition to the natural park, an area adjoining on the west was proclaimed a national monument by President Hoover in 1932, under the supervision of the National Park Service;[33] and this national monument was reduced in area by proclamation in 1940.[34] At times there have been a variety of reservations on the canyon. For instance, from 1908 to 1919 there were sections of two national forests, a game preserve, and a national monument in the area. There are still the national park and the national monument, and Kaibab National Forest on each side.

Efforts to create a national park began early, when Yellowstone was the only national park, for Senator Benjamin Harrison of Indiana introduced a bill to set aside Grand Canyon as a public park in 1882, and two other bills later in the eighties. The first bill was reported from committee but got no further attention.[35] John Muir urged establishment of the park in 1898.

There was no further congressional interest in the matter for nearly twenty years. In 1905, however, Senator Penrose of Pennsylvania and Delegate Wilson of Arizona brought up bills granting a right of way and ferry privileges across the Colorado—really for the

27 Hans Huth, *Nature and the American* (Berkeley and Los Angeles: University of California Press, 1957), 159-61, 181.
28 Stat. 27, 1064.
29 Stat. 34, 607.
30 Stat. 34, 3263.
31 Stat. 35, 2175.
32 Stat. 40, 1175.
33 Stat. 47, 2548.
34 Stat. 54, 2692.
35 S. 1849, 47 Cong. 1 Sess. S. 541, 48 Cong. 1 Sess. S. 863, 49 Cong. 1 Sess.

benefit of a mining claimant named Bass. Fortunately these bills got no attention.[36] Two years later Senator Smoot tried to get the preserve enlarged, but without success.[37] In the next Congress Senator Smoot introduced a bill to establish a game preserve covering a part of the canyon area, to be designated by the President, and this passed both houses without argument and was signed by President Roosevelt on June 29, 1906.[38]

In the 60th Congress, Delegate Smith of Arizona, probably incited by railway promoters, tried without success to get a right of way in the area for the Grand Canyon Scenic Railroad Company, and Delegate Cameron tried the same trick two years later, without success.[39] There had been a number of bills providing for railroad rights of way through the Grand Canyon Forest Reserve, two of which passed.[40] In the same Congress Senator Flint of California introduced two bills to set aside a part of the canyon area as a national park, but neither of them got a committee report.[41] Representative Hayes of California also tried in 1911 to set aside the park under the name "Carnegie National Park," "in commemoration of the name of the founder of one of America's greatest institutions and the benefactor of mankind by the promotion of everlasting peace among all nations of the earth without the use of arms"; but although this bill was favored by Secretary Fisher in 1912, and later by Lane, neither the new name nor the idea of peace was potent to call forth a committee report.[42] Some, for instance the Geological Society of America, thought the park should be named after Major Powell. In the meantime Smoot concluded that his game preserve was not large enough and tried without success to get it enlarged.[43]

Beginning in 1912, the Department of the Interior took an active interest in the creation of Grand Canyon park. The Sierra Club, of course, worked actively for it, Secretary of Agriculture David F. Houston favored it, and the legislature of Arizona adopted a resolution favoring it, although for years certain Arizona business interests and politicians were the main obstacle to its creation,

[36] S. 6565, 58 Cong. 3 Sess. H. R. 10411, 58 Cong. 2 Sess.
[37] S. 5010, 60 Cong. 1 Sess.
[38] S. 2732, 59 Cong. 1 Sess. Stat. 34, 607.
[39] H. R. 22093, 60 Cong. 1 Sess. H. R. 2258, 61 Cong. 1 Sess.
[40] See Stat. 29, 253; 30, 418.
[41] S. 5938, 61 Cong. 2 Sess. S. 10138, 61 Cong. 3 Sess.
[42] H. R. 6331, 62 Cong. 1 Sess.
[43] S. 417, 62 Cong. 1 Sess.

particularly an influential and unprincipled Arizona political boss, one Ralph Henry Cameron, later elected to the Senate. In 1915, although the roads were very poor, there were 106,000 tourist visits to the Canyon, many of the visitors coming by rail. The Santa Fe Railroad had the only good accommodations in the area.

In the 64th Congress Grand Canyon park bills were fathered by Senator Ashurst and Representative Hayden of Arizona, and Ashurst's bill received a favorable report from the Committee on Public Lands and Surveys, but no further attention. In the next Congress he was up again with his park bill. Among the main provisions of it were the following:

1. Concessions were to be let "at public bidding to the best and most responsible bidder."

2. Proceeds from leases and concessions were to be spent for administration, maintenance, and improvement.

3. Valid existing land claims were not affected, and the tolls on the Bright Angel toll road, or trail, were not affected, but the Secretary was to negotiate with Coconino County, which owned the trail, for its purchase, and report to Congress as to possible terms.

4. Power and reclamation projects, and prospecting and mining were to be allowed by the Secretary whenever consistent with the primary purposes of the park.

5. No building or other structure was to be built between Hearst's lands and the rim.[44]

In the House, the Committee on Public Lands offered several amendments: (1) protecting the rights of the Havasupai Indians living in the beautiful Havasu Canyon west of Grand Canyon, (2) allowing the Secretary to grant easements or rights of way for railroads across the park, (3) repealing the executive order of January 11, 1908, creating the Grand Canyon National Monument, and (4) excluding from the Grand Canyon National Game Preserve the lands included in the new park. The Senate concurred in these amendments, and the bill was signed by President Wilson on February 26, 1919.[45]

The act as passed made a national park of most of the lands formerly included in the Grand Canyon National Monument, which had been proclaimed by President Roosevelt in 1908,[46] and the

44 S. 8250, H. R. 20447, 64 Cong. 2 Sess. S. 390, 65 Cong. 1 Sess.
45 Stat. 40, 1175 ff.
46 Stat. 35, 2175.

Grand Canyon National Game Preserve. As usual in establishing acts, all valid land claims were recognized, and the rights of the Havasupai Indians in the Canyon of Cataract Creek were carefully guarded, even to the point of permitting members of the tribe, at the discretion of the Secretary, to farm land elsewhere in the park. The right of Coconino County to collect tolls on Bright Angel Trail was recognized, but the Secretary was authorized to negotiate with the county for the purchase of the trail and report possible terms to Congress.

Some of the provisions of the act were compromises with commercial interests, and did not represent true national park standards. Rights of way for irrigation canals, power lines and railroads were permitted; and reclamation projects were authorized, and prospecting and mining permits. These provisions were thought necessary because a dam on the Colorado was being considered— and was authorized in 1928—[47] and the area was thought to be of value for minerals. William Randolph Hearst owned two parcels of land on the South Rim, and to avoid opposition from him the act included an extraordinary provision that no building, fence, "or other structure" could be erected between his property and the rim —to cut off his view.

A significant but rather nebulous section of the act provided that concessions should be let "at public bidding to the best and most responsible bidder"—not necessarily the highest bidder. Just what this meant is not clear, for it suggested an auction of the concessions, and at the same time appeared to permit the Secretary to choose the "best and most responsible" bidder. It is also not clear whether it meant that all the concessions or each of the concessions should go to one bidder; but at any rate it seemed to authorize monopoly in each or all concessions—a wise provision. Many concession troubles had arisen because of earlier efforts to inject competition into a business that should have been recognized as a monopoly.[48]

The Park Service faced a sea of troubles in administering the new park. At first there was no money, and the Park Service could not take over from the Forest Service until August 1919, but Congress presently granted $40,000 for 1919 and $60,000 in 1920. The roads were barely passable; grazing livestock sometimes invaded the park,

[47] Stat. 45, 1057.
[48] Stat. 40, 1175. Shankland, op. cit., Chap. XVII.

the water problem on both rims was really difficult, for water for the hotel and camp grounds had to be hauled more than 125 miles. Worst of all, the park was infested with private mining and power site claims, mostly fraudulent. Ralph Cameron had located a number of claims beginning in 1902, two of them covering land where the Santa Fe planned to build its hotel, one on Indian Gardens, a wide place half way down the Bright Angel Trail where there was a spring and resting place for tourists going down into the canyon. Just before the national monument was established, in 1908, Cameron and associates had plastered the South Rim with forty-five claims strategically placed to control tourist business, at the head of Bright Angel Trail and on both sides of the Santa Fe terminus. From 1908 to 1919 the Forest Service, which administered the national monument, carried on a continuing fight with him. For several years he managed to hold control of the trail and of the Indian Gardens, which he kept in filthy condition, and charged $1.00 for every tourist riding down into the canyon, much to the distress of the Forest Service, the Santa Fe, and tourists. He was pried loose from the trail in 1912, which then reverted to Coconino County, Arizona; but he was hanging onto his other claims when the Park Service took over.

This was the mess that the Park Service inherited in August 1919. Sued by the government, Cameron defended his claims on the ground that the Grand Canyon area was not an object of such scientific interest that it could be established as a national monument under the Antiquities Act of 1906, and that although he had found no minerals, his claims were valid.

The District Court held against him, the Circuit Court of Appeals sustained the decision, and when he carried his case up to the Supreme Court that court affirmed the decision against him, on April 19, 1920.[49] But he still had about eighty-five mining claims, and claimed some sort of rights in power sites down in the canyon, as did several other men. He entered into negotiations with eastern power interests and apparently got a large sum of money for his campaign for the Arizona senatorship, which he won in 1920, greatly to the distress of Mather and the Park Service. As Senator, a good friend of President Harding's notorious Attorney General, Harry Daugherty, with much of the judicial and law-enforcing machinery of the state under his control or even in the hands of his

49 *U. S. Reports*, Vol. 252, 450.

friends or relatives, Cameron was a puissant nuisance to the Park Service for several years. He was able to manipulate cuts in the appropriations for the parks. In 1920, before he took his seat, he got a provision into the appropriation act forbidding any expenditure "for maintenance or improvement of any toll road or toll trail." He was working to regain control of the Bright Angel Trail, and wanted no interference or competition with it. In the appropriation for 1922 this prohibition was repeated, with an additional prohibition of any improvements on the North Rim—a prohibition injected by Representative Cramton of Michigan, chairman of the House Subcommittee, who tried in this way to stir up Senator Smoot and other political forces of Utah—the North Rim was accessible from Utah.

Cameron was disregarding a United States Supreme Court decision in hanging onto some of his claims, and was treading thin ice on some other matters, and generally overplaying his hand. Finally in March 1924 Cramton outlined some of his unsavory record before the House in a speech that brought headlines and editorials in newspapers. About the same time Harry Daugherty left the Cabinet; and Harlan Stone, a man of very different character, became Attorney General, and he presently cleaned the Arizona stables. In January 1924, Representative Hayden had introduced an amendment to the appropriation bill granting $100,000 to build a trail down the canyon or buy the Bright Angel Trail from Coconino County. There were three trails down the canyon at the time: the Bright Angel Trail, the Grand View Trail, twenty miles east, and the Hermit Trail, eight miles west, none of them in very good condition.[50] When the question of purchase was referred to the voters of Coconino County, they turned it down, and for two years the Park Service did nothing to improve the trail. Finally the Park Service was able to buy the trail, and the County put the money into a road leading to the canyon.[51]

There were other than Cameron's claims in the park, some alleging copper and asbestos deposits, even a few that were once worked a little, and some claims to power sites; and it took years to clean

50 *Congressional Record*, Jan. 29, 1924, 1640.

51 Stat. 41, 918, 1407; 42, 590; 43, 423. *Report, Director, National Park Service*, 1920, 128. For a very interesting account of Cameron's activities, see Shankland, *op. cit.* Chap. XVII; *The Nation*, Oct. 28, 1925, 481; and Edwin Corle, *Listen Bright Angel* (New York: Duell, Sloan and Pearce, 1946), 206-10.

them out. In 1931 the provision authorizing prospecting and mining was eliminated.[52]

The Park Service and the concessioners proceeded with the development and improvement of the park as rapidly as funds permitted. Already in 1919 there was a Wylie camp on the North Rim,
and in 1920 the old suspension bridge was built; two years later
Phantom Ranch was completed, at the bottom of the canyon. By
1922 stage trips were available every other day, from Lund and
Marysville alternately, to see Cedar Breaks, Bryce Canyon, Zion
and the North Rim of the Grand Canyon. In 1923 Congress granted
$40,000 to complete the Hermit road, and the Park Service hired an
architect to outline the future development of the South Rim, to
be followed by development of the North Rim the next year. In
1927 the boundaries of the park were changed, adding fifty-one
square miles of the Kaibab Forest on the north; and the Laura Spelman Rockefeller Memorial gave $10,000 for a museum. The next
year the Kaibab Trail was completed to the North Rim, where on
September 14, the Utah Parks Company, a Union Pacific concern,
opened a new lodge, 100 standard log cabins and 20 deluxe cabins.
This was expensive construction, for some of the materials had to
be hauled 200 miles from railroad points up in Utah. The operation of this concession was expensive too, for some supplies had to
be hauled this same distance, and water had to be pumped up 3,870
feet from Roaring Springs Creek. This was often referred to as one
of the finest concession developments in the park system.

The opening of the North Rim to tourists was a very important
advance. The North Rim is more attractive than the South Rim in
many ways, about 1,200 feet higher, cooler, with larger trees and
more attractive surroundings, and less congestion. Also the road to
the North Rim from Utah is itself of great scenic beauty, through
the aspen and pine forests of Kaibab Plateau. From one high point
on this road the view looking northward to the red mountains and
plateaus of Utah is almost as fine as the view of the canyon itself.
In 1928 a new suspension bridge was built in the canyon, and a
bridge over the Colorado east of the park at Lee's Ferry. This was
a great convenience, for it enabled tourists to drive from one rim
to the other without using the ferry at Lee's Ferry—a distance of
some 240 miles—although for years the road was very rough. Lee's
Ferry was named after a man, John D. Lee, who was a leader in the

52 Stat. 46, 1043.

Mountain Meadows Massacre in September 1857, in which a party of more than a hundred emigrants were massacred by Mormons and Indians. Lee had hoped to remain undetected in this isolated place, but United States troops ferreted him out and executed him. Navajo Bridge now marks the place where the ferry once was.[53]

There was a persistent overpopulation of deer in the Kaibab forest north of the canyon during these years. The Grand Canyon is really a gorge cut through mountains, and much of the area on the north is high land, at one point nearly 9,000 feet high, a high plateau partly surrounded on the south, east, and west by impassable canyons, and on the north by a hot desert which was also almost impassable to animals. So the deer were imprisoned within this area, which was high in altitude and subject to heavy snows, with no surrounding range to which they could resort when the heavy snows came and the forest leaves on which they lived in winter were gone. Mather was always a wildlife enthusiast, and the Park Service carried on a persistent war against predators, mainly mountain lions and coyotes; already in 1920 there were signs that the deer population of the Kaibab forest of the park and game preserve was excessive—perhaps nearly 50,000—and they were killing the little aspen trees by eating all the leaves. By 1924 many were reported starving in winter.

ACADIA PARK   Grand Canyon and Lafayette—later Acadia —national parks were created on the same day. Acadia—established by President Woodrow Wilson as a national monument in 1916 under the name Sieur de Monts, named Lafayette National Park in 1919, and the name changed to Acadia in 1929—included a part of what is called Mount Desert Island, although the word "Desert" has not the usual significance, for the island is decidedly not a desert. The first national park set up in the East, the first seacoast park, historically interesting and unique among coast points, rich in fauna and flora, Lafayette was a worthy addition to the park system, a gift to the government from a few devoted men, including George B. Dorr, who spent much of his fortune and life in promoting the park and served many years as its Superintendent, and John D. Rockefeller, Jr., who contributed much of the money needed.

53 See S. Ex. Doc. 42, 36 Cong. 1 Sess.

Acadia had been visited in 1604 by the French explorer Champlain who called the island the "Isle des Monts Deserts"—Sieur de Monts was an early French explorer, agent of Henry of Navarre—and in 1613 French colonists settled on the island. A century or so ago wealthy men began to build summer homes there, at first around Bar Harbor then at other points, until the area was threatened with the ugly commercialism of most summer resorts. In 1901 a group of men, including Charles W. Eliot, President of Harvard University, William Lawrence, Bishop of Massachusetts, and George B. Dorr, a Boston Brahmin of means and burning idealism, conceived the idea of preserving the beauty and the varied wildlife of the island—some of the wildlife was disappearing—adding as fast as possible to the area under protection. They got a charter from the state of Maine, and Dorr undertook the task of securing additional land, financed by himself and by a few other men, particularly by John D. Rockefeller, Jr. He was able to add Sieur de Monts Springs, the Summit of Cadillac Mountain—1,532 feet high—and much later Schoodic Point.

Dorr and his associates had no plans for getting the federal government to take over their lands until 1913, when the state legislature threatened to repeal their charter, but on this threat Dorr went to Washington and persuaded President Wilson to set the area aside as the Sieur de Monts National Monument, on July 8, 1916. The procedure followed, as reported in the proclamation, was that the association—the Hancock County Trustees of Public Reservations—conveyed the lands to the state of Maine, which conveyed them to the United States. Dorr and his associates followed the precedent set by William Kent and wife, who a few years before had given the Muir Woods to the government for a national monument. The new monument was reported to include about 6,000 acres: today it covers nearly 42,000 acres, and includes not only much of Mount Desert Island and Schoodic Point but a part of Little Cranberry Island and of Isle au Haut. Every year or two following the establishment of the monument the Hancock County Trustees would give more land.[54]

54 Shankland, *op. cit.*, 167-70. Stat. 39, 1785. *Outlook*, Aug. 23, 1916, 935; Apr. 28, 1917, 750; July 12, 1922, 153. *Scribner's Magazine*, Apr. 1917, 484. *National Geographic Magazine*, July 1914, 74; June 1916, 623. *Mentor*, Aug. 1923, 17. *Nature Magazine*, May 1929, 315. *American Forests and Forest Life*, Aug. 1929, 495. *American Forests*, Feb. 1957, 29.

The new monument was a fine addition to the park system, and two years later Congress gave $10,000 for administration and protection which enabled the Park Service to organize a small ranger force. Dorr and Mather wanted the monument raised to park status, and enlisted the interest of Senator Hale and Representative Peters of Maine, who brought up bills in Congress in 1918 to effect this; Senator Hale's first bill was to establish the Mount Desert National Park, but then it occurred to him that since France was our ally in the war that was going on and since the island had first been settled by Frenchmen, it would be a fine gesture to name it Lafayette; so he introduced another bill to create the "Lafayette" National Park. This passed both houses with no opposition except from Representative Mann of Illinois who pointed out that the park across from the White House was also called Lafayette Park, and that the advocates of woman suffrage often built bonfires on that park. President Wilson signed the bill on February 26, 1919.[55]

The act creating Lafayette had none of the familiar and unfortunate concessions to commercial interests. There were no railroads, reclamation promoters, cattle and sheep men and mining prospectors pressing for concessions, and the act created a real national park. There was one unusual provision in the creating act—the Secretary was authorized to accept for the government any lands on Mount Desert Island, or easements or buildings or money for extension and improvement of the park. This provision was used often in the years following.

Two years later a great marine and land biological station was established on the border, and in 1927 a museum of stone-age antiquities was built near the entrance—through the generosity of Dr. Robert Abbe, who also provided an endowment for it. The next year an auto camp ground was completed, but no concessioner has been given a lease for either hotels or cabins.

Lafayette Park seemed to present a very good set-up: a beautiful granite-bound island park, costing the government nothing but the annual appropriations for administration, which began at $10,000 and rose by 1933 to $55,000, allowing Dorr a salary of $3,000. But when Schoodic Point was donated to the park, the donors, who lived in England, did not relish the name "Lafayette," and since Dorr preferred the name "Acadia" anyhow, he induced Senator Hale and Representative Nelson to introduce bills to change the

55 S. 4569, S. 4957, H. R. 11935, 65 Cong. 2 Sess. Stat. 40, 1178.

name to "Acadia." Nelson's bill passed both houses without debate, and was signed by President Coolidge on January 19, 1929. The bill also provided for an extension of the boundaries of the park.[56]

ZION PARK   Zion Canyon, in southern Utah, one of the most magnificent of our national parks, was discovered in 1858 by Nephi Johnson, a Mormon scout. In 1861 Joseph Black explored the canyon and later a few settlers came in, led by Brigham Young, who, seeing the amazing coloring and height of the canyon walls, called it "Zion." Major Powell, explorer of Grand Canyon, visited the region in 1872, and gave the name "Mukuntuweap" to the North Fork of the Virgin River, which flows through the canyon, and "Parunuweap" to the East Fork which flows across the southeast part of the park. The Mormons valued it as a place of retreat when threatened by Indians, but not much was done with the canyon for thirty years, and it was known to very few because there were no passable roads anywhere in the area. On July 31, 1909, however, President Taft proclaimed the Mukuntuweap National Monument, which covered little but the Mukuntuweap or North Fork River and valley.[57] The new status of the canyon kept further entries out but nothing was done for the new monument until 1916 when Congress appropriated $15,000 to repair and extend fifteen miles of road into the canyon.[58] The next year the Park Service began modest improvements and gave the Wylie Camp concern a five-year concession to provide camp facilities and transportation to Lund. In 1917 Senator Smoot introduced a bill to change the national monument to a national park and the name from Mukuntuweap to Little Zion.[59]

On March 18, 1918, President Wilson proclaimed an enlarged national monument, enlarged from 15,840 acres to 76,800 acres, to include not only the North Fork canyon but the Great West Canyon, the Coal Pits Wash, Horse Pasture Plateau, and some other areas. In his proclamation he also changed the name from Mukuntuweap to Zion.[60] Soon, as the scenic magnificence of the area came

56 Shankland, *op. cit.*, 170. S. 4823, H. R. 15088, 70 Cong. 2 Sess. Stat. 45, 1083.
57 Stat. 36, 2498.
58 Stat. 39, 818.
59 S. 8282, 64 Cong. 2 Sess.
60 Stat. 40, 1760.

to be known, efforts were made to make it a national park. In 1918 Senator Smoot introduced a bill for this, but it was not reported. A similar bill brought in by Senator King of Utah likewise failed of a report.[61] In the next Congress, Senators King and Smoot and Representative Welling of Utah tried again, and this time Smoot's bill passed the Senate without discussion, but was questioned in the House. The bill had a provision authorizing the Secretary to buy eighty acres of private lands—the only private holding in the park— and the House amended this to limit the purchase price to $5.00 an acre. There was some discussion as to the wisdom of establishing another park so soon after a costly war. The Senate disagreed with the House amendment on land purchase and in a conference committee it was eliminated and the bill was passed and signed by President Wilson on November 19, 1919.[62] Congress gave $7,300 to start the new park off.

A fantastically beautiful canyon, similar to Yosemite Valley, Zion had not at the time been seen by Mather, but Albright had told him of it and he was more than delighted when he saw it two years later. Since it had been set aside as a national monument before, there was little settlement and few attempts at commercial developments; the establishing act created a true national park with no concessions to commercial interests.

The $15,000 road grant was not enough to do much, for there was rough land in the park and the road leading up the canyon called for expensive work. For the time the park was almost inaccessible, although in 1920 there were 3,692 visitors, 3,206 of whom were Utah residents. To get to the park from the east it was necessary to drive down through central Utah on a road, some of which was good for the times but toward the southern part of the state was usually covered deep with dust. The tourist was obliged to drive south to Fredonia in northern Arizona, then west past Pipe Spring to Hurricane on a mere faint trail where there was some danger of getting lost and perishing.[63] From Hurricane to Rockville and the park entrance, there was a rough road. In the summer of 1922 a flash flood washed out all the bridges in the canyon, making it ac-

---

61 S. 5039, S. 5048, 65 Cong. 2 Sess.

62 S. 38, S. 425, H. R. 6644, 66 Cong. 1 Sess. Stat. 41, 356.

63 The writer traveled this trail in 1922 and nearly lost the trail at one point. Occasionally a tourist would get lost in the desert at this time and a few deaths were recorded.

cessible only by horse or afoot for a while. From the west the park
was perhaps a little more accessible, but the drive from either north
or south was over poor roads, usually very dusty. There were few
good roads in the West at this time.

In 1922 the Park Service began a serious study of the road system,
and the next year got $133,000 for roads. A visit to the park by
President Harding helped to advertise the park and get this appropriation. The next year the West Rim trail was completed. In 1925
Congress voted the Park Service a round sum of $1.5 million for
roads and trails in the parks, and two years later the Mount Carmel
road was begun.[64] This road, with its mile-long tunnel, one of the
greatest pieces of road construction in the United States, made the
park easily accessible from the east, through red-rock scenery almost
as remarkable as the canyon itself.

There were other improvements. In 1922 the Union Pacific Railroad completed a line from Lund to Cedar City and the next year
the Utah Parks Company, the Union Pacific agency, was granted a
concession for touring accommodations in Zion and nearby Bryce
Canyon and the North Rim of Grand Canyon. Tourist traffic was
increasing rapidly, in spite of poor roads.

Like so many other parks, Zion was presently found not large
enough, *really* not large enough, and in 1928 seven sections were
withdrawn from the public domain for examination with the purpose of adding them. These studies went on for a year or two, and
in 1930 Senator Smoot and Representative Colton secured a considerable addition to the park.[65] The park was still too small. There
were gorgeous red canyons to the north and northwest—Kolob Canyons among them—which were of national park grandeur; and on
January 22, 1937, they were proclaimed as Zion National Monument.[66] This arrangement persisted until 1956 when the monument
was made a part of the park.

64 Stat. 43, 90.
65 S. 4169, H. R. 11699, 71 Cong. 2 Sess. Stat. 46, 582.
66 Stat. 50, 1809.

CHAPTER XII

The Mather Administration

1917-1928

HOT SPRINGS PARK, BRYCE CANYON PARK,

GREAT SMOKY MOUNTAINS PARK,

SHENANDOAH PARK, MAMMOTH CAVE PARK

HOT SPRINGS RESERVATION   Hot Springs Reservation, a health resort rather than a scenic park, is not really within the scope of this book, but since it called for more of the attention of Congress than perhaps any other park, almost more than all the other parks at times, it must be discussed very briefly. For some reason Mather wanted to make it a national park. This he succeeded in doing in 1921, through an amendment to a sundry civil appropriation bill.[1] There may well be some question as to the wisdom of this, for Hot Springs was just hot springs, supposed to have great curative powers in baths, but with no particular scenic merit. The springs had been set aside in 1832, the government had properly reserved with them four sections of land, but the area was largely in private holdings, with titles that were in process of litigation for years. The Hot Springs *Reservation* was not recognized until 1870, when Congress tried to set up legal procedure for settling some of the titles and claims to titles. For fifty years Congress was wrestling with the problems of land titles and disposition of the healing waters. The springs, really remarkable springs, were located in Hot Springs, a

[1] Stat. 41, 1407.

fair-sized town, and a national park in a town seems something of a misnomer. It should have remained a reservation.[2]

BRYCE CANYON PARK   After Zion, Congress rested from its park labors. For five years no more national parks except Hot Springs were created; but on June 7, 1924, Bryce Canyon National Park, not very far from Zion, a varicolored jewel of a little park, was added, as a result of promotion by Albright and Mather and Congressional efforts of Senator Smoot of Utah.[3]

Like the other scenic wonders, Bryce Canyon was no doubt known to the Indians long before white men ventured into Utah, although it is not certain that they paid much attention to it. It was visited in 1872 by a party of geologists who must have been rather insensitive to its beauty or they would have proclaimed it to the world. In 1875 the nearby settlements of Escalante and Cannonville were established, and Ebenezer Bryce, for whom the park is now named, settled in the lower gateway to the so-called "canyon." Incidentally Bryce "Canyon" is not really a canyon, but a horseshoe shaped bowl or amphitheater, remarkable not for its size or grandeur but for its fantastic beauty. It is only about two miles across and a thousand feet deep, with hundreds of minarets standing up in the bowl, of many shades of red, pink, yellow, and saffron—a jewel-like little amphitheater. However, to follow common usage, we shall call it a canyon.[4] This canyon is particularly pleasant as a summer vacation spot because at the rim it is more than 8,000 feet in altitude and therefore pleasantly cool, even almost cold at night.

Considering the fact that everyone who sees Bryce is entranced by its beauty, it may seem strange that it was little known outside the locality for many years after the first settlers came. Doubtless this was due largely to the fact that the region was highly inaccessible. No railroad ran near, and the roads in southern Utah were ex-

2 Stat. 4, 505; 16, 149.
3 S. 668, 68 Cong. 1 Sess. Stat. 43, 593.
4 The writer remembers vividly the time when he first saw Bryce Canyon in 1922. After some days of wandering about on bad desert roads he and two companions drove up a slight incline, and there the delicately intricate and brilliantly colored canyon lay before them like a scene from another world. Not one of the party spoke for several minutes!

ecrable.[5] It was something of an adventure to drive to Bryce, and as late as 1919 half of the people in Panguitch, only 18 miles from the canyon, had never seen it. In 1923, a road was built through Red Canyon to the rim of Bryce.

Photographs were published as early as 1916, and in the early twenties some interest began to appear. Albright had seen Bryce Canyon as early as 1917, and he induced Mather to go to see it two years later. Mather was of course tremendously impressed and immediately vowed that it should be made a part of the park system. The next year Secretary Payne, no doubt at Mather's and Albright's promptings, reported that it was worthy of national monument status, and that there was much wonderful scenery in southern Utah.

As a result of the strong recommendations of Mather, and of the Secretaries of the Interior and Agriculture, President Harding proclaimed *Bryce Canyon* a national monument on June 8, 1923.[6] The Secretary of Agriculture was favorable to the monument because the canyon was in the Paunsaugunt Plateau which had been set aside as the Powell National Forest in 1905, and it would therefore be under his jurisdiction as before, and could be easily administered. As a national monument it would be safe from further land entries. The proclamation did not prohibit the use of the monument for forestry purposes, that is, for the same purposes for which the Powell National Forest was used, but the monument reservation was declared to be dominant—a common provision in the creation of monuments—and there was to be no use which would interfere with its preservation or protection as a national monument.

The monument was highly inaccessible at first, and little known, but the fame of its gorgeous colors and myriads of pinnacles soon spread, and the next year its establishment as a national park was provided for under the name Utah National Park. Before this could be established, however, all the land within the boundaries had to become the property of the United States, and the Secretary was authorized to exchange for private lands in this park and Zion unappropriated public lands of equal value and approximately equal area in the state of Utah.[7]

5 In 1922 the writer found a small lodge at the canyon rim, but there were no tourists there.

6 Stat. 43, 1914.

7 S. 668, 68 Cong. 1 Sess. Stat. 43, 593.

Unfortunately there were 640 acres of land in the park owned by the state and by the Union Pacific Railroad. The Secretary was able to trade for the state lands without difficulty, but at first the Union Pacific was reluctant to exchange. Finally, however, the railroad agreed to a trade, and—before the land transactions were completed—Congress passed a law, on February 25, 1928, changing the name to Bryce Canyon National Park, and adding a considerable acreage from the Powell National Forest and from the public domain.[8] Three months later, on May 12, 1928, Congress passed an act to correct the description of the land, and on September 15 the last deeds to private lands were delivered, and the next day the park was dedicated.[9] On June 13, 1930, Congress authorized the President, on recommendation of the Secretaries of the Interior and Agriculture, to add a couple of townships to the park;[10] and on January 5, 1931, President Hoover made a considerable addition.[11]

The park still did not seem large enough, and Director Albright, Mather's successor, and his men, after some scanning of the boundaries managed to get Congress to pass another bill on February 17, 1931, authorizing the President, on recommendation of the Secretaries of Agriculture and the Interior, to make further large additions, and a small excision.[12] Again President Hoover was obliging, and issued a proclamation on May 4, adding 22,068 acres and eliminating 1,266 acres, which were returned to the Powell National Forest.[13]

So was Bryce Canyon National Park established and brought up to its present area of more than 36,000 acres. It was easy to establish, because everyone who saw it recognized its superlative national park quality; it was small, and had little that commercial interests would fight for, little commercial timber or grazing lands, no mineral or power or irrigation values—only scenery. After being established and enlarged to its present size it was large enough, and there was no occasion for trying to expand its boundaries much farther. There is remarkable scenery in surrounding areas that would be well

8 Stat. 45, 147.
9 *American Forests and Forest Life,* Jan. 1929, 37.
10 Stat. 45, 502; 46, 582.
11 Stat. 46, 3042.
12 Stat. 46, 1166.
13 Stat. 47, 2455.

worth national park or monument status, but it should probably be in separate administrative units. Bryce Canyon is destined to grow in popularity.

NATIONAL PARKS IN THE EAST   Mather had for some time wanted national parks in the East, partly because he thought the people there should have recreation areas near and partly because he could see that a few parks in the East would bring better support for the national park system. In the attacks on the western parks the western spoilsmen had some support from eastern men who resented the expenditure of money for western parks which were enjoyed mainly by the people of the West, while the money for their support came mainly from the more populous East. There was some logic in this. In 1916, for instance, of the total of 10,780 visits to Sequoia Park, 10,521 were from California—more than 97 per cent. The percentage of local visitors was lower in most of the other parks, but the truth was that the parks were maintained mostly for the benefit of the people of the West, while the costs, as far as they were met by appropriations, were born mainly by the people of the rest of the country. A few parks in the East would redress this injustice to some extent.

But eastern parks would cost a great deal, for the land was almost all privately owned. The creation of the western parks cost little or nothing, because most of the land already belonged to the government, in forest reserves or general public domain. Congress had seldom been willing to appropriate money for the purchase of privately owned land there, and it would appropriate little for the eastern parks, so the lands would have to be bought by the states and by private donors.

The demand for eastern parks arose along with a demand for national forests. The Forest Reserve Act—really only a few lines in an omnibus public lands act—passed in 1891, authorized the President to set aside as forest reserves, later called "national forests," timber lands on the federal public domain. Forest reserves thus established required no Congressional action and called for no appropriations, and the succeeding Presidents, particularly Theodore Roosevelt, set aside vast areas in the West covering much of the unappropriated timber lands. The purchase of privately owned timber lands was an entirely different matter, yet within less than ten years after the enactment of the Forest Reserve Act agitation arose for the purchase of timber lands, mostly cut-over lands, in the East; and very soon this agitation shaded over to a demand for national parks, although there was often no clear perception of the difference between national forests and national parks. That this confusion was widespread is indicated by the fact that the California parks, Yosemite and General Grant, were originally set aside as "forest reservations," and that even as late as 1910 Glacier Park and in 1916 Lassen Volcanic were established more as national forests than national parks.[14]

National forests serve some of the same purposes as national parks—recreation and watershed protection; and although timber cutting, mining, power and irrigation development, and hunting are allowed in national forests, there is more or less careful regulation, designed to protect the future interests of the country. The demand for forest reserves was logically related to the demand for national parks.

At any rate, even as early as 1900 there were attempts in Congress, supported by Secretary of Agriculture Wilson and President McKinley, and later President Roosevelt, to provide for the purchase of forest reserves or forest reserves and national parks in the Appalachians. On January 16, 1900, Senator Butler of North Carolina offered a Senate Joint Resolution calling for an investigation in western North Carolina and eastern Tennessee to determine the feasibility of establishing a "national park and forest reserve" there.[15]

On January 10, 1901, Senator Pritchard of North Carolina brought in a bill which was reported;[16] two days later Representative Pearson of the same state introduced a bill which was not reported.[17] In the next Congress, Senators Pritchard and Burton of Kansas and Representatives Brownlow of Tennessee and Moody of North Carolina fed several bills into the hopper to create a forest reserve, or the McKinley National Park and Forest Reserve, or the

14 See the author's *United States Forest Policy* (New Haven: Yale University Press, 1920), Chapter VI.

15 S. R. 69, 56 Cong. 2 Sess.

16 S. 5518, 56 Cong. 2 Sess.

17 H. R. 13502; 56 Cong. 2 Sess.

McKinley Appalachian National Park and Forest Reserve; and the
Burton Bill (S. 5228), passed the Senate with little opposition,
authorizing $10 million for purchase.[18] During the next four Con-
gresses more than a score of bills were introduced to get a forest
reserve or national park or both established, so many that they
need not be enumerated here.

The attitude of southern senators and representatives is easy to
explain: some were really interested in the preservation of Appalachian forests, others wanted the federal government to come in
and buy up timber lands, mostly cut-over lands of little or no value,
and reforest them at federal expense. Presently came also a crusade
for national forests in the White Mountains, but bills for these
did not pass either house; so the Appalachian and White Mountain
advocates joined forces to present a more effective front. In 1906
Senator Brandegee of Connecticut introduced a bill for the expenditure of $3 million for forest reserves in both sections, which
passed the Senate without comment.[19] The House was not usually
as favorably disposed toward these reserves as the Senate.

Other efforts followed, and soon forest reserves were being called
for in other sections of the country: the Potomac Watershed, the
Ozarks, the head of the Mississippi River, the Highlands of the
Hudson, the head of the Red River; but none of these made any
headway. On July 23, 1909, however, Representative Weeks of
Massachusetts introduced a bill "to enable any state to co-operate
with any other state or states or with the United States, for the protection of the watersheds of navigable streams, and to appoint a
commission for the acquisition of lands for the purpose of conserving the navigability of navigable streams."[20] This bill was debated
at great length. Navigability of streams was stressed in the bill to
justify federal rather than state action, although it was not really
an important point. Protection of the watersheds was much more
important. The phrase about co-operation of states with each other
and with the United States government was no doubt put in to
make the bill more attractive to those who thought the states should
manage their forests, particularly to Joe Cannon, Speaker of the
House, who was opposed to federal action. Most of the present-day

18 S. 492, S. 5228, H. R. 3128, H. R. 6543, H. R. 12138, H. R. 13523, 57 Cong.
1 Sess. *Congressional Record*, June 7, 1902, 6429-32; June 24, 1902, 7281-87.
19 S. 4953, 59 Cong. 1 Sess. *Congressional Record*, June 22, 1906, 8952.
20 H. R. 11798, 61 Cong. 1, 2 and 3 Sess.

arguments for forest conservation, in addition to navigation and watershed protection, were heard. Future scarcity of timber was predicted, the flood control and recreational value of forests was pointed out. A few men argued that since the government was spending money on forest reserves in the West it should do as much for the East.[21]

There was plenty of vocal opposition, but the bill had the support of dozens of conservation and scientific organizations, of President Taft, Secretary of Agriculture Wilson and others; and the combination of New England and Appalachian forces was able to push it to a favorable vote—57 to 9—in the Senate, on February 15, 1911. It provided $1 million for the current year and $2 million a year until 1915, to be spent by the Forest Reservation Commission. Under this law a number of forest reserves were established in the Appalachian Mountains and a few in the White Mountains and elsewhere. Purchases are still being made.[22]

National parks in the East were called for about as early as forest reserves. In March 1894 Representative Henderson of North Carolina introduced in the House a memorial of the North Carolina Press Association asking Congress to consider the establishment of a national park in North Carolina.[23] In November 1899 the Appalachian National Park Association was organized at Asheville, North Carolina, with members from various parts of the country; and early in 1900 memorials from this association, from the Appalachian Mountain Club of New England, from the American Association for the Advancement of Science—always in the forefront in any conservation movement—and from the American Forestry Association, were presented in Congress asking for the establishment of a national park somewhere in the Southern Appalachian region.[24] Specifically, the memorial called for the creation of an Appalachian park as a place for experiments in "scientific forestry," thus indicating a confusion as to the proper functions of national parks and national forests. This same confusion was shown in some of the earliest bills to create a "national park and forest reserve."[25]

[21] See the author's *United States Forest Policy*, cited above, Chap. VI.
[22] Stat. 36, 961.
[23] *Congressional Record*, March 27, 1894, 3260.
[24] S. Doc. 84, 57 Cong. 1 Sess., 158-63.
[25] *Congressional Record*, Jan. 4, 1900, 3848. S. Res. 69, S. Doc. 58, 56 Cong. 1 Sess. H. R. 3128, 57 Cong. 1 Sess. H. R. 18808, 58 Cong. 3 Sess.

In the following years there were many bills in Congress to create an eastern national park somewhere, in the Appalachians, in Shenandoah Valley, along the Potomac watershed or elsewhere.[26] In the sundry civil bill of June 12, 1917, Congress authorized the Secretary of the Interior to "accept for park purposes any lands and rights of way, including the Grandfather Mountain, near or adjacent to the Government forest reserve in western North Carolina." The owners of the mountain had made some kind of offer, and Congress opened the way to its acceptance. Secretary Lane, in his 1917 report mentioned it as "Grandfather Mountain National Park," but it never materialized, according to one story because the offer was of only the top of the mountain, and the owners wanted the government to develop it and build roads, which would enhance the value of their other lands. At any rate after some discussion nothing more was heard of it.[27] In 1922 Senator Swanson and Representative Slemp of Virginia introduced bills to establish "Appalachian National Park" in Virginia, an area around Big Knob. The cost was to be met by private donation, and the bill was approved by Secretary Fall. In his letter to the House Committee on Public Lands Fall attacked with some acerbity certain conservationists—he did not name them—who had criticized his conception of national parks. He had sometimes favored areas which were not of national park splendor but adapted to recreation only, and had in this way attracted severe criticism from some national park lovers. The Appalachian bill was reported by the House Committee on Public Lands but got no further.[28]

The eastern park promoters presently saw that they would accomplish more if they were to unite on several parks and thus secure the support of men from the various sections of the East and South. They usually joined forces on two, Great Smoky Mountains and Shenandoah, and sometimes but not always supported Mammoth Cave; but the promoters of Mammoth Cave tagged along, and finally got their park three days after the others were established.

Mather had urged the creation of eastern national parks at least as early as 1919, and in his 1923 report he again called for them.

26 See for instance, H. R. 13995, H. R. 18808, 58 Cong. 2 Sess. H. R. 3124, 59 Cong. 1 Sess.

27 Stat. 40, 152.

28 H. R. 12953, H. Rept. 1729, 67 Cong. 3 Sess. S. 4496, 67 Cong. 4 Sess.

Early the next year he persuaded Secretary Work to appoint a Southern Appalachian National Park Commission, with Representative H. W. Temple of Pennsylvania, an able and indefatigable friend of conservation and of national parks, as chairman, to survey possible park areas. The commission chosen was a distinguished group: W. A. Welch, general manager and chief engineer of the Palisades Interstate Park Commission of New York; Col. Glenn S. Smith, division engineer of the United States Geological Survey; Harlan P. Kelsey, a former president of the Appalachian Mountain Club, and William C. Gregg, of the National Arts Club. They had no government funds, but some of their expenses were paid by Gregg, John D. Rockefeller, Jr., and Mather. No commission ever served more faithfully.

They decided first just what they should be looking for, and laid down certain requirements for any area to be recommended:

1. It should cover not less than 500 square miles, so that visitors could be accommodated without confusion or overcrowding.

2. A substantial part of the area should have forests, shrubs, flowers, streams and cascades, all in a natural state.

3. It should have springs and streams for camping and fishing.

4. It should offer opportunities for wildlife protection, and should be a natural museum preserving the outstanding features of the Southern Appalachians as they appeared in early pioneer days.

5. It should be accessible by rail and by highways.

The commission sent out a letter, asking for suggestions, and received letters from some twenty-three localities in Tennessee, Kentucky, Virginia, North Carolina, West Virginia, Georgia, and Alabama, recommending many different areas: Great Smoky Mountains; Mount Mitchell, North Carolina, 6,684 feet in elevation, the highest mountain in the eastern states; Blowing Rock, North Carolina; Linville Gorge, North Carolina; Roan Mountains, North Carolina; White Sulphur Springs, West Virginia; Blue Ridge Mountains, Front Royal to Waynesboro; Massanutten Mountains, Virginia; Skyland, Virginia; Muscle Shoals Dam, Alabama; Shenandoah Valley; Grandfather Mountain; Cumberland Gap, Tennessee, Kentucky and Virginia.

The commission traveled for weeks, by rail, automobile and horseback, held meetings with local boosters and state officials, and finally decided that the Great Smoky Mountains, about equally in Tennessee and in North Carolina, came scenically first, because of

the "height of the mountains, the depth of the valleys, the ruggedness of the area, and the unexampled variety of the trees, shrubs
and plants," some 200,000 acres of forests of primeval character,
and because of the fact that a park here could be extended. There
were almost 1,400 varieties of flowering plants in this area.
The Great Smoky Mountains had another great advantage in that
they were largely an unknown and almost unexplored wilderness,
although the lands were all privately owned, mainly by lumber
companies. There were, however, scattered primitive houses of
mountain dwellers; farmers, moonshiners, ballad singers, living in
much the same way as their pioneer ancestors a hundred years
before. This land was the original home of the Cherokee Indians,
and there are some Cherokees here yet, descendants of the few who
escaped from the military forces which drove the Cherokees out and
to Oklahoma. The white men wanted their land. Yet it was clear
that road-building would be expensive in these mountains and
maintenance costly because of the heavy rainfall.

As early as 1911 the Forest Reservation Commission, established
under the Weeks Law, had authorized the purchase of the Great
Smoky Mountain area for a national forest, but the titles were
found clouded and negotiations were dropped in 1916. In 1925 the
owners resumed talks with this commission, and the commission
was on the point of resuming negotiations when it learned of the
national park plans and considerately withdrew.[29]

The Blue Ridge in Virginia was rated inferior to Great Smoky
Mountains in scenic qualities, but since it was near heavily populated areas it was recommended for first establishment, under the
name "Shenandoah," which was suggested by Harlan Kelsey. The
commission saw the possibility of a "sky-line drive" along the crest
of the mountains. Mammoth Cave was not mentioned, but was included in the bill which passed later.

In the 68th Congress, a spate of bills were introduced relating to
the Appalachian park, and in one case to Mammoth Cave. Senator
Harris and Representative Bell of Georgia proposed merely to in-
vestigate.[30] Senator Shields of Tennessee proposed to establish
Great Smoky Mountains National Park, but got no attention.[31]
Representative Weaver of North Carolina wanted to provide "for

29 American Forests and Forest Life, Apr. 1925, 240.
30 S. J. Res. 94, H. J. Res. 213, 68 Cong. 1 Sess.
31 S. 3012, 68 Cong. 1 Sess.

the perpetual preservation of the forests and wildlife of the Appalachians and for recreational purposes," evidently confused as to the distinction between national forests and national parks, and his proposal was debated briefly.[32] Representative Reece of Tennessee wanted an Appalachian national park, and Senator McKellar of Tennessee wanted a Smoky Mountains national park, but neither was awarded a committee report.[33] Representative Temple of Pennsylvania called for an Appalachian national park, and his bill was reported, debated a little and laid on the table in favor of a bill proposed by Senators Swanson of Virginia and McKellar, which included not only a national park in the Southern Appalachians, but also Mammoth Cave.[34]

The Swanson-McKellar bill passed both houses without debate and was signed by President Coolidge on February 21, 1925, "To provide for the securing of lands in the southern Appalachian Mountains and in the Mammoth Cave regions of Kentucky for perpetual preservation as national parks." The act authorized and directed the Secretary to determine boundaries and areas of these proposed parks and "to receive definite offers of donations of lands and moneys, and to secure such options as in his judgment may be considered reasonable and just for the purchase of lands within said boundaries and to report to Congress thereon." The Secretary was authorized to appoint a commission of five members, composed of a representative of the Department of the Interior and four "national park experts" to carry out the provisions of the act, without compensation; but $20,000 was provided for the expenses of the commission. This sum might cover a salary of $2,000 for one clerk, and $10.00 a day for subsistence cost of the members of the committee on the job. Although the bill seemed to make this as a definite appropriation, there must have been some slip-up, for twelve days later a bill was passed making the appropriation.[35]

Temple and his commission set to work with energy, called meetings in the various areas and discussed the problems ahead, particularly the problem of raising money, for the federal government was committed to the policy of appropriating nothing for purchase of lands; and, as usual, money was hard to get. Various difficulties

32 H. R. 10893, 68 Cong. 2 Sess.
33 H. R. 10891, S. 4081, 68 Cong. 2 Sess.
34 H. R. 11980, S. 4109, 68 Cong. 2 Sess.
35 Stat. 43, 958, 959, 1331.

were encountered. Much of the land, particularly in Great Smoky Mountains, was owned by lumbermen, who were cutting the good timber and were unco-operative; some of the other landowners did not like to leave their homes, and the commission considered the possibility of allowing them to live on their land for a few years; a considerable number of the people in North Carolina were hostile to the proposed Great Smoky, so hostile that the commission considered the possibility of establishing the park mainly in Tennessee.[36]

Not raising enough money by having the various states work separately, the commission considered the advisability of getting the states involved to work co-operatively and divide the receipts on some basis, but gave this up. They then decided to hire five men experienced in money-raising, but this plan proved too expensive.

The act of February 21, 1925, indicated that Congress definitely intended to set up parks in the East; and while the Temple Commission was wrestling with its various problems, a half-dozen senators introduced a bill to establish Great Smoky Mountains and Shenandoah National Parks, when certain amounts of land should be secured by the states and presented to the federal government. The bill was not clear as to the areas covered, but the areas suggested by Secretary Work—521,000 acres for Shenandoah, and 704,-000 acres for Great Smoky—were intended to be maximum areas that might finally be acquired; and there was a further provision "that the minimum areas to be administered and protected by the National Park Service" should be 250,000 acres for Shenandoah and 150,000 acres for Great Smoky Mountains, but no development of either area should be undertaken until "a major portion of the remainder"—presumably more than half—should be turned over to the Secretary—a rather nebulous provision. It appears to have meant that the National Park Service might assume the task of administering and protecting the areas when the amounts of land presented were 250,000 and 150,000 acres, but should spend no money in *developing* (building roads, camps, and other facilities) until a "major portion"—more than half—of the remainder should be acquired. For Shenandoah this would have been 250,000 acres plus more than half of the remaining acres (521,000 minus 250,000

---

[36] For the story of the Appalachian parks see *Final Report of the Southern Appalachian National Park Commission to the Secretary of the Interior, June 30, 1931* (Washington: U. S. Government Printing Office) .

leaves a "remainder" of 271,000 acres, and one-half of 271,000 acres, or 135,500 acres, added to 250,000 acres is 385,500 acres, or rather a "major portion" or "more than" that). For Great Smoky Mountains the remainder would have been 704,000 minus 150,000 or 554,000 acres, and half of this would have been 277,000 which, added to 150,000 would have been 427,000 or rather, more than that. Somewhat more than 385,500 acres and 427,000 acres were apparently the minimum acres necessary before there could be any development of the new parks.

Another provision of the act was that the Federal Water Power Act of 1920 should not apply to these parks—that there should be no invasion by water power projects; and a further provision was that the Secretary might retain the commission set up under the act of February 21, 1925.[37]

There was little debate on this bill, although a few senators were mildly opposed to the establishment of the parks before the entire areas were in government possession, pointing out the common trouble with privately owned lands in national parks. The bill passed both houses and was signed by President Coolidge on May 22, 1926.[38]

Although the parks were not yet established, the conditions of their establishment were thus laid down, in rather indefinite terms, and the Secretary and the commission were left with the onerous task of raising more money. At the time the bill was introduced $1.2 million had been subscribed by the state of Virginia and the Shenandoah National Park Association of Virginia for Shenandoah Park, and $1,066,693 had been subscribed by the state of Tennessee, the Great Smoky Mountain Conservation Commission, and the Great Smoky Mountains, Inc. of North Carolina for Great Smoky; but much more was needed. In 1927 Congress appropriated $5,000 for the expenses of the Commission; in 1928, $4,500; in 1929 and 1930, $3,000. This was not generous, and purchases lagged.

In January 1928 the commission went to Richmond for a dinner and reception given to the members of the Virginia legislature, and as a result of the discussion there and at the request of the Shenandoah National Park Association, Representative Temple and Senator Swanson of Virginia introduced identical bills in the House and Senate "To establish a minimum area for the Shenandoah Na-

37 S. 4073, S. Rept. 824, H. Rept. 1380, 69 Cong. 1 Sess.
38 Stat. 44, 616.

tional Park, for administration, protection, and general development. . . ," which passed both houses promptly and was signed by President Coolidge on February 16, 1928. This act reduced the minimum acreage of Shenandoah for "administration, protection and general development" from "more than" 385,500 to 327,000 acres. There was no change in the minimum for Great Smoky Mountains. To meet the difficulty of getting landowners to sell and move off their lands, this act also allowed the Secretary to lease such lands back to "persons and educational or religious institutions" for two years. This last provision applied also to Great Smoky Mountains.[39]

GREAT SMOKY MOUNTAINS PARK   Money-raising still lagged. On February 25, 1927, the North Carolina legislature had authorized the issue of bonds for $2 million to buy lands with, and in April a similar bill for $1.5 million had passed the Tennessee legislature—Virginia officials said that the state could not issue bonds for internal improvements. These sums were not enough. It was estimated that Tennessee and North Carolina had raised less than $5 million and $10 million would be needed. Early in 1927 the legislatures of North Carolina and Tennessee adopted a joint resolution requesting Representative Temple, Welch, and Assistant Director Cammerer to address the legislatures on the critical problem of raising money. This was a happy inspiration, for Cammerer set to work with his accustomed diligence and the next year induced John D. Rockefeller, Jr., through the Laura Spelman Rockefeller Memorial, to offer $5 million to be matched by other donations. Cammerer decided to give the donation to Great Smoky Mountains because there were about 200,000 acres of fine virgin forests there which he wanted to save. Both Tennessee and North Carolina immediately enjoined all lumber cutting. Cammerer selected the boundary for Great Smoky Mountains, to allot Tennessee 228,500 acres and North Carolina 225,500 acres.

Rockefeller's generous gift put new life into the Great Smoky Mountains Park movement, but there was still much to do, and the task was made a bit harder by a law passed in 1930. A large lumber company had extensive timber holdings, all but 10,729 acres of

39 S. 2656, H. R. 8526, 70 Cong. 1 Sess. Stat. 45, 109.

which were in Great Smoky Mountains Park, and the Park Service
decided that it would cost little more to add to the park this outside
acreage lying along the east boundary; so they asked Representative
Temple to introduce a bill to accomplish this, and this bill passed
and was approved on April 19, 1930.[40] On June 1, 1931, Representative Temple wrote Secretary Wilbur asking that the commission
be dissolved, and the Secretary complied, although the financing of
the parks was not yet completed, even with Rockefeller's princely
donation, which was used in buying lands for Great Smoky Mountains and not Shenandoah. In the depths of the Great Depression
money was hard to find.

We need not follow step by step the accumulation of the funds
needed for the new parks, but in 1929 Director Albright reported
that one-half of the minimum area of 427,000 acres for Great
Smoky Mountains had been bought or optioned for purchase, and
a little over half of the funds needed for Shenandoah had been
pledged. In February 1930 a large delegation from North Carolina
and Tennessee called on Secretary Wilbur and presented to him
158,799 acres in North Carolina and 158,799 acres in Tennessee.

The state purchasing commission worked hard, but in 1933 Cammerer reported that for Great Smoky Mountains there were still
three large tracts in North Carolina to be acquired, one covering
33,000 acres for which condemnation proceedings had been instituted, and two other large tracts and some forty scattered small
holdings. The total area acquired was only 400,000 acres, of the
704,000 acres specified as needed by the Secretary, on April 14, 1926,
and of the 427,000 acres called for by the act of May 22, 1926; but
on June 15, 1934, Congress decided that 400,000 acres was enough
to start with and established Great Smoky Mountains "as a completed park for administration, protection and development," and
decreed further that any lands acquired then or later within the
original specified limits of the park should become a part of it.[41]

Four years later, on February 12, 1938, Congress relaxed further
and appropriated $743,265.29 for the acquisition by purchase or
condemnation of additional lands.[42] The act providing this was
entitled "An Act to provide for the acquisition of certain lands for

40 H. R. 16715, 70 Cong. 2 Sess. H. R. 6343, 71 Cong. 2 Sess. Stat. 46, 225.
41 H. R. 7360, 73 Cong. 2 Sess. Stat. 48, 964.
42 Stat. 52, 29.

and the addition thereof to the Tahoe National Forest, in the State of Nevada, and the acquisition of certain other lands for the completion of the acquisition of the remaining lands within the limits of the Great Smoky Mountains National Park, in east Tennessee." The bill was introduced by Senator McCarran of Nevada—some distance from Great Smoky—in August 1937, with the purpose of getting eastern support for a project to add to Tahoe National Forest 100,000 acres of privately owned cut-over lands on the shore of Lake Tahoe, between California and Nevada, as a recreation area. This land was thought to be worth about $3.25 per acre and $325,000 was specified for its purchase. There was a great deal of debate on the bill, a few of the senators and representatives voiced fears of national bankruptcy, and the Lake Tahoe appropriation was eliminated, leaving a rather misleading title to the bill.[43]

The appropriation of $743,265.29 provided for a good-sized park, but there were still some adjustments to be made with the Cherokee Indians, whose lands adjoined the park;[44] and on April 29, 1942, Congress accepted jurisdiction.[45] The Park Service had already assumed administrative control after the passage of the act of 1934, but administration was made more effective by federal acceptance of exclusive jurisdiction.[46]

When the Great Smoky Mountains Park was finally established, there arose in Congress some interesting debates as to who should have credit for the new park. Senator McKellar of Tennessee was ambitious for the distinction of being largely responsible, but he did little more than many other Appalachian senators and representatives. If anyone in Congress should have major and very generous credit it would be Representative Temple, who did a vast amount of hard work with his commission. Among government officials, Secretary Work has often been cited as largely responsible for the creation of the park, but he would have to share credit with Albright and Cammerer. A mountain in the park is named Mount Cammerer.[47] Without the generous contribution of John D. Rocke-

43 S. 2583, 75 Cong. 1 Sess.

44 H. R. 5472, S. 2330, 75 Cong. 1 Sess. Stat. 54, 299, 300.

45 Stat. 56, 258.

46 On the general story of the southern parks see Robert Shankland, *Steve Mather of the National Parks* (New York: Alfred Knopf, 1951), 282, 283. *Congressional Record*, Dec. 11, 1929, 493 ff; Apr. 22, 1930, 7499 ff.

47 See debates, *Congressional Record*, Apr. 19, 1926, 4604-6.

feller, Jr., it is not certain that Great Smoky Mountains could ever
have been established.

This is of course not the end of our story, for much happened to
Great Smoky Mountains after it was finally established as a park.
Some lands were added from time to time; but the most important
addition was one of 44,000 acres being purchased for addition in
1944, by agreement among the Tennessee Valley Authority, the
state of North Carolina, Swain County, and the National Park
Service, in consideration of postwar road construction by the Park
Service. These lands were situated between the Fontana Dam reservoir on the Little Tennessee River and the park. This addition was
reported by Director Drury as "rounding out Great Smoky Mountains in accord with the original concept."[48] Years later, in February 1952, Representative Redden of North Carolina tried to get
this area turned back to Swain County, so that it could be reopened
to bear hunting, but without success.[49] The present area of the park
is over 500,000 acres.

It might have seemed that in contributing $743,265.29 to the pur-
chase of lands—in contradiction of its expressed resolution to contribute no money—and in providing funds later for administration,
protection, and development of the park—this expense rose from
$22,270 in 1934 to $125,100 in 1941—the federal government had
done quite enough; but in 1939 Representative Weaver tried to get
compensation for Haywood and Swain Counties for their loss in
taxable valuation from the creation of the park. There was no justification for such a demand, for, even allowing for the cost of buying the land, the states, and particularly the adjacent counties, have
profited greatly from the establishment of the park. Not only has
the tourist traffic brought a great deal of money into the area, but
the people living there have easy and free access to the park, and
they go there often. Many of the people who visit the park live not
very far away.[50]

In April 1939, when the appropriation for Great Smoky Mountains came up in the Senate, McKellar made a violent attack on
Superintendent Ross Eakin, accusing him of various improper
practices, one of which appeared to be that he was a Republican,

48 *Report, Secretary of the Interior, 1944,* 227.
49 H. R. 6784, 82 Cong. 2 Sess.
50 H. R. 4752, 76 Cong. 1 Sess. H. R. 4136, 77 Cong. 1 Sess.

although that was not the worst charge. Eakin was a high-class superintendent, but perhaps he had refused to consider McKellar in making appointments in Great Smoky. At any rate the Senate did not take the McKellar charges seriously.[51]

Some Tennessee people thought that they could not get a good enough view of the mountains, and on February 22, 1944, the President approved a law authorizing the acceptance of donations of land for the construction of a scenic parkway to provide a good view of the park from the Tennessee side, "generally parallel to the boundary of the park." This apparently referred to the Foothills Parkway which was started but never finished. Very recently the Park Service has revived this project and plans to finish it.[52]

Great Smoky Mountains is a worthy national park, the only one of the three mid-eastern parks that was fully approved by Robert Sterling Yard, of the National Parks Association. It has been kept as a wilderness park, with few roads, aside from the road across the mountain, with camp grounds but only one lodge in the park, accessible by trail. Except for these, tourists must use hotels and cabins outside the park. President Roosevelt formally dedicated the park on September 2, 1940.

SHENANDOAH PARK   Shenandoah was given a modest Rockefeller donation, but no congressional appropriation; money was scarce in Virginia as in North Carolina and Tennessee, and it required nearly ten years to raise enough. Some of the lands to be acquired had become valuable. In 1931 Director Albright reported only a little over half of the needed funds had been raised, and in 1933 there were still lands that needed to be bought or secured by condemnation. For Shenandoah, Congressional encouragement took the form of reduction in minimum requirements. It will be remembered that the minimum set in the creating act of 1926 was 385,500 acres or somewhat more than that; and that in 1928 this was reduced to 327,000 acres. On February 4, 1932, Congress again reduced the minimum acreage for administration of Shenandoah to 160,000, and in the same bill, to meet the difficulty of acquiring lands that owners wished to hold for homes or other use, authorized the Secretary to grant leases to the sellers for life, or in some cases

51 Congressional Record, Apr. 17, 1939, 4308, 4315, 4341 ff.
52 H. R. 1388, 78 Cong. 2 Sess. Stat. 58, 19.

for twenty years. The Secretary might even accept lands subject to easements and rights of way. These provisions applied not only to Shenandoah but also to Great Smoky Mountains, Mammoth Cave, and another park being promoted, Isle Royale in Michigan.[53]

In 1935, Virginia completed her purchases and the removal of some squatters, and on December 26 presented to Secretary Ickes the deeds to 176,429 acres, exceeding the minimum required by 16,429 acres. The Shenandoah National Park was thus established without a specific act of Congress; and on July 3, 1936, President Roosevelt dedicated the new park. More land has been added since the dedication, some with federal appropriations, and the present area is more than 200,000 acres.

Shenandoah Park covers mainly a little more than a hundred miles of the irregular crest of the Blue Ridge Mountains, along which the Skyline Drive and foot and horse trails have been built to afford many beautiful views of the surrounding country. As a matter of fact, the Skyline Drive comes rather close to *being* the Shenandoah Park. President Hoover had conceived the idea of the drive when he spent vacations in his camp on the Rapidan, in the area that was being bought for Shenandoah Park, and the drive was planned by the Park Service and the Bureau of Public Roads in 1931 and begun in 1932 with relief funds. It was completed in 1940 and has been a spring, summer, and fall vacation drive for vast numbers of people from the nearby cities.

On August 19, 1937, Congress assumed jurisdiction over the park,[54] and five years later, on June 5, 1942, amended the act to provide proper jurisdiction over liquor sales and to allow the state of Virginia to levy taxes on sales of liquor, oil and gasoline, and on "individuals, associations, and corporations, their franchises and properties, on said lands, and on their businesses conducted thereon."[55] Here, as often in national park administration, the federal government assumes the cost of development and administration and the state gets the tax revenues—a very profitable business for the state.

The tax provisions were quite too generous to the state of Virginia, but the statesmen of that commonwealth have tried at various times to load the federal government down with the additional

53 S. 2656, 70 Cong. 1 Sess. Stat. 45, 109.
54 Stat. 50, 700.
55 Stat. 56, 321.

burden of maintaining local roads in the park; and in 1939 a Senate Joint Resolution to accomplish this passed both houses, but was vetoed by President Roosevelt, on the valid ground that this would subordinate park standards to local considerations, and encourage local communities to call for purely local roads.[56]

MAMMOTH CAVE PARK   Mammoth Cave National Park was sometimes but not always included in bills and acts relating to the other two parks. Although Mather called for it in 1918 and 1920, and Secretary Lane, and later Payne, seemed to favor it, there was obviously some doubt as to whether it was of national park quality. The Temple Commission did not include it in their recommendations, yet the act of February 21, 1925, included Mammoth Cave with Shenandoah and Great Smoky Mountains. The act of May 22, 1926, did not mention it.

There had been efforts to give Mammoth Cave National Park status as early as 1911. On January 27, 1911, in the 61st Congress, Representative Thomas of Kentucky introduced a bill to achieve this, which was not reported.[57] Thomas tried again in the next Congress, and in nearly every Congress for the next fifteen years he was up with his Mammoth Cave bill, or in a few cases others introduced the bill.[58]

Finally, on May 8, 1926, in the 69th Congress, Representative Thatcher of Kentucky introduced a bill, and about the same time Senator Ernst, also of Kentucky, brought up an identical bill, which was considered in lieu of the Thatcher bill and passed both houses.[59] This bill provided that the Secretary of the Interior might acquire by donation 70,618 acres for the park. This was the maximum area, and the minimum area for administration and protection was fixed at 20,000 acres, including all the caves in the area,

56 S. J. Res. 160, 76 Cong. 1 Sess. Similar Senate Joint Resolutions were introduced in 76 Cong. 3 Sess., 79 Cong. 2 Sess., 80 Cong. 2 Sess., and 81 Cong. 1 Sess.

57 H. R. 32173, 61 Cong. 3 Sess.

58 H. R. 1666, S. 4997, 62 Cong. 1 Sess. H. R. 9822, 63 Cong. 2 Sess. H. R. 11781, 64 Cong. 1 Sess. H. R. 3110, 66 Cong. 1 Sess. H. R. 11493, 66 Cong. 2 Sess. H. R. 130, 67 Cong. 1 Sess. H. R. 168, 68 Cong. 1 Sess. H. R. 12020, 69 Cong. 1 Sess. See also S. 4997, 62 Cong. 2 Sess., by Bradley, and S. 4209, 69 Cong. 1 Sess., by Ernst.

59 H. R. 12020, S. 4209, 69 Cong. 1 Sess.

but no development should be undertaken until a "major portion" of the remainder (more than half of 50,618 acres, or 25,309 acres) should be acquired. Thus the minimum area necessary before development could be undertaken was 20,000 acres plus "more than" 25,309 acres, or a total of more than 45,309 acres. Like Shenandoah and Great Smoky Mountains, the park was exempted from the Federal Water Power Act of 1920.

The Ernst bill passed both houses with very little debate. The only objection expressed was that when the state began purchasing, prices of land would rise and make the cost prohibitive. This was a real difficulty faced in the establishment of all the eastern parks, as in the purchase of privately owned land in the western parks; but where private owners were too greedy the buyers sometimes used condemnation proceedings to have values set in court, but the proceedings often resulted in excessive prices too.

The passage of this bill was marked by certain irregularities which established a bad precedent. Usually when a national park was under consideration the Secretary of the Interior was asked to report on it—presumably with the advice of the Director of the National Park Service; but in this case no such report was called for. Neither the Secretary nor the Director had ever seen the cave, but they offered to examine and report on it. The Public Lands Committee apparently did not want a report, perhaps because they feared that it might be unfavorable. This was a bad precedent, for only if the Secretary and the Director have an opportunity to pass on proposed parks can the inferior areas be screened out and national park standards be maintained. It has been said that the Thomas-Ernst bill was pushed through to promote the political campaigns of certain members of Congress, and that the votes were lined up before the bill appeared.[60] The bill passed three days after Shenandoah and Great Smoky Mountains were provided for, on May 25, 1926.[61]

To purchase the lands required two associations were formed, the Kentucky National Park Commission and the Mammoth Cave National Park Association; and these agencies proceeded to scour the country for donations of land and money. The cave itself had been owned by private interests and, widely known as it was,

60 *National Parks Bulletin*, No. 49, Mar. 1926.

61 Stat. 44, 635. *American Forests and Forest Life*, July 1926, 413, 434; Aug. 1926, 485.

yielded a very good income; so it was acquired at high cost. The state voted parts of the funds needed, $1.5 million, private subscriptions covered a smaller share, and some lands were bought with funds provided by the Work Relief Act; but in 1939, 10,000 additional acres were still needed.

At first donations came in rather slowly, partly because many of the people in the vicinity of the cave were indifferent or even hostile to the proposal for a national park, some of them fearful of government interference with private rights; but the Kentucky Geological Survey made an investigation of the cave and published information widely, and this brought some change in public attitude. Yet, on May 14, 1934, Congress deemed it wise to pass an act relaxing requirements a little. The act of 1926 had required a minimum area of 20,000 acres, *including all the caves,* before the Park Service should assume administration and protection. In 1934 the minimum area remained at 20,000, but it did not have to include all the caves. Before the Service could begin general developments it must acquire a "major portion of the remainder," which meant "more than" 25,309 acres, including all the caves. The Park Service might assume administration and protection sooner, but the final requirements were the same as in the act of 1926.[62]

Three years later, in the Act of August 28, 1937, there was further relaxation in requirements as to the caves, in authorizing the Secretary to exclude the Great Onyx and Crystal caves, or either of them, from the required *maximum* final area of the park. In the same act, the lands bought with federal Work Relief funds were legally added to the park, despite the earlier prohibition of federal purchases.[63] Here, as in Great Smoky Mountains and Isle Royale, the federal government finally reneged on its pledge to contribute no funds.

In 1941 land purchases were completed, and on July 1 Mammoth Cave became a national park. On June 5, 1942, Congress accepted jurisdiction in the customary jurisdiction act, prescribing careful rules and regulations and providing penalties for their violations. The act also authorized the Secretary of the Interior to acquire additional lands, up to the maximum boundaries prescribed, including the caves—there were still caves in the area that had not been acquired; and to provide the money for such lands, a special

62 Stat. 48, 775.
63 Stat. 50, 871.

fund of $350,000 from the annual net revenues of the park was to be set up in the United States Treasury. A final provision authorized the Secretary to accept donations or to purchase lands for a "proper and suitable entrance road" to the park. There was no provision for state taxation of liquor and oil sales, or of property and incomes in the park.[64]

Apparently, the Secretary did not have enough money in the special fund to buy the "proper and suitable" entrance road, and on June 30, 1948, Congress authorized $350,000 for this purpose.[65] The special fund seems to have been insufficient even to buy the caves, whose value has been estimated at $800,000, so on March 27, 1954, the special fund was again authorized, and the Secretary was authorized to enter into contracts for the purchase of Great Onyx and Crystal caves. No money was appropriated, but there was some implication that an appropriation might be forthcoming if the special fund proved inadequate to meet the obligations incurred.[66] These privately owned caves were the subject of some discussion in Congress at times, Kentucky statesmen contending that they were subject to unfair competition from Mammoth Cave, which belonged to the government and paid no taxes. Two of them were surrounded by park lands and, like all privately owned lands on national parks, presented difficulties in administration. Several caves in the vicinity (including the Collins Cave, in which Floyd Collins had become wedged when chasing a rabbit and had died there—a sensational story in the newspapers of the time) advertised their wonders on flamboyant billboards that suggested a circus rather than a national park.[67]

THE QUALITY OF THE NEW PARKS   The establishment of the three eastern parks raises a question as to Mather's policy. Mather appeared to have favored all three parks at one time, although of the three only one, Great Smoky Mountains, was of such scenic splendor as to merit national park status. Mammoth Cave might have deserved status as a national monument, as the National Parks Association said, but not that of national park; Shenandoah

64 Stat. 56, 317.
65 H. R. 2096, 80 Cong. 2 Sess. Stat. 62, 1165.
66 S. 79, 83 Cong. 2 Sess. Stat. 68, 36.
67 See H. R. 2096, 80 Cong. 1 Sess.

is not of superlative scenic grandeur, although it would rank high as a recreation area, with its beautiful Skyline Drive and its nearness to centers of population. The truth is that Mather was perhaps too ambitious for more parks, and not quite discriminating enough as to their quality. This was shown not only in his approval of Mammoth Cave, but in his approval of Hot Springs, in his desire to add Mount Evans, and perhaps in his moderately favorable report on Indiana Sand Dunes and Mississippi Valley National Park.[68]

On the other hand, there was some logic in his approval of the eastern parks. He was not only a nature enthusiast, a lover of great scenery, but an eminently practical man who understood practical politics. He needed more support for the national parks of the West, knew that if he could get parks in the East he would have better support for the entire national park system, better support for appropriations, stronger defense against park raids by commercial interests. Mather had been fighting off livestock, lumber, irrigation and power interests, in some cases winning by a margin so narrow that he could see clearly the need for more support for the parks, and the danger that in some battle he might not have enough. The eastern parks, including Mammoth Cave, would make the people there park-conscious, would educate them in national park matters.

The fact that the people of Virginia, North Carolina, Tennessee, and Kentucky would devote so much money and energy to the creation of these eastern parks shows what an asset the western states have, free of all cost, in their national parks. Some of them have not been properly appreciative of this.

In the early years there were some surprisingly generous donations: Tioga Road, in 1915, by Mather and a few other men; funds to help rescue a grove in Sequoia, in 1916, by the National Geographic Society; an administrative site in Glacier, in 1917, by Mather; Sieur de Monts, in 1916, by George B. Dorr, John D. Rockefeller, Jr., and a few others.

It was assumed that the final establishment of the eastern parks would not bring an end to donations of land and money, so an agency was called for, which would accept and care for such donations. On February 28, 1935, Senator Byrd of Virginia introduced a bill to set up a National Park Trust Fund Board, consisting of the Secretary of the Treasury, the Secretary of the Interior, the Director of the Park Service, and two others, to serve for five years, without

68 *Report, Secretary of the Interior, 1920*, 82, 84.

compensation except for expenses. This board was authorized to accept gifts and bequests for the Park Service, but no gift was to be accepted that called for any expenditures. The Secretary of the Interior was also authorized to accept gifts and bequests. This bill passed with no debate and was signed by President Roosevelt on July 10, 1935. Every year the board makes a report—usually of rather modest donations.[69]

Mather got twelve new national parks, all but two of them splendid. He really wanted a few more, but was unable to get them. He thought Bandelier would be a good national park, and he seemed mildly favorable to a Sand Dunes National Park south of Lake Michigan, but recognized that it would be costly, since the land was privately owned and expensive. He and Albright would have been happy to get a coast redwoods national park, to save some of the great coast redwoods, but these were practically all owned by lumber companies and they made excellent lumber, so none were ever acquired by the federal government, in spite of the persistent efforts of the Save-the-Redwoods League, organized in 1917, and the indefatigable Sierra Club.

Strangely, there were few efforts in Congress to establish a coast redwoods national park, although the redwoods are about as impressive to view as the giant sequoias. In 1911 Representative Raker introduced a House joint resolution providing for a committee to investigate the "advisability and necessity" of establishing such a park, but it disappeared in committee.[70] Eight years later Representative Lea of California presented a House resolution "To direct the Secretary of the Interior to report upon the suitability, location, cost, if any, and advisability of securing a National Redwood Park." The resolution was agreed to, and Secretary Payne asked Forester Paul Redington of the Forest Service to make the investigation.

Redington's report recommended the purchase and establishment of a redwoods national park of 64,000 acres on the lower Klamath River drainage basin in Humboldt County, and in addition a separate unit of 1,800 acres of particularly fine redwoods on the Eel River, to be donated by the Save-the-Redwoods League, which had been raising money for this purpose. It was a splendid report, bold enough to meet the needs of the situation, and brought a favorable committee report and passage by the House without debate; but to

69 S. 2074, H. R. 6734, 74 Cong. 1 Sess. Stat. 49, 477.
70 H. J. Res. 284, 62 Cong. 2 Sess.

the everlasting loss of the nation, no further action was taken. Representative William Kent and wife presented Muir Woods to the government and the state of California bought several fine groves for state parks.[71] At the solicitation of Senator Perkins and Representative Hayes, Congress did give 4,000 acres of practically worthless land to California to add to one of the state's coast redwood parks for fire protection.[72]

Agitation for Grand Teton National Park had begun before Mather assumed office, but it was not established until February 26, 1929, after Mather's last illness had come upon him, and it will be considered in a later connection.[73] In 1919 he suggested that the Park Service could care for the military parks splendidly, but they were not turned over until after his death.

[71] H. Res. 159, 66 Cong. 2 Sess. *Report, Secretary of the Interior, 1919*, 138. *National Parks Bulletin*, No. 21, July 12, 1921.

[72] Stat. 37, 134.

[73] Stat. 45, 1314. See Chap. XV.

CHAPTER XIII

The Mather Administration

1917-1928

BOUNDARY REVISIONS; NEW NATIONAL

MONUMENTS; STATE PARKS

BOUNDARY REVISION FOR YELLOWSTONE PARK   Quite as much
needed as new parks were extensions of existing parks, particularly
Yellowstone, Yosemite, Sequoia, Rocky Mountain, Crater Lake, and
Mount Rainier. Yellowstone needed expansion along three sides:
along the west part of the north line to include more of the Gallatin
River and Specimen Creek valleys, lower land for winter grazing,
and, also important, petrified trees; along the east line, to add high
scenic areas mainly, and make the high divide the park boundary;
along the southeast boundary to include what was called the Thorofare region, the high headwaters of the Yellowstone and Snake
rivers; and, most important, along the south boundary line, to take
in the magnificent Grand Teton Mountains and the Jackson Hole
country for winter grazing land. The efforts at revision present a
confusion of bills and proposals to change one or more of those
boundary lines.

There had been revision bills in Congress for many years. In 1892
Senators Sanders of Montana and Warren of Wyoming introduced
bills to increase Yellowstone by about one-third, adding areas on
the south and east, but excising areas on the north and west to leave
the park entirely in the state of Wyoming, and cutting off a corner

271

on the north for the Cinnabar-Cooke City railroad. This was really a mining railroad bill, and Senator Vest of Missouri promptly opposed it, but it passed the Senate and was favorably reported by the House Committee on Public Lands, but got no further. In the debates, Senator Berry of Arkansas urged that the park be divided into 160-acre tracts or sold as a whole, since it was only "a playground for the rich."[1]

In 1916 Horace Albright, assistant to Mather, made an inspection of the Yellowstone region with a party of leading citizens and on this trip he was so impressed with the Grand Teton and Jackson Hole region that he resolved to make it a part of the national park system. He had no idea what a long-drawn task this would be, but he never gave it up as long as he was in the Park Service. At the time, Senators Warren and Clark and Representative Frank Mondell were favorable to the project. Two years later Albright again visited Jackson Hole, and found many friends of the idea of giving it park status. A little later, at Mondell's request, Chief Forester Graves visited the area and he and Mather and Mondell agreed on an extension of Yellowstone to include the headwaters of the Yellowstone and Thorofare rivers, the Grand Teton Mountains, and the part of Jackson Hole north of Buffalo Fork. Mondell introduced a bill to achieve this, which passed the House but was objected to in the Senate by Senator Nugent of Idaho, who thought the west line of the park would extend all the way to the Idaho line and cut off Idaho sheep range. In the next Congress Mondell tried again, but failed.[2]

When Albright first went into the Jackson Hole country he found most of the local people friendly to the idea of a national park, thinking it would bring more and better roads, which they were greatly concerned about, as was also Governor Robert Carey. Believing that roads were what the people wanted, Albright and some of his friends drew up a plan for additional roads, even made a map of them, which proved to be a serious mistake, for they presently found out that the dominating political force in the area was the dude ranchers, who wanted no more or better roads. At his next visit in 1919 Albright found himself in a hornet's nest of hostility to the park proposal—a rather peculiar situation, for Albright

1 S. 667, S. 2373, 52 Cong. 1 Sess.
2 H. R. 11661, 65 Cong. 2 Sess. H. R. 13350, 65 Cong. 3 Sess. H. R. 1412, 66 Cong. 1 Sess.

really did not want more roads either, but favored rather the retention of much of the area in wilderness condition—just what the dude ranchers wanted. But within the next two or three years Albright and his men found a somewhat different situation: the people of Casper and Lander demanded a Wind River Road, a road running southeast from Moran, over Togwotee Pass, to Dubois, Lander and Casper; and the people of Jackson began to demand road improvement on the Hoback Road and the road over Teton Pass to Idaho.

The road-builders won, and new roads were built and old ones repaired, but there was no progress on the new park or addition to Yellowstone, although Albright was working for it all the time, with encouragement from some local people who thought the new park or extension could be set up if enough money could be raised to buy out private owners. All efforts to raise money failed. Albright did a most important service, however, in inducing Secretary Payne to cancel Carey Act applications to dam Jenny and Leigh lakes with dams twenty and ten feet high. He and Payne also prevented Idaho interests from erecting *high* dams on Emma Matilda and Two Ocean lakes. Governor Emerson of Wyoming wanted to dam all the Jackson Hole lakes.[3]

There had been some changes in adjoining areas to provide better for wildlife in winter. Between 1908 and 1927 the Forest Service closed increasing areas in the national forests north and west of the park to livestock grazing so that the range would be available to the wild animals.[4] In 1912 Congress authorized the Secretary of Agriculture to purchase 2,000 acres of land south of Yellowstone for a winter game reserve and appropriated $45,000 for it.[5] On April 16, 1917 and February 28, 1919, President Wilson withdrew lands north of the park for better winter forage for the elk, but these lands were merely withdrawn from entry, apparently, for the withdrawals do not appear among the Presidential proclamations.[6]

Proposals for enlargement of Yellowstone soon brought up the old rivalry between the Park Service and the Forest Service. Some changes, as for instance the shift of the eastern boundary to the

---

3 For the later Jackson Hole story, see Chap. XXIII.
4 *American Forests and Forest Life,* Feb. 1929, 94.
5 Stat. 37, 293.
6 *Report, Secretary of the Interior, 1919,* 961 ff.

crest of the Absaroka Range, would have hurt the Forest Service very little, for in these high slopes there was little commercial timber, and that highly inaccessible. The timber immediately on the slopes of the Grand Tetons was not of great value either, but there was fairly valuable timber and grazing land south of Yellowstone and some in the Jackson Hole country, and the Forest Service was determined to keep it. The expansion of Yellowstone southward to include Jackson Hole would cost the Forest Service about 800,000 acres of land. Finally the feud between the two services became so bitter that in the winter of 1924-25 the President's Committee of the National Conference on Outdoor Recreation appointed a committee of five, called the President's Co-ordinating Committee on National Parks and National Forests, to survey and make recommendations regarding park expansions—of all parks, not just Yellowstone. The Co-ordinating Committee was an able and distinguished group of men: Representative Temple of Pennsylvania, a tireless and devoted friend of conservation, Charles Sheldon of the Boone and Crockett Club, Major W. A. Welch, of the Palisades Interstate Park, and Mather and Greeley.

THE CO-ORDINATING COMMITTEE   In the hearings before the Co-ordinating Committee the Forest Service did not object to the extension of Yellowstone to the east, to follow the crest of the mountains, or to the north, or to the southeast to take in the Thorofare and Upper Yellowstone country, but was adamant against the southward extension to take in Jackson Hole. Officers of that service urged that the timber in the south part of Yellowstone and south of Yellowstone should be subject to logging, and the logs should be floated down to saw mills on Jackson Lake. Albright contended that this country was more valuable in its virgin state than as a cutover forest. The Forest Service men argued that there were valuable minerals in the area—coal, phosphate, and asbestos—but Albright denied that these were of any considerable value. The Forest Service was solicitous of the cattle industry in the area and about the summer homes, but Albright and his men thought the summer homes should be restricted to the south part of Jackson Hole where they would not be a desecration of the scenery. The Forest Service had generally more local support, and won in this contest. Jackson Hole and the Grand Tetons were saved for the Forest Service, but

Albright continued his campaign, and a few years later got Grand
Teton National Park.

The Co-ordinating Committee held three meetings in March and
reached agreement on several points. In August they held a meeting in Cody, Wyoming, and arranged for a trip through the Rocky
Mountain region, to include Yellowstone, Grand Teton, Bryce
Canyon, Zion, and Kaibab and Tusayan national forests, Bandelier,
and the Mount Evans region near Denver. Early in September
1925 they finished their inspection trip and made their recommendations as follows:

1. That Rocky Mountain be expanded to the south to add
Arapahoe Mountain and Glacier, but be reduced in the vicinity of
Estes Park to exclude private lands, and in the area south of Grand
Lake. The Forest Service and the Park Service agreed here.

2. That Mount Rainier be expanded modestly.

3. That Sequoia be expanded greatly to take in Mount Whitney
and the Sierra crest and Kern Canyon.

4. That Grand Canyon be extended on the north to take in some
of the Kaibab National Forest.

5. That Yellowstone be expanded a little at the east and west
ends of the north line, that the Thorofare region and the Upper
Yellowstone be added on the southeast, and that the east boundary
be changed to follow the crest of the Absaroka Range, adding at
some points and subtracting at others. The committee recommended the creation of the Grand Teton Park as a separate park,
but did not approve the addition of Jackson Hole, and suggested
that the country south of Yellowstone, except the Grand Teton
Range, should continue to be managed by the state of Wyoming as
a wildlife preserve. The Yellowstone addition recommended was
about 300,000 acres, less than half of what Mather wanted.

For Yosemite the committee at first recommended that the
boundary be moved inward to eliminate private lands owned by
lumber companies, but there was some opposition to this and the
recommendation was withdrawn.

As usual with compromises, no one was greatly pleased, but the
Secretaries of the Interior and of Agriculture approved the report,
and early in March 1926 Senator Stanfield and Representative
Sinnott of Oregon introduced administration bills (Stanfield's "by
request"), to effectuate the recommendations of the committee; but
Representative Smith of Idaho promptly announced that he would

offer an amendment cutting out the Bechler Basin, in the southwest corner of the park, and would hold up the bills if this were not conceded. Whether as a result of his opposition or for other reasons, neither bill was given any attention.[7] Two years later, early in 1928, several bills were offered, to create Grand Teton National Park—or "Kendrick" National Park—or to revise the Yellowstone Boundaries. Senator Norbeck of North Dakota brought up two boundary revision bills, embodying generally the recommendations of the Coordinating Committee, and approved by Albright, Secretary Work of the Department of the Interior, and Acting Secretary Dunlap of the Department of Agriculture.[8] The bill (S. 3001) provided for a great improvement in the boundaries, but Dr. Willard Van Name, of the American Museum of Natural History, attacked it with acrimony in a letter which he sent to all members of Congress. He objected to the elimination of a small area on the east boundary—allowed to make the boundary line follow the mountain crest—and to other items that were really not in the bill. It took much of Cramton's time to explain the questions raised in Van Name's letter. Cramton was chairman of the House Committee on Appropriations for the Department of the Interior and a staunch friend of the parks. The Norbeck bill was reported favorably on January 17, 1929, and a month later was recommended for passage by the House Committee on Public Lands, passed both houses with little debate, and was signed by President Hoover on March 1, 1929.[9]

CHANGES IN YELLOWSTONE BOUNDARIES   The Norbeck Act revised the northwest, northeast, and east boundaries, adding 157 square miles and excluding 79 square miles. Among the additions were: (1) 43 square miles adjoining the northwest corner in Gallatin National Forest, primarily to protect a petrified forest; (2) 4 square miles in the northeast corner, to include the headwaters of Pebble Creek and provide a natural administrative boundary; and (3) an area of 110 square miles adjoining the east boundary in the Shoshone National Forest to include the headwaters of the creek's

7 S. 3427, H. R. 9917, 69 Cong. 1 Sess. *National Parks Bulletin*, Dec. 1926.
8 S. 2571, S. 3001, 70 Cong. 1 Sess.
9 Stat. 45, 1435.

tributary to the Lamar River, and to establish a natural administrative boundary along the crest of the Absaroka Range and the divide between the headwaters of the Lamar River and the North Fork of the Shoshone River. This was good summer range for elk and buffalo and contained the weird Hoodoo region of volcanic phenomena. The first elimination was an area of 50 square miles in the east central part of the park, establishing a natural administrative boundary along the divide. Nearly all this area was above 8,000-foot altitude, of little value as elk range and of no value for domestic grazing, with timber of no commercial value even if it had been accessible. The second elimination was an area of 29 square miles adjacent to the east boundary, including the headwaters of Eagle Creek and establishing a natural administrative boundary along the crest of the divide between Eagle Creek and the drainage flowing into Middle Creek and the southeast arm of Yellowstone Lake. This area was all above 8,000 feet in altitude, too high for elk or livestock grazing, with no commercial timber.

The Co-ordinating Committee had considered the south and southeast boundaries and recommended the addition of 340 square miles on the southeast to include the headwaters of the Yellowstone River. This was a logical part of the park, of minor importance as elk range but of major importance to moose, with no timber of commercial value; but it was not included in the act because of the opposition of a few professional guides and packers who conducted hunting parties into the area.

The Co-ordinating Committee also recommended the excision of 40 square miles between the Snake River and the South Boundary, but this was not included in the act, although the Snake River was the natural boundary of the park, for the area south of the river was difficult to administer. The committee did not study the Bechler Basin and the Idaho statesmen were unable to effect its elimination.[10] They had got a Senate resolution through the Senate in 1926, appropriating $3,500 for an investigation of the area, but nothing came of it.[11]

But the Norbeck Act was not exactly what Cramton wanted. The provision forbidding the construction of roads or hotels in the high country added on the east had got into the bill against Cramton's

10 Letter of Albright, Jan. 16, 1930; *Congressional Record,* Feb. 14, 1930, 3677.
11 S. Res. 237, 69 Cong. 1 Sess.

wishes, by a clerical error. The Park Service had no intention of allowing roads or hotels in this area, but did not wish to have its hands tied, and Cramton suggested the possibility that the provision was wanted by hotels outside the park to avoid too much competition with their business; and on May 31, 1929, he introduced a bill to eliminate this provision. In the discussion of this bill, Representative Connery of Massachusetts said that the Mayor of Lynn, Massachusetts, after a trip through some of the parks had charged that conditions were a "disgrace," that there was "graft," and the guides were practically "grafters." Cramton was unable to convince Connery that the charges were not valid, but the bill passed the House anyhow, without further discussion, passed the Senate without debate and was signed by President Hoover on April 19, 1929.[12]

YELLOWSTONE BOUNDARY COMMISSION   The Norbeck Act provided most of what Mather and Albright wanted on the northwest, northeast, and east boundaries, but nothing on the south and southeast. The Co-ordinating Committee had done a fairly thorough job of investigation, but on the south and southeast a more careful study was needed;[13] and soon afterward, while the Norbeck bill was being discussed, Nye of North Dakota brought up a Senate resolution authorizing the President to appoint a Yellowstone Boundary Commission to study these areas. The resolution passed both houses promptly and was signed by President Hoover on February 28, 1929, two days before the Norbeck bill was signed.[14]

President Hoover promptly appointed a five-man commission of able men familiar with park problems, and the commission held hearings at Cody and Jackson, Wyoming, Ashton, and Idaho, and spent fourteen days in field inspection. Final hearings were held in Washington on February 3, 1930.

The hearings were decidedly interesting. On the question of adding the Thorofare region and the headwaters of the Yellowstone and Snake rivers southeast of the park there was vigorous disagreement. Those who favored this addition argued that this high area was of national park quality, a natural part of Yellow-

12 H. R. 3568, 71 Cong. 1 Sess. *Congressional Record*, Feb. 3, 1930, 2959, 2960. Stat. 46, 220.
13 *Congressional Record*, Feb. 9, 1929, 3140.
14 S. J. Res. 206, 70 Cong. 1 Sess. Stat. 45, 1413.

stone Park, that there was little commercial timber there, and that
as a wilderness area it could be better administered by the Park
Service than by the Forest Service. The opinion was expressed by
several witnesses that the Wyoming Game and Fish Commission
was inefficient and indifferent to the protection of game, as for instance in permitting the "senseless and atrocious slaughter" of
thousands of antelope in one season—"a disgrace alike to the state
of Wyoming and to the self-styled hunters who took advantage of
the blunder of the Wyoming State Game Commission in opening
the season on antelope." It was also argued that this area was needed
for the moose. Albright believed that most of the people of Wyoming
favored the addition.

Against the addition were the cattlemen, woolgrowers, and hunters, of course, and the dude-ranch owners, the State Game and Fish
Commission and the State Izaak Walton League, the Wyoming
"boosters" who wanted to "see Wyoming grow," and others, who
pointed out that the state would lose all jurisdiction, could not tax
hotels as it did those in national forests, and would lose the 25 per
cent of gross timber and grazing receipts that were paid to the state
by the Forest Service. There was some fuzzy thinking on this point.
A Mr. Cooper, of the Woolgrowers' Association, did not think
that even the 25 per cent of timber receipts paid by the Forest
Service was enough: "If I take a dollar away from you I am perfectly willing to give you 25 cents back if you will let me keep the
75 cents." In other words, even the Forest Service was short-changing
the people of Wyoming in giving them only 25 per cent of the gross
receipts—which was probably more than the total net receipts above
the cost of guarding and administering the national forests, and
was more, in the long run, than the state would have received if the
forests had been turned over to private exploitation! Many of those
who opposed the addition liked Forest Service administration better
than that of the Park Service, because it allowed them more privileges—grazing livestock, hunting and trapping, prospecting for
minerals and even sometimes stealing timber and land under the
mining laws, cutting timber under certain circumstances, and building summer homes in the forests.

On the elimination of the Bechler Basin and the area south of
the Snake River along the south boundary of the park, little was
said—pro or con—in the hearings on the bill of Senator Nugent and

Representative Addison Smith. The general consensus was against these eliminations.

The Boundary Commission made five final recommendations:

1. That 52,480 acres be added on the south to southeast boundary from the Teton National Forest, to include the Bridger Lake area.

2. That the area east and southeast of this, the headwaters of Thorofare Creek and Yellowstone River, 165,000 acres, be made a wilderness area by the Forest Service.

3. That a biologist be appointed to study the elk and moose conditions in the upper Yellowstone regions in the southeast area in and adjoining the park.

4. That the small area south of the Snake River just inside the south boundary of the park be retained.

5. That the Bechler River meadows in the southwest corner of the park be protected from dams, and that a road should be constructed through this area from Ashton, Idaho, to Old Faithful station.[15]

A few weeks after the Norbeck Act was passed the Cramton Act made further changes in the boundaries, but of no great importance.[16] The Park Service never got any addition to the southeast but did get a little hump on the north boundary west of Gallatin, and it retained the Bechler Basin or Falls River Basin.[17]

Throughout these years, the Yellowstone elk were getting attention in other ways than in the boundary revision proposals. In the 69th Congress of 1925-27, Senator Wheeler and Representatives Evans and Leavitt of Montana pushed bills for better feed conditions, and the Leavitt bill passed both houses, "To make additions to the Absaroka and Gallatin National Forests and the Yellowstone National Park, and to improve and extend the winter feed facilities of the elk, antelope, and other game animals of Yellowstone National Park, and adjacent lands," etc.—by buying winter feeding range north of the park with donated money or by trading other land or timber for it. The animals had once ranged down the Yellowstone Valley in winter as far north as Livingston, but much of this land had been taken up by settlers; and the Leavitt bill was designed to turn over to game animals a narrow strip along the

15 *Report of the Yellowstone National Park Boundary Commission, 1931.* *American Forests,* June 1931, 378. *Nature,* Apr. 1930, 213.

16 H. R. 3568, 71 Cong. 1 Sess. Stat. 46, 220.

17 *Outlook,* Dec. 29, 1926, 553.

Yellowstone River, partly within Gallatin and Absaroka national forests, partly public domain lands, partly lands covered by a Northern Pacific land grant, and partly owned by settlers. It was understood that a sum of $100,000 in private funds was available to buy private lands, and the bill at first provided an appropriation of $150,000, to be matched from other sources; but this appropriation was eliminated in committee because "in conflict with the financial program of the President."[18] The bill authorized the President to add by proclamation land north of the west part of the northern boundary of the park. It was said to be approved by the people in the locality, and it passed with little discussion.[19]

President Hoover availed himself of the authorization in the Leavitt Act and proclaimed an addition of 7,600 acres in October 1932.[20]

On the first day of the 70th Congress, on December 5, 1927, Representative Leavitt had introduced a bill to appropriate $150,000 for the purchase of lands, to be matched by private or other agencies, and Senator Norbeck introduced two similar bills. Leavitt's bill passed without discussion, and was signed by President Hoover on May 18, 1928; and on the first day of the session Representative Addison Smith of Idaho tried to get a bill through the House cutting out of the park the Bechler Basin, in the southwest corner, as a site for irrigation dams, but the bill was not reported. His efforts to get this excision by an amendment of the Yellowstone boundary revision bills were similarly unsuccessful.[21]

BOUNDARY CHANGES FOR OTHER PARKS   Mather and his men wanted enlargement of several other parks. They wanted a great enlargement of Sequoia, to include Mount Whitney, then the highest mountain in the United States, and the Sierra crest and Kern

18 S. 3791, S. 3320, H. R. 10659, H. R. 10733, 69 Cong. 1 Sess.

19 H. R. 10733, 69 Cong. 1 Sess. Stat. 44, 655. *American Forests and Forest Life*, Feb. 1929, 93 ff.

20 Stat. 47, 2537.

21 H. R. 15, S. 2571, S. 3001, H. R. 17, 70 Cong. 1 Sess. Stat. 45, 603. See also Robert Shankland, *Steve Mather of the National Parks* (New York: Alfred A. Knopf, 1951) , 172, 173, 178-79. National Parks Bulletin No. 43, May 24, 1925. *Review of Reviews*, Mar. 1926, 322. *Yellowstone National Park Boundary Commission*, 1931. *American Forests and Forest Life*, Apr. 1925, 240, 241; Aug. 1925, 500; Nov. 1925, 701; Dec. 1925, 768.

Canyon to the east, and the Kings River Canyon on the north. The Sequoia that Senator John F. Miller proposed in 1881 was a big Sequoia, covering much of the western slope of the Sierra, but the Sequoia that was established in 1890 was a rather stingy little park, with little to recommend it but some groves of giant sequoias. It really needed enlargement badly. The enlargement of Sequoia had been urged by almost every Secretary of the Interior from Hitchcock, in 1900, for the next twenty years, and there were many efforts in Congress to secure this extension. But against the effort were arrayed the sheep and cattle men, lumbermen, power, and irrigation interests, and ranchers, sportsmen, and much of the time the Forest Service, which saw a danger of losing some of its domain.

The Forest Service was not opposed to the enlargement of Sequoia if it did not take in too much national forest land, but it did not believe that there was anything particularly scenic in the south part of Sequoia Park. The position of the Forest Service was generally that it could administer most forest land better than the Park Service, according to the principle of "multiple use"—using the land for timber production, grazing, perhaps also for mining, water power, irrigation, hunting and recreation, whereas the Park Service could use it for only two purposes—scenery and recreation. Foresters did not think that timber cutting, properly regulated, injured scenic values much, except in the case of trees of very exceptional value such as giant sequoias—and there were some giant sequoias in the national forests of the Sierra. Even the giant sequoias many foresters thought they could protect as well as anyone. The Forest Service employed landscape architects to work out a plan for the Kings River region which it thought about as good as any that the Park Service could provide. There was, however, one advantage in park administration for areas that demanded absolute protection—park rules were laid down by Congress, could be changed only by Congress, and therefore had stability and permanence, whereas Forest Service rules were largely departmental orders, which might be changed at any time. A giant sequoia grove in a national park, for instance, *must* be protected unless or until Congress passed a law authorizing cutting; but such a grove in a national forest might be cut at any time if the Secretary of Agriculture and the Chief Forester decided to do it, although it is almost inconceivable that they would do this.

This was the general situation when Mather assumed office. In March 1916 Mather's friend, Representative Kent of California, introduced a bill to enlarge Sequoia, excluding the Kings River watershed and establishing a game refuge in the Mineral King region, which was favored by the Forest Service, but it did not pass.[22] On June 5, 1919, Senator Phelan introduced a bill to increase the area of Sequoia about 400 per cent, which was reported but was not considered in the Senate. A bill introduced by Representative Elston had no better luck. The House Committee on Public Lands allowed the inclusion of the High Sierra—which had no grass or timber—but cut out a big slice of timber lands, *reducing* the park by about 150,000 acres.[23] These bills would have called the new park the "Roosevelt" National Park, in an attempt to capitalize on the fame of Theodore Roosevelt, who had died in January 1919.

The next year, June 1921, Representative Barbour of California introduced and fought for a "Roosevelt-Sequoia" enlargement, which would have given some land in the southwest part of the park to the Forest Service, to keep that service in good humor, but would have added much more along the northern and northeastern boundaries, to include mountain peaks and some giant sequoias. W. B. Greeley, of the Forest Service, defended this bill ably, but the old combination of livestock men, power and irrigation interests and sportsmen defeated it.[24]

In every Congress for several years Barbour, and several other men, pushed for an enlarged Sequoia, usually under the name Roosevelt-Sequoia, but long without success. In the fall of 1925 Temple's Co-ordinating Committee reported favorably on most of the provisions of the Barbour bill, to take in a large area of the western slope of the Sierra, including Mount Whitney and other high mountains, and running north beyond and including magnificent Tehipite Valley and Kings River Canyon—an increase of some 400 per cent in the size of Sequoia. The Barbour bill that finally passed, in 1926, fell far short of this. It doubled the size of the park, including the Kern and Keweah sections and Mount Whitney, but omitting the Kings River area—where there was coveted water power—and surrendering some land in the southwest

22 H. R. 13168, 64 Cong. 1 Sess.
23 S. 2118, S. 1391, H. R. 5006, 66 Cong. 1 Sess.
24 H. R. 7452, 67 Cong. 1 Sess.

part of the park to the Forest Service. It was debated at some length in the House. Most of the debate centered on the name, some of the representatives objecting to the name Roosevelt, others wanting Sequoia spelled "Sequoyah," like the name of the Indian chief after whom the park was named. The name "Sequoia" was retained in the bill that President Coolidge signed on July 3, 1926.[25]

The Barbour Act of 1926 did more than change the boundaries. It authorized renewable leases to concessioners for up to twenty years, and authorized continuance of leases made by the Forest Service on land shifted from it. It also authorized the Secretary to issue permits to bona fide claimants to cut timber for the improvement of their land, and to grant grazing permits at fees not above those charged by the Forest Service, so long as such permits were "not detrimental to the primary purpose for which such park is created." No permits for dams, conduits, reservoirs, etc. were permitted without special authority of Congress. Finally, the act set up the Sequoia National Game Refuge covering land adjoining the park, and prohibited all hunting and trapping in it.

The Barbour Act was good, but not enough for the Park Service and park supporters, who continued their efforts for expansion, the expansion to take place as the Kings Canyon National Park, adjoining Sequoia on the north. This was not to come until 1940, after years of hard fighting, particularly against the power and irrigation interests.

There were privately owned timber lands along the road in Glacier Park which Mather and Albright wanted, and they were able to trade for them within the next few years under a law passed in 1917. The 1917 act was the result of a bill introduced by Senator Walsh in the 64th Congress. It authorized the Secretary to get patented or state lands by exchanging dead, decadent, or matured timber of equal value in any part of the park where it would not injure scenic values in the park or, on approval of the Secretary of Agriculture, timber from national forests in Montana. The cutting was to be regulated by the Secretary, the private owners or the state were to pay any damages incident to the removal of timber, and the Secretary must report to Congress in detail the factors on which the valuations were made. Here Congress showed a proper concern

25 H. R. 9387, S. 4258, 69 Cong. 1 Sess. Stat. 44, 818.

regarding the terms of these exchanges, for without doubt the government was often short-changed in trades with private owners.[26]

Mather wanted and needed an extension of Mount Rainier to the eastward to the crest of the Cascades and southward to take in Ohanepecosh Hot Springs, to cover the road to Paradise Valley into the park, and to acquire Longmire Springs, where there were some shabby hotel accommodations. The President's Co-ordinating Committee recommended in favor of most of these, and some extensions were secured in 1926. Early in 1926 Senator Stanfield and Representative Sinnott of Oregon brought in bills for them and the Sinnott bill passed both houses without debate and was signed by President Coolidge on May 28, 1926.[27] This act made important additions to the park, but more were needed and were added in January 1931, in Albright's administration.[28]

Mount Rainier needed other things during these years—more and better roads, more and better hotels, more camp grounds, better sanitary facilities. The Yakima Park road was being built in 1928, which called for more camps; but the north part of the park and three alpine park areas in the southwest were designated "roadless areas" to remain free of roads and hotels. In 1924 the Superintendent reported the purchase of a snow plow to keep the road open in winter, and soon there was a development of winter sports.

Mather and Albright also wanted an extension of Grand Canyon northward to take in a part of beautiful Kaibab National Forest, and southward to include a chunk of Tusayan National Forest. The Co-ordinating Committee recommended two additions on the north and other minor changes. The Kaibab and Tusayan extensions were to come later. They wanted to get back about 60,000 acres in Yosemite, including Devils Postpile, Red Meadows, Rainbow Falls, and the Minarets, which had been cut from the southeast corner in 1905; and Mather always wanted to add to Crater Lake the lovely Diamond Lake and a couple of mountains—never to be achieved in spite of efforts by Senator McNary. He also wanted an extension eastward of Glacier to include some lower land for winter range for the wildlife, but this was never to be acquired.

26 S. 778, 64 Cong. 1 and 2 Sess. Stat. 39, 1122.
27 S. 3428, H. R. 10126, 69 Cong. 1 Sess. Stat. 44, 668.
28 Stat. 46, 1047.

INFERIOR PARKS   The Park Service would have been glad to get rid of two inferior national parks, Sullys Hill and Platt, and perhaps, but not certainly, Wind Cave. Sullys Hill was to be abolished in Albright's administration, but Platt is still a national park; and at any proposal for turning it over to the state, Oklahoma politicians arose in righteous wrath to defend their splendid national park. The early superintendents were apparently chosen by the state and were political appointees unfit for such a position. In the consideration of the appropriation bill, in January 1924, the Oklahoma men tried to get the appropriation raised from $10,000 to $25,000, and Louis Cramton, chairman of the House Subcommittee on Appropriations, used some plain language in fighting them off: "I say that before the people down there in that little local park can expect an increase in the appropriation from the Federal Treasury they have to get away from the idea that their little local park is local on everything except appropriations from the Federal Treasury." This seems reasonable, but Oklahoma Representative McKeown in retaliation spent much of a half-day of the time of Congress trying unsuccessfully to get reductions in the appropriations for every other park as it came up. If Platt is ever abolished it will be over the dead bodies of Oklahoma politicians.[29]

THE FEDERAL WATER POWER ACT   At this point it is necessary to divert attention to the story of water power legislation, which was of particular pertinence in relation to the enlarged Sequoia. The Right-of-Way Act of 1901 has been considered in the chapter on Yosemite Park. It will be remembered that the rights of way might be revoked at any time, and that therefore they did not establish a very firm basis for business investment. For some years there were efforts in Congress to permit water power developments and grant rights of way for electric lines through public lands; and finally, on July 10, 1920, an act was pushed through Congress creating the Federal Power Commission and giving it the authority to permit water development in publicly controlled lands, *including national parks and monuments.* This bill had been concocted by water power interests, with the co-operation of Secretary Lane, who was a reclamation enthusiast and a somewhat unreliable friend of the parks and of conservation generally, and was introduced by

29 *Congressional Record,* Jan. 29, 1924, 1645-49.

Representative Esch of Wisconsin early in 1919. The bill was a long one—covering seventeen pages in the Statutes when enacted—with a great complexity and confusion of details. Whether intentionally or not, it was so drawn as apparently to omit national parks; but a careful reading revealed that this was not true, as Esch admitted when asked. The bill was debated for days, but the matter of its application to the national parks was scarcely mentioned, and it was headed for passage before conservation forces noticed that it opened the parks and monuments to power developments.[30]

Lane's record should be traced briefly. His record on the national parks was generally good although, as we have seen, he helped to despoil Hetch Hetchy, and he tried to open some of the parks to grazing in the First World War. In 1919 he approved the invasion of Yellowstone by irrigation interests, and demanded that Mather make a report favoring this. Mather was determined not to do this and would probably have resigned if Lane had not himself resigned for personal reasons. Lane's record on oil is worse than his national park record. He had a hand in drawing up the unwise Ferris bill for exploitation of public oil lands, in 1914; and on the question of treatment of claimants on naval oil reservations in California, a burning issue from 1914 to about 1917, Lane was consistently lined up with the oil men, against Pinchot, Secretary Daniels of the Navy, and Attorney General Gregory. Pinchot criticized him bitterly for his attitude, and said "he could not be trusted." His record on the management of the Indian lands was, however, exemplary.[31]

On the enactment of the Federal Water Power Act, Los Angeles plastered the Kings Canyon area with power applications. On June 5, 1920, Congress passed a bill giving the city the right to cross national forests with water mains and power lines.[32]

The failure to exempt the national parks and monuments would not necessarily have been disastrous. The Federal Water Power Commission at the time was composed of men who could be trusted, Meredith, Payne and Baker; and the law did not *require* them to issue power permits but only authorized them to do so. But it was quite conceivable that a future commission of men of different character might gut some of the parks with dams and aqueducts and tun-

[30] H. R. 3184, 66 Cong. 1 Sess. Stat. 41, 1063.

[31] See the author's *United States Oil Policy* (New Haven: Yale University Press, 1926).

[32] Stat. 41, 983. *Science*, Jan. 23, 1921, 73.

nels and power lines that would do vast damage; and as Payne pointed out, there was a clear possibility that future commissions might construe the law as *instructing* them rather than *permitting* them to grant power permits. Mather was gravely concerned and immediately called on Secretary Payne, Lane's successor. Payne hurried over to see President Wilson, who called in Senators Jones of Washington and Walsh of Montana, and told them he would veto the bill unless they promised to exempt the parks and monuments from the act at the next session. They agreed, reluctantly, and when the next Congress convened in December, Senator Jones and Representatives Esch of Wisconsin and Rogers of Massachusetts introduced bills to exempt the parks and monuments.[33]

There were strong forces working for the park exemption—Mather and Albright, the Sierra Club, of course, and other conservation organizations; and George Horace Lorimer with his puissant *Saturday Evening Post*. Several state legislatures adopted memorials in favor of the bills. But these bills exempted only the parks already established; any parks established in the future would have to be separately exempted. How did this happen?

A man named Henry J. Pierce, president of the Washington Irrigation and Development Company of Seattle, and representative, according to his own statement, of Pacific Coast power interests and of the "people of California," appears to have told the Public Lands Committee that he would not allow the bill to pass unless future parks were left out—a rather illuminating commentary on American politics. This provision was tailor-made for a future enlarged Sequoia, or "Roosevelt-Sequoia," or "Roosevelt" park. The power interests were of course interested in power development in some of the parks already established, but their hopes were not roseate for this: their main ambition was for development in the area which was planned for the enlarged Sequoia—later to be partly realized in Kings Canyon Park—particularly in Tehipite Valley and Kings River Canyon. They could see that an enlarged Sequoia was likely to be established eventually, and they wanted the power sites in it. At any rate, future parks were not exempted, and in that form the bill passed both houses with very little discussion, although Senator Borah objected to the whole bill on the ground that the parks, in

33 S. 4554, H. R. 14469, H. R. 14760, 66 Cong. 3 Sess. *National Parks Bulletin*, No. 22, Nov. 8, 1921; No. 23, Dec. 14, 1921.

his opinion, were safer protected by the Federal Water Power Commission than by Congress. President Wilson signed the "Jones-Esch" bill on March 3, 1921, just before leaving office.[34]

NEW NATIONAL MONUMENTS   A large number of national monuments were proclaimed or authorized by Congress in Mather's administration, three of which—*Bryce Canyon, Carlsbad Cave,* and *Zion*—were later raised to national park status. It will be pertinent to list the national monuments proclaimed by each of the three presidents under which Mather served—Wilson, Harding and Coolidge—bearing in mind that the moving spirits behind these proclamations were almost always Mather, Albright, and the Park Service, often encouraged by the Secretary of the Interior in office at the time.

In February 1916, before the Park Service had been organized, President Wilson proclaimed the *Bandelier* National Monument in New Mexico, a red-canyon area with fine archeological ruins, named after a famous Swedish archeologist, Adolph Bandelier, who had explored the area from 1880 to 1886 and later wrote the famous romance of the life of the prehistoric inhabitants.[35] There had been several attempts in Congress to make this a national park, and Lane and Mather seemed to be mildly favorable. When Lacey introduced his Mesa Verde bill he had really wanted two cliff-dwelling parks, Mesa Verde and Pajarito—the latter to include Bandelier and the area west of it—but he feared that Congress would not establish two archeological parks, so he did not press for Bandelier. It was scarcely of national park importance anyhow. Several months later President Wilson proclaimed the *Sieur de Monts* National Monument, on the Maine coast, later to become the Acadia National Park. In August 1916 the President proclaimed the *Capulin Mountain* National Monument, a recently extinct volcano of perfect symmetry in northeast New Mexico.

In October 1916 President Wilson proclaimed the *Old Kasaan* National Monument, covering an abandoned village in Alaska, with

34 Stat. 41, 1353, 1354. *National Parks Bulletin,* No. 10, June 25, 1920; No. 15, Feb. 10, 1921; No. 23, Dec. 14, 1921. Shankland, *op. cit.,* 214, 216. *American Forests and Forest Life,* Jan. 1921, 5.

35 *The Delight Makers* (New York: Dodd, Mead and Co., 1918).

totem poles and other historic objects. The Casa Grande ruin, at one time often classified as a national park, had been set aside as a "reservation" in June, 1892, the only ancient ruin to get an early appropriation for protection ($2,000). With this a roof was built over the ruin. Seventeen years later the proclamation order was found not to include the ruins, and in 1909 President Taft issued a new proclamation covering it. In August 1918 President Wilson proclaimed it a national monument. A few weeks later, on recommendation of Secretary Lane and Mather, Wilson proclaimed the great *Katmai* National Monument in Alaska, the "Valley of the Ten Thousand Smokes," volcanic territory including the great active volcano Katmai and an area of "smokes," somewhat similar to the geysers of Yellowstone, now the largest area in the park system— 2,697,590 acres. Katmai Monument has been declared by some to be the greatest national monument, even "the greatest natural-wonder playground in America," or even indeed "in the world." At any rate, Katmai staged a terrific explosion in June 1912, one of the greatest volcanic eruptions of recorded history, and the National Geographic Society made investigations of the area in 1914 and the years following, as a result of which it was made a national monument. The *National Geographic Magazine* reported that the stream of hot, glowing sand covered more than 53 square miles of the valley floor, that the fallout was so dense at Kodiak Island, 100 miles away, that people had to shovel ashes off their roofs to avoid cave-ins, and that evidences of dust were seen all over the world. Fifteen hundred feet of the top of Katmai were blown off.[36]

In December 1919 Wilson proclaimed *Scott's Bluff* in western Nebraska a national monument. Scott's Bluff has an interesting history as a landmark and resting station on the Oregon Trail, and as the place near which Hiram Scott's skeleton was found about 1828. The story is that Scott, coming from the west with companions, fell ill about sixty miles west of the Bluff, was abandoned by his companions and crawled sixty miles to the Bluff before he died. (It may have been less than sixty miles!)

President Wilson's last monument, in December 1919, was *Yucca House* near Mesa Verde, a pueblo almost completely covered by earth and rubble. It was donated to the government by Henry Van Kleeck, of Denver.

36 *National Geographic Magazine*, June 1956, 749.

President Harding's record on national monuments is better than his record on oil reserves, and he was in office only a few months when he added to Muir Woods, and in January 1922 proclaimed beautiful *Lehman Caves,* in Nevada. In October 1922 he set aside *Timpanogos Cave,* an interesting cave high up in the side of Mount Timpanogos, near Provo, Utah. The *Fossil Cycad* National Monument, proclaimed a week later, contained fossil remains of fernlike plants that grew in early geological epochs—perhaps 120 million years ago, in the Mesozoic era. Some scientists have been deeply interested in these fossil cycads.[37] In January 1923 Harding proclaimed *Aztec Ruins,* pueblo ruins in northwestern New Mexico, presented through the generosity of Archer Huntington; and on March 2, 1923, he proclaimed the *Mound City Group* in Ohio, ancient Indian mounds used for the disposal of the dead; but since Congress was not yet voting adequate funds for the protection of national monuments, the Ohio State Archeological and Historical Society assumed care of the mounds until 1946. On the same day Harding proclaimed the *Hovenweep* Monument on the Colorado-Utah border near Mesa Verde, a monument covering remarkable square, circular, oval, and D-shaped towers which had apparently been built around springs from which the ancient Indians got their water. In May 1923 he enlarged Pinnacles Monument, and proclaimed the *Pipe Spring* Monument in northern Arizona, a Mormon fort, enclosing a spring, with an interesting history running back a century or more.[38]

President Coolidge began in October 1923 with a magnificent addition to the monument system, Carlsbad Cave National Monument (called Carlsbad "Caverns" in 1930, when it was made a national park). In April 1924 he proclaimed *Chiricahua* National Monument in southeastern Arizona, an area of "grotesque and arabesque" rock formations, once the retreat of the fierce Apaches, under Chiefs Cochise, Geronimo, and Massai, who fought off United States troops for many years. In May 1924 he proclaimed another recently extinct volcanic monument, the *Craters of the Moon* in Southern Idaho, so named because of its resemblance to pock marks on the moon. *Lava Beds* National Monument in northeastern California was proclaimed in November 1925, an area of extinct

37 *Science,* Oct. 23, 1936, 367; Mar. 19, 1937, 287.
38 The name "Pipe Spring" is said to have arisen because an expert marksman shot a pipe from the mouth of a friend here.

volcanoes and caves and peculiar volcanic formations where the Modoc Indians made a brave and for a time amazingly successful stand against United States troops in 1872 and 1873. In December 1924 Coolidge proclaimed *Wupatki* National Monument, pueblo ruins in Arizona, and in February 1925 proclaimed *Glacier Bay* National Monument, a bay on the Alaska coast into which flow some twenty mighty glaciers, including the Muir Glacier, named after John Muir, who visited this area in October 1879 to study glacial action.

A few years earlier Muir had become convinced that Yosemite Valley had been scoured out by glaciers in the ice age, whereas Professor Josiah Whitney argued that the valley was formed when its bottom dropped down into the earth, and that there had never been ice in Yosemite Valley. "The bottom never fell out of anything God made," declared Muir. The controversy raged long and heated, and finally Muir went to Alaska to study glaciers in action, to find of course that what had happened in Yosemite Valley was now happening in Alaska, and most clearly in Glacier Bay. Glacier Bay is also a good place to study climatic changes—the rising temperatures in Alaska and over all the world. The glaciers are receding. John Muir's camp, which was near the face of the glacier in 1879, is now thirteen miles from the face. Muir thought Glacier Bay was magnificent, and many observers rate it one of the noblest park areas that we have.

Congress got into the reservation of national monuments only a little during Mather's time. In August 1922 Congress authorized the Secretary of the Interior to set aside Palm Springs Canyon, an area of palms in Riverside County, California, if satisfactory arrangements could be made with the Agua Caliente Indians. Nearly all the land was owned by the Indians, and the money to purchase the lands was never found, so the monument was never established.[39]

PROTECTION OF THE ARCHEOLOGICAL MONUMENTS   The establishment of these national monuments did not do very much for their protection, for Congress voted only stingy sums for them, beginning with $3,500 in 1916 and rising to $35,000 in Mather's last year, 1928. In an effort to make the money go as far as possible

[39] Stat. 42, 832.

Secretary Work appointed Custodian Frank Pinkley, of Casa Grande and Tumacacori, as Superintendent of Southwestern Monuments (Arizona, New Mexico, and Utah) in 1924.

Frank Pinkley was one of the great characters of national park history, personally kind, genial, understanding, and wholeheart-edly devoted to the archeological parks. He began his career as custodian of Casa Grande, for some years the only ruin that had a custodian; developed a burning interest in archeology, and learned much from Dr. J. W. Fewkes with whom he did excavating work at Casa Grande in 1906-8. When the National Park Service was or-ganized in 1917, Tumacacori was also entrusted to him, and he was asked to keep an eye on several others, including Montezuma Castle. By 1924 he was supervising fourteen national monuments and other reserves, including Carlsbad Cave, and in 1934 six more were handed to him; giving him a total domain covering a part of three or four states. This he tried to police and supervise in his Model T, with appropriations which he correctly termed "microscopic." He tried hard not only to provide protection but to stabilize the ruins that needed stabilization—as most of them did—and to build up a staff of contented and zealous men, and also con-tented wives, most of whom had to live in primitive quarters; and he worked hard to get the national park men to understand the great importance of the archeological ruins in the park system. After thirty-five years in the Service he died in the line of duty, after delivering a talk at a long-planned training conference. Asso-ciate Director Scoyen described him as the "best loved man in the National Park Service."[40]

Recreation outside the parks and monuments was getting in-creasing attention during Mather's administration. In 1925 the National Conference on Outdoor Recreation, the American For-estry Association, and the National Parks Association co-operated through the Joint Commission on Recreational Survey of Federal Lands to study the recreational opportunities on the federal lands. Recreation in the national forests had been recognized by Secretary of Agriculture James Wilson as a desirable use of the forests as early as 1905, but for some years the Forest Service was too busy with other chores to give much attention to recreation. In 1924, however, Chief Forester W. B. Greeley reported that recreation had become scarcely less valuable than timber production, and was rising in

40 *National Parks Magazine*, July-Sept. 1958, 101; Oct.-Dec. 1958, 161.

value faster. The Forest Service often reserved uncut timber along roads, around camp grounds, and as a setting for vacation homes to assist in this development, in this way assuming some of the functions of the Park Service.[41]

The whole broad problem of land use was getting more and more attention. In February and April, 1927, the Joint Subcommittee on Bases of Sound Land Policy, organized at a conference called by the Federated Societies on Planning and Parks, took up the problem of land utilization in all its various aspects. This was a movement which expanded greatly in the next few years.[42]

STATE PARKS　　　One of the earliest promoters of state parks was J. Horace McFarland, of the American Civic Association, who saw that city people would want and need open spaces where they could get away from the dust and smoke and clangor of the cities. Mather was from the first much interested in state parks as a needed complement to the national parks. Yosemite had been a state park for years, but the movement for the establishment of state parks really had its beginning in the middle eighties. In 1885 the New York legislature passed the Forest Preserve Act and in that year the Niagara State Reservation was dedicated. In 1889 Minnesota established the Birch Coulee State Memorial Park and soon afterward the well-known Itasca State Park. About this time several civic groups began to agitate for state parks, but before 1900 only two states, New York and Massachusetts, had administrative agencies to manage state recreational areas. In 1895 New York and New Jersey created the Palisades Interstate Park covering the Palisades on the Hudson, and in 1900 set up the Palisades Interstate Park Commission to administer it, and appropriated $15,000 for a survey. Within the next ten years $8 million was subscribed for the purchase of lands and for other expenses, by individuals and by the two states, and 30,000 acres had been acquired.

The California state parks loom large in our history because California reserved about the only coast redwoods that were saved from the lumbermen. The beginning of interest in California dates from 1901, when the state bought the State Redwood Park in the

41 *National Parks Bulletin*, No. 42, Dec. 25, 1924; No. 44, May 26, 1925. *Review of Reviews*, July 1924, 65.

42 *National Parks Bulletin*, No. 53, July 1927.

Santa Cruz Mountains south of San Francisco, but the great interest in the coast redwoods came more than a decade later. California's
state park system grew out of the work of the Save-the-Redwoods
League, organized in 1918 under the leadership of John C. Merriam
and Newton Drury, to save not only coast redwoods but giant
sequoias. The State Park System was set up by the legislature in
1927, and in the same year a gift of $2 million from John D. Rocke-
feller, Jr., made possible the purchase of the Bull Creek—Dyerville
forest, to be added to the Humboldt Redwoods State Park previously established. In 1928 the people of California approved a $6
million bond issue to buy state parks, to be matched by private
funds; and by the end of Mather's administration California had
several redwood state parks and others. The Save-the-Redwoods
League was assisted by the Sierra Club in this work, of course, by
Drury and by Mather and Albright personally, for Mather and
Albright had long been interested in saving the big trees, both
redwoods and sequoias.[43] The work of planning the California
state park system was done largely by the great landscape architect,
Frederick Law Olmsted, Jr., whose father had planned Central
Park in New York and had had much to do with early Yosemite.
Both father and son were dedicated conservationists, particularly of
scenic values.[44]

Between 1917 and 1930, twenty-nine states were reported to have
established state agencies, but some of these were not of a high
order, being inefficient and politics-ridden.[45]

In his 1920 Report Mather pointed out that some states were
already setting up parks, and suggested a conference of all who were
interested in park development—national, state, county, and city—
and characteristically set about to arrange for the conference, which
was held in Des Moines in 1921, and almost every year thereafter.
His interest in this matter never lagged. He even suggested that
federal lands might be given to the states for parks. As early as 1914
Congress had authorized the Secretary to withdraw from other disposition, and reserve for county parks, public playgrounds, and

43 *Nature Magazine*, Oct. 1928, 236. *National Parks Bulletin*, No. 47, Jan.
1926.

44 See an article by Newton B. Drury, *National Parks Magazine*, Apr.-June
1958, 59.

45 Clifford Hynning, "State Conservation of Resources; a Study Made for the
National Resources Committee," 1939, 32.

community centers such tracts in reclamation projects as seemed to him advisable, not exceeding twenty acres in any township.[46] In 1926 Congress authorized the Secretary to withhold from entry all unreserved nonmineral public lands chiefly valuable for recreational purposes, and to sell or lease them to the states or exchange them for other lands. All minerals were reserved, and if the states failed to use them as parks for five years they reverted to the federal government.[47] In 1928 Congress gave some public land to the state of Wisconsin for a state park.[48]

PROPOSALS FOR NEW PARKS   While working for new parks, the Park Service was obliged to fight stubbornly against the establishment of inferior parks that it did not want. In the year 1916 sixteen proposed national parks were reported, a few of them more or less worthy, but most of them quite unfit for national park status. As an early state park official put it: "A little city park of bubbling mineral springs [Platt], a city-side group of hot springs with an ancient tradition of cures [Hot Springs], a limestone cave through whose small vent the wind whistled mysteriously [Wind Cave], a lake in a dry country on whose borders Indians had once fought [Sullys Hill]—the wonder is that many more manifest blunders were not perpetrated in the early making."

The worst of these proposed parks, and the one that caused most trouble, was a "park" called for by Albert Fall—"Mescalero Park" or "All-Year Park," or, as dubbed by its critics, "Spotted Park" or "Mexican Freckles." This was to be a park of a dozen or so small isolated tracts of little scenic value, mostly from the Mescalero Indian Reservation in New Mexico. The project had been cooked up by several chambers of commerce in the area, and was to be open to mining, grazing, power and irrigation development, and hunting, in true broad-minded western fashion. It was true that some of the land would have to be taken from the Mescalero Indians without compensation—but Indians were accustomed to having their land taken, and would presumably be "willing." As early as 1911 Senator Fall and several of the New Mexico delegation in

46 Stat. 38, 727.
47 Stat. 44, 741.
48 Stat. 45, 417.

Congress had put on a campaign which lasted about ten years to set up national parks in New Mexico—Rio Grande, Cliff Cities (Bandelier and surrounding cliff-dweller areas), Pajarito (somewhat the same area), and Mescalero. Fall's ambitions were for Rio Grande and Mescalero, and he worked for these through three Congresses. Of course he wanted Mather to report favorably on the Mescalero bill, and this Mather would not do, but instead stalled and went into retirement for a time without having made any report. Finally, in July 1922, Senator Bursum, who had succeeded to Fall's position in the Senate, got the Mescalero bill through the Senate without debate, perhaps because it was so worded as to be misleading to the senators. It was a bill "creating the Mescalero National Park in New Mexico, and providing for the allotment of certain lands in severalty to the Mescalero Apache Indians," and was assumed to apply to Indian affairs. In the House this might have been assumed from the fact that the bill was referred to the Indian Affairs Committee.[49]

The Senate vote awakened conservationists, who began a fusillade of criticism of "Mexican freckles." A number of New Mexico organizations joined in the attack, much to Senator Bursum's embarrassment, and the bill was not reported in the House. One factor that helped to defeat the bill was the fact, as revealed in the hearings, that a part of the park would adjoin Fall's ranch.

Appalachia National Park in Virginia was another bad dream that won Fall's approval. He had no conception of national park standards. Mescalero was not his only offense, for he had a notion that any patch of soil that might serve as a camping place or recreation spot might properly be made a national park. "National park or nothing" was his answer to a protest against one of his wild proposals.[50]

In the latter part of his administration Mather narrowly missed being presented with another lemon in the form of an Arkansas park. The first proposals were for a Mena National Park, by Senator

49 S. 3519, 67 Cong. 2 Sess.

50 Shankland, *op. cit.*, 221-24. *National Parks Bulletin*, No. 32, Feb. 7, 1923. S. 6659, S. 6714, H. R. 24123, 62 Cong. 2 Sess. S. 4185, S. 4187, S. 5176, H. R. 14739, H. R. 16546, 63 Cong. 1 Sess. S. 4537, 63 Cong. 2 Sess. S. 2508, S. 2542, S. 3114, 64 Cong. 1 Sess. S. 2291, H. R. 3215, 65 Cong. 1 Sess. S. 666, S. 2374, 66 Cong. 1 Sess.

Joe Robinson and Representative Wingo of Arkansas, in the first session of the 68th Congress, but these got no attention.[51]

In 1928 Robinson, who was a very influential senator, introduced a bill for the same tract under the name Ouachita National Park, which was debated at considerable length and passed both houses although it was opposed by the Forest Service, the Park Service, the Secretaries of Agriculture and the Interior, the National Parks Association, the American Civic Association, indeed by almost every conservation organization in the country, by a majority of the House Public Lands Committee—after an investigation of the area by a subcommittee—and by national park friends in Congress such as Temple, Colton of Utah, and Cramton. Frederick Law Olmsted, chairman of the Committee on National Parks and Forests of the American Society of Landscape Architects, issued a strong warning against Ouachita and other inferior parks: "There is great danger these and other such projects will be renewed and pressed at this winter's session of Congress, and society should be prepared to stand firmly against the tendency, which such bills indicate, toward a new and dangerous policy to the creation of National Parks, one concerned with regional needs rather than with proper national purposes."[52]

It seems strange that a bill to make a national park of an area so clearly unworthy of park status, although of modest scenic beauty, should have passed both houses; but of course there was a scent of pork about the bill and Congress is often attracted by that. The central states had no national parks and they should be given parks whether they had any scenery or not—to the dogs with national park standards! Also many men in Congress had not yet grasped the distinction between national parks and recreation areas, and thought of Ouachita as a recreation area, a playground for the people in the area.[53] But Colton, chairman of the Public Lands Committee, wrote a special letter to President Coolidge, urging him to veto the bill, which Coolidge did. Colton advised the President that if the Ouachita bill were signed the committee would have to report twelve other bills providing for inferior parks.[54]

---

[51] S. 3309, S. 3375, H. R. 9174, H. R. 9426.
[52] American Forests and Forest Life, Apr. 1930, 240.
[53] S. 675, H. R. 5729, 70 Cong. 2 Sess.
[54] American Forests and Forest Life, Apr. 1929, 229; Aug. 1929, 524.

Park standards were saved by President Coolidge's veto, but Robinson continued his efforts for some time, in the 71st, 72nd and 73rd Congresses. The Park Service and conservation organizations were on guard and squashed every bill. There was a fear that Robinson might propose his park as a "memorial," which would have made it harder to fight, but he did not do this.[55] The proposal for a Roosevelt memorial national park, covering some of the scene of Theodore Roosevelt's ranching days in North Dakota, was of this sort, and from 1925 it was a recurrent threat for years.

One of the really "democratic" park proposals was that of Socialist Representative Victor Berger of Wisconsin, to establish a national forest and a national park in every state, to promote reforestation, and for other purposes.[56]

The work of fighting for worthy parks and fighting off unworthy parks became so arduous that in May 1928 Senator Nye of North Dakota introduced a resolution in the 70th Congress providing expenses for an investigation as to the advisability of establishing certain additional national parks and changing boundaries of others. The resolution was agreed to, and a subcommittee of the Senate Committee on Public Lands and Surveys visited Yellowstone, Rocky Mountain, Wind Cave, and proposed parks in North Dakota, taking officials of the Park Service along; but the report of the committee, approving Roosevelt, Grand Teton, and Teton (Badlands) national parks, was something of a jolt to the Park Service, which had been fighting against the Roosevelt project, and was not thirsting for Badlands as a national park. Perhaps the approval of the Roosevelt project was due to Nye's influence. The committee was also favorable to boundary changes in Yellowstone, which were of course acceptable to Mather and the Park Service.[57]

During these years, indeed since 1910, the problem of liquor sales in the parks was raised in Congress repeatedly, particularly after automobiles were allowed in the parks and the problem of drunken drivers arose. One bill prohibiting the sale of liquors in the parks was reported favorably by the House Committee on Public Lands in 1916, but a similar bill applying to both national parks and national forests was opposed by Secretary of Agriculture

55 *National Parks Bulletin,* No. 60, 1934. *Science,* July 8, 1932, 33.
56 H. R. 12416, 69 Cong. 1 Sess.
57 S. Res. 237, 70 Cong. 1 Sess.

Houston on the ground that his staff of rangers was too small to enforce such a prohibition. Saloons and barrooms were not permitted on government lands in the parks, but where hotel privileges had been leased, concessioners were permitted to supply guests with liquors. The park rule at the time was that liquor bottles carried in the park must be sealed. Unfortunately there is a strong propensity on the part of some tourists to associate vacation with liquor.[58]

58 S. 2386, H. R. 3134, H. R. 5292, 59 Cong. 1 Sess. S. 915, H. R. 12405, 60 Cong. 1 Sess. S. 2846, 61 Cong. 1 Sess. S. 230, 62 Cong. 1 Sess. S. 4862, H. R. 6814, 64 Cong. 1 Sess. H. R. 150, 65 Cong. 1 Sess. H. R. 9284, 65 Cong. 2 Sess.

CHAPTER XIV

The Mather Administration

1917-1928

ATTACKS ON THE PARKS

New parks and additions to parks seemed important, but Mather was barely seated in his new chair when he saw that he had another job of equal importance and almost greater difficulty: the job of keeping what he had, of fighting off business interests, livestock, mining, lumber, power and irrigation, and hunters.

THE WAR AND THREATS TO THE PARKS   Only a few days before Congress appropriated money for the establishment of the National Park Service, the United States plunged into the First World War, and the war brought serious hazards to the parks, particularly the threat of opening the parks to grazing, hunting, and lumbering. With the excuse of adding to the food supply, western livestock interests insisted that the parks should be opened to cattle and sheep, and sportsmen even demanded that the elk and buffalo herds of Yellowstone be killed for meat, that the game preserves be opened to hunters; and in various parts of the country they called for suspension of the game laws to increase the food supply. A state official in Washington wanted to take sheep into Mount Rainier Park, and when the Park Service denied his application, he appealed to Food Administrator Herbert Hoover, who also turned him down. The sheepmen of California demanded grazing permits in Yosemite, the Oregon woolgrowers sought permits in Crater Lake; but Mather objected, pointing out that some twenty-five years before, before the park was created, sheep had so denuded the lower slopes of Mount Mazama—the mountain in which the lake is situated—that flowers were still very rare. The Montana woolgrowers wanted sheep permits in Glacier, insisting that because of drought thousands of sheep would die if they had not the park lands.

Lumbermen wanted to get a foothold in the parks, to help win the war by "developing" the forests there. The whole business was very silly, but Secretary Lane, although a supporter of the parks generally, was intoxicated with patriotism like most of the people in the country, and wanted to do his heroic best to win the war. To the livestock men, hunters, and lumbermen, the proposals were not silly but shamelessly selfish. They saw a chance to make some quick unearned profits and get a foothold in the parks: if they despoiled the parks that was not an important matter.

Mather was ill, but Albright fought off the spoilers as well as he could without the support of Secretary Lane, and was successful in keeping livestock out of most of the parks. A few cattle were grazed in Glacier and 5,000 cattle were admitted to Yosemite at a fee of 50 cents per acre—only a fraction of what it was worth. The defeat of the spoilers was largely due to the firm stand of the United States Food Administrators, Ralph Merritt and Herbert Hoover, who declared that food requirements could be met without violating the parks. At the same time the spoilers assaulted the national forests and achieved somewhat greater concessions there.[1]

The problem of grazing in the national parks and forests is a knotty problem at best, never solvable in precise terms. How much grazing should be allowed? The general rule is that *any* grazing of a forest is injurious, whether by domestic or wild animals, although there may be exceptions to this. Any animal will eat some wild flowers or shrubs, trample other flowers, shrubs and little trees; any animal will eat the best grass, leaving the undesirable plants to take over, and overgrazing may kill the best forage. Some animals are more injurious than others, sheep and goats being the most destructive. Much depends on the climate, the amount and character of

[1] Robert Shankland, *Steve Mather of the National Parks* (New York: Alfred A. Knopf, 1951), 201-6. *The Nation*, Feb. 1, 1919, 157.

the rainfall. Where summers are very hot and dry and vegetation in bad condition anyhow, as in much of the West, grazing can be much more destructive than in regions where there is abundant and regular rainfall, as in the higher mountain areas and in the East. Abolition of all grazing by domestic livestock is not always a solution of the grazing problem either, for wildlife, if too abundant, can ruin forage as truly as domestic animals. Aside from this, the problem of the Park and Forest services often is: How much damage are we justified in inflicting on the land for the sake of promoting wool or meat production?[2]

Miners and prospectors were always a threat to some of the parks, although the parks were a little more secure from mining interests after 1920, when the act providing for mining on public lands specifically excluded the national parks.[3]

The brazen and persistent machinations of Ralph Henry Cameron have been discussed.[4] He was able to make some trouble for the Park Service but much more for the Forest Service. He joined forces with Senator John B. Stanfield, an Oregon stockman who was trying to get for the stockmen who had grazing permits in the national forests the practical equivalent of titles to the leased lands. Stanfield had a personal grievance against the Forest Service because the Service had cancelled his grazing permit because of misrepresentation, and as chairman of a subcommittee of the Senate Committee on Public Lands and Surveys he was in a position to cause the Forest Service a great deal of vexation, in which the Park Service shared.

The subject of grazing fees had been a controversial subject for some years. In 1916 the Forest Service announced plans for raising the fees, which were very low, and made increases in 1917 and 1918, but Congress thought they were still too low. The Forest Service ordered an intensive study of the subject, which was made by C. E. Rachford, whose study showed that the fees should be raised 60 or 70 per cent to bring them up to the level paid on private lands. Announcement of plans to raise them brought violent opposition in Congress in 1924 and 1925. In the 68th and 69th Congresses several western men were up with bills and resolutions, fixing, regulating, reducing, or even waiving fees, or raising the states' share of the fee

2 *American Forests and Forest Life*, Mar. 1926, 167.
3 Stat. 41, 437.
4 See Chap. XI, p. 235 ff.

receipts from 35 per cent to 50 per cent. Cattlemen in the West were really in distress; and some of the western men painted the picture worse than it was.

A fundamental issue in the debates was whether the grazing fees on national forest lands should be on a demand and supply level, about the same as fees on private lands, or whether they should be lower, to give the leasing stockmen an advantage over others—really a subsidy from the government. Senator Kendrick of Wyoming pointed out that forest reserve fees were the lowest anywhere, and that as a result there were five times as many applicants for permits as could be accommodated, and those given permits were thus granted a special privilege.[5]

This was the general situation when Stanfield and Cameron began their campaign to "clean up" the Forest Service and take over the grazing lands. Stanfield was trying to loot the national forests of their grazing lands, and as chairman of a subcommittee of the Senate Committee on Public Lands and Surveys was engaged in a junket in the West in 1925 and 1926, under pretext of making a "probe" of the various misdemeanors of the Forest Service. Stanfield and Cameron were up for re-election, with no assurance of success, and needed an attractive campaign issue. They were Republicans, the Senate was controlled by Republicans, and it looked like a good time to grab off a large area of the public lands.[6]

The campaign began with a Senate resolution introduced by Stanfield on June 7, 1924, calling for an investigation of the laws relating to lands administered by the Department of Agriculture and the Department of the Interior, and the regulations and practices followed. This resolution thus covered the national forests, public domain, and national parks, although Stanfield as a stockman was mainly interested in grazing lands in the national forests and on the public domain.[7] The resolution got no attention, and on February 26, 1925, Cameron introduced a similar resolution which was agreed to promptly on March 4.[8] During the spring, summer, and fall of 1925, 49 hearings were held in 38 cities and

5 See the debates on Cameron's S. J. Res. 169, 68 Cong. 2 Sess., particularly *Congressional Record*, Feb. 19, 1925, 4123. Cameron's bill authorized the Secretary to *waive* grazing fees.

6 Shankland, *op. cit.*, 238-41. *American Forests and Forest Life*, Feb. 1926, 73, 203.

7 S. Res. 257, 68 Cong. 1 Sess.

8 S. Res. 347, 68 Cong. 2 Sess.

towns, and 583 witnesses testified.[9] The investigating subcommittee was composed of Stanfield (chairman), Cameron, Oddie of Nevada, Dill of Washington, Gooding of Idaho, and Kendrick of Wyoming, with several foresters sitting in and testifying as much as they were permitted to. Stanfield and Cameron did much of the probing into the various sins and delinquencies of the Forest Service; but some of the committee members did not seem to relish the proceedings very keenly.

The probe continued through much of the summer of 1925, with much tub-thumping by grazing tycoons; and on August 24 and 25, hearings were held in Salt Lake City at a joint meeting of the National Woolgrowers' Association and the American National Livestock Association. This was a sort of shotgun marriage of two groups that had always fought each other bitterly, sometimes with guns to the point of homicide, for the cattlemen hated sheep because of their destructive grazing habits and had occasionally killed them by the hundreds in range wars; and the sheepmen naturally reciprocated in kind. This situation ran back some years to the time when grazing was not regulated, and neither group really wanted to go back to those conditions; but they joined forces to try to dismantle the national forests and take over the grazing lands.

At the Salt Lake City meeting the two associations drew up recommendations for the disposal of more than 275 million acres of publicly owned lands in the West. In the national forests the grazing lands should be controlled on an "area basis," meaning that the Forest Service should lose its control over its grazing lands, which would be divided up and allotted to the men who held the leases, under the practical equivalent of title deeds, definite and transferable like any other land titles. These rights would even have had one great advantage over titles, for not being precisely titles, they would not be taxed. No charges should be made for grazing "which results in depreciating investment values in the privately owned dependent properties of the holders of such rights." This meant that grazing fees should not be raised if the increase reduced the value of the ranches adjoining the national forests whose owners had leases in the forests; which meant that grazing fees could never be raised at all, although they were much too low. All grazing fees were to be handed over to the states, although the federal government paid for the protection of the forests. Most of

9 S. Rept. 517, 69 Cong. 1 Sess.

the grazing leases were held by the big ranchmen, and therefore
they would get the land rights, but they generously included a
provision: "We favor equitable protection to communities, to the
small farmer and stock raiser, to the wild life, and to recreational
facilities." If the small farmer wanted some land he might buy it
from some large rancher if he had enough money.

This was the brazenly selfish plan of the big livestock men to get
free land rights for themselves to some 90 million acres of national
forest land—no land taxes, no cost of range upkeep, no limits on
buying and selling and speculation, no real responsibility for damage to range or forests. It might have been the entering wedge to
the destruction of the whole national forest system, with the national parks perhaps to follow.

For the public domain the general scheme was somewhat the
same: the equivalent of a title to the leaseholder who had priority
rights, and no grazing fees that would depreciate investment values
of the ranchers' lands, as in national forest grazing lands, and local
option in management.

As to the national parks, there were to be no new parks and no
further extension of existing parks in the West.[10]

On January 16, 1926, Stanfield introduced a bill in the Senate
which followed in some respects the resolutions of the stockmen at
Salt Lake City. The bill provided that grazing should be put on a
par with forestry in the use of the national forests, that leases should
run for ten years, with the lessees given preference in renewals, for
life, and to their heirs forever, with the right of sale or transfer like
any real title; there was to be no increase in grazing fees for ten
years; and the Forest Service was not to change the size of lease
areas or number of animals grazed more than 5 per cent in any
year; and where the contracts were made on the "area basis,"
lessees would have exclusive right to determine the kind and number of animals grazed, and the length of the grazing season. The
sole appeal from Forest Service decisions was to be to a board of
three who had knowledge of the industry—that is, livestock men.
Such a bill would have shut out settlers and small livestock men,
for most of the land leased was controlled by large operators, would
have deprived the Forest Service of almost all control of its grazing
lands, and would have brought irreparable damage to some of the

10 *American Forests and Forest Life,* Nov. 1925, 666, 667; Dec. 1925, 715.

western watersheds. It was an utterly selfish attempt to grab a large area of grazing lands, fortunately not successful.[11]

In December 1926 Stanfield brought up another bill to "promote development, protection and utilization of grazing facilities on national forests," but it was not reported.[12]

The Park Service did not escape the probe. Stanfield, Cameron, *et al.* even descended to an attempt to frame Albright, using as witnesses a group of men, every one of whom "had been arrested at some time or other for breaking laws, usually the prohibition law, in the park; many had served jail sentences for it." On the witness stand Albright defended his administration in an effective summary: "I have been on trial all morning with convicted bootleggers, a quack doctor, a disgruntled ex-road foreman, an ex-ranger with a bad record, and other men with personal grievances testifying against me through the convenient method of leading questions from a man who assembled this group of malcontents." Fortunately Albright and the Park Service had influential backing: the *New York Times,* the *Salt Lake Tribune,* George Horace Lorimer of the *Saturday Evening Post,* Harry Chandler of the *Los Angeles Times,* and a host of others. Recognizing that the Yellowstone hearings would add no glamour to his name, Cameron did not want them printed, but was finally forced to allow it. The upshot of the probe and of the many bills introduced was that Congress did nothing. Stanfield and Cameron had caused the Forest Service and Park Service a great deal of trouble but had gained nothing. In the next election Cameron was defeated by Carl Hayden, and Stanfield was also defeated.[13]

DAM THREATS   Mather had been in office only a short time when he encountered head-on a determined and persistent campaign by western men to get dam sites in Yellowstone. The campaign was spearheaded by Senator Nugent and Representative Addison

11 S. 2584, 69 Cong. 1 Sess. *National Parks Bulletin,* No. 45, Oct. 24, 1925; No. 48, Feb. 1926. Shankland, *op. cit.,* 238-41. *American Forests and Forest Life,* Feb. 1926, 73, 203.

12 S. 4865, 69 Cong. 2 Sess.

13 See Shankland, *op. cit.,* 238-41, and Samuel T. Dana, *Forest and Range Policy* (New York: McGraw-Hill, 1956), 229-34. So many bills and resolutions were introduced in this Congressional melee that they need not be cited.

Smith of Idaho, in an attempt early in 1920 to get two dams into the southwest corner of Yellowstone, one on the Bechler River and one on the Mountain Ash Creek, both in the Falls River Basin, to irrigate land in Idaho southwest of the park.[14] These bills provided that the Secretary should have the power to authorize the dams if they would not interfere with the use of the land for park purposes, apparently assuming that a complaisant Secretary might come to office soon. Nugent and Smith really had greater ambitions than their bills indicated: they really hoped to take over Yellowstone Lake, Shoshone, Lewis and Heart lakes, and Jenny and Leigh lakes in the Tetons. They argued that the Idaho farmers southwest of the park, some 20,000 people, were suffering severely from drought, and needed more water, that the roads to the reservoir would make that part of the park more accessible in case of forest fires, that the land inundated was swampy and of little value for park purposes, and that it was necessary to build the dams in order to help feed the nation and the world. There was also a suggestion that the water "now going to waste" would help to build up "an empire of happy, hard-working Americans who would solve life's problems in peace and prosperity."[15] Truly the state of Idaho had got perhaps more federal irrigation funds than any other state, but this would be private construction.

Smith had a deep sympathy for the people of Idaho in their trials and tribulations: "It is just a question of whether the Congress is willing to allow the farmers in eastern Idaho to build reservoirs at their own expense to save for irrigation purposes the snow and rain which God Almighty sends for all of us or whether a few splendid but overly esthetic people, so far as the western country is concerned, who are living in luxury in Boston, New York, Philadelphia, and other eastern cities, and who apparently have little interest or sympathy for those of limited means who are trying to build homes for themselves and families on the arid lands, are to be permitted to make it possible by defeating this legislation for these hardy pioneers who are reclaiming the desert to lose ten or fifteen million dollars worth of crops each year. These worthy people are just as much entitled to the use of this water as they are to air and sunshine."[16]

14 S. 3895, H. R. 12466, 66 Cong. 2 Sess.
15 Literary Digest, Oct. 23, 1920, 88.
16 Congressional Record, Apr. 19, 1920, 5856, 5857.

Nugent and Smith were working with the Yellowstone Irrigation Association of Livingston, Montana, an organization of somewhat nebulous character, which was trying to get Idaho, Oregon, Washington, Montana, Wyoming, and Utah into a political combination for raiding the national parks. Utah was reported willing to cooperate. Unfortunately they had the support of the Bureau of Reclamation, although the Bechler Meadows project was not represented as a Reclamation project.

It is not clear just what interests were to profit from some of these bills, other than the irrigation farmers, whether it was to be the Yellowstone Irrigation Association, or a few insiders in the Association, or the states Idaho and Montana, or whether, as one man suggested, the real beneficiary was to be a hydroelectric power monopoly which controlled the power industry in Montana and planned to develop power at the Yellowstone Lake dam.[17]

Secretary Lane was favorable; in fact he had apparently drawn up one of the bills. When the Idaho crowd had asked him for permission to build the dam he replied that he doubted his authority to permit it, and helped work out the bill for them. Of course Mather and Albright were staunchly opposed, and when ordered to make a favorable report on the bill Mather stalled as long as he could. His 1920 report was an eloquent plea for preservation of the parks, and he wrote in the *Independent* in November 1920: "Is there not some place in this great nation of ours where lakes can be preserved in their natural state; where we and all generations to follow us can enjoy the beauty and charm of mountain waters in the midst of primeval forests? The country is large enough to share a few such lakes and beauty spots."[18] Mather was on the point of resigning, rather than approve the project, when Lane himself resigned, and for a short time Alexander Vogelsang officiated as Acting Secretary. Asked by Senator Smoot, chairman of the Senate Committee on Public Lands and Surveys, to report on the Nugent bill he made a report which was a classic of evasiveness and nebulousness: "I have carefully examined this measure in the light of the policies of this department with respect to the protection of the natural conditions of the national parks, and I have reached the conclusion that no objection to the passage of the bill should be interposed by me for the reason that no easements for irrigation

17 *Outlook*, Sept. 8, 1920, 68.
18 *Independent*, Nov. 13, 1920.

purposes in the Falls River Basin, Yellowstone National Park, must be granted by the Secretary of the Interior under the provisions of this legislation unless he first finds that such easements will not bring detriment to or interference with the uses of the land involved for park purposes."[19]

John Barton Payne was soon afterward appointed Secretary. A staunch conservationist, he promptly moved against the bill and refused even to permit any survey of the irrigation possibilities of Yellowstone Park.

Albright, who knew more about Yellowstone than anyone else, made a report denying most of the allegations of the promoters. He said that the land in the Bechler Basin was not swampy but was fine meadow and forest land, with forty waterfalls and cascades, the best grazing grounds in Yellowstone for a large herd of moose, and that the dam could be built outside the park at somewhat higher cost. The National Association of Audubon Societies sent William C. Gregg to make an investigation of the area, and he too reported that it was a splendid park area. The association collected $4,000 to be used in a publicity campaign to save the national parks from spoliation. George Bird Grinnell wrote a letter to the *Sun and New York Herald* protesting against the bills, and Mather wrote a strong protest for the *Independent*. The *Outlook* carried on a persistent campaign against the dams.[20]

It was clear that these bills were to be only an entering wedge, that once the park defenses had been breached, the park was to be rather completely gutted, for there were a number of irrigation schemes for accomplishing this. The Bruneau project covered the waters of Yellowstone, Shoshone, Lewis and Heart lakes, and the Falls River Basin; the DuBois project was aimed at the Falls River Basin and Shoshone and Lewis lakes, and perhaps Yellowstone Lake; the Carlisle project, hatched in Cheyenne, Wyoming, was to build a dam at the outlet of Yellowstone Lake to raise the water level twenty-nine feet and conduct the water into the Snake River for use farther down the stream; the Falls River Basin project aimed at dams only in the Falls River Basin, at first, but later also

19 S. Rept. 500, 66 Cong. 2 Sess.

20 *Bird Lore*, Jan. 1921, 64. *Literary Digest*, June 5, 1920, 90. *Independent*, Nov. 13, 1920, 221. *Outlook*, July 7, 1920, 448; July 28, 1920, 578; Sept. 8, 1920, 68; Oct. 6, 1920, 255; Jan. 12, 1921, 44; Nov. 23, 1921, 469; July 11, 1923, 357.

Yellowstone Lake; the Montana project called for a dam across the outlet of Yellowstone Lake near Fishing Bridge, to raise the water level five to eight feet, and to conduct the water into the Yellowstone River. Some of these schemes were not clearly outlined and varied from time to time as told by different men. There were also plans to invade Yosemite and other national parks. In Yosemite the city of Los Angeles wanted a reservoir in Virginia Canyon and one in Tuolomne Canyon, also several dams in Sequoia. Mather and Albright could see that the only way to keep the camel out of the tent was to keep his nose out, that no *precedent* must be set for invasion of the parks.[21]

The Nugent bill passed the Senate on April 6, 1920, but got no further, for Secretary Payne wrote House Majority Leader Mondell a letter of protest, and Mondell headed it off. The promoters next tried to tack it onto an appropriation bill, but failed; then tried to get a special rule adopted which would call for action after an hour's debate. The Rules Committee held hearings on May 27, at which the promoters presented resolutions of both houses of the Idaho legislature, but strong opposition was shown. Among the organizations represented against the bill, by letter or telegram, were the American Civic Association, the Boone and Crockett Club, the Museum of Natural History, the New York Zoological Society, the American Game Protective Association, the Appalachian Mountain Club, the Campfire Club, the Forest Service, the Field Museum of Chicago, and the National Parks Association; and of course Mather and Albright were there. These protests and another letter from Payne scared the House out of further consideration of the bill.

Smith persevered, however, and the state of Idaho tried to help him by setting aside the Fremont State Game Preserve, adjacent to the park, to be altogether closed to hunters but to become effective only when Bechler Basin was turned over to the irrigation dam and reservoir—a rather clumsy bait for the conservationists which they did not take. Emerson Hough's article in the *Saturday Evening Post* of September 25, "Pawning the Family Heirlooms," and William Gregg's article on the Bechler River Dam in the same magazine of November 20, got enough attention to influence Congress, and Smith's project had to be dropped for a while. Smith then an-

21 *Report, Director of Park Service, 1920,* 21 ff.

nounced that he would try next time to have the Bechler Basin cut out of the park.[22]

For a while, in 1920, the looters considered trying to get dam sites through the Federal Power Commission, which was authorized to grant sites in the national parks, but at the time a majority of that commission were not willing to grant any permits, and the next year, in the Jones-Esch Act, the national parks already created were exempted from the Federal Water Power Act.

The weakness of the Nugent and Smith bills was that their scheme was for the benefit of Idaho alone, and Montana wanted some pie too; Wyoming was not reaching for anything at this time. There had to be a division of the spoils—Idaho to get Bechler Basin and Montana a dam at the outlet of Yellowstone Lake. On December 7, 1920, the day after the Senate convened, Senator Tom Walsh of Montana, an able, clever, indefatigable and unscrupulous spoilsman and enemy of the parks, introduced a bill to permit the state of Montana to dam the Yellowstone River near the outlet of Yellowstone Lake (near Fishing Bridge).[23] The bill did not make clear just who would actually build the dam and who would get the profits; but it appeared that the real builders and owners were to be the Yellowstone Irrigation Association, a group of Livingston promoters, and that the state of Montana was a dummy set up to hide the real purpose.[24]

The Walsh bill should normally have been referred to the Committee on Public Lands and Surveys, but Walsh had it referred to the Irrigation and Reclamation Committee of which he was a member. On Washington's birthday, 1921, he sprang a surprise hearing, with five members of the Livingston crowd in attendance and none of the conservationists invited. At the close of the hearings Senator McNary announced that the opposition hearings would be held at the next session of Congress, but Walsh insisted that they be held

22 *National Parks Bulletin*, No. 15, Feb. 10, 1921.

23 S. 4529, 66 Cong. 3 Sess.

24 Walsh's record on conservation is not quite as uniformly bad as this discussion would indicate. He did try in one Congressional session after another to despoil Yellowstone Park, but on one other conservation problem he did well. It was he who by his able and pertinacious conduct of the Teapot Dome investigation disclosed the corruption of the Harding Administration and saved the naval oil reserves. (See the author's *U. S. Oil Policy* [New Haven: Yale University Press, 1926], Chap. XXV.)

while the Livingston promoters were there to listen, so the conservationists were summoned for February 28. The hearings lasted four days. The formal statement of the promoters was submitted in a printed engineering report which none of the park defenders had yet seen; but from a copy of it Albright, then Superintendent of Yellowstone, and George E. Goodwin, Chief Engineer of the Park Service, by working much of the night, prepared their answer.

The promoters argued that the dam was feasible, that it would prevent much of the damage from floods in the Yellowstone Valley, would improve low-water navigation on the Mississippi, would reclaim 250,000 acres; that it would not raise the level of Yellowstone Lake above the ordinary high-water mark; in fact that it would really improve Yellowstone Park and that it was the only way to accomplish so much. Albright insisted that the dam would do great damage to the park.

On March 28 the conservationists held hearings before the Senate Irrigation and Reclamation Committee, with twenty-six organizations represented, and made such a shambles of the arguments of the promoters that the Walsh bill was not reported.[25]

At various times park defenders pointed out the devastating results of damming lakes. A dam usually raises the level of a lake reservoir in the spring of the year, killing trees along the shores; but this water is for irrigation use, and by the end of the summer the level of the lake is far down, perhaps to the point where there is scarcely any water left, and there is revealed a broad shore strip of dead trees, black stumps, trash, mud, or dry earth. A dammed lake is usually damned scenically. For many years Jackson Lake, in the Grand Tetons, was an example of this. In 1931 Congress voted $100,000 to clean up the lake, but it is still badly blemished.[26] Another horrible example at times is Lake Mead, formed by Hoover Dam, but there the level does not vary so much from season to season as from year to year, with the rain and snowfall in the Colorado watershed. In 1956 the water level was down 137 feet from the top of the spillway gates and there was a wide fringe of ugly mud around much of the lake.

In the next Congress, the 67th, Walsh came up, on April 12, 1921,

25 *National Parks Bulletin*, No. 15, Feb. 10, 1921; No. 16, Mar. 20, 1921; No. 17, Apr. 9, 1921.
26 Stat. 46, 1149 ff.

with two identical bills, reworded to make them look more palatable.[27] He sent a circular around to every member of Congress defending the dam, but omitting the facts that had been submitted by the Department of the Interior, and omitting the original argument that the dam would control floods in the lower Yellowstone Valley. At the hearings on the bill the new Secretary of the Interior, Albert Fall, who had assumed office on March 4, opposed the bill, declaring that if dams should ever be allowed in the parks they should be built by the federal government and not by the states or by private interests. This was a somewhat equivocal attitude, for the conservationists of course wanted no dams in the national parks, but they were moderately happy anyhow to get support against the Walsh bill.

The Fall regime calls for a bit of special attention here. When Warren Harding was elected President the Park Service shivered, for Harding's reputation was not good, and when he proceeded to live up to his reputation by making some very bad appointments, including Fall's, a "hack politician from deep in the land-grab belt,"[28] as Shankland describes him, Mather and his boys trembled in their boots. The western irrigation interests had been calling for a western man in the Department of the Interior, and Fall looked like the answer to their prayers. But Fall was after the oil reserves, not the national parks, and soon evinced a strong liking for Mather and promised not to disturb the parks. Following Mather's advice, he made excellent appointments in the Park Service—suggesting only that the men should be Republicans, which Mather quietly ignored. For a while the National Parks Association was most happy about Fall's splendid record. His position on the Walsh bill was not all that could be desired, for it indicated that he did not grasp the principle that must govern national parks—they must not be invaded by commercial developments—but his stand was better than might have been feared. Later, as we have seen, he brought Mather and Albright plenty of gray hairs.[29]

Finally, Fall called for an investigation by the Bureau of Reclamation and the Geological Survey—not by the Department of the Interior or the Park Service. This would have cost about $100,000, which would have been difficult to raise. Walsh, however, thought

27 S. 274, S. 275, 67 Cong. 1 Sess.
28 Shankland, op. cit., 217.
29 National Parks Bulletin, No. 26, Mar. 6, 1922.

$10,000 would be sufficient, and he and a man named Jerome Locke, said to be the originator of the Yellowstone Lake bill and a candidate for the House of Representatives, stumped the district for money to make the investigation, but with little success. In the election Locke was defeated two to one by Scott Leavitt, a friend of conservation and of the park, and so the Walsh bill was again lost. The election of Leavitt indicated that the people of Montana were not as favorable to the desecration of Yellowstone as some of the events in Congress might have suggested. This is often true in politics. A small, vocal minority can often make a noise that sounds like the voice of a multitude of people.

The story of Albert Fall would be incomplete without an account of his scheme for taking the national forests over into the Department of the Interior from the Department of Agriculture, to which they had been shifted from the Department of the Interior when the Forest Service was established in 1905. This scheme was actively promoted by livestock interests in the West, who were in revolt at livestock reductions the Forest Service had ordered in an effort to restore some of the overgrazed range in the national forests. The plan also had the support of the power interests, who were incensed because Gifford Pinchot, Chief Forester, had withdrawn the important power sites in the national forests from private appropriation. The national forests of Alaska were to be attacked, as an example of Forest Service "bottling up" resources and preventing development, and this brought support from lumber interests.

In the spring of 1922 Fall began to trumpet his intention to get the forests into his Department of the Interior and fire the whole caboodle of theorists who had been blocking the development of America's resources; but the conservation press and organizations and the farmers' organizations soon began to erupt protests. At this time Harding was planning his trip to Alaska, but before he left, Fall's connection with the Teapot Dome bribe began to leak out, and he left the Cabinet. The whole scheme blew up overnight. In Alaska a little later, President Harding gave a speech outlining a policy for the Alaska forests which was all that conservationists could have wished for.[30]

Yellowstone was thus saved for a while, and national parks looked up a bit. There was some cheer in the fact that on March 4, 1923, Fall resigned as Secretary of the Interior, and Hubert Work, defi-

[30] *American Forests,* May 1951, 10. Shankland, *op. cit.,* 217.

nitely a friend of the parks, took his place. It was only a reprieve, however, because in December 1923 Senator Walsh came up with two bills, one to authorize the Yellowstone Lake "regulating weir"— "weir" sounded better than dam—and another to appropriate $10,000 for a survey of Yellowstone Lake.[31] In this Yellowstone Lake bill the clause about water power being reserved to the United States and revenues to Montana had been dropped, but Secretary Work, on May 23, reported adversely on it, and it got no further attention.

For a year or so there was quiet on the dam front but when bills appeared to revise Yellowstone boundaries Smith was ready with an amendment to cut Bechler Basin out of the park. On March 2 and March 5, 1926, an administration bill for boundary revision was introduced by Representative Sinnott and Senator Stanfield of Oregon, and Smith sprang his amendment at the hearings before the House Committee on Public Lands.[32] It is unnecesary to trace all the devious maneuvering of Smith and his spoilsmen; sufficient it will be to say that their efforts were unavailing.[33] In the next Congress, while Norbeck was trying to get a revision of Yellowstone boundaries, Smith was on hand to "revise" Bechler Basin out of the park, again without success.[34]

In October 1921 there was a threat of dam building that would have spoiled a part of Glacier Park. One proposal, of the International Joint Commission of Canada and the United States, was for a dam at the outlet of Lower Saint Marys Lake, to raise the water level about forty feet and back the water about ten miles to Upper Saint Marys Lake, making both lakes one reservoir, the water to go three-fourths to Canada and one-fourth to the United States, for irrigation. Such a dam would have ruined two of the most beautiful lakes in the United States. Canadian promoters offered another threat in a proposal to dam the Canadian end of Waterton Lake—which extends across the boundary—to raise the level of the lake sixty feet. On the American side this would have flooded the floor of Kootenay Valley, destroyed hotel sites needed

31 S. 311, S. 313, 68 Cong. 1 Sess.

32 H. R. 9917, S. 3427, 69 Cong. 1 Sess.

33 For the story of Smith's strategy see *National Parks Bulletin*, No. 54, Nov. 1927.

34 S. 3001, S. 2571, H. R. 17, 70 Cong. 1 Sess.

for future developments and blocked a long-planned international highway. Of course it would have largely spoiled beautiful Waterton Lake. Fortunately the International Joint Commission refused to consider this project.[35]

During Mather's administration the stage was set for serious future trouble with power proposals. In 1921 Congress passed an act to permit a compact among the states of Arizona, California, Colorado, Nevada, New Mexico, Utah, and Wyoming, for the disposition and apportionment of the waters of the Colorado River; and on December 21, 1928, the construction of Boulder Dam—later named Hoover Dam—was provided for. This raised no park problems, but the later efforts of the states of the Upper Colorado to secure a series of dams brought a threat of power development in Dinosaur National Monument.[36]

ATTACKS FROM ZEALOUS CONSERVATIONISTS   Mather and the Park Service had to fight the power interests while under fire from men who should have been supporting them, Dr. Willard Van Name and Enos Mills, for instance. Van Name objected to practically every cut in park boundaries, however well justified; and in 1926 he announced that there was "every reason to fear and believe" that "high administrative officers of the government" had agreed to cut off the southwestern part of Crater Lake for the lumbermen. If there was anything to this rumor it does not appear in the official records.[37] Enos Mills was an innkeeper in Rocky Mountain Park, something of a naturalist, lecturer, and writer, the "Father of Rocky Mountain National Park," and the "Rocky Mountain John Muir," as he rather fondly pictured himself, an implacable enemy of the Forest Service and for some years a friend of Mather and the parks. But when Mather gave exclusive transportation rights in Rocky Mountain to someone else he incurred Mills' bitter animosity. Mills published articles in various newspapers and journals attacking

35 *National Parks Bulletin*, No. 26, Mar. 6, 1922. On these various attempts to invade Yellowstone, see Shankland, *op. cit.*, 212-17; *Report, Director of Park Service, 1920*, 22 ff.; *The Nation*, Aug. 21, 1920, 209; *The Outlook*, Dec. 29, 1926, 553, and Jan. 19, 1927.

36 Stat. 42, 171 ff.; 45, 1057 ff.

37 *Science*, n.s., July 23, 1926, 91.

Mather and the administration of the parks. In an article in the *New Republic* on "Exploiting our National Parks" he exploded a characteristic bomb. "Our twenty large and magnificent national parks are not under the laws of Congress nor under control of the people. They are under the autocratic rules and orders of a non-resident King."[38] Writing in some respectable journals, Mills had influence and brought Mather some anxiety, while confusing the public mind.[39]

PRIVATE LANDS IN THE PARKS   Private land holdings in the national parks were perhaps the worst problem of the Park Service, and Mather tried hard to get Congress to appropriate money to buy these lands, but with little success. The two exchange acts for Yosemite have been discussed. Mather did some trading under these laws, consolidating the timber holdings along the Big Oak Flat and Wawona roads. Before the Park Service was organized he bought one private holding, the Tioga Road, with his own and a few friends' money. Much more important than this, for the long run, was the grant of $50,000 in the sundry civil act of July 1, 1916, to buy a grove of 667 acres of giant sequoia trees in Sequoia Park. These trees stood on private lands patented before the park was established, in several tracts owned by different parties, who could cut them at any time. Conservationists had been gravely concerned about this possibility for some years, and had importuned Congress to provide the $50,000 demanded by the owners for the trees. By the time Congress got around to the appropriation, the owners had raised their price to $70,000, and for a while lovers of great trees were in a state of great depression; but the National Geographic Society presently came up with $20,000 to help save the grove.[40]

Congress early showed a generous willingness to accept donations. In 1916 Congress authorized the Secretary to accept donations of land or rights of way in Yosemite, and in June 1920 this authorization was made general for all parks.[41]

Trading was often approved, if it called for no money. In 1923 the Secretary was authorized to trade publicly owned lands in Mon-

38 *New Republic*, Nov. 10, 1920, 272.
39 Shankland, *op. cit.*, 186-88.
40 Stat. 39, 308.
41 Stat. 39, 308; 41, 317.

tana for private holdings in Glacier;[42] and in the ensuing years some trades were approved.

The Congressional appropriation of $50,000 for the purchase of the sequoia grove in Sequoia was the last generous gesture of Congress for ten years. An act of May 26, 1926, making additions to Absaroka and Gallatin national forests and Yellowstone Park was followed two years later by an appropriation of $150,000, to be matched fifty-fifty from other sources.[43] In 1927 Congress made its first general appropriation for the purchase of privately owned lands in the parks; $50,000, to be matched fifty-fifty by money from other sources. Mather was able to buy two holdings, one in Sequoia and a small one in Zion. This grant was repeated in 1928.[44] In March 1929, after Mather had resigned, Congress voted $250,000 to be matched fifty-fifty by other funds, and authorized the Secretary to contract up to $2,750,000, this to be matched too.[45] Congress was fond of this matching game, seeming to think that there were likely to be private philanthropists who would be glad to match Congressional grants. Sometimes there were such men.

WILDLIFE PROBLEMS   The wildlife in the parks presented a baffling array of problems from the very beginning of the Mather administration. Predators were being systematically destroyed by traps, strychnine, and rifle. R. B. Marshall reported in 1916 that two special rangers were hired in Yellowstone to kill predators, and that they had shot and trapped eighty-three coyotes, twelve wolves, and four mountain lions, while other park employees killed ninety-seven coyotes. As early as 1924 the National Parks Association saw that the extermination of predators was generally unwise,[46] but there was no general recognition of this until later, although it was already apparent that in Yellowstone the predator-reduction program was quite too effective. The fear of extinction of elk and bison was already changed to a problem of surplus that the Park Service was quite unable to solve. The bison that had numbered twenty-five were now four hundred, and the Service was working

42 Stat. 42, 1923.
43 Stat. 44, 655; 45, 603.
44 Stat. 44, 963 ff.; 45, 233 ff.
45 Stat. 45, 1526.
46 *National Parks Bulletin*, No. 40, June 10, 1924.

hard to raise enough hay to feed them. There were so many of these animals, and especially of elk that in severe winters many of them died. In the hard winter of 1916-17, 25 to 30 per cent of the Yellowstone elk died. In the winter of 1919 the record was worse. On October 22, 1919, a severe snow storm made it necessary to begin feeding. Snows and frigid weather persisted until May, and supplies of hay soon ran low. The Park Service worked hard to get more. Congress voted money to buy more, but in spite of all efforts thousands of elk died of starvation and cold in Yellowstone.

The tragedy of this was reported in the newspapers, and there were repeated demands that the park be extended to the south and north to provide lower winter grazing grounds, that the adjoining states set up wildlife refuges, and that more feed should be raised for the teeming population. The extension of Yellowstone was not to come in Mather's time, but Wyoming and Montana did set up refuges, and some feed was provided. Mather loved wildlife and was happy to see it increasing. He did not see the scientific relationship between predators and prey and it was not yet understood that the feeding of wildlife was not good except in extreme urgency. It was not until late in Mather's administration that the Park Service came to see that wildlife, like everything else in a national park, should be maintained in as nearly natural conditions as possible.

The surplus of elk, buffalo, and at times deer brought grave consequences other than the starvation of the animals, which were little noted in the early years of Mather's administration. The hungry and starving elk and deer ate the browse, even including the bark of trees, so closely that some of it did not recover for years, some of it never; and a further result of this was that with vegetation destroyed, the soil eroded, reducing or destroying productive value for the indefinite future. Soil erosion received little attention at this time.

On the other hand, some other species were not doing well and appeared to face possible extinction. The trumpeter swan and the whooping crane, among the birds, were becoming very scarce, and in the early twenties there were repeated reports that the antelope was so scarce as to indicate possible extinction. In 1924 Congress set aside 25,000 acres as an antelope reserve. Bighorns were at various times reported in bad condition as to health and numbers, but no one knew what to do about it. In some of the parks other than Yellowstone the problem of extinction of certain species still existed and had not been fully met, although there was a growing surplus of other animals.

Enlargement of the parks being difficult to secure, the states often unwilling to provide enough wildlife refuges, and the Park Service unwilling to open the parks to hunters, the Service was obliged to resort to live-trapping of animals and taking them to areas of scarcity or giving them to zoos, etc. This, however, was a very difficult task, even dangerous, and at best it reduced the teeming herds so little as to make little difference. It was even of questionable legality until January 1923, when Albright persuaded Congress to make it legal, for Yellowstone only, by an amendment to an appropriation bill.[47] The problem persisted throughout Mather's administration, and for years afterward.

THE END OF THE MATHER PERIOD   This brings us to the end of the Mather epoch—not to the end of Mather's influence, which we may well hope will never end—for on November 5, 1928, he was stricken with paralysis. During his illness letters of sympathy poured in from friends and acquaintances and strangers all over the country, from the President, from Justices of the Supreme Court, from officials and captains of industry everywhere—a beautiful letter from John D. Rockefeller, Jr.—from the great, the near-great, and from modest people grateful for his noble and unselfish services to the country. On January 15 Representative Louis C. Cramton who had perhaps done more than anyone in Congress to help Mather in his work, arose in the House to "pay tribute to this outstanding figure in the public service who has sacrificed his money, his health, his time, his opportunity for wealth, in order that he might promote that which will mean so much to the people of this country in the future." In his tribute Cramton used the words, *"There will never come an end to the good he has done,"* which were later inscribed on memorial plaques that were erected at some of the national parks.[48]

In spite of all that medical services could do, Mather died on January 22, 1930. A noble career, fourteen years in the service of

[47] *Congressional Record,* Jan. 12, 1923, 1688. Stat. 42, 1214.
[48] *Congressional Record,* Jan. 15, 1929, 1734-36.

the parks—a period short in time, great in achievement—was ended; a great man was gone.[49]

The record of Mather's twelve years as Director of the National Park Service is imposing, and more imposing the more one studies it. During these years he did a spectacular job of promoting the parks, making them known to millions of people; he developed a devoted and efficient force from almost nothing, improved concessions and facilities in the parks, fighting vested interests at every step. Twelve new parks were established in his regime—four of them in the East, and he fought off dozens of inferior parks. Nearly all efforts to despoil the parks with commercial business were warded off in a running battle against power, irrigation, livestock, mining and lumber interests, and hunters; such spoliation as Hetch Hetchy and the 1905 haggling of Yosemite came before Mather's time. The acts setting up new parks did indeed often make unfortunate concessions, but most of these were later erased. On the other hand Mather was able to get important extensions of some existing parks. He recognized the importance of state parks, and did much to promote their extension; he saw the educational function of the parks and developed the interpretive work from the very beginning.

Not all that was achieved was due to his personal efforts, of course. Other able men worked with him—Albright, Cammerer, and others in his own Park Service, and such men as Lacey, Mondell, Leavitt, Kent, Raker, Phelan, Cramton, Barbour, Kendrick, Nye, and Norbeck, in Congress; various men in the publishing field, as for instance George Horace Lorimer of the *Saturday Evening Post,* and such generous philanthropists as John D. Rockefeller, Jr., William Kent, Gilbert Grosvenor of the National Geographic Society, and George B. Dorr. Our national park system would lack some of its finest features if it had not been for the generous financial support of John D. Rockefeller, Jr.

In a few matters Mather did not achieve success. He was never able to do much in the elimination of private lands from the parks. He did not get all the parks he wanted, the coast redwoods park being perhaps the most unfortunate failure. He did save some species of wildlife from decimation, or even perhaps from extinction; but he never was able to solve the problem of animal surpluses which soon emerged. He did not understand the balance-of-nature principle of wildlife; but not many others understood it at the time.

49 Shankland, *op. cit.,* 284-91.

MATHER AND PINCHOT COMPARED   The work of Mather in the Park Service and Gifford Pinchot in the Forest Service present a striking parallel. Both men were wealthy, Pinchot much wealthier than Mather, however; both were generous and gave freely of their own money to promote the public interests—Pinchot gave thousands to the promotion of conservation in gifts that only he and the present writer ever knew anything about. Both were able organizers, wholeheartedly devoted to their "causes" and worked without stint; both started with a government department that had been poorly financed, badly managed or mismanaged, shot through with politics, staffed with some able men but too many incompetents; and both built up an efficient, loyal and devoted service. Both had to wage a continuing battle against greedy business and sectional interests and against Congressional inertia, indifference and even some hostility. Mather was the more singlehearted in his zeal, for he was almost entirely devoted to the conservation of scenic values in the parks; Pinchot worked for the conservation of the forests, power sites, streams, soil and minerals—about every natural resource, except the parks. Strange as it may seem, he had apparently little or no interest in the parks, and was indeed partly responsible for the worst disaster that any park suffered—the spoliation of Hetch Hetchy Valley; and so it was that these two men, so alike in their circumstances, their ideals and their careers, came to be enemies and fought each other with something approaching bitterness. Yet perhaps it was not strange. The parks and the forests were in natural opposition: many of the parks had to be excised from the national forests; whatever was given to some of the parks had to come from the national forests. It was natural that each of these men, so devoted to the promotion of his own domain, should fight hard for it and therefore against the other. If they had been time-serving and indifferent political appointees they would not have fought so hard.

CHAPTER XV

The Albright Administration

1929-1933

GRAND TETON PARK, CARLSBAD CAVERNS

PARK, ISLE ROYALE PARK

꘏ The Albright Administration is marked off from the Mather Administration here largely as a matter of convenience rather than logic, for in a sense the administration of Mather was also that of Albright, who worked loyally with him; and the Albright Administration was largely a continuation of that of Mather, who with Albright's assistance, had major policies pretty well formulated and in action when he died.

By mid-December 1928 Mather realized that he would not be able to resume active work and named Albright as his successor, subject of course to the approval of Secretary West and President Coolidge. Albright was named Director on January 12, 1929.

ALBRIGHT MOVES IN   Albright had been born and reared in Owens Valley, just east of the high Sierra, and there developed a love for wild, unspoiled mountain scenery. Like Mather, he graduated from the University of California—that nursery of national park talent—as a mining lawyer. In 1913 he went to work in Washington, in the office of Secretary Lane, specializing in legal work connected with the national parks. In 1915 he became assist-

324

ant to Mather, who was then Assistant to the Secretary in Charge of National Parks; and two years later, when the National Park Service was established, Albright became Assistant Director. In 1919 he was appointed Field Assistant to Mather and Superintendent of Yellowstone Park, the first civilian superintendent since 1886 when the Army took over.[1] Succeeding a man of Mather's genius, energy, personality, and private wealth was something of an undertaking, but Albright was quite equal to it. He conceived of his job as "to consolidate our gains, finish up the rounding out of the park system, go rather heavily into the historical park field, and get such legislation as is necessary to guarantee the future of the system on a sound permanent basis, where the power and the personality of the Director may no longer have to be controlling factors in operating the Service."[2] He was able, tireless, devoted to the parks; in fact he sacrificed heavily in his private fortunes to serve the parks. He knew many of the senators and representatives, was liked and respected by them, and by Representative Louis Cramton who had great influence with his appropriations subcommittee, and by President Coolidge's Secretary of the Interior, Roy West, and President Hoover's Secretary, Ray Lyman Wilbur; and he started with a well-selected group of men in the Park Service. He accomplished a great deal in his short administration—from January 12, 1929 to August 9, 1933.

Albright's term coincided roughly with the Presidential term of Herbert Hoover who, like his Secretary of the Interior, Ray Lyman Wilbur, was a strong supporter of the national parks. Hoover had been president of the National Parks Association, and Wilbur had served on the California State Park Commission. Wilbur was one of the early advocates of extensive wilderness areas in the national parks. Albright was fortunate in having such backing in his administration.

On some other public land questions, Hoover and Wilbur advocated policies which were not wise. Wilbur had a wild notion that the public domain should be given to the states, and he seemed to think that the national forests might be better off under state control or in the Department of the Interior. He had a reactionary hope that we were "in the midst of a movement back to local responsi-

[1] *Scribners Magazine,* June 1929, 621.
[2] Robert Shankland, *Steve Mather of the National Parks* (New York: Alfred A. Knopf, 1951), 295, 296.

bility," failing to see that state and local units were not equal to the task of managing areas of grazing lands that extended over several states. Apparently he knew little of the generally sad record of state administration of such lands.

THE DEPRESSION STRIKES   Albright became Director on January 12, 1929, and in early October an economic hurricane struck the stock market, to spread quickly to the nation's business and bring the most severe and persistent depression in the history of the country. Prices tumbled to new lows every week, investment houses and business firms toppled like rows of dominoes, laborers by the million lost their jobs and turned to the streets hunting work or handouts at kitchen doors. The outlook for the parks, for appropriations and for visitors, was depressing; but the situation proved not unfavorable, for Congress voted money to provide work in the parks and elsewhere. The appropriations for 1930 were up more than $3 million, and the number of visitors remained the same. For the next year the appropriations were nearly doubled, and again no decline in the number of visitors, although the character of the visitors was changing steadily—fewer coming by rail and more by automobile. Since the rail visitors more generally used the hotels, some hotel concessioners were in trouble during these years. Much of the work provided was on park roads, for which the grants were particularly generous. In addition to appropriations, there were cash donations in 1930 amounting to $1,015,740, used largely to buy private lands.

BUILDING ROADS AND FACILITIES   With generous funds, Albright and his men were able to accomplish a great deal, particularly in road building and improvement. Some roads were oiled to eliminate the dust so often complained of, and a number of important new roads were built: the Zion–Mount Carmel road and tunnel, one of the most impressive scenic roads in the world, the Wawona tunnel and road in Yosemite, the Cape Royal road in Grand Canyon, the Paradise Valley and Yakima Park highway in Mount Rainier, the Sylvan Pass road in Yellowstone, the magnificent Going-to-the-Sun road in Glacier. A new road was built across the divide in Rocky Mountain, the highest road in the park system, and indeed one of the highest in America. The Bright Angel Trail in the Grand Canyon was rebuilt. In the building of roads and all park structures and facilities the Service followed master plans which had been drawn up for each park by an expert landscape architect. Fortunately for our park system, Mather and Albright were both committed to careful planning by expert planners.

There was a new departure in the road-building appropriations of 1931. Before this, appropriations had been marked only for roads *in* the parks; now the Park Service was authorized to spend part of its funds for "approach roads," roads outside the parks, between the park entrances and nearby highway points. It was argued that the adjoining states were subject to a heavy burden in building such approach roads. At the time, most of the towns and cities along roads in the West provided free camp grounds for tourists, some of them not well cared for, and the cost of these, added to that of the approach roads, was appreciable, even in some cases onerous, for in some states the cost of new paved roads was assessed, at least in part, against the adjoining property owners. Also, some of the roads ran through national forests, but the Forest Service shared its revenues with the states in building roads through the national forests.

The burden was not as great as some of the western politicians tried to make it appear. After all, in many areas the roads were used mostly by people from the adjacent states, and in such cases the states should have paid practically all the costs of the approach roads. The western states were profiting handsomely on national park traffic, but they were always glad to load onto the federal government as many expenses as possible. The Leavitt appropriation bill of January 31, 1931, granted $7.5 million for roads and trails, $1.5 million of which was for approach roads, and on March 4 of the same year $2.5 million more was given for roads and trails and approach roads in and to national parks *and monuments*.[3] On July 21, 1932, $3 million more was given to provide work on national park and monument roads, including approach roads.[4]

Various expansions in the facilities in the parks and in the Park Service administration were possible. Several museums were added; the Indian museum at Acadia was deeded to the government; the Mesa Verde museum, one of the earliest built, was enlarged. The epochal discovery by A. E. Douglass of a way to date the cliff

3 Stat. 46, 1053, 1570.
4 Stat. 47, 717.

dwellings, by comparison of tree rings in the beams, brought more intensive study of the ruins of the Southwest. Extensive archeological excavations and studies were made at Chaco Canyon National Monument in New Mexico. An elevator was built in Carlsbad, a lighting system was installed in Wind Cave, and in Mesa Verde an effort was made to get more water by drilling a well 4,109 feet deep. The Division of Wildlife Studies was established in the Park Service as a full-time government activity, and a number of research projects were launched—one, for instance, on the damage done to trees by deer, bear, and porcupines. The wildlife in the parks was proving a baffling problem and wildlife research was expanding.

GRAND TETON PARK   Three new parks came in during Albright's administration. Only a few weeks after he took his new office Congress established Grand Teton National Park, in an area rich in the historic lore of Indians, trappers, and traders, a park covering the most scenic side of one of the most magnificent mountain ranges in the United States, or indeed in the world.[5]

The Grand Tetons had been wanted for years, as an addition to Yellowstone or as a separate park, often joined with Jackson Hole. We have already seen how the indefatigable Albright worked for Grand Teton and Jackson Hole throughout Mather's administration, but failed because of the opposition of the dude ranchers, the livestock men, the Forest Service, the hunters, and various other classes lined up differently at various times.[6] Always deeply in love with the Grand Teton–Jackson Hole area, however, Albright never gave up. Jackson Hole was not to be secured until years later, but the Grand Tetons were added to the park system on February 26, 1929.[7] Their addition was one of Albright's greatest achievements.

In January 1928 Senator Norbeck of South Dakota introduced a bill to establish the "Kendrick National Park," honoring an able and distinguished friend of the national parks, but it was not reported.[8] In December Senator Nye of North Dakota and Repre-

5 On the early history of this general area, see B. W. Driggs, *History of Teton Valley, Idaho* (Caldwell, Idaho: Caxton Printers, 1926).

6 See Chap. XIII.

7 Stat. 45, 1314.

8 S. 2570, 70 Cong. 1 Sess.

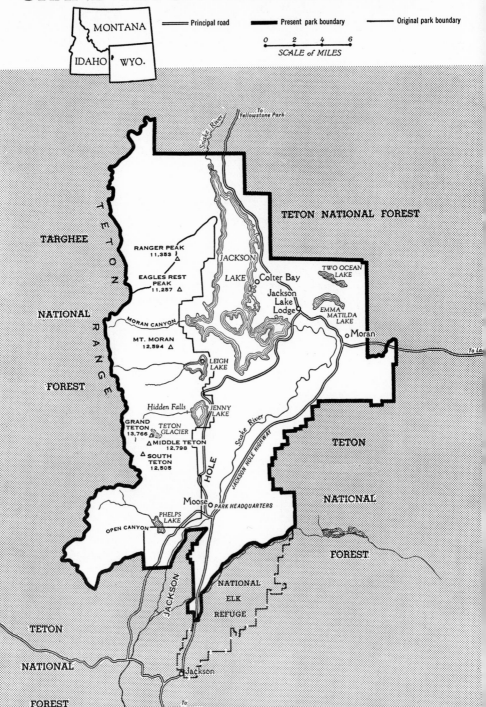

GRAND TETON NATIONAL PARK

MONTANA

IDAHO   WYO.

Principal road ▬▬▬ Present park boundary ▬▬▬ Original park boundary

0   2   4   6
SCALE of MILES

To Yellowstone Park

TETON NATIONAL FOREST

TARGHEE

RANGER PEAK
11,353 △

EAGLES REST
PEAK
11,257 △

JACKSON

LAKE   Colter Bay

TWO OCEAN
LAKE

NATIONAL

MORAN CANYON

MT. MORAN
12,594 △

Jackson
Lake
Lodge

EMMA
MATILDA
LAKE

o Moran

To La—

FOREST

LEIGH
LAKE

Hidden Falls

GRAND
TETON
13,766 △

JENNY
LAKE

TETON
GLACIER

△ MIDDLE TETON
12,798

△ SOUTH
TETON
12,505

Snake River

JACKSON HOLE HIGHWAY

TETON

HOLE

NATIONAL

Moose o PARK HEADQUARTERS

PHELPS
LAKE

OPEN CANYON

FOREST

NATIONAL

ELK

REFUGE

TETON

JACKSON

NATIONAL

Jackson

FOREST

To
Rock Springs

sentative Addison Smith of Idaho introduced bills to create Grand
Teton and revise the boundaries of Yellowstone, but neither got any
attention.[9] Smith had been trying for some years to get the Falls
River and Bechler Basin cut out of the southwest corner of Yellowstone, and here he was trying to tie this in with the creation of
Grand Teton. In the same session, on January 24, 1929, Senator
Kendrick of Wyoming brought in a bill to establish Grand Teton,
which was approved by Secretary West, by Acting Secretary Dunlap,
and by the President's Committee on Outdoor Recreation, and was
passed by both houses with very little debate.[10]

The new park was a stingy, skimpy, niggardly little park of only
about 150 square miles, from three to nine miles wide and twenty-
seven miles long, covering only the east side of the Grand Teton
Range, the grandly magnificent side. It did include two lovely lakes,
Leigh and Jenny—the latter sometimes acclaimed the most beautiful
lake in the park system—and a few smaller lakes; but it omitted the
much larger Jackson Lake, which had once been a very beautiful
lake but had been converted into a less beautiful irrigation reservoir; and it covered little of the lower land to the east which was
needed for winter elk range and as an area from which to view the
mountains. Perhaps as a result of the pressure of local interests,
Grand Teton was set up as a strictly wilderness park. There were
to be no roads—apparently the dude ranchers insisted on this. No
hotels or even permanent camps were to be established—perhaps a
concession to the hotels of Moran and Jackson. Bona fide land
claimants or owners were allowed to graze as many cattle or sheep
as they had grazed before, or as many as "may be reasonably necessary to the conduct of their business," and were permitted to take
dead and down timber. But the park was excepted from the Federal
Power Act of 1920. The appropriations for Yellowstone Park were
made available for administration also of Grand Teton, but two
years later a separate appropriation was voted. Two years after the
park was set up Congress appropriated $50,000 for cleaning up
Jackson Lake, although the lake was outside the park.[11] Fifty
thousand dollars more was secured from another source.

Since the creation of Grand Teton Park did little or nothing to
solve the problem of winter range for the Yellowstone elk, it did

9 S. 4674, H. R. 15475, 70 Cong. 2 Sess.
10 S. 5543, 70 Cong. 2 Sess. Stat. 45, 1314.
11 Stat. 46, 1149.

not end the agitation for the southward extension of Yellowstone to include the Jackson Hole area, east of the park; and in 1927 John D. Rockefeller, Jr., organized the Snake River Land Company to buy up private lands in the Jackson Hole country, with the purpose of presenting them to the government for the proposed addition. It was over twenty years before this problem was settled. But this story must come later.[12]

CARLSBAD CAVERNS PARK   To some park enthusiasts it seemed that with the establishment of Grand Teton we had reserved about all the outstanding scenery, but the next year, on May 14, 1930, one of the most fantastically beautiful of all was elevated to park status. Carlsbad Cave was known as Bat Cave to cattlemen in the 1880's, but was apparently not explored. The deposits of bat guano in the bat room presently attracted attention, however, and in a few years thousands of tons were taken out by a mining company. Among the miners was a local boy, Jim White, who devoted several years to the exploration of the cave. His reports of the marvels did not stir much public interest, but in 1923 Robert Holley, of the General Land Office, reported on the beauty of the cave; and in the same year Dr. Willis T. Lee, of the United States Geological Survey—trying to learn why dams on the Pecos River would not hold water long—explored the cave, employing Jim White as guide, and took pictures. Before his report was published, President Coolidge, on October 25, 1923, proclaimed the Carlsbad Cave National Monument, embracing 719 acres.[13]

Dr. Lee's report, published in the *National Geographic Magazine* in January 1924, immediately attracted attention, and in the spring the National Geographic Society sent an exploring party under Dr. Lee to make an extensive survey of the cave. These men spent six months at the cave, made maps and took many pictures, and published their report in the *National Geographic Magazine* in September 1925. Carlsbad soon became famous, tourist visits increased from 1,280 in 1924 to 46,335 in 1928, and Congress treated the new monument with unusual generosity, appropriating $5,000 for improvements in 1924, and $25,000 in 1925, to be available as soon as New Mexico surrendered title to a school section in the

12 See pp. 489 ff.
13 Stat. 43, 1929.

monument. Some of these and later appropriations were made for lighting the vast cave. It was fortunate that the cave was lighted electrically at an early date, for much use of lamps would have blackened the walls, as the Davy lamps long used in Mammoth Cave did there. In 1929, while still a national monument, Carlsbad was given $100,000, $85,000 of which was to be used to begin construction of an elevator from the floor of the cave to the surface.[14] Before the elevator was built visitors entered the cave by means of a miner's bucket lowered by a windlass to the floor several hundred feet below.

For some reason Carlsbad remained a national monument for several years, but early in 1930 Representative Simms of New Mexico introduced a bill to make it a national park, and this bill passed both houses without opposition, and was approved by President Hoover.[15] Among the reasons why there was no opposition was the fact that the revenues of the monument were above the expenses, so it made a net profit. This act, changing the name to Carlsbad *Caverns* National Park, provided that on recommendation of the Secretary of the Interior the park might be enlarged by presidential proclamation to include certain designated lands. This authorization was soon used, for on February 21, 1933, President Hoover proclaimed an addition of 9,239 acres to allow room for building a better road.[16] Carlsbad Cavern was not the only cave in the vicinity; there were several other openings, one of them—the New Cave, known since the 1880's—containing a great room and some extraordinarily massive stalagmites. To make certain that these other caves would be protected and for other reasons, President Roosevelt proclaimed a further addition on February 3, 1939, of 39,488 acres— about fifty-five times the original area of the monument.[17]

No park ever seems quite large enough to satisfy some park lovers, and there has been agitation for the addition of the Guadalupe Mountain region to Carlsbad, to provide above-ground scenery and wildlife. Secretary Ickes and Director Cammerer urged this addition in 1933 and in 1934, but such an addition would have had to come from the Lincoln National Forest, and the Forest Service seldom shows any enthusiasm for giving up its lands. The 3 million bats in Carlsbad do of course afford some wildlife interest.

14 *Congressional Record*, Dec. 11, 1929, 297, 298.
15 H. R. 9895, 71 Cong. 2 Sess. Stat. 46, 279.
16 Stat. 47, 2556.
17 Stat. 53, 2523. *Natural History*, Jan. 1954, 16.

New Mexico had a school section in the monument at first, but Carlsbad was little plagued with private holdings. There was, however, one small privately owned tract in the park on which there were guano deposits, and on May 4, 1934, Congress authorized the Secretary to exchange for this land a permit to mine guano on this tract or "any guano located within or on Government lands adjacent to said deposits."[18] Early in 1954 surveyors for the New Mexico State Land Office raised the question whether some of the Carlsbad caverns were not under land belonging to the New Mexico Education Association.[19]

ISLE ROYALE PARK   Most national parks were established in areas long known to be of superb scenic value, and after some years of agitation and promotion, of pertinacious pressure on Congress. Not so Isle Royale. This island, the largest in the Great Lakes, was considered for a national monument as early as 1923, when Secretary Work set aside 9,121 acres of land owned by the federal government, and the Detroit *News* undertook to get the privately owned lands; but the project was not carried through. There was not much agitation for national park status until 1931 when, on March 3, its establishment was provided for. Its interesting history runs back to ancient times, when aborigines mined the copper which here was found in pure form. In early American history it was the land of trappers, hunters, fishermen, and copper miners, the latter still at work as late as the 1880's. Isolated by surrounding waters, it remained largely a wilderness, and as such it was wanted as a wilderness national park by Mather, Albright, and others.[20]

On February 21, 1931, Senator Vandenberg of Michigan introduced a bill to establish Isle Royale National Park, which was favorably reported and debated a little. When Vandenberg asked for unanimous consent for consideration of the bill, Senator Blease of South Carolina objected, saying that he had been pushing without success a bill to set up a national park at King's Mountain, South

18 H. R. 5397, 73 Cong. 2 Sess. Stat. 48, 664.

19 *Kansas City Times*, Mar. 26, 1954. For really gorgeous pictures of Carlsbad Caverns, see the *National Geographic Magazine*, Oct. 1953.

20 George A. West, *Copper: Its Mining and Use by the Aborigines of the Lake Superior Region* (report of the McDonald-Massee Isle Royale expedition, published by Board of Trustees, 1929).

Carolina, and therefore objected to this park in the North. Blease's objection sent the bill back to the calendar, but a little later Vandenberg brought it up again, asking that the Cramton bill, H. R. 17005, which had passed the House the day before, be substituted for it.[21]

Louis Cramton of Michigan, chairman of the subcommittee on appropriations of the House Committee on Public Lands, a staunch friend of Mather, Albright, and the national parks, introduced an Isle Royale bill on February 10, 1931, declaring that it was an emergency bill, that it could not become fully effective unless the lands were ceded and that the legislature of Michigan was in session and would not meet again for two years. There was some questioning as to the emergency, and some sniping at the bill by southern Democrats. Representative Green of Florida thought there had been unfair treatment of an Everglades Park bill a few days before: "It seems very strange to me that only a few days ago my State desired a bill passed very similar to this. We purported to give to the Federal Government 1,300,000 acres of land in the southern portion of Florida for a national park. . . . When we offered to give that land we found on the other side of the aisle a legion coming to protect the Federal Treasury and to prevent the Everglades National Park from being established. Now, then, we find the gentleman from Michigan coming up with all of the lions and lambs lying down together to help him pass his park bill. . . . Why not also pass our Everglades Park Bill?" Cramton explained that he would have been glad to vote for the Everglades bill, and so no objections were raised and the bill passed the House,[22] and later the Senate, without debate.[23]

The establishment of Isle Royale Park had been favored by Mather, Albright, Gilbert Grosvenor, president of the National Geographic Society, by the Izaak Walton League, and by other conservationists and conservation organizations. Albright's recommendation was unequivocal: "It's a type of scenery utterly distinct from anything now found in our national-park system; its primitiveness, its unusual wildlife and interesting flora, its evidence of possible prehistoric occupation, all combine to make Isle Royale and its neighboring islands of national-park calibre."[24]

21 S. 6221, 71 Cong. 3 Sess.
22 H. R. 17005, 71 Cong. 3 Sess. *Congressional Record,* Mar. 2, 1931, 6790 ff.
23 Stat. 46, 1514.
24 *Congressional Record,* 71 Cong. 3 Sess. 6791.

The Isle Royale Act followed the pattern of the acts setting up the Appalachian parks, in requiring the state of Michigan to acquire the lands on Isle Royale and such "immediately surrounding islands as shall be designated by the Secretary of the Interior in the exercise of his judgment and discretion as necessary and desirable for national park purposes." The federal government was to spend no money for lands, the Secretary was given wide discretion, and whenever he thought enough land was acquired the park was to be established without further action of Congress. The new park was exempted from the operation of the Federal Water Power Act of 1920. In a section which was unfortunately unusual in park establishment, the act required that the park should not be established until exclusive jurisdiction should be ceded to the federal government. The next year, on February 4, 1932, Congress authorized the Secretary, in accepting title to lands, to lease them back to owners for their lives, or in some cases for twenty years. This provision also applied to Shenandoah, Great Smoky Mountains and Mammoth Cave.[25] The Island Copper Company of New York owned some 45,000 acres, much of which it agreed to deed to the government for the park; 72,000 acres of the remainder were owned by one lumber company. There were some owners of smaller tracts—sufferers from hay fever, etc.—and they were not disturbed.

Acquisition of needed lands was something of a task. Governor Brucker of Michigan promptly appointed a strong commission to acquire lands and the legislature appropriated $100,000 for purchases. The Michigan Conservation Commission was directed to turn over some 2,200 acres of state-owned lands. The federal government gave 10,266 acres of public domain lands. Some private owners agreed to give their lands to the government, but of course most of such lands had to be bought or secured by condemnation.

There was some reason for expedition, for there was a threat of timber-cutting by lumber companies; but land acquisition proceeded rather slowly, and in 1936 President Roosevelt allocated $705,000 of emergency funds appropriated the previous year, to buy lands in Isle Royale and a number of the small adjacent islands for CCC camps. Two years later Director Cammerer reported 20,723 acres still to be acquired. The land bought with federal money raised a question. The creating act had provided that no federal money

25 Stat. 47, 37.

should be spent and there seemed to be some question whether lands
bought with federal money could legally be added to the park. On
June 20, 1938, President Roosevelt signed the De Rouen bill making
such lands a part of the park.[26]

Finally, on April 3, 1940, with the acceptance of the last lands
required, Isle Royale was announced as an established park, a wilderness park, although one condition necessary to its completion was
not yet fulfilled—the acceptance of jurisdiction which was called for
by the establishing act. The establishing act did not make it a wilderness park, as in the case of Grand Teton and the later Kings
Canyon, but the Park Service has kept it so with no roads and few
hotel accommodations.

As usual in the establishment of national parks, Isle Royale was
barely set up when it was found too small; and efforts were made
to enlarge it by adding some of the hundred or more nearby islands.[27]
Finally on March 6, 1942, a law was approved adding a part of Passage Island, controlled by the Navy and not all needed for naval
purposes, abolishing the Siskiwit Islands Bird Reservation and adding the land to Isle Royale, and authorizing the Secretary of the
Interior to "include any submerged lands within four and one-half
miles of the shore line of Isle Royale and the immediately surrounding islands," these islands to be acquired by donation.[28]

On the same day that the addition of these islands was provided
for, Congress assumed jurisdiction in the usual comprehensive act
defining jurisdiction, crimes, and punishments. The act also reserved
to the state of Michigan the right to tax persons, corporations, and
property in the park.[29]

Isle Royale was thus established as a national park, with little
opposition or debate, perhaps partly because it was promoted in
Congress by two able and influential men, Senator Vandenberg and
Representative Cramton. It has presented some difficult problems
of administration. There were conflicting reports on wildlife at the

26 H. R. 7826, 75 Cong. 3 Sess. Stat. 52, 785. *Science*, n.s., May 31, 1940, 517.
American Forests, May 1940, 229.

27 S. 3317, H. R. 8648, 76 Cong. 3 Sess. H. R. 2614, H. R. 4386, S. 1248, 77
Cong. 1 Sess. H. R. 3014, 77 Cong. 2 Sess.

28 H. R. 4386, 77 Cong. 1 Sess. Stat. 56, 138. This act incorrectly attributed
control of Passage Island to the Secretary of the *Treasury*, and it was necessary
a little later to change the Treasury to the Navy (Stat. 56, 722).

29 H. R. 3014, 77 Cong. 2 Sess. Stat. 56, 133.

time its establishment was authorized, but apparently there had been a surplus of moose for more than ten years, and a dense population of beaver. It is a great moose country.

The problem of tourist accommodations has always been a vexing one. A wilderness park does not attract a large enough flow of tourists to justify heavy concessioner expenditures for facilities, in boats running from the mainland to the island—a distance of twenty miles —and in hotel accommodations. The boat service has often been poor and undependable.

ENLARGEMENT OF PARKS　　Albright also secured the enlargement of a number of other parks. In 1929 Congress authorized the employment of experts to examine lands proposed for new parks and monuments and for additions to them, which expedited the work of the Park Service. An extension of Mount Rainier to the east and southeast to the crest of the Cascade Range and Chinook Pass had long been needed, to include more low land for winter range for wildlife and for a road from Paradise Valley to Yakima Park. Like Yellowstone, Mount Rainier had been outlined along rectangular lines—almost a perfect square—which made practically no allowance for topographical lines, for rivers, valleys, and mountain ranges. Late in 1930 Senator Jones and Representative Summers of Washington introduced a bill for extension of the park, supported by Albright, the Forest Service, and the Secretary of the Interior, which passed with no opposition and was signed by President Hoover on January 31, 1931.[30]

There had been several extensions of Bryce Canyon, but the important extension was of 22,068 acres on February 17, 1931.[31] There were less important extensions of Crater Lake, Wind Cave, Rocky Mountain, Mesa Verde, Lassen Volcanic and Acadia. Some land was added to Acadia almost every year, largely through the generosity of George B. Dorr and John D. Rockefeller, Jr. During these years the Appalachian parks and Mammoth Cave were adding land from time to time; and Albright and a few other men made a careful study of Everglades, under authorization of an act of March 1, 1929. The bill to provide for this had been introduced by Representative

30 S. 5250, H. R. 15008, 71 Cong. 3 Sess. Stat. 48, 1047.
31 Stat. 46, 1166.

Yon of Florida to make an investigation of "Tropic Everglades National Park."[32] On May 2, 1932, Glacier Park was proclaimed as a
part of the Waterton–Glacier International Peace Park.[33]

GIANT SUGAR PINES NEAR YOSEMITE   There were about 13,000
acres of privately owned giant sugar pines—up to eight feet or even
ten feet in diameter—along the Big Oak Flat Road and Wawona
Road in Yosemite, and in the late twenties and early thirties some
of these forests, which were being threatened by lumbermen, were
saved for the park. In 1928 Representative Carter of California got
a bill through Congress authorizing the exchange of 1,010 acres in
the park for 1,350 acres of private timber along the west boundary,
valuable as feeding grounds for the park deer.[34] Almost a year later
Senator Johnson and Representative Englebright of California
brought up bills to authorize the President to proclaim an addition
of 9,000 acres along the western boundary of the park, and the Johnson bill passed without discussion.[35] On April 14, 1930, President
Hoover made the proclamation.[36]

On May 9, 1930, Congress authorized the President to proclaim
an addition of 960 acres of fine timber to Yosemite adjacent to Hetch
Hetchy Valley, and on February 14, 1931, appropriated $1 million
for this and also authorized the Secretary to obligate the government
for another $1 million for the purchase of the lands—$2 million altogether—to be matched fifty-fifty from other sources.[37] On August
13, 1932, President Hoover proclaimed the addition of 8,784 acres
and the most needed of the sugar pines were saved. John D. Rockefeller, Jr., contributed nearly $2 million called for by the purchase
act.[38] The exact amount of Rockefeller's contribution has been
variously stated—at $2 million, at $1,709,237.88, and at $1,750,000.[39]
Negotiations and purchases were going on for several years here,
and approximately $3.3 million was spent, half of it contributed by

32 Stat. 45, 1443. S. 4704, 70 Cong. 2 Sess.
33 Stat. 47, 145. Shankland, *op. cit.*, 296.
34 H. R. 12038, 70 Cong. 1 Sess. Stat. 45, 784.
35 S. 5880, H. R. 17221, 70 Cong. 2 Sess. Stat. 45, 1486.
36 Stat. 46, 3017.
37 H. R. 10581, 71 Cong. 2 Sess. Stat. 46, 265, 1154.
38 Stat. 47, 2527.
39 See *Congressional Record*, Dec. 8, 1930, 348.

Rockefeller. A man from Indiana, George A. Ball, had given $8,000 earlier, to buy an important private holding on the Glacier Point Road.

The purchase of these great sugar pines and the protection of the scenery along the park roads was due not only to the generosity of Rockefeller and to persistent efforts of Albright and various conservation organizations, but to the help of Representative Louis Cramton.[40]

Credit should be given some of the lumber companies for a generous and co-operative attitude in the negotiations for the sugar pines. The Sugar Pine Lumber Company sold its land on the basis of actual cost, leaving out all consideration of future profits, arranged for selective cutting along the outside part of the road where it still retained ownership, and agreed to save the finest individual specimens and selected groves along the highway.

Albright was able to get modest amounts of money for the purchase of other private lands in the parks. There had been dribbles of $50,000 each year since 1927, to be matched fifty-fifty from other sources, but in 1929 Congress raised the grant to $250,000, and also authorized the Secretary to contract up to $2,750,000, both sums to be matched from other sources. The next year, $200,000 was granted, to be matched, plus $1,750,000, part of the $2,750,000 appropriated in 1929. In the same bill $75,000 was appropriated for additions to Absaroka and Gallatin National Forests and Yellowstone Park "to improve winter-feed facilities of the elk, antelope and other game animals of Yellowstone Park and adjacent land," to be matched from other sources.[41]

---

[40] See an article by Albright in *Nature Magazine,* June 1930, 367; also *Science,* n.s., Dec. 23, 1932, 591.

[41] Stat. 46, 313, 319.

CHAPTER XVI

The Albright Administration

1929-1933

NEW NATIONAL MONUMENTS, HISTORICAL
PARKS, TRANSFERS TO THE PARK SERVICE

The important extension of Yellowstone boundaries has been discussed in connection with Mather's administration although the Norbeck Act was passed a few weeks after Albright became Director. Before the end of Albright's administration Yellowstone had reached somewhat its present proportions, with a bulge on the northwest corner, a smaller bulge on the northeast corner, and the east line following the crest of the Absaroka Mountains. The extension southeast to take in the high Thorofare region should have been but was not made, and the Jackson Hole country was added years later but to Grand Teton and not Yellowstone.

NATIONAL MONUMENTS   Albright was able to get a number of national monuments of scenic distinction. In March 1929 it was Congress, however, that provided for the establishment of the *Badlands* National Monument, in South Dakota, a large area of weirdly eroded and sculptured hills, fossil-bearing in places. There had been a number of efforts in Congress to establish the Badlands as a national park. Senator Peter Norbeck of South Dakota was much interested in the project, and it was largely through his efforts that

339

the monument was established. His Senate bill proposed a national park, the "Teton" national park, but in a conference committee the name was changed to "Badlands" and the status was reduced to national monument. The bill as passed provided that when the privately owned lands should be acquired free of cost to the government, and when the state of South Dakota should have built thirty miles of road through the area, the President might proclaim it as a national monument. These conditions were met in about ten years, and on January 25, 1939, the monument was proclaimed.[1]

Two years after Badlands, in February 1931, Congress again moved at Albright's and Wilbur's recommendation, to establish the *Canyon de Chelly* National Monument, in northeastern Arizona, with the consent of the Navajos who owned the land. This spectacular red-rock canyon—really *three* canyons, de Chelly, del Muerto, and Monument—up to 1,000 feet deep, has some 500 ancient cliff ruins, some of them small, and a tragic modern history, for in the Canyon del Muerto, in 1805-6, a hundred women, children, and old men were massacred by Spanish troops while the Navajo warriors were away. Canyon de Chelly was a most worthy national monument.[2] About this time Congress authorized the exchange of lands in Chaco Canyon, Craters of the Moon, and Petrified Forest, to eliminate private holdings.

The southwestern archeological monuments were still subject to vandalism in spite of all that the Park Service and the Departments of Agriculture and War could do. Artifacts and archeological materials were being stolen by vandals and were even offered for sale in shops. The appropriations to the Park Service in 1928 and 1929— $35,000 and $46,000—had been utterly inadequate to protect more than a score of these monuments. In April 1932 a conference was called of representatives of the Departments of War, Agriculture, and the Interior, and the Smithsonian Institution to consider the better protection of American antiquities. The conference recommended a standard application form for permission to conduct archeological excavations, and a standard form for issuing permits, to secure better information regarding applicants and the particular areas covered by permits, for there had been occasional violations of the terms of permits. The conference also recommended authorization of arrest of persons found on the public lands in possession

[1] S. 4385, 70 Cong. 1 Sess. Stat. 45, 1553; 53, 2521. See p. 411.
[2] Stat. 46, 1161.

of archeological material, the seizure and impounding of the material, and the prohibition of shipment of it without a permit. Wilbur and Albright had been insisting that Indian traders and operators of stores and trading posts should be prohibited from buying, bartering, or exposing archeological materials for sale.

Even some of the excavation work done by archeologists was not done carefully enough. As we have noted, some of the early work was done by Dr. Fewkes of the Smithsonian Institution, and with too little care.[3] In such work care must be taken not to mar the specimens; note must be made as to where found, with what other artifacts, wood, charcoal, bones of men and animals, and the like. Some of the early archeological work was not done with sufficient attention to such details.

A number of other national monuments were established. *Arches,* near Moab, Utah, included a number of natural bridges and fantastic rock formations; and *Sunset Crater,* in northern Arizona, is a symmetrical volcano cone 1,000 feet high which in a historic eruption some centuries ago scattered lava and cinders over the surrounding region, fertilizing the land so that the Indians could raise bigger crops for a few years, and attracting immigrants from other regions.[4] The *Great Sand Dunes* National Monument, covering an area of sand dunes in southern Colorado was proclaimed in March 1932, and the *White Sands* National Monument, covering dunes of white gypsum in New Mexico, was proclaimed a year later. In the story of White Sands we see the record of devotion of some men to the parks and monuments. A man named Tom Charles was the first custodian, at $1.00 a year, and he furnished his own car, gasoline and stamps.[5] *Grand Canyon* National Monument, covering 273,145 acres northwest of Grand Canyon National Park, was set up in December 1932, and *Death Valley* was proclaimed in February 1933, a monument of more than a million acres of about the driest and hottest desert in America, about 500 square miles of it below sea level—the scene of terrible hardship and tragedy in the days of the gold-seekers who tried to cross the valley.

In March 1933 another great canyon monument was proclaimed by President Hoover—the *Black Canyon* of the Gunnison in western Colorado, Albright and Secretary Wilbur suggesting it. The Gun-

3 See pp. 168, 169.
4 Stat. 46, 2988, 3023.
5 *Natural History,* May 1950, 228.

nison River was named after Captain J. W. Gunnison, who with
some of his surveying party was massacred by Indians in 1853. The
"Black" Canyon is black in two respects, being of dark-colored
rocks and also dark at the bottom because of its depth and narrow-
ness. This canyon is comparable with Zion, almost as deep and
narrower, but lacks the bright colors of Zion; and the visitor looks
down and not up. If a road could be built along the bottom of the
gorge it would enhance the interest of the monument.[6]

Several national monuments were enlarged: Aztec Ruins, Bandelier, Craters of the Moon, Colorado, Pinnacles, and Scotts Bluff.
Petrified Forest was expanded several times, adding 53,309 acres,
obtained by exchange with the Santa Fe Railroad and private individuals to take in some of the Painted Desert, including the Black
Painted Desert; and Katmai of Alaska was expanded several times
by the addition of 1,609,600 acres, to provide more protection for
the Alaska brown bear, moose, and other wild animals.[7] On the
other hand, one national monument, the Papago Saguaro, set aside
by President Wilson in 1914, was abolished in April 1930, and part
of it was reserved as a rifle range for the National Guard of Arizona,
part of it granted to the state of Arizona and the city of Tempe
for park use, and part of it to a water users' association, with a
reservation to the federal government of mineral deposits on the
land.[8] Three years later President Hoover proclaimed another
Saguaro National Monument, partly in the Catalina Division of the
Coronado National Forest, in Arizona.[9]

The Mountain of the Holy Cross in Colorado had been a famous
landmark for many years. Near the peak of the mountain a likeness
of a cross was outlined by snow-filled crevasses. William Jackson, a
widely known photographer with the Hayden geological survey
party, secured photographs of the mountain in 1873, and in 1876
Thomas Moran exhibited a painting of it which won public acclaim
and advertised the mountain widely. President Hoover proclaimed
Holy Cross National Monument on May 11, 1929. Years later the
monument was abolished when the conformity of the cross was
ruined by rock falls.[10]

6 Stat. 47, 2558.
7 Stat. 46, 3040; 47, 2486, 2552; 47, 2453.
8 Stat. 46, 142.
9 Stat. 47, 2557.
10 Stat. 46, 2993.

In Mather's and Albright's administrations there was agitation for a Quetico-Superior wilderness area, to include part of the Superior National Forest in northern Minnesota, on the Canadian border, extending over into and including the Quetico Provincial Park in Ontario. This area, abounding in clear lakes and connecting streams, was splendid canoeing and fishing country; but unfortunately much of the land on the United States side was owned by the state of Minnesota and by private interests. On May 26, 1928, President Coolidge issued an executive order temporarily withdrawing the lands to prevent the filing of further private claims, but the final establishment of this wilderness area was not achieved for years. It was to be under Forest Service administration, but the Park Service men and conservationists everywhere were greatly interested in it.

Like Mather and many others, Albright greatly desired a coast redwood park in California and worked hard for it, but the state of California did about all that was ever done to save the coast redwoods, except for the Muir Woods National Monument, given to the government in 1907 by Mr. and Mrs. William Kent.

NEW PARK PROPOSALS   Like Mather, Albright had a hard job fighting off inferior park proposals. In 1931 he reported fifty-five national park projects and forty-four national monument projects awaiting investigation. Most of these were quite unworthy, but some were pushed persistently. Some, on the other hand, were introduced by senators and representatives under pressure of local boosting orders, but without enthusiasm or even in the hope that they would be ignored. Two inferior parks got as far as Congressional authorization of investigation—Apostle Islands, in Lake Superior, off the coast of Wisconsin, and Upper Mississippi, along the Mississippi River in Iowa, Illinois, Wisconsin, and Minnesota. Neither achieved park status.[11] Senator Joe Robinson's Ouachita National Park proposal had passed both houses in President Coolidge's administration but, as we have seen, Coolidge had vetoed it.[12] That did not end the threat, however, for the Ouachita bill was up in every Congress for several years. One of the most troublesome of the park prosposals of these years and later was for the Theodore

11 Stat. 46, 264, 588.
12 See pp. 298, 299.

Roosevelt Memorial National Park in North Dakota, covering Roosevelt's ranch. It was pushed with persistence by North Dakota men in Congress.

The Park Service was happy to get rid of Sullys Hill National Park in North Dakota, in March 1931. It was made a game preserve, under the jurisdiction of the Secretary of Agriculture.[13]

HISTORICAL PARKS   Albright was deeply interested in historical records, sites, and buildings, and early in his administration achieved a beginning in the establishment of historical national monuments, which were to become an important part of the park activities in later years. *George Washington's Birthplace* National Monument was provided for by Congress in January 1930, with an appropriation of $65,000 to buy the land and build a replica of the house (surprisingly enough, with no requirement that the funds should be matched from other sources); and in July 1930 the *Colonial* National Monument was authorized, later Colonial National Historical Park, to cover roughly Jamestown Island, parts of the town of Williamsburg, and the Yorktown battlefield. The sum of $500,000 was granted for the expenses of setting up the monument, again with no provision for matching the grant from other sources. Thus Congress showed a more generous disposition toward historical monuments than toward scenic parks and monuments.[14]

Albright was much interested in building up the best possible personnel, and in offering promotion for merit. Mather had at first wanted to be free from civil service restrictions until he could weed out some of the political appointees of earlier years, but in 1925 the rangers went under civil service, and in 1931 Albright got the superintendents and the custodians of national monuments covered into civil service. That had its disadvantages, of course. The Civil Service Commission took up some time prying into the affairs of the Park Service, but it provided more security of tenure for employees, and is generally good administration.

CONGRESS SMILES ON THE PARKS   Mather and Albright had been interested in the interpretive or educational work of the Park Service during Mather's administration, and when Mather retired

13 Stat. 46, 1509.
14 Stat. 46, 58, 855.

Albright continued this work, with the support of Secretaries Work and Wilbur. Albright created the Branch of Research and Education in 1930, under the direction of Harold C. Bryant, with a staff historian; and on April 22, 1932, Congress voted $22,500 for field employees examining land and "for developing the educational work" of the Service.

In April 1932 Congress provided for an improvement in the payment of the commissioners before whom offenses were tried. Before this time the commissioners had been paid a small salary but had received the fees paid in the cases brought before them. The fee system was fairly common in early judicial procedure, but it was not good administration for it tended to encourage arrests. In the act of 1932 salaries were raised "in lieu of all fees and compensation heretofore authorized."[15]

In various ways Congress evinced a friendly spirit and confidence in the Albright regime. An act of April 18, 1930, authorized the Park Service to maintain central warehouses in providing for the needs of the Service.[16] The appropriation bill of May 14, 1930, included an allowance of $25,000 for attendance at meetings, photography, etc., and $23,300 for fighting tree diseases, which were a serious menace to the forests in the parks;[17] and in 1931, in an act of general application, Congress authorized mileage payments for the use by civilian officers and employees of their own cars.[18] In February 1931 fire lookouts were covered by the appropriation.[19]

THE ACT TO FACILITATE ADMINISTRATION   A year or so after Albright assumed office, on May 25, 1930, he managed to get an act through Congress "to facilitate the administration of national parks . . ." Senator Nye, of the Committee on Public Lands and Surveys, and a friend of the parks, introduced the bill, under which the Secretary was authorized:

1. to purchase personal equipment and supplies for employees and deduct the cost from their salaries;

15 Stat. 47, 126.
16 Stat. 46, 219.
17 Stat. 46, 317.
18 Stat. 46, 1103.
19 Stat. 46, 1154.

2. to pay 3 cents a mile for the use of motorcycles or 7 cents for the use of a car—or 10 cents where roads were poor—if it was cheaper to rent than buy; (For a short three-month park season it was often cheaper to rent.)
3. to contract for services, supplies and materials without advertising; (In case of fire or other emergency this was desirable.)
4. in emergencies to sell supplies, etc. to concessioners;
5. to cash travelers' checks for automobile license fees;
6. to care for indigents, and in case of death bury them, or to pay transportation costs for not over fifty miles;
7. to reimburse employees for loss of property in their work—from fires, etc.;
8. to require field employees to furnish horses, motor and other vehicles and equipment needed in their work, and to provide care and housing for them;
9. to hire or rent property from employees if in the public interest;
10. to hire work animals and vehicles without written contract;
11. to pay expenses of employees moving from one station to another.[20]

Some of these provisions were related to the peculiar conditions under which some of the parks operate. In some of the parks the tourist season is from three to four months and the real flood of visitors only about two months—July and August—and it is often cheaper to hire and rent men and equipment for that short period than to employ men for the full year and buy equipment, which would merely accumulate rust for most of the year. Particularly in case of forest fires or other emergencies, the park management needed a free hand, and could not be tied down by too much red tape.

UNIFORM ADMINISTRATION OF THE PARKS   On the same day that Nye presented his bill to facilitate the administration of the parks he offered another bill, "to provide for the uniform administration of the national parks"—also no doubt at the request of Albright—which passed with almost no debate. As passed, and approved—January 26, 1931—the act provided for the following:

1. Mineral prospecting in Mesa Verde and Grand Canyon was prohibited.

20 S. 195, 71 Cong. 2 Sess. Stat. 46, 381 ff.

2. In Mount McKinley the Secretary was authorized to prescribe regulations for surface use of any mineral locations already made or thereafter to be made, and to require registration of prospectors, but prospecting was not prohibited.
3. No further permits might be issued for summer homes in Glacier or Lassen Volcanic, but the Secretary might renew any permits already made. (In his letter of instructions to Mather, in 1918, Secretary Lane had already forbidden leasing of summer homes, so this merely confirmed the policy of the Secretary.)
4. Hereafter no rights of way might be granted for steam or electric railways, automobile or wagon roads in Lassen Volcanic.
5. No more rights of way might be granted for steam or electric railways in certain valleys of Glacier.
6. No rights of way might be granted in Mount Rainier for railways or tramways (as permitted in the act of 1899), but the Secretary might authorize easements or rights of way for tramways or cable lines for the accommodation of visitors.
7. The provision in the act creating Rocky Mountain, authorizing the Secretary to grant rights of way for steam or electric transportation, was repealed.[21]

Thus were some of the unfortunate provisions of establishing acts finally removed, to justify the park administration in accepting parks with such provisions.

GRAZING LANDS   The grazing lands of the West presented a most critical land problem in Albright's administration, and must be given brief consideration. They had never been protected in any way and were being overgrazed and eroded by cattle and sheep that ranged on the public lands without any restriction. This was important not only in relation to conservation generally but in relation to some of the parks and monuments, particularly those in the Southwest which were located on grazing lands and were surrounded by areas of abused and eroded grazing lands. Hoover's and Wilbur's plan for turning the lands over to the states was not wise. The political administration of most western states was on a low level, quite inadequate to the management of grazing lands. Some western states were largely controlled by livestock associations, which were

21 Stat. 46, 1043.

often hostile to any sort of control, and would have been very likely to turn the lands over to the stockmen, whose record in management of their own lands had often been far from glorious. Also, grazing areas often covered several states, and would have had to be managed through interstate agreements, which are difficult to secure; and, finally, most of the western states could scarcely have afforded to engage in a rigorous policy of protecting and restoring their grazing lands.

In April 1930 Congress authorized an appropriation of $50,000 to enable the President to appoint a commission to study and report on the conservation and administration of the public domain,[22] and President Hoover set up a Public Lands Commission, with James R. Garfield as chairman, to work out a plan for managing the grazing lands. Garfield had formerly favored cession of much of the public lands to the states, and apparently still favored that, for the commission reported in favor of it.

In its report the Public Lands Commission stressed the seriousness of conditions on the grazing lands: "Overgrazing of many areas has not only greatly reduced the carrying capacity for livestock generally but has greatly injured the land. In many sections it is now practically worthless. Erosion has been increased by the destruction of all vegetation and the silting of streams and rivers has added to the serious problem of range and farm and reclamation. Reservoirs are being rapidly silted and the costs of maintaining canals have been greatly increased."[23]

Important as protection of the grazing lands was to some of the national monuments, reservoir recreation areas, and to the entire economies of western states, it will be unnecessary to follow in detail the Congressional maneuvers in the early thirties in the efforts to do something for these lands. Some of the western men wanted the lands ceded to the western states, others wanted federal administration and protection. Finally, after long discussion, Representative Taylor of Colorado brought up a bill to establish federal protection, which passed both houses to become the Taylor Grazing Act of 1934.[24]

The Taylor Grazing Act authorized the Secretary of the Interior to establish grazing districts on not more than 80 million acres of

22 Stat. 46, 153.
23 H. Rept. 1710, 72 Cong. 1 Sess.
24 Stat. 48, 1269.

the unreserved public domain and regulate grazing on them. Two years later the act was amended to increase the area covered to 142 million acres. It was fortunate that the federal government was able to keep these lands, although the provisions of the act were quite too generous to the states which, for the counties in which the grazing districts were located, received 50 per cent of the receipts for grazing fees. In spite of all the government could do the grazing lands were and still are too heavily grazed.

REORGANIZATION OF GOVERNMENT SERVICES   Early in the Albright Administration there arose a considerable interest in a reorganization of the government services, to centralize in a new executive department, to be known as the Department of Conservation, the administration and development of the forests, parks, and wildlife resources owned by the government. At the time, the Forest Service and the Biological Survey were in the Department of Agriculture, the National Park Service was in the Department of the Interior, and the Bureau of Fisheries was in the Department of Commerce; and it appeared to some men that these services should be combined in one bureau or department. There had been efforts to create such a bureau at least as early as 1921, and on February 24, 1927, Representative Garrett of Tennessee introduced a bill to establish it.[25] At the annual meeting of the American Forestry Association on January 28, 1927, George B. Pratt, president of the Association, voiced approval of the plan: "I want to stress the importance of conservation as a major policy in federal stewardship. In the United States, exclusive of Alaska, the Federal Government is custodian of over 365,000,000 acres. This represents a land area of more than 570,000 square miles, title to which rests in the people of the United States. This land is divided among a score or more of uses and administered by many different bureaus, some of which are following definite conservation policies, but largely unrelated and unco-ordinated one with another. Others have no conservation policy or authority. The situation is inconsistent and a reproach upon national economy.

"I believe the time has come in the economic development of our country when we must demand that our Federal Government adopt an all-inclusive conservation policy and co-ordinate its activities

25 H. R. 17321, 69 Cong. 2 Sess.

into a separate department to be known as the Department of Conservation, or one equally well named. The natural resources owned by the people of the United States are far too valuable and too important to the permanent development of our country to permit any part of them to be dissipated by the traditions of departmental administration."[26]

The Garrett bill fell short of real needs in omitting important resources—the public lands, oil, gas, coal and other minerals, and water and water power. It is broadly true that there are not *many* land problems, *many* conservation problems, but *one* land resource problem, *one* conservation problem, for all kinds of natural resources are related to each other in many ways. But the Garrett bill was a threat to enough commercial and vested interests so that it did not pass.

In the 1928 political campaign proposals for government "reorganization" were given much publicity, Herbert Hoover already displaying his penchant for reorganizing government bureaus; and on December 3, 1929, in his message to Congress he outlined broadly and rather vaguely a scheme of reorganization, the main purpose of which was to bring the various bureaus and departments together that were concerned with the conservation of natural resources. He pointed out that conservation work was scattered among eight agencies in five departments, and suggested that they should be under one roof, but did not say just where that should be. He did however appoint a Commission on Conservation of the Public Domain with a membership representing the major public land states and the public, and hinted that it might be well to transfer the public lands to the states for school purposes.[27]

About this time William Hard, a widely known journalist, suggested that the best reorganization would place the "Department of Public Domain and Public Works" in the Department of the Interior, taking in the General Land Office, which controlled the public domain, the Bureau of Indian Affairs, the Geological Survey, the Coast and Geodetic Survey, the Forest Service, the Federal Power Commission, the Bureau of Fisheries, the Biological Survey, the National Park Service, and the National Forest Reservation Commission. This appeared to be somewhat the idea of the Hoover Administration, but it was poison to the Forest Service. The idea

[26] *American Forests and Forest Life*, Apr. 1927, 227.
[27] *American Forests and Forest Life*, Jan. 1930, 11.

of a new Department of Conservation was bad enough, but the Forest Service did not want to be shifted over into the Department of the Interior. The Park Service, in the Department of the Interior, was indeed devoted to the *preservation* of lands, scenic lands, but the Land Office, in the same department, was traditionally devoted to the *disposing* of lands to settlers. The lands remaining under the jurisdiction of the Land Office were the arid and semi-arid grazing and desert lands which were not adapted to ordinary farming and for that reason had not been disposed of. These grazing lands were not protected or managed in any way, were open to all who wanted to use them, and as a result were scandalously overgrazed and eroded.

Since the time when Gifford Pinchot first organized the Forest Service it had been a first-class, efficient service, and it did not want to be transferred to the same bailiwick with the Land Office. That office had historically a rather bad reputation, under some early administrations a rendezvous of speculators, land sharks, and land thieves. Some of the worst scandals of early administrations centered in the Land Office.[28] The record of the Land Office in later years was not bad, and on some questions it was and had been very good. Among the earliest and most active workers for the reservation of archeological sites in the Southwest were Commissioners Binger Hermann (1897-1902) and W. A. Richards (1903-6). Secretary of the Interior Harold Ickes strongly resented the criticisms of the record of the Land Office as if they were still pertinent.

Furthermore, the Forest Service did not think of its functions as mere ownership and protection of land, as some of the reorganizers apparently did, but as an active and constructive function, of growing, protecting and harvesting a tree crop, of gathering and promoting knowledge "in the growing, care and utilization of trees as plant crops," a function similar to that of ordinary farming, and therefore properly carried on in the Department of Agriculture. That was the reason the forest reserves had been shifted from the Department of the Interior to the Department of Agriculture in 1905. The Forest Service, furthermore, had its own grazing land problem, which it was solving with some success, in spite of the

28 For a discussion of the record of the Land Office, see an article by H. H. Chapman, *American Forests and Forest Life*, April 1930, 211, and the author's *United States Forest Policy* (New Haven: Yale University Press, 1920).

efforts of some of the livestock men to get control of these lands.[29]

Nothing came immediately out of all the discussion of reorganization, but the subject was brought up from time to time, and in the F. D. Roosevelt Administration, Secretary of the Interior Harold Ickes launched a determined effort to get the national forests over to his department, apparently with the approval of President Roosevelt; but again no change was made, largely because of the opposition of the Forest Service.

TRANSFER OF NATIONAL MONUMENTS, ETC. TO PARK SERVICE

Albright had some ideas on a different sort of reorganization. He feared that a small agency like the Park Service might be buffeted about in the interdepartmental rivalries in Washington, and conceived of a future Service with control over national parks and monuments, historic sites and buildings, national military parks and the national monuments that had been in the Department of Agriculture. He had come to believe that the national military parks—Gettysburg, Chattanooga, nearly a dozen of them—national battlefield sites, etc., could be more efficiently administered by the Park Service; and various men had ventured the same opinion. As early as 1919 Mather had suggested that these parks should be under the Park Service. In 1928 Secretary West had secured an agreement with the Secretary of War for the transfer to the Park Service of the military and historical parks and national monuments controlled by the War Department, and got a bill introduced into Congress by Senator Nye to effect this transfer, but the bill did not pass.[30] In 1932 President Hoover made a proposal to Congress for reorganization, but it was ignored. He then asked Director of the Budget Lewis W. Douglas to draw up a plan, and Douglas' plan gave the Park Service everything that Albright wanted.

On March 3, 1933, Congress authorized President Roosevelt to reorganize by executive order the executive and administrative agencies of the government, and on June 10 Roosevelt issued the executive order for reorganization, to take effect sixty-one days later. The order was spaciously inclusive: "All functions of administration of public buildings, reservations, national parks, national monuments, and national cemeteries are consolidated in an

29 *American Forests and Forest Life,* June 1929, 357; Jan. 1930, 3, 33.
30 S. 4173, 70 Cong. 1 Sess.

Office of National Parks, Buildings, and Reservations (a new name for the National Park Service) in the Department of the Interior. . . ." The Park Service did not like its new name, and on March 2, 1934, the old name was restored.[31] Also transferred to the Park Service were the Arlington Memorial Bridge Commission, the Public Buildings Commission, the Buildings and Public Parks of the National Capital—about seven hundred of them—the National Memorial Commission and the Rock Creek and Potomac Parkway Commission.[32] It has been said that the Park Service agreed verbally to take only four of the Forest Service's national monuments, but that at the end of sixty days it took all, including Oregon Caves, Bandelier, Chiricahua, Lava Beds, Mount Olympus and some others in the heart of national forests. Relations between the Forest Service and the Park Service had for several years been strained, and this was said to have made them even more unfriendly.

President Roosevelt, apparently after thinking the matter over for a while, decided he had not been explicit enough and issued a second order on July 28, 1933, making more explicit the reservations to be transferred: eleven national military parks, such as Gettysburg and Vicksburg; two "national parks," Abraham Lincoln and Fort McHenry; ten "battlefield sites," such as Antietam and Appomattox Court House; ten national monuments, mostly military and historical; four "miscellaneous memorials"; and eleven "national cemeteries." Quite an assortment, really, and Albright was greatly pleased to have the park system so well rounded out.[33]

ALBRIGHT MOVES OUT　　Albright did a splendid job as Director. Among his significant achievements were the efficient organizing of the Service, the expansion into the field of historical sites and monuments, the establishment of notable new parks and monuments, particularly Grand Teton, and finally, only a few days before he resigned, the addition of many areas from the Department of Agriculture and the War Department. But he had several times been tempted by lush offers from business corporations. He did not wish to leave the Park Service, however, until he was sure it was safe

31 Stat. 48, 389.

32 No. 6166, June 10, 1933 (5 U.S.C. Secs. 124-32).

33 No. 6228, July 28, 1933 (5 U.S.C. Secs. 124-32). Robert Shankland, *Steve Mather of the National Parks* (New York: Alfred A. Knopf, 1951), 299-301. *American Forests and Forest Life,* Jan. 1928, 62. Stat. 48, 385 ff.

from the politicians and commercial interests. It had been secure during Hoover's administration, and the election of Franklin Roosevelt was reassuring, for Roosevelt had long been an ardent conservationist.

As a boy Roosevelt had been a member of the American Museum of Natural History, with an interest in the protection of birds, and as a New York state senator from 1910 to 1912 he worked hard to protect the Adirondack Forests from lumbermen and power interests, and to protect wildlife. His interest in conservation was strengthened by association with Gifford Pinchot, whom he greatly admired; and in the years before he was elected President he devoted a great deal of energy to almost every aspect of conservation—soil, forests, power, wildlife, parks, and the prevention of stream pollution; but, like Pinchot, he was not interested in saving Hetch Hetchy Valley, perhaps because of the influence of Pinchot. His general record on conservation, as President, was to be quite comparable with that of the earlier Theodore Roosevelt. When he chose Harold Ickes for Secretary of the Interior it was clear that the Park Service was to have all the support and protection that an honest, intelligent and valiant Secretary could provide; and Albright felt free to leave. On July 17, 1933 he tendered his resignation—his resignation from the office of Director only, not from his position of active and constructive leadership in the conservation movement. That position he has held untiringly down to the present time.

The resignation of Albright really ended a period, an epoch in national park history—the epoch in which the main scenic parks were established and standards of administration were formulated. It was the period in which most of the attention was given to scenic national parks and scenic and archeological monuments. In the years following, the activities of the Park Service were to expand into various other fields, particularly into the fields of history and recreation, in co-operation with states and local government units.

The problem of a successor presented some difficulty. Albright favored Arno B. Cammerer, who had been Associate Director, but some others favored Newton B. Drury, who had been for twenty years the secretary of the Save-the-Redwoods League. Ickes appointed a committee, headed by Albright, to make the choice, and against the chairman's advice, the committee chose Drury, but Drury refused the appointment and Cammerer was given the job. He assumed office on August 10, 1933.

CHAPTER XVII

The Cammerer Administration

1933-1940

HISTORICAL PARKS AND SITES,

RECREATION AREAS, EVERGLADES PARK

Cammerer was a worthy successor of the able and indefatigable Mather and Albright. He had entered the National Park Service as Assistant Director in 1919, succeeding Albright who at that time went to Yellowstone as Superintendent; and when Albright succeeded Mather in January 1929, Cammerer became Associate Director. So he had long experience in the Park Service, and his record was impeccable.

DEPRESSION PROBLEMS   Cammerer took over a Service of carefully selected men who had been covered into civil service. Permanent rangers must have had eight years of common school, were chosen after examination on personality, appearance, and fitness, and entered at $1,860 a year, with deduction for quarters, food, and other allowances. Temporary rangers were selected by park superintendents and paid $1,680 a year. Salaries and classifications had been raised all along the line, so it was possible to keep good men; and good men were needed in the years just ahead.[1]

The situation of the parks did not appear very heartening when Cammerer took office. The country was at the gravelly bottom of

1 See *Congressional Record*, Feb. 9, 1931, 4422.

the worst depression in its history, and some men thought the economy never would revive; banks were failing; business was stagnant; unemployment was at fantastic figures; and the number of tourists was down, although not much lower. The Great Depression lasted all the years of the Cammerer Administration.

Some concessioners were in dire financial straits. In 1930 the Park Service had asked them to submit plans for operation and expansion over a five-year period, and most of them complied, but with the deepening of the depression many of them were obliged to drop plans for expansion, and some had to curtail service or even close down. The Park Service tried to help, encouraged changes in the type of service, substitution of cafeteria service for regular service, for instance, and low-priced cabin accommodations for hotel rooms, special rates for longer visits and "club" rates for groups. Attacking the problem from a different angle the Park Service, in 1937, forbade any advance in salaries of concession managers or officers who were receiving more than $5,000. In 1934 the Park Service put on a big travel promotion campaign through the co-operation of concessioners, railroads and other transportation agencies, automobile associations, oil companies, chambers of commerce, and civic associations. The press helped and the radio companies gave free time to the enterprise. The railroads, also suffering from reduced traffic, helped by offering reduced rates. Even so, the concessioners had tough pulling for several years. In 1933 the Mammoth and Lake hotels in Yellowstone, the Cut Bank and St. Marys chalets in Glacier, and the Prince of Wales Hotel in Waterton were closed. There was some discussion of government operation of the services—a plan favored by Secretary Ickes.[2] The private concessioner at Mount McKinley Park was not prospering. He had a small hotel at the railroad station, built by the government, and operated buses to a tent camp at the foot of the mountain, and there were complaints of excessive charges for the bus trip. Early in 1940 Representative Magnuson introduced a bill for government purchase of his property, in buses, tents and other facilities, reported to be worth perhaps $20,000–$40,000, and purchase of new facilities, but in the debates there were objections from many of the defenders of private enterprise, and the bill finally passed the House by the narrow margin of 173 to 170.[3] A similar

2 See the reports of the Secretary of the Interior from 1932 to 1939.
3 H. R. 4868, 76 Cong. 1 Sess.

bill introduced by Senator Bone was debated a little and passed the Senate, but was passed over in favor of the Magnuson bill.[4] A bill for government purchase of facilities in all national parks by Representative Voorhis of California was not reported.[5]

HISTORICAL PARKS AND SITES   Historical parks were becoming a more and more important element in the activities of the Park Service. Between 1890 and 1900 a number of battlefield sites had been set aside under the War Department and, as we have seen, were transferred to the Park Service in 1933;[6] but there had been growing interest in historic sites before this. The Antiquities Act of 1906 had authorized the establishment as national monuments of "historic landmarks, historic or prehistoric structures, and other objects of historic or scientific interest"; but it had been applied almost altogether to archeological structures, mostly cliff dwellings and pueblos in the southwest, and to areas of scenic or scientific value. Of about eighty-five national monuments established between 1906 and 1933, only nine were historical—related to events of the past two or three hundred years.[7]

On February 28, 1935, Senator Byrd of Virginia introduced a bill in the Senate "To provide for the preservation of historic American sites, buildings, objects, and antiquities of national importance," and this bill passed with little discussion and was signed by President Roosevelt on August 21, 1935.[8] Representative Maverick of Texas also introduced a bill for this purpose in the same session, which was passed over in favor of the Byrd bill.[9] This Historic Sites and Buildings Act declared it a national policy to preserve such things for the inspiration and benefit of the people. The Park Service was instructed (1) to secure drawings, plans, photographs and other data; (2) to make surveys of historic and archeological sites and the like; (3) to make necessary investigations to learn the truth about them; (4) to acquire such sites or objects in the name of the United States by gift, purchase or otherwise, if advisable; or

4 S. 1785, 76 Cong. 1 and 3 Sess.

5 H. R. 5502, 76 Cong. 1 Sess.

6 See pp. 352, 353.

7 *National Parks Bulletin*, No. 66, Dec. 1938. *Glimpses of Historic Areas East of the Mississippi River*, issued by the National Park Service, 1937.

8 S. 2073, 74 Cong. 1 Sess. Stat. 49, 666.

9 H. R. 6670, 74 Cong. 1 Sess.

(5) to contract and make co-operative agreements with states, cities, associations, and individuals to protect, preserve, and maintain them, even to restore or reconstruct, whether or not the United States had title; and (6) to erect tablets, to operate and manage historic and archeologic sites and the like, to charge fees for admission, and to carry on appropriate educational programs.

An "Advisory Board on National Parks, Historic Sites, Buildings and Monuments" of eleven eminent historians, archeologists, architects, and experts in "human geography," was provided for and was established in February 1936 to advise on the formulation of policies, without salary. No appropriation was made, but the next year $24,000 was provided for expenses.[10] The Advisory Board was clearly intended to advise only with regard to historical and archeological sites, but in recent years it has members who are naturalists and students of national parks and devotes much of its attention to the national parks and to wildlife problems. Proposals for new parks are referred to this Advisory Board.[11]

On the same day that he brought in the Historic Sites bill, Byrd also introduced a bill to set up a National Park Trust Fund Board, composed of the Secretary of the Treasury, the Secretary of the Interior, the Director of the Park Service and two other persons, to accept and administer gifts and bequests to the Park Service.[12]

Four years later, on July 18, 1940, Congress proved that it was in dead earnest in trying to preserve historic values, by passing an amendment to the Historic Sites Act requiring that before any federal building was demolished the Secretary of the Interior must be consulted as to whether the building had historic value.[13]

In its application to archeological sites the Historic Sites Act had something in common with the Antiquities Act of 1906, but it was used mostly to secure information, take pictures, and to protect sites and buildings of national historic significance—Harpers Ferry, the Old Philadelphia Customs House, Saratoga Battlefield, Old Main Building of Knox College, Illinois, Old Fort Laramie in Wyoming, the Chesapeake and Ohio Canal, the Subtreasury in New York, the Old Mint at San Francisco, and the like.

10 Stat. 49, 1795.

11 *Congressional Record*, Feb. 3, 1936, 1371; May 11, 1938, 6646.

12 S. 2074, 74 Cong. 1 Sess. Stat. 49, 477. Maverick also introduced a bill for this purpose (H. R. 6734).

13 Stat. 54, 765.

The Advisory Board moved with expedition, and three years later had assisted in gathering information on 7,000 early American buildings. Some of the work was in co-operation with the states, as for instance in reconstructing the old Hopewell Furnace, used in making iron in colonial days. The Smithsonian Institution, the Library of Congress, and the National Archives also assisted. Using largely Civil Works Administration money—money for relief employment—the Park Service made a valuable collection "of exact graphic records, 24,000 measured drawings and 26,000 photographs of antique structures important historically or architecturally."[14] These historical records were divided into six categories: Colonial Period, Revolutionary Period, Early Republic, Civil War, War in the West, and Recent Era.

GOVERNMENT EMPLOYMENT APPROPRIATIONS   With so many activities, so much to do, the Park Service would have been swamped if it had not been for the funds distributed by the various government relief and employment agencies set up by President Roosevelt and Congress, for in 1934 direct appropriations for the Park Service were cut more than 50 per cent, from $10,820,000 to $5,085,000. Congress had been wavering between a balance-the-budget program and a "prime-the-pump program," and there were some men in Congress and outside who believed that with the budget in balance the economy would recover naturally. Even Roosevelt, in his 1932 campaign, promised to balance the budget. But this was impossible. Even without any theory of priming the pump, millions of the unemployed would not for an indefinite time peaceably beg handouts from back doors; and relief payments were necessary, the better if coupled with opportunities for useful work.

President Hoover was wedded to the theory of balancing the budget, but in the last year or more he was obliged to distribute relief money, some of which was used to begin the Skyline Drive in Shenandoah National Park.[15] When Roosevelt came in, he set up a bewildering array of agencies to provide work. On March 21,

14 Robert Shankland, *Steve Mather of the National Parks* (New York: Alfred A. Knopf, 1951), 303. *Report, Secretary of the Interior*, 1936, 114; 1937, 45; 1938, 15; 1939, 241; 1940, 269 ff.

15 See p. 263.

1933, just seventeen days after his inauguration, he sent a message to Congress urging legislation to provide employment in forest and land reclamation; and on March 31 Congress passed the Emergency Conservation Act, giving the President authority to establish a series of camps for this purpose—the Civilian Conservation Corps (CCC).[16]

Five days later the President issued an executive order establishing the Office of Emergency Conservation Work and naming Robert Fechner as Director. The Department of Labor chose the men, the War Department moved them to the camps, in the "most rapid mobilization of men in the country's history." Within a little over two weeks after the law was signed, the first camp was set up, in a national forest. An Act of May 12, with later amendments, provided funds for relief of unemployment, to be used for forestry and other conservation activities.[17]

The word "conservation" in Civilian Conservation Corps had a double meaning here, for the agency was designed to conserve not only the resources but the character and morale of unemployed young men by providing productive work in the national forests, national parks and monuments, and in the state and local parks and related areas. In the first year as many as 300,000 men enrolled in the CCC.

The CCC boys did a vast amount of useful work, in reforestation, building ranger cabins and other needed buildings, fire trails, bridges, camp grounds, dams, water and sewer systems, telephone lines, and in clearing out forests to reduce fire hazards, clearing up along roads, and fighting fires, tree diseases and pests. Much of the work was greatly beneficial not only to the forests, parks, monuments, state parks and wildlife refuges—there were thirty-six camps working on wildlife refuges in 1941—but to the boys themselves, who profited from the healthful work, and from educational work offered at the camps. The CCC was generally regarded as a distinct success, and Roosevelt had thought that it should be a permanent agency, but by 1942 the demands of World War II removed the necessity for employment relief and it was abandoned.

Fortunately the Park Service was in a position to take prompt advantage of relief work funds. Beginning under Mather the Service had been constantly busy with planning, and under Albright's

16 Stat. 48, 22.
17 Stat. 48, 55.

direction master plans had been worked out in 1931 and 1932 for many of the parks; so the Service was able to put the men to work without delay. This was also true of the Forest Service but not of the state parks and wildlife refuges, where there were few or no plans, and where the work was often badly managed, with some work done that was of no value or even detrimental finally. As one writer, Albert Atwood, expressed it, there was in some cases too much of "cleaning up, after the manner of city parks; of smoothing, rounding, straightening, manicuring, landscaping." In wildlife refuges the CCC boys drained some marshes along the east coast to kill the mosquitoes, to find presently that they had destroyed the homes of wildlife. At a conference of wildlife and conservation societies in Albany, in October 1935, a resolution was adopted asking that all further work of the CCC be done outside the Adirondack and Catskill parks.[18]

The Emergency Conservation Act of March 31, 1933, also authorized funds for forest research and for the acquisition of land by purchase, donation, condemnation or otherwise. Under this and other acts a considerable amount of land was bought for CCC work, some of it for park use.

In May 1933 the Emergency Relief Act[19] set up the Federal Emergency Relief Administration (FERA) which started with $500 million from the Reconstruction Finance Corporation. Not all the work done was manual: there were seven white-collar projects— assembling, preparing, and disseminating information on travel and recreation facilities; mapping forestry data; in research, museum displays, guide service, and preparing material for publication.[20]

An important by-product of the CCC was the purchase of more than 7 million acres of forest lands for the boys to work on. Roosevelt was a forestry enthusiast, and he spent over $44 million for additional forest lands, largely in the East. Under the Weeks Law of 1911, and the later Clarke-McNary Act of 1924, there had been some purchases each year of forest lands in the East, but Roosevelt more than doubled the area of such lands.[21] He also gave $705,000

18 *Saturday Evening Post*, May 16, 1936, 18; Sept. 9, 1944, A 19.
19 Stat. 48, 55.
20 *Report, Secretary of the Interior*, 1941, 306.
21 Samuel Dana, *Forest and Range Policy* (New York: McGraw-Hill, 1956), 250.

from an emergency fund to buy land in Isle Royale, and $743,365 for land purchase in Great Smoky Mountains, some for rounding out Mammoth Cave National Park.

Soon afterward the National Industrial Recovery Act (NIRA)[22] set up the Public Works Administration (PWA) with an appropriation of $33 million to promote building. This agency spent $2,668,166 on federal recreation projects, loaned $7,997,000 to states and local communities and made grants of over $7 million to such units for recreational developments. This agency spent $20 million on park improvements such as buildings, and $34 million on roads and parkways; it built over 1,000 miles of park roads and 249 miles of parkways. In August 1933, under this act, the Soil Erosion Service—later changed to the Soil Conservation Service—was established in the Department of the Interior, one of the most significant developments in the history of conservation. Roosevelt had been interested in soil conservation for many years.

Depressions often speed up social progress, and in May 1933 Congress set up the Tennessee Valley Authority, largely as a result of persistent efforts of Roosevelt and of Senator George Norris of Nebraska, one of the great figures in the conservation movement and in progressive government generally. The Tennessee Valley Authority has promoted conservation on every front, including recreation, and has attracted the attention of conservationists all over the world; in fact it is one of two great outstanding land policies established by the United States. Our national park system is the other one.[23]

To speed up re-employment, Congress in 1935 again made heavy appropriations for a second public works program, and the President set up the Works Progress Administration (WPA)—later called the Works Projects Administration—to co-ordinate the whole work-relief program. This agency used CCC camps and spent about $13 billions before it was liquidated in 1942, most of it contributed by the federal government but some by local governments. It built buildings, bridges, parks, playgrounds and many other things for municipal, state, and county park projects, mostly municipal. A large proportion of the WPA, CWA (Civil Works Administration) and FERA money was spent on local areas, most of the CCC funds on state areas. In a few cases states set up small roadside parks,

22 Stat. 48, 195.
23 Stat. 48, 58.

where travelers could stop for a short time for rest and lunch. Texas established one of the best systems of roadside parks in the country using National Youth Administration labor.[24]

The expenditure of such vast sums of money called for careful surveys and planning, and in July 1933 the Administrator of Public Works appointed the National Planning Board, which did valuable work during the next several years. Roosevelt was always much interested in planning, particularly land planning.

Work relief funds were spent on other areas than national parks and monuments and state and local parks. As we have seen, much was spent on national forests. In addition to this the Forest Service was increasing its outlay for recreational uses of the national forests —from $65,028 in 1929 to $588,892 in 1938. Some, although not much, was also spent on state forests, the number of which was increasing. Roosevelt wanted more state forests. In 1935 state forests represented a total value of about 15 million dollars. Pennsylvania had 1,650,000 acres, Massachusetts 171,000 acres, and Vermont, New Hampshire, Connecticut, Indiana, Ohio, Illinois, Michigan, Wisconsin, and Minnesota had some state forest areas which to a limited extent were used for recreation. There were some state forests in the West which represented mostly federal grants and were generally not used much for recreation. In 1935 Roosevelt persuaded Congress to pass a bill to authorize co-operation with the states in acquiring state forests, and in co-ordinating federal and state activities in carrying out a national program of forest land management, appropriating $5 million for the project.[25] The Tennessee Valley Authority used some CCC labor, and in addition spent $184,490 up to 1938 for the development of recreational facilities.

Like Mather and Albright, Cammerer was interested in the state parks, and there was a rapid development of these parks in his administration, partly the result of the lush relief work funds available and the work of the CCC camps. In January 1939 the total number of these parks and related areas was reported at 1,397, covering 4,342,863 acres, and serving 75 million visitors. Of particular importance were developments in California. Late in Cammerer's administration the California State Park Commission completed arrangements for the acquisition of 6,772 acres of the Mill Creek

24 *Recreation*, Sept. 1936, 300.
25 Stat. 49, 963.

coast redwoods, the Save-the-Redwoods League contributing the money. The commission and the league immediately proceeded with plans for further purchases.[26]

The state park movement was given a strong push by President Roosevelt when he created the National Resources Board by Executive Order of June 30, 1934, to study the problem of natural resources, including national and state parks and related recreational activities. To prepare the report, the recreational division of the board was set up in the Park Service with George M. Wright, Chief of the Wildlife Division, as director, and Herbert Evison, Supervisor of State Park Emergency Conservation Work, as assistant director.[27] As a preliminary step to wise land utilization in the United States, $25 million was provided by the Federal Surplus Relief Corporation to acquire lands of low productivity or lands not in their proper use, described as submarginal lands, to reallocate them to their best use. Of this amount, $5 million was to be used to acquire certain lands for recreational use, with the Park Service developing this part of the program. Three types of areas were studied: (1) a few well-located regional areas of from 10,000 to 15,000 acres to be used by a large number of visitors, (2) smaller tracts of 1,500 to 2,000 acres near large industrial centers, for use by lower-income people and underprivileged children for family camps and organization camps, and (3) small wayside tracts, or picnic areas.[28]

STATE PARKS AREA STUDY   On March 9, 1935, Representative Robinson of Utah introduced a bill to aid in providing adequate facilities for park, parkway, and recreation-area purposes, but it got no attention.[29] In the same session Senator Wagner of the Committee on Public Lands brought in a bill for the same purpose which was reported and debated briefly.[30] In the second session, Robinson introduced a similar bill "To authorize a study of the park, parkway, and recreation-area programs in the United States,"

26 *American Forests*, Mar. 1940, 134.
27 Shankland, *op. cit.*, 302 ff. *Report, Secretary of the Interior, 1934*, 171.
28 *Report, Secretary of the Interior, 1934*, 172.
29 H. R. 6594, 74 Cong. 1 Sess.
30 S. 738.

which was taken up by Congress in place of the Wagner bill.[31] This second Robinson bill not only authorized a study but provided for the transfer of lands chiefly valuable for park purposes to the states and subdivisions of the states, and it was reported favorably by the House Committee on Public Lands. The bill aimed primarily at providing a comprehensive study of lands suitable for state parks and parkways, but authorized the Secretary to aid the state and local governments in planning, establishing, improving, and maintaining park areas. Subject to the President's approval, it even authorized transfer to any state or local unit by lease or patent the right or title to such lands on the public domain, with reservation of the minerals, the titles to revert to the United States if any state failed to use its land for the purposes designated. If Congress did not affirmatively oppose any transfer of lands made by the Secretary within sixty calendar days, the transfers should become effective. Lands controlled by the Department of Agriculture were not included because the Forest Service wanted no national forest lands transferred to the states.[32]

The bill was approved by the National Conference on State Parks, by the American Planning and Civic Association, the Association of State Foresters, and other organizations interested in conservation; and it passed the House with little opposition, but in the Senate some sniping showed a measure of hostility to the Park Service and to further expansion of the park system. Senator Chavez of New Mexico was concerned lest the establishment of more parks would reduce areas available for grazing. He wanted the public lands in New Mexico turned over to the state, as did also Senator Hatch. The bill provided that land transfers to the states for parks should become effective in sixty days *unless Congress objected,* and this provision met objection from Senator Connally, who saw that Congress could not often act in time to prevent transfers, however unwise they might be. Senator Adams of Colorado, usually an active friend of the parks, was in ill humor, perhaps because the Park Service had objected to the construction of a diversion tunnel through Rocky Mountain Park. Adams criticized what he called the "tremendous propaganda machine" of the Park Service and declared that there was "no limit to their ambition."

31 H. R. 10104, 74 Cong. 2 Sess.
32 *Ibid.*

His hostility sat awkwardly upon him, for Rocky Mountain Park was established more for the benefit of people in the near vicinity than perhaps any other national park.

The main objection to the bill was aimed at the provision authorizing the transfer of lands to the states, and that provision was eliminated by amendment. The bill as passed provided merely for a comprehensive study of the entire park situation.[33] The author is unable to understand the rather heated discussion of the transfer section of the bill, for, as we have seen, a law had been passed in 1926 "To authorize acquisition or use of public lands by states, counties or municipalities for recreational purposes," apparently designed to accomplish the same purpose as was intended here.[34] In 1906, twenty years before this, Congress had given the Royal Gorge to Canon City, Colorado, for use as a park, with a reservation of the right to recover it at any time.[35] In 1938, in the Small Tracts Act, Congress authorized the Secretary to sell or lease for not over five years not more than five acres of public lands as home, cabin, health, convalescent, recreation, or business sites, with a reservation of minerals to the federal government.[36]

The purpose of the Park, Parkway and Recreation Area Study Act of 1936 was to get data for a plan for co-ordinated and adequate public park facilities; and the Park Service was directed to cooperate with other federal agencies and with state and local government units and agencies, and was authorized to aid the states and local units in planning their parks and parkways if they wanted help. The study authorized by the act required several years, and the report was not published until 1941.[37] It was a careful and complete study of the whole problem of recreation, and of national, state, municipal and county parks.

The state park movement got a strong impetus from this act, and another result of it was the Mississippi River Parkway project. Under the act the Park Service reviewed and advised on $100 million worth of park and recreation applications. The advice was helpful in many ways. Most of the state park agencies were staffed with in-

33 Stat. 49, 1894.

34 Stat. 44, 741. See p. 296.

35 H. R. 4546, 59 Cong. 1 Sess. Stat. 34, 238.

36 Stat. 52, 609.

37 *A Study of the Park and Recreation Problem of the United States* (Washington: National Park Service, 1941).

competent, untrained men, often political appointees; whereas the Park Service had trained men, who could assist in planning the landscaping, the buildings, and the administration. Thanks to this help, some of the state parks are artistically planned and a few are well administered.[38]

There had been some interest in national, state, and city planning, particularly land planning, but the movement toward planning received a great impetus from the various work-relief grants early in Roosevelt's administration. The Public Works Administration set up the National Planning Board in July 1933, and this Board and the National Resources Board, and later the National Resources Committee, made and caused to be made a number of significant reports on planning and on conservation; but conservatives in Congress came presently to see that such reports might result in interference with private business and stopped the appropriations. The Parks, Parkway and Recreation Area Study Act of 1936 followed the recommendations of the Recreational Division of the National Resources Board.

RECREATIONAL DEMONSTRATION AREAS   Under the land program of the Federal Emergency Relief Administration a program was instituted in 1934 for the purchase of submarginal land—at a cost of $30 million—and the next year President Roosevelt set up the Resettlement Administration to shift farmers from such lands to better lands. Some of the lands bought were of recreational value, and these, the "recreational demonstration projects," were shifted from the Resettlement Administration to the Park Service for administration in 1936. These recreational demonstration projects, areas of land submarginal for agricultural uses but valuable for recreational uses, particularly for state, local, and municipal parks, had been authorized in the National Industrial Recovery Act of 1933, to be bought and developed as parks and later turned over to the states and municipalities for permanent administration. Later, in 1937, the Bankhead-Jones Farm Tenant Act provided $50 million for the purchase of submarginal lands, but these were under control of the Secretary of Agriculture.[39]

38 See *Park Use Studies and Demonstrations,* issued by the National Park Service, 1941.
39 Stat. 50, 522, 525.

The money needed for the recreational demonstration areas was provided by the various Federal Emergency Relief Appropriation Acts, to be spent by the Federal Emergency Relief Administration under its land program, but the Park Service was to do the developing. By Executive Order of April 27, 1935, the submarginal land acquisition program, of which the recreational demonstration projects were an integral part, was transferred to the Resettlement Administration of the Department of Agriculture.

The Park Service studied the recreational demonstration program, approved a number of projects, and set up CCC camps to begin development. By 1936 forty-six projects had been set up in twenty-four different states, and 397,056 acres of land were acquired for them, mostly to serve people in the major metropolitan areas, for camping, picnics, hiking, swimming and boating. On November 14, 1936, they were transferred to the Department of the Interior, that is, to the Park Service, for land acquisition as well as for development.[40] The visitor use of these areas increased at an amazing rate, doubling every year for the first three years; and by 1940 some 600 rural and urban organizations from 200 communities used the group camping facilities, which were then developed to accommodate 7,500 at a time. Summer camps were operated by counties, Community Chest agencies, city boards of education, Y organizations, youth organizations and other agencies. This testified to the great need for more recreational facilities in the metropolitan areas.

It was not the intention of the Park Service that it should control these areas indefinitely, except perhaps three or four of them. Once planned and developed they were to be turned over to the states or municipalities. In 1939 an act passed Congress authorizing the Secretary to convey or lease them to the states or local government units when they were adequately prepared to administer them; but President Roosevelt vetoed the bill on August 11, 1939, on the ground that some of the projects might be of use to other federal agencies.[41] In 1942, however, a bill was passed providing that the Secretary, with the approval of the President, might convey or lease to the states or political subdivisions thereof any or all of the

40 Exec. Order 496.
41 *Report, Secretary of the Interior, 1939*, 296, 297. H. R. 3959, 76 Cong. 1 Sess.

projects, or convey to other federal agencies; but the grantees must use them exclusively for public parks, recreational and conservation purposes, and if they failed to do so for three years the lands would revert to the federal government.[42]

This act did not end the recreational demonstration area activities of the Park Service, but it marked the beginning of the end which, as we shall see, came within the next few years.

NATIONAL RECREATION AREAS   Akin to the recreation demonstration areas were the "national recreation areas," which, however, differed in being of such national importance that the Park Service planned to keep some of them. The most important of the national recreation areas was the Boulder Dam project—later named "Hoover" Dam. Already in 1930 Lake Mead, above the dam, was reserved with the idea of making it a national monument, and on June 22, 1936, Congress appropriated $10,000 for a study of its recreational possibilities, to be done by the Park Service in co-operation with the Bureau of Reclamation. The recreational possibilities were found good, and development was begun the next year. Appropriations climbed to more than $100,000 in 1940.[43]

Under the agreement with the Bureau of Reclamation, that bureau administers Boulder City, Hoover Dam and Davis Dam below, and the Park Service supervises all recreational activities. Lake Mead is 115 miles long, with 550 miles of highly scenic shore line, several ancient Indian sites, good fishing, and swimming beaches; and it has been developed into a popular recreation area. It is true that the lake falls short of the highest standards in some ways. In summer it is very hot, and the level of the water varies widely—as much as 137 feet—which means that at times there is a wide strip of sand, rocks, or mud around the water. Boulder City has grown to a fair-sized little town, well planned. In its land planning the city has employed the principle of the "single tax," leasing rather than selling urban sites to businessmen.

Other areas followed Lake Mead: Millerton Lake in California, Coulee Dam (Franklin D. Roosevelt Lake), and Shadow Mountain Lake in Colorado. These will be considered later.

42 H. R. 2685, 77 Cong. 1 Sess. Stat. 56, 326.
43 Stat. 49, 1794; 50, 607.

WILDERNESS PARKS   A few of the parks established in Mather's and Albright's administrations had been to some extent "wilderness" parks—with few or no roads or tourist facilities—Acadia, Great Smoky, Grand Teton, and Isle Royale. In Cammerer's administration all the new parks added were wilderness parks. Everglades was the first one.

But the term "wilderness" must be defined and explained for it is subject to serious misunderstanding. Horace Albright and other national park authorities insist that *all* national parks are "wilderness" parks because in every national park, even Yellowstone and Yosemite, the area developed with roads and tourist accommodations is only a very small fraction of the total area of the park, almost all of which is left in its original wilderness state, accessible only by trail. Viewed in this way, the national parks are indeed all wilderness parks; yet it seems necessary to make a distinction, because some parks are more largely developed with roads and accommodations than others. In Yellowstone nearly all the scenic wonders are accessible by automobile, there are accommodations at the important points, and these points swarm with tourists; in Isle Royale there are no roads and only a few tourist accommodations; in Acadia there are roads but no accommodations, at Great Smoky there is one road and practically no accommodations (except campgrounds, which are provided in practically all national parks). There is no clear line dividing wilderness parks from others; it is always "more or less." These new parks were not established as wilderness parks because of any changes in the policy of the Park Service, but because conditions in the areas suggested that as the most appropriate policy. It had been Mather's plan to build one road through each of the national parks, or at least many of them, which would enable visitors to see the great scenery, but no more. This plan was followed in such parks as Yosemite, Glacier, Rocky Mountain, Shenandoah, and Great Smoky Mountains—a wise and reasonable plan.

The distinction, vague as it is, has been the basis of much controversy among the park lovers, the National Park Service usually taking the position that most of the parks should be reasonably accessible although not "developed" too much, while the "purists" or wilderness enthusiasts want few roads or none at all.

EVERGLADES PARK   Everglades National Park, a subtropical park in the extreme southwestern point of Florida, perhaps more important for its rich wildlife resources than for anything else, was authorized on May 30, 1934. The land situation in this general area had not been good for some decades. Under the Swamp Land Act of 1850, the state had got 20 million acres of federal land which was grossly mismanaged in the following years. About 16 million acres of this land was taken over in devious ways, by railroad, canal, and drainage companies.[44] In 1904 the state of Florida launched a drainage program in this area which did great damage—as it has done in many other swampland areas of the country. Only about 25 per cent of the area was suited to agriculture, and the drainage resulted in serious loss of top soil, in some salt water intrusion, and in many disastrous fires. A fire in 1952 burned over 42,984 acres of the Everglades areas, 40,214 acres of which were grassland—not grass such as northerners are accustomed to, but a tough grass that grows shoulder high.

The Everglades area was the home of about 163 varieties of birds, some of them of striking beauty: egrets, spoonbills, Everglades kites, white-tailed kites, Florida sandhill cranes, flamingoes, and many others; and some of these, especially the egrets, were prized for women's hats and as a result were threatened with extinction. As early as 1902, the National Committee of Audubon Societies raised money to employ a warden, but the warden was shot by poachers, and when the man accused of killing him was acquitted the neighbors burned his house. Two of the Society's wardens were killed. In 1910 Governor Hughes signed the Audubon Plumage Bill, outlawing the sale of most wild-bird plumage in New York where the trade was centered, but plumage continued to come into other states, and hunters killed the Florida birds for sale abroad. The 1913 tariff act forbade the importation of plumes. For about forty years, however, the only protection the birds got was provided by the National Association of Audubon Societies.[45]

The massacre of the Florida birds continued down to rather recent times. As an example of this, around 1910 and 1911 Cape Sable was the home of a thousand full-grown flamingoes, but they

44 See the author's *U. S. Forest Policy* (New Haven: Yale University Press, 1920) , 46, 330.

45 *National Parks Magazine,* No. 91, Oct.-Dec. 1947; No. 99, Oct.-Dec. 1949, 28.

were slaughtered and no more were seen for years. In 1941, a large male was seen there, but for five years he came alone. In 1946 he came with a mate but was shot and the mate disappeared.

There was also a great variety of tropical fishes which were being caught by seines and whatever means would yield the largest catch; some of these fishes were becoming hazardously scarce. Seines several miles long were reported to be used. The decimation of some kinds of fish was also a threat to the birds for which they served as food.

For years there was agitation by the Boone and Crockett Club, the Audubon Societies and other conservation societies, and by a few men in Florida and in Congress for an Everglades National Park. President Roosevelt had been interested. The National Parks Association, always deeply interested in primitive and wilderness parks, wanted an Everglades park as early as 1920, and Mather called for it in his 1923 report. In 1925 Barron G. Collier, owner of the Royal Palm Hummock, a short distance north of the Everglades on the west coast of Florida, indicated a willingness to present the area to the United States for a national park.

The first Congressional interest in the Everglades area was concerned with drainage and not the establishment of a park. In June 1906, in the 59th Congress, Senator Mallory of Florida introduced a resolution in the Senate calling upon the Secretary of Agriculture to have a survey made to determine the feasibility of draining the land here, but fortunately it did not pass. Too much land had already been drained. One of the arguments for the resolution was that the western states were getting money for irrigation and that therefore the East should be entitled to some money for drainage.[46] Years later, in April 1926, Senator Trammell of Florida brought up a bill for the establishment of a park in Florida under the name Ponce de Leon National Park, but it got no attention.[47] The next year some Miami boosters decided that it would be good for business to have a national park in the Everglades and put on a campaign to achieve this, but with no success. Early in 1927 Trammell and Representative Drane of Florida tried to get a reclamation survey of the Everglades, but fortunately failed.[48] In the next Congress,

46 S. Res. 65, 59 Cong. 1 Sess.
47 S. 3877, 69 Cong. 1 Sess.
48 S. 5075, H. R. 16084, 69 Cong. 2 Sess.

the 70th, Trammell introduced two Everglades Park bills, one to set up the park and the other to provide for an investigation of the area, but both were lost in committee.[49] In the last session, however, he succeeded, on March 1, 1929, in getting an investigation authorized, without any debate. The Secretary of the Interior was directed to investigate the desirability and practicability of establishing the "Tropic Everglades National Park," the character, ownership, and value of the lands and the cost of acquiring them.[50] In the same session Fletcher tried again to get Everglades Park established, and his bill passed the Senate but got no further.[51]

Secretary Wilbur appointed a committee with Albright, Cammerer, and other men of scientific distinction, and the following year the committee reported favorably, rating the area of definite national park quality, of high educational value, and recommending that it be established to preserve the primitive character of the region and the rich and varied wildlife.[52]

Representative Ruth Bryan Owen, of Florida, promptly introduced a bill in the House to establish Everglades, which was reported.[53] In the next Congress Senator Fletcher and Mrs. Owen brought in park bills, and the Fletcher bill passed the Senate, with amendments.[54] The park was not to be created until Florida turned over the lands needed—2,000 square miles, as recommended by the Secretary. After the bill (S. 475) had passed, someone happened to recall that the Seminole Indians had some rights in the area, so the bill was reconsidered and amended to protect their rights better and then passed again.

In the meantime, the National Parks Association appointed Frederick Law Olmsted and William P. Wharton to study the Everglades, and after they had reported favorably the Association voted its approval of the Fletcher bill.[55]

There was some opposition to this bill on various grounds: first, by creating the national park before the lands had been selected, the bill turned over to the Department of the Interior responsibili-

49 S. 2740, S. 3103, 70 Cong. 1 Sess.
50 S. 4704, 70 Cong. 2 Sess. H. Doc. 654, 71 Cong. 3 Sess. Stat. 45, 1443.
51 S. 5410, 71 Cong. 3 Sess.
52 *Science*, n.s., June 13, 1930, 597. *Report, Secretary of the Interior, 1930*, 83.
53 H. R. 12381, 71 Cong. 2 Sess.
54 S. 475, H. R. 5063, 72 Cong. 1 Sess.
55 S. Doc. 54, 72 Cong. 1 Sess. *American Forests*, Mar. 1932, 188.

ties that belonged to Congress; second, the bill virtually cut off the right of the people to revise the boundaries once they were chosen; and third, the bill failed to stipulate that preservation of the primitive should be the foremost objective of the park. The Wildlife Committee of the House was asked to grant a special hearing on the bill, and agreed to do so. George Collingwood of the American Forestry Association presented a substitute bill, and Director Cammerer agreed on two amendments, one forbidding any federal appropriation for five years, and another decreeing that the park should always remain a wilderness, clear of all developments.[56] The bill, however, did not make any further progress.

The report of the Albright survey committee gave publicity to the Everglades project, and there was strong interest in Congress. Early in 1933 Senators Fletcher and Trammell brought up a park bill in the Senate and Representative Wilcox of Florida introduced one in the House, supported by President Roosevelt.[57] The Senate bill passed the Senate with little debate but the Wilcox bill was debated with some spirit and heat if with less light than might have been desired, and it was the bill that passed both houses in the second session, in spite of an acrimonious attack on it by the Republican minority.

When the Wilcox bill came up in the House, Representative Cox of Georgia called up a house resolution for the House to be resolved into a Committee of the Whole to discuss the bill. The yeas and nays were called for on the resolution, and the vote showed 244 yeas, 87 nays, and 99 not voting. It was recognized from the first that it was largely a Democratic-Republican fight, with few holds barred.[58]

Lehlbach of New Jersey opened the attack on the bill: "This bill is to create a snake swamp park on perfectly worthless land in the State of Florida, so the fact that it would not cost the Government anything for the initial acquisition of this worthless swamp is the height of irony, but if the Government takes this and builds a road at a cost of $1,000,000 to get to it because it will take $1,000,000 to make it accessible, and then pours countless millions into that swamp, it will do something that adds value to the surrounding real estate in Florida. This is the most perfect example of super-

56 *National Parks Bulletin,* No. 60, Spring, 1934.
57 S. 324, H. R. 2837, 73 Cong. 1 Sess.
58 *Congressional Record,* May 24, 1934, 9495 ff.

salesmanship of Florida real estate, although we have seen many of them, that has ever yet been made public."[59]

Taber of New York, seasoned fighter against parks and parkways, insinuated that Henry Doherty, the oil tycoon, who owned hotels in Florida, was a big force behind the bill, and that it was likely to cost the government $100 million in the end. Treadway of Massachusetts suggested that Mrs. Owen had been defeated because she failed to get the park, and that Wilcox had been elected on his promise to get it, which Wilcox denied. McFadden of Pennsylvania went further to suggest that Henry Doherty, in appreciation of Mrs. Owen's efforts, had used his influence to have her appointed Ambassador to Denmark. Martin of Massachusetts conceded that there was much politics in the debate, but insisted that it would cost a great deal of money, and that if the land were of any value Florida would want to keep it. Reed of New York also thought the land worthless and would not "get away," and suggested that such states as New York, Pennsylvania, Michigan, and Ohio were developing their own park systems; why could not Florida do the same? Rich of Pennsylvania was very hostile: "It is time to put a stop to foolish legislation, it is time we woke up and use our own gray matter, and cease to follow some professor who is telling us to enact certain bills into law because some secretary wants it or some department head may have a fancy for the law."[60] On the statement of the promoters of the park that it would be presented by the state of Florida and would cost the federal government nothing, Rich suggested: "Whenever you are offered a gift horse you should look him in the mouth because he is going to require food, and that will cost you money before you get through with it."[61] Several men argued that the House should be devoted to the problem of the depression rather than to the creation of new parks. The opposition paid practically no attention to the real reason for prompt establishment of the park—the threatened extinction of some of the wildlife.

There was some rather frivolous discussion of the alligators and snakes that infested the Everglades—snakes weighing 40 pounds—to which Wilcox replied by quoting from Dr. Raymond Ditmars

59 *Ibid.*, 9497 ff.
60 *Ibid.*, 9510 ff.
61 *Ibid.*, 9507 ff.

of the New York Zoological Park to the effect that there were no more snakes in the Everglades than in New York or Pennsylvania, indeed not so many.[62]

The park advocates replied by pointing to the birds and fishes that were in danger of extermination and to the unique Royal Palms that were about gone. De Rouen of Louisiana, of the Public Lands Committee, listed the government departments and bureaus that favored the bill: the Department of the Interior, Park Service, Bureau of Indian Affairs, Geological Survey, Department of Agriculture, Biological Survey, Forest Service, Bureau of Plant Industry, and the Smithsonian Institution, as well as many conservation organizations and eminent scientists. The Florida representatives asserted that the park would not cost much as a wilderness park, that road-building was cheap in the area because the materials were right at hand, and there would be little road-building anyhow; but there was support from other parts of the country. Willford of Iowa was blunt in his appraisal of the opposition: ". . . When I listened to some of the asinine statements made in derogation of this bill I was not impressed with their soundness. I did not like it when the attack was made on one of our colleagues. Frankly, I wonder if a Republican is trying to beat him. . . . Let us come out in the open, let us fight in the open, let us see things as they are, let us not present counterfeit arguments. Let us get away from personalities."[63]

THE EVERGLADES ACT   In spite of what Blanton of Texas called the "Republican filibuster," the Wilcox bill passed the House, 222 to 145, with an amendment precluding any appropriations for protection and administration for five years. This amendment was thought necessary to get the bill passed. In the Senate the bill was substituted for the Fletcher-Trammell bill, which had already passed, and so it passed with no debate.[64]

As finally passed and approved on May 30, 1934, the Act provided for a park within an area of approximately 2,000 square miles—1,280,000 acres—to be presented to the United States by the state of Florida—the usual provision for eastern parks; and when this area was turned over to the Secretary and exclusive jurisdiction was ac-

62 *Ibid.*, 9504 ff.
63 *Ibid.*, 9508.
64 Stat. 48, 816.

cepted from Florida, the park should be established without further action of Congress. The Federal Water Power Act should not apply, and the act was not to "lessen any existing rights of the Seminole Indians which are not in conflict with the purposes for which the Everglades National Park is created"—which apparently meant that rights of the Seminoles which *did* conflict with the purposes of the park might be ignored. The plan of the Park Service was to use the Indians as guides. The provision that there were to be no appropriations for five years was unfortunate, for the wildlife, especially some of the birds, gravely needed protection.

A few months after this act was passed President Roosevelt issued a proclamation withdrawing all public lands in the area for possible inclusion in the park.[65]

Like most Congressional pledges as to the time or size or appropriations, this one was promptly attacked and soon revoked. The next year Senators Fletcher and Pepper and Representative Wilcox tried to remove the five-year restriction, and Fletcher's bill passed the Senate on August 22, 1935, but that was all.[66] In the next Congress Senators Andrews and Pepper and Representative Wilcox tried to get the restriction removed, and the Wilcox bill passed, and was signed by President Roosevelt on August 21, 1937.[67]

As in the Appalachian parks, the raising of money proved an arduous task. Soon after the authorizing act was passed in 1934 the Governor of Florida appointed an "Everglades National Park Commission" to organize the campaign for land and money, and the legislature passed a law in 1941 authorizing the state to exchange state lands anywhere for private lands in the park. The lands to be acquired were all owned by the state or by private interests. The exact area contemplated for the park seems to have changed from time to time, and to have been very indefinite at any given time. The establishing act called for "all the lands within boundaries to be determined by the Secretary of the Interior within the area of approximately two thousand square miles"—or 1,280,000 acres. This apparently meant that the Secretary might outline a smaller area within these maximum boundaries. The Secretary clearly had wide powers. In 1938 Director Cammerer reported that the park project

65 Exec. Order 6883, Oct. 22, 1934.
66 S. 3197, H. R. 8741, 74 Cong. 1 Sess.
67 S. 2830, H. R. 2014, 75 Cong. 1 Sess. Stat. 50, 742.

involved "more than" 1,000,000 acres, of which 759,520 acres were owned by the state. In 1940 he reported the authorized area at 1,545,092 acres, and in 1941 Director Drury stated it at 1,454,092 acres.

The acquisition of land for Everglades was long drawn out, and since the park was not finally established until late in Drury's administration, in 1947, further consideration of it will be postponed until later.[68]

68 See pp. 508 ff.

CHAPTER XVIII

The Cammerer Administration

1933-1940

BIG BEND PARK, OLYMPIC PARK

⚜ BIG BEND PARK   Big Bend National Park, in Texas, along the Rio Grande River on the Mexican border, was provided for on June 20, 1935. It covers three magnificent canyons, the Chisos Mountains, nearly 8,000 feet high, a few prehistoric cave dwellings, and some reminders of early Indian and pioneer six-shooter and mining days. The creation of this park was largely the result of persistent agitation by two or three men. Captain E. E. Townsend, sometimes called the "Father of Big Bend National Park," became interested in this area as a possible national park as early as 1894. He talked of it for some years to all who would listen, and roused a considerable interest, as a result of which, in March 1933, a bill was introduced and passed the state legislature to make the area a state park, a rather feasible project since much of the land—about 132,107 acres— was owned by the state.[1]

Townsend, who was a member of the state legislature, persuaded Representative R. E. Thomason to come to see the area, and Thomason was so impressed he introduced a bill in the 74th Congress to make it a national park, as did Senators Sheppard and

[1] Virginia Madison, *The Big Bend Country* (Albuquerque: University of New Mexico Press, 1955), 229 ff.

Connally. Conrad Wirth and others of the National Park Service also came to inspect the area and approved it for national park status, supported by a group of visiting scientists.[2]

With almost unprecedented promptness the Sheppard-Connally bill, one of the first presented, approved by Secretary Ickes, Acting Secretary Theodore Walters, and the Senate Committee on Public Lands and Surveys, passed without debate and was signed by President Roosevelt on June 20, 1935. It followed the precedent of the Appalachian, Isle Royale, and Everglades parks in providing for establishment before the exact area was determined. When "title to such lands as may be determined by the Secretary of the Interior as necessary for recreational park purposes within the boundaries to be determined by him within the area of approximately one million five hundred thousand acres . . ." and when jurisdiction was ceded by the state of Texas to the entire area the park was so established, but at no cost to the federal government. The Federal Water Power Act was not to be applied to the park.[3] Texas ceded jurisdiction four years later, on May 12, 1939. Ickes wanted the park to be named the "Jane Addams National Park," after the great social worker Jane Addams, and Roosevelt and even Vice-President Garner agreed to this suggestion. In 1935 Ickes reported in his diary that he was drafting a bill to change the name, but nothing came of it.[4]

Big Bend was intended to be an international park like Glacier-Waterton, and an invitation was extended to the Mexican government to set aside an area on the Mexican side of the boundary. The invitation was received favorably and a joint survey was made by the two governments and tentative boundaries agreed on, 800,000 acres in Texas and 700,000 acres in Mexico. Mexico has not yet created her part of the park, but at last reports still looks upon the project favorably.

Texas proceeded to see what she could do toward acquiring the necessary lands. Early in 1937 a bill was introduced in the state legislature appropriating $1.5 million for this purchase, but in the

2 H. R. 6373, S. 2131, 74 Cong. 1 Sess. Also *Congressional Record*, 2822, 6709, 10464.

3 H. R. 6373, S. 2131, 74 Cong. 1 Sess. Stat. 49, 393.

4 *The Secret Diary of Harold L. Ickes* (New York: Simon and Schuster, 1954) , Vol. I, 385.

paralyzing depression of the time this was reduced to $750,000 and even this amount was vetoed by Governor James Allred on the ground that there were no funds in the treasury to pay it. So the promoters, led by President Morelock of Sul Ross State College at Alpine and a State Park Board of prominent men, proceeded to beat the brush for donations, with rather indifferent results. In May 1939 the state provided for the transfer of jurisdiction over 132,107 acres of state school lands, and reported a total of 145,567 acres of the total of 788,682 acres ready for transfer—not an impressive achievement. On January 16, 1941, however, Governor O'Daniel recommended to the legislature an appropriation of $1.5 million and in July the appropriation was made.[5]

With funds available the State Park Board proceeded to buy land. Most of the land was cheap, of little value even for grazing, but as in the Appalachian parks there were difficulties enough in buying and in securing satisfactory titles. The land was owned by about three thousand individuals, only fifty-five of whom were resident, so the owners had to be found. Over half, however, was owned by only twenty individuals. It was difficult to clear titles, and the state was often obliged to use condemnation suits for this purpose.[6]

The State Park Board proceeded with vigor, and on September 5, 1943, Governor Coke Stevenson presented deeds to 691,338 acres to the Regional Director of Region Three of the National Park Service; and on June 12, 1944, the Secretary of the Interior accepted the deeds, thus establishing the park, with 707,895 acres.[7] Congress voted funds for administration and protection of the new park, but little for development.

The park was established, but there was no legal protection for it except such as might be afforded by the courts in adjacent areas, which were pretty far away. The park needed a commissioner before whom cases could be tried—the story of Yellowstone and the California parks over again, but only for a short time. The park was barely established officially when Representative Thomason brought up a bill to appoint a commissioner, which passed the

5 *Report, Secretary of the Interior, 1941*, 280.
6 See Madison, *op. cit.*, 229 ff.
7 *Report, Secretary of the Interior, 1944*, 223, 224. *National Parks Magazine*, July-Sept. 1944.

House without objection but got no further. The next year he tried again, with the same result; but in 1947 he got results.[8]

In administering and protecting the park the Park Service has had various troubles, rounding up or fencing out trespass stock, some of it from Mexico, occasionally infected with the foot and mouth disease. In Big Bend, as in Grand Canyon and Death Valley, there were some wild (feral) burros, not native to the area, that did damage to the forage. There were and still are few facilities available for tourists, although there are camp grounds and some simple accommodations; and the roads are poor and inadequate. It is not the intention of the Park Service, however, to develop the park very extensively, but to keep it largely a wilderness park.

The relatively small amount of privately owned lands within the boundaries of the park are being acquired as rapidly as funds become available to the Park Service.[9]

OLYMPIC PARK   Three years after Big Bend, on June 29, 1938, the Olympic National Park was established, in the Olympic Peninsula of northwestern Washington, after a checkered history as forest reserve under the Secretary of the Interior (1897-1905), and under the Secretary of Agriculture (1905-9)—all forest reserves were shifted to the Department of Agriculture in 1905; national monument under the Secretary of Agriculture (1909-33), and under the Secretary of the Interior (1933-38); national park in 1938; with its area changed several times.

The Olympic Mountains were first seen by a white man when a roving sea captain, Juan Perez, saw them in 1774 as he sailed along the Pacific Coast. He named them "La Sierra de la Santa Rosalia," or Saint Rosalie Mountains; but the name did not stick, and fourteen years later an English captain, John Mears, saw them from the coast and named the highest mountain "Mount Olympus"—believing it deserved the dignity of association with its great namesake, the home of the Greek gods. The name was accepted and today we have Mount Olympus, the Olympic Mountains—the entire range— the Olympic Peninsula, the Olympic National Forest, and the city

8 H. R. 4697, 78 Cong. 2 Sess. H. R. 1705, 79 Cong. 1 Sess. H. R. 490, 80 Cong. 1 Sess. Stat. 61, 91.
9 H. R. 1527, 83 Cong. 1 Sess. Stat. 67, 497.

OLYMPIC NATIONAL PARK

WASH.

OREGON | IDAHO

═══ Principal road ▬▬▬ Present park boundary

─── Former Mount Olympus National Monument ─ ─ ─ Boundary of Olympic National Park, 1938

0   5   10   15
SCALE of MILES

Neah Bay

JUAN DE FUCA STRAIT

Port Angeles

OZETTE LAKE

Soleduck River

OLYMPIC NATIONAL FOREST

MT. ANGELES
6,454

BLUE MT.
6,007

HURRICANE RIDGE

Elwha River

OLYMPIC

Lapush

Hoh River

MT. CARRIE
7,018

MT. OLYMPUS
7,954

MT. TOM
7,180

MT. FERRY
6,220

MT. QUEETS
6,525

NATIONAL

Dosewallips R.

OLYMPIC OCEAN STRIP

Queets River

QUEETS CORRIDOR

FOREST

HOOD CANAL

PACIFIC OCEAN

Quinault River

OLYMPIC NATIONAL FOREST

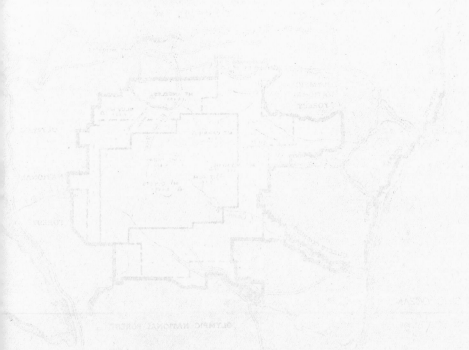

of Olympia, the capital city of Washington.[10] This region was not much explored until fairly late, but from the 1880's on there was the usual procession of hunters, trappers, mining prospectors, settlers, lumbermen, speculators, and land grabbers.

Much of the Olympic area was established as the Olympic Forest Reserve on February 22, 1897, by executive order of President Cleveland.[11] In April 1900 President McKinley restored a large part of it to the public domain;[12] in 1907 it was enlarged.[13] In 1909 some was restored to the public domain on demand of mining proprietors who claimed that there were rich deposits of minerals there, especially manganese;[14] but much of the land restored found its way into the hands of lumbermen and land speculators.

There were early attempts to make a wilderness national park of what was left of the forest reserve—or "national forest" as it was called after 1907. In 1904 Representative Cushman of Washington introduced a bill for an "Elk National Park" here, which was honored with a report; and Representative Humphrey made an effort to protect the game, which was not reported.[15] In 1906 and 1908 similar bills also failed.[16] National park advocates were concerned about the Roosevelt elk, along with the scenery and some of the magnificent "rain forests." In this area were some of the largest trees in the world, next to the Sequoias—the largest specimens of Douglas fir, red cedar, Alaska cedar, western hemlock and Sitka spruce in the world; and the trees grew in dense stands because of the heavy rainfall—nearly 160 inches annually, the highest in the United States.

Near the end of President Theodore Roosevelt's administration Representative Humphrey easily persuaded him to proclaim the Mount Olympus National Monument in the Olympic National Forest, covering 615,000 acres, to assure protection of the Olympic elk, or "Roosevelt" elk, and some of the splendid forests.[17] This

10 Irving R. Melbo, *Our Country's National Parks* (Indianapolis & New York: Bobbs-Merrill, 1941), Vol. II, 121 ff.

11 Stat. 29, 901.

12 Stat. 31, 1962.

13 Stat. 34, 3306.

14 Stat. 35, 2247.

15 H. R. 10443, H. R. 13291, 58 Cong. 2 Sess.

16 H. R. 15335. 59 Cong. 1 Sess. H. R. 14037, 60 Cong. 1 Sess.

17 Stat. 35, 2247.

proclamation did not change the administrative agency of course, and it did not prohibit forest use but merely decreed that the monument use should be dominant. Although an important purpose in the proclamation was to protect the Roosevelt elk, the monument was not closed to hunting and trapping until October 5, 1927, by President Coolidge. The monument proclamation brought strong protests from various commercial interests, particularly from mining prospectors, who saw manganese as a very important resource in the area, although none had been found in the monument.

The complaints of the miners led Humphrey to introduce a bill in 1911 to change the monument to Mount Olympus National Park and permit mining and timber cutting, but this bill was not drastic enough to please the miners, lumbermen, chambers of commerce, and industrial development fanatics, who refused to support it and killed it.[18] A similar bill introduced by Senator Jones also failed.[19] A few years later Senator Jones and Representative Johnson presented bills which were also ignored.[20]

In the meantime, however, in 1912 President Taft proclaimed a small reduction in area to permit certain land claimants to secure titles, and on May 11, 1915, President Wilson proclaimed a reduction of nearly one-half to release minerals claimed to be in the monument. We had not yet entered the First World War, but were providing war supplies for England and France.[21] This reduction, blamed partly on the Forest Service, reduced the monument to only 299,340 acres; and stripped it of most of its timber.

This "rape of 1915" was a blow to the park promoters, and for several years not much was done. In 1933 President Roosevelt transferred the monument, along with all others, to the National Park Service, and this had important consequences. Park devotees began to wonder why, since Mount Olympus was already in the Park Service, it should not be a national park. The Emergency Conservation Committee was organized, with Mrs. Rosalie Edge, a New York leader in the conservation movement, as chairman, and Irving Brant, well-known writer, as secretary; and this committee published a pamphlet, *The Proposed Olympic National Park,* which created a great deal of interest for and against the park. Brant had

18 H. R. 12532, 62 Cong. 1 Sess.
19 S. 5257, 62 Cong. 2 Sess.
20 S. 3486, H. R. 6864, 64 Cong. 1 Sess.
21 Stat. 37, 1737; 39, 1726.

the ear of Roosevelt and also of Secretary Ickes, and doubtless had much to do with the final establishment of the park.

As in so many of the parks—Yellowstone, Yosemite, Rainier, Crater Lake, and Glacier—Mount Olympus had her wildlife problems, particularly that of lack of low ground for winter forage for the Roosevelt or Olympic elk. The closely trimmed monument was nearly all high land, much of it alpine, with private ranches between this and lower grazing grounds, and the elk would not or could not go down past these ranches, in some cases because the settlers kept packs of dogs that drove them back to the high lands. In some places elk were starving, although in other places there was plenty of feed. There were investigations, by the Park Service, the Forest Service, and the Boone and Crockett Club of New York, and proposals that the private lands be bought and that a large national park be created, but for some time nothing was done.

In 1933 the Forest Service and the State Game Commission declared a four-day open season and 150 elk were killed. This brought outcries from the conservationists, gave impetus to the park movement, and scared the Forest Service out of further open seasons for two years. In 1936, 1937, and 1938 certain areas were opened again, and the 1937 eight-day open season in west Jefferson County proved good ammunition for the park advocates. *"Four thousand hunters* concentrated in the area, used great quantities of intoxicating liquor, had six accidents, two fatal, perpetrated many law violations, killed more than 800 elk and let a great deal of meat spoil. What was more, a study revealed that many of the elk were killed on the understocked portions of the drainages, below the overgrazed areas."[22]

It was not elk, however, but timber that proved the most controversial problem. The great forests of the Pacific Northwest were approaching their end, and lumbermen were determined to get the remnant proposed for the park, while the conservationists were as stubbornly determined to save the last stand of the great Washington forest. As early as June 1926, Representative Johnson had brought in a park bill, but it was not considered.[23] His failure discouraged further attempts for several years, but on March 28, 1935,

22 Ruby El Hult, *Untamed Olympics: The Story of a Peninsula* (Portland, Oregon.: Binforde and Mort, 1954), 219. See this very interesting book for the whole story of Olympic.

23 H. R. 13069, 69 Cong. 1 Sess.

Representative Wallgren made a determined effort to get the Mount Olympus National Park established, adding 400,000 acres to the monument, the Roosevelt elk coming in as an added recommendation for the bill. It was reported favorably, without amendment, approved by the Educational Conservation Society and various other conservation organizations and, of course, by Ickes and Cammerer of the Park Service; but in the haste and confusion of the last days of the session it failed of further consideration.24

During the summer there were further surveys of the area, and the Park Service asked Wallgren to introduce another bill, which he did, but this time for an addition of 320,000, not 400,000 acres, to make a park of 642,000 acres, provide better range for the elk, and include some timber. The 80,000 omitted covered much inferior land, but also some fine Douglas fir as well as Lake Quinault, which Cammerer wanted included. The National Parks Association sent two representatives to the Olympic to study the area, and on their report decided to support the measure. The association, always favorable to strictly wilderness parks, wanted an amendment to prevent any commercial development "or plan for the entertainment of visitors" if it would interfere with primitive natural conditions, but Wallgren refused to include this lest he encounter objections from his constituents.25

Wallgren's discussion on H. R. 4724 was wise and farsighted: "Today in Washington State the logger is moving into the last virgin stands of timber. Until recently these stands were ignored for the timber near the seacoast could be cut at greater profit. What now if this timber is turned over to the logger? What will be the future benefit to our State and the Nation? Will payrolls boom in some sections for a few years and then disappear? Will only charred stumps be left to remind us of former grandeur?

"The story of the lumber industry is one of slashed and burned-over forests, of low wages, of stranded populations and of eventually useless lands. What proof have we that it will be different in the future? Only the promise of a not very reliable industry. When logging and milling is in process settlements are built. Homes, schools, churches, and stores represent the investment of workers who thought the timber assets were everlasting. Then suddenly the

24 H. R. 7086, 74 Cong. 1 Sess.
25 H. R. 4724, 75 Cong. 1 Sess. *National Parks Bulletin*, No. 64, Dec. 1937, 10 ff.

timber in the area is exhausted and assets become liabilities. The result is a ghost town amid fire-blackened snags and stumps, the unburied skeletons of forest beauty."

Wallgren saw that the practice of selective cutting was not perfectly adapted to forest conditions in Washington: "Selective cutting means that the big tree will be felled and the smaller ones left for the future. Can you evaluate the efficiency of such a system where a tree 14 feet in diameter stands closely flanked on all sides by smaller trees? You who have never seen logging operations in such a forest cannot visualize the felling of a giant Douglas fir 200 to 300 feet tall. . . . Never does one know what other trees will be crushed, mangled, and hurtled through the air by the falling giant."

Wallgren quoted from the National Resources Committee to the effect that available timber supplies would be largely depleted in twenty-five years and argued that the tourist industry would last longer: "The tourist industry may not be as definite as the lumber industry, yet it is a real industry. With only a vague set of promises as to the foundation for sustained yield on the timber side of the argument, I think that definite experience can show that the real sustained yield for this area is to be found in the tourist trade which cannot but be attracted to such a unique recreational area."[26]

Proponents of the park faced strong opposition during these years. Of course lumber interests were opposed, and the lumber business was the most important business in the locality, with many employed in it. As usual in national park problems, there were a few miners or would-be miners who conjured up visions of mineral wealth and opposed the creation of the park. Many of the newspapers and a considerable number of the local citizens were opposed, yet there was some support even locally. The Forest Service furnished some of the most tenacious opposition. Under the Roosevelt Reorganization Order of 1933, the Mount Olympus National Monument, along with other national monuments administered by the Forest Service, had been turned over to the Park Service; and any enlargement of the monument must come from the Olympic National Forest. The hearings on these bills were a several days' battle between the Forest and Park services before the House Committee on Public Lands, with Ickes and former Director Albright furnishing much of the fireworks. Finally the American Forestry Association made the suggestion that a committee of disinterested

26 *Congressional Record*, 75 Cong. 1 Sess., Appendix, 1416 ff.

experts study the problem. Secretary Wallace of the Department of Agriculture agreed, but Secretary Ickes refused. President Roosevelt favored the park and his influence was persuasive, but neither of the Wallgren bills was ever debated in the House.[27]

In the summer of 1936, in an effort to forestall the new park, the Forest Service designated certain lands adjacent to the national monument as "Primitive Areas"—kept as wildernesses free of roads or improvements—somewhat like wilderness national parks, such as Olympic was to be. To give this arrangement the appearance of permanence it was done through a Departmental Order of the Secretary of Agriculture, rather than by mere administrative regulation. This method of undercutting the demand for more parks had been used widely by the Forest Service, and there were some fifty such "Primitive Areas" in the scenic regions of western national forests.[28]

In September 1937 President Roosevelt, in one of his characteristic dramatic moves, visited Port Angeles. He gathered together in the Lake Crescent Tavern the Washington senators and representatives, with representatives of the Forest Service and Park Service, and turned on the Roosevelt charm for a couple of hours, dissipating some of the bellicosity of the warring groups. The next April he held another conference at the White House in Washington where he tried to get further agreement. Encouraged by Roosevelt's support Wallgren ventured another park bill in March 1938, this time to establish the *Olympic,* not *Mount Olympus* National Park, of 860,000 acres, plus a 50,000-acre parkway along the Pacific Ocean from Cape Flattery to the Queets River. Governor Martin of Washington promptly challenged the size of the park, said 450,000 acres would be about right. Roosevelt wanted a park bill passed that session and suggested as a compromise a reduction to 680,000 acres, with a provision that would permit the President later to expand the area to 892,000 acres by proclamation, after consultation with the Governor of Washington, the Secretary of the Interior, and the Secretary of Agriculture. There was agreement on these provisions, and with a special message from Roosevelt to Congress urging passage and with the approval of many conservation organizations, the Wallgren bill moved promptly through Congress with

27 *National Parks Bulletin,* No. 62, Feb. 1937, 7; No. 64, Dec. 1937, 10 ff.
28 *National Parks Bulletin,* No. 62, Feb. 1937, 7.

little debate, but with committee amendments and changes which
need not be considered here.[29]

The act as approved by President Roosevelt, on June 29, 1938,
abolished the Mount Olympus National Monument and established
the Olympic National Park, of 648,000 acres. A small area covered
by the national monument and omitted from the park was returned
to the Olympic National Forest. Mining entries were permitted for
five years in the east part of the park, and of course all valid land
claims were protected. Counties that were partly in the national
forest and partly in the park were to get national forest revenues in
the proportion that the area in both national forest and national
park bore to the total areas of the counties—the Forest Service paid
to the states or counties 25 per cent of all revenues from the sale of
timber. The provision authorizing the President, after eight months,
to add to the park by proclamation any lands in the Olympic National Forest or lands acquired by gift or purchase, after consulting
the Governor, the Secretary of the Interior, and the Secretary of
Agriculture, was a concession to state interests and to the Forest
Service, but it was largely a gesture, for if the President found the
Governor and the Secretary of Agriculture opposed he could nevertheless make the additions in conformity with the law.[30]

With the park established, there were eight months for President
Roosevelt and the Governor and Secretary of Agriculture to get
together on the additions—Secretary Ickes, of the Department of the
Interior could be trusted to agree to any additions, the more the
better, for Ickes was much interested in Olympic. There was the
usual tussle between the Forest Service, which wanted the least
possible addition, and the Park Service, which wanted as much as
possible, the lumber interests siding with the Forest Service and the
citizens divided. Finally, on January 2, 1940, Roosevelt proclaimed
an addition of 187,411 acres, to take in the great rain forests of
Bogachiel, Hoh, Queets and Quinault river valleys on the west side
of the park extending down toward the Pacific Ocean; the great
Elwha River Valley on the north, with the "panoramic country"
behind it—Hurricane Hill, Obstruction Point and Deer Park, famous winter sports regions which in summer afforded magnificent
outlooks over the Strait of Juan de Fuca and the snowcapped peaks

29 H. R. 10024, 75 Cong. 3 Sess. Hult, *op. cit.*, 224 ff. Stat. 52, 1241.
30 Stat. 52, 1241.

around Mount Olympus; the "Seattle Skyline" of high peaks and the valley of the Dosewallips on the east; part of the valley of the Skokomish on the southeast; and the north shore of the beautiful Lake Quinault. These additions brought the area of the park up to 835,411 acres—62,881 short of the maximum allowed by Congress.[31]

President Roosevelt also authorized the Public Works Administration to acquire a strip down the Queets River Valley to the ocean, and a strip along the ocean—altogether 47,000 acres. The Queets Corridor had some fine stands of timber and the Ocean Strip covered a beautiful stretch of the coast where there was good fishing and clam digging. The Park Service set about to make appraisals and plans for buying, for much of the land was privately owned. There was some local opposition to further additions to the park, yet the people of Port Angeles and local officials asked that a 20,600-acre area known as the Morse Creek Watershed, including Mount Angeles, Lake Angeles and some fine Douglas fir timber, should be added to protect the city water supply; and Roosevelt proclaimed the addition on May 29, 1943.[32]

During these years the Olympic was up for a great deal of discussion, in Congress and in the Olympic locality. In the first session of the 76th Congress, in 1939, several Olympic bills were offered in Congress by the Washington delegation. Senator Bone and Representative Wallgren wanted to provide for the acquisition of non-federal lands in the park; Representative Wallgren wanted the government to accept jurisdiction; Representative Smith wanted to authorize the acquisition, rehabilitation, and operation of facilities in the park.[33] Wallgren's bill (H. R. 6559), to accept cession of jurisdiction was debated at some length but did not pass. In the next Congress Wallgren, risen to the dignity of Senator, offered the bill again, and Representative Jackson introduced a similar bill, which passed without debate and was signed by President Roosevelt on March 6, 1942. This act contained the usual provisions for the protection of wildlife, property, and scenery and for the appointment of a commissioner with jurisdiction over offenses. The act accepting jurisdiction did not specifically give the state the right to

31 Stat. 54, 2678. *1940 Yearbook, Park and Recreation Progress* (National Park Service), 19.

32 *Report, Secretary of the Interior, 1943*, 211. Stat. 57, 741.

33 S. 1511, H. R. 3660, H. R. 4928, H. R. 5446, 76 Cong. 1 Sess.

tax persons, their franchises and property in the park, but the state had ceded jurisdiction with that reservation so it had that right. There had been commercial fishing in the park, and the act provided for regulation of fishing: "nor shall any fish be taken out of any of the waters of the park, except at such seasons and at such times and in such manner as may be directed by the Secretary of the Interior."[34]

Senator Bone's bill to provide for the acquisition of private, state, and county lands, introduced in 1939, did not get any attention, but in 1942 Representative Jackson offered a similar bill which passed both houses without debate, and was signed by President Roosevelt on December 22, 1942.[35]

There were some privately owned vacation facilities in the Olympic area owned by the Olympic Recreation Company and the Olympic Chalet Company, built before the park was established. The Park Service wanted to get and rehabilitate or scrap them, and persuaded some of the Washington delegation in Congress to try to get a bill through Congress to permit this. Representative Smith tried it in the first session of the 76th Congress, but without success. Four years later Representative Norman brought up a bill which passed Congress without debate.[36]

World War II came in December 1941, and presently there were demands on the park, which was believed by some of the mining fraternity to have valuable minerals. Representative Jackson brought up a bill in 1942 to extend the mining section of the establishing act of 1938, which had provided prospecting rights for only five years—now nearly expired—but it was not reported. In the next Congress Representative Magnuson introduced a bill to provide prospecting and mining rights for the indefinite future, but it also failed of a report.[37]

During the war the War Production Board called upon Secretary Ickes to open the park to lumbering of some of the Sitka spruce, the best lumber for airplanes. This put Ickes in a tight place, where he had to choose between despoiling the park and holding

---

34 H. R. 6559, 76 Cong. 3 Sess. S. 1333, H. R. 4336, 77 Cong. 1 Sess. Stat. 56, 135.

35 S. 1511, 76 Cong. 1 Sess. H. R. 7191, 77 Cong. 2 Sess. Stat. 56, 1070.

36 H. R. 4928, H. R. 5446, 76 Cong. 1 Sess. H. R. 1654, 78 Cong. 1 Sess. Stat. 58, 793.

37 H. R. 7449, 77 Cong. 2 Sess. H. R. 3084, 78 Cong. 1 Sess. S. 1470, 79 Cong. 1 Sess.

up the prosecution of the war. He declared that he would turn over some of the timber if it were absolutely necessary, and did allow some cutting; but before very great damage had been done the War Production Board found that it could get Sitka spruce from Canada, and that aluminum was better anyhow.

At the end of the war, however, the Olympic ran into rough seas. Soldiers came home from the war to find insufficient housing; and the lumbermen pointed to Olympic as the very best place to get the lumber to build more houses—for soldiers mainly, of course, because it was a patriotic duty to build homes for returning heroes, and here patriotism and profits could be served at the same time. For several years the Park Service fought off the lumbermen and the Forest Service, both of which believed that standing mature timber should be cut. The sight of so much beautiful timber, some of it mature or even partly down and rotting was something to stir a forester's soul to battle, and to inspire a lumberman to start filing his saws. The lumber market was good; and the lumbermen were determined that Olympic should disgorge some of its timber.

In the 79th Congress, in 1946, Senator Magnuson introduced a bill to eliminate some privately owned land, but failed.[38] The next year he introduced a bill to eliminate 18,185 acres, mostly private lands on which there had been lumbering, and Norman offered a House Joint Resolution calling for a nine-member commission to study the boundaries of the park and recommend needed changes. The commission was to consist of one representative each from the Washington State Conservation Commission, the National Parks Association, the National Park Service and the Forest Service; and five from the local towns. Such a commission would have been heavily weighted against the park, for only the National Parks Association and the Park Service would have been likely to oppose drastic reductions. Such a commission would certainly recommend drastic reductions, and its recommendations might have great weight in Congress; so Secretary Krug and the Park Service opposed strongly.

It appeared likely however that action of some kind would be taken in Congress, and to stave off something worse as a result of the joint resolution Secretary Krug at first agreed to support bills introduced by Representatives Norman and Jackson, reducing the park by 56,000 acres with one-seventh of the commercially valuable

38 S. 2266, 79 Cong. 2 Sess.

timber, including the 18,185 acres of private lands that Magnuson had proposed to eliminate. Krug believed it would be better to lose this than run the risk of losing much more; but it presently became apparent that the lumber interests of Olympic Peninsula and Gray's Harbor were determined to eliminate much more anyhow, after they had got this, so Krug withdrew his approval. The lumbermen were organized for a knock-down, drag-out fight, and by this time the conservation organizations of the country were alert too, and many of them had representatives at the hearings at Lake Crescent in September 1947, hearings on several of the bills that had been presented. It was expected that there would be further hearings in Washington, D. C., later, in order that the views of individuals and organizations in the East might be presented; but no further hearings were held, and none of the bills was reported from the committee.

Concurrent resolutions were presented late in the 1948 regular session of Congress by Representative Mack and Senator Cain to establish a joint investigating committee from the House and Senate, but they were not reported. So the Olympic National Park came through a tough battle unscarred; but it was obvious that in the next Congress the fight would be on again. The fact that so many of the Washington delegates were working so persistently for reduction of the park indicated that they had strong popular support at home, but the fact that none of the measures introduced was even reported showed that the Public Lands Committee was friendly to the park.[39]

In the next Congress, in 1949, Mack and Cain were up again with concurrent resolutions to establish a joint Congressional investigating commission, but Cain seemed rather apathetic about the business and nothing came of it.[40]

In the meantime, the Park Service had been busy acquiring private lands in the Queets Corridor and Ocean Strip as a Public Works Project; and on January 6, 1953, President Truman proclaimed an addition of 47,754 acres in these areas and in the so-

[39] S. 711, S. 1240, H. R. 2750, H. R. 2751, H. R. 4053, H. R. 4054, H. J. Res. 84, 80 Cong. 1 Sess. S. Con. Res. 55, H. Con. Res. 203, 80 Cong. 2 Sess. *Report, Secretary of the Interior, 1947*, 319, 337. *National Parks Magazine*, July-Sept., Oct.-Dec. 1947.

[40] S. Con. Res. 5, H. Con. Res. 11, 81 Cong. 1 Sess. H. R. 8160, 81 Cong. 2 Sess. *American Forests*, Dec. 1946, 568; Dec. 1947, 535, 537; Mar. 1948, 98 ff.; July 1948, 324.

called Bogachiel Strip in the northwest part of the Olympic area.[41] These additions brought the total area of the park near the limit set by the establishing act of 1938. The Park Service got 470 acres more by exchanging wind-blown timber in the park for it—a trade of somewhat questionable wisdom, for it was said that the lumbermen doing the clearing, not very punctilious as to what they took, sometimes cut trees that were standing rather firmly. The Park Service had been generally opposed to such exchanges.

Here was a pretty mess—the park enlarged instead of reduced! There was much criticism of Truman's action—"another example of power-hungry federal bureaucrats usurping State rights," as Representative Mack described it. An editorial in the Aberdeen *Daily World* declared: "The enormity of the steal cannot be judged without taking into account the people of the Queets Valley who have been dispossessed, the removal from public use of the lands on the western slopes of the Olympics, the locking away of tremendous wealth in forests and minerals and water power, and the removal of the best tree-growing land on the globe."[42] There was criticism of the policy of leaving dead and down timber as likely to lead to forest fires, of what Mack called the "socialization" of the tourist business, and of the failure to develop the park to attract tourists, of the closing of the land to mineral development, and of the purchase of agricultural land with PWA funds. As to wildlife, it was argued that a dense forest is not good for game—which is generally true. More than half the workers in the area were employed in the lumber industry, and local boosters wanted full employment as long as the timber would last.[43]

Supporters of the large park area answered that the interests of the entire country should be weighted more heavily than the interests of a small locality, and that in the long run the community itself would gain from the preservation of these magnificent forests, for the lumber business as usually carried on was a temporary, exploitive business that left only dreary cut-over lands; that there was plenty of timber outside the park if the lumbermen would cut less wastefully, and that we could afford to preserve a wilderness area with trees growing, maturing, dying, and falling to the ground.

---

41 Stat. 67, C27. *Report, Secretary of the Interior, 1953,* 293.

42 *Congressional Record,* 83 Cong. 1 Sess., Appendix, 140.

43 *Congressional Record,* 83 Cong. 1 Sess., Appendix, 118, 140; Jan. 7, 1953, 243, 244. *American Forests,* Sept. 1954, 30 ff.

That was the natural cycle of birth, growth, and decay. It was true that there were some very valuable trees here, but as one writer said, "so are there very valuable lands in Central Park, New York." Even if the plan had been to lumber these trees finally, their preservation might have been a good business proposition, for stumpage values have usually tended to rise; we have always cut our forests too fast.

In 1954 the park boundaries were again examined by a special committee appointed by Governor Arthur Langlie. After the examination was completed, the Governor was reported as reconciled to the boundaries existing.

To fend off some of the criticism, the Park Service began a road into the park to extend as far as Hurricane Ridge, in 1950, and made plans for the development at Hurricane Ridge of dining facilities and a ranger station. From this point there is a magnificent view of the Olympic Range and of the ocean. There are several other roads in the park but they do not penetrate far, and there are tourist accommodations at several points. The plan still is, however, to keep most of the park a wilderness.

CHAPTER XIX

The Cammerer Administration

1933-1940

KINGS CANYON PARK, NEW NATIONAL

MONUMENTS, MOUNT RUSHMORE

KINGS CANYON PARK   Kings Canyon National Park in the
Sierra Nevada, enclosing magnificent mountain and canyon scenery
like that of Yosemite, grew out of agitation for enlargement of
Sequoia park, which it is, essentially. John Muir visited the region
in 1875 and was vastly impressed with it, always insisting that it
was as fine as Yosemite. When he saw it the next time, in June 1891,
the lumbermen were blowing giant sequoias to bits with dynamite,
sheep were skinning the mountainsides, sheepmen were shooting
and poisoning the wild game and setting many fires. Muir thought
the region should be made a national park, and at the request of
Robert Underwood Johnson, editor of the *Century Magazine*, wrote
an article with illustrations, on "A Rival of Yosemite, the Canyon
of the South Fork of the Kings River," which was reproduced in
summary in *Planning and Civic Comment*. Johnson and his *Century Magazine* did much to stir up interest in this region.[1]

The bill introduced by Senator John F. Miller in 1881 could be
classed as a Kings Canyon bill, for it covered a much larger area
than that of Sequoia Park as it was set up. Beginning in 1879,

[1] *Century Magazine,* Nov. 1891, 77. *Congressional Record,* 76 Cong. 3 Sess.,
Appendix, 3390.

Secretary of the Interior Carl Shurz under President Hayes, one of the great Secretaries in our history, took a deep interest in the preservation of the giant sequoias of California; and in 1885 Secretary L. Q. C. Lamar, in the Cleveland Administration, suspended land entries in eighteen townships in Fresno and Tulare counties, including many of the sequoia groves. In 1889 there was planned a withdrawal of the entire forest region from Yosemite (then a state park) southward to Kern County; but there was much pressure on the Secretary to rescind the withdrawals. Commercial interests were strong, but Colonel Stewart and his friends got the closely clipped sequoia and General Grant parks,[2] and two years later the Sierra Club was organized by John Muir and other devoted men to fight for a big Kings Canyon, for the next half-century as it turned out. In 1906 the Sierra Club sent a report to the President, the Secretary of Agriculture, and the Chief Forester, urging better protection of the Kings Canyon area.

In 1891 Secretary John W. Noble had submitted a report of the California Academy of Sciences urging park status. In 1893 and 1894, Captain James Parker, Acting Superintendent of Sequoia under Secretary Hoke Smith, called for a park here, as did Secretary Hitchcock in 1900, 1903, and 1905. In 1910, Secretary Ballinger urged that the boundaries of Sequoia be extended; in 1911, Secretary Fisher declared they should be extended "very greatly." From 1915 to 1918, every report of Secretary Lane called for an extension to take in Kern Canyon, Kings River Canyon to the north, and Mount Whitney on the east—somewhat the same area covered later by Kings Canyon park. Sequoia had been established to protect the giant sequoia trees, and Lane pointed out that it had no remarkable scenery and needed that of the Kings Canyon country. In 1916 R. B. Marshall, Superintendent of National Parks, urged expansion of Sequoia to include more scenery and also more giant sequoias.

Beginning in 1910, there were efforts to extend Sequoia by Senators Flint, Sherman, and Phelan, and by Representatives Kent and Elston.[3] Phelan's bill (S. 2021) "to add certain lands to Sequoia National Park and change the name to Roosevelt National Park"—the name "Roosevelt" carried weight at the time—passed the Senate,

2 See Chap. III.

3 S. 10895, 61 Cong. 3 Sess. H. R. 13168, 64 Cong. 1 Sess. H. R. 21104, 64 Cong. 2 Sess. S. 2875, 65 Cong. 1 Sess. H. R. 10929, 65 Cong. 2 Sess. H. R. 14332, S. 2021, 65 Cong. 3 Sess.

amended by the Senate Committee on Public Lands and Surveys to permit mining, but in the House committee it fell among assassins. A majority of that committee decided that since there was disagreement between the Forest Service and the Park Service as to the proper boundaries of the park, it should not be expanded but only the name changed. A minority report urged expansion, but to no avail. In opposition to this measure, as to most measures for expanding Sierra park areas, were the sheepmen who had profitable grazing privileges and were tearing up the mountain slopes with their "hoofed locusts." The Phelan bill got no further.

In the next Congress, the 66th, there were several bills for the enlargement, by Senators Johnson and Phelan, and by Representative Elston.[4] Phelan's bill, to increase Sequoia's area by about 400 per cent—a real Kings Canyon bill with the name Roosevelt—introduced on June 5, 1919, elicited a committee report but was not considered in the Senate; and Elston's bill, also for enlargement and change of name to Roosevelt, was cut to ribbons in the House Committee on Public Lands. The Forest Service objected to the inclusion of some forest lands, the ranchers and livestock men wanted no restriction of their grazing permits, and the lumbermen and the farmers of the San Joaquin Valley wanted the timber from the forests; so the bill was amended in the committee to effect a *reduction* of the park by 150,000 acres. Mount Whitney and other high mountains were to be included—they had no grass or timber on them—but a big slice of timberland in the south part of the park was to be cut out. Fortunately the bill as amended did not pass.

In the next Congress, on June 29, 1921, Representative Barbour of California decided to make a stab at a Kings Canyon Park—called Roosevelt-Sequoia, however, with the Sierra Club working to iron out the differences between the Forest Service and the Park Service. The Barbour bill would have eliminated 97 square miles of forest land along the southwest boundary—to please the Forest Service— but would have added 953 square miles along the northern and northeastern boundaries, to take in mountain peaks and some giant sequoias of ten-foot diameter or more. Unfortunately, the San Joaquin Light and Power Company and the city of Los Angeles had filed applications for six power sites in the area. In the debates in the House the sheep and cattle men, the sportsmen, and the irrigation

4 S. 2118, S. 1391, H. R. 5006, 66 Cong. 1 Sess.

farmers of the San Joaquin Valley, who looked forward to irrigation dams and reservoirs up in the mountains, were opposed. Representative Mann of Illinois, ever-vigilant guardian of the Treasury, objected to a provision in the bill which would have abolished the act of 1900 authorizing the use of troops in park protection, although troops were no longer used. Representative Frothingham was concerned about the bears that had been "killing and wounding" people in the parks, and there was some opposition to the change in name. On the other hand, W. B. Greeley, of the Forest Service, defended the bill with vigor, declaring that ordinary timberlands, mineral lands, and grazing lands had been excluded, and that there was no justification for water power developments in the new park.[5]

Among the opponents of the Barbour bill was the conservation zealot, Willard Van Name, of the American Museum of Natural History, who objected to the elimination of timber lands in the south part of Sequoia, lands which under the bill were transferred to the Forest Service. On these lands there were some 550 giant sequoias of which 140 were privately owned. Van Name argued that the lands added were mostly bare rocks needing no protection whereas the forest lands eliminated, including the giant sequoias, should be preserved—but the Forest Service promised to preserve the sequoias. Writing in such reputable journals as the *New Republic, Science,* and the *Outlook,* Van Name attracted a considerable amount of attention and bolstered opposition to the new park.[6]

The Barbour bill ran into too strong opposition and did not pass the House, but agitation for enlargement of Sequoia continued, the Sierra Club leading. Mather and Albright and Secretary Work called for it again and again; but against it were the commercial interests and the city of Los Angeles. There was something devious about the demands of Los Angeles. The city government was said to have a thirty-year partnership agreement with the Southern Edison Company dividing the power sales market. The company guaranteed the city enough power to fill its needs in emergency, and the city in turn agreed to turn over to the company any surplus power it might acquire from its increasing number of plants. It was expected that

5 H. R. 7452, 67 Cong. 1 Sess. *National Parks Bulletin,* No. 22, Nov. 8, 1921; No. 23, Dec. 14, 1921; No. 24, Jan. 30, 1922.

6 *Science,* Dec. 22, 1922, 705; Jan. 19, 1923, 82. *New Republic,* Feb. 7, 1923, 286, 288; Feb. 14, 1923, 322. *Outlook,* Mar. 28, 1923, 567.

within ten years Hoover Dam would meet all possible needs of the city, and then the power from the Roosevelt-Sequoia dams would go through city wires to the company for sale in the general market outside Los Angeles.[7] On June 15, 1923, the Federal Power Commission rejected Los Angeles filings in Tehipite Valley and Kings River Canyon.

In the 68th Congress, on December 20, 1923, Representative Barbour brought up another bill to enlarge Sequoia and change the name to Roosevelt-Sequoia, but it was not reported from the committee.[8] Undeterred, Barbour introduced another bill in the next Congress, as did also Senator Shortridge, also of California. Barbour's bill, more than doubling the size of the park—including the Kern and Keweah sections and Mount Whitney but omitting the Kings River area, and so falling far short of the aspirations of the conservationists—and surrendering some lands to the Forest Service, passed and was signed by President Coolidge on July 2, 1926. It was debated at some length in the House, most of the debate, however, centering on the name. Some representatives objected to the name "Roosevelt," others wanted Sequoia spelled "Sequoyah" like the name of the Indian chief.[9]

The Barbour Act was just hors d'oeuvre to the park expansionists, who continued to press for further additions. In the very next Congress, in February 1928, Representative Crail of California tried to get further additions but failed.[10] Senator Johnson of California brought up a bill in 1935, in the 71st Congress, to establish the *Kings Canyon National Park,* which was supported by the Educational Conservation Society and other conservation organizations, but was not accorded a committee report.[11] In 1938 Senator Murray of Montana introduced a bill to add the Redwood Mountain giant sequoia grove to Sequoia Park, and Representative De Rouen of Louisiana brought up a Kings Canyon bill, but neither was reported.[12] On February 7, 1939, Representative Gearhart of California presented a bill for the "John Muir-Kings Canyon National

7 *National Parks Bulletin,* No. 33, Mar. 8, 1923.
8 H. R. 4095, 68 Cong. 1 Sess.
9 H. R. 9387, S. 4258, 69 Cong. 1 Sess. Stat. 44, 818.
10 H. R. 11189, 70 Cong. 1 Sess.
11 S. 2289, 74 Cong. 2 Sess.
12 S. 3973, H. R. 10436, 75 Cong. 3 Sess.

Park," later changed to "Kings Canyon Wilderness National Park," and still later to the "Kings Canyon National Park" as the bill moved through committees and Congress.[13] In the same Congress Murray introduced another bill to add to Sequoia.[14]

The Gearhart bill covered much of the mountain area north of Sequoia, but to the disappointment of the National Parks Association and other conservation organizations, omitted the beautiful Tehipite Valley and the majestic Kings Canyon, left for possible reservoirs which might, however, be used by the Park Service as recreational areas. On the other hand, about 5,763 acres of the Redwood Mountain giant sequoias, privately owned with taxes in default, were taken in and soon afterward were bought. The General Grant National Park was abolished and added to Kings Canyon as the General Grant Grove section.

On June 2 the bill was reported by the House Committee on Public Lands with several evil amendments: allowing dams and reservoirs in the park, allowing road construction without limitation and hotels and recreation facilities with little limitation, and authorizing the Secretary to extend grazing permits for the lifetime of present permittees and their heirs. The name was changed to Kings Canyon. In the House, on July 18, a House Resolution presented by Representative Sabath of Illinois brought the bill up and it was debated at considerable length, and with vigor.

Representative De Rouen of Louisiana, of the Public Lands Committee, befriended the bill from the start and explained and defended its provisions. Englebright of California argued that the bill provided nothing that had not already been provided and might "prevent the development of natural resources." He said that some twenty water users' associations were opposed, and that the bill was opposed by the legislature of California, the California State Chamber of Commerce, the Farm Bureau organizations and the livestock associations. He declared that the park would cut down power development needed by the farmers who irrigated from wells. O'Connor of Montana said that the Park Service protected forests against fire better than the Forest Service; Elliott was concerned about the hunters and fishermen and thought that in a bad drought the live-

13 H. R. 3794, 76 Cong. 1 Sess.
14 S. 631, 76 Cong. 1 Sess.

stock men would need the land for grazing. He also said that the park would cost Tulare County $850.29 in taxes! The Forest Service was favorable to this bill, and Elliott ventured the opinion that pressure had been brought to bear—presumably by President Roosevelt— to get the foresters lined up. Horton of Wyoming argued that the multiple-use principle of the Forest Service was better than the single use of park lands. Rich of Pennsylvania, usually hostile to the western parks, objected to the federal government providing playgrounds for everybody, thought most people needed work more, and that the federal government was going bankrupt. Shafer of Wisconsin was opposed. Cochran of Missouri objected to dams in the park. Gearhart presented an editorial from the *Los Angeles Times* asserting that most Californians favored the park, that it had always been defeated by the power interests; and he listed a number of daily newspapers that favored it. Englebright of California tried to get the bill recommitted but failed by a vote of 205 to 140, and the bill passed the House.

On February 19, 1940, in the third session of the 76th Congress, the bill came up in the Senate. Pittman of Nevada pounced upon it— said the legislature of California was strongly against it, as were some seventy-two organizations in the state, and that the Forest Service was doing a very good job of conservation and a better job on recreation than the Park Service. Ashurst of Arizona thought the federal government was getting too much power, and that the President had set aside too many national monuments. There was not very much opposition in the Senate, however, and with President Roosevelt's backing the bill passed without difficulty, and was signed by the President on March 4, 1940, to include an area of 454,600 acres.

THE KINGS CANYON ACT   The Kings Canyon Act as finally passed did not please anyone entirely. The park advocates were disappointed because Tehipite Valley and the canyon of the South Fork of Kings River were cut out by sliver-shaped excisions, but there was consolation in the fact that the act said nothing about dams and power projects in the park, and in the fact that the Bureau of Reclamation indicated that it had no designs on Tehipite Valley or Kings River Canyon but preferred dams at Pine Flat and on the North Fork of the Kings, the latter in the distant future, both outside the park. At the same time that Gearhart introduced his park bill he introduced also a bill to provide for the construction of the Pine Flat Reservoir and other works in the Kings River Basin, outside the park, and also a bill to authorize construction of distributing systems for irrigation in the Central Valley Project, near Mount Shasta, perhaps hoping to divert reclamation activities away from the park.[15] Grazing permits already in force were not affected, but were to be subject to regulation by the Secretary to protect the land. The General Grant National Park was converted into the General Grant Grove as a part of Kings Canyon park, and the President was authorized to add to it the Redwood Mountain Grove, one of the finest of the giant sequoia groves, a part of which had been acquired by the Park Service. This addition was proclaimed by President Roosevelt on June 21, 1940.[16] Through this grove section the General Grant Grove was connected with Sequoia Park, and it should have been made a part of Sequoia. It is about six miles from the nearest point in Kings Canyon.

Kings Canyon was to be a wilderness park, and the Secretary was authorized in his discretion "to limit the character and number of privileges" granted, none to be for more than five years. The bill had originally included a provision that no structure should be erected except by federal funds, but this had been struck out in the House Committee on Public Lands. The original bill had provided that no roads should be built except in the lower part of the canyon of the South Fork of Kings River, but this had also been cut out in the House Committee. Appropriations for the park were made, however, subject to this provision—a provision inserted in the appropriation bills by Representative Albert Carter of California. A road runs up the South Fork of the Kings River only as far as the Copper Creek area; otherwise there are no roads in the park. It is a wilderness park.[17]

Kings Canyon National Park was thus finally established, after a sixty-year struggle against power and irrigation interests, lumbermen, ranchers, cattle and sheep men, hunters, and at times the Forest Service. Hundreds of men and women, including a number of

15 H. R. 3792, H. R. 3793, 76 Cong. 1 Sess. See also H. R. 9046, 76 Cong. 3 Sess.
16 Stat. 54, 2710.
17 Stat. 54, 41.

Senators and Representatives and scores of organizations worked tirelessly for it—one of the finest national parks. Credit should go to so many that it seems invidious to point to any, but probably Secretary Ickes, behind him President Roosevelt, and Representatives Barbour and Gearhart, and, of course, Director Cammerer and his Park Service, especially Regional Director F. A. Kitridge, may be mentioned. Ickes worked very hard on this project.

A few things have happened since the park was established. The five-year limit on permits did not prove satisfactory and ten years later, on August 17, 1950, Congress eliminated this provision to make the term of permits twenty years, the same as in other parks.[18]

In 1948 the city of Los Angeles filed several applications for water and power development, but the Sierra Club filed briefs in protest before the Federal Power Commission, and the Commission rejected the applications. In the next two years several bills were introduced to develop water power not only in the Tehipite Valley and Kings Canyon, which had been carved out of the park, but also in the park. In 1952 Los Angeles filed applications for power developments in Tehipite Valley and Kings Canyon and several places within the park. These applications were protested by Secretary Chapman, Director Wirth, and by the Sierra Club and the Fresno Chamber of Commerce; and Secretary Chapman requested a joint survey by the Park Service and the Bureau of Reclamation to see if there were not sites outside the park and excluding Tehipite and Kings Canyon that would serve reasonably well.[19]

THE SOUTHERN PARKS   Great Smoky Mountains, Shenandoah, and Mammoth Cave, had been authorized earlier, but two of them were finally established early in the Cammerer administration: Great Smoky Mountains on June 15, 1934, and Shenandoah on December 26, 1935. Isle Royale was finally established on April 3, 1940, not long before Cammerer resigned, but Mammoth Cave was not established until July 1, 1941, after Cammerer's resignation. There had been much difficulty in raising the money to complete Mammoth Cave, partly because of the high prices asked for the Great Onyx Cave and Crystal Cave; and in 1937 Congress passed an act authorizing the Secretary to exclude these caves from the

18 Stat. 64, 458.
19 *Report, Secretary of the Interior, 1950,* 306; 1952, 355.

maximum boundaries.[20] An act of June 5, 1942, authorized their inclusion, and efforts are still being made to acquire them.[21] For several years lands were added to these southern parks from time to time.

ADDITIONS TO PARK AREAS   Additions were made to several other parks. In June 1935 the Wind Cave National Game Preserve was added to the Wind Cave National Park.[22] In May 1938 Congress appropriated $30,000 for the addition of lands to Rainier.[23]

On June 20, 1938, Congress enlarged Hawaii National Park to take in a fine beach and primitive Hawaiian village, additions wanted by the Park Service to preserve an area of Hawaiian culture. Under this act, the Kalapana seacoast extension was declared open to home sites for Hawaiians only, and fishing in the area was also open only to Hawaiians.[24] On the same day Congress added to Isle Royale 100,000 acres that had been bought with emergency relief funds.[25] On February 12, 1938, Congress appropriated $743,265 for the purchase of lands in Great Smoky Mountains; in February 1939 President Roosevelt proclaimed an addition of 39,488 acres to Carlsbad Caverns[26]; and on January 2, 1940, as we have seen, he proclaimed an addition of 187,411 acres to Olympic.[27]

The campaign for the extension of Yellowstone southward to include Jackson Hole was not forgotten during these years. As long as he was Superintendent of Yellowstone, and later Director, Albright worked hard for this, but Jackson Hole was not made a national monument until 1943, and added to Grand Teton in 1950. Discussion of the long-drawn battle to achieve this will be postponed until later.[28]

Like Mather and Albright, Cammerer always wanted the restoration to Yosemite of the Minarets region which had been cut out in 1905, but this was never achieved.

20 Stat. 50, 871.
21 Stat. 56, 317.
22 Stat. 49, 378, 383.
23 Stat. 52, 330.
24 Stat. 52, 781.
25 Stat. 52, 785.
26 Stat. 53, 2523.
27 Stat. 54, 2678.
28 See Chap. XXIII.

THE SUGAR PINES NEAR YOSEMITE   Some giant sugar pines and other trees bordering Yosemite had been bought by the government and John D. Rockefeller, Jr., in Albright's administration, as we have seen,[29] but there were still nearly 8,000 acres of these giant trees in private ownership along the Big Oak Flat Road, which Cammerer wanted to add to the park. In particular, the Carl Inn tract, owned by the Yosemite Sugar Pine Lumber Company, would soon be cut. This tract had originally been in the park but was taken out. In 1932 and 1933 Senator Nye, chairman of the Public Lands and Surveys Committee, introduced bills "To provide for the restoration, through exchange, of certain timber lands to Yosemite," but they got no attention.[30] Early in 1936 he tried again but again without results.[31] Early the next year, undeterred by the opposition of the Forest Service, Senator McAdoo and Representative McGroarty of California brought in identical bills to provide for the purchase of the lands, and the McAdoo bill passed the Senate with little debate. The McGroarty bill encountered more opposition in the House. The timber was in Englebright's district and he saw nothing good in the bill. It would throw a thousand men out of work, he said, would bankrupt the logging railroad built into the area and take the jobs of the 125 men working on it, and deprive other industries of transportation facilities. O'Malley of Wisconsin very properly asked if the operations would not have to stop anyhow when the timber was cut. Englebright thought that there were as good sugar pines elsewhere, that California had plenty of parks and forests, that the purchase of these trees would not bring more people to the park, and by taking this property off the tax rolls would levy a heavy burden on one of his counties. To compensate for this burden, he insisted on an amendment compensating the county, even including delinquent taxes that the lumber company had been unable to pay. There was strong opposition to this amendment, and it was voted down, and the bill passed by a vote of 183 to 128. In the Senate there were minor amendments which called for a conference committee, but the conference committee report eliminating the compensation to Tuolumne County passed both houses without debate, and was

29 See pp. 337 ff.
30 S. 4472, 72 Cong. 1 Sess. S. 19, 73 Cong. 1 Sess.
31 S. 615, 74 Cong. 2 Sess.

signed by President Roosevelt on July 9, 1937.[32] The act authorized the Secretary to buy or condemn the lands, and pay for them "under any fund of moneys available for such purpose . . . except from the general fund of the Treasury." The money was to come from available relief funds.

The McGroarty bill passed after the end of the fiscal year, however, and the money had to be reappropriated, and soon, if the sugar pines were to be saved, for the lumber company had begun cutting. The company, like most lumber companies at the time, was in financial straits and likely to grab at any possible income, therefore likely to cut the trees soon; so McAdoo offered an amendment to the deficiency appropriation bill, which was accepted, and on August 25, 1937, $2,005,000 was made available for purchase, which was consummated early in 1939.[33]

The acquisition of these sugar pines should be credited partly to a newspaperman, Irving Brant, who thought the sugar pines more magnificent than any other trees but the giant sequoias and coast redwoods, and called on President Roosevelt to see if some way could not be found to save them. Naturally the President was interested, as was also Ickes, and they helped to get the money needed.[34]

NEW NATIONAL MONUMENTS   Some splendid national monuments were established. Less than two weeks after Cammerer assumed office, President Roosevelt proclaimed *Cedar Breaks* National Monument in Utah, an amphitheater-shaped escarpment, 2,000 feet high, of rich and brilliant colors. Here some forty-seven shades, mostly of pinks and reds—are displayed with an effect as brilliant as that of Bryce Canyon, although the minarets that make Bryce Canyon so unique are lacking. An elevation of 10,400 feet at the top provides cool weather all summer and plenty of rain for fine forests, particularly aspens, which grow in amazingly crowded

[32] S. 1791, H. R. 5394, 75 Cong. 1 Sess. Stat. 50, 485.

[33] Stat. 50, 485. *Report, Secretary of the Interior, 1938,* viii. *Congressional Record,* Aug. 20, 1937, 9433. Carl Russel, *One Hundred Years in Yosemite* (Yosemite National Park: Yosemite Natural History Association, 1957), 163. *Nature Magazine,* June 1935, 327.

[34] *The Secret Diary of Harold L. Ickes* (New York: Simon and Schuster, 1957), Vol. II, 32.

stands.[35] On June 14, 1934, Congress authorized the Secretary to establish the *Ocmulgee* National Monument in Georgia, covering ancient Indian mounds, presumably burial mounds, when the lands should be presented to the government without cost; and, in 1936, the required lands having been vested in the government, President Roosevelt proclaimed the monument.[36] Here was a case where Congress provided for the establishment of a monument. In 1941 Roosevelt proclaimed the addition of an area thought to cover an ancient Indian stockade.[37]

In January 1935 President Roosevelt proclaimed the *Fort Jefferson* National Monument, including the *Dry Tortugas Islands* south of Florida, mainly to preserve the massive old fort—the largest all-masonry fortification in the western world—built in 1846 to control the Florida Straits. In this fort was later imprisoned Dr. Samuel Mudd, the man who, probably in entire innocence, had set John Wilkes Booth's leg after Booth had shot Lincoln, and who later when "pardoned" had much to do with the discovery of the relation of mosquitoes to yellow fever. The Dry Tortugas Islands are the home of a wide variety of bird and marine life, somewhat like Everglades Park.[38]

On August 10, 1936, *Joshua Tree* National Monument in southern California was proclaimed to preserve what was named by the Mormons "Joshua Tree"—a many-armed giant species of yucca of the lily family, growing to a height of forty feet—and other desert plants and animals, including a type of desert bighorn.[39] The establishment of Joshua Tree was at least partly due to the interest and efforts of a wealthy Pasadena woman, Mrs. Sherman Hoyt, "friend of the desert," who by personal interview got F. D. Roosevelt interested. There was so much private land in Joshua Tree Monument that for several years it was impossible for the Park Service to provide protection and development. *Organ Pipe Cactus* National Monument, on the Mexican border in Arizona, was proclaimed in April 1937, in spite of the opposition of local prospectors, who saw vast mineral wealth just beneath the surface. The organ pipe cactus grows in bunches, without arms like those of the

35 Stat. 48, 1705.
36 Stat. 48, 958; 50, 1798.
37 Stat. 55, 1654.
38 Stat. 49, 3430. *National Parks Magazine,* July-Sept., 1957, 112.
39 Stat. 50, 1760.

Joshua tree, to a height of twenty feet. In the proclamation, the Papago Indians were granted the right to pick the fruit of the organ pipe and other cacti.[40] In addition to this and other species of desert plants found nowhere else in the United States, the monument also protects the Gaillard bighorn sheep.

One of the most beautiful areas in the entire park system, *Zion National Monument*, was proclaimed by President Roosevelt on January 22, 1937, to include red rock Kolob Canyons and other canyons and adjacent areas northwest of Zion National Park. Just before 1930 several homesteads and a dude ranch had been considered for this area, and in March 1930 an article by Dr. George Middleton in *Touring Topics* directed attention to the scenery here. National Park Service officials were asked to explore it, which they did, and, as a result of their exploration and recommendations, the area was reserved from entry and later established as a national monument. The canyons here are like Zion Canyon but narrower, perhaps more brightly colored, and not quite so deep. They are inaccessible by automobile, however, for the monument has been maintained as a wilderness area. It was quite worthy of national park status and in July 1956 was added to Zion park.[41]

Another national monument of very great beauty was proclaimed by President Roosevelt on August 2, 1937—*Capitol Reef* in Utah, an area of red and multicolored cliffs, canyons, and one natural bridge—an area once known as the Wayne Wonderland. The place was advertised and promoted for years by a Mormon bishop of Torrey, Ephraim Pectol, who finally got the Park Service interested. The colored cliffs are as fine as can be seen almost anywhere, and there are two very narrow canyons through the "reef" from west to east, Grand Wash and Capitol Gorge. In both the road follows the bed of a dry wash between almost perpendicular walls hundreds of feet high, so narrow in places that two cars cannot pass. Only the Capitol Gorge road goes all the way through the "reef"—about four miles—and cars caught in the gorge by a sudden heavy rain have occasionally been dashed to pieces. Capitol Reef, almost more interesting than Bryce, in the opinion of the writer, is quite worthy of national park status.[42]

40 Stat. 50, 1827. *Natural History,* Mar., 1952, 120.

41 Stat. 50, 1809; 70, 527. *National Geographic Magazine,* Jan. 1954. *National Parks Magazine,* July-Sept. 1957, 115.

42 Stat. 50, 1856.

Later in August, Congress established *Pipestone* National Monument, in Minnesota, covering catlonite or red pipestone from which the Indians had long made smoking pipes. The quarries were reserved exclusively to the Indians.[43]

In April 1938 President Roosevelt proclaimed the *Channel Islands* National Monument, off the coast of southern California, where were found a large rookery of sea lions, nesting sea birds, and fossils of Pleistocene elephants, ancient trees and various other scientific values.[44] The next year, in May 1939, *Santa Rosa Island* National Monument, in Florida, was proclaimed, valuable for geological and scientific reasons, but was abolished in 1946. In July *Tuzigoot* National Monument was proclaimed, a monument of ancient Indian ruins in Arizona.[45]

A number of interesting historical monuments were set up in the Cammerer regime that can only be mentioned: *Andrew Johnson* in Tennessee, *Fort Laramie* in Wyoming (the state of Wyoming appropriated money to buy the land for Fort Laramie), *Ackia Battleground* in Mississippi, and *Homestead* in Nebraska. Homestead National Monument, which marked the first claim homesteaded under the Homestead Act of 1862, was set up by Congress on March 19, 1936, with an appropriation of $24,000 to be used for suitable buildings for a museum on pioneer life. Pioneer life always had a strong appeal in Congress. *Whitman* National Monument in Washington, was authorized by Congress on June 29, 1936, to mark the site of the place where missionaries Marcus Whitman and his wife and twelve others were massacred by the Indians in 1847. The land was donated by two local organizations. The *Cumberland Gap* National Historical Park, of both scenic and historical value, was authorized by Congress on June 11, 1940; and the *National Cemetery of Custer Battlefield* Reservation was granted $25,000 for a museum in 1939, and transferred from the War Department to the Department of the Interior on July 1, 1940. Six years later the name was changed to *Custer Battlefield* National Monument.

The *Chesapeake and Ohio Canal* was purchased by the federal government in 1938 with $2 million of public works funds; and another $500,000 of public works money was given for surveys, re-

43 Stat. 50, 804.
44 Stat. 52, 1541.
45 Stat. 53, 2542, 2548. Stat. 60, 712.

search, and some development, the Civilian Conservation Corps and the Public Works Administration doing much of the work under the supervision of the National Park Service. President Roosevelt was much interested in the restoration and preservation of the canal.

ADDITIONS TO THE MONUMENTS   During Cammerer's term a number of the monuments were enlarged. A little was added to Muir Woods; Death Valley had needed some land with springs, and in 1937, 305,920 acres were added; Montezuma Castle got an accretion as did Tonto and Wupatki. Presidential proclamations added 203,885 acres of scenic canyons to the small fossil-bearing area of Dinosaur, a large acreage to Black Canyon of the Gunnison, a modest amount to Walnut Canyon, and 29,160 acres to Arches. Chiracahua, Tuzigoot, and Big Hole Battlefield were expanded a bit, an island in the Platte River was added to Scotts Bluff; and 904,960 acres were added to Glacier Bay, to include more glaciers and more land for the Alaska brown bear and other wildlife.

On the other hand, the Lewis and Clark Caverns were turned over to Montana in August 1937. For some years they had been closed to the public because the Park Service could not afford a custodian, but the gate could be forced open, and there was much vandalism. Grand Canyon National Monument was reduced considerably.

The Badlands National Monument in South Dakota had been authorized in 1929, the land to be acquired by the state of South Dakota; and in June 1936 Congress authorized the President to add more land to it by proclamation, to bring it up to a maximum of not over 250,000 acres. On January 25, 1939, President Roosevelt used this authorization to add more than 150,000 acres.[46] The creation of Badlands Monument was largely due to the efforts of Senator Peter Norbeck, of South Dakota.

MOUNT RUSHMORE NATIONAL MEMORIAL   In the same year that Badlands was authorized, 1929, Congress took a step for the creation of one of the most controversial additions to the park system—the Mount Rushmore National Memorial, the faces of

[46] Stat. 45, 1553; 49, 1979; 53, 2521.

Washington, Jefferson, Lincoln, and Theodore Roosevelt carved in giant relief in the granite of Mount Rushmore, in the Black Hills, South Dakota.

The sculptor, Gutzon Borglum, had been working on a memorial to the Confederacy on Stone Mountain, near Atlanta, Georgia. This memorial attracted the attention of Doane Robinson, South Dakota state historian at Pierre, in 1923, and he wrote to Borglum, who was having trouble with his southern sponsors, inviting him up to the Black Hills to look over a possible memorial there. Borglum came, was impressed, and chose Mount Rushmore for the memorial. Senator Norbeck, who had become interested in the project, at first objected to this choice, but later became reconciled to it. The Rapid City chamber of commerce paid the expenses of this survey.

The state assumed responsibility for the project but failed to provide funds. With some help, Rapid City then raised money for houses for the workmen, and Samuel Insull gave a power plant for the work; but there was not enough money to go ahead. In the summer of 1927, however, President Coolidge was induced to come to the Black Hills for his vacation, and he became interested. He introduced Borglum to Andrew Mellon, Secretary of the Treasury, who used his influence to get Congressional legislation to help with finances. The state, not a populous or wealthy one, had bitten off more than it could chew and, as with some of the eastern parks, the federal government was called on to bail out the enterprise.

On January 19, 1925, Representative Williamson of South Dakota had introduced a bill in the House "To authorize the creation of a national memorial in the Harney National Forest," the memorial to be the faces of Washington and Lincoln only, carved on a high rock at no expense to the federal government; and this bill passed Congress with almost no discussion. Since the memorial was to be in a national forest the authorization by Congress was necessary.[47] On March 29, 1928, Williamson brought in a bill "Creating the Mount Rushmore National Memorial Commission and defining its purposes and powers"—really to take charge of the work—and on the next day Senator McMaster of South Dakota introduced an identical bill in the Senate.[48]

The Senate bill passed both houses after some debate. The faces or figures of Jefferson and Theodore Roosevelt had been added to

47 H. R. 11726, 68 Cong. 2 Sess. Stat. 43, 1214.
48 H. R. 12521, S. 3848, 70 Cong. 1 Sess.

the project, and there was a rumor that the figure of Calvin Coolidge was to be added to the others on the mountain, whereat there were a few jocose remarks. Discussing the House bill, Representative Black of New York—a loyal Democrat—declared that the inscription on the memorial should be: "The farmers asked of Coolidge bread, and he gave them this stone. . . ." "However," he added "future generations may decide that a bust of Cal should be erected. That would be a bust. The statues of the other patriots would fall off their pedestals laughing at Cal in a Tom Mix suit, riding an iron horse with the sofa only 20 feet away. Or, perhaps there will be a frieze (or freeze) of Cal, couchant, a la Big Chief Pain-in-the-Neck, making funny faces at a couple of little brook trout rampant."[49] Black thought there would be more logic in erecting a statue of Woodrow Wilson, but was informed that there was no intention to add Coolidge or anyone else. There was some questioning as to the policy of carving statues or figures of presidents in particular states at federal expense—there had been a proposal for such a memorial in Tennessee—but the bill withstood all criticism, and with various amendments passed both houses and was approved by President Coolidge on February 25, 1929.[50]

The Mount Rushmore Act of February 25, 1929, provided for the appointment by the President of a Mount Rushmore National Memorial Commission of twelve members to serve without salary, which should supervise the work according to Borglum's plans; $250,000 was authorized for this, to be matched fifty-fifty by funds from other sources. It was apparently believed that this sum would be enough to complete the enterprise, but private sources did not provide much money, so little of the appropriation could be used and not much was done. In 1934 $250,000 was granted with no matching requirement, and, in 1935, $200,000 more. In each case, the amount appropriated was believed to be enough to complete the job; but, in 1938, $300,000 more was granted and the project was turned over to the National Park Service. Even this was not enough, and when Gutzon Borglum died on March 6, 1941, there was still some work to be done. His son Lincoln was appointed to finish the job but it was never really completed. The original plans had called for completion of the figures down to the waist, but the faces were about all that were done.

49 *Congressional Record*, May 28, 1928, 10391.
50 Stat. 45, 1300.

The work had cost nearly a million, $836,000 of which was contributed by the federal government, and was far short of Borglum's original grand plans. He had envisioned a grand staircase leading up to the base of the great figures, with a great hall carved in the rock in which there should be placed historic records and bronze busts of great Americans. These projects were not even started, and there were thousands of tons of rock debris piled up around the monument. To finance the completion of some of the unfinished work, Senator Gurney and Representative Case tried in 1947 to get Congress to authorize the issue of not more than 2 million special silver 50-cent coins, but with no success. There was a rash of these special "coin" bills before Congress at the time and Senator Fulbright objected to all of them. His objection stopped consideration of the Gurney and Case bills.[51]

Mount Rushmore has probably been dedicated more often than any other park area. There were ceremonies when the work was started, in 1927, and unveiling ceremonies when each of the heads was completed. Whether the memorial was worth so much ceremony is a question on which there is no agreement. Some artists find the memorial quite inartistic, artificial, incongruous, even a bit blatant, particularly at night when the floodlights play upon it; others insist that it is really impressive, grand in conception, big, as befits a nation that has many big things. It is perhaps the biggest thing of its kind in the world—the faces alone are about sixty feet high, and with the possible exception of Roosevelt's face, they are surprisingly well done. Surely our government has spent a million dollars for many things that were worth less.

In recent years there has been some cleaning up of the area around the memorial and considerable improvement in roads and tourist facilities, for Mount Rushmore is a popular tourist attraction. Gutzon Borglum and his wife were buried in the monument area in accordance with an act passed in 1941.[52]

51 S. 1042, H. R. 2278, 80 Cong. 1 Sess. S. 1657, 83 Cong. 1 Sess. There was some objection to government striking of medals in another case, as recorded in 1926. Longfellow's early home in Portland, Maine, was owned by a private individual, and the federal government was reported striking off 500,000 medals for him which he could sell for any price that seemed profitable. (*Congressional Record*, May 14, 1926, 9459.)

52 Stat. 55, 584.

CHAPTER XX

The Cammerer Administration

1933-1940

PARKWAYS, SEASHORE AREAS,

PROBLEMS OF PARK ADMINISTRATION

PARKWAYS   An important result of the depression and the distribution of money for relief work was the building of several parkways, mainly in the South. One or two of them were scenic. This movement began late in President Hoover's administration. Hoover had a camp on the Rapidan River, in the area being acquired for the Shenandoah National Park, and while there he conceived the idea of the Skyline Drive along the crest of the Blue Ridge, and in 1932 gave some relief money for the construction of the drive.[1]

This was the beginning of the era of federal parkways. The parkways were built and later maintained at federal expense, but the states provided the rights of way. There was nothing in the laws establishing the parkways stipulating the width of the rights of way, but in Congressional debates it was stated that it was to be 200 feet, or even 1,200 feet in some cases. This must have been a requirement of the Secretary.

In November 1933, $50,000 of public works money was allotted for a study of a parkway through the Green Mountains in Vermont,

1 Robert Shankland, *Steve Mather of the National Parks* (New York: Alfred A. Knopf, 1951), 298.

but nothing came of it. The conservative Vermonters had no strong yearning for such embellishment of their mountains. About the same time, studies were made of a Natchez Trace Parkway, to run from Nashville, Tennessee, to Natchez, Mississippi.[2]

The second parkway to be considered and the first to be provided for, on June 30, 1936, was the Blue Ridge Parkway, to connect the Skyline Drive in Shenandoah National Park and the Great Smoky Mountains National Park with a road running along the crest of the Appalachian Mountains, a distance of 477 miles. This parkway had been started under authority of the National Industrial Recovery Act of 1933, without specific Congressional authorization. Early in 1936, in the second session of the 74th Congress, Senator Byrd of Virginia and Representative Doughton of North Carolina brought up bills to establish this parkway; and the Doughton bill was debated at some length, largely on political lines, the Republicans, led by Taber of New York, Rich of Pennsylvania, and Wolcott of Michigan opposing, and the Democrats lined up in favor.[3] In spite of all opposition, the Doughton Bill, H. R. 12455, passed the House by a vote of 145 to 131, and passed the Senate with little discussion.[4]

Under the Doughton Act the states of Virginia and North Carolina were to provide the right of way except where the road ran through national forests, and the federal government, that is, the Bureau of Public Roads, would build and maintain the road—an expensive job, along the crest of the mountains. The road might be connected with national forest roads, and in proximity to national forests the Forest Service and the Park Service were to co-operate in providing recreational facilities—there were some national forests in this region, purchased under the Weeks Act of 1911, and with emergency relief funds. In 1937 and 1940 bills were passed to make proper adjustment with the Cherokee Indians for encroachments on their lands;[5] and in June 1940 Congress amended the act of 1936 to authorize the Secretary of the Interior to issue revocable permits to owners of adjacent lands to use the parkway, and author-

2 Stat. 48, 791.
3 S. 3988, H. R. 10922, H. R. 12455, 74 Cong. 2 Sess.
4 Stat. 49, 2041. *National Parks Magazine,* Apr.-June 1949.
5 Stat. 50, 699; 54, 299.

izing him to accept lands and interests in lands in the Blue Ridge and Natchez Trace parkways.[6]

Some of the most spirited debates were on the question of appropriations to build the Blue Ridge. On May 19, 1937—before Natchez Trace had been established—there was a tussle in the House when the appropriation bill came up, granting $3 million for the Blue Ridge. Taber of New York offered an amendment to strike out the appropriation, arguing that the federal government should not pay all the cost of the roads. Woodrum of Virginia pointed out that the parkway had been authorized by Congress, and that Virginia and North Carolina had gone ahead with the purchase of the right of way at a cost said to be $6 million, which may well have been an exaggeration. After some argument, Taber's amendment failed, 21 to 123. Doughton offered an amendment to increase the appropriation to $5 million, but Rich of Pennsylvania promptly opposed this, pointing out that the parkway would parallel other good roads, yet the amendment passed 141 to 59. Ditter of Pennsylvania called the bill a "pork barrel" program. Jenkins of Ohio got down to political realities in his speech: "Mr. Chairman, we have listened with a great deal of interest to the conflict between the members on the Democratic side over these amendments. Sometimes some of them show signs of a desire to practice a little economy, but they are afraid to come out in the open for they do not want to get out too far from the money pots. They want to be in a position to drag all the political bacon they can back into their districts. They are afraid to follow the President when he talks economy, for they know he does not mean it, and they are afraid to vote against the President's pet extravagances, for they know that it was by virtue of these huge sums that most of them were elected to their present positions."[7]

Jenkins declared: "I said at that time and I say now that it was the most gigantic and stupendously extravagant and unreasonable expenditure made by the most extravagantly expensive administration in the history of the world. Think of it—477 miles of parkway 800 feet wide." Jenkins thought they needed a flood-control dam on the Ohio more than this parkway.

6 Stat. 49, 2041; 54, 249.

7 *Congressional Record,* 75 Cong. 1 Sess., 4807.

In the debates there was, as it would appear today, too much concern about budget-balancing, no understanding of the principle that unemployed labor and capital put to work produce wealth which fundamentally costs nothing. To the extent that Blue Ridge was built by unemployed labor and capital it did cost nothing. The value of such expenditures in stimulating economic recovery was not discussed. Too little attention was paid, furthermore, to the value of the product—the very beautiful scenic Blue Ridge Parkway. Since it had not been built no one could know how beautiful it would be.

In 1944 an organization, the Grandfather Mountain Park Association, was established to acquire Grandfather Mountain near the parkway, for addition to it. In 1945 the association was reported as having acquired much of the land, but Grandfather Mountain is still private property, visible from the parkway. In 1948 the National Park Service and the Forest Service made an agreement for integrated use of park and forest lands in the Grandfather Mountain-Linville Gorge section of the parkway, setting up a special administrative area of about 55,000 acres, some of it privately and some publicly owned, some of the privately owned land to be acquired by the Park Service when possible. The Linville Gorge was to be kept a "wild" area, and on the national forest land there were to be special regulations as to cutting, to preserve the aesthetic aspects of the area.[8] In 1950 two fine donations were made, the Moses H. Cone Memorial Park, and the Julian H. Price Memorial Park; and in 1951 John D. Rockefeller, Jr., gave money for Linville Falls and Gorge.

Tourist accommodations have been something of a problem in Blue Ridge. Unable to attract the interest of concessioners for enough hotel and cabin accommodations, the Park Service built a 24-room lodge, coffee shop and gasoline station at Doughton Park in 1949, and very limited facilities at a few other points. The Bluffs Lodge and coffee shop in Doughton Park are operated by National Parks Concessions, Inc., which also operates concessions at several other points and at several national parks, and offers high-class service.

The next parkway established, two years after Blue Ridge, was the Natchez Trace. Early in 1934 Senator Stevens of Mississippi introduced a bill providing $50,000 for a survey of the route, which

8 *Report, Secretary of the Interior, 1948,* 353.

passed and was signed by President Roosevelt on May 21.[9] The
survey was begun in February 1935, and completed in June; and on
February 6, 1936, Representative Ford of Mississippi introduced a
bill authorizing an appropriation of $25 million for construction
and maintenance of Natchez Trace; but it did not pass; neither
did bills by Representative McGhee and Senator Harrison of Mississippi. On February 2, 1938, a bill to build the Natchez Trace
Parkway was introduced by Ford and debated with some acerbity
and at length in the House in Committee of the Whole. The right
of way was to be provided by the states, and the federal government
was to build the road, which was to follow an old Indian trail, the
same trail Jackson had followed on his way to defeat the British at
New Orleans, and it had been "marked by handsome boulders with
suitable inscriptions by the Daughters of the American Revolution
at great expense"; but Washington was not reported to have slept
here, and the road had no great scenic value.[10]

The debates on this bill were largely along political lines, the
Republicans opposing and the southern Democrats favoring. Various arguments were used against the bill. First was the expense.
Lord of New York thought it would cost about $20 million, or
finally as much as $200 million. Wolcott of Michigan said the bill
was merely a scheme to give southern states $20 million of tax-
payers' money, while elsewhere the states had to match federal road
money dollar for dollar and maintain the roads afterward, and
that the President had started these southern parkways and spent
$1,250,000 on them before they were called to the attention of
Congress. Hook of Michigan hoped that in granting concessions
the Secretary would not establish big monopolies as in the western
parks.

The defense of the bill was vigorous, and not altogether lacking
in logic, although there was a strong odor of the pork barrel in
some of the arguments. Reece of Tennessee pointed to the $12
million spent on the Cape Cod Canal in Massachusetts; Whitting-
ton of Mississippi pointed to the millions spent in western parks and
for access roads to the parks—1,000 miles of them, according to his
figures; Vincent of Kentucky argued that defense appropriations
went largely to the eastern states, as did river and harbor and naval
and army expenditures; and the parkway expenditures would not

9 S. 2825, 73 Cong. 2 Sess. Stat. 48, 791.
10 H. R. 6652, 75 Cong. 3 Sess.

even balance them. There was some discussion of the odious fact that not all states had national parks, as if it were due to unfair discrimination in Congress and not to the lack of scenery in most states. The Democrats had a strong preponderance of votes, and the bill passed the House by a vote of 200 to 118, passed the Senate without debate, and was signed by President Roosevelt on May 18, 1938.[11]

While the Democrats were in the saddle in Congress they decided to do well for the South, and a month after Natchez Trace was authorized Congress passed an act providing $10,000 for a survey of an "Oglethorpe National Trail and Parkway" to run from Savannah to Augusta, Georgia. According to the bill, this parkway project had many recommendations: it was an Indian trail; General Oglethorpe had followed it when he returned from a Creek Nation Treaty conference; it passed many historic and prehistoric sites, and sites where fossilized oysters five by twenty-four inches were found; it passed creeks where bass, perch and bream abounded, and dogwood, laurel and magnolias; and Washington had once traveled this trail, and very likely had slept somewhere along the way. Despite these many attractions, the Oglethorpe National Trail and Parkway never received any further attention.[12]

Other parkways were demanded. Representative Hendricks of Florida wanted a survey for a parkway from the Augusta terminus of the Oglethorpe National Trail and Parkway to the Blue Ridge Parkway at Tennessee Bald, North Carolina, and an extension of the Blue Ridge to the vicinity of Saint Augustine, Florida, by way of Stone Mountain, and Atlanta, Georgia.[13] Representative Collins of Mississippi wanted a survey of the old Jackson Military Road, with the idea of building a parkway; Representatives Reece and Jennings of Tennessee wanted to extend the boundaries of Great Smoky Mountains, without federal appropriations, to include a right of way for a proposed scenic highway along the top of Chilhowee Mountain and the slopes of Cove and Webb Mountains from the Little Tennessee River to Cosby, and this was approved by the Department of the Interior but made no headway.[14] Representative Taylor of Tennessee threw caution to the winds and pro-

11 Stat. 52, 407.
12 Stat. 52, 752.
13 H. R. 4014, 77 Cong. 1 Sess.
14 H. R. 9464, H. R. 9679, 76 Cong. 3 Sess.

posed an appropriation of $100 million for an eastern national park-to-park highway, through Virginia, North Carolina, Tennessee, Kentucky, West Virginia, and the District of Columbia.[15]

These parkway projects did not materialize, but several others did. The Washington Memorial Parkway, in the District of Columbia; the Baltimore-Washington Parkway; the Colonial Parkway, from Yorktown to Jamestown Island; and the Suitland Parkway, from Washington to Silver Hill Road, Maryland. The Foothills Parkway, north of Great Smoky Park, designed to afford a view of the Great Smokies, was planned and begun, but the state had difficulty getting titles to the land, and for years little was done on it. Recently, there has been renewed interest in it and definite plans are being made for its completion. The Chesapeake and Ohio Canal was partly restored with public works funds in 1939, and for some years there were plans for building a parkway along the canal. The state of Oregon had built her own parkway—a highly scenic road from Portland up the Columbia to the Dalles—as early as 1915.

Some of these parkways or roads are of such scenic or historical value that they belong under control of the Park Service; others are just roads, which should have been built and maintained by the states.

Congress recognized the difference between Blue Ridge and Natchez Trace by appropriating more for Blue Ridge, which now has more than 400 miles of road completed, whereas Natchez Trace has only a little more than 200 miles completed. Skyline Drive and Blue Ridge are worthy units in the national park system, as Foothills will be when completed, and they have been splendidly built and wisely administered. The roads are well built, with many parking "overlooks" where the tourist can stop and enjoy lovely vistas of the distant valleys and blue, hazy mountains; there are attractively planned picnic areas, campgrounds and comfort stations, set properly back from the road; the speed limits are low enough so that the leisurely driver is not likely to feel in the way; here and there are seen beautiful rhododendron, azalea, shadblow, dogwood—a wilderness of gorgeous flowers, each in its season, and many kinds of trees luxuriant in the moist climate of the Appalachians. The altitude of the parkways—from about 2,000 feet to more than 4,000 feet—means comfortable summer weather, with cool nights. No billboards scream the virtues of cigarette brands or the hotel

15 H. R. 1964, 75 Cong. 1 Sess. H. R. 286, 76 Cong. 1 Sess.

at the next junction which is "run nice for nice people," or the restaurant where the "food is good"; no lumbering trucks tear up the roads and perhaps the people—everything is fine and artistic on these parkways. They are wonderful places for a leisurely driver to spend a few days in unhurried enjoyment of lovely mountain scenery, although at times they are crowded like some of the parks. The total money cost of Blue Ridge to the present has been less than $50 millions (to the extent that it was built by unemployed labor and capital its fundamental cost was nothing); and at either cost it is a fine bargain. It is enjoyed by more visitors than any other unit in the park system—over 4 million a year.

There is an inconsistency in the naming of Blue Ridge and Shenandoah National Park. Blue Ridge, somewhat the finer of the two, is a national parkway, while Shenandoah, which is essentially Skyline Drive, is a national park. They should both be either national parks or national parkways.

It is true that these parkways were built and are used rather largely for the benefit of the people in the surrounding regions. They have added greatly to the value of farm land and land in the towns along the way. The people from miles around come up frequently for weekends and vacations, partly at the expense of the federal government which maintains the roads and services; but this is similarly true of some national parks, particularly those such as Yosemite, Sequoia, and Rocky Mountain, which are near large centers of population. The people of the surrounding states exploit the parkways by taxing sales and concessions while the federal government pays the bills, but this is true also of most national parks.

AREAS CONSIDERED FOR ADDITIONS TO PARK SYSTEM   The Park Service was always studying new areas for possible additions to the park system. In 1936 the Service investigated many areas, and as a result recommended, in addition to ocean beaches, a number of areas in the West as parks or monuments: Yampa and Green River canyons in northwestern Colorado and northeastern Utah; Wayne Wonderland in Utah, a part of which was soon to become Capitol Reef National Monument; an Organ Pipe Cactus area, soon to become a monument; Kofa Mountains in Arizona, later to become a game range; and Kolob Canyons northwest of Zion Park, to be established as Zion National Monument in 1937. The Park Service also approved of a Green Mountain national park in Vermont and Mount Katahdin national park in Maine, and there were several attempts in Congress to establish them, but they all failed. Mount Katahdin was later given to the state of Maine by Governor Percival Baxter as Baxter State Park.[16]

For several years there was some interest in archeological ruins near Manuelito, New Mexico. The state bought the private holdings except the Indian allotments and had agreed to exchange state lands for federal lands elsewhere; but the monument has not materialized.[17] Travertine Bridge, also in New Mexico, a natural bridge of travertine, was proposed in a number of bills in Congress and praised by some observers, but it was never established. Representative Murdock of Arizona worked hard for it.

One of the most attractive areas considered was known as a proposed Escalante national park, to include a large area in southern Utah and northern Arizona. The Park Service was greatly interested in this, but it was held up by grazing, mining, and power interests. Several other canyon areas in Utah were considered but likewise failed to materialize for one reason or another. Some of the lands involved belonged to the Navajos, who deferred their approval.[18]

As usual, park standards were threatened by the efforts of various men and groups to establish new parks and monuments of inferior merit. In 1936 the Park Service reported 224 projects on the list to be investigated, which preliminary investigation reduced to 156 active projects. From 1933 to 1940 the Service investigated 353 proposed areas, and in the same period 420 additional park and monument proposals were made but not investigated.[19] Some of these were of course offered by senators and representatives under pressure from local constituents or in the hope of pleasing them, but without great enthusiasm or persistence. There were several

16 *Report, Secretary of the Interior, 1936*, 111. H. R. 5864, H. R. 6599, 65 Cong. 1 Sess. S. 2622, H. R. 2961, 76 Cong. 1 Sess.

17 *Report, Secretary of the Interior, 1941*, 314.

18 *Report, Secretary of the Interior, 1933*, 165; 1936, 111; 1937, 64; 1938, 32; 1939, 292; 1940, 191.

19 *Report, Secretary of the Interior, 1944*, 212, 213.

efforts to raise Petrified Forest to national park status, always unsuccessful until 1958 when Congress authorized it.[20]

The examination of so many proposed parks and monuments,
most of them unworthy, was a considerable task for the Park Service, and Congress was somewhat helpless in appraising the areas that
were being proposed at every session. It was apparent, too, that
there was always a chance that inferior areas might slip through;
so in March 1935 Senators Wagner, Ashurst, Norbeck and Nye introduced a Senate Resolution providing that the Committee on
Public Lands be authorized to investigate the advisability of establishing additional parks and monuments.[21] Four years later, Representative De Rouen of Louisiana introduced a House Resolution
authorizing a survey and study of the national parks, monuments,
and shrines, and another resolution providing expenses for the
study, which was agreed to.[22] Two years later the study was not
completed, and Representative Robinson of Utah brought up a
resolution extending the time to January 3, 1943.[23]

Perhaps it may be worth while to note some of the proposed
areas investigated in one year (1938): Coast Redwoods national
park, California; Columbia Gorge recreational area, Oregon; Cumberland Gap national historical park, Tennessee, Kentucky and
Virginia; Flathead national park area, Montana; Fort Peck recreational area, Montana; Gila national park area, New Mexico;
Glacial Grooves national monument, Ohio; Grand Coulee recreational area, Washington; Grasslands national monument, South
Dakota and Nebraska; Hart mountain national monument, Oregon; Luquillo national park, Puerto Rico; Newberry Crater national monument, Oregon; Northern Cascades national park area,
Washington; Palmyra Island national monument, near Hawaii;
Palm Canyon national monument, California; Porcupine mountains national park, Michigan; Roosevelt Badlands national monu-
ment, North Dakota; San Juan national park area, Colorado; San
Juan national monument, Puerto Rico; Ship Island national monu-
ment, Mississippi; Superior national park, Minnesota; Waimea
Canyon national park, Hawaii; and Wind River national park,
Wyoming.

20 Stat. 72, 69.
21 S. Res. 102, 74 Cong. 1 Sess.
22 H. Res. 284, H. Res. 285, 76 Cong. 1 Sess.
23 H. Res. 242, 77 Cong. 1 Sess.

Altogether a bewildering array of historical park areas were shifted to the Park Service on June 10, 1933. These are outside the scope of this book, however, and enough has been said about a few of them. The classification of such areas was more confusing than it need have been. There is no reason, for instance, why Gettysburg should be a national military park and Antietam a national battle-field site. The Park Service has worked on the problem and in 1940 made a beginning at a reclassification. It has been working since and hopes soon to achieve some simplification. Anything done would have to have Congressional approval because Congress gave the names to most of them in setting them up.

SEASHORE AREAS   In Cammerer's administration, the Park Service became much interested in seashores as recreation areas and tried to get some of them reserved before they were all turned over to private ownership. In June 1936, apparently concerned about beach erosion, Congress had declared it to be "the policy of the United States to assist in the construction, where federal interests are involved, but not the maintenance, of works for the improvement and protection of the beaches along the shores of the United States."[24]

In 1936 sixteen seashore recreation areas were being studied by the Park Service and two years later several more were being sur-veyed. Most of them were on the Atlantic and Gulf coasts and the Great Lakes, but one in Curry County, Oregon, was considered favorably. The Atlantic Coast was better situated, being near large populations and warm enough for swimming in summer. The Pacific Coast was better in other respects, with less private owner-ship and more rugged and scenic topography, but usually too cold for swimming, and many of the areas rather far from population centers. At any rate, only the Cape Hatteras National Seashore, on the coast of North Carolina, made the grade. It was authorized by an act of August 17, 1937, to cover approximately 100 square miles with provisions customary for eastern park areas. The state of North Carolina was to acquire the lands, except in the villages, in an area up to 100 square miles, and turn them over to the federal government free of cost; and the Secretary was authorized to accept donations. There were some peculiar provisions, too. Residents of

24 Stat. 49, 1982.

the villages might make a living fishing, under rules of the Secretary; and except for certain parts of the area deemed especially adapted to swimming, boating, sailing, and other recreational activities the Seashore was to remain a primitive wilderness area, to preserve the unique fauna and flora. There were four federal areas included: the Kill Devil Hill National Memorial, the Cape Hatteras Lighthouse, the Fort Raleigh National Historic Site, and a federal migratory bird refuge; but these were not to be disturbed.[25]

This act did not *establish* the Cape Hatteras Seashore—it only authorized its establishment when the state of North Carolina should turn over the lands; with due caution the act provided that if the state did not get the land within ten years the Secretary might abandon the project. The state set up the Cape Hatteras Seashore Commission two years later to direct acquisition of state and private lands, but the Cape Hatteras National Seashore—changed to Cape Hatteras National Seashore Recreational Area in 1940[26]—was not completed for a number of years.

Other areas were studied: Rehoboth-Assateague in Delaware, Maryland, and Virginia; Barnegat Inlet in New Jersey; Anastasia Island in Florida; and Padre Island in Texas; in fact some twenty sites were being studied in 1938. But nothing definite was accomplished, largely because the most desirable beaches along the Atlantic and near the large cities were already privately owned. This is a major national crime, comparable with the failure to save in a national park some of the finest coast redwood groves. An effort was made in Congress in May 1940, by Senator McNary of Oregon, to set up a coast national park along the rugged, scenic coast in Curry County, Oregon, but without success.[27]

At the dedication of Dr. Edmund A. Babler Memorial State Park in Missouri, on October 10, 1938, Ickes put his case for seashore reservations rather effectively: "When we look up and down the ocean fronts of America, we find that everywhere they are passing behind the fences of private ownership. The people can no longer get to the ocean. When we have reached the point that a nation of 125,000,000 people cannot set foot upon the thousands of miles of beaches that border the Atlantic and Pacific Oceans, except by permission of those who monopolize the ocean front, then I say it

25 Stat. 50, 669.
26 Stat. 54, 702.
27 S. 4064, 76 Cong. 3 Sess.

is the prerogative and the duty of the Federal and State Governments to step in and acquire, not a swimming beach here and there, but solid blocks of ocean front hundreds of miles in length. Call this ocean front a national park, or a national seashore, or a state park or anything you please—I say that the people have a right to a fair share of it."[28]

Cammerer had plenty of work and plenty of problems throughout his administration. Some activities developed in normal fashion. The interpretive work so heavily stressed by Mather and Albright continued to develop satisfactorily, with Congressional approval. In 1934 interpretive lectures were specifically authorized, and the next year $20,720 was granted for field employees examining land and for developing educational work. These grants were secured against the opposition of several conservatives in Congress—in the House, Taber of New York, Rich of Pennsylvania, and Lambertson of Kansas. State parks were growing, with some Park Service guidance. Before 1934 only nine states had provided annual appropriations of any considerable amounts; between 1933 and 1941 eleven more had established fairly well-financed systems.

WILDLIFE PROBLEMS   Wildlife still presented many difficult problems, but the Park Service had come to a more scientific view of wildlife than that of Mather; in fact the principle of the "balance of nature" had been gaining acceptance in the latter years of the Mather administration. With the light afforded by the survey of the fauna of the national parks which Albright had ordered but which appeared early in Cammerer's administration,[29] the Service had some factual basis for a better wildlife administration. Soon after Cammerer assumed office Congress authorized the Bureau of Biological Survey and the Bureau of Fisheries to make surveys of wildlife resources on federal lands, and to establish "game farms" and fish-cultural stations, in co-operation with the Park Service or other federal agencies, the game farms to be established only with the consent of the states concerned.[30] President Roosevelt pro-

28 *A Study of the Park and Recreation Problem of the United States* (National Park Service, 1941) , 125.
29 *Fauna of the National Parks of the United States* (Washington: National Park Service, 1933, 1935, 1938, 1940) .
30 Stat. 48, 401, 402.

claimed "Wildlife Week" in 1938, and this "week" has been observed every year since. Of course, wildlife problems are never
"solved" in the sense that they do not require constant attention
and constant reconsideration and perhaps alteration of policies.
Senator McCarran's plan for authorizing hunting and selling of
wildlife meat was not popular with most authorities, for instance.

During this period naturalists were coming to a clearer appreciation of the value of swamps in wildlife conservation. For years
there had been a widespread campaign for the drainage of swamps,
to increase the amount of agricultural land; but it presently appeared that this not only destroyed the breeding places for some
species of waterfowl and other wildlife, but had other ill effects,
as for instance in the lowering of the ground-water level. Some of
these swamps were later restored.

INSECT PESTS AND FOREST FIRES   The problems of fighting
insect pests and diseases of forest trees were always serious. In 1937,
for instance, the mountain pine beetle was working in Yellowstone
and Teton, where the control program had been abandoned several years before because of the large area infested; the needle miner
was spreading in the lodgepole forests of Yosemite; and the Black
Hills beetle was on a rampage. The Saguaro cacti were found to be
infected with bacteria spread by a moth, which makes the survival
of the great cacti quite uncertain. Three years later the white pine
blister rust was reported a serious menace in California. Insect
and disease threats have been perennial in the parks and forests,
and the two services have co-operated in the control work.

Forest fires were always a very serious danger and sometimes did
immense damage. In 1937 the Heavens Peak fire in Glacier destroyed 7,642 acres, and three disastrous fires burned over 33,000
acres in Isle Royale, killing the trees and much of the wildlife. Isle
Royale was still only a project and no fire protection had been
organized.

Since Mather's time, when the admission of automobiles was first
discussed, technological developments often have presented problems of more or less difficulty. In Cammerer's time trailers and
airplanes began to call for consideration. Airplanes were not common enough yet to raise a serious question as to airport construction, but the Park Service itself was finding them very useful for

some purposes. In the Mount McKinley Park they were used in patrol work and in hunting predators, vastly increasing efficiency. The radio was coming into use, increasing the efficiency of park administration, particularly in forest fire protection. By 1935 the Park Service had developed small sets which proved almost indispensable.

TOURIST VISITS   When Cammerer came in in 1933 the number of tourist visits was down a little, to 3,481,000, and many concessioners were in trouble; but visitor figures began to climb the next year, and in 1936 were up to 11,989,000, then on up to 16,-755,000 in 1940—about five times as many as in the boom year 1929, before the depression. Such an impressive gain in tourist visits might well have suggested that the real danger was of such a tide of tourists as the facilities could not accommodate; but in 1937 a United States Tourist Bureau was set up in the Park Service with emergency funds, to co-operate with the states in promoting travel; and when in the fall of 1939 World War II brought an end to European travel, Congress the next year passed "An Act to Encourage Travel in the United States," authorizing the Secretary to co-operate with public and private tourist agencies in promoting travel and to set up an advisory committee to assist in the work of promotion. An appropriation of $100,000 was authorized for expenses.[31] The next year $75,000 was given for encouragement of touring, then no more until 1947. Whether as a result of this work or merely because Europe was off-limits to tourists, the national park system had 21,236,000 visits in 1941.

The government facilities in the parks were not at first seriously inadequate for this flood of visitors. There were lush work-relief funds in the early years of Cammerer's regime, and after 1934 appropriations were fairly generous. There were always some donations, in some years $200,000 or more, mostly for the purchase of private lands, or even occasional generous contributions such as John D. Rockefeller, Jr., often made.

As visitor figures climbed, the concessioners found themselves in better situations, some of them to the point where they could not handle the crowds that came; but that was for others to worry

31 Stat. 54, 773.

about. Yet the concessioner in Mount Rainier was in trouble, and in 1939 Representative Coffee and Senator Bone of Washington tried unsuccessfully to get a bill through Congress for government purchase, rehabilitation, and operation of the facilities there.[32] These bills were reported adversely by the Bureau of the Budget as involving too much expense, and were given no consideration. Representative Magnuson of Washington tried to do something for Mount McKinley. The government had built the facilities at Mount McKinley and had leased them to a private concessioner, who found his business unprofitable and himself unable to provide accommodations for the tourists who came. The Magnuson bill authorized the President to "construct, reconstruct, maintain and operate" the lodges and other facilities, paying for the personal property of the Mount McKinley Tourist and Transportation Company, and operating it directly or through a concessioner"; and the bill passed and was signed by President Roosevelt on March 29, 1940.[33] Representative Voorhis of California wanted government ownership and operation of concessions in all parks.[34]

The rapid increase in the number of automobiles and the relative decline in the number of visitors coming by rail brought a marked change in the character of concession services demanded and provided, a change to which the depression contributed. In Mather's time the hotels provided a high-class and fairly expensive service, and the sight-seeing transportation afforded most of the concessioners' profits; in Cammerer's administration there was a change to more low-priced cabins, cafeterias, coffee shops and grill service which yielded more and more of the revenues.[35]

Winter use continued to grow, and this presented difficulties. To what extent could the parks and the hotels be kept open for winter guests, how could park employees be retained to care for the facilities and for the skiers who got lost or broke their legs, etc. etc.? Some of these problems are still unsolved. So too, mountain climbers sometimes presented problems, for the Park Service rangers were occasionally called on to rescue climbers who had encountered disaster, or even bring in the bodies. This did not happen

32 H. R. 3705, S. 2055, 76 Cong. 1 Sess.
33 H. R. 4868, 76 Cong. 1 Sess. Stat. 54, 80.
34 H. R. 5502, 76 Cong. 1 Sess.
35 Report, Secretary of the Interior, 1938, 24.

often, but the Service had to adopt a rule discouraging mountain climbing without official permission.

With the increase in the number of visitors, the Park Service faced the problem of the adequacy of water supplies for some parks, and in 1936 persuaded Congress to vote $25,000 for the investigation and purchase of water rights.[36] This appropriation, raised to $50,000 in 1938, was continued each year until 1941, and the Park Service has been looking out for its water supplies right down to the present. In fact, the Park Service has a rather amazing record of foresightedness on many problems.

STATE EXPLOITATION OF PARKS   The states in which there were national parks, especially the western states, always hankered after more of the park revenues, and in Cammerer's administration they made a little progress toward getting more. In ceding jurisdiction most of them had reserved the right to tax sales, persons and corporations and their franchises and properties, as a compensation for the taxes they would collect if the parks had not been established. They chose not to understand, perhaps really did not understand, that the taxes levied in the states were used to provide services in the states—roads, schools, justice, protection—and that the parks called for no such services from the states. The federal government built the roads; there were almost no public schools in the parks; the commissioners, paid by the federal government, afforded justice and protection in ordinary cases.

There was no justification for state taxation of business in the parks, yet in nearly all the parks the adjacent states had got this right; and in 1936 and 1940 the right was made general. The Federal Aid Highway Act of 1936 was amended to authorize state taxation of gasoline sales in the parks and other federal reservations, excepting gasoline used by the government; and in 1940 the states were authorized to tax sales, use, and incomes in federal areas. Although the federal government was paying nearly nine-tenths of the cost of maintaining the parks, it was handing over a part of its meager revenues to the states which were the main beneficiaries of the park system.[37]

36 Stat. 49, 1795.
37 Stat. 48, 1519, 1521; 54, 1059.

For Yellowstone, this tax exploitation is particularly unjustifiable, a clear violation of the law of July 10, 1890, under which Wyoming was admitted to the Union. That law stated: "Provided, that nothing in this act contained shall repeal or affect any act of Congress relating to the Yellowstone National Park, or the reservation of the park as now defined, or as may be hereafter defined or extended, or the power of the United States over it; and nothing contained in this act shall interfere with the right and ownership of the United States in said park and reservation as it now is or may hereafter be defined or extended by law; but exclusive legislation, in all cases whatsoever, shall be exercised by the United States, which shall have exclusive control and jurisdiction over the same. . . ."[38]

Surprisingly enough, the bill to make this exploitation general, introduced by Representative Buck of California, passed with practically no opposition in Congress, although Acting Secretary of the Interior E. K. Burlew objected to it on the ground that it might be applied to Indian reservations and the Secretary of the Navy opposed its application to naval lands.[39]

But some of the western statesmen wanted ever more from the parks. Early in 1940, in the 76th Congress, Representative Robinson of Utah and Senator Hayden of Arizona introduced bills providing for state participation in park revenues—gifts of 25 per cent of the revenues for the benefit of the counties adjacent. Robinson's bill was reported favorably by the House Committee on Public Lands and Hayden's bill passed the Senate with no debate. This attempt at exploitation was defended by McCarran with the argument that the states have to police park areas—which was not true—and have to provide for sanitation etc., etc.—which was also not true. Hayden argued that his bill did in the parks what was done in the national forests and grazing lands, which turn over to the states a percentage of their revenues; but this was a fallacious argument, for the national parks are not operated to yield any net revenues, but on the contrary a net deficit of nearly 90 per cent. The Department of the Interior was said to favor the bill.[40] In 1939 the Park Service raised some of the fees in an effort to reduce the deficit.[41]

38 Stat. 26, 222.
39 H. R. 6687, 76 Cong. 1 Sess.
40 H. R. 9535, S. 3869, 76 Cong. 3 Sess.
41 Report, Secretary of the Interior, 1939, 268.

THREATS TO THE PARKS   Like Mather and Albright, Cammerer had to fight off the irrigationists who wanted to invade Yellowstone. Idaho men were insistent on the damming of Yellowstone Lake. The Idaho and Montana legislatures presented memorials favoring it,[42] and on April 28 and May 2, 1938, Senator Pope and Representative White of Idaho presented bills for a "weir" at Yellowstone Lake. It was only a few weeks before the end of the 75th Congress and, apparently, they thought one of the bills might pass in the hurry and confusion of the closing days of the session; but neither bill got any attention.[43] Failing in this, White tried to get a bill through to build an Idaho entrance to the park, through the southwest part, but this also failed.[44]

About this time, Wheeler of Montana and Horton of Wyoming brought up bills to authorize the states of Wyoming and Montana (South Dakota was included in one bill and in some discussions) to enter into a compact to divide the waters of the Yellowstone River; but whether this was planned as a sort of entering wedge for the spoliation of Yellowstone Lake is not quite certain. Probably it was not so intended, but the National Parks Association protested it and a provision was added that it should not apply in Yellowstone Park. As so amended, it passed both houses and was signed by President Roosevelt on August 2, 1937.[45] Wyoming was defending Yellowstone at this time, and Horton offered a House joint resolution prohibiting any water or power development in the park.[46] On the other hand he wanted no new parks or additions to parks in Wyoming.[47]

Representative O'Connor of Montana was apparently working for mining interests when he introduced a bill to reconvey to Montana 3,000 acres along the north boundary of Yellowstone. His bill was reported adversely by the Department of the Interior, but favorably by the Public Lands Committee. Soon afterward, however, he withdrew the bill.[48]

42 *Congressional Record,* Jan. 27, 1939, 907.

43 S. 3925, H. R. 10489, 75 Cong. 3 Sess. *American Forests,* July 1938, 293; Sept. 1938, 422.

44 H. R. 3841, 76 Cong. 1 Sess. H. R. 3395, 77 Cong. 1 Sess.

45 Stat. 50, 551. See also S. 1759, H. R. 6116, 76 Cong. 1 Sess. Stat. 54, 399.

46 H. J. Res. 348, 76 Cong. 1 Sess.

47 H. R. 9220, 76 Cong. 3 Sess.

48 H. R. 6975, 76 Cong. 1 Sess.

THE ROCKY MOUNTAIN TUNNEL   Rocky Mountain National
Park was invaded by irrigation and power interests in 1937. Already in 1935 there had been some interest in a proposal for bringing water from the west slope of the Rocky Mountains to the east
slope by a tunnel through Rocky Mountain Park; but it was held
up by a disagreement between the people on the two sides of the
Rocky Mountain divide. In June 1937, peace having been established between the two sides of the divide, Senator Adams introduced a bill to authorize the project. His bill appropriated $900,000,
but carried a provision that no construction should be commenced
until the repayment of all costs of the project, in the opinion of
the Secretary of the Interior, should be assured by contracts with
water conservancy districts or irrigation districts or water users'
associations.[49] The Park Service, the National Parks Association,
and many conservationists were opposed to it.

The National Parks Association, at its annual meeting on May
14, 1937, outlined its reasons for opposition: (1) The building of
the project would create a precedent which might result in further
invasion of the parks. (2) The building of the tunnel would alter
natural conditions on the surface and impair or destroy primitive
values in the park. (3) Other routes were available which could
be used.[50]

Secretary Ickes was not enthusiastic about the project but finally
gave his reluctant approval. His approval cannot be attributed to
any lack of loyalty to the parks but to the peculiar situation in
Colorado. Most of the Colorado population and most of the irrigated lands are east of the divide, and the heaviest rainfall is on the
west side; and the reclamation project was designed to bring water
from the west side at Grand Lake through the mountains to the
towns and irrigation farmers north of but not including Denver—
altogether some 140,000 people. This could have been done outside
Rocky Mountain Park, but at considerably greater expense. Ickes
may well have concluded that the conduit or tunnel would not
seriously injure the park, and that the expense of going around it
would not be justified. Furthermore, he had no choice, for Congress
provided for the tunnel. The mountains here are 12,000 feet high,
and the tunnel was to be built at an elevation of 8,000 feet, so there
should have been little injury to the mountain except at the tunnel

49 S. 2681, 75 Cong. 1 Sess.
50 *Science*, July 16, 1937, 48.

entrances, and the Reclamation men promised to take good care to clean up around the entrances. They have done this.

The Adams bill passed the Senate without opposition, but in the House there was considerable debate, on a fairly high plane, although Adams and the other Colorado promoters were overly enthusiastic about the gains to be expected from the tunnel and about the repayment of costs. Reclamation projects seldom repay costs, except by the wierdest calculations known in accounting—deferring interest charges for fifty years on irrigation costs, for instance. Taber of New York was opposed to building more reclamation projects, with farm crops in surplus. Taylor, seasoned conservationist of Colorado, had formerly been opposed when the people on the two sides of the divide were in disagreement; but they had come to an agreement on this bill, and so Taylor favored. Most of the debate was pointed at the reclamation question, but Dirksen of Illinois objected to *any* invasion of any national park, in this representing the view of the Park Service.

In spite of fairly vigorous opposition the Adams bill passed the House, 174 to 154, and was signed by President Roosevelt on August 9, 1937.[51] The Reclamation Bureau did not begin work until 1940, and the tunnel was finished four years later, but the work proceeded for years afterward for the project covered several dams as well as the tunnel.

MINING INTERESTS AND PARK AREAS   Mining interests were always scheming to get into some of the parks. Mining had been allowed in Death Valley in Albright's administration and on June 13, 1933, and in 1934, Representative Floyd of Washington tried to get all the parks opened to prospecting.[52] In June 1936 President Roosevelt issued a proclamation validating land claims in Katmai National Monument that were in force when the monument was proclaimed, claims that had since been maintained; but this did not seem to add appreciably to the rights of claimants.[53] In the same year, however, Congress opened Glacier Bay to mining, in spite of a chorus of opposition from conservation organizations and a strong editorial in the *Saturday Evening Post*. This spoliation

51 Stat. 50, 595.
52 Stat. 48, 1396. H. R. 9156, 73 Cong. 2 Sess.
53 Stat. 49, 3523.

was partly due to efforts of the novelist Rex Beach and of Delegate Dimond of Alaska, who was never friendly to Alaska parks and monuments and national forests; but the bill to exploit Glacier Bay was pushed by Senator Schwellenbach of Washington, and it passed with practically no discussion. President Roosevelt at first agreed with Rex Beach and approved the bill, later backed off from this position and suggested a survey first, then still later swung back to approval.[54] The exploiters argued that mining would not injure the glaciers but there was no doubt that it would injure the plant and animal life.[55]

There were other efforts to open some of the parks and monuments to mining. Senator Hayden of Arizona tried to open up Organ Pipe Cactus, and Representative Sheppard worked persistently for the mining "development" of Joshua Tree.[56] Magnuson, as we have seen elsewhere, tried to extend for the indefinite future the mining rights in Olympic.[57]

Senator McCarran just didn't like the parks or any federal reservations, and he called for and got an investigation of the administration of the public lands.[58] In California, the oil fever struck so hard in 1940 that the state was reported considering a constitutional amendment to give the legislature power at any time to sell or lease for commercial purposes any or all state parks when in the opinion of the legislature they became more valuable for oil and gas than for recreation.[59]

Early in 1939 there was an effort by Senator Pittman and Representative Scrugham of Nevada to get 8,000 acres of land in the Lake Mead Recreation Area transferred to the state of Nevada for the use of Las Vegas.[60] Although Secretary Ickes was opposed, the Pittman Bill passed both houses, but it was vetoed by President Roosevelt who thought the Hoover Dam area should be kept intact.

54 Edgar B. Nixon, ed., *Franklin D. Roosevelt and Conservation* (Hyde Park, N. Y., National Archives and Records Service, Franklin Roosevelt Library, 1957) , Vol. I, 480, 517.

55 H. R. 9275, S. 4784, 74 Cong. 2 Sess. Stat. 49, 1817. Natl. Parks Bul. 62, Feb., 1937. Sat. Eve. Post, Aug. 15, 1936, 22.

56 S. 4083, 76 Cong. 3 Sess. H. R. 7558, 75 Cong. 1 Sess. H. R. 3827, 76 Cong. 1 Sess.

57 S. 1470, 79 Cong. 1 Sess.

58 S. Res. 241, 76 Cong., 3 Sess.

59 *American Forests*, Nov. 1940, 509.

60 S. 2, H. R. 6692, 76 Cong. 1 Sess.

Something seems to have been wrong with the administration of Yosemite, for in 1934 Congress included in the Yosemite appropriation the expenses of a "comprehensive study of the problems relating to Yosemite National Park," and this was in almost every Yosemite appropriation until 1942.[61] During some of these years Yosemite had quite too much "entertainment"—swimming pool, outdoor stage for evening shows, liquor store and dance hall, in addition to the facilities found in most parks—but whether this was the matter to be investigated or whether there was some design for paring down the park for commercial exploitation the writer is unable to say.

PURISTS ATTACK PARK SERVICE   While fighting off the spoilsmen and the advocates of inferior parks, Ickes, Cammerer, and the Park Service were under heavy fire from the purists of some of the conservation organizations, particularly the National Parks Association and the Wilderness Society, which charged the Park Service and Ickes with violation of "true national park standards," accused them of giving too much attention to historical, military, and recreational areas, to recreation generally, and to state and local parks, as opposed to the great scenic national parks and monuments.

Some of the purists wanted only the most splendid parks in the system, the "primeval" parks as they called them, and wanted them kept largely in primeval condition, with few roads and facilities, untouched by any commercial exploitation. They criticized the Park Service for having approved national parks set up with provision for any kind of commercial use, or parks that had been commercially exploited—timber cut, for instance, as in Mount Katahdin, or reservoirs constructed as in Jackson Hole; they criticized what they called the "excessive and unnecessary" road-building in some of the parks and the variety of amusements permitted in Yosemite. They criticized Ickes' approval of the Colorado–Big Thompson tunnel in Rocky Mountain, and condemned the opening of Glacier Bay to mining. In February 1936 the National Parks Association pointed up some of these criticisms in a quotation from a speech of Secretary Work, made in 1925: "Municipal and state parks and National Forests together offer outdoor opportunities in countless numbers, and easily accessible. The Government finds

61 Stat. 48, 385, 387.

itself duplicating these areas down to the smallest picnic park. We have gotten away from the fundamental principle that the government should do nothing an individual municipality or state can do for itself, and we are competing in little things, benumbing public spirit and thwarting local pride of possession and development."[62]

In December 1937 James Foote, executive secretary of the National Parks Association, published a letter voicing some of these and other criticisms: "Mr. Ickes—Your National Parks: An Open Letter to Secretary Ickes." Foote also asserted that under the new regional administration, too many positions were going to state-park men. The next June Ickes replied in the *National Parks Magazine,* explaining and defending his and Cammerer's administration. In the same issue of the magazine, William Wharton, president of the National Parks Association, published an article headed "Park Service Leader Abandons National Park Standards," criticizing Cammerer's presentation of his policies at a National Park conference held on January 21, 1938, under the auspices of the American Planning and Civic Association. Cammerer had said, referring to Katahdin, that he would not object to the inclusion of an area with cut-over timber if in fifty or a hundred years it seemed likely to reach park standards, that he would rather have a little mining in Glacier Bay than have Congressmen refuse to set aside needed parks. He pointed out that many commercial uses permitted in setting up national parks had later been eliminated. He thought it wise to take a practical view, rather than a rigidly doctrinaire attitude. Albright got some criticism, too, for what was called his "departure from national park standards."[63] To differentiate the truly scenic parks from the many unworthy recreational areas in the park system, the National Parks Association proposed that they be called "national primeval parks" and administered by a separate agency; but the name never caught on.

As to the justice of these criticisms, there can be no definitive conclusion. Some of the purists simply wanted one kind of park administration, the Park Service believed in a somewhat different sort of administration; and they were both informed, enlightened, and sincere. To some extent the difference was due to their different respective positions: the purists were free of all responsibilities

62 *National Parks Bulletin,* No. 61, Feb. 1936.

63 *National Parks Bulletin,* No. 64, Dec. 1937, 3; No. 65, June, 1938, 3, 7; No. 68, July, 1940.

and could speak and write without fear or inhibitions; the Park Service, on the other hand, had a job to do, the job not only of protecting the parks but of making them accessible—as required, by implication at least, by the act of 1916—and of winning friends and public support for them.

At the same time that the purists were criticizing Park men for being lax in their devotion to "national park standards," many others, including some influential politicians, were assailing them from the other side for too rigid adherence to those principles. The Park Service was following a middle course generally, and was the target of missiles from both sides. It was of course unfortunate that park lovers should have been quarreling among themselves.

One criticism often aimed at the Park Service was that it was devoting too much attention to recreation and other "side issues." There was no question that the Service, and other federal agencies, were up to their necks in the field of recreation. In 1938 thirty-five administrative units attached to departments and independent agencies of the federal government were engaged in the promotion of sixty to seventy different programs affecting the citizens' use of leisure time, the Park Service taking a goodly share of this activity.[64] But there was a rapidly growing need for recreation areas, and the Park Service was probably better qualified to do this work than any other agency.

The National Parks Association criticized the confusion in the classification of park areas: "State parks, recreation areas, national parks and primeval national parks have been shuffled and jumbled until today a confused American public scarcely knows which is which."[65]

REORGANIZATION THREAT AGAIN   Throughout the Cammerer Administration, there was a great deal of discussion of possible reorganization of government departments, one element of which was to be a transfer of the Forest Service from the Department of Agriculture to the Department of the Interior, which would be called the Department of Conservation. Ickes was an honorable man, but like Caesar he was "ambitious," and he had apparently sold the idea to President Roosevelt. For several years he worked

64 *1938 National Park Yearbook*, 11.
65 *National Parks Bulletin*, No. 64, Dec. 1937.

with the greatest persistence to get the national forests, fought the Forest Service men and Secretary Wallace of the Department of Agriculture bitterly, even threatened several times to resign if Roosevelt did not get the national forests for him; but Roosevelt always put him off, apparently sensing political complications if he made the change.[66] Ickes argued that the only major land administration activity not in the Department of the Interior was the Forest Service, that half of the area of the national forests was really grazing lands, which should be in the Department of the Interior, along with the Grazing Service which managed the grazing lands, and with the Park Service. The transfer was opposed by Henry S. Graves, Gifford Pinchot, and other foresters. The Park Service, however, was not greatly concerned about the transfer, so it will be unnecessary to discuss it further here. It still bobs up once in a while.

In the parks, two or three problems called for particular consideration. As the number of visitors increased so did the number of park employees, some of whom lived in the parks throughout the year and had children who needed educational facilities. To help in meeting this problem, the Secretary asked Senator Adams and Representative De Rouen to introduce a bill to permit the use for elementary school purposes of government-owned buildings in the parks and monuments and Indian reservations when the buildings were not needed for other purposes; but the bill did not pass.[67] In the next Congress, Senator Wheeler of Montana and Representatives Horton of Wyoming and O'Connor of Montana tried again and the Wheeler bill passed.[68]

COST LIMIT ON PARK BUILDINGS RAISED   Late in his administration Cammerer managed to get the cost limit on park buildings raised. The limit had been fixed at $1,000 in 1912 and raised to $1,500 in 1918. With price inflation, a vast increase in the number of tourists, and the amount of business to be attended to $1,500 was proving a very skimpy allowance. In March 1937 Secretary Ickes wrote a letter to the Vice President requesting that this allow-

66 See *Secret Diary of Harold L. Ickes* (New York: Simon and Schuster, 1954). many references.

67 S. 2935, H. R. 7825, 75 Cong. 1 Sess.

68 S. 29, H. R. 2881, H. R. 4097, 76 Cong. 1 Sess. Stat. 54, 761.

ance be raised, and Representative De Rouen of Louisiana introduced a bill to raise it to $3,000 but Taber of New York managed
to prevent it from coming to a vote.[69] In the same Congress, Senator Adams of Colorado introduced a similar bill which passed the
Senate but did not reach a vote in the House because of the objections of the anti-park trio, Taber, Wolcott of Michigan, and Rich
of Pennsylvania. These men thought that the Park Service was very
extravagant, and Wolcott objected to the delegation of so much
power to the Executive. This was the sort of difficulty that the Park
Service often faced in the early years—the disposition of Congress
to tie the Service up with petty regulations and restrictions, as if
the members of Congress, not half of whom had ever seen a western
park, could know better how to manage the parks than the Park
Service itself.[70]

In the next Congress, in 1939, De Rouen and Adams brought in
administration bills again to raise the limit to $3,000 and the Adams
bill passed both houses in spite of some opposition from Wolcott
and Rich, and was signed by President Roosevelt on February 13,
1940.[71]

There were other laws which in various ways gave the Park Service greater freedom in some of its work, but we need not consider
them here. For the benefit of the states rather than the Park Service, Congress passed an act in June, 1940, providing that where a
given act was a crime under state law but not under federal law in
the parks, the state law should prevail, and the state could punish
offenders in the parks.[72]

With the establishment of new parks, historic sites, recreational
demonstration areas, recreation areas—involving a total expenditure
of more than $200 million—the work of the Park Service mounted
to back-breaking proportions, and Cammerer had to call some of
his men in from the field to help at the Washington office. As a
further means of meeting all the demands of the time, he and Ickes
set up four regional offices, in Richmond, Omaha, Santa Fe, and
San Francisco, each with a regional director and branch chiefs.[73]

69 H. R. 6350, 75 Cong. 1 Sess.

70 H. R. 6350, S. 2056, 75 Cong. 1 Sess.

71 H. R. 6657, S. 2624, 76 Cong. 1 Sess. Stat. 54, 36.

72 Stat. 54, 234.

73 Shankland, *op. cit.*, 304. *Report, Secretary of the Interior, 1936*, 101. *National Parks Bulletin*, No. 64, Dec. 1937, 25.

END OF CAMMERER'S CAREER   All the responsibilities and multiplied tasks of the hectic years of the Great Depression and the heavy relief and employment expenditures were too much for Cammerer, and he developed heart trouble which forced his resignation in 1940. Probably his break in health was due not only to hard work but partly to the difficulty of getting along with his chief, Ickes. Ickes was an honest, honorable man and a devoted public servant, but a crusty, crabbed "curmudgeon"—as he described himself—not an easy man to get on with. Cammerer remained with the Service as regional director at Richmond, but still worked too hard and died on April 30, 1941, the second Director to die of overwork—the second Director to "give his life for the parks." In commemoration of his work in securing Great Smoky Mountains National Park, Mount Cammerer and Cammerer Ridge were named after him.[74]

74 Shankland, *op. cit.*, 306.

CHAPTER XXI

The Drury Administration

1940-1951

THE WAR AND POSTWAR YEARS,

THE TOURIST INVASION

Cammerer resigned effective August 9, 1940 and Newton B. Drury accepted the Directorship. Like Mather and Albright, he was a graduate of the University of California—in the same class as Albright. His interest in park problems and his ability were attested by the fact that for twenty years he had been executive secretary of the Save-the-Redwoods League, which had accomplished wonders, and also an executive in the California State Park Commission, one of the most energetic and successful of the state's commissions. He was the first director who was not a Mather-trained man; but he had had some contacts with Mather in his work for the redwoods. He was of a somewhat different disposition from Mather and Albright—a less aggressive promoter, yet his record of achievements was impressive; more retiring, more philosophical; less at home before appropriation committees and in the hurly-burly of politics, in fact he was said to dislike that part of his job. But he was well and broadly educated, conscientious, indefatigably devoted to the parks, and courageous and stubborn in defending them or in defending any principle that he regarded as important. Probably he was a little more sympathetic with the purist view of

443

park management than any of the other Directors, which might be the reason that Albright did not regard him as highly as many other men did.

Aside from the fact that the Director's job was a back-breaking job, Drury found conditions favorable. As a result of work relief funds, the parks were in better condition than ever before; visits were at an all-time high of 16,755,251; appropriations were reasonably generous at $21,098,282, with considerable emergency relief funds still available and some CCC men still working. Roosevelt was President and Ickes Secretary, both friends of the parks, and Congress was well disposed.

On April 3, 1940, Isle Royale National Park was finally established, on July 1, 1941 Mammoth Cave, and on June 12, 1944 Big Bend. In the cases of Isle Royale and Mammoth Cave, Congress reneged on its promise not to grant federal funds. Great Smoky Mountains, which had been established for full development on June 15, 1934, was dedicated on September 2, 1940. Everglades was not finally established until 1947.

FOREST PESTS, DISEASES, AND FIRES   Of course, there were many problems, sometimes it seemed little but problems. The number and virulence of forest insects and disease seemed to increase from year to year, and the battle between the Park Service and the beetles and bugs and diseases shifted back and forth with never a decisive victory. About 1941 the Service noticed that a bacterial necrosis was attacking the Saguaro, Organ Pipe and Senita cacti in the Southwest, and for some years there was doubt whether these plants would survive indefinitely, in fact there is still some doubt. There had been steady improvement in methods and equipment for fire fighting, but forest fires were always a serious danger. On November 15, 1941, Congress passed a law imposing a heavy penalty for setting fire to timber on any federal reservation, which perhaps helped in the southern parks and forests, where some natives found a kind of happiness and self-fulfillment in setting forest fires.[1] Incendiarism has been such a serious problem in southern forests that it sometimes seemed hardly worthwhile to try to grow timber—

1 Stat. 55, 763.

on large areas of land that were adapted to little but forest growth. In October 1956 an entire issue of *American Forests* was devoted to this problem. On October 17, 1947, a fire started outside the limits of Acadia National Park, spread to the park, and in a fire which burned for several days, destroyed 17,188 acres of timber on the island and 8,750 acres in the park. Congress promptly appropriated $400,000 to clean up and reforest the land.[2]

ECONOMICS OF THE TOURIST BUSINESS   The Park Service was always concerned about the question of fees for entrance, and in 1939 changed some of the fees. There had been some study of the economic aspects of the tourist business in Cammerer's administration, but Drury went further with these studies, to find out the amounts spent by tourists, and even their income groups and vocational and social classifications. To some extent, these studies were slanted at the question of the value of the parks to the people of the surrounding states. A study of Yellowstone in the late forties revealed that 4,200 people were employed in the park, most of them from three to five months, who earned from $1,250,000 to $1,500,000 a year. At least one-fourth of these were residents of the three surrounding states. This study showed that in 1941 tourists had spent $3,000,000 in the park and $6,500,000 in the states outside the park.[3] In 1949 the Park Service, in co-operation with the Bureau of Business Research of the University of Montana, made a pilot survey of Glacier Park visitors to determine the economic value of the park to the state, and came up with the conclusion that 75 per cent of the visitors who came to Montana came primarily to see Glacier National Park.[4] A 1950 study of Yellowstone indicated that tourists left $6,000,000 in the park, $6,076,055 in Wyoming, $4,790,710 in Montana, and $2,116,536 in Idaho.[5] There is something fanciful about such studies, but they served a useful purpose in helping the western people to see how profitable the parks were to them.

2 *National Parks Magazine*, No. 92, Jan.-Mar. 1948. Stat. 62, 222.
3 *National Parks Magazine*, No. 93, Apr.-June, 1948.
4 *Report, Secretary of the Interior, 1950,* 335.
5 *Report, Secretary of the Interior, 1951,* 345.

BROAD PROBLEM OF LAND USE   The Park Service had become a rather large organization, more and more interested in the whole problem of land use and conservation, and in late 1940 Secretary Ickes set up the Office of Land Utilization to formulate and direct an over-all and completely integrated program of land use and conservation.[6] In the late forties considerable sums were spent on soil and moisture conservation—$80,000 in 1948. With such funds the Service planted willows in the arroyo of Chaco Canyon to retard erosion; seeded, limed, and fertilized worn-out fields in Mammoth Cave Park; worked on soil erosion control along the Blue Ridge and Natchez Trace parkways, and did needed work elsewhere. In 1949 the Service spent $95,000 on this soil and moisture conservation, and stated that it should have $300,000 for it.[7]

Many activities proceeded much as before. The educational or interpretive work of the Service was growing rapidly. In 1941 the Service had thirty-four permanent naturalists, and small staffs of geologists, biologists, historians, and museum experts. An increasing number of students came to the parks for study. In 1941 over a hundred college and university classes entered the parks and monuments for study in the natural sciences, history, and archeology, and ninety-seven groups visited the parks for research. There were 115 museums altogether, about half of them historical. There was still a little criticism of the educational work in Congress, but the criticisms did not get much support. In March 1939, when Taber was objecting to the Service's "propaganda" expenditures, Representative Rankin of Mississippi answered rather well: "Mr. Chairman, if that (propaganda) is what the gentleman is after, he is in the wrong place. He should jump on the newspapers and the radio and the Power Trust, if he wants to stop propaganda in this country. To pass them up and then try to stop the educational work of the Park Service on the ground that it is propaganda is too far-fetched to be seriously considered."[8]

There was a considerable amount of construction in the parks and monuments in Drury's administration. Roads were built or reconstructed, campgrounds improved, with special attention, in

6 *Report, Secretary of the Interior, 1941,* XXVIII.
7 *Report, Secretary of the Interior, 1948,* 355, 356; 1949, 307.
8 *Congressional Record,* 76 Cong. 1 Sess., 2890.

some areas, to the growing number of trailers. At Lake Mead Recreation Area, a campground and lodge were built; at Olympic trails were improved and trailside shelters and administrative buildings were begun; at Arches administrative headquarters were started; at Mesa Verde a library was built, and a new water supply system was provided to replace the inadequate deep well, at a cost of $362,000.

There was occasionally some question as to what functions and activities were permitted the Park Service, and in 1946 Congress passed an act "to provide basic authority for the performance of certain functions and activities of the National Park Service," which enumerated the various parks and the purposes for which appropriations might be used.[9] It did not make any very significant changes, but perhaps it was well that certain acts should be specifically authorized, as for instance the plan of the Park Service to go outside Mesa Verde boundaries in search of water.

There was a growing interest in historic sites and buildings, which extended to archeological sites, and in the protection, stabilization, and even restoration of some such sites, the work of studying and protecting usually carried on in co-operation with various organizations. Under the guiding hand of the Park Service, state parks were growing in number, and standards of administration were rising somewhat. These were mainly recreational, but some were scenic, even beautiful, and there were a growing number of state historical parks.

WAR BRINGS NEW PROBLEMS   In December 1941 the attack on Pearl Harbor plunged the country into the Second World War and brought critical problems to the Park Service. With a war to finance, Congress cut park appropriations more than 50 per cent, although visits for 1941 were at an all-time high of over 21 million—war was declared after the touring season was over. With the imposition of gasoline rationing, there was no further reason for promoting travel and the travel bureau closed the field offices in New York and San Francisco, and abandoned all promotion. The railroads also abandoned their policy of putting on special supplemental trains and reducing rates to the parks. In 1942 the visitor

9 Stat. 60, 885.

total was down 55 per cent, although the average stay was longer—in Yosemite, more than doubled.

Reduced travel of course meant trouble for concessioners. By June 1943 no accommodations were offered at Crater Lake, some hotels in other parks were closed, and in some parks only "minimum service" was offered—cabins and simple meals. There had been three lodges at Isle Royale; two were closed. The Park Service tried to make adjustments to save the concessioners, but there was no real substitute for tourist business. Many concessioners would have been glad to unload their properties onto the government but, of course, Congress could not see the wisdom of buying them.[10]

The Park Service soon had a serious employment problem. In 1942 the CCC camps were ordered abandoned, with June 30, 1943, as the final liquidation date; but in 1943, the final liquidation date was postponed until 1944, although the camps were largely abandoned by August 15, 1942.[11] The military services were taking even the regular, trained employees of the Service, which was obliged to use various makeshifts, hire inexperienced men on a temporary basis, use women as rangers and fire lookouts, and skimp some protection services, with the result that vandalism increased. The Park Service tried to keep minimum staffs of engineers, landscape architects, and historians in the Washington office and in the four regional offices, in an effort to put the basic functions on a permanent rather than temporary basis, but such activities as the Historic Sites Survey, the Historic American Buildings Survey, road and trail building, and land acquisition were discontinued or cut drastically. Between June 30, 1942, and June 30, 1943, the number of permanent, full-time positions was reduced from 4,510 to 1,974—more than 55 per cent. There was a very modest compensation for the loss of CCC help in the establishment of camps where conscientious objectors worked. The work of the headquarters staff was made more difficult by the fact that the offices of the National Park Service, along with two other services, were moved from Washington to Chicago in 1942 to make room for military functions in Washington. They were not moved back until 1947.[12]

10 *Business Week,* June 19, 1943, 32.
11 Stat. 56, 562, 569; 57, 494, 498.
12 *Report, Secretary of the Interior, 1943,* 217, 218.

RECREATION AND THE ALASKA HIGHWAY   Notwithstanding
the stringency of war, the Park Service was given the difficult task
of assaying the recreational resources along the new Alaska highway. This highway was essentially military in its conception and
purpose, and on July 20, 1942, at the request of the Secretary of
War, Secretary Ickes withdrew from entry a strip of land forty
miles wide along the route of the highway to facilitate location and
construction and to provide military protection. The Canadian
government reserved a strip two miles wide along the 1,360 miles
of the Canadian part of the highway. Ickes saw the recreational
value of the road and asked President Roosevelt to approve the
allocation of enough of the highway funds to finance a study of
recreational values, and on January 8, 1943, approval was given.
The survey was pushed vigorously, and the report was completed
the next year.[13]

The Service continued its work of planning. During the year
1942 it completed master plans for all the 166 units of the national
park system, and submitted them to the National Resources
Planning Board as the basis of a six-year advance plan and program
of construction.[14]

WAR THREATS FROM COMMERCIAL INTERESTS   As in the First
World War, commercial interests promptly tried to capitalize on
the war spirit, anxious to help win the war for human freedom, at
a profit. On December 16, 1941, Secretary Ickes called upon the
various bureaus in his department for "full mobilization of the
Nation's natural resources for war . . . upon a basis best suited to
serve our military and naval forces without waste, and with a view
to saving all that we can of such resources for future generations."[15]
With respect to the demands for war materials and uses in the
national parks Ickes announced as a basic policy that all reasonable
alternatives must be exhausted, and that the demands must be
based on critical necessity rather than on convenience; but it seemed
necessary to compromise somewhat with national park principles.

---

[13] *Recreational Resources of the Alaska Highway and Other Roads in Alaska*
(National Park Service, Dec. 1944.) .

[14] *Report, Secretary of the Interior, 1942,* 169.

[15] *Ibid.,* 160.

Livestock men, always patriotic in war time and anxious to do their full part to feed the nation, again tried to get their cattle and sheep into the parks, but Ickes and Drury managed to keep grazing in the major parks down to prewar level. In national monuments, recreational demonstration areas, and historical areas, they allowed an increase from 20,000 to 25,000 cattle and from 74,000 to 82,600 sheep. There had been a small amount of grazing in ten of the national parks and a considerable amount of grazing in ten other national parks and in thirty-three of the national monuments and other areas; but it had long been the fixed aim of the Park Service to reduce the amount of grazing gradually and eliminate it ultimately.[16] A drought in the spring of 1944 brought new demands from stockmen, and Drury advised Ickes to consider limited grazing in some park areas in California as a war emergency measure if it could be shown to be necessary to save pure-bred stock from starvation. Ickes set up a grazing committee, including representatives of the Sierra Club, the California Council, the Western Federation of Outdoor Clubs and the Forest Service; but the committee reached the conclusion that there was no necessity for more grazing in the parks. In Yellowstone Park, in 1943, government hunters killed 691 elk and gave the meat to eleven Indian agencies and to the Montana Fish and Game Commission, and hunters killed 7,230 outside the park, but these were not mainly patriotic gestures. There were too many elk in Yellowstone.

The war threat to national park forests was quite as serious. There was a shortage of the Sitka spruce used in airplanes, as we have seen, and there were magnificent spruce trees in Olympic Park. Ickes and Drury held that none should be cut "unless the trees were absolutely essential to the prosecution of the war, with no alternative and only as a last resort"; but they could not well stand out as "slackers" in the war, so they made available some 4 million feet of spruce in the Coastal Strip and Queets Corridor. These areas were not yet a part of Olympic, but much of the land had been bought with the purpose of adding it. Before much damage had been done, the War Production Board got some Sitka spruce from Canada, Washington, and Oregon and found ways of using aluminum more. The War Production Board and lumbermen also wanted spruce and hemlock in Great Smoky Mountains, but

16 *Report, Secretary of the Interior, 1943*, 204.

found other wood. Manufacturers of tannin extract demanded dead chestnut trees along Blue Ridge. For a while there was a largely imaginary threat to all the country's timber—the threat of arson by traitorous sympathizers with the enemy. With the CCC workers disbanded and park employees greatly reduced, this looked like a real danger; but no clear evidence of such arson was ever seen.

A war calls for vast amounts of various minerals, and although the parks and monuments had few minerals, there were demands that they provide whatever they had that was needed. A deposit of tungsten in Yosemite was opened to mining, on recommendation of the Bureau of Mines, the Geological Survey, and the War Production Board; copper was reported in Grand Canyon and Mount Rainier, but the reports proved false; manganese was said to be found in Shenandoah, but this report was also false; some 15,000 tons of salt were mined in Death Valley; in the Olympic Acquisition area and in the Sitka National Monument thousands of tons of sand and gravel were mined for construction uses; in Mount McKinley Park the Park Service allowed the owner of an antimony mine to build a short-cut road across the park to get the crude ore out; operators of manganese mines adjacent to Olympic were allowed to use park lands for truck trails to reach the highways; and in Death Valley four access roads were allowed to reach sources of manganese, lead, tungsten, and talc. Some of these mines and roads disfigured the parks and monuments to some extent but the Park Service wished to do its loyal part in the war.[17]

MILITARY USE OF PARK AREAS   Military uses of the parks, monuments and related areas, including wildlife refuges, were extensive and in some cases detrimental. In 1942 the Secretary reported 125 permits to the War and Navy Departments to use national park lands, buildings, and facilities, and the next year 403 such permits were issued. The Paradise section of Mount Rainier was used for training troops in mountain warfare, the equipment for arctic warfare was tested in Mount McKinley, and various types of equipment and clothing were tested in Shenandoah, Mount Rainier, and Yosemite. At Joshua Tree National Monument desert warfare training units were permitted to build a road across the

17 *Report, Secretary of the Interior, 1943*, 203.

monument; at Hawaii extensive military training and defense installations were built, but they damaged the natural features badly and the Army repaired the damage and made other arrangements. In 1940 Congress withdrew 6,400 acres in Hawaii National Park for a bombing target range.[18]

In Yosemite the Navy took over the famous Awahnee Hotel for use as a convalescent center; in Mount McKinley the McKinley Park Hotel, operated by the government, was turned into a recreation center for soldiers; and on the South Rim of the Grand Canyon a former CCC camp was turned into a training camp. In Hot Springs the Eastman Hotel and Bathhouse was bought by the War Department for use as a hospital. Practically all the national park and monument areas along the Pacific, Atlantic, and Gulf coasts were used for defense installations, aircraft warning service posts, or for training, but they did little damage. Even some of the military and historic sites were used for the study of military maneuvers. In addition to this, a great deal of equipment was turned over to the armed forces by the Park Service to be used for clearing Army airfields.[19] The Park Service also waived all entrance fees for members of the armed forces, and many visited the parks—1,655,720 in 1943. In 1946 all the military concessions were turned back to the Park Service.

The first half of the Drury Administration was dominated by the war and the many problems brought by the war. Appropriations declined from $21 million in the fiscal year 1940 to $5 million in 1943, stuck at near the latter figure until 1947. The number of visits, 21 million in 1941, declined to 6 million in 1942; and did not get back to the 1941 level until 1946. Work on the parkways continued, but more slowly. The Park Service maintained its interest in state parks, but could do little for them, just as it retained a keen interest in interpretive work but had to restrict its activities. The guided trips in private cars were eliminated and hiking trips substituted. The Yosemite School of Field Natural History, which had been operating for more than a quarter of a century, was discontinued; publications were reduced and radio programs abandoned.[20] Some of the museums, now numbering 115,

18 Stat. 54, 761.
19 *Report, Secretary of the Interior, 1943*, 200 ff.
20 *Report, Secretary of the Interior, 1942*, 170.

were closed. In 1941 the Service had on its staffs 34 permanent naturalists and 114 temporary ranger naturalists, and small staffs of geologists, biologists, and museum experts; and over 100 college and university classes and 97 research groups visited the parks for study. In the next few years this personnel dwindled and the work declined.[21]

WILDLIFE PROBLEMS   The Service was still plagued with a host of wildlife problems. There was, for instance, the problem of the relation of predators to the Dall Sheep in Mount McKinley. The sheep seemed not to be doing well, and there was a suspicion that the wolves were killing too many; but some of the naturalists believed that the trouble was mostly something else, and a careful study by Adolph Murie tended to show that the wolves were not the main cause of the decline in sheep population.[22] Mountain sheep in Rocky Mountain, Death Valley, and Joshua Tree also called for study. Many of them were at times thin and mangy, and the problem was what caused this? In Death Valley and Grand Canyon an overpopulation of burros proved difficult to overcome, and in Yellowstone the surplus of elk and bison continued unabated, in spite of efforts of the Park Service to secure a reduction. During much of this period Zion was plagued with a great surplus of mule deer which was little affected by hunting outside the park. The canyon was a fine, sheltered wintering ground, largely free from predators, and the deer did not venture out much, with the result that they multiplied to a point where they destroyed much of the food plants, while the deer themselves suffered grave deterioration. In 1944 park rangers in co-operation with the Utah State Department of Fish and Game, killed 300 of them, but the forage in the canyon did not recover for years.

In Rocky Mountain a similar situation developed. There the elk and deer had been heavily overgrazing the forage for years. They were restricted to the higher elevations by domestic livestock which used the lower pastures. The Park Service finally, in the winter of

21 *Report, Secretary of the Interior, 1941,* 286.
22 Adolph Murie, *The Wolves of Mount McKinley* (Washington: National Park Service, 1944).

1943-44, planned a reduction of one-third—200 deer and 300 elk—but managed to kill only 12 elk and 14 deer. One of the problems in Rocky Mountain was the deer-beaver relationship—the deer killed the aspens which the beaver needed, and vice versa.

For some time the Park Service policy had been to permit each species of wildlife to carry on its struggle for existence without artificial help, in the belief that this would ultimately be good for the species and conform to the purpose of the parks, although if a particular species appeared to be on the point of extinction it might be given help by control of predators, artificial feeding, treatment for diseases, or whatever proved necessary. One difficulty often encountered was that distress for one species might mean trouble for another. In Yellowstone, for instance, a persistent surplus of elk sometimes meant starvation for the elk and depletion of the forage for both elk and antelope, with the antelope threatened with extinction.[23]

Late in Drury's administration there was a great deal of interest in the preservation of the little key deer of the Florida Keys, which seemed to be on the verge of extinction. These little deer—only twenty-six to twenty-nine inches high and weighing only about fifty pounds—had never been very numerous, and by 1947 were estimated at only about seventy, declining to twenty-five or fifty in 1950 as a result of the intrusion of "sportsmen," the building of homes in the area, and the destruction of forage by hurricanes. There were a number of efforts in Congress to set aside a small refuge for them, all of them unsuccessful; but the Boone and Crockett Club for some years maintained a warden for their protection.[24] In August 1957 a refuge was finally set aside for them.[25]

With reduced revenues and depleted manpower as the emergency relief work was eliminated, some of the work of the Park Service suffered. The CCC boys had done much of the fire fighting, and when they left fires became a worse menace, as did also the forest insects and diseases. The ever-present problem of sanitation was perhaps less serious, with declining numbers of visitors, but maintenance had to be neglected.

23 *Report, Secretary of the Interior, 1943*, 208, 209; 1944, 220 ff.
24 *National Parks Magazine*, July-Sept., 1950, 100.
25 Stat. 71, 412.

THE END OF THE WAR AND NEW PROBLEMS: TOURIST INVASION

The end of the Second World War, in August 1945, brought an end to one kind of troubles and a beginning of another. Already in the summer of 1945 tourist visits began to climb and the next year reached an all-time high of 21,752,000—to the park system—and continued to climb. Appropriations proved not so buoyant, remaining at war levels through 1945 and 1946, leaped nearly 500 per cent in the fiscal year 1947, to $26 million, then dropped to $10 million in 1948, and did not rise to a fair level until 1950. Throughout much of his administration Drury had to worry along with inadequate appropriations. When he came in in 1940 the parks were in good condition as a result of relief work camps and funds; but in the next five years there was serious depreciation of facilities, and the park personnel force was badly shattered. Ranger forces were short, and the forty-hour week and other labor regulations made the situation worse.

In 1949, near the close of his administration, Drury reported discouragingly on "The Dilemma of Our Parks."[26] He stated that on some days as many as 30,000 visitors invaded Yosemite, that there was heavy wear and tear on the vegetation, carelessness with trash, especially in Yellowstone, that the crowds were quite too great on naturalist-led walks, that sanitation was a serious problem, that more camping space was needed, that some parks, particularly Big Bend and Olympic, needed roads, that more museum space was needed. He estimated the financial needs of the park system at $140 million for physical improvements, $175 million for roads and trails, and $181 million for completion of the parkways that Congress had already authorized. The appropriation for 1949 was a little over $14 million.

There were insistent demands that the appropriations be increased, but for some time, under the weight of the vast war debt left by the Second World War, Congress was in no mood to spend lavishly, particularly for the protection of natural resources. Indeed in the 80th Congress—the "worst" Congress, President Truman called it—the livestock and other interests of the West were making a pertinacious drive to take over the national grazing lands and national forests. They succeeded only in reducing appropriations for protection—under the pretense of economizing. In the discus-

26 *American Forests*, June 1949, 6 ff.

sion of the appropriation bill in 1947, Senator Taylor of Idaho struck at the "penny wise and pound foolish" policy of Congress and at the "Republican economizers," and made a strong plea for larger appropriations. He stated that some of the parks were on a self-supporting basis at the time.[27]

The tourist invasion at the close of the war was hard to care for in many ways. There were not enough hotel and cabin accommodations, particularly cabin accommodations, which many of the visitors wanted. The Service had tried to secure expansion of cabin service, but had not been able to get enough. This shortage of accommodations was worse at some points than others, worse at Yosemite Valley and Old Faithful, for instance, than in some of the less frequented canyon parks, such as Zion. In 1946 there were numerous complaints of inability to get sleeping accommodations— all, taken by eleven in the morning; of bad roads; of restaurants closed because of lack of meat; of shortages of many things.[28]

Perhaps the worst result of shortages of rangers was the increase in vandalism, which had been serious during the war and was quite as bad or worse afterward. The vast majority of tourists are of course decent, law-abiding people, but there are always a few vandals and hooligans who, if they are not watched, appear to find satisfaction in destroying or mutilating beautiful natural objects so that others cannot enjoy them. At Yellowstone they threw rocks, beer bottles, banana peelings, trash of all kinds, into the lovely pools, even jammed limbs of trees into them so they could not erupt naturally, and wrote their names on formations. At Grand Canyon they wrecked three cases at a trailside exhibit, damaged the binoculars at Yavapai observation station and destroyed or stole various exhibits. At Hawaii they destroyed some of the silversword plants which the Park Service had been trying to save from extinction. At Petrified Forest they stole petrified wood and cut dates and names over prehistoric Indian pictures at Newspaper Rock. At Zion they wrote names on natural features; at different points they damaged comfort stations and buildings, hacked trees and shrubs, even burned in their camp fires the tables at camp grounds, the signs and amphitheater seats. In Joshua Tree two teen-age boys started a fire that destroyed most of the Washingtonia palms in the 49 Palms Oasis. In various of the ruins of the South-

27 *Congressional Record*, May 12, 1947, 4984.
28 *Congressional Record*, 79 Cong. 2 Sess., Appendix 3495.

west vandals stole artifacts, and damaged some of the walls, as did also grazing cattle and rodents.

One cannot fail to agree with Mark Twain's strictures on the vandals at Baalbec: "It is a pity some great ruin does not fall in and flatten out some of these reptiles, and scare their kind out of ever giving their names to fame upon any walls or monuments again, forever." Many of the ruins needed strengthening and stabilization, and such work had been largely abandoned during the war.[29]

In a few parks there were not even enough rangers to man the checking stations, and in 1948 several of the parks were estimated to have lost altogether $100,000 from this. It would not have helped the parks to shift labor from other essential work to the checking stations, even if they had been able to collect twice or five times their wages, because the increased revenues would have gone to the United States Treasury, and the other services would merely have suffered more.

One investigator drew a disheartening picture of conditions in Yosemite in the late forties. He found that there were altogether 492 buildings in this park, half of them from sixteen to seventy years old, and that $5,000 was allocated to maintain them where $150,000 was needed; that the amounts of investment by the government and by the largest concessioner were about equal, but that as a permanent maintenance crew the government had one carpenter, the concessioner eleven, the government had one painter, the concessioner seven, the government had altogether ten men and the concessioner sixty. The telephone system was so poorly constructed that it broke down in almost every storm; the power plant, completed in 1918, was subject to frequent failures, and the current was so poor at times that radios and electric razors would not work. The sewage disposal system, built in 1931, was overloaded, and there were 100 privies in the park. Klamath weed—poisonous to animals—and thistles were spreading. Entrance stations were unmanned at night. The museums were crowded and attendants sometimes did part-time work for nothing. Yet the park revenues exceeded expenditures: the park was operating at a profit.[30]

There were too many tourists not only for the cabins and facilities but for a few of the parks themselves. The crowds that often

29 *Report, Secretary of the Interior, 1945,* 207 213; 1947, 322, 323; 1948, 322.
30 *National Parks Magazine,* No. 101, Apr.-June, 1950, 43.

descended into Yosemite Valley could not all find hotel rooms or cabins. They could scarcely find space to throw down a camp bed. At Old Faithful in Yellowstone the tourist cars swarmed like Japanese beetles, with parking spaces hard to find, and at meal times hungry visitors formed a line a block long in front of the cafeteria. The hordes of tourists were becoming a problem, and for the indefinite future would be growing worse.[31]

PLANS FOR MEETING TOURIST INVASION   Various plans were discussed for meeting the situation. As early as 1945 Drury considered moving the concession facilities and administration buildings out of congested areas in several parks; but this was a long-run program which would provide no relief for several years. Also considered was the establishment in crowded areas of a limit on stays at campgrounds and hotels and cabins at the height of the season. S. E. Brady, managing director of the Tri-State Yellowstone Park Civil Association, suggested that earlier opening and later closing of the parks might relieve congestion. Yellowstone, for instance, was open officially from May 1 to October 15, but the hotels were open only from May 20 to September 14. Whether this extension would have helped may well be doubted, for Yellowstone is sometimes a very cold and snowy place in early May and late September.[32] Where the difficulty was not lack of room but only lack of facilities and unwillingness of concessioners to build facilities, it was thought advisable to have the government build the facilities. This is what was done with success at one point on Blue Ridge Parkway. It would have been easier to induce a concessioner to operate a government-built concession than to build one himself and operate it. Proposals for government building of concession utilities, however, had the unfortunate effect of scaring concessioners and so of making it more difficult to get them to expand accommodations. Notwithstanding the surplus of visitors, Congress on July 25, 1947, voted $75,000 for a revival of the Tourist Bureau.[33]

In the meantime the Park Service did its best, skimping on its ranger force. In Mesa Verde one ranger sometimes had to care for

31 *Report, Secretary of the Interior, 1947*, 17.
32 *Congressional Record*, May 12, 1947, 4885.
33 *Report, Secretary of the Interior, 1946*, 35, 334, 335.

300 people in four hours. In some cases restrictions were imposed
on tourists to protect park objects. In Mesa Verde visitors were no
longer allowed to wander freely through Cliff Palace; at Yellowstone certain routes were prescribed among the formations to limit
wear and curb vandalism; at Montezuma Castle only those engaged
in serious study were encouraged to enter the castle.[34] Yet the
Yosemite School of Field Natural History, abandoned during the
war, was reopened in June 1948.[35]

NATIONAL PARK CONCESSIONS, INC.   There were some important new developments in park policy, one of which was in the
concession policy. The general policy of the Park Service had been
one of regulated private operation of concessions, with some kind of
division of profits, although there were variations. In Mount Mc-
Kinley the government operated the concession, but only because
it had not proved profitable to private enterprise. When Ickes came
in he had a theory that the government should build, own, and
operate the concessions, although he said little about government
operation, perhaps recognizing that it would be politically impossible to get such a radical policy through Congress. In 1941, however, Ickes was able to break away from the old profit-motivated
concession policy in Mammoth Cave Park. For a century or more
the facilities at Mammoth Cave had been managed in various ways,
but not on a conventional profit-seeking basis; and when Mammoth
Cave was finally established as a national park in July 1941, Ickes
and Drury were able to set up a new kind of concession principle
in the National Park Concessions, Inc., a nonprofit distributing
membership corporation, with no capital stock, which furnished
accommodations at reasonable rates and developed facilities solely
in the interest of the public welfare. Any profits made went to the
development of additional facilities. In the event of liquidation or
dissolution of the corporation, its assets would be sold and the
proceeds, with all other money belonging to this corporation, would
be donated to the government to be spent by the Secretary of the
Interior for the benefit of the National Park System. The Park
Service maintained the same relationship to this agency as to other

34 *Report, Secretary of the Interior, 1947,* 17.
35 *Report, Secretary of the Interior, 1946,* 330; 1948, 340; 1949, 308, 309.

private concessioners in other parks, in supervision over prices of food, sanitation, and wages and hours of employees.[36]

National Park Concessions, Inc., was given all or some of the concessions in several other parks, monuments, and other areas— Isle Royale, Big Bend, Everglades, Olympic, F. D. Roosevelt Home, Vanderbilt Mansion, and Blue Ridge Parkway. It also entered into a sub-agency agreement with the Lassen National Park Company to operate the concessions in Lassen Volcanic for the duration of the war.[37]

PRIVATE CONCESSIONERS AND THEIR PROBLEMS   Rather naturally the problem of concessions came up for serious consideration. The concessioners had plenty of business, but for a year or two after the end of the war they worked under great difficulties. After five hungry years they had insufficient supplies, labor, buses, and many other things; especially they lacked experienced help and accommodations for their help, and had to pay much higher wages for such inexperienced help as they could get. With many requests for advance reservations some were obliged to limit stays of guests— at the South Rim of Grand Canyon, for instance, to three days.

They needed more facilities, but after the lean war years they naturally were reluctant to add heavily to their investments. Like Mark Twain's dog that would not chase the coyote, they had "had some of that pie." In 1947 there was rumbling in Congress at the services rendered and prices charged in the parks, and the House Appropriations Committee demanded that the Park Service make a study of concessions, insisting that prices should be reduced, that the Treasury should get a greater revenue, and that concession "monopolies" should be ended.

Drury decided that he could not direct the study in such unbiased fashion that the conclusions would command the respect of Congress and the public, so Secretary Krug—Ickes' successor—appointed an outside committee, an advisory group, headed by Clem Collins of Denver, past-president of the American Institute of Accountants. The report was made February 19, 1948, approving the general policy of the Service in the preceding thirty-one years, approving the policy of government ownership of concessions, but not gov-

36 *Report, Secretary of the Interior, 1941*, 291, 292.
37 *Ibid.*, 217.

ernment operation, and suggesting that Congress should establish a definite policy of acquisition and maintenance. Unsympathetic with criticism of monopoly in concessions, the advisory group ruled that contracts to a single concessioner for all operations in a given area represented sound policy, considering the hazards involved in many concession operations and the need for adequate and continuous service, and that the Director should be free to select operators on the basis of known qualifications, not only as to adequate financing but also as to sympathy with the objectives and policies of the National Park Service.

The advisory group ruled that while "service at cost," with a reasonable return on investment included in cost, was sound in principle, it was not actually practicable; that a franchise or contract fee should be levied against net profits; that the concessioner should get a fair minimum return of perhaps 6 per cent on investment, and should get a fair percentage of the profits above this to offset occasional lean years. The group did not believe that the concessioners generally made excessive profits.

This study might have seemed enough, but in 1948 Representative Dawson of Utah presented a House resolution authorizing the House Public Lands Committee to study concessions, and Senator Butler of Nebraska offered a Senate resolution for the same purpose, but neither was reported.[38]

The advisory group reported that the facilities provided by the federal government as well as the personnel in the parks were "taxed beyond capacity." "All this results in situations for which the Service is often criticized but over which it has little control. Much of this criticism would not arise if the appropriations for the Service were more nearly commensurate with responsibilities on it and the public service expected from it."

Under-Secretary Chapman wrote to Albright asking him to comment on the reports of the advisory group, and in his reply Albright, whose judgment was about the best that could be got, said that he found little in the report that he disagreed with. Albright thought that ultimately it would be well for the government to own the facilities, but that this could not come soon.[39]

The work of the advisory group, and of the Park Service, would have been easier if the Service had been able to keep up with its

[38] H. Res. 639, S. Res. 254, 80 Cong. 2 Sess.
[39] *Congressional Record*, 80 Cong., 2 Sess., Appendix, 4149, 4150.

auditing of concessions, but it was not able to hire enough auditors and at times was years behind. In 1949 there were 671 unaudited reports, and the number was increasing. The task of auditing the reports of 250 concessions doing a gross business of $25 million was beyond the Service's financial resources.

While the advisory group was studying the concessions, a number of contracts expired, and a few of the concessioners showed little interest in renewal. At Mount Rainier, for instance, the Rainier National Park Company, which had operated since 1916, tried to "throw in the sponge" in 1948. This company had been organized and financed by a group of public-spirited citizens of Seattle and Tacoma at the solicitation of Mather, but operating at a loss in the war years and unable to replace its old and inadequate plant, it had induced Representative Tollefson to introduce a bill for government purchase of its assets, excluding transportation facilities, which passed without discussion, appropriating whatever was "necessary" for the purpose.[40] Senator Mitchell had already brought up a bill to make appropriations for construction of facilities in Rainier, but it got no attention.[41] Similarly the Lassen National Park concession company found itself unable to finance needed new developments, and decided it had had enough of national park business, and asked to be relieved of its obligations; but Drury induced the company to continue operations for another year. In Glacier, the Glacier Park Company was not interested in a twenty-year renewal of its lease, but was willing to continue on a year-to-year basis until it could dispose of its facilities. The company had several hotels, and the decline of railroad tourists—to only 2 per cent of the total—spelled red ink in its operations.[42] A number of concessioners found it difficult or impossible to secure the capital for the expansion that was so imperatively needed, or even for rehabilitation. Sale of a business that had been losing money was naturally difficult to manage. In a few cases there were men who were willing to take over surrendered contracts, but most of them lacked capital and experience.

Early in November 1948 Secretary Krug announced new policies aimed at greater uniformity in contracts, the elimination of inequities, encouragement of investment, and a more clear-cut defi-

40 H. R. 1662, 81 Cong. 1 Sess. Stat. 64, 895.
41 H. R. 6473, 81 Cong. 1 Sess.
42 *Report, Secretary of the Interior, 1949,* 301.

nition of contractual obligations of both government and concessioners. Krug's new policies did not elicit any enthusiasm on the
part of concessioners, however, because, like Ickes, he believed in
government construction and ownership of concessioners' facilities.

When Oscar Chapman succeeded Krug as Secretary, in 1949, he
suggested certain new principles which he thought would make
concessions more attractive:

1. A policy of canceling existing contracts prior to their expira-
tion and granting new contracts for up to twenty years.

2. Options to purchase the concessioners' facilities to be exercised
only at the end of the contract period. This option had of course
not been popular with concessioners.

3. The requirement that the concessioner must set aside 10 per
cent of the gross receipts from rental of overnight facilities to be
used to maintain and repair such facilities was to be eliminated.

4. Revision made in regulations governing labor conditions, providing for a forty-eight-hour work week, with time and a half for
overtime, to put concessioners on a par with competitors outside the
park.

5. For most concessioners a flat franchise fee with a tax based on
gross revenues above a "break-even" point, rather than on net
profits.[43]

This had several advantages:

1) The government would be assured of a small rental payment.

2) The amount due the government would be easily determined, without extensive computations.

3) The Park Service would be relieved of the necessity of making audits of the concessioner accounts to ascertain the
correctness of the net profit as reported.

4) Disputes concerning the amounts charged for salaries and
expenses of officials and the correctness of other charges for
expenses would be avoided.

Some progress was made in securing extensions and improvements. The 100-room Lake Hotel in Yellowstone, closed for several
years, was rehabilitated and modernized and 50 new cabins were
added. At Shenandoah, a 10-room guest building was erected at
Big Meadows; on Blue Ridge Parkway a 24-unit lodge, a gasoline
station, and coffee shop were erected by the government; at Yosem-

43 *Report, Secretary of the Interior, 1950,* 301.

ite, Zion, and Bryce Canyon there were considerable additions, in some cases of rooms and cabins with baths, a new luxury in park services and one which was adding to the responsibilities of the Park Service in providing water and sewer facilities. New concessions, mostly minor, were also set up at various other points.[44] In 1948 the Park Service, long experienced in training its own men in providing interpretive services, though these had suffered along with everything else during the war, began a policy of training also the employees of concessioners.

WINTER USE OF PARKS   Winter use of parks had been growing rapidly, but suffered more during the war than summer use. After the war, however, there was a strong demand that some of the parks be opened in winter, and the Service would have been glad to accede to that demand; but there were many difficulties in the way. If skiers were to come to the parks in winter the roads must be kept open, and in areas where the snowfall was from six feet to as much as twenty feet this was expensive. The hotels and cabins in such parks as Mount Rainier, Crater Lake, Lassen Volcanic, Yosemite, and Sequoia were built for summer use, and were scarcely fit for winter use. It was hazardous to house large numbers of guests in timber buildings covered with snow and with few exits—snow nearly covered buildings in Mount Rainier and Crater Lake; and heating costs were high, as indeed were all costs. Most of the visitors came on week ends or holidays, yet it was often necessary to keep up operations throughout the week, and it was difficult to get dependable employees without a heavy payroll for the rest of the week. The Rainier National Park Company furnished winter accommodations for several years and consistently lost money doing it; and most other concessioners were not anxious to try it. The solution of the problem came partly with the development of ski runs outside of the parks.[45]

STATE PARKS   Assistance to the states in the creation and administration of state and local parks was skimped. While recognizing that its main function was the protection and management

44 On concessions, see *Report, Secretary of the Interior, 1946*, 35 ff, 310; 1947, 330; 1948, 345 ff.; 1949, 297 ff.; 1950, 319 ff.
45 *Report, Secretary of the Interior, 1946*, 36, 317; 1950, 323.

of the great scenic parks, the Park Service assumed some responsibility in furnishing advisory and consultative assistance to the states on park questions, particularly planning and administration; and under its encouragement and guidance the number of state parks, and the use of them, increased greatly even in the postwar period. From 1946 to 1951 the number of state parks increased from 1,550 to 1,725, the attendance from 57 million to 120 million, and the expenditures from $10.5 million to $38.5 million.[46] Senator Pepper of Florida wanted the federal government to do more for state parks, but failed to interest Congress.[47] Many of the state parks were not well managed.

On June 10, 1948, Congress provided for some additional help to the states, and more work for the Park Service, by an act providing for the disposition of surplus federal real property to the states and their political subdivisions for use as public parks, recreation areas, or historic monuments—the determination as to what areas were suitable to be made by the Park Service. Areas for public park and recreation use could be sold to the states for 50 per cent of fair value; those valuable as historic monuments were to be given free. In the following years a considerable number of such areas were conveyed on the recommendation of the Park Service.[48]

Two years before this, in the appropriation bill of July 1, 1946, Congress helped the Park Service out a little by authorizing the transfer of war surplus equipment and materials up to $2.5 million worth, and on June 29, 1948, added $3 million worth to this. The Service got $322,000 worth of supplies under these acts, mostly road and trail equipment and materials, but some of it was not in good condition and it was difficult to get parts for some of the equipment.[49]

RECREATIONAL DEMONSTRATION AREAS   The recreational demonstration area activities of the Park Service, which had their beginning in 1936, were gradually abandoned, following the Act of 1942 which allowed the Park Service to divest itself of the

[46] *Years of Progress, 1945-1952* (U. S. Dept. of the Interior), 126, 127.
[47] S. 2043, 79 Cong. 2 Sess.
[48] *Report, Secretary of the Interior, 1948*, 354; 1949, 324, 325; 1950, 330. H. R. 5125, 78 Cong. 2 Sess. S. 2277, 80 Cong. 2 Sess. Stat. 58, 765 ff.; 62, 350.
[49] Stat. 60, 378; 62, 1142. *Report, Secretary of the Interior, 1949*, 306.

projects.[50] In 1946 only six remained to be disposed of, and by 1948 appropriations were down to $10,000, for the distribution was about concluded. In a few instances projects were turned over to national parks and monuments. Lands acquired for Acadia, French Creek, Shenandoah, and White Sands were turned over to Acadia National Park, Hopewell Village National Historic Site, Shenandoah National Park, and White Sands National Monument, respectively, under the act of 1942.

The recreational demonstration projects, conceived partly as a way of providing work relief, proved to be of great public value, as the heavy use of them proved; indeed it is now clear that there should have been many more of them, and of other submarginal land purchases, with vastly greater acreage, for within a few years more parks and recreation areas were needed, and are still needed. It would have been farsighted statesmanship to buy not 397,056 acres of submarginal land, but 50 to 100 million acres. Some would have been developed for recreational use and the rest could have been reforested, to be turned to recreational use when needed or used as forest land. If we had done this we would have less eroded and ruined land and our agricultural economy would be in sounder condition.[51]

50 See pp. 367-69.
51 *Report, Secretary of the Interior, 1946,* 342; 1947, 338, 339.

CHAPTER XXII

The Drury Administration

1940-1951

THREATS TO THE PARKS: DAMS, MINING, STATE INTERESTS, MECHANIZED TRAFFIC

Under the Park, Parkway, and Recreational Area Study Act of 1936, the Park Service had made studies of the recreational resources at reservoir sites, but early in the Drury Administration these studies took a new turn; the Bureau of Reclamation and the Army Engineers began to ask the Service to study recreation possibilities before the reservoirs were created.

RECREATION ON RESERVOIR PROJECTS   The Boulder Canyon Project was authorized in December 1928. In June 1936, $10,000 was appropriated for administration, protection, and maintenance of the recreational activities, and the next year $45,000 was granted for these purposes.[1] In November 1940 the Bureau of Reclamation requested the Park Service to study the scenic, scientific, and recreational resources of the Colorado Basin as part of a comprehensive plan for the utilization of the water resources of the region, and on January 27, 1941, Secretary Ickes approved the request. The work was done by the Branch of Lands of the Service, headed by Conrad

1 Stat. 45, 1057; 49, 1794; 50, 607.

467

L. Wirth, with Frederick Law Olmsted as consultant, and the report was completed in 1946—an excellent report.[2]

Other areas followed Hoover Dam—Lake Mead. In 1940 the Park Service, co-operating with the Reclamation Service and using PWA funds, made a study of the recreational possibilities along the impounded waters of the Colorado River in Texas, and the next year Congress appropriated $27,000 for an investigation of the recreational resources of Denison Dam and Lake Texoma on the Texas-Oklahoma border. Other areas were developed—Lake F. D. Roosevelt above the Grand Coulee Dam, Millerton and Shasta Lakes in California, and Shadow Mountain Lake in Colorado.

The intention was to keep these as recreation areas, but the Millerton Lake area was later turned over to the state of California, Shasta Lake was transferred to the Forest Service, and, after struggling for some years with the problem of financing, Lake Texoma was transferred in 1949 to the Army Engineers who had built the dam. There were large tracts of private lands along the shore, which the Park Service with its limited appropriations was unable to buy, and there was some local dissatisfaction with the slow progress in development. To some of these people it seemed likely that the Army Engineers, with their more adequate funds, might be able to proceed more rapidly; of course the states themselves were not inclined to buy the land. Furthermore, administration proved difficult because of an unsatisfactory division of authority between the Park Service and the Army Engineers. The story of Texoma illustrates well the difficulties encountered in some of these inter-agency projects.[3]

Most dams are "multiple-purpose," providing irrigation, hydroelectric power, and flood control, or perhaps only two of these, and it may be difficult to single out the most important purpose. Almost all dams do to some extent provide flood control, but in recent years there has been a proliferation of dams whose primary purpose is flood control. In 1936, as a result of a number of floods and droughts, Congress passed an act declaring it to be a policy of the government to control floods, employing the Army Engineers, and under the act of 1936, and later acts of 1938 and 1944, many dams

2 *A Survey of the Recreational Resources of the Colorado River Basin*, published in 1950.

3 *Report, Secretary of the Interior, 1949*, 327.

were built.[4] On some of these various dams the Park Service was asked to study recreational resources and make plans for their development. In 1947 the Service was reported studying 12 reservoir projects, making two sub-basin reconnaissance surveys covering 21 other reservoirs in the Missouri River Basin, and also studying 128 existing and proposed projects outside the Missouri River Basin. The next year the Service continued its study of the Missouri River Basin and turned out 55 reconnaissance, project, and sub-basin reports, an atlas of archeological sites in reservoir basins, and 27 evaluations of recreational benefits of reservoir sites. Some of the surveys were not completed because of lack of funds.[5] Yet Congress had been fairly generous in appropriating funds for this work—$260,400 in 1947, $300,000 in 1948, and $227,000 in 1949.

SCENIC, SCIENTIFIC, HISTORICAL, ARCHEOLOGICAL, AND PALEONTOLOGICAL STUDIES   In these reservoir surveys the Service was instructed to study not only the recreational resources but also the scenic, scientific, historical, archeological, and paleontological resources. When dams were built they sometimes inundated archeological and paleontological ruins and articles of value, particularly in regions of the West, and the task was to save these before the water covered them. The work was to be carried on in co-operation with the Bureau of Reclamation, the Office of Indian Affairs, the Army Engineers, and the Smithsonian Institution, with state universities, historical societies and museums assisting. The Service began such archeological studies early in Drury's administration, made studies in the Yampa and Green river basins in Dinosaur National Monument in the early forties, when it seemed likely that these basins would be inundated by dams; and during the decade of the forties the amount of this work increased. In 1948 the Service reported archeological surveys of 38 reservoir areas in 18 states, 14 of them in the Columbia River Basin, and 68 paleontological surveys, four of them in the Missouri River Basin. Using bulldozers to dig up the soil, they reported finding new data on the pre-Columbian inhabitants of Nebraska, which indicated that their cultural existence ran back much earlier than had been believed.[6]

4 Stat. 49, 1570; 52, 1215; 58, 887, 888.
5 *Report, Secretary of the Interior, 1947*, 334; 1948, 352.
6 *Report, Secretary of the Interior, 1948*, 352.

As more dams were built and more land was inundated, it came to be seen that such dams could have a serious influence on wildlife, particularly on fish. Dams on the Columbia River have interfered with the migration and spawning of salmon, to a point where there has been some concern regarding the future of the salmon packing industry; and in some other dam reservoirs fish have not prospered for some reason. Land wildlife has sometimes suffered too because the best grazing land has been covered by the reservoirs.

RECLAMATION SERVICE AND ARMY ENGINEER THREATS TO PARK
AREAS   Unfortunately, the Reclamation Service and the Army Engineers were not punctilious as to where they planned to build their dams; the national parks looked as good to them as anywhere, or perhaps a bit better than most other places, because there were good power sites in the national parks. These two dam-building agencies caused the Park Service more trouble than almost any group of private interests; they always had fat purses and strong political influence. In the late forties they were making tentative plans for spending $9 billion for dams, a few of them in the national parks and monuments. In 1947 the Bureau of Reclamation was planning 134 irrigation and power projects on the Colorado and its upper tributaries, to cost $3,460 million. Several of the senators and representatives from Arizona—Hayden, McFarland, Murdock, Harless, and Patten—were pushing a bill, introduced by McFarland and Hayden, for the Bridge Canyon Dam, which passed the Senate on February 21, 1950. This dam would have made a reservoir of much of Grand Canyon National Monument and eighteen miles of the national park. Urged by the National Parks Association and other conservation organizations, Hayden reduced the height of the dam to 1,877 feet above sea level so it would not flood so much of the national park, but the Park Service was still opposed to it, and it did not pass the House. This dam was to cost $234 million.[7]

Another dam scheme in the Grand Canyon area, the Kanab Tunnel, an Army Engineers' scheme, called for a dam in Marble Canyon, upstream from the park, and the diversion of water through

7 H. R. 1616, H. R. 1598, 80 Cong. 1 Sess. S. 75, H. R. 934, H. R. 935, 81 Cong. 1 Sess. S. 75, H. R. 1500, H. R. 1501, 82 Cong. 1 Sess.

a tunnel under the Kaibab Plateau to a powerhouse on Kanab Creek. No part of this weird engineers' delirium would have been in the national park, for the tunnel would have detoured around north of the park, but it would have robbed the Canyon of some of its water within the park and would have changed the nature of the stream—from a violent, turbulent flow of dirty, silt-laden water to a small, more placid flow of clear water. To those unschooled in park principles this might have seemed an improvement, but to the Park Service it was desecration. The Colorado had always been a violent, turbulent, silt-laden stream, that was why it was able to grind its way down into the mighty canyon; and to reduce it to a pretty little river would have been to change its fundamental and natural character. The Park Service wants things *natural,* as nature made them. It might have tolerated a power dam above, which would merely have caught the silt and cleared the water, because the silt in the river is gradually filling the Hoover Dam Reservoir— Lake Mead—but a reduction in the amount and character of the flow was contrary to national park principles.[8]

The Army Engineers wanted to invade Glacier Park, build a dam at Glacier View on the Flathead River, which would have flooded 20,000 acres of winter range of moose and elk and white tail deer. They defended this dam as needed in flood control—there had been a disastrous flood on the Columbia the preceding spring—and they argued further that some industries should be moved back from the coast, where they were vulnerable to enemy attacks, and would need electric power from the dam. Irrigation was a minor point. Drury objected to this in rather eloquent terms: "Civilization is encroaching on the wilderness all over our land. What remains of it becomes increasingly precious to present-day Americans, and will be in even greater degree to Americans in the future. Here, threatened with permanent destruction, is an extraordinarily fine example of 'original America.' We cannot afford, except for the most compelling reasons—which we are convinced do not exist in this case—to permit this impairment of one of the finest properties of the American people."[9] Various conservation groups joined the Park Service in protest, and in 1949 the Army Engineers abandoned the project. In August of the next year, however, Representative

8 *Report, Secretary of the Interior, 1949,* 294.
9 *Report, Secretary of the Interior, 1948,* 339.

Mansfield of Montana revived the project with a bill in the House, which fortunately did not pass.[10]

There was of course a need for flood control in all parts of the country, and the Army Engineers planned a dam at Mining City, on the Green River in Kentucky, which the Park Service reported would periodically flood the Echo River Channel in Mammoth Cave. The project hung fire for several years, but the Omnibus River and Harbors flood control bill of May 1950 was amended to prohibit construction if it would have any adverse effect on Mammoth Cave.[11]

There were also threats of dams in Kings Canyon and Big Bend national parks, in Dinosaur National Monument, and across Lake Solitude in the Cloud Peak Wilderness Area of the Bighorn National Forest in Wyoming; but none of these was successful. The Army Engineers investigated the possibility of building flood control dams on the Potomac too, which might have done injury to the Chesapeake and Ohio Canal, now in the National Capital Park System under the jurisdiction of the Park Service.

Water power, irrigation, and flood control projects might have been regarded with more tolerance if they could have been more nearly justified in accounting terms; but very few of them were worth what they cost. They had their inception in the Reclamation Act of 1902, which provided that the receipts from the sale of public lands in the West might be used to build reclamation dams. The reclamation fund—the amount received from the sale of public and reclaimed lands—was supposed to be a revolving fund, to be used for more and more dams; but unfortunately this fund did not revolve, because few of the projects were worth what they cost, or perhaps were worth nothing, in the sense that the farmers using the lands could pay nothing toward cost. This was understood by western senators and representatives at the time the Reclamation Act was passed. They regarded the reclamation fund as a pork barrel, just as some of them still do. As the sales of public lands dwindled, the westerners came to rely more and more on the federal Treasury. A few of the dams, such as Hoover, Grand Coulee, and Bonneville,

10 H. R. 6153, 81 Cong. 1 Sess. *Report, Secretary of the Interior, 1947,* 336; 1949, 294; 1950, XX, 306; 1952, 355; 1954, 319.

11 Stat. 64, 175. *Report, Secretary of the Interior, 1947,* 336; 1949, 294; 1950, XX, 306; 1951, 319.

have been quite worth their cost, but most of the irrigation dams have not justified their cost, particularly in recent years when the best sites have already been used and when there have been more farm products than were needed. Multiple-purpose dams also produced electric power, but usually at high cost. Flood control dams were really less needed than soil and forest conservation.[12]

Secretary Chapman finally decided that he had enough of fighting the dams, and in 1951 issued an order barring the Bureau of Reclamation from surveys and investigations in national parks and monuments, wilderness areas, and wildlife areas.

Meantime there had been some agitation for the establishment of a Missouri Valley Authority, a Columbia Valley Authority, and several others, patterned after the Tennessee Valley Authority; and these proposals worried the Park Service lest such organizations might bring water-control dams into the parks. The first bills had no provisions exempting Yellowstone, Glacier and other park areas in the Missouri basin from water control structures.[13]

STOCKMEN THREATEN GRAZING LANDS   In the early forties the western stockmen launched a bare-knuckle fight for the grazing lands on the national forests and public domain, which was presently expanded to cover other federal resources. The fight began in 1941 when the Grazing Service tried to raise the grazing fees—which were much too low. There was a lull for a couple of years, but in early January, 1945, Senator McCarran, a Nevada stockman and lawyer, introduced a bill "relating to the management and administration of national forest grazing lands" which passed the Senate but not the House.[14] A year later Senator Robertson, a wealthy Wyoming rancher, brought in a bill which was a masterpiece of grandiose cupidity, "To provide for the granting of public lands to certain states, for the elimination of lands from national forests, parks, monuments, reservations and withdrawals in connection with such grants, and for other purposes." The bill was designed to give many of the federally owned resources in the West to the states and finally to the big stockmen, but it was too large a pill for Congress

12 *Report, Secretary of the Interior, 1948,* 338 ff.
13 H. R. 2203, 79 Cong. 1 Sess. H. R. 4287, S. 1631, 81 Cong. 1 Sess.
14 S. 33, 79 Cong. 1 Sess.

to swallow.[15] The stockmen did, however, manage to get Congress to cut appropriations so drastically that the Bureau was unable to guard the range, which was for a while gravely abused. A complicating factor in this tussle was the fact that certain officials in the Grazing Services were playing improper politics. The threat was not to the parks directly, although if the stockmen had been able to gut the grazing lands on the range and in the national forests, they would surely have invaded the parks next.[16]

MINERS AND OTHERS REACH FOR PARK AREAS   Both the miners and the lumbermen were after Olympic. Representing the miners, Representative Magnuson of Washington tried in June 1943, in the 78th Congress, to get the park opened to mining, but failed. In the next Congress, promoted to the Senate, he tried again and failed.[17] The lumbermen made persistent efforts to get some of Olympic cut out for lumbering but never succeeded. Senator Hayden and Representative Murdock of Arizona strove mightily to get Saguaro opened to mining, but failed, although their efforts were not altogether unreasonable. Saguaro had been set aside too hastily and included some land that could have been left out.[18] These two men had better luck with Organ Pipe Cactus. Without much trouble they succeeded, in 1941, in opening the monument to mining, in spite of the protests of conservation organizations.[19] Ten years later there was one mine in the monument. Hayden and Murdock also tried to secure the establishment of Coronado (at first International, later National) Monument, open to grazing and mining, and succeeded in August 1941.[20] Representative Englebright of California wanted to open Death Valley to mining; later Representative Clair Engle wanted to permit grazing in all national parks and monuments.[21]

15 S. 1945, 79 Cong. 2 Sess.
16 Report, Secretary of the Interior, 1948, 32. National Parks Magazine, Jan.-Mar., 1948.
17 S. 1470.
18 S. 7, 76 Cong. 1 Sess. S. 259, S. 394, H. R. 2676, 77 Cong. 1 Sess. National Parks Bulletin, No. 69, Feb. 1941.
19 S. 260, H. R. 1064, H. R. 2675, 77 Cong. 1 Sess. Stat. 55, 745. American Forests, July 1941, 349; Nov. 1941, 534.
20 Stat. 55, 630.
21 H. R. 1398, 78 Cong. 1 Sess. H. R. 5058, 78 Cong. 2 Sess.

Joshua Tree National Monument had a long record of assaults from mining interests. In 1942 Drury reported that the monument was so shot through with private holdings that it was impossible to administer it properly. Mining interests were trying to get in, and in 1946 the Park Service agreed to eliminate about one-third of the monument, the part thought to be valuable for minerals, but the miners wanted all but 50,000 of the 825,340 acres in the monument eliminated. Representative Sheppard of California introduced a number of bills to eliminate a part of the park, but none passed. Other men picked up the ball, and finally Phillips of California got the bill through in September 1950. This act eliminated 289,500 acres, and directed the Secretary to make a mineral survey to determine if the monument was more valuable for minerals than for national monument purposes. A joint survey by the Bureau of Mines, Geological Survey, and Park Service disclosed that the remaining lands were of most importance for national monument purposes; but that did not end the threat, for five years later the miners were still banging at the monument gate.[22]

Several years later Senator Barrett of Wyoming brought up a bill to grant mineral rights to those who had acquired or should later acquire land under homestead entry. On some of the public lands the subsoil minerals were reserved to the federal government and Barrett did not approve of this. Particularly he did not like the fact that the federal government owned 70 per cent of the minerals in Wyoming and paid only 37½ per cent of the royalty receipts to the states. The government also paid 52½ per cent into the reclamation fund, however, and kept only 10 per cent to cover cost of administration. Barrett's effort was fruitless.[23]

The miners' senators and representatives pursued their goal with persistence worthy of a better cause. In House discussions of the appropriation bill, in June 1941, several western men tried to tack on an amendment forbidding the acquirement of land for park or monument purposes in Arizona except by act of Congress, and some of the mining men were eloquent in their approval. Representative White of Idaho announced it as the "birthright of the American

[22] *Report, Secretary of the Interior, 1942,* 177; 1946, 322, 339; 1951, 340. H. R. 2795, 80 Cong. 1 Sess. H. R. 4116, 81 Cong. 1 Sess. H. R. 7934, 81 Cong. 2 Sess. Stat. 64, 1033.

[23] H. R. 8781, 81 Cong. 2 Sess.

citizen to discover, locate, and own mining claims under the public-land laws, a birthright certain departmental officials assiduously seek to take away from the people of the United States. . . . If we seek to Russianize this country, the policy these departments seek to impose on our people by stripping our citizens of their remaining birthright is a good way to go about it. . . . We must be vigilant, and see to it that our laws protecting our rights are not repealed or nullified." The amendment to an appropriation bill was of course out of order and was held to be so.[24]

In a bill for the admission of Alaska to the Union, Delegate Bartlett of Alaska tried on March 2, 1948, to abolish Katmai, Sitka, and Old Kasaan, reduce Glacier Bay, and eliminate all national forests, wildlife refuges and other federal reservations in Alaska, but the National Park Service got these provisions eliminated from the bill, which did not pass anyhow.[25]

THE DAM THREAT TO DINOSAUR   By far the most controversial attempt at a park raid was, however, the effort of the Bureau of Reclamation to build two dams in the Dinosaur National Monument. This monument, originally (1915) an 80-acre dinosaur graveyard, was enlarged by President Roosevelt in 1938 to 209,744 acres of some of the most scenic canyon land in the West. The proclamation adding this land contained a provision which was later cited as permitting the building of dams: "this reservation shall not affect the operation of the Federal Water Power Act of June 10, 1920, as amended, and the administration of the monument shall be subject to the Reclamation Withdrawal of October 17, 1904, for the Brown's Park Reservoir Site in connection with the Green River Project." Opponents of the Dinosaur Dam insisted that this provision conferred no rights but there was dispute about it. The Jones-Esch amendment to the Federal Power Act, passed in 1921, forbade power developments in *existing* parks, but at the time Dinosaur covered only 80 acres, and there was some question whether the Jones-Esch Act should be construed to forbid power developments in the 203,885-acre addition made by Roose-

24 *Congressional Record,* 77 Cong. 1 Sess., 5375.
25 H. R. 5666, 80 Cong. 2 Sess.

velt's proclamation of 1938.[26] At any rate David Madsen, Superintendent of Dinosaur, later testified that at public meetings at Vernal, Utah, and Craig, Colorado, he had told the people that grazing and power development in the enlargement that was being considered would not be interfered with.

Congress had passed an act in August 1921, authorizing Arizona, California, Colorado, Nevada, New Mexico, Utah, and Wyoming—the states in the Colorado drainage area—to make compacts for the disposition and apportionment of the waters of the Colorado, and the states in the Lower Colorado area came to an agreement; in 1931 Boulder Dam was begun, and completed in 1935. The states in the Upper Colorado Basin came to an agreement later on dams to be built on the Upper Colorado.[27]

The 1946 report on the recreational resources of the Colorado River Basin was definitely critical of the two dam sites suggested for Dinosaur—Echo Park and Split Mountain. "Construction of dams at these sites would adversely alter the dominant geological and wilderness qualities and the relatively minor archeological and wildlife values of the Canyon Unit so that it would no longer possess national monument qualifications."[28]

Three years later, notwithstanding this report, Commissioner Straus of the Reclamation Bureau wrote to Secretary of the Interior Chapman asking him to approve the dam, and ten days later Drury addressed a memorandum to Chapman urging him to deny the application. Early in 1950, without consulting the Park Service and before Chapman had approved, the Bureau of Reclamation laid its plans before the administrative agent for the Upper Colorado states; and soon afterward the Upper Colorado Association urged immediate construction of the Echo Park Dam, with several others to follow later. With lush funds at its disposal, the Reclamation Bureau put on a very effective propaganda campaign which

26 There is a discrepancy here in the areas given for Dinosaur. The original area was stated at 80 acres, and the 1938 addition at 203,885—so stated in the proclamation. This should make an area of 203,965, which is 9,744 acres less than reported after the addition, and now reported as the gross area of the monument. Later, more accurate surveys resulted in the revised figure of 213,709 acres.

27 Stat. 42, 171.

28 *A Survey of the Recreational Resources of the Colorado River Basin* (Dept. of the Interior, National Park Service, 1950), XXII.

won over many of the people of Utah and western Colorado. It represented the dams as being for water power and irrigation, although Echo Park Dam was for power only; it argued that the dams would not injure this monument scenically, but would really improve it, would bring in roads and accommodations and make the monument more accessible; that there was no other satisfactory site for the dams, and that the Echo Park and Split Mountain dams were the essential keys to the whole Upper Colorado Project. The town of Vernal, near the monument, and the home of Senator Watkins, made much of the noise in favor of the dams, hoping for a real estate boom and rapid "development."[29]

But the dams had to be approved by the Secretary and by Congress; Drury and the Park Service were of course opposed to it. Secretary Chapman called for hearings on April 3, and at the hearings he announced: "It is my purpose in holding these hearings to try to determine from you people which you think is the more important to the country, the largest number of people who can be served and the greatest good that can be served. . . . I am sincerely and honestly trying to get a record that I intend to review carefully and personally. I want to make a decision in this case that will stand in the interest of the people when I have made it. I don't expect to make everybody happy when I make this decision. . . . I only hope that I am right, and I want to be right."[30]

The hearings were not altogether amicable, for Drury and the Park Service were resolute in their opposition to the dams; but on June 27, 1950, Chapman announced his decision to approve, on the ground that if built in Dinosaur the dams would be more economical of water than they would if built elsewhere—less evaporation. He argued that he was not providing any dangerous precedent for other park areas. Drury was, of course, unhappy, and reported with the slightest touch of sarcasm: "Ultimate decision on the proposals rests with the Congress. The Secretary's assurance that his decision was based upon special circumstances, and his reaffirmation of long-established policy as to the integrity of national park areas is gratifying to the National Park Service."[31]

29 Article by Bernard De Voto, *Saturday Evening Post*, July 22, 1950. *National Parks Magazine*, Jan.-Mar. 1952.
30 *National Parks Magazine*, July-Sept. 1950, 110.
31 *Report, Secretary of the Interior, 1950*, 305, 306.

There is a tradition in Washington to the effect that when the boss says anything, his subordinates should say "yes, yes, yes." Chapman, as Secretary of the Interior, was Drury's administrative superior, and when Chapman approved the Dinosaur dams the traditional bureaucratic thing would have been for Drury to agree that dams in Dinosaur were absolutely necessary and good and holy. But Drury, by all reports, was not a bureaucratic, time-serving, rubber stamp; he was a man of courage and strong convictions, very staunchly devoted to his task of protecting the parks and monuments. He had spoken out against the dams that Chapman approved, and it appears that Chapman did not forget or forgive such "insubordination." In early December 1950, he offered Drury a lower position than that of Director, a newly created post as special assistant to the Secretary of the Interior, at a lower salary. Within hours, it was said, this was followed by a peremptory demand that he accept or resign as of January 15, 1951. Chapman explained that on November 30, 1951, Demaray had asked to be retired and as a matter of sentiment he wanted to reward him with the Directorship for a short time. This explanation might have held marbles but not water, and on January 10, 1951, Drury declined the demotion and offered to state his reasons, but was told that it was unnecessary. On April 1 he presented his resignation and went back to California as Chief of the Division of Beaches and Parks of California, where he had served for years with distinction.[32]

This was bad administration in various ways. For one thing, Chapman's announcement of Drury's resignation was followed almost immediately by the appointment of the new Director. This was in unpleasant contrast with the procedure of Ickes when Albright resigned. Ickes formed a special committee to advise him on the selection of a successor; Chapman did no such thing. Chapman's treatment of Drury was not even calculated to help the dam promoters if that was what he wanted to do, for inevitably the mess would come up in the Congressional debates and would hurt Chapman and the cause he had espoused.

32 *National Parks Magazine*, No. 105, Apr.-June 1951, 42. *American Forests*, Mar. 1951, 48. *Congressional Record*, 82 Cong. 1 Sess., Appendix, 1241.

Chapman's action represented a vindictive and inglorious anti-climax to an otherwise good administration as Secretary of the Interior. Aside from the discourtesy of his treatment of an able and conscientious public servant—who was right, as Chapman implicitly conceded later when he changed his mind and testified against the Dinosaur dams—there was the question as to the effect of his action on park administration. There was no question as to Demaray's capabilities or devotion to the parks, but in his short term—and it was to be a short term, for he had already indicated his intention to retire—he could not pick up the innumerable administrative tasks and manage them as well as the man who had been handling them for ten years. Furthermore, as the editor of *American Forests* pointed out: "At stake, however, is much more than the disposition of one man's job. Of basic concern is the question of a new principle in casting off and selecting administrative leaders. Certainly conservation, or any other cause, will suffer if we abandon the custom of seeking out the most qualified man in the nation to direct our vital land use programs. Nor will government be able to entice such caliber of man into a position subject either to pressure or politics."[33]

Various organizations presented petitions to President Truman, protesting against Chapman's action, but without effect.

Drury was out, but Dinosaur was not lost. The fight was just shifted to Congress, where it was to be decided in the next Congress, the next presidential administration, the next park administration.

THE PARK SERVICE AND NON-PARK AREAS   The Park Service, along with conservation organizations, not only tried to protect the national parks and monuments but took an interest in attempted desecration of state parks and other areas. During these years, for instance, there were persistent attempts to get a power dam in the splendid Adirondack Forest Reserve of more than 2 million acres—really a state park too—in New York; but the protests of conservation organizations stopped it. Protests were not so successful with San Jacinto Mountain in southern California, dedicated as a federal-state primitive area in 1930 through agreement of the Forest Service and the California State Park Commission. In the forties

33 *American Forests*, Mar. 1951, 48.

certain recreation interests began to agitate for an aerial tramway to the top of the mountain. Various conservation organizations, including the Park Service, tried to prevent this, but in 1945 a law passed the California legislature permitting it, and was signed by Governor Warren.[34] When the term of the tramway contract with the Winter Park Authority expired in December 1956, the State Park Commission refused to renew it, so San Jacinto appears to be safe for the present.[35]

Canada also has had troubles with power invasions of her parks. During the Second World War power interests succeeded in damming Lake Minnewauka in Banff National Park.[36]

PROBLEMS RELATING TO ARCHEOLOGICAL RUINS   Research and the stabilization of structures in the archeological national monuments, neglected during the war and for some time afterward, was resumed in the late forties, the Smithsonian Institution taking an active part in the work. These structures were subject to destruction from rain, from wind erosion, and from freezing and thawing, as well as from vandalism and from grazing animals. In some places the ground water disintegrated foundations. There were many ruins that still had to be excavated, and many ancient structures that needed stabilization to prevent them from falling or disintegrating further. In 1949 the Park Service reported fourteen scientific-educational agencies conducting sixteen separate field research programs, one of which uncovered in California evidence of the earliest known type of American dwelling, dating back to a time between 3000 and 2000 years B.C., and the earliest known ancestor of Indian maise, a diminutive pod corn of about 2500 B.C.

Dr. Jesse Nusbaum, at one time superintendent of Mesa Verde, served as consulting archeologist to check plans and qualifications of research groups and to guard against violations of regulations. Stabilization work was carried on at Tumacacori, Casa Grande, Canyon de Chelly, Hovenweep, Aztec Ruins, Bandelier, Mesa Verde and Chaco Canyon. The usual policy of the Service was to

34 *National Parks Magazine*, No. 97, Apr.-June 1949, 21.
35 *National Parks Magazine*, Apr.-June 1957, 63.
36 *National Parks Magazine*, July-Sept. 1949, 10.

make repairs so obvious that even a novice could see that they were repairs, using steel posts to support roofs in Montezuma Castle and Tonto, and sometimes using steel angles, rods, and turnbuckles.[37] Two months after Chettro Kettle ruin in Chaco Canyon was stabilized, a flash flood swept down and destroyed twenty-five rooms and deposited six to eight feet of mud and debris over other parts of the ruin.[38]

PRIVATE AND STATE LANDS IN PARK AREAS   Non-federal lands in the national park and national monument areas still presented one of the greatest problems of the Park Service. There were about 600,000 acres of non-federal lands in the park system—150,000 acres owned by states, 150,000 by railroads, and 300,000 acres by several thousand private owners. The state lands were school lands, given the states when they were admitted to the Union, and were a problem in twenty-six areas, particularly in Glacier, Carlsbad, Dinosaur, Great Sand Dunes, Joshua Tree, Saguaro, and White Sands, practically all in the West. In the East and in Texas the states had to contribute their state lands and large sums of money to get their parks; in the West the states often did pretty well in trades with the federal government. The state of Montana had tracts of about 10,000 acres of timber land in Glacier Park which for thirty years the Park Service had been unable to secure. The lands were state school lands and if the state wanted to dispose of them it must sell at public sale at not less than $10.00 an acre. It was said that the state was willing to contribute half the value of the lands if a sale could be arranged to the federal government; and in January 1948 Representative D'Ewart introduced a bill to authorize such a sale, which passed without debate.[39] Another trade was made in 1954, and five years later 9,353 acres of Montana land were acquired.

The railroads had originally been granted a total of 190 million acres of public land to encourage railroad building, more than 500,000 acres of which were later included in national parks and

[37] National Parks Magazine, No. 85, Apr.-June 1946. See also James A. Lancaster, Jean M. Pinkley, Philip F. Van Cleave, and Don Watson, Archeological Excavations in Mesa Verde National Park, Colorado (Washington: National Park Service, 1958).

[38] Report, Secretary of the Interior, 1948, 342, 343; 1949, 316.

[39] H. R. 4980, H. Rept. 1306, 80 Cong. 2 Sess. Stat. 62, 80.

monuments, chiefly Grand Canyon, Yellowstone, Bryce Canyon, Joshua Tree, Grand Canyon National Monument, Petrified Forest, and Wupatki. About 350,000 acres were released under the Transportation Act of 1940 leaving 150,000 acres, much of which was in Joshua Tree. This railroad land was in checkerboard grants with alternate sections (square miles) remaining in government ownership. In some cases real estate promoters bought railroad sections to develop as desert homesteads or for other purposes, much to the disadvantage of the Park Service; but in most cases the railroads were co-operative in exchanging their lands. In Mount Rainier, for instance, the Northern Pacific, which owned 300 acres of primeval forest, sold its land to the Park Service in 1945 for a fraction of its market value.

The personally owned lands, scattered among several thousand owners, were the worst nuisance, used in lot subdivisions, as homesites, ranches, cabin sites, resorts, soft drink stands, and cafes, auto junk yards, sawmills, gravel pits, many of them eyesores. The most troublesome were the subdivisions, in Glacier, Kings Canyon, Lassen Volcanic, Olympic, Rocky Mountain, and Yosemite. Particularly were they troublesome where they were owned by senators and representatives—in Glacier, Senators Walsh and Wheeler owned summer homes at the foot of Lake McDonald. Often the buildings were poorly designed, some lots sold and resold, some were tax-delinquent and abandoned. A few private owners donated their lands to the government, but purchase was the only way to get most of them, and the Park Service had never had enough money to buy much.[40] In the early fifties the Supreme Court of the United States helped the Park Service a little in its decision that the federal government, since it had been ceded jurisdiction over Sequoia and Kings Canyon by the state of California, had jurisdiction over private lands in those parks and could regulate their use.[41]

Prior to the thirties, some funds were voted occasionally, conditioned on equal amounts being donated by private or other donors. Just before the Second World War Congress made several small grants for specific parcels, and after the war $25,000 for Montezuma Well and, in 1947, $30,000 for George Washington Carver National Monument. About the end of the war the Park Service began to

40 See an article by Newton Drury in *National Parks Magazine*, No. 89, Apr.-June, 1947. *Report, Secretary of the Interior, 1946*, 34.

41 *Report, Secretary of the Interior, 1952*, 382.

formulate definite plans for land acquisition, set up in its Lands Division a Real Estate Branch, to analyze all data regarding private lands. This analysis was fairly well completed by 1946, and priorities were set up for acquisition.[42]

In the appropriation act of July 25, 1947, the first important general grant for land buying was made, of $200,000, $30,000 of which was to be used for lands for the George Washington Carver National Monument, and the rest for certain specified areas. This was a beginning, enough, as Drury said, to buy all the private lands in the parks in 100 to 150 years if prices did not rise.[43] The next year another $200,000 was granted, to be used for certain specified parks, and in 1949 $300,000 was voted for private lands and Mammoth Cave—the amount for Mammoth Cave not specified.[44]

In the 1950 appropriation act the Park Service was given greater latitude in the expenditure of moneys, and one item of $19,667,000 was granted for roads, trails, buildings and other facilities "and for the acquisition of lands and water rights" etc., etc. This enabled the Park Service to buy private lands if that seemed more important than other uses of the money. Of course, the Service could sometimes trade public lands outside the parks for private lands within, but this was increasingly difficult to do as more and more of the best land on the public domain was taken up by private individuals; yet there was some trading. Director Wirth traded the Southern Pacific out of 30,000 acres in Joshua Tree in 1952. In the middle forties the Park Service tried to get a law passed authorizing exchange of lands within the parks for other lands within the parks in order to get lands that were situated along the roads or otherwise strategically located.[45]

There was some progress in reducing the amount of private lands. Between 1946 and 1951 the amount was reduced from 609,000 acres to 510,000 acres.

42 *National Parks Magazine,* Oct.-Dec. 1951, 125.
43 Stat. 61, 483 ff.
44 Stat. 62, 1140; 63, 793.
45 In his "Secret Diary," Ickes says that apparently the Park Service had been for several years engaged in some rather questionable practices in purchasing private lands in the parks. Congress commonly appropriated money for this purpose with the proviso that it should be matched 50-50 by funds from other sources. This was a niggardly policy, for there were few private individuals willing and able to match federal funds; and the Park men, according to Ickes, found a way around this. They employed an appraiser who "would

WESTERN MEN REACH FOR PARK REVENUES   Some of the western men presently conceived the idea of getting a slice of the national park revenues by tying it in with appropriations for the purchase of private lands. No matter how much they were exploiting the parks, some of them were reaching for more in about every Congress. In the forties a number of bills were offered to secure state participation in park revenues, some of them offering the bait of funds for purchase of private lands. Some of these bills were brought up by real friends of the parks, others by western men whose main interest was in getting revenues for their states.

In 1948 Senator Butler of Nebraska introduced a bill which would have given 25 per cent of the national park revenues to the states as a compensation for loss of tax revenues, and would have given the Park Service $20 million to be used $1,250,000 a year for purchase of private lands.[46] The Park Service, and also the National Parks Association favored the bill, because it would reduce the hostility of some western people to the parks and to the expansion of park areas, and at the same time would provide funds for buying private holdings. This was understandable, but there was no real justification for a division of park revenues as long as the expenses of administering the parks were so much greater than the revenues. In 1950 the appropriations were over $30 million and the revenues a little more than $3.5 million, which meant that the taxpayers of the United States were paying about 85 per cent of the cost of maintaining the parks while the people of the western states were getting far more benefit from the parks than people elsewhere. This was brought out in clear relief recently by figures of visits to Yosemite. California and Illinois paid about equal amounts in taxes for the support of the parks, but California provided 74.19 per cent of the visits and Illinois 2.53 per cent—California people used the park thirty times as much as Illinois people. Naturally, the more the western states got out of the parks, and the

determine the value of the property to be purchased, then double that value on the basis of an understanding with the owner that half of the doubled value would represent a contribution to the National Government. The net result was that the Government would be paying the full, fair and reasonable values of the property instead of fifty per cent of it." The Park men were not doing this for any personal profit, of course, but to build up the parks; but Ickes was gravely concerned about it. (*Secret Diary of Harold L. Ickes* [New York: Simon and Schuster, 1954], Vol. II, 582 ff.)

46 S. 2132, 80 Cong. 2 Sess.

more the government appropriated, the more reason there was for hostility on the part of middle and eastern states that had no national parks within their borders.[47]

PROBLEMS OF MECHANIZATION   In the early forties trailers began to assume the dignity of a real problem, growing steadily. In the years after the Second World War airplanes became another problem. The Park Service had begun to wonder what to do about airplanes as early as 1920, and by 1944 there was a demand that airfields be built in the national parks and that airplane services be developed. Some people argued that the planes gave a better view of some scenery than could be got from the ground, and saved time too; perhaps in the deep recesses of their minds some were moved by the common American notion that the use of planes would enable them to get past the scenery more quickly. The Park Service conceded that sight-seeing planes might be desirable in some places, but insisted that they could use outside airfields, and stood adamant against the building of airfields in the parks, arguing that airplanes would alter the landscape, create excessive noise, frighten wildlife, and perhaps increase the fire hazard. Airplanes do create excessive noise, as city residents near airports can testify. A further result of airplane touring over the parks would be a reduction in park and concessioner revenues, for the planes would pay no entrance fees and would patronize no park hotels or cabins; but of course on the other hand they would make no demands on park facilities.

The Service was willing to have airports built outside the parks, and co-operated with the Civil Aeronautics Administration in trying to get them, even encouraged the introduction of a bill in Congress to allow the Department of the Interior to sponsor or co-sponsor such developments. In 1950 a law was passed granting the Secretary authority, in co-operation with the Administrator of Civil Aeronautics and perhaps other agencies, to develop airports *in or in close proximity to* national parks and monuments and recreation areas. The first one built was near the west entrance of Yellowstone, where facilities existing were unsatisfactory.[48]

47 *Congressional Record*, 77 Cong. 1 Sess., May 14, 1941, 4057.
48 *Report, Secretary of the Interior, 1950*, 336. H. R. 4587, 81 Cong. 1 Sess. S. 1283, 81 Cong. 2 Sess. Stat. 64, 27.

Drury and his men were generally opposed to visitor use of planes in the parks. Yet some planes did fly over the parks, sometimes at low altitudes. In February 1947 the Park Service adopted regulations forbidding the landing of planes in any national park area except in emergencies and except at a small number of existing airports and landing strips, but was unable to control the height at which planes must fly, although the Service tried to keep all planes above a 2,000-foot minimum. At Grand Canyon the Arizona Helicopter Service began helicopter flights over the canyon in June 1950, from Tusayan Auto Court, just outside the park. There was no law to prevent this, and safe height limits did not apply to helicopters, but there were many irritating incidents, and low-flying helicopters disturbed visitors and residents until one machine was wrecked and the flights were abandoned.[49]

But airplanes and helicopters have been useful, in policing, in fire protection, in taking wildlife censuses, in the rescue of mountain climbers, and in other activities. The first Park Service use of a helicopter in rescue work was in Yosemite in 1950.[50]

Another machine whose invasion of the parks has sometimes been criticized is the outboard motor. This sputtering creature of the devil does disturb primeval quiet and doubtless scares the fish. It is a considerable nuisance on Yellowstone Lake. Aquaplaning in Grand Teton gives the park a bit of a honky-tonk flavor. Radio sometimes disturbs the quiet of campgrounds, but is indispensable in park work. Jeeps are sometimes said to be injurious to the ground cover, but they too are about indispensable in some areas.

DANGERS IN THE PARKS   There are always a few visitors to the parks who like to climb mountains, and sometimes get into precarious situations. In seven areas the Service requires those who plan to climb to register before they start, and insists that they be fit for such adventure, even talks some of them out of it; but some get into trouble, and a few are killed. Five mountain climbers were killed in 1949. The record of the Service in the matter of fatalities is rather good, however. In 1949 there were forty-four

49 *Report, Secretary of the Interior, 1946*, 328; 1947, 339; 1949, 328; 1950, 336; 1951, 346; 1952, 437.

50 The Forest Service reported in January 1957 that its use of airplanes, mainly in fighting fires, had increased 1,000 per cent in five years.

fatalities in the national parks and monuments, with over 33 million visitors—not a bad record. Of these fatalities, eighteen were in motor vehicles, thirteen were due to drowning, seven in mountain climbing, one from electrocution, two from scalding in the thermal areas, one in skiing, and two unknown. Probably people are safer in the national parks than outside.[51]

INTERNATIONAL INTEREST IN THE PARKS   More and more the national park system was attracting the attention of leaders in foreign countries. In 1946 Secretary Krug reported park visitors from Belgian Congo, Brazil, France, Great Britain, China, Denmark, Spain, Finland, Netherlands, Sweden, Uruguay, India, Honduras, and elsewhere. Some of these visitors came to study our national park system, with the purpose of developing something like it at home; and we shall see that some of them did this, although no countries except Canada and New Zealand have national park systems comparable with our own.[52]

51 *Report, Secretary of the Interior, 1950, 332.*
52 *Report, Secretary of the Interior, 1946, 343.*

CHAPTER XXIII

The Drury Administration

1940-1951

JACKSON HOLE

Two national parks that had been authorized before were established in Drury's administration—Big Bend (1944) and Everglades (1947). There were also several important additions to park areas.

In 1942 Isle Royale was enlarged by the addition of much of Passage Island, the Siskiwit Islands Bird Reservation, and "any submerged land within four and one-half miles of the shore line of Isle Royale and the immediately surrounding islands."[1] The Park Service was steadily adding to the Ocean Strip and the Queets Corridor in Olympic. More important was the proclamation of *Jackson Hole* National Monument in 1943 and its final addition to Grand Teton in 1950.

Jackson Hole is a valley, not precisely defined, lying south of Yellowstone Park but not immediately adjoining it, and southeast of Jackson Lake, some of it timbered and under Forest Service administration, some of it grassland, and some desert. Some of it was included in a wildlife refuge. The "settlers" were mostly cattlemen and dude ranchers, but there were some summer homes, refreshment stands, filling stations, dance halls, and other tourist

1 Stat. 56, 138.

accommodations of the sacrilegious type commonly provided by private enterprise in scenic areas. It was lower in altitude than Yellowstone, with a milder winter climate, more suitable to winter grazing for wildlife.

EARLY INTEREST IN JACKSON HOLE   As indicated in the discussion of Grand Teton, the problem of the addition of Jackson Hole to Yellowstone or later to Grand Teton goes back to early national park history.[2] It was the national park perennial, almost constantly before park officials and Congress for fifty years. In 1898 the Senate directed the Secretary of the Interior to report on the question whether the area south of Yellowstone—described as the Yellowstone Forest Reserve, now the Teton National Forest—should be added to prevent "extinction of the large game roaming therein."

The Secretary sent Dr. Charles D. Walcott, director of the United States Geological Survey, to explore the Grand Teton and Jackson Hole country, and he recommended national park status for the area north of the Gros Ventre River—an area larger than had been proposed before—either as an addition to Yellowstone or as a separate park, but nothing came of his recommendation. The Secretary reported favorably on the extension and outlined a bill to achieve it, but the bill was not introduced.[3] On February 4, 1898, the indefatigable conservationist, Representative Lacey of Iowa, introduced a bill to extend the limits of Yellowstone, and a few days later Senator Hansbrough of North Dakota brought in a bill, but neither got any attention.[4] Early in 1902 the Secretary sent to Congress the draft of a bill for the extension of Yellowstone, but it was not introduced.[5]

In 1905 the Wyoming legislature provided some alleviation of the elk range situation by establishing a state game preserve south of Yellowstone, known as the Teton State Game Preserve. This preserve provided good summer and early fall range, but left the winter range problem largely unsolved. To protect the elk further, Congress appropriated $45,000 on August 10, 1912, for the estab-

2 See pp. 328 ff.
3 S. Doc. 39, 55 Cong., 3 Sess.
4 H. R. 7703, S. 3638, 55 Cong. 2 Sess.
5 S. Doc. 500, 57 Cong. 1 Sess.

lishment of a winter game reserve south of Yellowstone, but nothing was said about the Grand Tetons.[6]

Almost every report of the Secretary of the Interior and of the Director of the Park Service, from the time it was organized in 1917 and for the next twenty-five years, called for the addition of the northern part of Jackson Hole to the national park system in one way or another. In his 1917 report Secretary Lane called for the addition to Yellowstone of the Grand Tetons and Jackson Lake, and the next year he reported that he was making an investigation of the Jackson Lake area. His report in 1918 revealed 1,910 acres of patented lands and 3,114 acres of pending entries, the owners and claimants of which were mostly opposed to the proposed addition. About this time Representative Mondell made several efforts to extend Yellowstone southward, fighting the Forest Service and the grazing interests at every step. Much of the land to be added was in a national forest, and the Forest Service fought hard to keep it.[7] Homesteaders began to come in about this time, some bona fide, some with the purpose of getting land titles that they could sell to large operators, and at first they were not anxious to be covered into a national park, although they presently found that the climate was too severe for successful farming.

In the next few years attempts were made in Congress to add at least the northern part of Jackson Hole to Yellowstone, by Representative Sinnott and Senator Stanfield of Oregon, but with no success. Early in 1926 Senator Gooding of Idaho brought up a Senate resolution to investigate the problem, which was agreed to, with an appropriation of $3,500 for expenses.[8]

In 1923 a group of Jackson Hole citizens had invited Albright to confer with them about the possibility of selling the private lands in the northern part of Jackson Hole to the government. In 1925 a hundred farmers, owning 32,000 acres of land, sent a petition to a Casper meeting indicating their willingness to sell their land for park use, but their petition was ignored; in fact land owners adopted several petitions favoring reservation of Jackson Hole.

6 Stat. 37, 293.

7 H. R. 11661, 65 Cong. 2 Sess. H. R. 13350, 65 Cong. 3 Sess. See also Robert Shankland, *Steve Mather of the National Parks* (New York: Alfred A. Knopf, 1951), 172, 173.

8 H. R. 9919, S. 3427, S. Res. 237, 69 Cong. 1 Sess.

The moving spirit behind most of the Jackson Hole agitation was Horace Albright, as we have already seen. He was deeply in love with the scenery and worked persistently to save it from commercial debauchery. All this time there was also much discussion of the southern Yellowstone elk herd and its need for winter range; and the Committee on Outdoor Recreation appointed an Elk Commission, composed of representatives of the federal bureaus interested in wildlife conservation, which carried on an investigation of the area and, at a meeting in Washington in February and March 1927, recommended that 12,000 acres of land be purchased and added to the Biological Survey refuge near Jackson, and that the remaining federal lands in the area be withdrawn from entry.

In this long struggle for the preservation of the Grand Teton and Jackson Hole region we see one of the vices of Congressional procedure with respect to the establishment of national parks—the weighting of small local interests above those of the people of the United States as a whole. In all their pertinacious efforts to save this unique and splendid area, Albright and his men had constantly to seek the approval of local interests for their plans; and the wishes of a few dude ranchers, hunters, ranchers, boosters, and developers were weighted more heavily than the interests of all the rest of the people of the United States who, as a matter of fact, already owned most of the land.

ROCKEFELLER IN JACKSON HOLE   In 1924 John D. Rockefeller, Jr., visited Yellowstone and Jackson Hole and, shocked by the unsightly dead and down trees and slash along the roadsides in Yellowstone, he gave the Park Service $50,000 with which to clean them up. In July 1926 Rockefeller and his family again visited Yellowstone, and Albright took them down to Jackson Hole, where they were greatly impressed with the scenery, thought it equalled or exceeded anything they had ever seen; but Rockefeller saw nothing to admire in the hot-dog stands, dance halls, rodeo grandstands, filling stations, billboards and assorted ill-planned architectural rubbish along the road—on private lands and therefore there legally. Albright sold the idea of buying this land to Rockefeller while he was there. Rockefeller asked Albright to send him a map of such lands indicating probable cost of acquiring them, which Albright did. After considering the maps and data, Rockefeller advised Albright and Director Mather that he was ready to proceed with the program of land purchase, to restore and preserve the landscape, and to preserve the wildlife by eliminating fences and other barriers to the natural drift to winter range, and by providing more winter feeding grounds.

It was no simple problem to figure out the best procedure in buying. It was obvious that Rockefeller could not do it himself, under his own name, for that would have led landowners to ask unreasonably high prices, even the many landowners who were in debt, making no profit, and anxious to sell. Albright suggested that a land or cattle company be organized to buy the land, and this was the plan followed. The Snake River Land Company was organized in 1927, and a Jackson banker named Miller was asked to do the purchasing. Miller was not Albright's choice, for he was unfriendly to the Park Service, perhaps because he had once been a local forester, but he was an able man and knew the country and the people well. Rockefeller instructed him to pay fair prices for land, and not to take undue advantage of those who were hopelessly mortgaged. Without doubt Miller paid more than fair prices for some holdings. In 1933 the Snake River Land Company reported that it had bought or had under contract for purchase 35,310 acres of land for which it had paid $1,400,310, an average of $39.00 per acre. The laws of Wyoming required that land should be assessed at its true value and for land which was assessed at $521,037 the Land Company had paid $1,316,672! In the depths of the Great Depression Jackson Hole land could not possibly have been worth $39.00 per acre. It was clear that a land-buying plan of this kind would encourage entrymen to file land claims with the purpose of selling later at a profit, so Secretary Work persuaded President Coolidge to withdraw the area from entry. The first withdrawal order, of July 7, 1927, did not cover enough land, and two were issued later. Albright took no part in the land buying, which began in 1928.

It was agreed at first that dude ranches should not be bought, but left as one of the unique and characteristic features of the area, but it presently appeared that dude ranches could be turned to other uses, perhaps subdivided and sold, to become serious nuisances. To meet this danger, Albright, Rockefeller, and their men later decided to buy the dude ranches and lease them back to their former owners to be operated as dude ranches only; but this proved unsatisfactory to some, who wanted to sell and get out of the business. It was depression time, and business was poor. There were some state lands in the area, and a privately owned hotel at Moran, which were rather difficult to arrange for. Buying the Jackson Hole lands proved a difficult task.[9]

At the time, it seemed that it should not be difficult to get the land added to Grand Teton—get the government to accept a gift of nearly $1.5 million worth of land—because the Rockefeller holdings, together with the land already owned by the government, constituted 92 per cent of the total involved. The remaining private holdings were not important and their owners were not prospering, for livestock prices were low. The men who sold their land, often for more than it was worth, must have been "willing sellers" and well satisfied. In early October 1929 a vicious recession struck the country, pulling prices of farm products down further—they had slumped precipitously in 1920 and had never recovered.

JACKSON HOLE IN CONGRESS   In 1929 Secretary Wilbur visited the Jackson Hole area and approved the park plan, as did President Hoover. In 1930 a special wildlife committee of the Senate visited the region, and the citizens presented their proposal for inclusion of land in a park, but to no effect. In June 1932 Senators Carey and Kendrick of Wyoming brought up a Senate Resolution "to investigate the activities in the Jackson Hole region, . . . of the National Park Service, Department of the Interior, and the Snake River Land Company, in connection with the proposed enlargement of the Yellowstone National Park and/or the Grand Teton National Park. . . ." This investigation was for the purpose of determining "the methods employed by the National Park Service to discourage persons from making entry and settlement, etc., etc.," and the "methods employed by the Snake River Land Company or any of its agents to harass residents and settlers on public lands and national forests in said region in order to bring about their removal from said lands."[10] Carey had turned sour on the park proposal—had conceived a notion that Rockefeller should give his land to the state of Wyoming for a *state* park. There is no evidence

9 On the Jackson Hole story, see *Mr. John D. Rockefeller, Jr.'s Proposed Gift of Land for the National Park System in Wyoming*, privately printed in 1933.

10 S. Res. 226, 72 Cong. 1 Sess. *Congressional Record*, June 10, 1932, 12512.

that Rockefeller representatives had agreed to such a plan; neither did Albright and the Park Service ever approve of it. Carey took a leading part in the investigation, and was apparently satisfied with the behavior of the Park Service and the Snake River Land Company, for, in May 1934, he brought up a bill to extend the boundaries of Grand Teton, which passed the Senate and was favorably reported by the House Public Lands Committee but too late to be considered.[11]

On June 3, 1935, Senators Carey and O'Mahoney of Wyoming introduced a similar bill, and the bill seemed likely to pass, but it allowed a $10,000 tax reimbursement for Teton County, and provided an appropriation of $350,000 for the acquisition of lands for the establishment of the Jackson's Hole National Game Refuge, and the Bureau of the Budget objected to these items, so the bill failed.[12]

OPPOSITION TO RESERVATION OF JACKSON HOLE   The Jackson Hole question became very confusing at this point. Apparently, there had been little opposition to the addition of the new area at first. The Mondell bill very nearly passed in 1919, and with very little debate, as did the Carey bill in 1934, and the Carey-O'Mahoney bill in 1935. Albright, who knew as much as anyone about the situation, believed that most of the people in the vicinity favored the project; but presently a powerful propaganda drive was inaugurated which threw a smoke screen of misrepresentation over the enterprise. Reports were pushed out that Rockefeller was trying to get control of the big game, trying to get a monopoly of the concessions; that Teton County would be bankrupted—although the Park Service was willing to allow the county an amount equal to the taxes lost (about $10,000 a year); that the Park Service would stop all grazing and cancel all summer home leases, although the Park Service had no intention of doing this for some years.

Who originated this propaganda? Of course the livestock men and associations must have had a hand in it, but just why they should have been galvanized into a fighting force for this area of

11 S. 3705, 73 Cong. 2 Sess.
12 S. 2972, 74 Cong. 1 Sess. *The Nation*, July 7, 1945, 13. Edgar B. Nixon, ed., *Franklin D. Roosevelt and Conservation* (Hyde Park, N. Y.: National Archives and Records Service, Franklin D. Roosevelt Library, 1957), Vol. 1, 508.

modest importance is not clear. The ranchers who sold their land to Rockefeller were presumably gone and those who did not sell were not a numerous host, also not prosperous. Yet the livestock men were strong in Congress—some of the senators and representatives from Wyoming and surrounding states were stockmen—and fought against the Jackson Hole proposal with pertinacity. One reason for this was doubtless that these western livestock men always harbored a hope that they might be able to grab more land titles or leases if the land was not securely tied up in the park system. The associations spent a lot of time scheming to this end, and their livestock men in Congress of course helped. They still had the old grab-bag theory, of the publicly owned lands. The livestock interests had been partly responsible for the stingy outlines of Grand Teton Park.

Some of the dude ranchers, the packers and outfitters who served hunters, and the hunters themselves were opposed. The sportsmen's organizations are puissant political pressure groups in western states.

The local Forest Service office was said to have taken an active part in this propaganda drive; in fact, the Jackson banker Miller, who had been Rockefeller's buying agent and a former local forester, was said to be a leader in the drive. Certainly the local national forest office seems to have fought bitterly against the transfer of Jackson Hole to park jurisdiction. It was reported that when President Roosevelt set up Jackson Hole as a national monument in 1943 and the local Forest Service staff turned their office and equipment over to the Park Service, they tore out all plumbing and telephone equipment, explaining later that they did it by mistake. The Forest Service headquarters intervened at one time to order less belligerency in the Jackson Hole office.[13]

There was opposition from other quarters: from politicians in other western states, from the Wyoming State Administration, from some of the people of Teton County, who feared a loss of tax revenues, from "boosters," who liked to "see Wyoming grow," and from Roosevelt-haters.[14] John Muir had once described the western land-grab attitude with some wit: "All our precious mountains, with their stores of timber and grass, silver and gold, fertile valleys

13 *The Nation*, July 7, 1945, 13.
14 See an article by Struthers Burt, who lived in this area, in *The Nation*, Mar. 3, 1926, 225.

and streams—all the natural resources of our great growing States are set aside from use, smothered up in mere pleasure grounds for wild beasts and a set of sick, rich, dawdling sentimentalists. For this purpose business is blocked and every current of industry dammed. Will our people stand this? No-o! Which in plain English means, 'Let us steal and destroy in peace.' "[15]

Some of the "purists" among the devoted park lovers were opposed. The National Parks Association referred to one of the Jackson Hole bills as adding to Grand Teton "a Biological Service game preserve, three irrigation reservoirs, large areas of national forests, commercial traffic ways, dude ranches and plain desert."[16] The association objected to the inclusion of three reservoir lakes—Jackson, Two Ocean, and Emma Matilda—because they were formed by dams built after the national park system had been established; and it also did not like the highway that ran through the Jackson Hole area, because it undermined the primitive character of Grand Teton. The association has always favored wilderness parks, roadless if possible. It was obvious too that if Jackson Hole were added, grazing permits and summer home leases formerly issued by the Forest Service would have to be continued, contrary to national park principles.[17]

The propaganda was effective, and for several years nothing could be done but investigate. There was more or less continuous investigation. Two years after the Carey Resolution was passed, Senator Robinson of Arkansas brought up a Senate resolution providing more money for this investigation, which was agreed to.[18] In May 1938 O'Mahoney introduced a Senate resolution calling on the Senate Committee on Public Lands and Surveys, with both senators from Wyoming, to investigate the feasibility of enlarging Grand Teton, which passed without comment.[19] In August, a subcommittee of the Senate Committee met at Jackson, Wyoming, with Park Service officials, and heard testimony. The next year Representative De Rouen of Louisiana, of the House Committee on Public Lands, introduced two House resolutions, one to authorize a study of the national parks, national monuments and shrines, and

15 *Harpers Weekly*, June 5, 1897, 563.
16 *National Parks Bulletin*, No. 61, Feb. 1936.
17 *National Parks Magazine*, No. 75, Oct.-Dec., 1943, 3.
18 S. Res. 199, 74 Cong. 1 Sess.
19 S. Res. 250, 75 Cong. 3 Sess.

one to pay $2,000 for expenses, which were agreed to without comment.[20] Two years later Representative Robinson of Utah brought up a House resolution extending the time of investigation to January 3, 1943, which was agreed to.[21]

There was plenty of investigation. Representative Horton of Wyoming, probably with the intention of scaring the Park Service out of further Jackson Hole proposals, brought up a bill in the House to abolish Grand Teton and transfer its lands to the Forest Service.[22]

THE NATIONAL MONUMENT PROCLAIMED   If Albright had not been a man of extraordinary tenacity and perseverance he would have given up his favorite enterprise, and had Rockefeller not been a very patient and generous-minded man he would have thrown up his land and walked off. Here he was, holding nearly 35,000 acres of land and paying taxes on it, unable to give it to the government—land which he had bought with the encouragement of Albright, Coolidge, and others. Some of the ranchers were not altogether unhappy, probably hoping that Rockefeller would get disgusted with the situation and dump his land on the market at bargain prices. Patient as he was, Rockefeller did finally urge the administration to take some action, and President Roosevelt, embarrassed by his inability to get Congress to act, set Jackson Hole up as a national monument by proclamation on March 15, 1943.[23]

WESTERN RESENTMENT   The reaction of the anti-park forces was prompt and violent. The cattlemen of the area, believing themselves deprived of grazing rights, staged a cattle drive across the Hole in defiance of the government. Ickes wrote a diplomatic letter to Senator O'Mahoney of Wyoming, assuring him that private rights in Jackson Hole would be protected, that grazing privileges, stock driveway privileges, and summer home permits issued by the Forest Service would be honored during the lifetime of holders,

20 H. Res. 284, H. Res. 285, 76 Cong. 1. Sess.
21 H. Res. 242, 77 Cong. 1 Sess.
22 H. R. 6959, 76 Cong. 1 Sess. See *Congressional Record*, 78 Cong. 2 Sess., Appendix 2593, 2894, 2895.
23 Stat. 57, 731.

that Teton County would for the present continue to collect taxes, including gasoline, use, sales and liquor taxes, and that the states and localities would be given ample opportunity to present their views before any changes were made; but his letter did not mollify the opposition appreciably.[24] In August court action was instituted by Wyoming at Sheridan to have the Roosevelt proclamation annulled, on the ground that the Jackson Hole area was not of such character as to come within the terms of the Antiquities Act, and that therefore the proclamation was invalid. The decision of the court was that the important historical incidents in the area were enough to bring it within the provisions of the Antiquities Act, and that the proclamation was valid.

A week after the monument was proclaimed stockman Representative Barrett rushed a bill into the House to abolish it and afterward he and stockman Senator Robertson of Wyoming offered bills to amend the Antiquities Act to prevent further presidential proclamations of monuments. To this purpose also were bills by Senators O'Mahoney of Wyoming and McCarran of Nevada, Representative Chenoweth of Colorado, and Delegate Dimond of Alaska. O'Mahoney also introduced a resolution in the Senate calling upon the Committee on Public Lands and Surveys, or a subcommittee of it, to make a study of the methods and purposes and administration of laws relating to the establishment or alteration of boundaries of national parks and monuments, national forests and Indian reservations, which was agreed to without comment.[25] Peterson of Florida, of the House Committee on Public Lands, called for a study of the problem.[26]

The Barrett bill was reported favorably by the House Public Lands Committee, and was debated at greater length and with more virulence than any park bill in years.[27] Dirksen of Illinois said the real question was whether a President could "dip into the solemn domain of a State and without what appears to be proper justification take over an area of 221,000 acres"—apparently under the impression that this land belonged to Wyoming; Ellsworth of Oregon thought the Antiquities Act was a great danger to the West; Fernan-

24 *Congressional Record*, 78 Cong. 1 Sess., Appendix, 1776.
25 H. R. 2241, H. R. 2591, S. 1046, S. 1056, S. 3884, H. R. 3864, S. Res. 134, 78 Cong. 1 Sess.
26 H. Res. 273, 78 Cong. 1 Sess.
27 H. R. 2241, 78 Cong. 2 Sess. The debates were in the second session.

dez of New Mexico suggested that the courts should decide whether the proclamation was legal. Peterson of Florida opposed the bill and presented a telegram from Ray Lyman Wilbur, Secretary of the Interior under President Hoover, objecting strongly to it; but his remarks had little effect on the House, which was clearly bent on chastising Roosevelt and Ickes. After some desultory debate, the House agreed, 103 to 41, to make the Barrett bill a special order, and resolved itself into a Committee of the Whole House for further debate.

O'Connor of Montana was incensed at the President's action in "by-passing Congress," although he absolved him of blame because he and Ickes too, had probably taken someone else's word in the matter. He rapped Rockefeller for buying the land "in a conniving way," and declared that the Antiquities Act did not contemplate this sort of monument. Fernandez was also incensed at the "secrecy" of Rockefeller's land buying. May of Kentucky thought that the "President could take in Daniel Boone's tomb and half of Kentucky to protect it." White of Idaho was concerned about mining rights and bureaucracy: "This thing is a plan to create among bureaucrats—not custodians of the land, for that is owned by the people and is directed by the policies of the Congress—but is a plan to create a bureaucratic owner, a bureaucratic proprietor. If you go on this land, you go with their permission and their tolerance, and if you do not have that permission and tolerance, you stay off.[28] White spoke feelingly of Jackson Hole as "a little island, a little oasis, where these old settlers have made their homes and built up a community."[29]

Mott of Oregon called the proclamation "one of the worst examples of executive usurpation of legislative authority that has ever occurred in the history of our Government," and pointed out that Congress had several times refused to give Jackson Hole national park status, and that Roosevelt should have been governed by the decisions of Congress.[30] Dirksen of Illinois followed the same line of argument: "Do we propose to be rolled back by the Secretary of the Interior or do we propose today in compliance with existing law to roll him back?"[31] Johnson of Oklahoma, too, saw as the para-

28 *Congressional Record,* 78 Cong. 2 Sess., 9095.
29 *Ibid.,* 9087.
30 *Ibid.,* 9183.
31 *Ibid.,* 9086.

mount question "whether or not the astute and ambitious Secretary of the Interior shall be permitted by subterfuge to bypass or circumvent the expressed will of the Congress."[32] Robertson of Wyoming, on the other hand, with apparently intimate knowledge of the history of the area, indicated that "Bureaucrat Albright" was the moving spirit behind the events leading up to and including the establishment of the monument.[33] Lemke of North Dakota was critical of Rockefeller for his "deception."

DEFENSE OF THE MONUMENT There were defenders of the proclamation. Peterson of Florida explained the terms of the proclamation at length, but the rebels did not want explanations; they wanted blood. LeCompte of Iowa praised Representative Lacey, the author of the Antiquities Act. Cochran of Missouri pointed out that seven or eight national monuments had been created that were larger than Jackson Hole. Cochran gave a long and careful analysis of conditions in the monument, and of the history of the efforts to give it park status. Peterson of Florida insisted that many of the private owners in the Hole favored the monument. Case of South Dakota could not see why an adjustment of interests could not be worked out, and said that the people of South Dakota were not opposed to their national monuments. Murdock of Arizona conceded that sometimes the Park Service took in too much land, but argued that the Barrett bill would solve nothing. He protested against the attacks on Roosevelt: "Don't slap the President of the United States squarely in the face," which was, of course, just what some of the belligerents were most interested in doing. He favored, rather, a bill prohibiting the establishment of national monuments except by acts of Congress.

Outland of California rather pertinently suggested that the real issue was whether Jackson Hole was of enough importance to be preserved as a national monument, a question that was ignored in the discussions. Outland's discussion of the general story of the national parks seems worth quoting: "Less than three quarters of a century ago, in 1872, the great Yellowstone region was set aside as our first national park—not as a Berchtesgarden for a Hitler nor for the 'princely delight and pleasure' of kings and nobles as were

32 *Ibid.*, 9195.
33 *Ibid.*, 7980.

the forests in the medieval ages, not for commercial or individual aggrandizement, but for the enjoyment of the people of the entire Nation, and for those of other countries able to visit them. I think it is significant of our American way of life that the men who stood to gain most, were the park not established, were the ones who were instrumental in bringing about the creation of Yellowstone National Park. Their vision and foresight—and their sense of public responsibility—were greater than that of many of us today. Surely the United States is big enough, and wealthy enough, to put aside and protect a small percentage of its area for this purpose."[34] Outland presented letters and telegrams from various conservation organizations against the bill, including of course the Sierra Club.

One of the ablest defenses of the proclamation was made by McCormack of Massachusetts. He pointed out that the President represented the people too, and that his repeated victories indicated that they believed that he represented them well. He pointed to such splendid monuments as Grand Canyon and Zion as examples of wise action on the President's part.

Leroy Johnson of California suggested that the Barrett bill was largely a party issue, that it was supported mostly by the Republicans. This was fairly clear. By the time the bill had been debated for several days Peterson of Florida had made it clear to all that the monument did little or no harm to the interests of anyone, even to Teton County, because Ickes had reassured the rebels that the county would be reimbursed for tax losses—only about $10,000 anyhow.

It was not a national park issue altogether, not West versus East, but Republicans versus Democrats, with some breaks in the ranks, although the western men made the most noise. A number of eastern men who could have had no particular reason for opposing Jackson Hole Monument favored the Barrett bill: May of Kentucky, Wright of Pennsylvania, Plumley of Vermont, Brown of Ohio, Keefe of Wisconsin, Rowe of Ohio, and Fish of New York. It is perhaps significant that Tom Dewey, Republican aspirant for the Presidency, went to Wyoming and in a speech there pronounced the monument "characteristic of the deviousness of the New Deal, which shows lack of respect for the rights and privileges of the people affected."[35] Since there was so much anti-Roosevelt and anti-

34 *Ibid.*, 9184.
35 Quoted from *Chicago Daily Times*, Dec. 14, 1944.

Ickes venom in the debates, little attention was devoted to one of the important reasons for establishing the monument—the addition of winter range for the elk. With a national election just ahead, Congress would naturally take to the great game of politics, but it was unfortunate that more attention could not have been given to the real issues.

The pertinacity of some of the Wyoming men in pushing the Barrett bill indicates that there were economic motives at work too, of course. Kenneth A. Reid, executive director of the Izaak Walton League, asserted that these men hoped that if the monument could be abolished, Rockefeller would get tired and sell his land and they and their friends might "make a killing" in the purchase of it. "The many dramatic stories about dispossessing the ranchers, ruining the cattle business, and taking upwards of 200,000 acres off the tax rolls amount to nothing but hysterical or malicious bunk," he concluded.[36]

It was a political fight, to some extent, but there was more than politics behind the Barrett insurrection. Barrett and his crowd must surely have known that the Jackson Hole project would benefit Wyoming, by attracting more tourists. They certainly knew that the stale old tax-loss argument had no pertinence, since an allowance had been made for that. But some of this crowd, including Barrett himself, were stockmen, and perhaps some of the lands that Rockefeller had bought were wanted because with them would go leases of adjoining national forest lands.

Many of the Republican papers of course favored the Barrett bill, but there was editorial opposition in a number of newspapers, some of them in the West. The *Capital Journal* of Salem, Oregon, outlined the general position of anti-park men clearly in an editorial on January 11, 1945: "The creation of every national park and monument has met with violent opposition unless the area was without other than tourist, recreational, and scenic values. Lumbermen, stockmen, hydroelectric and commercial interests lead the opposition as a rule, backed by local officials fearing loss of tax revenues in the future—few of them ever on record for conservation of natural resources and most of them practicing a depletion that has made similar regions a desert waste."

After extended debate, the Barrett bill passed the House by a vote of 178 to 107, with 142 not voting. The vote ran largely but

36 *Congressional Record*, Mar. 7, 1945, 1877 ff.

not altogether on party lines. Fernandez of New Mexico also introduced a bill in the second session of the 78th Congress, to amend
Section 2 of the Antiquities Act, and Peterson of Florida brought up
a bill to provide for payments to Wyoming for rights of way of
various kinds.[37]

In the Senate the bill was reported favorably by the Senate Committee on Public Lands and Surveys and passed without discussion
on the last day before the Christmas recess; but Roosevelt pocket-
vetoed it.

An interesting aftermath of the furor over the Barrett bill was
recorded in the *Salt Lake Tribune* of January 4, 1945. A group of
local taxpayers appeared before the Teton County Commissioners
in Jackson and demanded that the commissioners reimburse the
county for the county money they had spent for "propaganda and
expenses in supporting the Barrett bill in the most recent session
of Congress." They questioned whether the county officials had the
authority to spend money for such a purpose when large numbers
of taxpayers believed that the monument was a great asset to the
country.[38]

REACTION TO ROOSEVELT VETO   Roosevelt's veto was accompanied by a memorandum saying that while he wished to keep
the monument he would favor proper adjustments, reimbursement
to Teton County for tax losses, and continuance of grazing privileges granted by the Forest Service for the life of the lessees and
their heirs and assignees. But Barrett and his friends were not interested, and Barrett promptly introduced three bills in the next
Congress, the 79th, one to abolish the monument, one to repeal
Section 2 of the Antiquities Act (the section under which national
monuments were set aside), and one to provide for the administration of all public lands in Jackson Hole by the Forest Service.[39]
Senator Robertson and Representatives Fernandez, O'Connor, and
Chenoweth also proposed to repeal Section 2 of the Antiquities
Act.[40] None of these bills passed. Peterson, on the other hand, tried

37 H. R. 4575, H. R. 5469.
38 *Congressional Record*, 79 Cong. 1 Sess., 1879.
39 H. R. 2109, H. R. 2110, H. R. 2691, 79 Cong. 1 Sess.
40 S. 664, H. R. 409, H. R. 112, H. R. 1507, 79 Cong. 1 Sess. H. R. 5859, 79
Cong. 2 Sess.

to save the monument by providing tax-loss payments to Wyoming and rights of way, including stock driveways, over and across federal lands.[41]

Early in the first session of the 80th Congress, in January 1947, Barrett arose as usual to demolish Jackson Hole, to repeal Section 2 of the Antiquities Act, to amend the Taylor Grazing Act, and by some sort of schizophrenic logic, to establish Old Fort Casper National Monument.[42] Robertson of Wyoming and Fernandez were intent on amending the Antiquities Act.[43] Barrett's Jackson Hole bill was referred to the Committee of the Whole House.[44] Peterson tried to pacify the western stockmen by getting payments for tax losses, and rights of way and stock driveways across Jackson Hole.[45] McCarran of Nevada offered a bill to abolish all national monuments, additions to national parks, wildlife sanctuaries, and additions to national forests established or added to by Presidential Proclamation, unless upheld by Congress within a certain time, and to remove the President's power to make such withdrawals.[46]

The second session of the 80th Congress convened on January 6, 1948, and the next day stockman Senator Robertson brought up the well-worn bill to abolish Jackson Hole National Monument.[47] Barrett was busy during this session doing some chores for the grazing and mining interests, and he did well for them.[48] Nothing came of the Robertson bill, but Barrett was able to get an amendment to every appropriation bill from 1944 to 1948 forbidding any expenditures for the administration and protection of the new monument. Cattle could roam without restriction and hunters had free range of the monument.[49] The lack of funds for administration of the new monument may have hurt some of the local people more than the Park Service. There were roads in the area, one of them

41 H. R. 1292, 79 Cong. 1 Sess.
42 H. R. 1330, H. R. 2438, 80 Cong. 1 Sess.
43 S. 91, H. R. 1676, 80 Cong. 1 Sess.
44 H. R. 1330, 80 Cong. 1 Sess.
45 H. R. 3035, 80 Cong. 1 Sess.
46 S. 32, 80 Cong. 1 Sess.
47 S. 1951, 80 Cong. 2 Sess.
48 H. R. 5833, H. R. 6073, H. R. 6302, H. R. 6335, H. Res. 604, H. Res. 612, 80 Cong. 2 Sess.
49 Barrett claimed credit for this amendment, but O'Mahoney once stated that it was he who injected it, on the theory that no money should be spent on the monument until its final status should be determined, which does not seem very reasonable. See *Congressional Record* May 27, 1948, 6633-6635.

the south road into Yellowstone, and it is likely that the neglect of these roads for several years may have brought hardship to the people in the locality, in rough roads and reduced travel.

THE COMPROMISE BILL   In the 81st Congress, 1949-50, Barrett, apparently convinced that he could not abolish the monument, talked of a settlement with Secretary Chapman; and on April 12, 1950, Senators O'Mahoney and Hunt of Wyoming, two of the less obstreperous of the western men, tried to effect some reconciliation of conflicting views in a bill "to Establish the Wyoming-Jackson Hole National Park"—later changed in the Senate to "A New Grand Teton National Park."[50] This bill was a long one with several detailed sections, the first of which prohibited the President from establishing or extending any national parks in Wyoming without express authorization by Congress. Since the President had no particular interest in establishing or extending any other parks or monuments in Wyoming this was not a severe restriction, and it gave some satisfaction to Barrett and his crowd.

Of the area in the monument, all but about 9,000 acres was to be transferred to Grand Teton, which was enlarged from 95,360 acres to 298,738 acres; 6,376 acres to the adjoining National Elk Refuge; and 2,806 acres to the Teton National Forest. This was satisfactory to the Park Service, for it made Grand Teton the kind of park it should have been in the first place. It will be remembered that it was established as a skimpy little park. Under the bill the east boundary was moved farther east, to take in Jackson Lake and the two smaller lakes farther east, Two Ocean and Emma Matilda, all of them reservoir lakes, covering also much of the highway running north from Jackson to Yellowstone Park, much of the Snake River and its valley—the area from which the mountains could best be viewed.

The O'Mahoney-Hunt bill was not debated much, although some of its provisions were changed in committees. As finally passed and signed by President Truman on September 14, 1950, it was about the best compromise possible, although on some points it yielded quite too much to the western spoilsmen.[51] The distribution of the

50 S. 3409, 81 Cong. 1 Sess.
51 Stat. 64, 849 ff.

Jackson Hole land was about as satisfactory as could have been hoped for. Rockefeller had conveyed his land—more than 33,000 acres—to the government on December 16, 1949, and it had been accepted. The tax loss concession to Teton County was changed. Instead of running forever, the tax losses were to run in full for five years, then decrease 5 per cent each year for twenty years, but the payments were not to exceed 25 per cent of the fees collected from Grand Teton visitors. This change was urged by Secretary Chapman, and also by F. J. Lawton, Director of the Bureau of the Budget. This tax loss reimbursement, reported at $10,000 at the time—the amount Rockefeller had paid for several years—but later reported at $25,000, was too much of a concession, but was necessary to get the bill passed. Doubtless Teton County has gained tax-wise and otherwise from the creation of the enlarged Teton, and would have gained without the tax-loss contribution.

The lease continuance provisions for stockmen and for owners of summer homes, were exceedingly generous to lessees, amounting almost to possible perpetual leases, but for the long run this was not critically important. The elk-control provisions, however, represented a most unfortunate concession to the selfish demands of Wyoming sportsmen. Co-operation with the Wyoming Game and Fish Commission might prove fairly satisfactory, but the deputization of Wyoming hunters as rangers, to kill elk in a part of a national park free of license costs, that was an insult to the Park Service and to ordinary decency. It came rather close to making a part of Teton Park, the game trails, a private hunting preserve for Wyoming, administered at the cost of the federal government; and it was of course a violation of park principles that the Park Service had always stubbornly opposed, a violation that might well set a precedent—as perhaps it was hoped that it would. Hunters' organizations were trying hard to get into the national parks, and here they were in, if they were Wyoming residents and had been anointed by the Wyoming Game and Fish Commission. It is true that the Park Service had not been able to effect an adequate reduction in the number of elk in the area, and more elk should be killed, but that did not justify setting up part of the new park as a hunting preserve for Wyoming sportsmen alone. Furthermore, as we shall see, the arrangement was almost entirely ineffectual in reducing the number of elk.

The elk problem requires a short explanation. From earliest days, before the monument was established, the Jackson Hole elk summered north and east of the Teton boundaries, in Teton National Forest and southern Yellowstone Park, except for a small herd which summered in the Berry Creek country in the north end of Teton mountains. In the fall they migrated southward to the lower lands of the national forest and the elk refuge, crossing a small area east of Jackson Lake that was included in the national monument. Hunters could shoot them in open season in the national forest or in the elk refuge, but they preferred to shoot them in this small passageway because it was near the road, and the "sportsmen" did not like to walk far. So when this passage area was included in the monument, where shooting was prohibited, they had to go farther for their elk, and objected to this interference with their freedom and their rights as American citizens.[52]

Not long after the new park was established the small dams on the lakes Two Ocean and Emma Matilda were destroyed and the lakes were restored to their original levels.

EVERGLADES PARK AGAIN   Acquisition of land for Everglades Park was proceeding slowly. By 1941 only a few small isolated tracts had been turned over to the Secretary, but Governor Spessard Holland was much interested in the park project and worked hard to get the money needed, assisted by the Everglades National Park Commission, the Florida State Chamber of Commerce, the Florida Federation of Women's Clubs, the Florida Parent-Teachers Association, the National Association of Audubon Societies, and of course by Secretary Ickes and Director Drury— Cammerer's successor. The Royal Palm State Park of 4,000 acres was deeded to the state for the park by the Florida Federation of Women's Clubs. There was need for expedition, for the area was still subject to depredation and destruction of wildlife.

In 1944 a new difficulty arose. Oil was discovered about twenty miles from the park, a modest flow of low-grade oil but enough to set local citizens afire with visions of oil millions. It became almost impossible to secure private lands at anything but prohibitive prices, except with reservation of the oil, which at first National

52 See an article by Olaus J. Murie in *National Parks Magazine*, No. 107, Sept.-Dec., 1951, 119.

Park officers were unwilling to grant; and yet there was urgent need for the establishment of the park so that the wildlife could be better protected.

Governor Holland, whose term was about to expire, tried to revive interest in the park and negotiated with Secretary Ickes and Governor-Elect Caldwell an agreement by which Florida would issue conditional deeds covering 847,175 acres of dry and submerged lands to the Secretary of the Interior in return for protecting the wildlife until the lands could be acquired, with a limit of ten years for acquisition of the lands; and Representative Peterson and Senator Andrews introduced identical bills in the House and Senate to confirm this agreement. The Peterson bill passed both houses without debate and was signed by President Roosevelt on December 6, 1944.[53]

The Peterson Act authorized the Secretary to accept any lands subject to such reservations of oil, gas or mineral rights as he might approve within the area of approximately 2,000 square miles that he had recommended in his report to Congress on December 3, 1930, provided that there should be no general development of facilities in the area and that the park should not be established until a "major portion" of the lands selected by him should be turned over to the government. This phrase is reminiscent of the laws setting up the Appalachian parks. Until the lands turned over to the government should be cleared of the oil, gas, and mineral reservations, the Secretary was authorized to furnish adequate protection. The act provided further that unless the park was established within ten years, or on abandonment of the park at any time, the title to lands accepted should revest in the state or other grantors. On the execution of these various provisions the Secretary might establish the Everglades National Park at any time.

The provision allowing acceptance of lands subject to mineral reservations was of course a bitter pill for the Park Service, a violation of national park principles; but some of the lands could not be got without it, and Secretary Ickes and Ira Gabrielson of the Fish and Wildlife Service decided that more should and could be done for protection, even with oil reservations. Until the park was established, the area was to be administered by the Fish and Game Service as the Everglades National Wildlife Refuge, but that Service

53 H. R. 5289, S. 2141, 78 Cong. 2 Sess. Stat. 58, 794.

had inadequate funds for protection from some of the local sportsmen and poachers.

During these years the federal government was spending money
every year on soil erosion control—in the Everglades region, not
only in the projected park—and on research and demonstration
work to reduce the fire hazard, beginning with $75,000 in 1939,
up to $1,278,000 in 1946, and more than a million annually until
1950; but the disastrous fires in 1951 and 1952 indicated that the
fire prevention work was not very effective, and there were recurrent
complaints of inadequate protection of the wildlife.

There was some agitation for the inclusion in the park of the
royal palm big cypress forest of Flakakatche Slough about eight
miles north of the town of Everglades—the only stands of these
majestic trees left in the United States, sometimes compared with
the California redwoods. Already in 1941, Dr. John H. Davis of the
University of Florida urged the reservation of these trees, which
were being logged; but nothing was done about them and most of
them were cut within a few years.[54]

The Everglades National Park Commission developed lethargy
in its money-raising, and the Florida State Chamber of Commerce
took over the business, but for several years with only modest success. On March 14, 1947, however, the state deeded to the federal
government 850,000 acres of land for temporary administration as
a wildlife refuge, and on June 20, 1947, on receipt of a check for
$2 million from the state for land purchase, Secretary Krug signed
the order establishing the park. Today the park has a gross area
of about 1.5 million acres.

With the $2 million grant from Florida, Ickes proceeded to buy
more land, for the park was still far from complete, but prices were
up and some titles were badly tangled. In the next two years he
bought 210,000 acres for $298,000 but was obliged to allow oil ex-
ploration for several years.

Early in 1949, Senators Holland and Pepper and Representatives
Smathers and Peterson made a concerted effort to get the oil reservation problem settled more definitely.[55] The Peterson bill passed
both houses with no real opposition although there was a difference
between the House and the Senate as to the time that the oil reservations should run. The House favored 1956 as the terminal date,

54 *National Parks Magazine,* Apr.-June 1948; Oct.-Dec. 1948, 32.
55 S. 285, H. R. 1254, H. R. 4029, 81 Cong. 1 Sess.

as did also the Park Service; the Senate favored 1958, or as long as oil should be produced. The Senate view prevailed in the act as passed. The act was needed not only to settle the duration of reservations but to enable the Secretary to spend the money he had got from Florida. If it had been appropriated by Congress, he would have had the right to buy land with it, but, under a statute of August 1, 1888,[56] he could not spend money given by Florida without Congressional authorization.[57]

By 1950 Secretary Chapman, successor to Krug, enlarged the park from 464,000 acres to 1,228,500 acres, including waters and submerged lands, but there were 128,000 acres of private lands within the enlarged park still to be acquired, and some were acquired by negotiations and some by condemnation. The Collier Corporation made a donation of 10,000 acres of valuable land on the west coast.[58] A Secretarial Order of February 22, 1950, extended the boundaries somewhat.

With the Park Service in control, better protection could be afforded the birds and fishes. In 1951 Secretary Chapman issued needed regulations, especially regarding the dragnet seines which were threatening the fisheries of Florida Bay. A few concessions have been granted for boat trips, etc., and there are overnight accommodations for tourist use at Flamingo Bay within the park.

PROPOSED PARKWAYS During Drury's administration one archeological national monument was created, the *Effigy Mounds,* in Iowa, to preserve ancient Indian mounds. In August 1949, $250,000 was voted for a survey of a proposed Mississippi River parkway. The Mississippi River parkway, to a limited extent scenic, and perhaps useful in some other ways, grew out of the Parks, Parkways and Recreational Area Study of 1936. Beginning in 1939, bills began to appear in Congress, but it was not until 1949 that Congress voted $250,000 to the National Park Service and the Bureau of Public Roads to make a survey of a parkway following the Mississippi River.[59] It required two years to make the study, which

56 Stat. 25, 357.
57 Stat. 63, 733. H. Rept. 428, 81 Cong. 1 Sess.
58 *Report, Secretary of the Interior, 1949,* 322; 1950, 325; 1951, 339. *Audubon Magazine,* Mar. 1949, 112.
59 Stat. 63, 626.

was completed in August 1951, and in 1955 several of the ten states involved were planning land acquisition.

Early in 1943, Victor M. Cutter, Chairman of the New England Region of the National Resources Planning Board, proposed the building of a parkway for New England to traverse the "high backbone" of New England, the Berkshire Hills, Green and White Mountains and Mount Katahdin to the lakes of Southeast Maine. It was to run along the sides of the mountains, not on the crest; but the New Englanders did not warm to it and the National Parks Association was opposed.[60]

BOUNDARY CHANGES   Boundaries of several national monuments were modified. In 1940 and again in 1943 exchange of lands in Death Valley was authorized. Montezuma Well was added to Montezuma Castle in October 1943, Congress providing the money —$25,000—without any provision for fifty-fifty matching.[61] In 1941, Pinnacles was enlarged—for the fifth time—by 4,589 acres, Ocmulgee was enlarged to take in an old Indian stockade; Craters of the Moon was reduced to provide land for a highway. Some of Wupatki was cut out to allow for a diversion dam on the Little Colorado for irrigation by the Navajos. In 1942 Katmai was enlarged to take in all islands in Cook Inlet and Shelikof Strait "in front of and within five miles of the Monument," to include some valuable marine life; Cedar Breaks boundaries were "adjusted"; White Sands Recreational Demonstration Project was added to White Sands; 10,511 acres were added to Hawaii.

HISTORICAL AREAS   Nearly all the new areas added were historical and some of them are worth a brief notice. In July 1943 Congress provided for the establishment of the George Washington Carver National Monument near Diamond, Missouri, the Secretary of the Interior to acquire the birthplace of the great scientist by gift or purchase or condemnation. In a burst of generosity that is difficult to understand, Congress appropriated $30,000 in the act, and later, in September 1950, appropriated $150,000 more and authorized the minting of a special 50-cent coin to honor Carver.[62]

60 *National Parks Magazine*, Jan.-Mar. 1943, 8, 13; July-Sept. 1943, 26.
61 Stat. 57, 572.
62 Stat. 57, 563, 64, 828.

About this time Congress also authorized a 50-cent coin in honor of Booker T. Washington. For a short time these honorary coins were rather fashionable. An act passed in August 1935, providing for the Patrick Henry National Monument, did not fare so well. It was repealed in December 1944.[63] Congress passed laws authorizing the establishment of two national memorials and monuments: De Soto National Memorial in Florida, and the Saint Croix Island National Monument in Maine, but the land for these had to be donated. Saint Croix was never established. In 1939 Congress had authorized the acceptance of the Franklin D. Roosevelt home as a National Historic Site, and on November 21, 1945, it became federal property. It was subject to life estates of the family, but these rights were surrendered by Mrs. Roosevelt and family.

Representative Lemke of North Dakota made persistent attempts to get Theodore Roosevelt's North Dakota ranch established as a national park. Early in 1945 he introduced two bills to achieve this, and in spite of the opposition of the Park Service and the National Parks Association, got a bill through Congress; but President Truman vetoed the bill on the ground that the project was not of national park calibre.[64] In the next Congress Lemke tried again; the House Public Lands Committee amended the bill to establish a national memorial park, and so it passed with little comment. It was to involve an expense of only $75,000, $35,000 for a statue of Roosevelt in Medora and $40,000 to reconstruct the original ranch house where he lived and did much of his writing.[65] A year later the memorial was enlarged.[66]

The most ambitious of the historical parks was the Independence National Historical Park in Philadelphia, provided for in 1948. This park included Independence Hall and surroundings, and millions were spent clearing out inappropriate buildings and restoring the area as it was in colonial times.[67]

Proposals for new parks and monuments continued to pour in. During the war the Park Service could do no investigating of proposed areas, and in 1946 several hundred proposals awaited study.

63 Stat. 58, 852.
64 H. R. 1441, H. R. 4435, 79 Cong. 1 Sess.
65 H. R. 731, 80 Cong. 1 Sess. Stat. 61, 52.
66 Stat. 62, 352, 384.
67 For a list of some of the historical parks and monuments see *Years of Progress, 1945-1952* (Department of the Interior), 117.

In 1949 twenty-nine proposals were presented, mostly historical, of which only four were worth investigating. The Service adopted a conservative attitude toward additions, but of course it could not control Congress. In 1949 the Hoover Commission called for an impartial board of review to check on proposed areas, but probably the most expert and unbiased board of review is the National Park Service.

Indicative of the growing interest in history was the formation of the National Council for Historic Sites and Buildings in April 1947, "to further the preservation, study, and interpretation of historic sites and buildings situated in the United States and its possessions and significant for American history and culture." This Council brought together the forces of thirty-six national organizations and agencies interested in historic preservation, and brought about the passage of an act by Congress in October 1949, authorizing the establishment of the National Trust for Historic Preservation in the United States, to receive donations of sites, buildings and objects significant in American history, and accept, hold and administer gifts of money, securities and other property. This National Trust was organized in May 1950, on the model of the National Trust of Great Britain, supplementing excellently the work of the Park Service.[68]

NEW AREAS CONSIDERED BY PARK SERVICE   The Park Service itself has indicated more or less interest in a number of areas as possible additions to the park system, perhaps not as parks or even monuments, but in some useful role. The Committee that surveyed the Colorado River Basin, in its 1946 report suggested as "areas that should be preserved and made available for recreation . . . the western slope of the Wind River Range in Wyoming; the San Juan–San Miguel-Uncompahgre Mountain area, the White River Plateau, the Elk Mountain area, and the Park Range in Colorado; the Uinta Mountains, the Aquarius Plateau–Boulder Mountain area, Monument Valley, and the Canyon lands of southeastern Utah; the Gila primitive area and Manuelito area in New Mexico; Meteor Crater, Fort Bowie, the Blue Range area, Mount Baldy-

68 *Ibid.* Also, *Report, Secretary of the Interior, 1947,* 334; 1949, 313 ff., 328; 1950, 316. Stat. 63, 927.

White Mountain area, the San Franciscan volcanic field, the Mogollon Rim area, Travertine Bridge, and the Kofa Mountains in Arizona; and Palm Canyon in California." Beautiful Glacier Peak in Washington was also considered. This committee thought that certain archeological sites should also be preserved: "Poncho House in Utah; and Kinishba Ruins, Clear Creek Ruins, Chavez Pass Ruins, and Awatovi in Arizona."[69]

Meteor Crater, south of Winslow, Arizona, is a really interesting natural wonder, a crater 500 feet deep and a quarter-mile across, estimated to have been made by a huge meteor perhaps 30,000 years ago. It is privately owned, with an ugly board fence around a part of it so the public can't see it without paying an admission fee. Drury had wanted it for years.[70] Travertine Bridge too was unusual, a natural bridge of travertine rather than of sandstone like most others. Representative Murdock of Arizona introduced a bill to make a national monument of this bridge, but with no results.[71]

The Park Service was also interested in two virgin forest areas: Tensas Swamp in Louisiana, a swamp with virgin bottomlands forest and rich bird and animal life, and a virgin timber tract on Porcupine Mountain in Michigan, one of the very few tracts of virgin timber in the Lake States. Tensas Swamp timber was logged, but Porcupine Mountain was saved by the state of Michigan in 1944 at a cost of $1 million, to be used as a sort of state park or forest museum. Virgin timber is nearly always expensive.

There were serious efforts by the state of California and in Congress to save some of the remaining coast redwoods in a national park or national forest. In April 1946 Representative Helen Gahagen Douglas of California introduced a bill in Congress to establish the "Franklin D. Roosevelt Memorial National Forest." Roosevelt had died on April 12 the preceding year, and he had been much interested in saving the coast redwoods. Part of the large area to be bought was to be under control of the Park Service, cooperating with the California State Park Commission, the rest was to be a national forest, but presumably with prohibition of cutting.

69 *A Survey of the Recreational Resources of the Colorado River Basin* (Washington: National Park Service, 1950), XXII, XXIII.
70 *National Parks Magazine,* No. 93, Apr.-June 1948.
71 H. R. 1102, 77 Cong. 1 Sess.

The bill carried an appropriation of $25 million, which no doubt was a factor in its defeat, but another factor was a memorial of the legislature of California against any more national parks in forested areas of the state, especially in coast redwood forests.[72] In April 1948 Representatives Johnson and Engle of California tried to get Congress to *lend* California the money to buy redwoods, but Congress was not interested in coast redwoods.[73] But the Save-the-Redwoods League, the Sierra Club, the Daughters of the American Revolution, and the California Department of Natural Resources were busy with plans for saving more of the coast redwoods during these years.[74]

The Park Service had still further ambitions. Cape Hatteras National Seashore had been authorized in 1937, and the Park Service was trying to get the state of North Carolina to provide the land, but without much success. Two other seashore areas, Beach Island, in New Jersey, and Rehoboth-Assateague, were being considered. There was some demand for a Great Plains national monument to preserve the natural conditions of an area of a million acres in the western plains. There was interest in the establishment of an Atomic Bomb national monument north of Alamagordo, New Mexico, the site of the first atomic bomb explosion. The Secretary of War promised to place as an exhibit here the airplane which had dropped the bomb on Nagasaki; but just why this unfortunate episode in American history should be memorialized is not quite clear.[75] The monument was not established.

While urging some new park areas, the Park Service managed to abolish or turn over to other jurisdictions several unworthy monuments: Father Millet Cross, Wheeler, and Holy Cross.

The manner in which Drury's term ended has already been discussed.[76] His successor, Demaray, assumed office in April 1951, but served only a short time and was succeeded by Conrad Wirth.

[72] H. R. 6201, 79 Cong. 2 Sess. H. R. 2876, 80 Cong. 1 Sess. *Congressional Record,* Feb. 27, 1946, 1697. *National Parks Magazine,* No. 89, Apr.-June 1947, 16.

[73] H. R. 6387, H. R. 6389, 80 Cong. 2 Sess.

[74] *National Parks Magazine,* No. 79, Oct.-Dec. 1944, 17; No. 88, Jan.-Mar. 1947, 13; No. 92, Jan.-Mar. 1948, 25; No. 93, Apr.-June 1948.

[75] *Report, Secretary of the Interior, 1946,* 341.

[76] See pp. 478 ff.

CHAPTER XXIV

The Wirth Administration

1951-

VIRGIN ISLANDS PARK, SEASHORE AREAS,

PETRIFIED FOREST PARK, CITY OF REFUGE

NATIONAL HISTORICAL PARK

When Chapman dismissed Drury on January 19, 1951, he immediately appointed Arthur E. Demaray as Director. Demaray was a worthy successor to the line of able directors. He had begun as a draftsman and on the strength of a vast versatility had "climbed up through a half-dozen posts" to the position of Associate Director, and then Director.[1] There was no question as to his fitness, but he served only a few months, and in December 1951 was succeeded by Conrad Wirth, who had had twenty years of experience in the national parks in many capacities and was well qualified for the position. Since Demaray served only a short time, it has seemed appropriate to refer to this chapter as the "Wirth Administration."

VIRGIN ISLANDS PARK   In the Wirth regime a number of park and monument areas were established, but only two national parks—the Virgin Islands National Park, and the Petrified Forest National Park, raised from monument status.[2] As early as 1939

1 Robert Shankland, *Steve Mather of the National Parks* (New York: Alfred A. Knopf, 1951), 245.

2 Stat. 72, 69.

Representative De Rouen had tried to get a recreation and conservation area in the Virgin Islands, but had failed.[3] Senator Jackson of Washington and Representative Engle of California introduced bills in 1955 to establish the national park, and Engle's bill passed both houses with little discussion and was signed by President Eisenhower in August 1956.[4] It is one of the smallest national parks in the park system—5,000 acres—but additions are being made. It is largely a wildlife and botanical park. The wildlife has been grossly abused on the Islands; there has long been a traffic in birds and their eggs, and some species are almost extinct. Plant life is rich and varied although neglected by the inhabitants, who have also devastated the habitat of wildlife and the land itself. It is not an area of outstanding magnificence, but is a lovely green island, with fine beaches and other attractions; and it is unique among national parks—there is nothing else in the system quite like it. It is a gift, and the administration expenses are very modest. The land for the park was given to the government by Jackson Hole Preserve, Inc., under Laurance S. Rockefeller, son of John D. Rockefeller, Jr., who has also built some excellent accommodations and is building more.[5]

There were modest additions to a few park areas. In 1953 President Truman added 47,753 acres to Olympic, including the Ocean Strip, the Queets Corridor, and nine sections elsewhere.[6] A little was added to Rocky Mountain to provide land for a new approach from the east, to replace the Big Thompson Road.[7] In the winter of 1951-52, John D. Rockefeller, Jr., gave $95,000 for the purchase and addition to Blue Ridge Parkway of beautiful Linville Falls and Linville Gorge. Kentucky has been trying for some years to acquire Great Onyx and Crystal caves for addition to Mammoth Cave, but so far without success.

SEASHORE AREAS   The Cape Hatteras National Seashore Recreational Area was finally established in the Wirth Administration. The project had been moribund because of oil prospects and

3 H. R. 9621, 76 Cong. 3 Sess.
4 S. 1604, H. R. 5299, 84 Cong. 1 Sess. Stat. 70, 940.
5 *National Parks Magazine*, Oct.-Dec. 1956, 163, 164.
6 Stat. 67, C 27.
7 Stat. 63, 626.

indifference on the part of the state of North Carolina; but in 1952 it developed new life with a $618,000 donation from the Avalon Foundation, a charitable trust established by Mrs. Ailsa Mellon Bruce, and from the Old Dominion Foundation, a charitable and educational foundation created by Paul Mellon, the donation to be matched by the state of North Carolina. The state matched the grant, and with the $1,236,000 the Service proceeded to buy land.

In December 1952 the state turned over to the Secretary 6,490 acres of previously state-owned lands which, with the 5,880 acres in the Pea Island National Wildlife Refuge (part of the seashore area), and 44 acres in the former Cape Hatteras Lighthouse Reservation that had been in the custody of the Park Service, brought the total lands in federal ownership in the Hatteras area to 12,414 acres. Since the act of 1937 creating the project had set 10,000 acres as the minimum acreage, the Secretary instructed the Park Service to assume jurisdiction; but purchases continued, and by 1956 the Service had acquired by purchase or had options on 25,000 acres of the 28,500 acres it had scheduled for inclusion. In one condemnation proceeding, however, the Service found itself embarrassed by the excessive award of the District Court—an award of $484,000 for a tract which it had appraised at $185,000. This often happens in condemnation proceedings.[8] In 1957 the Avalon and Old Dominion Foundations gave $200,000 more to complete land acquisition.

Professor Raymond Hall, of the Advisory Board on National Parks, Historic Sites, Buildings and Monuments, and some others have objected to some of the developments on Cape Hatteras, as too much like those on resort beaches. The Park Service has planned to spend $1.4 million for beach erosion and sand fixation work to prevent shifting of the beach, and Hall objects to this particularly, as interfering with nature's processes and therefore a violation of national park principles.

In 1954 the Park Service, with funds donated by generous friends of the parks, launched a study of the remaining seashore areas on the Atlantic and Gulf coasts, in co-operation with the states involved. In this study full consideration was to be given to areas valuable for unique or rare plant and animal life. The study was carried on in 1954 and 1955, and the report was not heartening. A

8 *Report, Secretary of the Interior, 1956,* 324.

similar survey in 1935 had revealed plenty of unspoiled seashore areas suitable for public recreation, and had recommended that twelve major strips with 437 miles of beach be preserved as national areas, only one of which, Cape Hatteras, was secured. Most of the others, by 1955, had gone into private and commercial developments; but after studying 126 undeveloped areas, the Service found 54 areas, with 640 miles of beach—17 per cent of the Atlantic and Gulf coasts—of which 16 were given highest priority for acquisition. These included: Great Beach, Cape Cod, Massachusetts; Shinnecock Inlet and Fire Island, New York; Popham-St. John and Crescent Area, Maine; Parramore Island, Virginia; Bogue Banks and Smith Island, North Carolina; Debidue Island and Kiawah Island, South Carolina; Cumberland Island, Georgia; Marco Beach, Mosquito Lagoon and St. Joseph Spit, Florida; Brazos Island and Padre Island, Texas.

In April 1959 the Advisory Board recommended the reservation of Oregon Dunes coast, in Lane and Douglas counties, and Padre Island along the Texas coast, and the Park Service wants a portion of outer beach, along Cape Cod. The Oregon Dunes would cost perhaps $4 million, and Great Beach as much as $16 million.

The Park Service report on beaches was criticized by the National Parks Association, as putting too much emphasis on recreation possibilities and not enough on possibilities of preserving coastal plant and wildlife habitats, but the Association approved the reservation of coastal areas anyhow. The Service promptly began planning for similar surveys of the Great Lakes shores and the Pacific Coast, and has recently issued several excellent reports.

The question might be raised as to the justification for government reservation and administration of coastal areas, at considerable expense, if private interests will provide the recreation at no public expense. The justification lies in the number of people who can enjoy the beaches and in the character of the recreation provided. To the extent that beaches are owned by individuals for summer homes, only a small number are accommodated, to the exclusion of the general public; and if the beaches are developed as resorts or amusement centers by private interests, the recreation is often of low character, vulgar, tawdry, even demoralizing. Mather once said that the people should have the Coney Island type of recreation if they want it, but he did not want it in the national park system. The Park Service, furthermore, can provide some protection for wildlife and plant life, and for aesthetic values. Coastlines and beaches should never have been permitted to pass into private ownership.

EVERGLADES A PERSISTENT PROBLEM   Senators Holland and Smathers and Representatives Fascell and Rogers of Florida tried to get an extension of the boundaries of Everglades Park,[9] and on March 12, 1954, an Order of Secretary McKay added 271,000 acres to the park.

In the last few years there has been some tension between the Park Service and certain interests and individuals in Florida, particularly real estate interests and sportsmen. With the spectacular growth of the resort business, and to some extent of fruit and vegetable production, some land values have reached fantastic levels; and here was the Park Service, as late as 1954, adding 271,000 acres to the park, taking it forever from speculation and "development"! The next year the legislature of Florida adopted a memorial objecting to this enlargement, and an "Association for the Best Use of Florida Lands, Inc." was formed "to save Florida's lands from the Everglades National Park for use and development." McKay's order of 1954 was said to have been followed by a threat of the Governor to call out the militia to prevent the taking over of state lands. Even the owners of land which was bought or condemned at prices which were fair at the time were likely to think that they had been cheated if the prices were now much higher; and some of the land had risen several hundred per cent. Everglades had been a "good buy."

Hunters and fishermen found national park regulations somewhat restrictive and irksome. Everglades was a wilderness park, and as such had to be carefully guarded. Some natives could not see the necessity for keeping out "gladesbuggies" (old Fords with oversize tires) and "airboats" (boats driven by fans operating in the air rather than in the water), where they once roamed freely. Some agricultural interests resented the prohibition of drainage canals in the park, but the Park Service wanted no more drainage. Some people thought the park had expanded too much anyhow, and boundaries were changed too often; and in 1957 several identical

9 S. 2642, 84 Cong. 1 Sess. S. 1790, H. R. 6641, H. R. 6643, 85 Cong. 1 Sess.

bills were introduced to fix the boundaries definitely and finally, one of which, by Senators Holland and Smathers, was the subject of hearings in June 1957. It was a compromise bill, favored by the Park Service and by several of the Florida men in Congress.[10]

BOUNDARY ADJUSTMENTS   There were boundary adjustments, mostly increases, for several national monuments. Hovenweep, Mound City, and White Sands were enlarged; Truman added Devil's Hole to Death Valley, and traded a perpetual right-of-way easement to Borax Consolidated, Ltd. for 230 acres of private lands in the monument. On the other hand, 29,118 acres were eliminated from Glacier Bay by Presidential proclamation, and in 1952 Badlands was reduced 32,000 acres, 12,000 acres of which were private lands. Wallace Pratt and wife have given 5,000 acres for an addition to Carlsbad Caverns. The Service made studies of the boundary lines of fifteen other areas.[11] In July 1956 Zion National Monument was very properly added to Zion Park.[12]

ELIMINATIONS SUGGESTED   The Advisory Board on National Parks, Historic Sites, Buildings and Monuments, set up in February 1936 after the passage of the Historic Sites and Buildings Act, has taken an increasingly active part in national park affairs in recent years.

At a meeting in March 1954 the Advisory Board received a report of a "survey team" which recommended that "the Service reexamine the areas it administers to determine those which are primarily of state significance rather than national significance with a view to transferring those not of national significance to the states," and named seven areas which they believed to be in this category: Millerton Lake Recreation Area, Platt National Park, Mound City Group National Monument, Moore's Creek National Military Park, Big Hole Battlefield National Monument, Natchez Trace Parkway, and Lehman Caves National Monument. At the

10 S. 1790, H. R. 6641, H. R. 6653, 85 Cong. 1 Sess. Stat. 72, 280.
11 Report, Secretary of the Interior, 1955, 358.
12 Stat. 70, 527.

same meeting the Board adopted a resolution tactfully suggesting that "certain areas now administered by the Park Service possess a degree of interest which would make them suitable for administration by appropriate agencies or political subdivisions of the states," and approved "the Department's efforts toward that end." Among those approved for transfer were: Hot Springs National Park, Platt National Park, Capulin Mountain National Monument, Mound City Group National Monument, Pinnacles National Monument, Shoshone Cavern National Monument, Verendrye National Monument, Moore's Creek National Military Park, Brices Cross Roads National Battlefield Site, Cowpens National Battlefield Site, Tupelo National Battlefield Site, White Plains National Battlefield Site, and Millerton Lake National Recreation Area.

Something was done in the matter of elimination or transfer: of Castle Pinckney in South Carolina and Fossil Cycad in South Dakota—the latter because it was found that the fossil cycads were no more to be seen in the monument than in some other places; Old Kasaan in Alaska was abolished because the totem poles and other curiosities were so badly depreciated as to be unworthy of protection; Verendrye National Monument was turned over to the North Dakota State Historical Society because careful research revealed no proof of the historical events it was supposed to commemorate. Millerton Lake National Recreation Area was turned over to the California State Park System in 1957, leaving only three national recreation areas—Lake Mead, Coulee Dam (F. D. Roosevelt Lake), and Shadow Mountain. Shoshone Cavern was given to Cody, Wyoming, to be used as a park, and White Plains was disposed of. The Park Service tried to make a national recreation area of Platt National Park, adding some land to it—a noble endeavor, worthy of success.

ADDITIONS AND CHANGES   Coronado International Memorial in New Mexico had been authorized in 1941, conditional on Mexico setting up a corresponding area across the line. Just why Mexico should be supposed to want to honor the Spaniard Coronado is not clear; but at any rate that country was slow to act, and in July 1952 Congress passed an act changing the area to a *national* memorial and prohibiting the establishment of the international memorial until Mexico had done her part. In November 1952, President Truman proclaimed the Coronado *National* Memorial covering the United States part of the area.[13] Fort Union was authorized in June 1954.[14]

Since its proclamation as a national monument[15] there have been many attempts to elevate Petrified Forest from monument to national park status, opposed by most conservationists and by the Park Service. About 8,600 acres were added in 1955. Senator Hayden of Arizona tried to raise the status of the monument in 1956 but failed;[16] but early in 1958 the Department of the Interior was reported to be favoring the change, and national park status was achieved on March 28, 1958, to become effective when inholdings are acquired.[17]

CITY OF REFUGE NATIONAL HISTORICAL PARK   Several historical parks were added in the Wirth regime. One of the most interesting to be authorized was the City of Refuge National Historical Park in Hawaii. This city, on the Kona coast, dates back two or three hundred years, and was long a safe refuge for Hawaiian fugitives and refugees of all kinds. The city was walled on the land side and the walls were badly disintegrated, in spite of some protection and restoration by the Bernice F. Bishop Museum of Honolulu.[18] Albright had visited the city as early as 1926 and later had recommended its establishment as a national monument, but the proposal remained dormant until 1947, when Delegate Joseph R. Farrington suggested to Superintendent Oberhansley of Hawaii National Park that the city be brought under federal protection. The Park Service sent Regional Historian Aubrey Neasham, Assistant Director Hillory A. Tolson, and Chief of Development Thomas C. Vint to Hawaii, and they strongly advised its establishment as a national historical park. Tolson and Delegate Farrington worked for its creation and got the authorization in July 1955. The Territory of Hawaii is now acquiring the land for the park.[19]

13 Stat. 55, 630; 66, 510; 67, C 18.
14 Stat. 68, 298.
15 See p. 156.
16 S. 4038, 84 Cong. 2 Sess.
17 Stat. 72, 69.
18 Stat. 69, 376.
19 Stat. 69, 376. Nash Castro, *The Land of Pele* (Honolulu: Hawaii Natural History Association, 1953), 68, 69.

THE QUETICO-SUPERIOR WILDERNESS AREA   There have been "wilderness" enthusiasts for many years—Muir was one of the first and most influential—but in recent years there has been a growing interest in the creation of wilderness or primitive areas, with few roads and facilities or none at all, in the national park system and in the national forests. The Quetico-Superior Wilderness Area, which was provided for in 1948, under Forest Service control, is one such area. In 1955 a Citizens Committee was formed to acquire 50,000 acres of private lands to complete the area, authorized by the act of 1955, and several of the Minnesota men in Congress tried to get appropriations for land buying. In January 1955 Senators Thye and Humphrey introduced a bill to add more lands to the area and to appropriate more money—$2.5 million—for purchase, which passed and was signed in June 1956.[20]

In very recent years a number of other areas have been considered for possible inclusion in the park system or for preservation in some other role. The Park Service will never be happy until the Minarets, cut out of Yosemite in 1905, are returned to the park system. The return of the Minarets is always given high priority in plans for the future. Albright believes that the Forest Service might be willing to return them if it were not for the pressure of mining interests.

WILDERNESS AREAS IN THE NORTHWEST   The Park Service has been deeply interested in the preservation of two splendid national forest primitive or wilderness areas in the northwest—the Three Sisters Primitive Area in Oregon and the Glacier Peak Limited Area in the northern Cascades in Washington, the latter one of the most magnificent primitive areas in the country. These areas are subject to logging at any time that the Secretary of Agriculture decides it is desirable, and many conservationists believe they should be made secure. When the Secretary of Agriculture cut 53,000 acres from Three Sisters it was evident that they were not secure.[21] There have even been suggestions that these areas, particularly Glacier Peak, might be worthy of national park or monument status. Glacier Peak is a magnificent scenic area quite comparable with

20 S. 2967, 84 Cong. 2 Sess. Stat. 70, 326 ff.
21 *Sierra Club Bulletin,* Apr. 1956, 5. *National Parks Magazine,* Oct.-Dec. 1956, 173.

some of our national parks. As in Olympic and Glacier parks, the mountains in Glacier Peak are not very high—the Peak only 10,528 feet high, and thirty others over 8,000 feet high—but in the cold and wet northern Cascades they carry a heavy mantle of snow fields and glaciers that enhance the beauty of the scenery. On February 16, 1959, the Forest Service announced a proposal to set up a 422,925-acre wilderness area here—but in the proposal the forested valleys were to be left out for possible logging, thus botching the scenery and spoiling the biotic balance of the area. Critics suggested that the project would create a starfish-shaped wilderness area covering only the high altitudes. In the same northern Cascade region, the Salmon La Sac area and the adjoining Alpine Lake Limited Area have been urged for wilderness status.[22]

Also considered for such status was Admiralty Island, along the Alaska coast, which was once considered as an alternative to Glacier Bay Monument.

In 1956 there was some excitement over excavations in Russell Cave in Alabama, which revealed civilizations running back perhaps 9,000 years. The cave was bought by the National Geographic Society which has offered it to the government for a national monument. Plans are being made to accept it.[23]

THE GRASSLAND NATIONAL MONUMENT PROPOSAL   There has been some agitation for the establishment of a grasslands national monument, or even two or three of them, in the Middle West. Following a survey by Drs. F. W. Albertson and G. W. Tomanek, of the Fort Hays Kansas State College, Professor Raymond Hall has been urging the establishment of at least one short-grass monument north of Cheyenne, Wyoming, or north of Scottsbluff, Nebraska, or along the Nebraska-South Dakota line; and a tall-grass monument in the flint hills area of Chase County, Kansas. The purpose of such reservations would be to preserve for its scientific and educational value an area of each type of grass, with its native fauna and flora. With a great surplus of farm products and with dust storms an intermittent threat in some of this area, there would be no loss and some gain in taking some of the land out of cultivation. In

22 *National Parks Magazine,* Apr. 1959, 6. *American Forests,* Mar. 1959, 12. *Living Wilderness,* Summer-Fall 1958, 23; Winter 1959, 23.
23 *National Geographic Magazine,* Oct. 1956, 542; Mar. 1958, 438.

1956 the Park Service reported that it had made a contract with the Fort Hays Kansas State College for the study of possibilities for a grasslands national monument. John D. Rockefeller, Jr., has given $20,000 for the purchase of original prairie land in Kansas. At its meeting in April 1959 the Advisory Board recommended the creation of a 34,000-acre tall-grass prairie national park or monument near Manhattan, Kansas, and a short-grass reservation of some kind farther west.

WESTERN WONDERLAND   Not long ago the Park Service became interested in Dead Horse Point, in Utah, not far from Moab, and entered into an agreement with the Bureau of Land Management for its possible inclusion in the park system. Dead Horse Point is a little promontory which juts out into the canyon of the Colorado, at its junction with the Green River Canyon. The Colorado Canyon is about fifteen miles wide here, only about half as deep as at Grand Canyon, but the view is almost as impressive. It should be in the park system, perhaps as a part of a "Western Wonderlands National Parkway"; but grazing, uranium, and oil activities present serious difficulties in the way of its inclusion. The name "Dead Horse Point" came from a pathetic occurrence of some years ago, when stockmen drove a herd of wild horses out onto the Point, selected the best and left the rest on the promontory. These horses, excited and confused, feared to cross the narrow neck to the mainland and ran about in a circle on the point until they died of thirst. This area is being considered for a Utah State park.

In eastern Utah and northern Arizona are to be found some of the most scenic lands in America, stark, bold, weird, fantastic, stupendous, and beautiful; indeed much of the Colorado River Basin, with its tributaries, is a wilderness of mighty red, pink, yellow, and multi-colored rocks, cliffs, escarpments, mesas, canyons, buttes, spires, and natural bridges the equal of which is perhaps not to be found anywhere else in the world. Some areas in this general region have been set aside as national monuments—Rainbow Bridge, Capitol Reef, Natural Bridges, Arches, and Navajo; but there are others that might be considered worthy: Chesler Park, Devils Lane, Cyclone Canyon, Lavender Canyon, Valley of the Goblins (wanted by the Park Service as a national monument), Monument Canyon, Monument Valley, San Rafael Swell, The

Needles, Navajo Mountain, Escalante Canyon, Cathedral Valley, Dead Horse Point, Circle Cliffs, Hole in Rock, Upheaval Dome Pasture, Standing Rocks, Elk Ridge, Gypsum Canyon, Fable Valley, Beef Basin Canyon, Land's End, Fisher Towers, Dark Canyon, Arch Canyon, Indian Creek Canyon, Crossing of the Fathers, Hite Area, and doubtless others. The present rather primitive road from Bryce Canyon through Escalante to Capitol Reef, one of the most scenic roads in the United States, should be included in any plan for development, as should also the scenic highway from Moab to Cisco, along the Colorado River.

The need is that some of these areas should be made accessible to the public, in such manner as the Park Service, in co-operation with other government bureaus, decides upon. Clearly a quarter of the state of Utah cannot be set up as a national park or monument. Although nearly all the lands are unsurveyed public lands, stockmen have leases, some of the area is infested with uranium and oil prospectors and miners, and there are plans for developing water power at various points. Planning will be difficult. Perhaps the best plan would be to reserve the most noteworthy sites as national monuments and connect them with roads running through the public domain in what could be called the "Western Wonderland." Tourist accommodations could not easily be made available in many of them, but would have to be found in towns not too far away. However done, the development of these magnificent areas would be expensive, for they are far from sources of some materials, and roads through some of the country will be costly; but it would be vastly worthwhile. A million people would visit these wonders every year if roads were available, relieving the congestion in some of the parks.

The Park Service has appreciated the scenic magnificence of this area for many years and has tried to do something for its development. In 1933 the Service approved the elevation of Navajo National Monument (established in 1909) to park status, to include Paiute Strip, Navajo Mountain, Rainbow Bridge National Monument, Monument Valley, and Navajo National Monument.[24] In 1936 Secretary Ickes reported that three new monuments were being considered—Green River, including Dinosaur, Escalante and Kolob Canyons. Kolob Canyons were included in Zion National Monument the next year. In 1937 Kofa Mountains in Arizona were

24 *Report, Secretary of the Interior, 1933,* 165.

added to the project, and for several years Escalante was being pushed. The park or monument or recreation area being considered would have covered 1,280,000 acres, in a narrow strip on both sides of the Green and Colorado rivers from the vicinity of their junction southwest of Moab, Utah, south to the Arizona line. In 1939 and 1940 it seemed likely that the reservation would be made, but Governor Blood asked that the proposal be held up pending a study of power possibilities in the area. Very little was said about it for some years, perhaps because of impending power developments on the Colorado and its tributaries.[25]

THE CHESAPEAKE AND OHIO CANAL   The Chesapeake and Ohio Canal, scenic as well as historic, has presented some perplexing problems which are still unsettled. Completed as far northwest as Cumberland, Maryland, in 1856, the canal had ceased operations in 1924, and in 1938 was acquired by the federal government. In 1948 Congress authorized the Secretary to have the Public Roads Administration and the National Park Service survey the canal between Great Falls, Maryland, and Cumberland, Maryland, and report on the advisability of constructing a parkway along the route of the canal, voting $40,000 for the survey.[26] Two years later Congress authorized the Secretary to accept lands and exchange Chesapeake and Ohio property under his jurisdiction for other lands, to increase the parkway width to an average of 100 acres per mile.[27] In 1953 the state of Maryland approved the acquisition of land for the parkway, but the next year surveying was still continuing. In 1950 a plan was announced for a motor highway from Washington to Cumberland, using the canal and towpath as a right of way. Protests came from many organizations and individuals at this desecration of the old canal, and Justice William O. Douglas and some thirty others made an eight-day hike along the canal to advertise their opposition to the highway. Wirth appointed a committee to study the problem of the disposition of the canal, and as a result

25 *Report, Secretary of the Interior, 1935*, 202; 1936, 111; 1937, 64; 1939, 292. *Yearbook, Park and Recreation Progress*, 1941, 4, 26, 27. *A Survey of the Recreational Resources of the Colorado Basin* (Washington: National Park Service, 1950), Chap. VIII. *Westways*, June 1953, 8 ff.
26 H. R. 5155, 80 Cong. 2 Sess. Stat. 62, 351.
27 H. R. 8534, 81 Cong. 2 Sess. Stat. 64, 905.

of the report of the committee Wirth decided not to build the highway. In February 1956 Secretary McKay announced that he would ask Congress to provide for the development of the canal as a scenic and historic park instead of parkway.[28]

But the Park Service will not have the final word; the final decision is up to Congress, and it will be difficult to make. There are some who believe the Potomac should be left for a dam and reservoir for a future water supply for Washington, with water power development. This brings support from the neighboring farm cooperatives, which would have first chance at electricity produced by federal projects. Of course the Army Engineers would enjoy building the dam. Balancing all the diverse interest groups will be a very difficult task.[29]

PROPOSED ADDITIONS TO THE PARK SYSTEM   Several Indian ruins should be set up as national monuments: Kinishba Ruins in Arizona and Manuelito in New Mexico, and perhaps others, as for instance some mentioned in the Survey of the Colorado River Basin discussed in the previous chapter. In the case of Manuelito, the state of New Mexico spent money buying the land for the monument, but it was never established.

It would be fortunate if some wealthy philanthropist should provide the money for the addition of one more historical park or monument—Virginia City, Nevada. This town, once the scene of Mark Twain's early journalistic activities, rated by some the most interesting town in America, was the scene of wild mining excitement in the 1860's and 1870's when the Great Comstock Lode was pouring out its millions in silver; but when the lode suddenly pinched out most of the people departed, leaving a most typical western mining town. In recent years it has lost some of its historic buildings and gained some desecrating modern buildings, but it is still a very interesting town.

Wirth and the Park Service would of course have been happy to have one coast redwoods park, but, except for Muir Woods National Monument, California has been left to struggle along with the problem of acquiring coast redwoods, and to some extent even giant sequoias. The State Park Commission got the North Cala-

28 S. 77, 85 Cong. 1 Sess.
29 *American Forests*, May 1959, 22.

veras Grove of giant sequoias in 1931 as we have already seen;[30]
and in 1954 the State Park Commission, the Calaveras Grove
Association, and John D. Rockefeller, Jr., bought the great South
Calaveras Grove of 1,000 giant sequoias for several millions,
John D. Rockefeller, Jr., contributing $1 million. Horace Albright
and the Save-the-Redwoods League were the prime movers in the
campaign to buy the grove, which was needed to fill out the Calaveras Grove. Late in 1956 the Save-the Redwoods League announced
that the League and the state of California had bought the famous
coast redwood grove, the Avenue of the Giants, the League and the
state each paying $600,000 of the purchase price. The League has
saved more than sixty memorial groves of the great trees, and the
League and the California State Park Commission are planning for
the purchase of more groves and additions to groves. In 1956 the
State Park Commission was budgeting $3,940,000 for coast redwood
park projects. Surely the people of the United States should be
eternally grateful to the Save-the-Redwoods League, the Sierra Club
and the state of California for doing this great national service
which the United States Congress always refused to do. Today
California has about 157 units in its park system, including a number of coast redwood groves and many beach areas.

There have been many suggestions for park areas of more or less
doubtful value. Utah promoters wanted a Golden Spike Monument
Site at Promontory, Utah, where the two sections of the Union
Pacific Railroad met and were joined by a golden spike. The Advisory Board approved it as a national historic site, but not in federal ownership, and this is what it now is.

There has been some interest in the establishment of Wheeler
Peak, in eastern Nevada, as a "Great Basin Range National Park,"
to include also Lehman Caves, now a national monument. Wheeler
Peak is only 13,061 feet high, but it is a beautiful mountain, the
next highest in the desert basin of Nevada and in that respect
unique, and there is a forest in the area of the bristlecone pines,
perhaps the oldest type of trees in the world. The area was explored
by Weldon F. Heald and Albert Marshall in September 1955, and
Heald was so impressed that he proposed that it be made a national
park or monument.

Since that time there have been several studies of the area. The
Sierra Club has seemed mildly favorable to its establishment, the

30 See p. 115.

National Parks Association has favored it, and in 1957 the "Great Basin Range National Park Association" was set up to promote the project. Although most of the people of Nevada favor the park, there is objection from a few stockmen who herd cattle and sheep here, and from miners—there are 1,460 acres of mining claims in the project, but no mineral production. The Forest Service, which at present controls it, may be assumed to have no yearning for a park here. That Service has already established picnic sites and camping units, and is reported planning for resorts, cabin camps, and summer homes, designating the area the "Wheeler Peak Scenic Area," perhaps to forestall the park. In the 85th Congress Senators Bible and Malone and Representative Baring introduced bills asking the Secretary to investigate the area with the purpose of appraising its suitability for national park status.[31]

There has been agitation for the establishment of Grant's Tomb on Riverside Drive in New York City as a national shrine. The Advisory Board has approved it as a memorial, but not as a historic site or national monument. Recent reports are that it will be transferred to the federal government.

Very recently Senator Paul Douglas of Illinois has revived interest in the establishment of an Indiana Sand Dunes National Monument covering up to 3,500 acres of the sand dunes on the south shore of Lake Michigan, and several bills have been offered for its establishment.[32]

PROPOSALS FOR A "HISTORICAL BUREAU"   With the growing number and importance of historical parks, there have been suggestions that there should be a separate bureau for them. Of the 180 areas administered by the Park Service, about 100—over half—are related to United States history. It is argued that the work of protecting Yellowstone or Yosemite is essentially different from the task of administering a battlefield or cemetery, or the Statue of Liberty; that the former calls for naturalists, whereas the latter calls for historians; and that the Park Service is growing extraordinarily complicated and bureaucratic, to the point of unwieldiness. The Di-

31 S. 3587, H. R. 11799, 85 Cong. 2 Sess. See also *National Parks Magazine*, July-Sept. 1957, 99; Apr.-June 1958, 71; Feb. 1959, 14. *American Forests*, Feb. 1959, 17; Apr. 1959, 4.
32 S. 3898, H. R. 12689, 85 Cong. 2 Sess. H. R. 6517, 86 Cong. 1 Sess.

rector is obliged to belong to so many boards and commissions that the attendance at their meetings and dedications is a full-time job. It is argued that in a separate bureau the historical parks would gain a higher dignity than they now have. On the other hand there are difficulties in the way of any such separation. Some units in the park system could not be easily and precisely classified. Some parks and monuments are both scenic and historical: Acadia, Death Valley, Grand Teton, Great Smoky Mountains, Lava Beds, Cumberland Gap, Canyon de Chelly, and others. Also it would weaken the Park Service to split it in two, and if it were split into scenic and historical bureaus, there would still be the problem of proper placing of recreation areas, which perhaps detract from the attention given to scenic parks more than do the historical parks. The Director has too much to do, and his duties, in scenic parks, historic areas and recreation areas run in different directions and call for different types of training; but the remedy for that is not easy to outline.[33] The establishment of a fifth regional office at Philadelphia, in July 1955, afforded some relief.

33 *National Parks Magazine*, No. 127, Oct.-Dec. 1956, 152.

CHAPTER XXV

The Wirth Administration

1951-

FINANCIAL AND CONCESSION PROBLEMS,

OVERCROWDED PARKS, MISSION 66,

CURRENT PARK SERVICE ACTIVITIES

⚒ SKIMPY FINANCIAL SUPPORT The postwar financial embarrassment of the Park Service continued with little abatement for several years. The number of visits increased by leaps and bounds—from 37 million in 1951 to 54,923,000 in 1956—but appropriations remained about the same during that time, and the Park Service and the concessioners were hard pressed to care for the invading hordes; in fact they could not care for them at all well.[1] The Park Service simply could not pay for the rehabilitation of roads, buildings, and facilities, or for enough rangers to attend to all the wants of the visitors, to guard the natural wonders, or at times even to man the entrance stations. The result was that rangers were overworked and yet the visitors ran wild. Vandalism flourished, even to the stealing of precious and irreplaceable objects.[2] There was some discussion of the "erosion" of our parks, and predictions that some of them, for instance Yellowstone, would be largely ruined in fifty

[1] The figures on visits refer to the visits to the entire park system. In 1955, for instance, the total number of visits was about 50 million but only 20 million of these related to the national parks.

[2] *Reader's Digest*, Aug. 1952, 125; *Harpers Magazine*, Oct. 1953, 49; Feb. 1954, 12. *American Forests*, May 1955, 24. *Natural History*, May 1952, 200.

years. Bernard De Voto, the able and tireless friend of the parks, urged as the only way to save them, "Let's close the national parks," because "so much of the priceless heritage which the Service must safeguard for the United States is beginning to go to hell."[3]

Some of the park facilities were antiquated and insufficient, and in 1954 Congress passed a law authorizing the Secretary to exchange the inadequate electric and communication facilities of Glacier and Grand Canyon for more modern and efficient facilities, "on an equal value basis."[4]

An adequate force of rangers could not possibly be hired without a considerable increase in appropriations. The general level of wages in the country was far above that of 1941 when the Service had about the same number of rangers. Park rangers, like forest rangers, are extraordinarily loyal to their jobs, difficult and even sometimes dangerous as the jobs are—in fire-fighting and rescue work, for instance. They love their work and stick to it under very adverse conditions; but their conditions of employment were becoming impossibly bad. Not only were wages low and hours of labor quite too long, but prices were high and rising, particularly after the onset of the Korean War in 1950. Many of the employees had to live in wretched quarters, "CCC barracks built of tarpaper in 1934 and intended to last no more than five years, old warehouses and cook shacks built of slabs, curious structures hammered together from whatever salvaged lumber might be at hand."[5] At a conference in September 1953 the wives of the Superintendents were asked to make a survey of housing conditions in the parks, and their report revealed really distressing conditions for employees —"barbarous," as several expressed it. The Service needed hundreds of new, decent houses for them.[6] In February 1956, Alfred Knopf, the book publisher, member of the Advisory Board and generous friend of the parks, sent a letter to every senator and representative, calling for better housing for park employees.

To make matters worse, the rents on these habitations were raised drastically, following a decree of the Bureau of the Budget that the rents of government housing must be equal to those of comparable housing outside. De Voto found rangers paying as

3 *Harpers Magazine*, Oct. 1953, 49.
4 Stat. 68, 771.
5 *Harpers Magazine*, Oct. 1953, 50.
6 *Report, Secretary of the Interior, 1953*, 288.

much as 23.5 per cent of their modest wages for rent. Furthermore, if rangers had children of school age, they were required, at least in some areas, to pay tuition and transportation costs to public schools outside. De Voto described this situation for Grand Teton Park: "The park pays Teton County, Wyoming, $26,000 a year in lieu of taxes; it produces God knows how much for the state in gasoline and sales taxes; the business brought in by its visitors is all that keeps the town of Jackson solvent or even alive. But a hangover from the controversy over Jackson Hole National Monument, a controversy created for profit by local politicians and the gamblers and the land speculators allied with them, has enabled the town of Jackson to pressure the state administration. By decree of the state Attorney General, park personnel are not residents of Wyoming . . . and must therefore pay for the transportation and tuition of their children who attend public schools."[7] For one ranger interviewed, this amounted to $158 per child.

Notwithstanding all this, Senators Barrett and Hunt and Representative Harrison of Wyoming introduced identical bills in 1953 to make sure that if the Jackson Lake Lodge should be given to the government it would still be taxable by the state of Wyoming. In the hands of Jackson Hole Preserve, Inc., it paid taxes like any other concessioner property, but if owned by the government these taxes would cease. The proponents of this measure argued that owing to the reduction in the number of cattle in the area and other changes made by inclusion in Grand Teton Park, the tax rate in Teton County was very high—four times the state average—and if the taxes were lost the county would be in dire financial straits. There was little sense in all this argument, but Assistant Secretary Orme Lewis approved the Senate bill and it passed both houses without comment. Rowland Hughes, of the Bureau of the Budget, opposed, however, and President Eisenhower pocket-vetoed it.[8]

To make matters worse, the Ferguson amendment to the 1952 appropriation act cut funds and forced reduction in employment; the Jensen amendment required the keeping of complicated records; and the Whitten amendment to the supplemental appropriation act of 1952 blocked many deserved promotions.[9] On the other hand

7 *Harpers Magazine,* Oct. 1953, 51.
8 S. 1706, H. R. 4770, 83 Cong. 1 Sess.
9 *Congressional Record,* 82 Cong. 1 Sess., 763, 1160, 1255, 8116.

the appropriations in 1951 and 1952 were less specific as to where money should be spent, giving the Service more latitude.

If the Park Service had been permitted to keep its receipts it would have gained by raising admission fees, but when the fees were raised in 1954, the increased revenues went to the Treasury; and the increase in fees did not reduce visitor use, and so did nothing to solve the problem of park poverty.

CONCESSIONER PROBLEMS   The concessioners were about as ill-equipped for the tourist invasion as the Park Service. They had been expanding and improving their accommodations somewhat, but not nearly enough to serve all the visitors, and some of what they had was fitter for the slums of Chicago than for national parks.[10] According to one report, on an August day in 1954, of 16,435 tourists who entered Yellowstone 6,000 had either to sleep in their cars or drive back out of the park. This situation was unsatisfactory to the public but not altogether bad for the concessioners, although they had their difficulties with rising costs during and after the Korean War.

There were some criticisms of the concessioners, some charges that although they were making handsome profits they were resting on their oars instead of rehabilitating and expanding their facilities. Anthony Netboy started a round of debate with an article in *American Forests* in May 1955, in which he asserted that some of the concessioners made up to 10 per cent or more on their investment, yet rendered poor and inadequate service, Yellowstone and Yosemite coming in for special criticism. To this H. Oehlmann, chairman of the Western Conference National Park Concessioners, made reply two months later, denying that the concessioners were responsible for the situation. He said that the concessions were not generally very profitable, that in some parks earnings were quite dismal, that several concessions were for sale, and that in one park (Mount Rainier) Congress finally authorized the purchase of the concessioner's facilities as the only alternative to closing them. He charged much of the responsibility to Ickes' threat of government ownership

10 The author had a room in Old Faithful Hotel in the summer of 1953— the cabins were all taken early in the day—a room without bath for $8.00, with a leaking toilet forty feet down the hall and ten men waiting in line to get in.

of facilities and restrictive policies of Ickes and Krug, which did not give the concessioners the confidence essential to long-run expansion. He also pointed out that there had been considerable improvements in facilities. The Park Service backed him up in his statements as to the profits of concessioners.[11] In 1953 the average rate of return was calculated at 6.87 per cent, which was not excessive considering the hazards of the business.

Not all the concessioners were having a wonderful time. In 1938 the government had been obliged to build a hotel and other facilities in Mount McKinley because no private concessioner could see a profit in it, and from 1953 on, the nonprofit National Park Concessions, Inc., managed the business on an emergency basis. In Isle Royale, too, the government owned the Rock Harbor lodge and other facilities but had trouble finding a private concessioner, so National Park Concessions, Inc., took over. The Park Service was obliged to build additional accommodations in 1955. In 1951 the Glacier Park concessioner was reported anxious to quit, but was induced to continue for a while on a year-to-year basis. At Mount Rainier the concessioner had been losing money and the government had been obliged to buy the facilities, which the concessioner was operating on a year-to-year basis.

At Big Bend, hot in summer and far from other national parks, the Service had difficulty finding a concessioner as late as 1957. At that time the concessioner at Lake Mead was reported to be wishing to get out. In 1954 the Santa Fe Railway Company did get out of its business on the South Rim of Grand Canyon, donating its power plants, boilers, water system (including pumps at Indian Gardens), and related property to the government, and selling its other properties, including El Tovar Hotel, Bright Angel Lodge, and the Auto Lodge, to the Fred Harvey Company which had been operating the business for years. The main difficulty with most concessioners was that they could not or did not wish to expand facilities enough to care for the crowds that came. Most of the concession renewals in 1954 were for short periods—from one to five years, mostly for one year.

In Everglades a different situation developed in 1955. There were two applicants for concessions, the Fred Harvey Company and a Florida group. Fred Harvey had a long record of efficient service, which the Park Service would have been glad to recognize; but on

11 *American Forests*, May 1955, 24; July 1955, 13.

the other hand the state of Florida had put up the money for the park, and it had been the policy of the Service to use local interests where possible. So the concession was awarded to the Florida group.

Concessioners did provide some expansion. In 1956 the Yellowstone concessioners were reported to be planning to spend $3.5 million in the next five years and $10 million in the five years following that. The Jackson Lake Lodge, built at an expense of $6.5 million, was opened at Grand Teton in 1955 by Jackson Hole Preserve, Inc., the Rockefeller nonprofit organization. The lodge is owned and operated by the Grand Teton Lodge Company, at cost. Any profit made is returned to Jackson Hole Preserve, Inc., to be used in its conservation activities. The Rockefeller organization also operates a lodge at Jenny Lake. Private concessioners were planning to spend $4 million at six points on Blue Ridge Parkway. In January 1957 concessioners were reported to have completed or to have under way a total of $10 million worth of new facilities. In that year total private investment in the parks was reported at $50 million—up $13 million from the $37 million reported in 1955.

There was some criticism in Congress of prices, service, and of concession policies, but there was little logic in criticizing the concessioners. A few no doubt were inefficient, but most of them were doing about as well as they could under the conditions existing. They had not forgotten the red ink of the war time and, on the reverse side of the booming prosperity, wages and costs were rising.

In the appropriation bill of July 1953 a section was added which made unnecessary work for the Park Service, a section requiring the Secretary to review concessions and thereafter report all concession leases and contracts to the President of the Senate and the Speaker of the House sixty days before awards were made.[12] This was a broad hint that the Park Service had been unwise or delinquent in its concession policies and needed the "vigilant supervision" of Congress. The only effect this provision could have was to increase the amount of paper work and expenses of the Park Service. The Service promptly set to work to get the provision at least modified to apply only to the more important contracts, finally succeeding in July 1956 in limiting the requirement to leases and contracts involving a gross annual business of $100,000 or of more than five years' duration.[13]

12 Stat. 67, 271.
13 Stat. 70, 543.

Debates in Congress threw little light on the concession situation. Barrett and Hunt of Wyoming thought the concessioners should have greater security and not less. Barrett admitted that some of the buildings were unfit for use, but said it was difficult to get anyone to invest in more and better facilities. There was no agreement as to whether competitive bidding or negotiation of concessions was best. Hayden of Arizona stated that sometimes it cost as much to administer and supervise a concession as it yielded; and on the other hand Bridges asserted that one concessioner with a gross income of over $6 million and a net profit of $239,309, paid the government only $7,550. He thought the government should get more from the concessioners. Nothing very helpful in these debates. Of course, the Wyoming men were generally favorable to more generous treatment of the parks, and there were rumors that the state of Wyoming wanted to operate the Yellowstone concessions, but these were unconfirmed. No one suggested that the real trouble was the policy of concessioner building of facilities, that if the government built the facilities it could have all that Congress wanted to provide.[14] Very recently Senator Murray and Representative Metcalf of Montana have tried to get the lease period increased to thirty years, and have succeeded.[15]

To an increasing extent the trouble was not Congressional stinginess, but too many people and too little space. In such areas as Yosemite Valley there has not been for years enough room for all the people who wanted to get in; in Zion Canyon and Mesa Verde the same condition was developing. As formerly, various remedies were suggested for this situation: larger appropriations, shift of facilities out of congested areas, elimination of resort-type of recreation, limitation of stays, increase in entrance fees, and other changes. These will be considered in Chapter XXIX on Financing the Parks.

REMEDIES FOR FINANCIAL SITUATION AND OVERCROWDING: CUT OUT SUPERFLUITIES   Some the purists have insisted that the appropriations would not be so painfully inadequate if so much were not spent on "superfluities"—recreation areas at dam sites, second-rate scenic areas, minor historical areas and parkways; that if these were turned over to the states and localities, there would be enough

14 *Congressional Record,* June 26, 1953, 7349 ff.
15 Stat. 72, 152.

money to care for the scenic parks.[16] There may be a question about this, however. It rests on the assumption that the Park Service would get as much money if it did not do these chores, which may not be true. The more areas there are in the country that profit from the work of the Service the greater support there is likely to be, not only in the matter of appropriations but also in the protection of the parks from commercial invasion. Furthermore, the number of visitors to the national parks has been somewhat less because of the existence of the recreational areas and some of the really fine state parks which the Park Service has helped to create and develop. Some of the state parks in New York, Pennsylvania, California, Tennessee, Louisiana, Utah, and a few other states are almost comparable in beauty with some of the national parks, and they doubtless accommodate visitors who, but for their existence, would go to national parks.

One way of meeting the shortage of facilities has been to limit the time of visits in the parks, even for campers. In Yosemite, in the summer of 1959, the limit was ten days in the Valley and fifteen days in Abawona, Bridalveil Creek, and Tenaya Lake. A remedy, if such it can be called, for park overpopulation is already operating. Tourists who have visited some of the more congested parks and have found them unpleasant go to other parks or the national forests, or stay at home.

REMEDIES FOR OVERCROWDED PARKS: THE NATIONAL FORESTS

Recreation areas in the national forests take care of some of the vacationers, and so help to relieve the congestion in the parks. There has been some such use of the national forests since they were first established, and by about 1932 recreation had come to be regarded as a major use of national forests. During the thirties many improved public recreation areas were built in national forests with emergency funds, but the outbreak of the Second World War prevented the completion of the planned program. There were 60 million visits to the national forests in 1957, and 39 per cent of the visitors camped and picnicked outside the improved areas because there was no room for them there or because conditions were unsanitary or otherwise unpleasant.[17] This was bad practice, both from the point of view of sanitation and fire hazard.

16 *Reader's Digest*, Jan. 1955, 50.
17 *American Forests*, Feb. 1957, 5, 78; Jan. 1959, 6.

In 1956, however, the Forest Service inaugurated a program similar to Mission 66 of the Park Service. "Operation Outdoors," as it was called, was a five-year program for improving recreation facilities, adding nearly 100 per cent to the number of camping and picnicking grounds, and also for improving the wildlife habitat. President Eisenhower called for an increase of $7,748,000 for national forest recreation. This is most commendable, for some of the camps in the national forests are quite equal scenically to those in some of the national parks.[18]

There were in the national forests in 1955, 4,400 camp and picnic areas, sufficient to care for 280,000 people at one time. Some popular areas have as many as 100,000 or more visits each year, others have scarcely 200. Most of them are free, but at a few a fee is charged for special provisions of various kinds, including trailer accommodations; and in a few cases length of stay is limited. There were also in the national forests 208 areas for winter sports, 461 resorts, and 79 wilderness, wild, primitive and roadless areas covering 13,768,267 acres, with 120,000 miles of trails for those who enjoy hiking or horseback riding. Of course everything in the national forests is as well managed as it could be with the limited funds available, for the Forest Service is a well-administered government agency with long experience in the recreation field.[19]

In addition to the recreation areas in the national forests, 63 of the 455 commercial timberland companies are operating 132 public parks covering 3,432 acres.[20]

In the 85th Congress, in 1957, there were several bills presented to establish national forest recreation as a policy of Congress, by Metcalf of Montana and by Neuberger, Morse, Murray, Humphrey, Clark, and Cannon. Representative Saylor introduced a bill to provide $3,500,000 for recreational facilities and wildlife preservation on forest lands on the public domain.[21]

Among the most attractive scenic areas in the national forests are of course the wild and wilderness areas; and there has been agitation, by wilderness enthusiasts and conservationists generally, for

---

[18] *American Forests*, Feb. 1957, 4, 78.
[19] *National Forest Vacations* (Washington: U. S. Forest Service, 1955), *American Forests*, Mar. 1955, 37.
[20] *National Parks Magazine*, July 1959, 10.
[21] H. R. 1245, H. R. 5189.

an increase in their number. At the present time there are eighty-two
of these areas, but they do not greatly reduce pressure on the national
parks because they are not accessible by roads and have no living
facilities.

REMEDIES FOR OVERCROWDED PARKS: INCREASE IN NUMBER

Increase in the number of national parks and monuments might
provide for some of the swarm of vacationists. Perhaps the most discussed has been the Glacier Peak, or Glacier Peak–Lake Chelan area,
in the northern Cascades, discussed above. The Forest Service has
been planning to make it a wilderness area, but many park men
think it should be a wilderness national park. The Western Wonderlands, urged by the writer in an earlier chapter,[22] would without doubt be popular and would appreciably reduce attendance at
some other parks, but it would cost heavily. There are some who
think that this should be left as a wilderness area, with few roads
or none, but to the writer this area does not seem to be well suited
to wilderness use. Distances are too great to be covered by hiking
or even by horseback, and it is mostly hot in summer, with little
shade or water.

REMEDIES FOR OVERCROWDED PARKS: USE OF OTHER AREAS

Some of the national monuments are as scenic and recreational as
the national parks. In 1956 they recorded altogether nearly 9 million
visits, compared with 20 million to the national parks. Recreational
areas attracted 5 million visits, parkways 7,438,000. National wildlife refuges, covering 17 million acres, recorded 7,555,000 visits.
Tennessee Valley Authority does not develop or operate recreational facilities, but sells or leases recreational sites to federal, state,
and local agencies for recreational use. In 1956 there were 30 million
person-days' use of the reservoirs and 9,636,000 visits to the dams.

The Corps of Engineers (Army Engineers) with 137 projects,
reported over 70 million visits in 1956. The Bureau of Reclamation,
which builds irrigation and power dams, largely in the West, usually
turns the administration of recreational areas over to other agencies
—the Park Service, in the case of Lake Mead behind Hoover Dam,

22 See pp. 527-29.

Franklin D. Roosevelt Lake behind Grand Coulee Dam, and others. There were nearly 10 million visits to the 140 recreation areas in the Bureau's system in 1955.

Laws to permit purchase of public lands by cities, towns, and individuals run back to 1890, when towns and cities were permitted to buy up to 160 acres of unreserved lands for park and cemetery purposes, with a reservation of minerals to the federal government.[23] In 1926, as we have seen, an act authorized the acquisition or leasing of public lands, not national park lands, by states, counties or municipalities for recreational purposes, the Secretary of the Interior to exchange such lands for state-owned lands. Leases were authorized for twenty years, but if the lands were not used for five years they would revert to the United States.[24]

Under the Small Tracts Act of June 1938, the Secretary of the Interior was authorized to sell or lease not more than five acres of certain unreserved public lands outside of Alaska which he might classify as chiefly valuable as home, cabin, health, convalescent, recreational, or business sites, with a reservation of the minerals to the government.[25] An act of October 17, 1940, authorized the sale or leasing of 160-acre tracts of land in Alaska to cities or towns for park or recreational purposes;[26] and five years later employees of the Department of the Interior were allowed to buy or lease small tracts in Alaska because there was so little privately owned land that employees often found it almost impossible to get even a dwelling site.[27]

In June 1954 the acts of 1938 and 1945 were amended to permit also nonprofit associations to acquire public lands and to broaden the authority of the Secretary in selling and leasing. The act was intended to apply to scattered tracts too small to be easily administered, and the amount allowed was limited to 640 acres to any one grantee in any year. It did not apply to national forests, national parks or monuments, wildlife refuges, or Indian reservations.[28] In September 1954 this was broadened to cover national forest lands, and to permit the Secretary of Agriculture or the Secretary of the

23 Stat. 26, 502.
24 Stat. 44, 741.
25 Stat. 52, 609.
26 Stat. 54, 1191, 1192.
27 Stat. 59, 467.
28 Stat. 68, 173.

Interior to issue permits for buildings or leases for not over thirty years.[29]

It is doubtful if these laws helped much in the accommodation of recreationists, for little of the public domain was suited to recreation.

REMEDIES FOR OVERCROWDED PARKS: THE STATE PARKS AND FORESTS   State parks have been increasing in number, area, and in the number of visitors in recent years. In 1956, there were 2,100 state park and related park areas, covering more than 5 million acres, spending $28 million annually for land and capital improvements and $38 million for operation and maintenance, hiring, 6,048 year-round employees to care for more than 200 million visitors.

New York and California were leading in expenditures. In 1957 and 1958 California had appropriations of $50 million and $22 million, largely from accumulations of off-shore oil royalties[30]— more than half as much as the entire National Park Service spends.

It is difficult to appraise the results of the Park Service's efforts to promote state parks. There is no doubt that through the work of CCC boys and through various federal programs, directed by the Park Service, some state parks are well improved, with fairly well-designed buildings; but some states have done little or nothing since the CCC camps left, and their parks are not well cared for. A few are well managed, with trained employees who enjoy security in their jobs and a chance of promotion for merit, but this cannot be said of most of them. In a few cases there has been even a measure of hostility to the intervention by the Park Service. In some parts of the country state parks cannot afford a very satisfactory summer vacation, because of the heat. Where the temperature ranges up to 100 degrees, and even above, the people are likely to seek the cool mountains or northern lakes rather than nearby reservoirs, lakes, streams, or other attractions. Yet at times there is a fairly good attendance of fishermen, swimmers, and others, even in the torrid states. The people of some states seem willing to use the parks moderately, but not pay for their upkeep and management. Perhaps it would be wise for the Park Service to abandon largely its services

29 Stat. 68, 1146.

30 Marion Clawson, *Statistics on Outdoor Recreation* (Washington: Resources for the Future, 1958), 69.

to the state parks and let the states furnish their own interest and enthusiasm and money.

In the use of some state parks and other recreation areas the problem of segregation has proved a troublesome one. In a few instances states have refused to administer federally developed areas if they were obliged to conform to the Supreme Court decision on desegregation.

There has been a considerable expansion of state forests too, some of which, mainly in the north-central and eastern states, were used to some extent for recreational purposes. In 1954 the states owned a total of 30 million acres, mainly acquired by federal grants, tax delinquency and purchase.

OUTDOOR RECREATION RESOURCES REVIEW COMMISSION   As the tourist crowds swarmed over the parks and forests and recreation areas, agitation arose for another survey of recreation areas, outlined in a bill, backed by the Administration, to create a national Outdoor Recreation Resources Review Commission. Albright questioned the wisdom of it at the time, thinking the Act of 1936 to be adequate, and Wirth was not enthusiastic, but since Secretary Seaton favored it, he went along. The National Parks Association also was in favor, and the bill passed in 1958. The Commission was appointed the same fall and, under the terms of the Act, is required to submit its report to Congress and the President by September 1961.[31]

MISSION 66   There had thus been an expansion of recreational facilities along many lines, but not enough to take much of the burden off the national parks. The simple fact was that the National Park System, designed for 25 million visits, was by 1955 having to care for twice that number. It was quite inadequate, quite outgrown, calling for an entirely new plan for the parks, not a piecemeal, year-to-year plan, but a broad master plan for ten years ahead when the Service expected 80 million visits. This plan was worked out largely in 1955, and to dramatize it it was called "Mission 66"—a plan looking forward to the Service's fiftieth anniversary in 1966.

31 S. 846, H. R. 3549, 85 Cong. 1 Sess. Stat. 72, 238.

The intent of Mission 66 was, first of all, to provide for a comprehensive study of the national park problem, rather than a definite fixed plan. Director Wirth defined it as "an intensive study of all the problems facing the National Park Service—protection, staffing, interpretation, use, development, financing, needed legislation, forest protection, fire—and all other phases of park management."[32] The general idea was to develop the parks so that they could properly accommodate the visitors expected. Some roads were to allow only one-way traffic to relieve traffic congestion; some parking space might be provided in multiple-level ramps in hillsides; some housekeeping functions of both concessioners and the Park Service—houses, shops, and warehouses—were to be removed from centers of visitor use, perhaps moved outside the parks. Wirth foresaw the possibility that all overnight accommodations would have to be moved out of some of the parks. In Rocky Mountain those on the east side of the park were greatly reduced, in spite of some protests from local people. The visitor use of the parks was generally to be spread over a wider area.

A longer season is envisaged, so that more people can see the parks in winter, and in some areas, as for instance the caves, a longer day—Carlsbad Caverns, which has a heavy visitor load, looks just as well at night as by day. Finally there were to be airports adjacent to the parks, but the Park Service is still hostile to airports *in* the parks, and doubtful about helicopters.[33] Yet there are airports in McKinley, Grand Teton, Death Valley, and Lake Mead, but not operated by the Department of the Interior.

Congress responded generously to the plan, granting $48,866,300 for the fiscal year 1956, over $68,000,000 for 1957, $76,004,000 for 1958, and $79,962,000 for 1959. Appropriations for the parks got strong support from the Eisenhower Administration and from many of the western men—Representative Engle and Senators Murray, Barrett, Neuberger, Goldwater, Jackson and O'Mahoney. The total cost of the ten-year program was estimated at $786 million.

Employee housing was rated so important that Mission 66 proposed that the building program for this should be carried out in five years rather than ten. A study in 1953 revealed that 26 per cent of the field employees lived in two-bedroom houses or apartments, only 13½ per cent in three-room houses or apartments, and 60½

32 *American Forests*, Aug. 1955, 16.
33 *Ibid.*

per cent in tents, one-bedroom houses or apartments, dormitories, single rooms, trailers and makeshifts. Better housing properly rated high priority.

Very important among the facilities planned are about a hundred "visitor centers," buildings near the centers of visitor activity, where visitors can get needed information about accommodations, travel routes, publications, exhibits, and about the park areas. Museums are often located in these visitor centers. Also high in priority was the purchase of private lands in the parks—about 700,000 acres.

To some extent the new plan involved changes, and to some extent it aimed mainly at more generous provision for existing activities and facilities. In a few parks the changes were to be rather drastic, as for instance in Mount Rainier, where there had been concession trouble for some time. In 1952 the government had been obliged to buy all concession facilities. The buildings had deteriorated seriously and were operated at a loss, but the old concessioner was retained on a year-to-year basis. The concessioner and the Automobile Club of Washington wanted the government to subsidize a new $5 million hotel at Paradise, along with a chair lift for skiers; but the Park Service planned to abandon all overnight accommodations at this point, not immediately but finally, and to have only meals, museum, visitor center, picnic areas, and limited camping facilities throughout the year. The plan was to move all overnight accommodations to two areas, one a strip adjoining the Longmire campground, partly in Snoqualmie National Forest, and the other in the northeast section of the park near Crystal Creek. Nearly $4 million was planned for visitors' accommodations and more than $4 million for roads. The general idea was to get the facilities on lower ground. Some were to be moved to Ashford, northwest of the park. Many of the people of Washington are opposed to these changes, and the Jackson Hole Preserve, Inc.—the Rockefeller organization—recommended that instead the government build a new hotel at Paradise, a 250- or 300-room hotel to cost $6,878,000; but Director Wirth has insisted that the accommodations should be on lower ground, because their construction and maintenance would cost less, they would be closer to sources of supply, closer to roads, water, and power, and would enjoy a longer operating season.[34]

In September 1957 the Park Service completed the Stevens Canyon

34 *National Parks Magazine,* Apr. 1959, 17.

Road, a highly scenic eighteen-mile road in Mount Rainier. The National Parks Association and some of the wilderness lovers did not like this road, but the Park Service hoped that it, and also the Hurricane Ridge Road in Olympic, would build up public support against the efforts of certain Washington politicians to carve timber out of Olympic.

At Yellowstone, with a Mission 66 allotment of $44 million, there were to be some changes, particularly a shift of concessioner facilities—not paid for by the Park Service—farther away from the Canyon. This new Canyon Village is now completed, with 500 guest rooms, lodge, stores, and campgrounds. The Park Service also plans a restoration of the road up Mount Washburn, which has been unusable for years. This, it is hoped, may tend to bring more of the Yellowstone crowd back to the Mammoth Hot Springs center and away from the more crowded centers. Mammoth Hot Springs has been somewhat neglected in recent years.

At Yosemite the plan was to move the Service's warehouses and other facilities and some of the personnel out of the Valley to El Portal, with the clear possibility that much of the concessioner's facilities would gradually be moved out of the Valley too. At Everglades, with $9 million allotted, plans covered a restaurant, cafeteria and snack bar, trailer parks, service stations, boat transportation, and a road between Flamingo and the Royal Palm area. At first the plans allowed no overnight accommodations here, except at Flamingo, but Director Wirth has found that for some of the boat trips overnight accommodations will be needed.

At Mesa Verde the Spruce Tree Point has become so crowded that the plan is to move camps largely to Morfield Canyon, five miles from the entrance, and the lodge, cabins, and information center to Navajo Hill, fifteen miles from the entrance. Spruce Tree Point would become only an archeological center.

Allotments for some of the other parks seem generous: the Utah parks, $16,900,000, $3,500,000 of which is to be used in opening up Dinosaur; Grand Canyon over $17,000,000; the Colorado parks, $18,000,000; Sequoia and Kings Canyon $9,942,000; Death Valley, $4,625,000; Glacier, $20,900,000; Crater Lake, $5,721,000; Great Smoky, $12,200,000; Acadia, $6,690,000, mostly for roads; Hawaii, $3,300,000; Isle Royale, $4,000,000; Big Bend, $10,720,000. Blue Ridge Parkway was expected to need $42,950,000 for completion and for facilities; and Foothills Parkway was to be awarded $24,380,000 for completion. Cape Hatteras was expected to need $4,375,000, and a modest amount was to be spent to make Katmai more accessible. Over $1,000,000 has been contracted for a ferry boat at Isle Royale.

All these were tentative estimates, subject to change, and of course conditional on adequate appropriations. For road building the amounts given the Park Service are given under authority of the Federal Aid Highway Act which in 1956 was $16,000,000.

GREATER FREEDOM FOR PARK SERVICE ACTIVITIES   The Park Service had been somewhat handicapped by the fact that its activities were limited strictly by park boundaries. Often it would have been convenient to be able to co-operate with owners of adjoining lands, and to arrange for use of adjoining lands for certain purposes, since topographical features do not always correspond with boundary lines. The Park Service needed more latitude here, and in January 1951 Representative Murdock of Arizona, at the request of Secretary Chapman, introduced a bill to allow the Secretary greater freedom in this and other matters.

Section 1 of the Murdock bill authorized the Secretary—really the Park Service—to render emergency rescue, fire fighting, and co-operative assistance to nearby agencies. This was needed not only because fires can be put out most easily before they gain too much momentum, but also because such a provision would build up good will in surrounding areas. Section 2 allowed him to acquire leases, easements, and rights of way outside park boundaries. This was needed for fire prevention, the establishment of water systems, and general administration. Section 3 authorized transportation of employees at Carlsbad Caverns where there was a shortage of housing, to quarters in the town of Carlsbad, thirty miles away.

Section 4 authorized the Secretary to furnish utility services to concessioners on a reimbursement basis. This provision would enable the Secretary to buy electric power from commercial sources to augment its own inadequate generating capacity, deliver the current to concessioners over the park distribution system, and collect the cost from them. There was a shortage of power in some of the parks, and the alternative to this was the building of additional government generating capacity, which would have been more expensive because of the short season for which current was needed. This also applied to communication facilities. For several years the Park Service had found that it could often buy current from commercial sources cheaper than it could produce it. Under Secretary McKay, who had a strong preference for private enterprise, this policy was extended to Grand Canyon, Bryce Canyon, Zion, Yellowstone, Yosemite, Sequoia, and Kings Canyon.

Section 5 provided authority to operate, maintain, repair, or relocate government-owned electric and telephone lines and other facilities, whether within or outside the park system—a provision designed to reduce costs in some instances. Section 6, an important section, authorized the acquisition of such rights of way as might be necessary, and the construction, improvement, and maintenance of roads within and adjacent to the parks.

Section 7 provided authority to operate, repair and maintain motor and other equipment on a reimbursable basis, and charge depreciation on equipment against the various projects on the basis of use, so that construction and maintenance costs would reflect actual cost.

Here was a bill to give the Park Service greater freedom and latitude in its work. There had been fairly steady progress in this direction for many years—since the days when the Service was limited to $1,000 for any building and Congress generously authorized the purchase of waterproof footwear for its employees! The House Committee on Interior and Insular Affairs amended the Murdock bill, striking out the right to acquire lands outside the parks, and requiring the Service to charge the Carlsbad employees fair rates for transportation, and then recommended the bill unanimously. The House passed the bill without comment, but it did not get much attention in the Senate.[35]

In the next Congress, in January 1953, Representative D'Ewart of Montana, at the request of Secretary Chapman, introduced a bill very similar to the Murdock bill, which passed both houses with no debate but with an amendment forbidding any acquisition of land without the consent of the local taxing body.[36]

An act passed by Congress in 1954 "To Create a National Monu-

35 H. R. 1638, 82 Cong. 1 Sess.
36 H. R. 1524, 83 Cong. 1 Sess. Stat. 67, 495.

ment Commission" had little to do with park administration, but was the fruit of the prevailing anti-communist hysteria. The function of the commission set up was "to display to the world the ideas of democracy as embodied in the five freedoms."[37] Few American institutions display to the world "the idea of democracy" as well as our national park system.

VARIOUS ACTIVITIES OF PARK SERVICE   Much of the work of the Park Service has proceeded somewhat as usual. In 1953 the Service was studying the Missouri, Columbia, and Central valleys; the Arkansas, White and Red River basins, and the New England–New York region, with the help of universities.[38] At the same time it was acting as agent for the Bureau of Reclamation in negotiating agreements with state, county, and local agencies for the administration and maintenance of reservoir recreation areas of less than national significance. In the financial stringency of the postwar period some of the interpretive functions of the Park Service were eliminated or changed in character. Some of the conducted hikes, bird, flower and tree walks, game stalks, beaver watches, and auto caravans were discontinued, and self-guiding nature trails and trailside exhibits with frequent guiding signs, were substituted. For lectures, recorded talks were more and more used. In recent years increasing attention has been given to the training of employees. In the fall of 1957, a special school for new rangers was started in Yosemite.

Research has expanded. In 1956, 22 state universities, 10 federal agencies, and 11 state agencies were conducting research in national park areas, and national park men were working on 160 research projects.

Museums have been enlarged and equipped better, although still inadequate to the increasing demands on them. In July 1955 a new law was passed for museums, authorizing the Secretary to accept donations, to buy collections with donated funds, to exchange properties for others of greater significance, to accept loans of museum objects and pay transportation costs on them, and to loan objects and collections to responsible public and private organizations without cost to the government.[39]

37 H. R. 6455, 83 Cong. 2 Sess. Stat. 68, 1029.
38 *Report, Secretary of the Interior, 1953,* 295.
39 Stat. 69, 242.

Archeological studies in the river basins and in the southwest archeological monuments have continued, in co-operation with universities, the Smithsonian Institution, the Geological Survey, the Corps of Engineers, the Bureau of Reclamation, and the Federal Power Commission; and the work of stabilization of ruins has been pushed with energy. The Service's real estate business—involving the disposal of surplus federal real property for public park, recreation, and historic monument purposes—was still operating in 1957 and business was fair.

PRIVATE AND STATE LAND IN PARKS   In the Wirth Administration the program of private land acquisition begun in 1947 has been pushed with vigor, and with some success. At the time the National Park System was established, in 1916, there were over a million acres of nonfederal lands in the system—one-fifth of the total acreage. By 1956 nearly 90 per cent of this had been acquired, leaving less than 150,000 acres within the original thirty-three park and monument units; but many new parks and monuments had been added and in 1956 there were still about 700,000 acres of private and state lands in the 23 million-acre total of the park system. There had been modest appropriations, beginning in 1947, and an act passed on August 31, 1954, authorized $500,000 for purchase, to be matched by donations.[40] This appropriation was repeated in the following years, and the Park Service, which had examined these lands and established priorities for purchase, was able to buy considerable acreages. Acreages of 92,750 in 1955, 46,000 in 1956, and 52,500 in 1957, were acquired by donation, purchase, and exchange. With $500,000 from the government, $500,000 from Jackson Hole Preserve, Inc. and $250,000 from other sources, the Service had $1,250,000 for purchase in each year 1955 and 1956, and in 1957 $1,300,000.

In January 1957 Director Wirth reported the receipt of fifteen gifts of land and water amounting to over 422,000 acres, and commitments of more than $1 million in donated funds. There were still some embarrassing private holdings in the parks, as for instance a tract of 100 acres in General Grant Grove, known as "Wilsonia," a cluttered-up summer colony resembling a deserted mining village.

40 Stat. 68, 1037.

State lands were sometimes hard to get. In 1957 there were still 10,000 acres in Glacier, which the Park Service had been unable to secure. The state of Arizona owned 5,900 acres of fine saguaro cacti in Saguaro Monument, and after years of negotiation the Park Service—through the Bureau of Land Management—managed to trade 36,750 acres of public land outside for this holding. There were also private lands in the monument, so many holdings that the monument was difficult to administer, and the Service had recommended that it be abolished; but the Tucson Chamber of Commerce protested against this and helped to get the holdings exchanged.

SALVAGING OLYMPIC TIMBER   Early in the 1950's the Park Service decided it would get some money to use for buying up private lands in Olympic by selling some of the dead, insect-infested, and down timber in the park to lumbermen. Under the National Parks Act the Park Service was authorized to dispose of timber when necessary to protect it from insects or diseases or conserve the scenery, and some of the timber apparently presented some hazard of fire and of injury to tourists. At any rate, Wirth authorized contracts with lumbermen to salvage some of the timber. The salvage operations presently brought criticism from the Wilderness Society and the National Parks Association. Both sent men to inspect the salvage operations, and their reports were highly critical of the contracts and of the way they were being carried out. It was asserted that the lumbermen did not follow good practices in their operations, did not take proper care of the soil, and that because the Park Service did not supervise the operations carefully enough the lumbermen cut sound trees as well as dead and diseased. The wilderness men objected altogether to the idea of selling timber—even dead, down, and infected trees—as contrary to national park principles, a worse evil than the existence of some private lands in the park. "The resources of the national parks should not be regarded as sources of potential revenues." Furthermore, these operations were likely to result in more insistent demands for the exploitation of the timber in the Olympic and other parks.[41] Soon afterward, Superintendent Fred Overly of Olympic Park replied to these criticisms, denying the

41 *The Living Wilderness,* Fall and Winter 1956-57, 42. *National Parks Magazine,* Jan.-Mar. 1957, 18.

soundness of most of them but admitting that some errors had been made. His defense seemed sincere and was rather convincing.[42]

On February 22, 1957, a heavy wind blew down many big trees in the vicinity of the North Fork Quinault road, and the Park Service sent four National Park experts in to study conditions and report as to the advisability of logging the damaged trees. The experts decided in favor of it, in the interest of fire prevention and insect control; and as a result the Service sold at auction the damaged trees in several sections. Not all experts agreed with the decision. Some thought that since storms were a part of nature's scheme and had always been so, any cleaning up was an interference with the natural order. The National Parks Association maintained as a principle that "Every alteration of the natural landscape, however slight, by such activities as logging . . . is a direct violation of a fundamental principle of national park management." The Advisory Board registered certain principles on the subject: "Salvage of forest products is simply incidental to removal and shall never be the reason for removal. . . . Preservation of the vegetation in its natural condition is paramount. Cutting or salvage in interior areas to reduce hazards from fires, insects or diseases, blowdowns, storms, floods, avalanches, etc. can be justified only under extreme or unusual conditions."[43]

Here, as often, we see two opposing points of view, both honestly held and both maintained with some tenacity.

THE TRAILER PROBLEM   The Park Service has been increasingly plagued by the growing number of trailers brought into the parks. Not only do trailers add to the hazards on mountain roads, but they are something of a nuisance in the parks. In recent years some trailers are almost as big as freight cars, for the owners must have all the comforts of home. Also some of them damage trees and shrubs and, still worse, dump sewage into lakes and rivers. This last practice became such a hazard that California was obliged to forbid trailers in courts where they could not be connected with sewers. The trailer owners stayed somewhat longer than any other class of visitors too, in fact a few of them made long visits in the national

42 *National Parks Magazine*, Apr.-June 1957, 91.
43 Report of Advisory Board, 1957 (mimeo.). See *National Parks Magazine*, Oct.-Dec. 1957, 149.

parks and forests, if allowed to do so. In some national forests, however, there is a 15-day limit. The Park Service began a study of trailers in 1953, during the Wirth Administration, and is still studying. The problem will not be easily solved.[44]

44 *American Forests,* Jan. 1957, 25.

CHAPTER XXVI

The Wirth Administration

1951-

DINOSAUR DAMS AND OTHER THREATS

TO THE PARK SYSTEM

The Eisenhower Administration has been marked by serious lack of fidelity to the general cause of conservation. The turning over to the states of the off-shore oil reserves—worth perhaps billions—and to private interests of the great Hells Canyon dam site on the Snake River; "political" appointments to a number of government positions formerly protected by Civil Service; the appointment to the Tennessee Valley Authority of directors unsympathetic with the purposes of the Authority; the Dixon-Yates affair; the attempt to gut Dinosaur National Monument with two dams: these actions were widely criticized by conservationists and by liberals generally.

On the other hand, aside from Dinosaur, the Administration's record on the national parks and some other federal reservations was good. Secretary McKay defended Olympic against the lumbermen who wanted to slice off a part of the park; he defended the Wichita Mountains Game Refuge against the Army; he defended the whooping crane's Aransas sanctuary against Air Force bombing planned for an area nearby; he opposed the Glacier View Dam in Glacier Park; and he worked for generous appropriations for the parks.

DINOSAUR DAMS AGAIN   It is unnecessary to follow exhaustively all the Upper Colorado Project bills. In the 83rd Congress, bills were introduced by men from the Upper Colorado region, one of which (S. 1555), sponsored by Millikin, Anderson, Barrett, Bennett, Chavez, Goldwater, Hayden, Hunt, Johnson and Watkins, was debated in the next session but failed to pass. Early in 1955, in the next Congress, a number of bills were brought in, one of them (S. 500) sponsored by eleven senators from the states concerned. This bill, approved by President Eisenhower, Secretary McKay of the Department of the Interior, former Commissioner of Reclamation Straus, and the then Commissioner Dexheimer, the Federal Power Commission, and the Corps of Engineers, passed in the second session of Congress. There was powerful opposition from all over the country, from California, dependent on the power from Hoover Dam and the water from the river below, and from conservationists. The latter were able to force the promoters to eliminate Dinosaur, and to insert a provision forbidding the building of a dam or reservoir within any national park or monument and prohibiting any impairment of the Rainbow Bridge National Monument.[1]

A brief examination of the Upper Colorado Project will reveal its folly and extravagance.[2] The Colorado River has flowed enough water to fill Lake Mead only once or twice since Hoover Dam was completed twenty-five years ago, and has ranged down to 137 feet below the rim. In July 1955 Hoover Dam's power output was cut back 35 per cent because of shortage of water. Yet here was a project to build seventeen to twenty-five dams—including the Dinosaur dams—which were calculated to produce 1,200,000 kilowatts of power, 48,000 acre-feet annually of water for municipal and industrial uses, a full supply of water to irrigate 132,000 acres of land, and supplemental water for an additional 240,000 acres of land.[3]

The Upper Colorado Project offered a threat not only to Dinosaur National Monument but also the possibility of flooding some of Rainbow Bridge National Monument, and of seriously injuring or ruining Lake Mead National Recreational Area. If the level of

1 S. 500, H. R. 3383, 84 Cong. 1 and 2 Sess. Stat. 70, 107.

2 For an interesting analysis, see Owen Stratton and Phillip Sirotkin, *The Echo Park Controversy* (University: University of Alabama Press, for the Inter-University Case Program, 1959).

3 *The Reclamation Era*, Feb. 1957, 1 ff.

Lake Mead were to fall 500 feet or more, it would not be worth much for recreation.[4]

In short, here was a proposal to spend perhaps $3 billion of federal money, spoil Dinosaur National Monument, perhaps gravely injure Rainbow Bridge National Monument, partly or entirely spoil Lake Mead National Recreation Area, to produce high-cost electricity where it was little needed, water for municipalities that needed it no more than the Los Angeles area did, raise more farm crops for the government to buy, and—the only favorable effect— catch some of the silt that otherwise would have settled in Lake Mead.[5]

One unit of the Upper Colorado Project, the Glen Canyon Dam above Grand Canyon, has been authorized and is being built, and the Reclamation Bureau and the Park Service are wrestling with the question whether the waters of the reservoir will damage Rainbow Bridge, or how much, or what means can be employed to prevent damage. This dam will create a reservoir which will extend 186 miles up the Colorado River, nearly to the mouth of the Green River, and 71 miles up the San Juan River. It is said that it will take ten years to fill the reservoir. Presumably Lake Mead will not flourish during that period.

Having saved the Dinosaur National Monument, conservationists, with Ira Gabrielson a leading figure, proceeded to try to make the monument more secure by raising it to national park status. A week after Eisenhower signed the Upper Colorado Project bill, Representatives Aspinall of Colorado and Saylor of Pennsylvania introduced identical bills for this. Aspinall's action is difficult to understand, for he had been one of the sponsors of the Upper Colorado Project bill which would have spoiled the monument, and his park bill looked like a way to commit political suicide, for apparently most Colorado people wanted dams in Dinosaur. It was too late in the session for either bill to make any headway.[6] In the next Con-

---

4 For a very able speech of Senator Paul Douglas against the Upper Colorado Project, see *Congressional Record*, Apr. 18, 1955, 4579.

5 One interpretation of President Eisenhower's support of this preposterous reclamation project is that it was a gesture of gratitude to Senator Watkins of Utah, a strong promoter of the project, for his service as chairman of the Senate committee which censured Senator Joseph McCarthy. Watkins lived at Vernal, a few miles from Dinosaur.

6 H. R. 10614, H. R. 10635, 84 Cong. 2 Sess.

gress Saylor and Senator Allott of Colorado brought up bills, but the Allott bill left the door open to the building of Dinosaur dams later.[7] In the next Congress Saylor and Allott again tried for national park status, but again Allott's bill left Dinosaur open to possible dams, and was therefore opposed by Secretary Seaton.[8] Some of the Dinosaur dam proponents are still determined to get Dinosaur, but perhaps when roads are built into the area and a million visitors go to see it every year, Utah and Colorado may be reconciled to a great Dinosaur national park.

OTHER THREATS TO THE PARK SYSTEM The Dinosaur attack was not the only threat to the national park system. Power interests were still trying to invade several of the national parks. The Bridge Canyon dam was still a threat to Grand Canyon National Park and Monument, and there was also a proposal to build a Marble Canyon dam, upstream from the park and forty miles downstream from Lee's Ferry, which would not have affected the park except through the flow of water. The Glacier View dam, and the Mining City dam were still under consideration, and there was some talk of a dam in Big Bend. The International Boundary and Water Commission had authority to build an international dam there, under the 1945 treaty with Mexico, on a site which would have backed water into the park; but in 1950 the executive officer of the Commission expressed his desire to protect the park.[9] In April 1949 Secretary Chapman had thought that the Army Engineers were abandoning the Glacier View dam, but a few months later, on August 26, 1949, Representative Mansfield introduced a bill to build the dam immediately.[10] When this failed it was succeeded by a proposal to build the Smoky Range dam, nine miles down the stream from Glacier View, to flood 8,700 acres in Glacier Park—whereas Glacier View would have flooded 20,000 acres; but Secretary Seaton has opposed the new project. In February 1952 the city of Los Angeles published notice of applications to build power dams in the Tehipite and Cedar Grove sites just outside Kings

7 H. R. 935, S. 2577, 85 Cong. 1 Sess.

8 H. R. 951, S. 160, 86 Cong.

9 Report, Secretary of the Interior, 1950, 307.

10 H. R. 6153, 81 Cong. 1 Sess. H. R. 6722, 83 Cong. 1 Sess.

Canyon, the two sites that had been sliced out of the park because of their power potential. These applications were protested by the Sierra Club and the Fresno Chamber of Commerce, and by the Park Service, which hoped to be able to include these sites in the park eventually.

In 1951 Representative Johnson of California tried to settle once and for all the question of dams in the national parks and monuments, by introducing a bill explicitly prohibiting their construction, but his proposal got no attention.[11]

There were other threats: of Army Engineer levees on the Snake River in Grand Teton; of a McKenzie River dam in Oregon, which the people of Eugene opposed; and of a dam at Sutter's Mill, Colona, California, a state park which was being considered as a national monument. The Chesapeake and Ohio Parkway, opposed by most conservationists, was again agitated. The Bruces Eddy dam, on the Clearwater River in Idaho was before Congress much of the time from 1954 to 1957, and the Army Engineers were given $500,000 to plan it. There were attempts to get storage dams on the Potomac, opposed by the Park Service. The lumbermen were trying to get lumber in Olympic. Early in 1956 Rayonier Inc. ran an advertisement in *Editor and Publisher* discussing the "waste" of lumber in the "hoarded" forests of Olympic, and sent a copy of the issue to many newspapers, but was unable to get into the park.

An ominous note came from the California State Water Resources Board in 1956, in a tentative $11-billion scheme to harness every stream in California and carry the water wherever it is needed most. Such a plan may seem quite necessary before many years have passed if the population and industries of California continue to grow at the present rate; yet it would inevitably spoil much fine scenery, perhaps ruin important national park areas, just as Hetch Hetchy did.[12]

Katmai National Monument, the largest unit in the national park system, larger than Yellowstone, was opened to the mining of siliceous volcanic ash (pumicite) in 1953. During the war an enterprising contractor who was building houses at Anchorage set up an illegal pumice operation in the monument, and persuaded Representative D'Ewart to introduce a bill authorizing the Secretary to permit such

11 H. R. 5023, 82 Cong. 1 Sess.
12 *Living Wilderness*, Spring 1957, 28.

business. The contractor presently found that the pumice was not, after all, good for building blocks and abandoned his enterprise; but Congress was not notified and proceeded to pass the D'Ewart bill.[13] The monument is now open to mining of pumice, and its wildlife is threatened by the salmon packing industry, representatives of which say that the beavers block the streams so that the fish cannot easily get up to their spawning grounds, and that the big brown bears especially, and also the eagles, gulls, cormorants, murres, hair seals, and otters kill many salmon. There are plans for building an airstrip for use of planes, which the purists object to.[14]

In filling out the Everglades Park, the Park Service encountered oil prospecting and had to buy some land with reservation to the owners of mineral deposits. Oil prospects in Cape Hatteras Seashore delayed the establishment of the project for several years. With the development of the atom bomb and with the Korean War, a flood of uranium mining claims was filed in the West, on the public lands and national forests; and in August 1954 the mineral leasing laws were amended to permit "multiple mineral development" and to provide for uranium development. Uranium exploration and mining have wrought havoc on some of the public lands and forest lands of the West.[15]

For several years Michigan's Porcupine Mountains were threatened by mining interests, but the threat has been defeated.

There has been a strong demand for a law to permit such claims in the parks. The Atomic Energy Commission called for the right to explore for uranium in Capitol Reef, Big Bend, Grand Canyon, Petrified Forest, and Fossil Cyead, and began explorations in Capitol Reef in 1953. The Service granted permission to explore Big Bend with Geiger counters. A mining claim on the South Rim of the Grand Canyon, which had passed to patent, is now yielding uranium ore. Nothing can be done about it, but several Arizona men in Congress did introduce bills to require that mining should be carried on properly.[16] Joshua Tree and Death Valley are being disfigured with diggings and all that goes with them.

13 H. R. 1529, 83 Cong. 2 Sess. Stat. 68, 53.
14 *National Parks Magazine*, Jan.-Mar. 1958, 10.
15 Stat. 68, 708.
16 S. 109, H. R. 1213, 82 Cong. 1 Sess.

THREATS FROM THE MILITARY   In recent years the military services have been reaching for large areas for range practice and other uses. In 1953 they had fifty-two defense use permits in the parks and monuments and some in the wildlife refuges—where they were presumably "exotic" and not welcome; but the Military are long accustomed to get what they want without much difficulty. Some of the wildlife refuges, set up by department decrees and not by Congress, could be erased in the same way. In 1956 the Military had a total of about 26 million acres—not all in the wildlife refuges —and were asking for 9 million more. When the Army tried to get 10,700 acres from the Wichita Mountains Wildlife Reserve, however, it encountered unaccustomed difficulty. This reserve, with its bison, deer, Texas longhorns, wild turkeys, prairie dogs, and other wildlife, was a popular resort for people from the surrounding regions. Senators Monroney and Kerr and Representative Wickersham of Oklahoma tried in the 84th Congress to get bills through to open up Wichita Mountains to the Army, but failed. The next move was to get the addition through the authorization and appropriation bills, enlarging nearby Fort Sill without even using the word "Wichita." The bills passed, but McKay refused to make the transfer of the lands. Representatives Engle of California and Fernandez of New Mexico tried to get bills through Congress to require Congressional approval for any military withdrawal of more than 5,000 acres, but failed. In the 85th Congress, in 1957, Engle and Bible of Nevada brought up similar bills, and the Engle bill passed.[17] In February 1957 the Department of the Interior announced an agreement giving the Army about one-third of the Wichita Mountains area demanded.[18]

ROADS IN THE PARKS   Recently there has been some fairly heated discussion of the problem of road building in the national parks, charges that too many are being built and that the roads are built too wide and straight, too much like speedways. The California

---

[17] H. R. 5538, S. 557, 85 Cong. 1 Sess. Stat. 72, 27.
[18] H. R. 5700, 84 Cong. 1 Sess. S. 3360, H. R. 9665, H. R. 10371, H. R. 10389, H. R. 12185, 84 Cong. 2 Sess. *Congressional Record,* 84 Cong. 1 Sess., 9712, 11040 ff. *National Parks Magazine,* July-Sept. 1956, 142; Oct.-Dec. 1956, 147. *American Forests,* July 1956, 14.

Highway Division has been thinking of building a new road across the Sierra, the Mammoth Pass Road, which would cut through the Devils Postpile and the Minarets area. There is a 170-mile stretch of the Sierra between Tioga Pass and Walker Pass east of Bakersfield without any roads, and it seems to some that it would be well to open some of this to automobile tourists; but the wilderness lovers object and are supported by the packers.[19] The Park Service suggested changes in the plans. Such a road would of course divert some of the Tioga Road traffic.

The Park Service itself has apparently been considering the construction of a road along the Ocean Strip in Olympic Park. As a protest against too much road building here, Justice William O. Douglas organized a hike along forty-three miles of the Strip, as he did along the Chesapeake and Ohio Canal.[20] Certain tourist-minded people around Great Smoky Mountains have been clamoring for a new road in that park, along the north shore of Lake Fontana, but Director Wirth has held them off, although he may have to compromise a little.[21]

DESECRATION OF PARK AREAS   The Park Service and all park conservationists have opposed the building of facilities that would mar the natural conditions of the parks unless they were absolutely necessary; and there have been threats of this since very early times. In 1890 Secretary Noble turned thumbs down on a proposal to build an electric elevator beside the Lower Falls in Yellowstone. In 1916 a man named Davol conceived the idea of running a cable across Grand Canyon so that tourists could cross without riding down into the canyon on muleback. There was something to be said for it or it could not have had the approval of Lane, Yard, and even Albright; but Mather would have none of it, and it was given up.[22] In President Hoover's administration there was a proposal to build a cable to Glacier Point in Yosemite so that the physically handicapped

19 *Living Wilderness*, Summer-Fall 1957, 31; Spring 1959, 32. *National Parks Magazine*, Apr.-June 1958, 80.

20 *National Parks Magazine*, Apr. 1959, 10.

21 *Living Wilderness*, Autumn 1958, 14. See also an excellent article in *National Parks Magazine*, Feb. 1959, 3.

22 Robert Shankland, *Steve Mather of the National Parks* (New York: Alfred A. Knopf, 1951), 207, 208.

might get to the Point and all might go up in winter when snow blocked the roads and trails. Hoover and Wilbur were inclined to favor it, but Albright turned it down. Yosemite has been threatened by several other schemes: one in 1933 to dam Yosemite Creek so that the falls would be in operation all year; one to build a small dam above Mirror Lake in the Valley to make a waterfall; one to throw floodlights on Bridal Veil Falls at night. The "firefall" has been on exhibition for many years. It is rather impressive, really, but has something of the Coney Island flavor. There was at one time a demand for a cableway up Mount Hood—in a national forest—but Chief Forester Greeley tactfully declined to approve it; and much later some enterprising boosters in Seattle and Tacoma wanted to build a tramway up Mount Rainier, but McKay stepped on that, as he did on a proposal for a tramway from the rim of Crater Lake down to the lake.

Reminiscent of the early Yellowstone buffalo corral are several animal shows set up in recent years, such as the Jackson Hole Wildlife Park, east of Moran, where several kinds of animals are kept. Some of the purists have objected to these exhibitions of wildlife.

At night floodlights are thrown on the sculptured heads in Mount Rushmore, but perhaps that may be permissible, for Mount Rushmore is man-made and not a natural wonder.

To encourage winter use, the Park Service has approved ski-lifts at Paradise Valley in Mount Rainier, in Rocky Mountain, Sequoia, Yosemite, Lassen Volcanic, and Olympic. The National Parks Association has opposed such "improvements," and the Advisory Board recommends that aids to skiing and other winter sports be limited and in any case be only such as are removable and will not encroach on natural features of the parks. Director Wirth insists that they do no appreciable damage. The lift at Hidden Valley in Rocky Mountain was called for by the Estes Park Chamber of Commerce which found business very poor after the Colorado-Big Thompson Water Diversion Tunnel was completed and the working force left. The Chamber of Commerce hoped to build up local business on an influx of skiers. The National Parks Association argued that use of the parks should not be determined by local interests, but of course the number of skiers is increasing rapidly, and the Park Service seemed to feel obliged to extend a friendly hand. Defending the Hidden Valley facilities Wirth said: "If the people can't use the areas, there is no use having them." There are five ski tows in Sequoia, and in a very few cases trees have been cut to open up ski runs.[23]

There was a request for a television tower on the top of Scottsbluff in Scottsbluff National Monument, but it was refused, and very recently there was a proposal for a Ferris wheel on the edge of Yellowstone Canyon, which was of course not considered. There is aquaplaning on Jackson Lake and hydroplane racing on Lake Mead, which some park lovers do not think proper; and power boats on Juniper Lake in Lassen Volcanic are now forbidden. Very recently there has been some discussions of the power boats on Yellowstone Lake—some six thousand of them. Many conservationists think these boats create too much noise and commotion, and the Park Service is considering a regulation to keep power boats out of the southerly arms of the lake and allow them in the rest of it. Perhaps they should not be allowed on the lake at all.[24]

There has been some criticism of the Wirth Administration by the National Parks Association, the Sierra Club, the Wilderness Society, by some members of the Advisory Board and by others of the purist camp who believe that he stresses recreation and development too much, to the neglect of fundamental national park principles and of rigorous protection of scenic values. It is easy to see how a Director might do this, for most of the forces operating push him in this direction, particularly if he is ambitious and anxious to see his department grow. Albright and Cammerer were accused of the same sin—if it is a sin. There may be honest differences of opinion on this point.

There have always been a few devout souls who wanted to combine the glory of the parks with religious observance of some sort, who have believed that the national parks were just the place for religious devotion; but most park men have not warmed to the idea. For years there has been agitation for the building of a "Shrine of the Ages" near the South Rim of Grand Canyon—180 feet or 250 feet from it, according to the man doing the surveying. Wirth was widely criticized for approving it, partly on the ground that the shrine was too ornate and pretentious and was to be too close to the canyon rim. Recent reports indicate that the funds have grown to a point where the shrine may at least be begun, perhaps

23 *National Parks Magazine*, Jan.-Mar. 1956, 3.
24 *Op. cit.*, Feb. 1960, 16. *Living Wilderness*, Winter, 1959-60, 42.

partly finished, the final completion to be delayed until the promoters have raised money needed by solicitation of visiting tourists. This would seem to be a rather cheap and unseemly business. The cost has been vaguely reported at a million dollars.[25] It is reported that religious groups are considering the erection of similar religious shrines in other parks.

Other shrines have been proposed. One proposal is to throw floodlights on the General Grant giant sequoias, which are now classified as a shrine. Another is to transfer the administration of Grant's Tomb on Riverside Drive in New York to the park system and call it a national shrine. Within the past few years, there has been agitation for the establishment of a *system* of shrines, but the Park Service has pointed out that there are already too many classes of areas in the park system, and no more should be added. On the contrary, the Service is trying to reduce the present twelve classes to six or seven—a most commendable effort.

As to religious structures, the general policy of the Park Service is to permit only one nondenominational church in the few parks where religious needs cannot be met from outside the park area. The Advisory Board has been rather hostile to over-emphasis on church building: "Any religious or other public structures erected in areas under control of the National Park Service should be built in modest and unpretentious style, of a size limited to normal visitor needs and the requirements of the local population and not of such a character as to constitute an artificial tourist attraction."[26]

Some conservationists see a threat to aesthetic values of the parks in a few of the new buildings being built. There has been some criticism of the diningroom at Skyland in Shenandoah, the museum-ranger station at Everglades, the new utility building at Big Bend, the new building at Saguaro, the new concessioner buildings at the Canyon in Yellowstone, the Jackson Lake Lodge at Grand Teton, and the sky post observation tower in Clingmans Dome in the Great Smoky Mountains. One observer has objected to the bright colors used by some concessioners in painting their buildings, as out of harmony with park surroundings. As to the appropriate style for buildings in the parks, there will no doubt be much debate. Styles of private residences have been almost completely revolutionized in

25 *National Parks Magazine*, Apr. 1959, 1.
26 Unpublished report of the Advisory Board.

the past ten or twenty years, and it is not surprising that the revolution should strike the parks too.[27]

The modern accommodations being added in some of the parks will add to the troubles of the Park Service. Room or cabin with bath is quite in accord with American living standards, demanded in most hotels and motor courts everywhere, and the parks are merely falling into line; but when such accommodations are available in the parks at reasonable rates is it not possible that an increased flood of foot-loose Americans may decide that the parks are just the place to spend much or all of the summer, with all the comforts of home? There was something to be said for the simple bathless cabins of yesterday—they did not strongly invite unreasonably long stays, they lent a touch of ruggedness to life, in their simplicity they were consonant with the mighty mountains and canyons; and for those who wanted great scenery and not luxury they were good enough. Every bathroom adds to the task of providing water and sewage disposal.

ATTACKS ON BILLBOARD ADVERTISING   Americans are generally rather indifferent to aesthetic values, and it is cheering to see a few signs of interest in the protection of our highways from billboard debauchery. There have been a few bills in Congress to prohibit the erection of billboards along highways built partly with federal funds. In the 85th Congress, Representative Hale of Maine and Senator Neuberger of Oregon introduced bills to require this prohibition in the Federal Highway Act of 1956.[28] But the bills encountered the stubborn opposition of the advertising lobby, one of the most powerful and arrogant lobbies in Washington, with fairly tight control over Congress; and many men in Congress are themselves believers in the stupid notion that advertising, including billboards, the worst form, is essential to business and prosperity, and democracy and the American way. The president of Outdoor Advertising, Inc. put his case in the following choice words: "I wonder if you will agree that freedom to communicate is basic to our society, and that freedom of speech—freedom to be heard—also implies freedom to be seen. The right to communicate visually in the outdoor area—in good taste and within the law—would seem to

27 *National Parks Magazine*, July-Sept. 1952, 135 ff.; Jan.-Mar. 1957, 24 ff.
28 H. R. 3977, S. 963, 85 Cong. 1 Sess.

be one of our essential freedoms." As if the billboards which debauch the scenery along our highways were ever in good taste!

When one of the billboard bills was in Congress, someone wrote: "The pusillanimity of Congress in the face of the strong tactics of a few Congressional spokesmen for the billboard industry and related lobbies was matched only by the weak-kneed attitude of the Administration in its failure to push for effective billboard-control legislation."

In spite of the opposition of the hucksters a bill did pass Congress and was signed on April 16, 1958, but it was watered down to throw the burden of initiative on the states, which must pass legislation enabling them to carry out the national policy of control. Any state which did this, however, would receive an additional one-half of one per cent of the cost of highways above the 90 per cent of construction cost which the federal government contributes for interstate and defense highways. President Eisenhower has asked Congress to strengthen the law.[29]

Some of the more enlightened nations do not permit roadside advertising and as a result have many beautiful roads. Even in the United States, the Union Oil Company recently abandoned roadside advertising, with the following explanation: "Two factors were of primary concern to the company in reaching the decision to abandon this type of advertising. First, was the traffic hazard which a great many experts have indicated billboards tend to increase. Second, is an apparent and growing resentment on the part of many people and residential communities to obscuring our natural beauties with this type of advertising."[30] In at least some areas the Standard Oil Company no longer uses billboard advertising.

Representative Blatnik of Minnesota would go even further and plant trees along the interstate highways. Most of our roads are very ugly, with bare clay banks here and there and no attention to aesthetic values. In a few places trees and shrubs have been planted, and it may be hoped that much more will be done to add beauty to the countryside. In a time of widespread unemployment this would make an excellent employment project.

29 Stat. 72, 94.
30 *American Forests,* Jan. 1958, 40. *National Parks Magazine,* Jan.-Mar. 1958, 7. *Living Wilderness,* Spring 1957, 29.

PART THREE

Special
Park
Problems

CHAPTER XXVII

Wildlife

When the European colonists came to America they found what they naturally regarded as an abundance of land, forests, minerals, and game. In the course of years they proceeded to waste the land and forests and minerals, and kill the game. They extirpated the prairie chicken (heath hen) in the eastern states, the elk in Arizona and New Mexico, the bison and elk east of the Mississippi River, the musk ox in Alaska, the bighorn along the Upper Missouri River, the grizzly bear in California and throughout much of its range, and the grayling fish in Michigan. In later years they managed to exterminate the big sea mink of New England, the Carolina paroquet, Eskimo curlew, and passenger pigeon.

Victor H. Cahalane, chief of the biology division of the National Park Service, stated in 1947 that "during the past 2,000 years, about 106 species and subspecies of mammals have become extinct in the world. Only 35 of these were lost in the first 1,850 years. Thirty-one died between 1851 and 1900. From 1901 to 1945, forty were wiped out. Thus the rate of extinction appears to be increasing."[1]

[1] Paper presented at the meeting of Chief Park Rangers, National Park Service, Mar. 19, 1947.

The stories of the disappearance of some of these animals and birds make interesting if often dispiriting reading. The mighty grizzly was once common in the hills and valleys of California, but was hunted persistently, by vaqueros, sportsmen, and professional hunters. In 1848 five professional hunters were engaged in this business, and one hunter claimed to have killed 200 grizzlies for their hides and for the $50.00 bounty offered by the state. It is true that there was reason for the public hostility to this animal, for he was not an amiable neighbor to the settlers, having a tendency to kill sheep and cattle and sometimes injure people. At any rate, by about 1925, or perhaps as early as 1922 according to Dr. E. Raymond Hall, he was only a memory for old-timers and an emblem for the California state flag. Seven or eight races of grizzlies have been exterminated in the past fifty years.

The story of the passenger pigeons is not flattering to the human race. At one time they were so numerous that they sometimes flew in clouds that darkened the sky, but they were slaughtered by the million, perhaps for the hogs to eat, or just for "sport." There were still many of them in 1872, but the last bird died in 1914.[2]

The heath hen, once an important game bird living along the North Atlantic coastal plain, was hunted almost to the point of extermination by 1890, but under rigorous protection increased a little and seemed likely to survive on Martha's Vineyard Island, its only refuge. But disastrous grassland fires swept the island and almost wiped the birds out. For a while a few were seen, but predators, disease, and hunters reduced these to two, which were watched anxiously and reported from time to time in the newspapers; then only one; then in 1932, none.[3]

The story of the ivory-billed woodpecker, the largest woodpecker in the United States, is similar. At one time it was seen in the Mississippi Valley from southern Illinois to the Gulf of Mexico; but as the virgin forests were cut its range was more and more restricted, for it lived on certain grubs found in the dead trees of such forests. As late as the forties two pairs were known to live in the Tensas Swamp in Louisiana, where there was primeval timber, but when the timber was logged they disappeared. This species is believed to be extinct.

2 *American Forests and Forest Life,* Feb. 1917, 103.
3 Devereux Butcher, *Seeing America's Wildlife in Our National Refuges* (New York: Devin-Adair Co., 1955) , 303.

Many other animals at various times have seemed to be approaching extinction, and some have been exterminated in certain areas but have survived in others. A few years ago there was some concern about the survival of the wolverine, fisher, marten, and black-footed ferret, but they are staging a fair comeback. The river otter was extirpated by trappers over much of its original geographic range, but has been brought back by government protection. The cougar was reduced greatly by hunters and trappers, but seems in no danger of extinction. The wolf, once so common in various parts of the country, is no longer found except in the Superior National Forest, in Isle Royale and Glacier parks, and perhaps two or three other places. It still persists in reduced numbers in Mount McKinley National Park where it has been subject to control.[4] The Tule or dwarf elk no longer exists in a wild state within the geographic area that it once occupied, but some are kept in a fenced area in Owens Valley. The bighorn sheep has been and still is in danger of extinction from diseases perhaps contracted from domestic sheep. The woodland caribou, which once ranged widely in the northern states, is threatened with extinction; and the elephant seal once reached a level of a dozen or so individuals. The walrus is still declining. At various times there has been fear that the antelope was headed for oblivion, but the government has done a good job of protecting it and the danger seems over. The little key deer of Florida came close to extinction but may yet be saved, owing to the 1,000-acre sanctuary granted them in 1957 by Congress, under a bill introduced by Representative Bennett of Florida.[5] The musk ox disappeared from Alaska a century ago, but some of the Greenland subspecies were introduced in 1930, and are doing fairly well on Nunivak Island. Canada has native musk oxen but only a fraction of what she once had, and is trying to save them. There is some concern about the future of the polar bear, and also the grizzly. We cannot class the Texas longhorn with wildlife, but it is an interesting brute with a romantic history. It would have perished but for a private refuge and a government refuge in Oklahoma. The exotic wild horse, once found in parts of the West, is seldom seen.

Among the birds threatened with extinction, the great trumpeter swan, the largest of the swans, has achieved the most publicity. It was estimated at only thirty-three in 1934, seventy-three in 1935,

4 *American Forests,* Jan. 1959, 17.

5 See H. R. 1058, H. R. 1127, 85 Cong. 1 Sess. Stat. 71, 412.

but it is now estimated at nearly six hundred birds—the result of the most careful protection by the Park Service and Fish and Wildlife Service. These swans live not only in Yellowstone Park but in Grand Teton Park, National Elk Refuge in Wyoming, Targhee National Forest, and in Red Rock Lakes Migratory Waterfowl Refuge in southwestern Montana, set aside especially for them; and there are other larger colonies in Canada. Some other places are good for nesting, but are subject to too much hunting and fishing or noise and disturbance. Year after year the Park Service counts the swans and reports the numbers. Unfortunately, the movement of the great birds from refuges comes at the time of legalized hunting, and some are shot, perhaps mistaken for snow geese, or even shot deliberately. Park rangers have given lectures to schools and organizations surrounding the refuges, trying to get the people to see the problem, and the survival of the swans seems fairly well assured. This cannot be said of the whooping crane, the largest migratory bird in America, which is down to about twenty-seven specimens, in spite of the establishment of a winter refuge set up for it on the Texas coast—the Aransas Refuge. The roseate spoonbill was once common along the Gulf Coast, but by 1890 had disappeared in Texas and was almost gone in Florida; but with protection by naturalist and conservation organizations and by the government, it was saved in both states along with the egret and other beautiful birds.

The California condor, a large vulture, the largest American bird—wingspread up to nine feet—although innocent of all bad habits, that is, habits contrary to man's interests, has been almost exterminated by wanton shooting by "sportsmen," by poisoners, followers of the manners of the Borgias, and by the gradual change to farm cultivation in some areas. To keep the number of predators down, especially coyotes, stockmen in the early days poisoned carcasses of dead livestock, and many condors are said to have been killed by eating these carcasses. On the other hand, when ranchers had large herds of cattle or sheep, a few died from time to time and provided food for the condors, There are perhaps only fifty to sixty of these great birds in the West, but a Condor Refuge established in southern California may save the species for future generations to admire.

For many years Alaska offered a bounty for killing the bald eagle because it ate salmon, but it was finally realized that the eagle was a part of the scheme of nature, and since 1940 has been protected by law, as it is in the other states. A sanctuary has even been set aside for it on an island in the Susquehanna River. The prairie chicken, whose courting "boom" was music to the pioneers on the plains, is now gone from much of its original range. The nene, a land-dwelling goose in Hawaii, was for a time thought to be extinct, but a few have been seen recently, and it may be saved. In the Florida Everglades several species of wildlife were in a stage of decimation when the Everglades National Park was established.

This discussion of the extinction or near-extinction of many species of wildlife suggests the great importance of the national parks in the conservation of wildlife. Although the Yellowstone establishing act was badly drawn for wildlife protection, and for years not well enforced, it was about the earliest attempt at protection of the wildlife that the government wanted to preserve—the prey animals, deer, elk, buffalo, antelope, and birds, but not the predators, which were killed in large numbers. Presently a more generous policy was adopted, and today all national parks—except a corner of Grand Teton—are wildlife sanctuaries in which no hunting is allowed, where special care is even sometimes given to preserve species threatened with extinction. In this work the Park Service co-operates with the Fish and Wildlife Service, but in some of the wildlife refuges, controlled by the Fish and Wildlife Service, hunting and trapping are allowed.[6]

WHY PRESERVE OUR WILDLIFE?   Perhaps the question may be raised, why should we be so solicitous about the preservation of every species of wildlife? We have fared very well without the passenger pigeon and the Eskimo curlew: could we not live well enough without the trumpeter swan and the whooping crane and the wolverine? The answer is that although we could indeed get along and prosper without some of these, there are strong reasons for preserving every possible native species of wildlife. In the first place, the birds and animals add greatly to the interest, richness, and beauty of life. We can see this in the crowds that go to the zoos in every city, and to some of the parks and wildlife refuges. People love to see the wildlife, even in captivity, and better free. The writer remembers as one of the finest sights of early childhood the great

6 *Bird Lore,* May 1929, 188.

flocks of geese, ducks, and cranes that winged their way north in
the spring and south in the fall, when these birds were more plentiful than they now are. The birds and animals are a part of nature,
and many men have a deep-seated love of nature. As Rachel Carson
has expressed it:

> But for all the people, the preservation of wildlife and of wildlife
> habitat means also the preservation of the basic resources of the
> earth, which men, as well as animals, must have in order to live.
> Wildlife, water, forests, grasslands—all are parts of man's essen-
> tial environment; the conservation and effective use of one is
> impossible except as the others also are conserved.[7]

In the second place, wildlife in its natural state is the essential
material for research in biology, as we can see from the use of the
national parks by research biologists. Every species has its place in
the great scheme of nature, and its loss might bring ill effects that
are unpredictable.

In the third place, some of the birds have a more immediate and
practical value in keeping down the number of insect pests. Insect
pests are a formidable threat to farm production, and a heavy expense, and some birds are man's indefatigable helpers in their sup-
pression.

Several of the national parks were established partly or even
largely to preserve certain species of wildlife: Mount McKinley, to
preserve Dall sheep; Everglades, to preserve many species of subtropical birds; Olympic, to preserve the Olympic or Roosevelt elk.
Some extensions of park boundaries have been made primarily to
provide better range conditions for wildlife. This was true of Yellowstone, for instance, and the Devils Hole section of Death Valley
National Monument was added partly to preserve a unique species
of minnow. About 283 national wildlife refuges, administered by
the Fish and Wildlife Service, have also been established for wildlife protection.

THE STORY IN ALASKA   For many years wildlife in Alaska
fared a little better than that of the other states because it was more
isolated, but the slaughter soon began, and in recent years there has
been some concern about the Alaska moose, the largest of the moose

7 *Guarding Our Wildlife Resources* (Washington: Department of the Interior,
Fish and Wildlife Service, 1948) , 1.

family, the caribou, and the mountain sheep, which were claimed to be threatened by wolves as well as by man, and certainly were gravely affected by great fires that burned their range. In recent years there has been concern about the Alaska brown bear, the largest terrestrial carnivore in the world. In 1908 Congress became enough concerned to pass a law forbidding the wanton destruction of game, except eagles, ravens, and cormorants; and beginning in 1909 made an annual appropriation of $10,000 or more for protection of Alaska game.[8]

An act of June 6, 1924, authorized the Secretary of the Interior to reserve fishing areas in any of the waters of Alaska over which the United States had jurisdiction and to establish closed seasons during which fishing should be limited or prohibited.[9] In 1925 the Alaska Game Commission was set up to establish regulations for the taking of various kinds of wildlife and to issue hunting and trapping licenses.[10]

About the time that the first game-protection law was passed there was some distress among the Eskimos, and Congress provided for the introduction of reindeer in 1892, hoping they might prove useful to the natives as they were to the Laplanders, and appropriated funds for their care every year for years thereafter. This may well have been a mistake, certainly it was a violation of one of the fundamental rules of game management—the general rule against the introduction of exotics. Recently there have been reports that the reindeer cross-breeds with the caribou to produce an animal that is inferior in stamina to the caribou.

In spite of the law for game protection, and in spite of the establishment of the Mount McKinley National Park in 1917, the destruction of Alaskan game continued. The law of 1908 was not well adapted to Alaska conditions, the population hostile, the game wardens inadequate in numbers and in loyalty. There was very little real game protection in Alaska until 1924, and a great deal of poaching has continued to the present time. In 1941 eleven Alaska agents investigated 224 cases, prosecuted 141 persons and convicted 139 of them. Their take had been 3,204 muskrats, 322 beavers, 141 minks, 70 foxes, 30 land otters, 16 martens, 9 brown and grizzly bears, 5 wolverines, and a few other animals, the pelts of which

8 Stat. 35, 102.
9 Stat. 43, 464 ff.
10 Stat. 43, 739.

were confiscated. In 1955 the record was about the same, and a number of guns, traps, and snares were confiscated.[11]

As early as 1934 President Roosevelt, incensed at the slaughter of Alaska bears, particularly the big brown bear which was being killed by hunters and cattle and sheep men, wrote to Secretary Ickes asking him to try to stop the slaughter. For several years the Secretary of the Interior had tried to provide better protection, and had secured enlargement of Katmai National Monument. He was planning a proclamation doubling the size of Glacier Bay National Monument to accomplish this. There were at the time over 6 million acres in parks and monuments where the bears were given total protection, and the Alaska Game Commission had given the brown bears some protection on several refuges. The Department of the Interior is planning to establish a 9-million-acre arctic wildlife range in Alaska, along the north coast for caribou, Dall sheep, moose, wolves, wolverines, polar, grizzly and black bears, and other arctic animals and birds. Recently Representative Bonner and Senator Magnuson have introduced bills to provide for this range.[12] Canadian officials are considering the establishment of a 5-million-acre refuge adjoining it.[13]

Now that Alaska has been granted statehood, it is possible that conservation of all resources may fare ill, for like the people of all young pioneer states, the Alaskans are intent on "development." Under the admission act Alaska will be granted 102.5 million acres of public lands which she can retain or sell, and whatever she does with it she will have a tremendous, perhaps impossible, job of protecting it, particularly from fire. With long, dry summer days, the vast forests of the state are subject to terrible, widespread forest fires, sometimes burning all summer and destroying more than 5 million acres of timber, killing wildlife and destroying—for perhaps half a century—the lichen on which some of it depends. The state will not have the resources to control such fires, but it will of course be helped by the federal protection afforded the huge areas of national forest and other public land that still will constitute a large part of Alaska. Fortunately, the federal government has retained

11 *Report, Secretary of the Interior, 1941,* 4-3; 1956, 287.

12 H. R. 7045, S. 1819, 86 Cong.

13 Edgar B. Nixon, ed., *Franklin D. Roosevelt and Conservation* (Hyde Park, N. Y.: National Archives and Records Service, Franklin D. Roosevelt Library, 1957), Vol. I, 284, 289, 295. *National Parks Magazine,* July-Sept. 1958, 117.

control of the Alaska wildlife until the state is ready and able to assume responsibility for it.[14]

FACTORS UNFAVORABLE TO WILDLIFE   Gunners and trappers were not the only factors tending to reduce the amount of wildlife in the United States. The mere growth of population tends to the same end—the more people there are, the less wildlife. Cities grew and expanded, railroads were built, and highways, which not only enabled hunters to range more widely but subtracted from the land available for wildlife. Land that had been the home of wildlife was turned to farming. This affected the wildlife even in some of the national parks, for some wildlife roams rather widely and finds its outside range more and more limited. A few species of animals and birds benefited from the cutting of forests and establishment of farms—the sagacious coyote, some foxes, the cottontail rabbit, skunk, opossum, white-tailed deer, bob-white and a few others. About 100 million acres of land were drained, and this was a serious blow especially to migratory waterfowl, as well as, in many cases, a policy of gross folly for other reasons. Hundreds of dams were built, flooding the best lands—best for animals as for man. Soil erosion, the result of wasteful lumbering on watersheds and wasteful farming on agricultural lands, reduced the forage for wildlife; many farmers conceived the idea of "clean farming"—cutting and burning shrubbery along the fences—and so spoiled the habitats of some wildlife. Soil erosion and stream pollution have affected fishes and aquatic life most seriously, but directly or indirectly some other wildlife as well. Finally, in very recent years, the use of DDT and other insecticides has brought the possibility of injury to birds, fishes and other wildlife from eating materials that have been poisoned. The Fish and Wildlife Service is studying this problem.[15]

THE STORY IN YELLOWSTONE   There was not much interest in the protection of wildlife at the time Yellowstone Park was established; in fact not very much was known about wildlife management, and this was reflected in the provisions of the establishing act. The Secretary, it will be remembered, was merely instructed

14 *American Forests*, Apr. 1958, 13; Aug. 1958, 10.
15 Ira N. Gabrielson, *American Forests*, Mar. 1949, 12 ff.

to "provide against the 'wanton' destruction of fish and game found within said park, and against their capture or destruction for the purposes of merchandise or profit." Under this provision, or in violation of it, there was gross exploitation of the fish and game in the park, sometimes, as we have already seen, for sale to the hotels in the park. Without funds for the employment of rangers, there was for several years practically no protection of the wildlife. Even after the detail of troops to protect the park in 1886, protection was inadequate and there was some poaching. Finally, the Lacey Act of 1894 provided adequate legal protection of wildlife.[16] Protection against poaching, it may be noted, was not a business for timid men, for in a few cases the poachers would use their guns on the rangers.

Even if the laws had been adequate for protection, Yellowstone was not well drawn as a wildlife refuge, or indeed, as we have seen, as a scenic park. In the first place, it was not a self-sufficient biotic unit for most animals, where they could live in natural conditions. It was mostly high terrain, good for summer forage but too cold for winter grazing. In the second place, the rectangular boundaries, drawn without regard to the topography of the land, cut across grazing areas without any respect for animal habits. Where a boundary line cut across a given grazing area, the elk, deer, and bison could not well discern the imaginary line which divided their refuge from their slaughter territory, and they were shot in great numbers.

When United States troops moved in, in 1886, there was better protection, and wildlife conditions improved, yet were not satisfactory at the turn of the century, particularly for the buffalo. The story of Secretary Hoke Smith's "corral" and the later "buffalo ranch" has been mentioned, but they call for a little further elaboration.

When the "corral" was abandoned in 1897 there were only about twenty-five buffalo in the park and for several years they seemed on the point of extinction, in spite of the fact that Montana, Wyoming, and Idaho forbade the killing of buffalo. In 1902 only twenty-two buffalo were reported. In that year President Roosevelt persuaded Congress to appropriate $15,000 for building an enclosure and buying more buffalo.[17] Whether they were put in the

16 See pp. 45, 46.
17 Stat. 32, 574.

old corral or a new one was built for them does not appear from the records, but Acting Director E. T. Scoyen says he is sure that a new corral was built, near Mammoth Hot Springs, and the small herd was kept in it and given the most meticulous care.

In 1907 "Buffalo Ranch" was built up in the Lamar Valley—barns and other buildings, corrals, pastures, chutes, runways, and traps—and the Mammoth Hot Springs herd was moved over to Lamar Valley, where again the animals were given all possible care. Shelters were provided against bad weather, cows were segregated from bulls except for breeding, calves were removed from their mothers at an early date to assure against accidental injury, and some were bottle-fed. To avoid a surplus of obstreperous, bellicose bulls, always likely to injure other animals, especially calves, in fighting, most bull calves were castrated.

There was a "wild" herd elsewhere in the park which had survived all hardships and poaching, but in winter the herd at Lamar Valley, along with some elk, deer, and antelope, were fed hay produced in the vicinity. From 1903 to 1942 there was an appropriation of $2,500 or more each year for the expenses of feeding the buffalo and paying the "buffalo keeper"—a man named "Buffalo Jones." By 1917 the appropriation was up to $5,000 for "feed for buffalo, salaries for buffalo keepers, seeding and fencing meadowlands, irrigation, etc."[18]

Under such care the herd prospered mightily, and in 1912 the Lamar herd was reported at 143, and in 1915 at 239. In 1918 Albright reported that Lamar Valley was a big bison range, with 400 bison; but the task of providing feed became more and more onerous. It was necessary to build an irrigation system, and in 1914 the hay crop harvested had risen to 200 tons, and in 1918 to 1,000 tons with 324 acres of land under cultivation, but this was for the northern herd of elk as well as for the bison.[19]

A small herd was moved from the Lamar Valley Ranch to the corral near Mammoth Hot Springs every spring so the tourists could see the bison, and was moved back at the end of the tourist season. There was also a corral on Yellowstone Lake, as we have seen, with a few buffalo, elk, and bighorn sheep, maintained by the Yellowstone Lake Boat Company, which provided boat trips across

18 Stat. 40, 151.

19 *Science Monthly,* Aug. 1935, 141. *National Parks Magazine,* Jan.-Mar. 1944, 26. *American Forests,* Oct. 1944.

the lake; but these animals were grossly neglected, and the Superintendent compelled the boat company to release them.[20]

The Buffalo Ranch at Lamar Valley was a sort of livestock business, but operated at a considerable loss and to the demoralization of the buffalo, who developed a habit of hanging around the hay stacks too much and foraging too little. The bulls also devoted too much energy to fighting, disturbing the herds and injuring the calves, and twice nearly killed the buffalo keeper. In 1915 Acting Superintendent Lloyd Brett recommended the disposition of 100 surplus bulls.

In later years there was some criticism of the buffalo show at Mammoth Hot Springs as contrary to national park principles, but at the time it seemed justified. The Park's Acting Superintendent was trying to popularize the park, and wisely too, for the park needed friends; visitors, who were much interested in the buffalo, perhaps developed an interest in wildlife preservation from seeing them. The Buffalo Ranch operations have also been criticized, but at their inception they were merely a very conscientious and determined effort to save the buffalo from apparently impending extinction. They did not seem as secure in 1907 as they do today. We must recognize the fact that this herd, and the "wild" herd, have furnished the bison that were used to stock other areas in various parts of the country.

Much later there were somewhat similar wildlife shows at Platt, Wind Cave, Colorado National Monument and near Grand Teton. In July 1948 a Jackson Hole Wildlife Park of 1,200 acres was set up east of Moran, where buffalo, elk, moose, antelope, white-tailed and mule deer were exhibited. In 1955 the Fish and Wildlife Service fenced in a pasture of 176 acres where a small herd of elk was kept in the summer. The wildlife enclosure at Wind Cave is well designed and much enjoyed by visitors, as is the one at Platt. Whether there should be such wildlife displays in or adjoining the national parks is a question on which there may be honest disagreement. Purists object to them, as artificial and inconsistent with national park principles; animals, they say, should be free, unrestrained, in their natural surroundings. On the other hand, the enclosures were introduced, in the case of Platt and Wind Cave at least, because those parks needed an additional attraction; the visitors take a great interest in the wildlife, and if the animals were not

20 *Report, Secretary of the Interior, 1907*, 533, 534.

fenced in they would not often be seen. In a large enclosure they are not seriously "restrained."

As a further means of saving the "approved" Yellowstone wildlife, predator elimination was carried on early in the history of the park. In 1877 Superintendent Norris reported that carcasses were being poisoned for wolves and wolverines. In 1889 Secretary Noble reported predators increasing, and thought they should be checked. The next year he reported bear and mountain lions increasing and killing many elk, deer, especially the calves and fawns, and even the calves of buffalo. He hesitated to use hunters to kill the predators, but in 1891 appointed one hunter. In 1893 a pack of hounds was brought in to help in hunting mountain lions, and was used for about ten years. In 1897 Acting Superintendent Young complained of the depredations of coyotes among the antelope and elk calves, reporting seventy-five antelope in Gardiner Valley killed by them during the winter. Rather interestingly, there were a few men, even as early as this, who believed it might not be wise to exterminate the coyotes, because the coyotes killed many gophers, and if they were eliminated the gophers would ruin the grass.

Ten years later the mountain lions were reported almost exterminated, but the coyotes were still active, and park men shot, trapped, and poisoned ninety-nine of them. By 1912 wolves were reported to be scarce, but in 1914 some were reported seen, and the next year even increasing, as were mountain lions. No doubt figures of numbers of these predators were subject to a wide margin of error, but the numbers killed were probably fairly accurate. In 1916 two special rangers were hired to kill coyotes, and they shot and trapped 83 coyotes, 12 wolves, and 4 mountain lions, while park employees killed 97 coyotes. In 1923 the Secretary reported 300 coyotes killed.

With predators under heavy pressure, the number of elk increased rapidly. As early as 1897, the Secretary estimated them at 20,000, which was too many; and very soon the prospect was not for extinction but overpopulation and starvation. From 1912 on a considerable number were shipped out to other parks and various points, but this did not keep the numbers down. In 1916 they were so numerous around Gardiner, where they were being fed, that the Northern Pacific ran special trains in January and February to see them, and nearly 2,000 people made the trip. From that time on there were usually more elk than the range could support, and in the severe winters of 1916-17 and 1919-20 thousands starved to death. More would, of course, have died had it not been for $5,000 of private gifts and deficiency appropriations of $43,026 for feed.[21]

In some of the other national parks established after Yellowstone the story was repeated. For many years there was usually a surplus of some species of wildlife, particularly elk in Yellowstone and some of the other parks, and the results were tragic. In any very severe winter thousands starved to death or barely survived. The death rate was particularly heavy for fawns and pregnant females. Particularly was this true when they were fed at certain stations. For years the Bureau of Biological Survey maintained a feeding station in the elk refuge south of Yellowstone, where hundreds of elk were fed in winter—1,923 tons of hay in the winter of 1919-20. It seemed a humane business to feed hay to starving elk, but feeding was injurious in some ways. It was finally learned that the hay, which was not their natural feed, was not good for them, neither was it for deer; also the animals tended to hang around the feeding stations to be fed and not bestir themselves to hunt their own food. In 1939 the Park Service definitely adopted as a policy, "Every species shall be left to carry on its struggle for existence unaided, as being to its greatest ultimate good, unless there is real cause to believe that it will perish if unassisted."

WILDLIFE DISEASES   Animal diseases have always been one of the most difficult problems faced by the Park Service and Fish and Wildlife Service, sometimes difficult to diagnose and more difficult to treat. Few people who see the lordly elk in the parks, the sedate moose, beautiful deer and bighorns, the swift antelope and massive grizzly, realize how much they are troubled with diseases of various sorts, sometimes to the point of death, and what a baffling problem they present. We have seen what a problem hemorrhagic septicemia and brucellosis in the bison herd in Yellowstone offered. It was later encountered in bighorns. In 1924 the Park Service had to kill some 20,000 deer infected with foot-and-mouth disease in the Tuolomne region in Yosemite. In 1942 the Service found the California mule deer in Yosemite, Sequoia, and Kings Canyon infected with wood ticks, lungworms, nasal botflies

21 Stat. 41, 512.

and eye worms. Bighorns have sometimes been infected with lungworms, scab, and as a result of the latter which destroys the skin
and wool, progressive pneumonia. Bears which were very thin and
showed bad temper have been found heavily infected with broad
tapeworm, which they got from infected fish. Rangers were able to
treat some of them successfully with kamela, mixing it with cocoa,
butter, honey, and powdered sugar. Elk often have ticks, and deer
are subject to ticks, lice, tapeworms, roundworms, and other parasites, to diseases of the eyes—occasionally blind deer and bear are
found wandering about—pseudo-tuberculosis, pneumonia, deer foot-
worm disease, grubs, liver flukes, and other diseases, some of them
difficult or even impossible to treat. Bighorns have sometimes contracted parasites from domestic sheep. Sometimes epidemics—called
"epizootics" in animals—would strike some of the wild animals:
encephalitis, mange, rabies, and various other diseases, some of them
not understood. Rabies in wild populations sometimes presented a
really terrific problem. The veterinarians of the Fish and Wildlife
Service, which co-operates with the Park Service on wildlife problems, earn their salaries.[22]

One of the worst results of animal overpopulation was the destruction of the range by hungry or starving animals, which ate the
forage so closely as sometimes to kill it, chewed off all the leaves
they could reach, including the needles of pines which were highly
injurious to them, even gnawed the bark off the trees. Some range
was so badly cut that it will not recover for decades; and this means
grave injury to the watersheds with all the evils that it entails. Excessive numbers of animals were thus inconsistent with all land
management principles. Of course excessive population of one
species and destruction of the range meant deficient forage and
distress for other species, even for species that were not numerous
enough.

A historic example of range destruction by starving animals was
seen in the Kaibab Plateau, north of Grand Canyon. The Forest
Service, which had jurisdiction, hired hunters to kill the cougars in
this region, and as a result the deer began to increase rapidly. This
was about 1910. By 1917 there was clear warning of famine; by 1923
the situation became so critical that Secretary Wallace appointed

22 See William M. Rush, *Wild Animals of the Rockies* (Garden City, N. Y.:
Halcyon House, 1947, reprint) , Chap. XXXII, 77, 160, 175.

a Citizens' Advisory Committee to make a study and suggest remedies. The committee reported that there were 30,000 deer in an area that could support only 15,000; that the animals were gaunt and thin already in August, and the range nearly destroyed. As remedies, the committee suggested that domestic cattle should be removed from the plateau; that owing to differences in seasons the game management should have power to change regulations from year to year; that 15,000 should be given away, or if this was impossible that as a last resort government hunters should be hired to kill about half the deer.[23] In the mid-twenties a man named McCormick conceived the idea of driving a few thousand deer down and across Grand Canyon to the Navajo Indian reservation, but the deer refused to be driven. By 1939 the herd had starved down to about one-tenth of its peak and the range had lost half or more of its feed value. In their hunger the deer had eaten all the aspen leaves as high as they could reach, killing the small aspen trees. For years there were no small aspens in many parts of the area, and this is true of some parts even today.[24] In such cases the animals that survived were as badly "eroded" as the range and the soil. In their weakened condition they were attacked by diseases and epizootics which weakened them further; in certain cases their average weight was said to have been reduced by nearly 50 per cent.

This overpopulation problem has not been confined to the national parks and national forests. In recent years there have been reports of excessive numbers of deer and a few other animals in various parts of the country. In Pennsylvania, for instance, deer have multiplied to a point where they are a serious nuisance to farmers. In Texas a considerable number of deer often starve to death in late winter. The cutting of timber has contributed to the increase, for deer and some other animals thrive on shrubs and shoots that grow up after logging rather than in dense timber.

The Yellowstone elk surplus has persisted down to the present time. In the fall of 1957 the Park Service reported that there were 8,200 elk in the northern herd, which was at least 3,000 too many. The Park Service has tried to meet the problem in various ways.

[23] Figures as to numbers of wild animals appear to be very inaccurate, for Aldo Leopold estimated that this herd had increased to about 100,000 by 1924, and that two severe winters had killed some 60,000 by starvation.

[24] See an article by Aldo Leopold, in *Audubon Magazine*, Vol. 45, 156. *National Parks Bulletin* No. 41, Oct. 23, 1924.

Winter feeding of the animals was found to be no remedy. It was expensive, bad for animal health, and condemned except in extreme circumstances.

Shooting of the elk outside the parks when they came down to lower land in the fall was relied on largely for many years, but this was not effective enough as the starvation in severe winters proved. In recent years, as more and more of the surrounding land was taken up by settlers, more of the elk herd have tended to remain in the park, except in severe winters, and the kill outside has been short of needs. The adjoining states have sometimes tried to help by altering the length of the hunting season, lengthening it when population was excessive and shortening it when there was need to reduce the kill; but such measures were often inadequate. For many years state fish and game commissions have co-operated with the Park Service in efforts to solve this and other wildlife problems.

One of the first proposals for meeting the problem of animal surpluses was the expansion of the parks to take in more of the lower land for winter grazing. As we have seen, almost every year from fairly early Yellowstone days the Secretary, and Mather after the Park Service was established, called for expansion of Yellowstone, but with only small success. Additions were asked for several other parks, but without much success. This would have helped, at least temporarily, but in the long run the surplus would have reappeared as long as the policy of predator control was maintained.

It was sometimes suggested that the adjoining states establish game preserves outside the parks where the animals could go in winter. Wyoming did establish three—the Hoodoo, Teton, and Shoshone reserves—and Montana established a small one, but Idaho hunters for years killed whatever game came into the state. The problem was somewhat the same for some other parks, and the adjoining states responded in various ways. California was urged to set up a game preserve west of Yosemite but did not do so. Colorado set up a state game preserve on lower land east of the Rocky Mountain Park in 1919. The elk had been exterminated here, but a herd was brought in from Yellowstone and the state wanted to see it prosper. Washington established a state game preserve south of Mount Rainier in 1923. In 1939 the Arizona State Game and Fish Association changed the boundaries of the game refuge adjacent to the South Rim of Grand Canyon. Hunters had been killing so many bucks that there were many barren does and few fawns, and the deer seemed to be headed toward extinction. State game preserves would have helped in some ways, but animal overpopulation would soon have appeared unless hunting was allowed in those preserves—as it usually was.

Even before the Park Service was established the Acting Superintendent of Yellowstone live-trapped a considerable number of surplus animals and sent them out to organizations and agencies asking for them. In 1916 Mather gave permission for the trapping and removal of 668 elk, 12 buffalo, 8 grizzly bears, and some other animals. Between 1913 and 1934, 3,007 Yellowstone elk were sent out to 24 different states and 307 to Canada. In the eight years from 1934-35 to 1942 the Park Service trapped and sent out 1,730 elk from the north Yellowstone herd, and it still sends out a number every year. These are given for various purposes in the following order:

    a) range stocking for federal and state agencies,
    b) stocking public zoos,
    c) stocking private farms and zoos,
    d) for release in various areas for public shooting.

Bears, both black and grizzly, are sometimes trapped and sent out, but only to public agencies or institutions. Applicants for animals are required to show that they have facilities for their care, must pay a small handling charge for each animal, cost of shipment, and of any veterinarian services needed, and the cost of crates needed for individual animals.

The number of animals thus live-trapped and sent out is never enough to reduce the surplus very much. The surplus elk in Yellowstone alone sometimes amounted to 10,000 animals, and it would have been a task for the United States Army to handle so many wild animals—very expensive too, and a few would die or be seriously injured in transit. Bears were dangerous to handle, and in traps and cages would sometimes break their teeth and claws trying to tear their way out, perhaps finally having to be killed.[25]

When all these measures fail, and after trying in various ways to get animals to move out of the parks, the Park Service as a last resort has been obliged to delegate rangers as hunters to shoot surplus animals in the parks, and give the carcasses to Indian agencies or

25 See Rush, op. cit., Chap. IV.

other federal agencies. This has often provided inadequate reduction too, as we have seen.

Something was done, however, in stocking other parks and in restocking those in which certain animals had been exterminated. In 1912 wild turkeys were introduced into Sequoia; in 1920 beaver and grouse and ducks were planted in Lafayette (later Acadia). Some years later twelve antelope kids were brought to Grand Canyon and planted in Hermit Camp, but they did not prosper. They had been raised on a bottle, were pampered and tame, and perhaps not fitted for wild life. It is not quite certain that the early stocking of animals was legal, but in 1923 Albright managed to get Congress to pass a law authorizing it and even authorizing the *sale* of surplus buffalo.[26]

In 1933 antelope were brought into Petrified Forest; a fence was built around the monument to keep livestock out, and water holes were provided. Bandelier was stocked with antelope about the same time. In 1934 the Park Service proposed that bison from Yellowstone be brought into the Blackfeet Indian reservation east of Glacier, but the Indians were suspicious of the plan and would not agree. Deer and beaver were sent to Shenandoah; antelope to White Sands; Merriam turkeys and bighorns to Mesa Verde; beaver, eastern wild turkeys, ruffed grouse, and white-tail deer to Mammoth Cave; antelope and white-tail deer to Big Bend; and bighorns to Rocky Mountain. The badger was returned to Wind Cave, where prairie dog towns offer an ample food supply.

It is the policy of the Park Service to restore to park areas all forms of life that have been extirpated, but this is often difficult or impossible to do. Some park areas were outlined too small to accommodate many of the mammals which originally inhabited the localities; the national parkways are too narrow to serve well as wildlife sanctuaries. In some cases there would be local opposition to stocking park areas with such species as grizzly bear, wolf or cougar, or perhaps even such inoffensive but prolific animals as prairie dogs. Prairie dogs were once very characteristic of the high western plains, their towns sometimes occupying considerable areas and, where still to be seen, are the object of great interest to tourists; but they eat the grass, and the farmers and stockmen who eradicated them would not like to see them return to their lands.

26 Stat. 42, 1214.

Where a species has disappeared from a given park area, restocking is not likely to be successful if the conditions still remain as they were when the species died out.[27]

PREDATOR CONTROL AS A POLICY   The predator-control policy long followed by Park Superintendents and later by Mather was partly responsible for animal overpopulation. There is something pathetic, something shocking, in the thought of the cougars, wolves, coyotes and other predators killing the beautiful deer, antelope and elk, something revolting to humane sentiments; yet, whatever views one may have as to human infant damnation or predestination, the truth is that the beautiful little fawns and calves were predestined to cruel death, by predators, hunters, or by starvation, and starvation was the worst of these. Abandonment of the policy of predator control was being considered by park and wildlife leaders in the late twenties. In 1931 Secretary Wilbur reported that the Park Service had established rules against extermination of any species of wildlife, including predators, against the use of poisons, and regulating the use of steel traps.

There had been more or less research into wildlife problems for many years, beginning with studies of bird migration made by the American Ornithological Union when it was organized in 1883. The Union turned its studies over to a committee headed by Dr. C. Hart Merriam of New York, who had been naturalist of the Hayden Survey at an early age. In 1885 Merriam persuaded Congress to give independent status to his work under the title "Division of Economic Ornithology and Mammalogy," in the Department of Agriculture, and did a great deal of valuable work on birds. An important survey of "life zones" was made in the San Francisco Mountain region of Arizona, where different types of life could be studied at different altitudes. In 1896 the name of the division was changed to the "Bureau of Biological Survey," and Merriam served as director until 1910. In 1900 the bureau was given the task of regulating traffic in game and fur animals under the Lacey Act, and later was charged with administering the Migratory Bird Treaty legislation. The hiring of a trained naturalist for each of the national parks was urged by Joseph Grin-

27 See Victor H. Cahalane, *A Program for Restoring Extirpated Mammals in the National Park System* (National Park Service, July 22, 1950).

nell and Tracy Storer as early as 1916, but it was not until ten years
later that much scientific research was done. In the late twenties
George Wright, a wealthy young ranger with a burning enthusiasm
for wildlife, made some studies, with two assistants, paying the costs
himself; in 1931 and 1932 the government shared the cost of a comprehensive study of wildlife in the parks. In 1933 the Division of
Wildlife Studies was established with Wright as chief. About this
time Thomas Cochran of New York gave money for a special survey
of the Yellowstone elk herds and the life habits of elk, to be made
by William Rush, and the Museum of Vertebrate Zoology of the
University of California made a study of the animal life in Mount
Lassen.

In the early thirties the predator problem began to get a great
deal of study, much of it done with CCC funds and personnel. Later,
in 1937, Adolph Murie began a study of the relationship of coyotes
to other species in Yellowstone, and later came up with some rather
surprising conclusions, one being that the absence of predator control for four years had had little effect on the number of coyotes.
Murie found from examination of 5,000 droppings and from other
evidence that in spring, summer, and fall field mice, pocket gophers,
and other rodents constituted the most important items of coyote
diet, with a small amount of insects and birds. In winter the coyotes
did feed mostly on the big game, but largely in the form of offal—
left by elk hunters—on newborn elk calves, and on deer, many of
them weakened by insufficient feed furnished by the depleted range.

A similar study of the Dall sheep–wolf relationship, in Mount
McKinley National Park, also by Murie, led to the conclusion that
although the wolves killed some sheep they usually killed the
weaker, older or diseased animals, and so tended to improve the
breed. The golden eagle has sometimes been regarded as the worst
predator of bighorn lambs and a wicked killer of the lambs of
domestic sheep, but naturalists do not regard their depredations as
seriously as they once did, and the eagles are protected in the parks.
At one time hawks and owls were hated by farmers and others because they took an occasional chicken or other fowl, and they were
shot indiscriminately on sight; today the naturalists rate all but two
of the hawks and all but one of the owls as generally beneficial to
farmers. The Audubon Society objects to the idea of drawing a distinction between beneficial and harmful species; all are part of the
scheme of nature.

PREDATOR CONTROL ABANDONED   A great variety of problems have been studied, so many that they cannot be even mentioned here, and a vast amount of information, needed for intelligent management of wildlife in the parks, has been garnered. Such information is useful not only to the Fish and Wildlife Service and the Park Service, but also to the Forest Service and other government departments, to managers of city parks and zoos, and even to private livestock interests. By the middle thirties predator control had been largely abandoned in the national parks, and in 1939 a policy statement of the Park Service and the Fish and Game Service was announced: "No native predator shall be destroyed, on account of its normal utilization of any other park animal, excepting if that animal is in immediate danger of extermination, and then only if the predator is not itself a vanishing form; when control is necessary it shall be accomplished by transplanting or, if necessary, by killing offending individuals, not by campaigns to reduce the general population of a species." A further provision was that "species predatory upon fish shall be allowed to continue in normal numbers and to share normally in the benefits of fish culture."

Protection of predators in the parks raises some fairly serious problems in the relation of the parks to surrounding areas. Farmers and stockmen sometimes accuse the Park Service of growing predators in the parks, which wander out of the parks and prey on their livestock; occasionally they even insist that the Service should build a fence around the parks to prevent this—a quite impossible task, of course.

Overpopulation is not the universal problem. In various parks and at different times there has been a serious decline of valued species, and various measures, including control of predators, have been taken to stop the decline. In 1921 there were few moose in Yellowstone, in 1933 the white-tailed deer were crowded out of Yellowstone by elk. In 1935 Rocky Mountain bighorns were reported declining, Dall sheep were down to one-third of the 1929 level, and reduction of predators was one remedy indicated. In 1939 there was still a scarcity of white-tailed deer in Yellowstone, moose had not recovered from the meat-hunting days in Mount McKinley, and the desert bighorns in Death Valley were fighting for survival. Overpopulation is not the universal problem, but sometimes a surplus of one species will bring such destruction of range that another species may be crowded out.

Students of wildlife were coming to the scientific principle of wild-life management—an approximation to primitive faunal relation-ships as far as the unnatural conditions in the parks permitted, sometimes referred to as the "balance of nature." An *approximation* only, for the unnatural conditions in the parks did not permit a reproduction of the primitive conditions. No park, with its artificial boundaries, is a self-sufficient biotic unit. "Balance of nature" does not mean a stable equilibrium, but a shifting balance of all the forces affecting wildlife, "a fluctuating balance like a teetering beam scales"—some animals are subject to more or less cyclical changes in numbers. All this makes the problem of wildlife administration very difficult, for when a species is declining it may not be possible to tell whether there is something seriously wrong which may bring decimation or extinction, or whether the decline will presently be reversed.

Even when animals become something of a nuisance in the parks, they are protected if they are a part of the natural order. In a few parks beavers do some damage—chew down trees, flood roads and meadows, and in places spoil the fishing—but they are generally use-ful in the mountains and are protected, and even promoted. Porcu-pines are a nuisance in some places, killing many trees, and getting quills into the faces of livestock, deer, and dogs. In Mount McKinley they developed a habit of trying to chew up the buildings, but their punishment was not death but deportation to another part of the park. In Mesa Verde the porcupines were for a few years a serious threat to the trees, in some areas destroying more than half the piñon pines and threatening to destroy them all. The loss was so great and the threat to park values so serious that the Park Service killed the porcupines in the areas where they were most destruc-tive.[28] At times skunks have made their homes under cabins, but the Park Service favors deportation for this offense too, if practic-able.

Bears cause more trouble than any other animals, injuring tour-ists, tearing up their cars, breaking into food lockers—which can scarcely be built so strongly that bears will not break in—upsetting garbage cans, and invading the tents of the campers. In 1956 bears caused seventy-three personal injuries in Yellowstone, and in 1957, ninety-three, along with considerable property damage; they caused

[28] *Fauna of the National Parks of the United States* (Preliminary Survey, National Park Service, May 1932), 61.

eighteen casualties in Great Smoky Mountains, and seven in Yosemite in 1956. But the personal injuries were due mostly to tourist violation of the park rules against feeding the bears. The bear problem has long been a vexatious problem for the Park Service, especially in Yellowstone. As someone once observed, "People come to see the scenery but stay to watch the bears"; really, many tourists who go to Yellowstone could get about all that they are after and save money by going to the nearest zoo. Wherever there are bears and crowds of tourists there will be trouble. The Service does not usually kill bears for the sins of the tourists, but a few of the worst offenders are killed almost every year. In 1943 eighty-seven bears were killed by rangers in Yellowstone, Yosemite, and Crater Lake.

The Park Service itself was for many years partly responsible for some of the bear troubles. For years bear-feeding grounds were maintained near the main tourist stations in Yellowstone, where garbage was fed to the bears while the people stood by to see the show. It was a pretty good show too, for even the grizzlies came to get their (more than proportionate) share of the garbage; but it tended to attract bears to these central points where they were likely to cause trouble. In the early thirties, however, Park Service naturalists began to question the policy, as well as the entire general policy of encouraging bears and other animals to stay around the hotels and camps where the tourists could see them; began to veer to the idea that animals should be seen in their natural conditions and not as half-tamed panhandlers around the camps. In the late twenties, Director Albright directed a survey of "Faunal Relations in the National Parks," to be made in the Branch of Education and Research of the National Park Service by George Wright, Joseph Dixon, and Ben Thompson. In their Preliminary Report, published in May 1932, they suggested that garbage feeding shows probably had a bad effect on the health and habits of bears, and that while formerly justified as a means of increasing the popularity of the parks, it should perhaps be abandoned.[29] Yet it was not until 1943 that the Director reported that the feeding "shows" had been stopped. In 1951 a regulation was adopted prohibiting tourists from feeding not only bears but deer, moose, buffalo, elk, and antelope. Tourist feeding of deer is somewhat dangerous, and is not good for deer health.

Wildlife management is difficult anyhow because various species,

[29] *Ibid.*

especially wide-ranging ones like the wolverine and fisher, wander in and out of the parks, and even if protected in the parks may be exterminated outside. Every year, furthermore, most of the parks are more closely circumscribed by the intrusion of man in the surrounding areas. It is not only that settlers on the land adjoining the parks may kill the animals that drift out of the parks—some of which, as for instance bears, may be predators of their livestock—but also that their sheep and cattle eat the forage needed by the park animals in winter. In some places domestic livestock, particularly sheep, have nearly ruined the range outside the parks, and so the biotic unit of the parks becomes more and more inadequate.

Outside the parks the predator policy has not changed much. It has been said that coyotes are beneficial in the parks but bad outside, but they wander a great deal, across park boundaries, and many are killed outside. In 1952 some 500 were ear-tagged in and near Yellowstone, and it was found that many, especially the young, left the park. Obviously predator control outside the parks may affect the number of predators *in* the parks. Predators outside the parks are still destroyed, by co-operative action of the Fish and Wildlife Service, the states, counties, and livestock and agricultural associations, for the predators sometimes kill chickens, turkeys, sheep, calves, even cattle, and they are occasionally responsible for epidemics of rabies. In recent years they have sometimes been hunted by airplane. In the fiscal year 1957 the total number killed by gun, trap and poison was 62,585 coyotes, 2,790 wolves, 22,198 bobcats and lynxes, 1,039 bears (reported as "stock-killing," whatever that may mean), and 267 mountain lions. There were also control operations on prairie dogs, ground squirrels, pocket gophers, jack rabbits, field mice, kangaroo rats, cotton rats, porcupines, woodchucks, and moles.[30] Some naturalists believe that there is too much killing of predators outside the parks, too much use of poison, and the present writer would like to protest against trapping—the cruelest, most infernally barbarous business in the world today.

The bounty system—payment of bounties for predators killed—once common in the states outside the parks, and still fairly common, has long been opposed by naturalists, and is being scrutinized with a more and more jaundiced eye by a growing number of state game wardens.

30 *Report, Secretary of the Interior, 1957,* 392.

DEMAND FOR HUNTING IN THE PARKS   Even with the abandonment of predator control there were for years too many elk in Yellowstone, and deer in some other parks; and finally the Park Service delegated ranger-hunters to kill certain numbers in the parks; but this was often ineffectual, the kill was often only a fraction of the number that must be eliminated to bring the total down to range-carrying capacity. In this situation there arose an insistent demand from hunters that the parks be opened to hunting. In 1944 the Western Association of State Game and Fish Commissioners adopted resolutions calling for hunting in the parks under licenses issued by the states, and for state rather than Indian tribal council control of fish and game on Indian reservations. They also demanded that no more lands should be turned over to federal reservation without the approval of the state where located.[31] More recently the International Association of Game, Fish, and Conservation Commissioners was reported drafting a law to achieve the same end. The legislature of Wyoming has memorialized Congress to permit hunting in Yellowstone under direction of the Wyoming Game and Fish Commission. There have been efforts to open the Great Smoky Mountains to hunting of "stock-killing" bears—probably "stock-killing" would have been interpreted loosely. In 1950 hunting was legalized in a part of Grand Teton Park, for Wyoming hunters, but Grand Teton is the only park any part of which is open to hunting.[32]

The Park Service is opposed to hunting in the parks, for various reasons. In the first place, the Service desires to keep the parks in as natural condition as possible, and the natural process is for the predators to kill the prey animals; the hunters should do their killing outside. In the second place, hunting would be an incongruous activity in the parks, perhaps would result in various sorts of violations of park principles and in disturbance of biological relationships. Some hunters are gentlemen, and would observe the rules of decorous conduct; others might behave as they do in other hunting areas: kill indiscriminately, perhaps each other—the death rate is fairly high in hunting outside; perhaps litter up the parks with whisky bottles and other trash. Bad manners of a few sportsmen have resulted in their being shut out of some privately owned hunt-

31 *Audubon Magazine*, July 1944, 246.
32 See p. 507.

ing land. The Park Service points out that the parks should be maintained in the interest of visitors rather than of the relatively few hunters. In the third place, if there were visitors in the parks they would be in some danger.

It must be conceded that the deputization of Wyoming sportsmen to kill the elk, under the act adding Jackson Hole to Grand Teton Park, did not accomplish much in elk reduction. When the act was passed, the Park Service, in co-operation with the Wyoming Game and Fish Commission, listed 1,200 hunters, 510 of whom reported for duty, and killed 184 elk—less than 10 per cent of the total kill for the Teton Management Area. The next year 1,200 hunters were again listed, 455 of whom applied for park permits and killed 27 elk—of a total of 3,500 killed for the herd as a whole. In 1954 only 109 were killed.[33] The Advisory Board calls insistently for the elimination of the hunting privilege in Grand Teton Park—for the conversion of a Wyoming hunting range to a national park. It has been reported that the elk population of the area is declining and that there was no necessity for hunting in the fall of 1959.

A fairly plausible argument might be made in support of the hunters. It is true that in nature the predators kill the prey, and the Park Service of course insists on the natural process; but this is of no advantage to visitors, who almost never see the predators, except the bear, and practically never see the natural operation of killing the prey. (A bus-load of visitors recently did see a bear kill an elk calf, and some of them were half-sick for the day as a result.) This is nature's way, but there is nothing beautiful about it, surely. How much worse would it be to kill off the predators and let the hunters kill the proper number of deer and elk and antelope? It would be more humane, the meat could be saved, and the visitors would miss nothing—so it might be argued. Indeed the argument might be stronger than this, for it might not be necessary to kill all the predators; there are too many prey animals anyhow, and the Park Service is unable to control the number. Why is it better to feed good venison to mangy coyotes and mountain lions than to people?

Finally, the Park Service has failed to solve the problem of excess numbers in Yellowstone and some other parks, after working at it for fifty years, with the result of starvation of the animals and devastation of the habitat. The shooting of animals outside the parks has

33 *Report, Secretary of the Interior, 1952,* 365; 1953, 300; 1954, 345.

been generally a failure. The hunters might argue that they could do no worse. Of course, no one would want any species exterminated.

EXOTICS   In the parks the introduction of exotics is forbidden. Even in outside areas this should be managed only by trained naturalists after careful consideration. In his constant "reshuffling of the fauna," as Durward Allen expresses it, man does prepare "niches which no native animal can fill adequately and for which there is something made to order on the other side of the world,"[34] and in such cases, the introduction of an exotic may possibly be wise and successful. According to Allen, examples of such success have been the pheasant, the Hungarian partridge, and the chukar from India. These he thought were excellent additions to our wildlife. Wild hogs from the Harz Mountains in Germany seemed for a time to be a worthwhile contribution, but recently there has been some doubt about this. Even if an exotic were apparently beneficial outside the park areas, the Park Service would not want it in the parks for the park policy is to maintain the park areas exclusively for native species.

Reckless introduction of exotics is likely to bring unpredictable evils, in parasites and diseases, in the possibility that an exotic may disturb the natural life equilibriums, or may in one way or another crowd out more desirable native species, or may interbreed with native stock to produce an inferior cross-breed. This was recognized in the Lacey Act of 1900, which prohibited the importation of any foreign wild animal or bird except under permit from the Department of Agriculture, with the mongoose, fruit bat, English sparrow, and starling specifically mentioned. As early as 1922 the Council of the American Association for the Advancement of Science adopted resolutions against the introduction of exotics.

We have several examples of the evils wrought by the reckless introduction of exotics, in the reindeer, the English sparrow, the starling—a nuisance of high priority—and in the Asiatic carp, which roots about in beds of vegetation, muddies the water, and crowds out more desirable fishes. The carp was brought in by the United States Commissioner of Fisheries in 1876, and has proved a nuisance

34 Durward Allen, *Our Wildlife Legacy* (New York: Funk and Wagnalls, 1954) , 176.

here as in other countries where it was introduced. Not many years
ago domestic rabbits were liberated on Santa Barbara Island, of the
Channel Islands National Monument, where they were exotics, and
in a few years became a serious pest. Some other countries have suffered more than the United States from exotics: Australia from the
introduction of rabbits and other animals, New Zealand and Hawaii
from many exotic plants, birds, and animals. The extent to which
exotics have added to the work of the Park Service may be seen
from the fact that in Hawaii Park, in the first ten months of 1949,
the Service killed 3,006 goats, 261 wild pigs, 44 mongooses, and 4
feral house cats. Exotic insects, such as the Gypsy moth, the boll
weevil, the corn borer, the White Pine Blister Rust, and recently
the fire ant, have caused vast and irreparable damage in this country. The exotic tree *Ailanthus,* from Asia, has been a nuisance in
Shenandoah Park and elsewhere. Where an exotic species has become established in a national park the rule, enunciated in 1939,
is that it "shall be either eliminated or held to a minimum provided
complete eradication is not feasible."

Domestic "exotics" present a different picture. The Park Service
and the Fish and Wildlife Service work consistently to shift animals
and birds into new areas or areas where they once thrived but were
exterminated; but this work is done by trained men who know what
they are about. This has already been considered. Some domestic
exotics, however, present difficult problems. The wild burro is an
exotic in Grand Canyon, Big Bend, Death Valley, and Lake Mead
National Recreation Area, and it is a serious nuisance. The Park
Service would like to maintain the conditions natural to every area,
which would call for the elimination of the burro, but when Service
men kill a few of the patient, sagacious little fellows, the burden-
bearers that carried prospectors into every corner of the West and
then escaped or were left to live or die, there is some public sympathy for them. Many have been killed, but some burros still live,
spoiling the range and the water holes for indigenous species. The
state of California has set aside a refuge for them adjacent to Death
Valley National Monument, but this presents difficulties too, for
the burros wander over to Death Valley to graze.

MIGRATORY BIRDS   Some kinds of wildlife, particularly
migratory birds, have been protected not only in the parks but in

special refuges and elsewhere. Today we have 205 of these refuges, covering 3,270,000 acres, and the Fish and Wildlife Service administers a total of more than 17 million acres of refuge land, nearly 8 million acres of which are in Alaska. To some extent these wildlife refuges supplement the national parks, for some of them are used for recreation and fishing. They may be used also, however, for trapping and hunting, and on some of them there may be grazing, farming, lumbering and other commercial operations.[35]

Migratory birds are still being threatened by too much drainage of wet and swampy lands outside the parks and refuges, with resulting destruction of the nesting places of waterfowl and homes of furbearers. The country once had 140 million acres of swamp or marshland, of which some 76 million acres are left, and of this only 23 million acres are of high or medium quality. About 4 million acres of the remaining wetlands are the potholes, marshes, and sloughs of the Dakotas and Minnesota, which in wet years produce some 20 per cent of the entire continental waterfowl population. These wetlands are being drained quite too fast, and often at a loss, at the expense of the government through the Soil Conservation Service, to add to the production of farm crops for the government to buy. It is estimated that 95 per cent of the American fur crop comes from wetlands.[36]

In recent years there is increasing distrust of some of the insecticide spraying campaigns carried on in the forests and elsewhere, fear of their effect on fish and other wildlife, on the balance of nature, and as applied to fruits and vegetables their effects on human health. There have been cases where spraying killed all the fish in small lakes, and considerable numbers of birds in the forests. It is at least clear that such spraying must be done under supervision of competent naturalists and that a vast amount of research must be done, and soon, on the various effects, direct and indirect, of lavish use of DDT and other insecticide sprays.[37]

35 See Butcher, *op. cit.*, 9 ff. *Report, Secretary of the Interior, 1957*, 372.

36 Will Barker, in *American Forests*, Apr. 1957, 42. See also *American Forests*, Feb. 1957, 22. Lester Errington, *Of Men and Marshes* (New York: Macmillan Company, 1957).

37 *American Forests*, Jan. 1958, 9; Feb. 1958, 4; Aug. 1958, 23; Nov. 1958, 7, 12, 14; Apr. 1959, 5. The July 1960 issue is devoted almost entirely to this question.

FISHING IN THE PARKS   The national parks are sanctuaries for terrestrial animals, but not for fishes, which may be caught under proper regulations unless fishing threatens to destroy the fish resource or do serious damage to the parks in some way; and many anglers fish in the parks. At one time this was very satisfactory sport but with the vast tourist invasions of recent years it has become less fruitful. Only in the more remote and inaccessible areas of most national parks is there usually good fishing.

Naturalists, including those in the Fish and Wildlife Service, Park Service, and also the general public, have been much slower to appreciate the importance of care of the fishes than of other wildlife. Not very many years ago there was little understanding of the biological processes in lakes and streams, because fishery research and practices lagged far behind game studies and techniques. As a result, although the general principles of national park management called for maintenance of the original conditions in the parks, fish conditions of nearly all park waters have been modified by long-time angling, by artificial stocking, or by migration of imported species to new waters. "In some instances, native races of fish have been exterminated. In others, haphazard fish cultural practices of earlier times have resulted in unfortunate biological legacies. Stocking of alien races or closely related species produced numerous hybrids. In a few areas, streams were modified by removal of forest cover prior to park establishment."[38] Even minor, well-justified restrictions proposed to conserve fish species often encounter the most determined opposition of fishermen—who are a rather numerous host.

To maintain the supply of catchable fish, park waters have for years been stocked more or less regularly from fish hatcheries, and this practice has been subject to much critical examination in recent years. The conclusion reached has been that hatcheries have at least been relied on too much. When the park waters or any waters outside are stocked with catchable-size fish, the ultimate in artificiality is reached. In June 1954 Director Wirth approved a statement of policy to the effect that "the use of catchable-size fish in stocking waters is not compatible with the fundamental concept of national parks," and should be resorted to only by permission of the Director. Where a species is gone or depleted the general policy of the Park Service is that "natural restoration to normal abundance and rela-

38 Victor H. Cahalane, in *Yosemite Nature Notes*, No. 5, May 1947.

tionship of species by protection and other encouragement is preferred to restocking and other artificialities."[39]

Professor Raymond Hall, of the Park Service Advisory Board, suggests as a possible program the closing of some park waters to fishing, the abandonment of fish planting, the reduction of number limits and the raising of size limits, the use of barbless hooks and the release of some fish caught, and perhaps the use of glass-bottom boats to see the fish. Former Director Horace Albright considers all this quite fanciful, but the trend of recent thought in the Park Service and elsewhere is toward at least one of Hall's proposals—the abandonment of fish planting. A few of the parks are about closed to fishing now, because they have too few fish to bother about.

In 1956 Director Farley, of the Fish and Wildlife Service, reported a vast amount of research and administrative work relating to fish: "Sampling of inland and marine fish populations, life history studies, selective breeding of hatchery stock, disease and nutrition studies, pollution investigations, as well as migration and harvest studies," selective control of rough fish, and the development of effective stocking methods. Thousands of acres of fishing lakes were bought, leased or developed, and studies were made in the improvement of habitat, by "streambank protection, gully control, tree and shrub planting, fencing, channel improvements, and barrier removals." Naturalists were coming to a clearer appreciation of the importance of habitat conditions in fish culture as in conservation of animals and birds. In fish culture as in all wildlife protection the naturalists were upsetting many traditions and building a more scientific theory of management.[40]

THE IMPORTANCE OF HABITAT   In recent years it is more and more recognized that in wildlife management perhaps the most important factor is the maintenance of good conditions in the habitat, which for fishes includes the watershed draining into lakes and streams. It appears that lakes and streams in areas of good, rich land, well conserved, support more and better fish than those in areas of poor and eroded lands; and the best way to maintain good fishing is to maintain good conditions on the land and in the

39 Unpublished report of the Park Service.
40 Stat. 64, 430. *Report, Secretary of the Interior, 1956*, 292. See also Allen, *op. cit.*

water. Fish are capable of an astronomical rate of increase, and if the habitat conditions are good there will be many fish without any supplement from hatcheries, although of course if there is too much fishing there may not be enough for all the fishermen. Capture of fish released from hatcheries is often extremely expensive, per unit captured—as high as $12.50 a pound. The maintenance of the supply of fish is extremely complicated, a problem for trained naturalists, who are working on it all the time.

All fishes and almost all animals have a high rate of increase if conditions are favorable; if conditions are unfavorable, *naturally* unfavorable or unfavorable because the habitat is too crowded, little can be done. The study of fishes proves again that conservation is largely *one* problem and not many unrelated problems. If there is to be an abundant supply of healthy fish and animals and birds, there must be good land management in a broad sense— preservation of forests, grass, and the soil itself on the watersheds. Soil, timber, and grass conservation affects all wildlife, streamflow, siltation of dams and therefore irrigation, water power, water supply for cities, floods, harbor maintenance, perhaps even navigation, and certainly the health of domestic animals and man himself, for crops grown on good, well-conserved land are more nutritious and more healthful than crops grown on poor and abused land. Conservation is *one* problem.

The story of wildlife presents a striking analogy to that of the human animal. Like the other animals, birds, and fishes, but to a lesser extent, the human race has a great capacity for multiplication, and in much of the world this has brought the people to the conditions similar to those of the elk in Yellowstone, there being no predators to keep the population in check. As with the elk, and with other wildlife in many places, this has brought malnutrition, poor health, disease, stunted bodies, and destruction of the land habitat. The Malthusian Doctrine, often pooh-poohed by cheerful sentimentalists, applies with relentless severity to wildlife and most human populations.

CHAPTER XXVIII

National Park Concessions

Concession problems have been discussed at various points in the preceding chapters, but it will be well here to draw together some of the loose strands and formulate a few tentative conclusions regarding concessions, from a broad economic point of view.

Accommodations for visitors in the parks may be provided in various ways: (1) by private construction, ownership, and operation of hotels and other facilities, with reliance on competition to keep prices down and quality of services up, or through monopoly, with regulation of prices and services; (2) by government ownership and private operation, again either competitive or monopolized; (3) by government ownership and operation; or (4) by government ownership and nonprofit or co-operative operation. There may be various conceivable arrangements under each of these. Not all these alternatives were considered at the time Yellowstone was established, for private ownership and operation was the only policy considered; in fact it will be remembered that a few private facilities were set up in Yellowstone, and also Yosemite, before those parks were established. In the early years Congress would not appropriate money even for protection and administration; government construction and operation of facilities were quite unthinkable.

PRIVATE OWNERSHIP AND PRIVATE OPERATION   There are many questions as to possible concession arrangements under private ownership and operation. First, should the concession be awarded by competitive bidding to the bidder who promises the highest returns to the government or should the concessioner be selected on the basis of known ability, character, and interest in the business? The answer is clear. Competitive bidding has no place here, for various reasons. It is likely to turn up incompetent, inexperienced, and uninterested men, often without enough capital to carry on the business properly. As Albright once said, there is not enough profit in any park enterprise to entice an experienced man to promise much for a concession; and on the other hand the income from concessions ought not to be a governing factor in granting them. Much more important are service to the public, protection of park features, and maintenance of park management ideals.

Should the Service rely on competition as a regulator of prices or should the business be monopolized and prices be regulated? The answer is not so simple here. Many years ago competition was often relied on in the general economy where it could not possibly produce anything but inefficiency or chaos: as in the early street railways, where different companies operated on alternate streets on the theory that they would compete and give good service; as in the railway system, when competition was allowed between railroads running from New York to Chicago (and in the rate wars the roads hauled passengers for nothing, and then combined to avoid bankruptcy); or as in the two telephone systems that operated in some cities forty or fifty years ago, and everyone had to pay for two telephones to get full service. Only after many years did the people see that some businesses are natural monopolies and cannot be made competitive.

The national park concessions are somewhat of this nature. If competition is to work well certain conditions must prevail. First, the total amount of business must be large enough to enable two or more competitors to operate at something approximating lowest possible costs. If there is not enough business to permit this, costs for both or all competitors will be higher than they should be and rates will have to be high or service poor—just the condition that prevailed in the early history of Yellowstone when competition was relied on. Under such circumstances the competitors are likely to combine in some sort of tacit agreement, but this will not correct the high costs. There are still two or more concerns in the field doing what one could do more cheaply.

Service to the public often suffers too. This was seen in the transportation of passengers in early Yellowstone and later in Rocky Mountain. In Yellowstone the various independent stage operators that met the trains were wont to set up a potpourri of barkers' appeals that was quite out of harmony with the splendor of the park, with sales appeals that had no resemblance to the treatment the tourists got once they were ensnared. At a later time this was true in Rocky Mountain Park. Worst of all was the fact that there was no reliable service that could be depended on in all kinds of weather and regardless of the number of passengers. The jitneys took only the cream of the business. It was necessary to monopolize the business to get reliable service. Mather saw the necessity of regulated monopoly from the first. In Yellowstone he found too many concessioners, and soon got government-regulated monopolies for one hotel company, and one transportation company, and persuaded the two camping companies to combine and drop their transportation business.

In the second place, conditions in the parks are not favorable to effective competition. Competition can be effective only if the public has time and opportunity to learn something about the services provided by the various competitors. There should be a fairly stable buying public. This is not found in the parks, where the average visit is for only two or three days, where the tourists are very busy, running hither and yon, with little time to appraise two or three or a half dozen restaurants or merchandise stores. Tourists are quite unable to make the decisions on which effective competition depends.

For yet another reason competition cannot work well in the parks. If the parks are to be properly and artistically developed, there must be effective co-operation between the concessioners and the Park Service; and this co-operation is much easier to secure from one concessioner than from several.

In many of the parks, however, whatever the situation within the parks, there is competition, perhaps fairly effective competition, from business concerns outside and from other alternatives open to tourists. With the development of better roads and cars, the visitors can often go outside for cabins, meals, or food or general merchandise if prices in the parks seem unreasonably high. Their admission tickets enable them to leave and re-enter at any time. Or they can camp in tents or in cars or trailers. It is very difficult to avoid competition in the present world, and probably this competition from outside and from other alternatives is quite as effective as regulation by the Park Service. It is surprising that the prices in most of the parks are so nearly on a par with prices outside.

This competition from outside has been increasing and seems likely to increase further as better transportation expands the area within which tourists can move and, more important, as more and more facilities are moved outside park limits. As already noted, there are long-run plans for moving facilities of most kinds out of certain congested areas within the parks and in some cases outside the parks. Where the latter policy is followed the Park Service will lose some control over hotels and cabins and other tourist facilities if they are surrounded by privately owned land. If the new locations are on public domain or on national forest land the Park Service might retain full control, as it might through control of such utilities as water or electricity, or in some other way. The Park Service will try to maintain some control over tourist facilities wherever located, to avoid the development of the ugly architectural hodgepodge characteristic of private enterprise, such as Grand Lake Village and Estes Park Village, but private facilities will be closer and will probably offer more effective competition.

Regulated monopoly is then generally preferable to competition in park concessions. But just how far should monopoly extend? Should one concessioner control all the business in a park, or only all business of a given kind? Should a single concessioner control all the hotel, or hotel and cabin, or hotel, cabin, transportation, and merchandising of all kinds, including gasoline sales? There is no hard and fast answer to this question, but the answer will vary with the amount of business in the parks. Where there are many visitors, perhaps each line of business may have its own concessioner, but in parks where there is not much business one concessioner may have to have all lines to make reasonable earnings. Most concessioners are obliged to furnish some services at a very small profit or at a loss. At times and in some cases, hotel companies would have failed if they had not also had transportation facilities—as in Yellowstone after the Northern Pacific withdrew and sold all its interests. In other cases, as for instance in Glacier, horse and pack animal transportation has been hazardous. This does not mean that a concessioner must have all the services in a park, but often he must have more than one; and he may need all. Personalized operations, such as photography and curio stands, are sometimes independent.

There is a further question, whether the general principle of monopoly should extend to more than one park. There are economies in such a policy, economies in management, in buying supplies, in hiring labor; and some concessioners do range over several parks. The Utah Parks Company controls at Zion, Bryce Canyon, Cedar Breaks, and the North Rim of Grand Canyon, and provides a better service than four different concessioners could afford. National Park Concessions, Inc. also controls at several parks, and affords high-class services, although at some points it operates under serious handicaps, for the concessions it was awarded were mostly those that business concessioners did not want.

If efficiency were the only ideal, it would probably be well to have all the services in all the parks under a single management, as a regulated monopoly. The examples of the modern chain stores, chain motels, and hotels, suggest that such an organization might fit the modern picture better than separate concessions for each park, and might afford cheaper and better service.

Regulation of prices and services in the parks is so difficult that it cannot be the main reliance in protecting visitors. The Park Service can set prices for most of the many goods and services, but how can it regulate quality? As in the case of public utilities of any kind, such regulation is not very effective. The service may set a maximum price of $2.00 for dinner at the lodge, but how will it specify just what kind of a dinner shall be served, what quality of food, how well cooked and how well served? It may set a schedule of rates for rooms or cabins, but what of the services going with the rooms or cabins? It is true that if visitors make too many complaints the concessioner's lease may be terminated, but that may be a slow and unreliable spur to good management. The reasonable prices and good quality usually found in the national parks are probably not due so much to regulation as to competition from outside and from the desire of most concessioners to do their jobs well. The Service tries to pick out concessioners who will have an interest in their jobs. Men whose interests are largely acquisitive are not likely to seek national park business.

The financial arrangements usually call for a franchise fee either based on a flat fee or a flat fee plus a percentage of the gross receipts. Previous to 1950 there was some sort of a division of profits between the concessioner and the government, with the government share rising as profits go up. The flat fee has been a traditional payment since early years, although for some of the smaller businesses it has been nominal or very modest. There has been some criticism in Congress of the smallness of some of the fees paid, and probably it would be politically unwise to eliminate them, but as a matter of logic flat fees should be abolished. Such a fee is a fixed charge, it must be paid whether the concessioner makes any profit or not; and any fixed charge adds to the hazards of a business which has enough hazards without it. A slight change in the division of the profits would yield the government as much revenue as the fee and would be easier for the concessioner to pay since it would be payable only when he has net revenues.

The division of profits above expenses and reasonable return on investment was for many years of *net* profits, but in 1950, as we have seen, Secretary Chapman substituted a division of *gross* revenue, above a "break-even" point, to avoid some of the expensive auditing required in computing net profits.[1] Albright regards this as a distinct improvement, and his judgment is probably the best that can be secured.

The idea behind the division of profits is that the concessioner should get his expenses, including a return on investment, but only as much above that as is necessary to make up for unprofitable years and give him an incentive for efficient management. Park business is a public utility, and as such should not yield high profits; yet since a concessioner, unlike an electric utility or telephone company which almost always makes a fair return, may lose money in unfavorable years, he may properly be allowed a share of profits in good years. In Congress and elsewhere at various times there have been complaints of high prices, poor service, and excessive profits of concessioners, but these complaints have not generally been justified. In 1948, a time of booming tourist traffic, Albright pointed out that in most cases there were no bidders for expired concessions; and this has often been true. At the time, a number of concessioners would have been quite willing to sell to the government. The Yosemite Park and Curry Company, one of the most profitable,

1 See p. 463.

reported earnings of 7 per cent. In 1953, a good year for concessioners, the average rate of return for 170 concessioners was reported at
6.87 per cent, the assets at $26 million, the gross income from all
sources at $32 million.[2]

There is fairly general agreement that the average return to concessioners is not excessive; some do well but others lose. The Park
Service does not of course want concessioners to make too much
profit, but they should make enough so that they can offer adequate
service, and make such additions to facilities as are needed. Over
some years in the past there has been a pressing need for expansion
of cabin facilities, and the money for expansion must come largely
from profits, for if the concessioner borrows much, his debts increase the hazards in a naturally hazardous business. All this puts
the Park Service in something of a quandary. It cannot allow the
concessioners to make too much profit in serving the visitors, yet
often wants them to have enough money for expansion. At one time
some contracts required concessioners to spend a percentage of their
gross receipts for better and additional accommodations; but this
did not work satisfactorily.[3]

As we have seen, for years the term of franchises was only ten
years—in Kings Canyon at first only five years—which was quite too
short to attract businessmen, although the right term depended
somewhat on the nature of the concession. A franchise to run stage
lines or rent riding horses would not have had to run as long as
one for building and operating a hotel, for horses and stages could
be taken out of a park at the termination of a lease without very
great loss; yet riding horse facilities in Glacier have often been inadequate and unsatisfactory. No careful businessman—and most
good businessmen are careful—would ordinarily invest his money
in a good hotel or cabins on a ten-year lease, with the possibility
of having to abandon his investment or perhaps sell to someone
else at the end of ten years; a verbal promise by the Secretary or
Director that if he gave good service his franchise would be renewed
could not give him adequate assurance, because Secretaries and
Directors and policies sometimes change. Even if a concessioner
accepted a ten-year lease, without adequate assurance of renewal,

2 *Congressional Record,* 71 Cong. 2 Sess., 3677, 3678; 72 Cong. 1 Sess., 2952;
June 17, 1948, Appendix, 4149. *American Forests,* July 1955, 13.

3 *Report, Secretary of the Interior, 1952,* 376.

he might have a strong incentive to "milk" the lease toward the end, to skimp on upkeep and on service and fudge a bit on prices, if possible, to get as much as possible out of the business before he has to close it out. Not infrequently the Park Service has awarded new concessions before the termination of the old, or in case there were problems to be ironed out, has sometimes given concessions of one year or more until final arrangements could be made. There is no strict rule on concessions.

For the building of good hotels and cabins even a twenty-year lease is not long enough. The concessioner should be able to earn not only a reasonable current return on investment but enough above this to amortize the investment during its reasonable life, which should be longer than twenty years. To amortize the investment in twenty years would call for too high earnings. It is true that the concessioner could plan for amortization over a longer period of thirty or forty years, and if his franchise was renewed he could complete it; or if for any reason his franchise is terminated he might leave a disposable value in his property. In 1958 the maximum term of leases was increased to thirty years.

The franchise should be granted with firm assurance of renewal; and of course the terms of renewal should be as specific as possible, as a matter of fairness and in order to attract the best concessioners. Along with this should go definite arrangements as to the disposition of the facilities in case for any reason—unprofitableness to the concessioner, or dissatisfaction with the service he renders, or any of a score of other reasons—the franchise is not renewed. The Park Service has fully recognized this in recent years, but there are many difficulties in the way of such agreements. To mention one, suppose a concessioner builds a hotel costing $100,000 in the depths of depression, and his franchise ends twenty years later when the cost would be $300,000. If he does not renew, what allowance should he have, cost of *production* or cost of *reproduction?* This question also arises in the allowance for returns on investment. It has never been definitely answered in the general field of public utilities. Many other questions arise: how much allowance should be made for depreciation, for obsolescence (going out of style), how much for shifts in the current of tourist traffic which may increase or reduce the amount of business, how much for the growth or occasionally the decline in tourist business? Generally tourist business has increased, but at the same time there have been declines, as for instance at Mammoth Hot Springs in Yellowstone. A thousand questions arise to plague the park administration.

Perhaps the fundamental difficulty in private ownership and operation of park concessions, as of other public utilities, is that it represents something of a paradox in its reliance on the profit motive to get business efficiency, in a business which should not yield appreciable net profit. We see this in privately operated utilities of all kinds, where some men insist that private operators, powered by the profit motive, do a better job than publicly hired managers, although there are supposed to be no net profits in the operation of such utilities. In the parks, logic would lead to the conclusion that a private concessioner might reach for profits by raising prices, if possible, or by skimping on services.

GOVERNMENT OWNERSHIP AND PRIVATE OPERATION

The government has provided some or all of the facilities in a few areas of the National Park System. In 1910 there were two hotels in Yosemite owned and operated by the government. In 1937 the government was reported as owning the Painted Desert Inn in Petrified Forest, and as operating it the next year because it could find no private concessioner; it was also building the hotel and utility plant at Mount McKinley, to be operated by the government-owned railroad. Two years later the government built facilities at Bandelier, but leased them to a private concessioner. It has also built facilities at Isle Royale and Blue Ridge Parkway, and it owns the facilities at Muir Woods. Usually the government has provided the facilities only when no private concessioner would tackle the job, where it was impossible to make a profit. Here we have a fairly common division of business—the profitable business to private enterprise and the unprofitable business to the government, and then perhaps loud complaints of the inefficiency of the government!

In 1934 Secretary Ickes began to talk about nationalization of concession facilities, and after the war he again took up the cudgels for that policy. In 1946 Ickes' successor, Julius Krug, and Director Drury announced it as a government policy to work for government ownership of all facilities with operation by nonprofit distribution companies or by private enterprise. In 1948 Albright stated that he thought this would be the best policy, but thought it would not come for a long time because of the expense involved. Certainly, government construction and ownership of facilities would offer some advantages. The government can get money at a lower interest rate, would not need to carry insurance—which costs about twice as much as the risk is worth—and could avoid some of the taxes paid by private concessioners to the states. It could sometimes plan better, build better, could maintain regulations more easily. More important, it would be much easier to secure concessioners to operate the facilities than to build and operate them, for buildings represent a long-run investment that is subject to some hazards, and they call for reserves of capital. The Park Service is often hard pressed to find concessioners for some of the parks, and has for years been trying with only fair success to get expansion of facilities. It cannot be said that the building and owning of the concession facilities is too delicate a job for the government: the Park Service is doing things that are quite as difficult—providing sewers and water for the parks. State park facilities are often owned by the state governments.

Government building and ownership of concession facilities would thus be better than private ownership, but it is unlikely that it will come soon, if ever. Not only is there the powerful general hostility to government activities, increasingly puissant in recent years, but with the rising costs of national defense and of the many government functions, and with our growing debt, there is little possibility that Congress will soon vote money for the purchase of present facilities and the building of more. The cost of concessioner fixed assets was reported at $60 million in 1957. It is true that such an expenditure, properly managed, would be an investment and not mere expense, for it should yield a return as it does under private ownership, but there might be a slip-up in this. Whether, if the government owned the facilities, it would be more or less difficult to secure expansion is anybody's guess. The record of Congress in providing for the parks has often been somewhat less than munificent.

One thing is certain: unless there is a definite and realizable plan to turn to government ownership of facilities, it is unwise to agitate for such a policy, for a threat of expropriation naturally frightens private concessioners out of further improvements. Without doubt, Ickes' and Krug's talk of government ownership, and even of operation, had such an effect on the private concessioners in the forties. At that time the Park Service was insisting on an "option to purchase" clause in leases, permitting the government to purchase without regard to the willingness of the concessioners to sell, which also dampened their enthusiasm for park business. Businessmen must feel confidence in the future if they are to do their best.

GOVERNMENT OWNERSHIP AND OPERATION   If government construction and ownership of facilities are impossible of realization, both government ownership and government operation are doubly or triply impossible. Whether such a policy would be wise or not is a difficult question. It would avoid some of the wastes and inconsistencies of private enterprise, just as it does in all public utilities. It would save on accounting and auditing. With private operation the concessioners are obliged to maintain accountants or accounting staffs, and the Park Service has to maintain a staff of auditors to check the accounts. At times the Service, with inadequate funds, has been years behind in its auditing. Under government operation this double expense would be unnecessary. Under government operation there could be better co-operation between concession management and other park activities, better control over the character of buildings constructed—although the Park Service must approve of the location and character of buildings built—better control over the activities sometimes engaged in by private concessioners, as for instance resort-type of activities. Government officials in a well-managed service like the Park Service usually have higher aesthetic standards than private businessmen, and often higher standards in other ways.

The assumption commonly is that private enterprise is more efficient, more progressive, more alert and dynamic than the government—presumably because private businessmen are after profits; but in public utilities they are not supposed to make net profits, only a reasonable return on investment. It is true that because of the ineffectiveness of utility regulation some utilities do make net profits, even handsome profits in some cases, but they are not supposed to earn so much. The park concessioners likewise should not and do not ordinarily make much above expenses and return on investment, and therefore the spur to efficiency is largely lacking. Where they are in a monopoly position there may be inefficiency for that reason also. There is little reason to believe that a private concessioner who is a monopolist and is limited to a modest return will be more efficient than a government employee. The Directors of the Park Service and Superintendents of the parks would probably stand up handsomely beside the leading concessioners, or any group of businessmen paid three or four times as much for their services; and it seems reasonable that they could choose managers to work for the government as well as they choose concessioners to work for themselves. The work in the national parks is very attractive to some men, who will accept employment and work very hard for less than they could earn in private business. Mather and Albright, Cammerer and Drury, Demaray and Wirth, and many others in the Park Service would be examples of this.

Yet there are some advantages in private operation. Private businessmen are perhaps more likely to watch costs carefully; they *may* be more alert to possible changes and improvements—the government often tends toward routine and inertia; businessmen are sometimes more exacting employers and may get more from their employees. More important, if the Park Service were operating the concessions it would have more work to do than when private concessioners are doing a good job. With such concessioners as the Utah Parks Company north of Grand Canyon, and at one time the Northern Pacific in Yellowstone, the Great Northern in Glacier, and the Santa Fe at the South Rim of Grand Canyon, the Park Service, with too much to do anyhow, did not need to devote much attention to concession problems—but of course these were the best of the concessioners. Unsatisfactory private concessioners can cause a great deal of unpleasant work and many headaches.

Whether, if the government ran the concessions as well as they are run by private concessioners, the service would be regarded as favorably by tourists is not certain. There is always some criticism of meals and room accommodations in the parks, as elsewhere; and if the government were providing the services there might be more grumbling—but perhaps not much more, because some park visitors believe that the government does provide the services.

If most private concessioners do not make more than a modest return—and there is fairly general agreement that they do not—the case for government operation does not seem very strong, unless it can be shown that it would be able to effect economies not available to private concessioners. Perhaps, as in the past, it may be adopted only when private concessioners cannot be found.

GOVERNMENT OWNERSHIP AND NONPROFIT OR CO-OPERATIVE OPER-
ATION   Another possible arrangement is government ownership
and nonprofit concession operation, such as we have had with
National Park Concessions, Inc. in Mammoth Cave, Olympic, Big
Bend, Isle Royale, Mount McKinley, Blue Ridge Parkway, Home
of Franklin D. Roosevelt, and Vanderbilt Mansion. It is impossible
to appraise this co-operative management for it has been employed
mostly in areas that private concessioners would not take; but it
should be given a trial in some of the larger parks. In some of the
Scandinavian countries, and indeed in some businesses in the
United States, co-operation has proved successful, not only financially but in the development of a fine civic spirit. It is free of the
logical inconsistency of private operation—reliance on the profit
motive in a business where there should be little or no net profits.
Ickes was actively interested in National Park Concessions, Inc. and
gave it assignments in several park areas; but in recent years Secretary McKay, with his partiality to private business, usually tried to
get private concessioners when he could, and only when there was
no interest was he willing to lease to National Park Concessions, Inc.
In Mount McKinley, for instance, after he found a business concessioner, who failed, his successor, Secretary Seaton, called upon
National Park Concessions, Inc., in 1957, under a temporary lease
which rather closely resembled government operation. The government paid $7,500 for the manager's salary, and made up any deficits
in the operation of the hotel and other services; and if National
Park Concessions, Inc. made any profits above disbursements they
were paid into the United States Treasury.

Another nonprofit distributing organization, Government Services, Inc., was in Ickes' time interested in possible operation of
national park concessions. For many years it has operated cafeterias,
newsstands and similar services for federal workers in government
buildings in Washington, and has provided very satisfactory services.

In conclusion it should be said that a study of concession policies
lends little support to criticism of the policies followed by the Park
Service. There have been mistakes, no doubt, but the Directors
have been able and conscientious men, who usually did the best
job possible under the conditions prevailing.

CHAPTER XXIX

Financing the Parks

Like all activities, private and government, the administration of the parks has to be paid for, financed in some way; and this problem of financing has been critically important since the time when Yellowstone was created in 1872. At that time and for several years afterward, as we have seen, it was commonly assumed that the new park would be self-supporting, that enough money could be got from concessioners to pay the expenses of protection and administration; and this assumption persisted with the establishment of Yosemite and later parks. As late as 1920 Mather still thought that the parks would finally be self-supporting.

In early Yellowstone history, the concessions yielded little or nothing. When some leases were finally made the fees charged were so small that they yielded very little. When the troops were brought in it was assumed that there would be little expense for protection and administration, although Congress appropriated modest sums, gradually increasing, for roads, protection, and administration, particularly for roads. It was still believed that when the roads and administration facilities were established the early parks would be self-supporting. There was as yet no charge for admission to the early parks. There was a gradual increase in concessioner facilities in Yellowstone, and they eventually yielded a small revenue; in 1910 investment by private concessioners in Yellowstone amounted to more than $1 million and total revenues from the concessioners in all the parks were $51,000. In all parks but Crater Lake, Mesa Verde, and Glacier, revenues could be used for administration, but in those three parks they had to be paid into the Treasury. Yellowstone at this time was the only park that had any considerable investment in visitors' facilities, or in roads.

By 1915 Secretary Lane reported the following sources of revenue for the parks:

1. Auto permits
2. Concessions
3. Receipts from public utilities operated by the government—light, telephone, etc.
4. Natural resources—sale of timber, stone, fuel, etc.

The first automobile admission fee was imposed at Mount Rainier in 1908, and in the next few years was used at General Grant (1910), Crater Lake (1911), Glacier (1912), Yosemite and Sequoia (1913), Mesa Verde (1914), and Yellowstone (1915). There were no automobile fees at any of the national monuments until 1939.

In 1917 Albright, reporting for Mather who was ill, outlined the principles that governed Congress in the financing of the parks as follows:

1. The parks, far from centers of population, are not visited by most people, and therefore the burden of maintenance should be shared by those who go there.
2. A large proportion of the travel is local, and therefore the local areas should share the costs.
3. Tourists must pay for the use of roads and streets and for public utilities at home, and should pay similar costs in the parks.

Albright did not approve of the second principle, on the ground that the people in surrounding areas *did* pay for the state roads leading to the parks, especially where the roads led through national forests, which paid no taxes, and on the ground that the towns on these roads provided campgrounds for tourists.

Albright outlined the sources of revenue for the parks at the time
as follows:[1]

1. Taxes on concessions, which might be:
   a) a fixed portion of the authorized rate for services;
   b) a reasonable, arbitrary tax based on the number of guests;
   c) a stipulated annual fee fixed by careful analysis of concessioners' gross revenues, operating expenses, net profits,
   etc.;
   d) a percentage of gross receipts; or
   e) a fair share of net profits.
2. Payments by public utilities, for water, electric power, telephone, etc. These were provided by the Park Service at this
   time.
3. Sale of natural resources—dead timber, stone, hides of predatory animals, etc.
4. Automobile and motorcycle permits.

These revenues were paid in proportion to benefits received rather
than ability to pay. Tourists who went to the parks by train, as most
of them did at the time, presumably paid indirectly in the taxes
paid by hotels and transportation companies, which must maintain
rates high enough to cover their taxes as well as other expenses.

The automobile fees were levied largely for the purpose of paying for roads and improvements. Albright construed the policy of
Congress to be the appropriation of an amount equal to the park
revenues for park purposes, and in addition funds for new construction and general maintenance. Yellowstone needed more roads
than other parks and the automobile fee was highest there—$10.00
in 1916. Since all the parks needed roads, the fees elsewhere were
also rather high—Yosemite $8.00, Mount Rainier $6.00, Sequoia and
Crater Lake $3.00, General Grant $2.50, Mesa Verde and Glacier
$2.00. In 1917 these fees were reduced considerably.[2]

When the Park Service was established in 1916, Mather and Secretary Lane assumed, as Congress and many park men had assumed,
that once the parks were provided with roads and facilities they
would be self-supporting. It seemed not an unreasonable hope.
Here were areas of natural wonders unsurpassed anywhere in the
world, visited by people from all parts of the country (although

1 *Report, Secretary of the Interior, 1917,* 803-7.
2 See *Report, Secretary of the Interior, 1917,* 803 ff.

mostly from the West) and from foreign lands in rapidly increasing numbers. Surely the visitors should and would pay the expense of maintaining and protecting those areas; in fact Yosemite made a profit in 1907, and Yellowstone in 1915 and 1916. In 1916 Mather stated that at least five parks could be made self-supporting—Yellowstone, Yosemite, Mount Rainier, Sequoia, and General Grant. In 1920 Secretary Payne reported that 40 per cent of the appropriation would be returned in revenues. In 1921 the balance was about the same. In 1923 Secretary Work reported that Yellowstone, with $320,000 appropriations and $290,000 revenues, lacked only $30,000 of being self-supporting, and predicted that other parks might approach this when built up. The next year Crater Lake was reported making a little profit.[3]

From about this time on appropriations generally rose faster than revenues—the deficits grew larger absolutely and proportionally, and never again fell to the levels of the early twenties. During the years of lush relief work payments in the Great Depression, appropriations lost about all relationship to revenues. In the late thirties Congress and the Bureau of the Budget voiced criticism of the smallness of the revenues and called for higher fees; and in 1939 Ickes and Cammerer revised the fees upward and assessed fees at some parks where there had been none and at some monuments. This, with more visitors, brought revenues up somewhat. In 1947 Secretary Krug reported that in a number of parks income exceeded expenditures, but for the park system as a whole revenues were only about one-ninth of appropriations. The next year, as a result of a drastic slash in appropriations and a fair increase in receipts, they were about one-third.

Again in 1953, as a result of suggestions from the Bureau of the Budget and the House Appropriations Committee, Secretary McKay and Director Wirth set up a new schedule of fees, differentiating between fifteen-day permits and season or annual permits, the fee for the latter to be double that for the fifteen-day permits. At Yellowstone the trailer fees were raised from $1.00 for fifteen days to $3.00, and for annual permits from $2.00 to $6.00. At Yosemite the fee for passenger cars and trailers was set at $3.00 for fifteen days and $6.00 for a year.[4] This was a move in the right direction. Wirth

---

3 These figures come from reports of the Secretary of the Interior which differ somewhat from recent statistics of the Park Service.

4 *American Forests*, July 1954, 46.

thought it would raise receipts about $1 million, but it fell short of that. In 1956 total appropriations for the park system were $48,866,300, and total receipts $5,065,784—close to one-tenth of appropriations. In the fiscal year 1959, under Mission 66, appropriations rose to $79,962,600 and receipts fell to $5,688,138—about one-fourteenth of appropriations.[5]

The total of 62,812,000 visits to the national park system in 1959 was shared by the various types of areas as follows:

National parks	22,392,000
National monuments	10,696,000
Historical areas	
nonmilitary	6,960,000
military	3,871,000
District of Columbia	4,607,000
Recreational areas	5,336,000
Parkways	8,952,000

THE PARKS DEFICIT   Thus, the deficit of the national parks has grown, both absolutely and relatively, for many reasons. In the first place, the fees charged are much lower than they were in 1916 when the Park Service was established, while the price level has risen greatly. The Yellowstone automobile fee, $10.00 in 1916, when the automobile itself was a luxury, would have to be about $25.00 today to represent the same purchasing power; it is actually $3.00 for a fifteen-day permit. Even if the Yellowstone fee had been left at $10.00, the park would probably be at least self-sustaining. But this would have been politically impossible, for Congress is no longer wedded to the theory of self-sufficiency, and a few men in Congress have even insisted that there should be no charge for admission to the parks.

Another reason for growing deficits is that the Park Service has been adding new areas requiring expenditures, heavy expendi-

5 In addition to automobile fees there are various charges in some of the national parks. Trucks and commercial vehicles pay more than automobiles in several parks, sometimes according to weight—up to $10.00 in Rocky Mountain. There are also guide fees in a number of parks and monuments, and small admission fees in some of the historical parks, elevator fees in a few places, and boat permit and wharfage fees. The fee policy is really fairly complicated. Fees for commercial vehicles, for instance, may be waived for educational, welfare, or scientific groups, for Boy Scouts, Girl Scouts, school children, church organizations and nonprofit organizations, under some circumstances. There are various regulations governing the operation of trucks and buses.

tures in some cases, without yielding a proportionate amount in revenues, or perhaps none at all: historic and military parks, and historic sites, many of which call for an admission fee of only 25 cents; national monuments, which exacted no fees until 1939, and now some of them only $1.00 for a season permit and 50 cents for a fifteen-day permit, and others only 25 cents for admission. For some of these the cost of administration is too low, so they may add little to the deficit. Our seashore project has been rather expensive; the Cape Hatteras National Seashore Recreational Area reported receipts of $5,541 in the fiscal year 1959 and appropriations of $762,853. The parkways add heavily to the deficits; in the 1959 fiscal year Blue Ridge and Natchez Trace reported receipts of less than $10,000 and appropriations of nearly $13 million.

Like many other government agencies, the Park Service has greatly expanded the number of services it affords. More than a hundred museums have been built since Mather's time, which must be maintained—and museums tend constantly to expand. Studies of river basins and reservoir sites, administration of recreation areas, surveys of historic sites—these add considerably to expense. Advice and assistance to the states and local governments on state parks; growing use of the parks for winter activities; research on wildlife, history and archeology—most of these cost more and more. Purchase of privately owned lands in the parks has been a fairly heavy expense in recent years—more than $1.5 million for land and water rights in 1959.

In some ways the quality of the services rendered in the national parks is far better—and of course more expensive—than it was long ago, with better and more roads, better sanitation, better-trained rangers, better protection against fire and insect pests, better accommodations in many ways. It is true that at times the services have been quite inadequate for the crowds that surged into the parks, but there has been general improvement. If we could go back and take a trip through any of the parks as of Mather's time, we would think some of the services very rough and primitive.

The deficit has been growing, and as Mission 66 gets into full swing it seems likely to grow further. Does this seem fair, equitable, and wise, or should the visitors to the parks pay a larger proportion of the expenses—more than about 6 per cent in 1959? Is it equitable to assess against the people of the entire country more than nine-tenths of the cost of the parks that relatively few ever see? The general policy governing this question is that "any service, benefit or privilege furnished by the federal government shall be self-sustaining to the fullest extent possible, taking into consideration such factors as the cost to the government, the value to the recipient, and the public interest served."[6] It hardly seems that the present park deficit represents conformity with this principle.

There is less inequity in this than there was at one time, because in recent years more of the park visitors come from far away and a smaller proportion from the states immediately adjacent to the parks. When, in 1916, of the 10,780 visits to Sequoia, 10,521 were from California; when, in 1920, of 8,143 visits to Mount Rainier, 7,383 were from Washington; and of 115,588 visits to Rocky Mountain, 84,542 were from Colorado, these parks were largely state parks as far as their use was concerned, maintained at the expense of the federal government. As late as 1932, 94 per cent of the Yosemite visits were reported to be from California. Today the percentage of local use is much lower, although still fairly high.

PARK SERVICE EXPENDITURES AND RECEIPTS   The deficit could be reduced either by reducing expenditures or by increasing revenues. Let us consider expenditures first. For the fiscal year 1959 the total appropriations for National Park Service activities amounted to $79,962,600, of which $16,056,200 went to management and protection, $12,477,100 to maintenance and rehabilitation of physical facilities, $50,000,000 to construction, and $1,429,300 to general administrative expenses. The management and protection appropriations were listed as follows:

Management of parks and other areas	$12,415,234
Forestry and fire control	1,122,680
Soil and moisture conservation	102,660
Park and recreation programs	2,103,956
Concessions management	311,670

Maintenance and rehabilitation of physical facilities expenses were divided into:

Roads and trails	$5,314,395
Buildings and utilities	7,162,705

6 Stat. 65, 290.

Construction appropriations included four main categories:

Parkways	$14,782,000
Roads and trails	15,218,000
Buildings and utilities	18,406,800
Acquisition of lands and water rights	1,593,200

Only a rash man would suggest that most of these costs are too high; most of them are too low, as anyone would agree who has been in the parks recently. Perhaps something could be saved in the cost of road construction and maintenance, but that would not be popular. In the parks, as outside, Americans want good roads so that they can drive past the scenery as fast as possible; but if they drove more slowly on somewhat poorer roads they would gain quite as much from a visit to the parks.

Something could be saved if a few of the least worthy parks and parkways could be shifted to the states or disposed of otherwise. In 1959 appropriations for Platt were $92,464, for Hot Springs $222,847, and for Natchez Trace Parkway $5,773,291. Platt and Natchez Trace Parkway should not be in the national park system, and Hot Springs should not be a national park. Disposal of these three units would save more than $6 million. Only three of the parkways should be in the park system—Blue Ridge, Colonial, and Foothills—and there should be a fee for driving on them. In 1955 the Park Service planned to establish a fee of $1.00 for a fifteen-day permit and $2.00 for an annual permit for Blue Ridge, but action was deferred at the request of the House Subcommittee on Appropriations. With about 4 million visitors using the parkway this would raise $2 million, or perhaps even more.

Turning now to the question of receipts, the sources of receipts for the National Park Service in 1959 were as follows:

Total receipts	$5,688,138
Entrance fees	4,741,158
Business concessions	444,206
Rents, royalties, and other earnings	85,265
Permits and licenses	25,136
Sale of government property and products	374,699
Fees for services	1,895
Fines, penalties, and forfeitures	3,882
Recoveries and refunds	11,713
Gifts and contributions	214

TAXES PAID THE STATES   This classification does not show
one of the important items in the national park deficit—the taxes
collected in the parks and paid to the states. Clawson and Held
make a rough estimate that the gasoline taxes alone amounted to
perhaps $1,722,600 in 1955.[7] There seems to be no uniformity in
state taxation of park property or business. The states do generally
tax sales of gasoline, liquor, and goods sold in the parks, personal
property of concessioners, and any equity they may have in buildings or other improvements, but not land, which is owned by the
government. Under the law, they tax franchises and the incomes of
park employees. The Rockefeller lodge and other properties in
Grand Teton, both real and personal property, belong to the company and are taxed by the state of Wyoming like any other property. Property and business in Yellowstone Park should not really
be taxed at all by the state, for the park was established before
Wyoming became a state.

There is no reason why most of the states should collect *any* taxes
in the national parks. When the roads were paid for by assessment
on adjoining property, or from the general funds of the states, or
when the roads ran through national forests which paid only modest
amounts toward their building and maintenance, there was some
justice in giving the states taxes from the national parks; although
from the time the Forest Service was set up in 1905 it has given a
part of its receipts to the counties in which the forests were located,
for roads and schools—10 per cent in 1905, 25 per cent from 1908 to
the present time.[8] Today, when road costs are met largely from
gasoline taxes and from federal subventions, there is no justification for state taxation in national parks. The states get the gasoline
taxes and the Park Service builds the roads.

The great argument for these taxes is that they are needed to
balance the loss in taxes incident to the establishment of the parks,
the argument resting on the assumption that the park land was a
part of the state, *belonged* to the state, which for most western parks
was not true. Most of the western parks were established on forest
reserve lands or on the public domain, which were the property of
the federal government. Occasionally western men show that they
do not understand this—when Wyoming senators, for instance,

7 Marion Clawson and Burnell Held, *The Federal Lands: Their Use and
Management* (Baltimore: The Johns Hopkins Press, 1957), 451.
8 *Ibid.*, 256.

speak of what they "gave" to Yellowstone. Wyoming had nothing to give to or for Yellowstone except political support—which the state did give sometimes, but not always. The western states that had lands in the parks very generally demanded full consideration for them, in money or exchange, when the Park Service wanted them. Yet they often wanted national parks established within their boundaries, for they knew that national parks brought business to the states. The scenery would presumably bring many tourists anyhow, but the stamp "National Park" helps. The states adjoining most of the parks would have profited handsomely from the establishment of the parks, without any tax contributions. This would not be so definitely true of a few wilderness parks, such as Olympic, Kings Canyon, and Everglades, which do not attract large crowds.

As noted in earlier chapters, the Park Service has made various studies as to the amount of money spent by national park tourists. A study in 1950 indicated that tourists spent $19,000,000 in and near Yellowstone Park, $10,965,000 in the vicinity of Great Smoky Mountains, $3,358,000 in and near Crater Lake.[9] It was estimated in 1955 that travel to the parks generated about $2 billion dollars in travel business, from which the state and local governments got about $150 million.

Assume that the states get no tax revenues from the parks: would they be better off if the parks were ceded to them so that they could levy state taxes? For such a park as Carlsbad Caverns this might be true, for Carlsbad Caverns has yielded a profit—only a small profit in 1958—and by raising the fee New Mexico might make a very handsome profit from it. As for most of the other parks, the states would be worse off if they owned them, unless they cut the expenses of operation and let them deteriorate (for the states are less rather than more efficient in government functions), or if they sold them to private interests, which would of course desecrate them. Yosemite, as a private recreation resort, might be made to yield a profit and might pay sizable taxes to the state of California, perhaps more than are now collected in the park; but it would lose some of its scenic qualities, and there would of course be considerable costs of various kinds.

There is no way by which some of the states could cover the expenses of most parks if they had them, and therefore their taxes are not higher because of the parks, but lower. The states gain from

9 *Years of Progress, 1945-52* (Department of the Interior).

them in three ways, without any tax contributions from the parks: from the amount of tourist business brought in, from the privilege of visiting the parks partly at the expense of the federal government, and from the lower taxes that they enjoy because the federal government cares for the parks. When the taxes from the parks are added to these benefits, the parks become very desirable neighbors indeed.

Western politicians are sometimes moved to eloquence when they speak of all that the states have done for the parks; but most of the states have done very little. Wyoming spent about $7,000 trying to protect Yellowstone in 1884—and was later reimbursed; Arizona spent $1,000 in 1923 to protect Tumacacori; Tulare County, California, gave $10,000 in 1921 to buy some giant sequoias, and the state of California gave $8,000 for a survey of Lassen Volcanic in 1923; Colorado built a road across the divide in Rocky Mountain, which she needed anyhow; South Dakota built a road across Badlands. Of course the eastern and southern states gave much of the money and lands for their parks. California, after doing her best to wreck Yosemite in 1905 and after spoiling Hetch Hetchy in 1913, turned to a really generous policy of conserving some of the giant sequoias and coast redwoods.

Most of the western states have done little for the parks. The park rangers protect them; the commissioners administer the law, except for felonies; the Park Service builds and maintains the roads, including some approach roads, the water, sewer, electric and telephone facilities, supervises the concessioners, and maintains such schools as there are in a very few parks. All the states do is take the tax money that should go to help pay for these functions. Then some of their statesmen try from time to time to get, in addition to all this, a 25 per cent cut of the park revenues!

COMPENSATION TO THE STATES FOR OTHER FEDERAL LANDS

The states are really treated too generously on most of the federal lands within their boundaries. The 25 per cent of national forest receipts is more than the states would get from taxes if the forest lands were privately owned, in the long run. One error in many discussions of this lies in the common assumption that if the land were privately owned the only result would be an increase in taxes, without any increase in state expenditures. If the forest lands were

privately owned, the state would have to build the roads, and if
farming, grazing, or lumbering were carried on there would have
to be regulatory and law enforcement agencies, reforestation, fire
control, insect control, watershed protection, wildlife protection and
promotion and, most expensive of all, schools in the area. In the
recreational use of the national forests the states do even better than
in timber sales, for most of the people who use these forests come
from adjacent areas, and fees are paid at only a few of the forest
areas and amount to very little compared with the cost of administration. In the eastern national forests, mostly cut-over forest lands,
purchased under the Weeks Act of 1911 and later acts, the payment
to the states was raised from 5 to 25 per cent in 1914. Here was the
federal government reforesting nearly worthless land that the states
did not want, and giving them 25 per cent of whatever receipts it
might get![10]

On mineral lands the states have fared well. The Mineral Leasing
Act of 1920 gave $37\frac{1}{2}$ per cent of the receipts to the states for roads
and schools, and $52\frac{1}{2}$ per cent to the Reclamation Fund—to be
spent in the West on irrigation. Only 10 per cent was reserved for
the federal Treasury. On grazing lands, the Taylor Grazing Act of
1934 gave 50 per cent to the counties in which the lands were located
but this was used for range improvement: 25 per cent was used
directly for range improvement, and 25 per cent went to the federal
Treasury. In 1947 the act was amended to give the federal Treasury
$87\frac{1}{2}$ per cent, but this was only about enough to pay the costs of
range administration and improvement. On the grazing lands the
federal government is exploited by the stockmen, who have usually
paid fees much lower than would have been fixed by the market.
In the reclamation (irrigation) of arid lands in the West, the receipts from the sale of public lands were used as a Reclamation
Fund; but in 1928 the federal government began to vote money for
reclamation, and so inaugurated one of the most wasteful policies
in our history—the irrigation of lands which when irrigated were
almost all worth less, often much less, than their cost, even with
the addition of water power produced.

The western states have apparently exploited the federal government in the reclamation projects in another way—in taxing the
reclamation facilities after they were built. At any rate, in 1940 the

10 Stat. 38, 415, 441. See Ellis Williams, "National Forest Contributions to
Local Governments," *Land Economics*, Aug. 1955, 204 ff.

states of Arizona and Nevada were authorized to tax the Boulder Canyon Project.[11]

The states have really exploited the federal government on almost all kinds of federal lands; yet some of the western men have been much given to complaints of the burden imposed on them by federal reservation of "their" lands, particularly forest lands. Illustrative of these complaints was a speech in the House by Representative Ferris of Oklahoma in July 1919: "There are 165,000,000 acres of forest reserve scattered through those [western] states. Those lands yield no taxes. Those lands are tax-free. They are to be held as a Government timber supply and it is a very great burden on these States of the West. In this regard the Western States bear the burden for the whole Republic. They furnish the timber supply. They carry the load of State government while these lands are tax free. . . . It is a tremendous draft on those people to have those great forest preserves go tax-free, to have them withdrawn and held in the interior of those states."[12] To this Representative Walsh of Massachusetts very properly replied: "Those of us who have had the honor to be permitted to follow legislation through the Congress in recent years have observed that the West is pretty well taken care of by Uncle Sam's Treasury—the Indians, reclamation projects, the forest reserves, and last but not least, the mighty farmer."[13]

Senator Stanfield of Oregon voiced the western complaint a few years later: "All Government property, which includes the national forests, is untaxable, and that leaves the Government owning these large national forests without contributing any taxes for State government, county government, or schools, yet holding the lands for the benefit of the people of all the States, their children and children's children yet unborn, that they may not want for the products of the forests in the future. The Federal Government is in the position of an absent landlord owning 18 per cent of our lands and paying no taxes. If these forest lands in the 11 Western States were privately owned and therefore taxable, they would pay over $25,-000,000 per year for State and county purposes alone."[14]

The truth is that the western states were living partly on federal subventions, on contributions from the other states, and that if all

11 Stat. 54, 775.
12 *Congressional Record,* July 1, 1919, 2236.
13 *Ibid.,* 2237.
14 *Congressional Record,* Mar. 4, 1925, 5505.

the federally owned lands had been turned over to them to care for, they would have been quite unable to assume the burden of adequate care. In Wyoming, for instance, at one time 34 per cent of the total state revenues came from federal subventions of various sorts, in Nevada 29 per cent, in Idaho 20 per cent, and in Montana 13 per cent. If the federal lands had been turned over to these states, such subventions would have ceased, and only by rapid and wasteful exploitation of the lands could the states have got so much income—for a while only, not for many years.[15] Many of the western people realize this, and in spite of the occasional fulminations of some of their politicians they would not want the states to take over these lands. In recent years some of the western senators and representatives have been leaders in the defense of the parks and in conservation generally—have come to see what Pinchot and Mather and the conservationists saw long ago.

State exploitation of federal lands seems to be inevitable, political forces operating as they do. As Clawson and Held have said: "Within government, pressures for higher prices and higher fees on federal land do, it is true, exist. But they are exerted only occasionally, not continuously, and hence not often effectively. Perhaps in part this may be because in these cases political influence is not sought as persistently as it is when industry and interest groups oppose higher prices and fees.

"The Bureau of the Budget and Appropriation Committees of the Congress may urge a federal agency to make higher charges and collect more for the sale or lease of the lands and their products. But these are only annual pressures and are usually very general in nature."[16]

From a different angle, we may say that the reason why the western men are able to exploit the federal lands in the West in so many ways is that the other men in Congress are usually less interested in guarding the federal Treasury than they are in getting something of a different sort for their own constituents. Congress is a sort of mart where different local economic interests engage in a scramble for local advantage, with little consideration for the general public interest.

15 *American Forests,* Jan. 1930; Mar. 1932, 158; Dec. 1932, 638. *New Republic,* June 1, 1932, 59.

16 Clawson and Held, *op. cit.,* 233.

WAYS OF REDUCING PARK DEFICITS   From the preceding analysis it appears that the most obvious and fair way to reduce the park deficit would be to eliminate the tax payments to the states. These payments were originally intended as compensation for tax losses, and for most of the parks there are no tax losses. Elimination of these tax payments is impossible politically, of course. It is much more likely that the national park states may some day be able to push through a bill giving them 25 per cent of the park revenues, which would be a wholly unwarranted gratuity. Some western men in Congress have been working for that for years, and the Park Service and in 1946 the Secretary of the Interior have approved it, on the ground that it would allay the opposition of western men to the further acquisition of lands for park areas—such as there was to the addition of Jackson Hole, for instance. This does not seem adequate grounds for such an imposition on the federal Treasury. If the western men have to be bribed so heavily to permit new park areas, it would be better to add no new areas, aside from private lands in the parks.[17]

An attempt was made very recently to eliminate the tax contribution in parks that were set up before the states were admitted to the Union—to Yellowstone and perhaps Platt. Nothing came of it.

There is also no reason whatever why the Park Service should build approach roads. These should be built by the states.

If abolition of the park tax contributions is impossible, the next best means of reducing the park deficit would be to raise the entrance fees, which furnish most of the park receipts. Clawson and Held have figured that for the park system the average park receipts per visit are and have been for a number of years about ten cents, while the appropriations are about a dollar per visit; and as they say: "A carload of people can enjoy the resources of one of these parks for many days for less than the cost of a movie or of a single meal."[18] An increase in admission fees would be paid disproportionately by visitors from the neighboring state or states which get

17 *American Forests*, Mar. 1948, 122. Senator Hayden of Arizona tried several times to get state participation in park revenues—S. 257, 77 Cong. 1 Sess. S. 380, 78 Cong. 1 Sess. S. 67, 79 Cong. 1 Sess. Representatives Peterson of Florida, Le Fevre of New York, and Senator Butler of Nebraska also sponsored bills to achieve this.

18 *Op. cit.*, 297.

the tax revenues. The Park Service would get back some of the tax revenues.

As pointed out in an earlier connection, even a considerable increase in the entrance fees—doubling them, let us say—would add little proportionately to the cost of a trip to the parks. The fifteen-day permit at Grand Canyon is $1.00 and the average visitor travels more than 4,000 miles, and spends $508 on the trip on which he sees the park; doubling the entrance fee would raise this total cost to $509. Even at Yosemite, where many of the visitors are from California, the average cost of the trip is $245, which would rise to $248 if the fee were doubled. At Shenandoah the average cost of a trip to the park would go up from $125 to $125.50. The entrance fee at nearly all national monuments is 25 cents or 50 cents, and doubling this should be practically painless, although it is surprising how easily pained some people are in such matters. The truth is that some tourists show unbelievable stinginess at the park entrances. One ranger told the writer that he always disliked to work at the entrance stations because there was so much complaint about the admission fees.

Dr. Marion Clawson, looking forward to a possible total of 300 million or so visits to the parks in the year 2000, suggests that the entrance fees be raised sharply—"to something in the order of $25 where they are now $3. . . ." There can be no doubt that fees as high as this would reduce the number of visitors, but the response to his proposal shows clearly that there would be a great deal of hostility to such a fee. For visitors who take in several parks on a trip, it would make a substantial increase in expense. Clawson suggests also the possibility of adopting a system of reservation requirements to get into the parks, but this would be very hard to administer and would also cause hostility. The states that have at least one national park or part of one within their borders have heavy representation in Congress, particularly in the Senate—all the western states except Idaho and Nevada and a number of states farther east—and it seems likely that they would unite in opposition to a $25.00 fee or to reservation requirements. It is difficult to conceive of 300 million visitors anyhow. How could they possibly get into the parks?[19]

However, entrance fees are so low that they could be raised considerably without reducing the number of visitors very much, but

19 *National Parks Magazine*, July 1959, 3; Oct. 1959, 16.

of course the visitors are of different natures and interests, of different financial and cultural resources, and they come to the parks for different reasons and in different ways. Each class would presumably react in a different way to higher entrance fees. Those who visit a park as the main purpose of their travel, who "go to see Yellowstone," or some other park, might be little affected. On the other hand, there are visitors whose main destination is beyond a park, who go through the park incidentally, willing to pay a small fee rather than take another road, but not enough interested to pay very much. Such parks as Great Smoky Mountains, Rocky Mountain, and Shenandoah have many such visitors, people who use the park roads as parkways and might use them considerably less at higher fees. The "repeaters"—the citizens of San Francisco who run up to Yosemite for frequent week-ends—presumably would react in the same way because they would have to pay often and because scenery seen often is likely to lose some of its attraction. In general, the average length of stay might tend to be longer.[20]

It is impossible to draw a "demand curve" for entrance to the national parks, to tell how much the number of visitors would decline if entrance fees were raised. If the number declined very little, the park deficit would at least be reduced; if the number declined considerably, that would be good in another way, for there are too many people in some of the parks, too many particularly who do not really care much for what they see.

Aside from the effect of higher fees on the number of visitors, there would doubtless be some increase in hostility to the parks among the people nearby. There might, however, be somewhat less hostility in other parts of the country, where the people have to pay for park maintenance yet cannot easily go to see the parks.

The deficit has been growing. Seemingly this is in accord with the trend of taxation over the years, for the benefit theory of taxation—assessing costs according to benefit received—is stressed less today than it was in Mather's time. In recent years there has been more emphasis on the ability to pay in assessing taxes (costs), and on the "general good" arising from government expenditures.

Yet there is some validity in the benefit theory, and visitors to the parks should pay more than 6 to 12 per cent of the expense of

[20] On this subject see a paper by Marion Clawson, *Methods of Measuring the Demand for and Value of Outdoor Recreation*, Reprint No. 10 (Washington: Resources for the Future, 1959).

maintaining them. Those visitors who would be willing to pay the full expense are getting a subsidy from the taxpayers of the United States which they enjoy to the full extent of the subsidy; those who would not be willing to pay more than the present fee are getting the same subsidy, but it means nothing to them. Here the subsidy represents mere waste of capital and energy, except to the extent that the park visit is educational; and the visitor who rates a trip through Yellowstone at $3.00 and no more is probably allergic to education. The visitor who would be willing to pay full cost is more likely to get educational value.

Not only should there be a general increase in entrance fees, but fees should be imposed at a few parks where there are none now. With the Park Service allocating $1,927,056 to Great Smoky Mountains in 1959 there should be an entrance fee, as on any turnpike. The cases of Everglades, Mount McKinley, Isle Royale, Olympic, and Big Bend are very different, and probably call for no entrance fees.

On the other side of this question there are those who think there should be no entrance fees at all. When Ickes raised fees in 1939 Senator Reynolds called it a "vicious practice," "an unjustifiable and unnecessary tax on the health and recreation of the American people. . . . Surely," he said, "we have not come to the point where there should be a tax on fresh air, scenery and history."[21] The answer to this is that there *is* a tax on the fresh air, scenery, and history in the national parks and monuments; the question is whether that tax shall be paid partly by the people who enjoy these things or altogether by the people generally. Air, scenery, and history, like salvation, are in a certain sense free, but someone must pay the cost of maintaining the parks—and churches. In January 1932 Senator Smoot of Utah introduced a bill to prohibit any charge for admission to the parks.[22] This was probably a popular gesture to make, although the fees at the Utah parks have been quite too low. Not many years ago the fee was $1.00 for Zion, Bryce, and the North Rim of Grand Canyon—for *all* of them—yet a park ranger told the writer that some people complained because it was so high.

The Park Service has been reluctant to impose fees that would make it difficult for people of small means to see the parks, and this is commendable; but some of the taxes paid in the east and central

21 *Congressional Record*, 76 Cong. 1 Sess., Appendix, 1287 ff.
22 S. 2762, 72 Cong. 1 Sess.

parts of the country are paid by people of small means too, most of whom do not see the parks. It is likely that park visitors have at least average incomes, perhaps above average, and the Park Service cannot establish its fees with much regard to economic inequalities. Furthermore, most of the people who spend hundreds of dollars cruising around in the national park country can afford higher park fees without taking bread from their children's mouths. They can just skimp a little on gasoline if necessary.

If the Service wished to make allowance for economic inequalities it could do so by imposing higher fees on the hotels and cabins with bath, which are used by visitors of generally higher incomes than the "cabins with path" and campgrounds. These higher fees presumably would be shifted to the visitors. It is doubtful if this would be wise, however. The hotels have had rough sledding in past years, and their rates are fairly high now. Furthermore, the public has everywhere turned somewhat away from hotels to cabins and motor courts, and it would be unfortunate further to burden the hotels.

Perhaps there should also be some distinction among automobile entrants, according to the number of passengers. Various schemes have been considered, but any such scheme would have to be approved by the Park Service, which would know how many complications would be involved and how much would be gained.

Thus, by elimination of a few of the least worthy parks, by abandoning responsibility for several of the parks and parkways and by charging a fair fee for admission to the others, by eliminating the tax gratuities to the states, and by raising the fees drastically, the national park deficit could be reduced very considerably. As suggested elsewhere, the fixed fee on concessioners should be abolished.

The national park deficit should be reduced drastically, but it should not be eliminated; visitors to the park system should not pay the entire cost of maintaining the *system*, for some of the work of the Service is for the general public good, and not for the benefit of visitors to the scenic parks alone—such activities as advice and assistance to state parks, planning of recreation areas, saving of archeological and paleontological objects, and research in many fields. Such scenic parks as Yellowstone, Yosemite, and Crater Lake might well be somewhere near self-supporting, but not the park system. Some of the activities—even the maintenance of the great scenic parks, and more definitely that of protecting and maintaining the archeological and historical areas—are educational and deserving of public support.

Whatever may be said as to the justice of reducing the national parks deficit, by eliminating the unfair state tax collections, by raising the entrance fees or otherwise, there can be little hope of accomplishing very much; too many states participate in the booty. There are over twenty states that have all or a part of a national park, or perhaps several, within their boundaries; and if national monuments, military and historical parks, parkways, and national recreation areas are included, many more than half the states have from one to several areas in the national park system, many of which share in the advantages of the federal subsidy. It is difficult to imagine Congress approving measures that would go very far toward balancing the park budget.

One thing might well be done in this matter. Perhaps visitors to the parks should be informed as to how little they pay of the total expenses of their visits, and how much is paid by the taxpayers of the country. On the admission slips this could be stated clearly, so that the visitors would know what a bargain they are getting. This might tend to reduce complaints and build up good will.

Granting that the federal government pays too much of the cost of maintaining the parks, the burden is not very heavy compared with some other items of expense borne directly or indirectly by the people. At $80 million, appropriations are only a little more than the *cost of advertising liquors*—about six-tenths of one per cent of the cost of liquors, one-third of the cost of outdoor advertising (billboards), six-tenths of one per cent of the total amount wasted in advertising, one-tenth of the cost of our tariff—which is for the benefit of particular industries, at the expense of all the people. Surely our national parks have a greater educational and cultural value than any of these! Viewed thus comparatively, our park appropriations are a bagatelle, and our national parks a splendid bargain; but of course they would be a still better bargain if they cost less, and the cost would be less onerous if it were fairly distributed.

CHAPTER XXX

Wilderness Areas

✣ The movement for the preservation or establishment of wilderness or primitive areas is not a development of recent years only; it began before Yellowstone was established, and became a fairly strong movement late in Mather's administration. In recent years, however, it has gained more and more support, from conservation organizations and from the general public.

The terms "wilderness," "primitive," "wild," "roadless," "natural," "scenic," "sacred," and "limited" have been used in somewhat confusing manner. At first the Forest Service used the term "wilderness," but later changed this to "primitive" and still later back again to "wilderness," while the Park Service at first used the term "primitive" and later changed this to "wilderness." Recent regulations of the Forest Service with regard to areas that are withheld from commercial exploitation use the term "wilderness" for areas of more than 100,000 acres, and "wild" for areas of 5,000 to 100,000 acres. In 1933 Albright recognized also "sacred" areas, set apart to safeguard unique features of national parks, with no buildings or roads permitted, and "research" areas in national parks and monuments, to be held unmodified in character and administra-

639

tively isolated from entrance (except in emergency or by special permit) and left undisturbed by man-made development, for purposes of scientific investigation and education. Years later it seems to have occurred to the Park Service that since nearly all of every national park was really wilderness the terms "sacred" and "research" had no definite meaning and they were dropped.[1]

Man has always had something of a hankering for the wilderness, a longing to get away from the artificialities of civilization and lose himself in natural surroundings that are unmarred by man; but in our earlier history this longing presented no problems, for the wilderness seemed illimitable. The frontier was itself something of a wilderness, and until about 1890 or 1900 America always had a frontier, moving steadily westward into the wilderness, converting it to settled habitations of men, or to a wasteland.

More than a century ago, however, there were expressions of interest in the preservation of wilderness areas, one of the first being from George Catlin (1832-39), the painter of Indian and frontier scenes. A decade or so later, Thoreau began to write of the joy of wilderness life as an escape from the artificialities of ordinary life and a source of physical, moral, and intellectual power.[2] The greatest of the lovers of wilderness, and the one who did most to promote the idea of wilderness preservation, was John Muir, who wandered about the Sierra in California, up into Oregon, Washington, and Alaska, as far east as Grand Canyon and down to the Gulf of Mexico, studying geology, wildlife, botany—almost everything—and writing of his travels and observations with poetic enthusiasm and power. A most remarkable man, John Muir knew perhaps more about the western wilderness than anyone else of his time, loved it, and tried to save the best of it. He had much to do with the creation of Yosemite Park, and in 1892 formed the Sierra Club, which became an amazingly active and effective organization, in the front ranks in every battle for the parks, the forests, and for conservation generally, more and more interested in wilderness preservation as the years passed.[3]

1 *Living Wilderness*, Winter-Spring 1958, 14.
2 There is a Thoreau Society in New England today.
3 See James P. Gilligan, "The Development of Policy and Administration of Forest Service Primitive Areas in the Western United States," a Ph.D. thesis at the University of Michigan, 1953. The writer has made extensive use of this scholarly work. On John Muir, see *American Forests*, Apr. 1958, 33.

John Burroughs, a little after Muir's time, was a naturalist and writer with some interest in nature and the wilderness. Still later, Enos Mills spent many years exploring the Rocky Mountains in Colorado, writing and drumming for the establishment of Rocky Mountain National Park—and later damning the Park Service. Theodore Roosevelt was from early life an ardent lover of the wilderness, something of a naturalist, and a writer of no mean ability.

Beginning at the time of the Civil War, a number of conservation, scientific, and recreation societies were established, and many of them favored the establishment of wilderness areas: the National Academy of Sciences (1862), the Alpine Club (1863), the White Mountain Club (1873), the American Forestry Association (1875), the Appalachian Club of Boston (1876), the Rocky Mountain Club of Denver (1875), the American Association for the Advancement of Science (1880), the Boone and Crockett Club (1885), the National Audubon Society (1886), the Sierra Club (1892), the Mazamas of Oregon (1894), the New York Zoological Society (1895), the Campfire Club of America (1897), the Society of American Foresters (1900), the American Civic Association (1904), the Seattle Mountaineers (1906), the National Conservation Association (1909), the Wildlife Protective Association (1910), the American Game Protective and Propagation Association (1911), and some others.

There were other organizations and institutions that took an active part in the wilderness movement from about 1920 on: The Ecological Society of America, the Roosevelt Wildlife Experiment Station, the Carnegie Institution, the New York State Museum, the Conservation Council, the American Society of Mammalogists, the National Parks Association, the National Geographic Society, the Geological Society of America, the American Nature Association, the Wilderness Society, the American Planning and Civic Association, and some of the federal bureaus, such as the Fish and Wildlife Service. The zoological and wildlife and botanical organizations usually supported proposals for wilderness areas because such areas were particularly useful for their studies.[4] Wilderness areas should be natural, not only with respect to the land and the forests and lakes and rivers, but also with respect to the wildlife, which should not ordinarily be subjected to shooting, trapping, poisoning or management; but this principle is sometimes violated. Wilderness men

4 *National Parks Magazine*, Apr.-June 1944, 3.

do not approve of killing wolves in Mount McKinley, or of poisoning prairie dogs in the parks.

The first wilderness areas were of course the early national parks, from Yellowstone on down; but even the early national parks were not quite pure wilderness. Most of them had to have roads and trails if the people were to see and enjoy them, as well as eating and overnight accommodations, which of course modified the wilderness character of the parks to some extent. Also, hunting was allowed in the Yellowstone Act, by implication at least, for the Secretary was merely authorized to provide against the "wanton destruction of the fish and game," and "against their capture or destruction for the purposes of merchandise and profit." These provisions were repeated in the acts setting up Sequoia and Yosemite. The wildlife in Yellowstone was not given adequate protection until 1894, in the Lacey Act. In yet another respect the parks, down to the early thirties, fell short of pure wilderness character; predators were being killed from fairly early times. In a pure wilderness there would have been no hunting and no killing of predators. No national forests were set aside until after Yellowstone, Mackinac, Sequoia, Yosemite, and General Grant had been established, and these national forests were open to hunting and various commercial uses.

The specific designation of wilderness or primitive areas, however, came first in the national forests. Until 1897 the forest reserves were really "reserves" with no provision for protection or use. In 1905 they were transferred to the Department of Agriculture and Chief Forester Gifford Pinchot, who had been appointed Forester in 1898, set about to winnow out the incompetents, establish an efficient Forest Service, and develop forestry—the management of forest lands primarily for timber production. Pinchot seemed strangely uninterested in scenic values, uninterested in the national parks, even hostile to the idea of wilderness preservation. In 1897 he had got into a quarrel with John Muir and the preservationists, and later, as we have seen, he was partly responsible for the rape of Hetch Hetchy.[5] He may have been wise in his opposition to wilderness areas, for such areas might have brought so much local hostility that the whole forest reservation policy would have been overturned. It was maintained by a rather precarious balance in some of the earlier years; in fact in 1907 the President's power to set aside

5 See pp. 86, 87.

forest reserves was taken away, for the six important timber states of the West.[6]

There was a powerful movement at the time, led by the western anti-conservationists, to abolish the forest reserves, and it very nearly succeeded. Pinchot's policy was generally (1) to get the support of the local people, and (2) to maintain the principle of multiple use—use of the forest reserves for timber, grass, water, minerals, and for hunting and recreation, although he did not stress recreation very much.

WILDERNESS PRESERVATION IN THE FORESTS   W. B. Greeley, who became Chief Forester in 1920, was more interested in recreation, and soon developed a considerable interest in wilderness preservation, spurred to it by the aggressive efforts of Mather to take more and more of his national forests for new national parks and additions to parks. Areas in the national forests which had little commercial timber, usually high in the mountains, scenic, and therefore what the Park Service might want, and inaccessible, could be established as primitive or wilderness areas, and so perhaps kept out of the hands of the Park Service. For some years there was a sort of race between the Forest Service in the establishment of primitive areas and the Park Service in adding to the park areas. Recurring proposals to take the national forests over into the Department of the Interior also encouraged the establishment of primitive areas.

Interest in wilderness preservation in the national forests got a fillip in 1921 from a proposal of Aldo Leopold for a Gila Wilderness Area in the Gila National Forest in New Mexico and Arizona, a scenic area, still largely a wilderness, with some cliff dwellings and historic associations running back to the time when it was a battleground of the Apache Indians. Leopold wanted one large wilderness area in each western forest, free of roads and modern developments, as a protest against motor recreation. There was not much immediate interest in his proposal; but in 1924, the Gila Wilderness Area of 695,000 acres was approved by the district forester of New Mexico and Arizona, and by 1925 five similar areas had been

6 Stat. 34, 1271. Senator Fulton of Oregon, who introduced the amendment to an appropriation bill taking away this right, had been heavily implicated in Oregon land frauds a few years before.

set up in the West. In October 1925 Leopold published a strong appeal in *American Forests and Forest Life*, "The Last Stand of the Wilderness," which brought out some discussion among foresters and conservationists. The sportsmen, too, presently saw that here was a good setup for them, for hunting was allowed in forest wildernesses, and the sportsmen's organizations were very strong politically in the western states. Hunters and fishermen helped substantially in balancing some budgets. In the year 1950-51 fishing licenses brought in nearly $12 million.

The dude ranchers also were enthusiastic. They saw that wilderness areas were good pasture, and there were quite a few dude ranchers. It will be remembered that the dude ranchers and packers were largely responsible for the fact that the Park Service was never able to add to Yellowstone the high Thorofare region southeast of that park. The High Sierra Packers' Association of California was formed in 1937, and the next year claimed 160 packers wholly dependent on wilderness areas, and 770 resorts with $30 million capitalization.

In allowing hunting the Forest Service had an advantage over the Park Service, which did not permit hunting. By 1926 Greeley saw that in the wilderness areas recreation would be a highly important if not dominant use, and in December of that year he set up regulations permitting not only hunting but grazing, some improved campgrounds where needed to prevent fire, and rough shelter cabins. These regulations were more liberal than those of the Park Service and so brought friendlier public relations. It is true that the Park Service allowed grazing in some parks, but always with an eye to its eventual elimination. Greeley's policy no doubt slowed down the spread of national parks.

As a further effort to popularize the wilderness areas in the national forests, the American Forestry Association in 1933 organized the Trail Riders of the Wilderness, groups of outdoor lovers who rode horseback through these areas under supervision of a forest ranger. This plan was first proposed by a railroad executive hoping to stimulate passenger business. He offered to find packers who would reduce prices on a two-weeks' trip if the Association would guarantee a minimum number of riders. The Association has done a fine public service in providing these trips, for the Trail Riders always remember their trips with deep appreciation.

Strongly influential in wilderness preservation in the national forests was one Robert Marshall, like Mather a millionaire with a burning, almost Messianic zeal for a wilderness policy. For some years he worked at wilderness exploration and in 1935, with Yard and a few others, established the Wilderness Society and published the *Living Wilderness,* which Marshall financed. At first the Forest Service paid little attention to him, but Chief Forester Silcox became interested and from about 1935 on gave more attention to recreation, and also to wilderness areas. Marshall persuaded the Commissioner of Indian Affairs to set aside twelve roadless areas of more than 100,000 acres and two wild areas in the Indian reservations, which were established by Ickes in October 1937. In May 1937 Silcox brought Marshall into the Forest Service as Chief of the Recreation and Lands Division where he worked with the zeal of a crusader, but became discouraged with the results of his labors. He would have quit the Forest Service, but in September 1939 the Secretary of Agriculture issued new regulations providing for "wilderness" areas of over 100,000 acres, which must have the approval of the Secretary of Agriculture, and "wild" areas of 5,000-100,000 acres, which required only the approval of the Chief Forester. Roads and commercial timber cutting were prohibited in these areas.

WILDERNESS PRESERVATION IN THE PARKS   Although the specific designation of wilderness areas came first in the national forests, it should not be assumed that the national parks lagged in wilderness preservation, for almost all of every national park was held in a wilderness state—wilderness in a stricter sense than the specifically designated wilderness areas in the national forests, because in the parks no commercial uses are allowed except a little grazing in some parks, and mining in a few park areas, authorized by Congress against the opposition of the Park Service. The roads and visitor accommodations even in the most extensively developed park in the system—probably Yellowstone—cover only a small fraction of the total area; and a fairly typical plan in several of the parks is of one road across the park. This is true of Yosemite, Glacier, Rocky Mountain, and Great Smoky Mountains. On the roads and at concession points the parks were presently to look like anything but wilderness as the crowds of people swarmed in.

The national parks were more rigorously guarded from all commercial developments than were the wilderness areas of the national forests, and they were more secure from boundary alterations or eliminations, because they were set up by actions of Congress and could be altered or eliminated only by Congress, whereas the national forest wilderness areas could be changed or eliminated at any time by departmental order.

The need for preservation of extensive wilderness areas in the parks was recognized by Mather, and in 1924 he stated it well:

> It is not the plan to have the parks gridironed by roads, but in each it is desired to make a good sensible road system so that the visitors may have a good chance to enjoy them. At the same time large sections of each park will be kept in a natural wilderness state without piercing feeder roads and will be accessible only by trails to the horseback rider and the hiker.[7]

More of the national parks established in recent years have been largely wilderness in character—Isle Royale, Olympic, Everglades, and Kings Canyon—but this does not signify any change in the park policy of Congress or the Park Service but is merely a recognition of peculiar characteristics of those areas, or of other circumstances.

Roads are generally frowned upon by the wilderness lovers. Trails, for hikers and perhaps for horseback riders, are more generally approved because they provide more intimate contact with nature, call for some exertion and effort, and do not scar the natural landscape so much. Serious erosion sometimes develops along mountain roads, particularly if they are badly planned. Along the trails there are sometimes shelters here and there for protection against rain and inclement weather. About 8,000 miles of trails have been built in the national parks, particularly in the more definitely wilderness parks—Olympic, Isle Royale, Acadia, Great Smoky Mountains, and in Kings Canyon where the famous John Muir Trail runs along the high Sierra.

There are thousands of miles of trails outside the national parks. In 1932 Clinton C. Clarke proposed a wilderness trail, for hikers and horsemen, from Canada to Mexico, through Washington, Oregon, and California. Much of this trail is now available to hikers. In 1932 the Federation of Outdoor Clubs was organized, soon to include about twenty-five hiking and mountain-climbing organizations. There is a Long Trail, a wilderness footpath along the ridge

[7] *Report, Director, Park Service, 1924,* 14.

of the Green Mountains of Vermont, from the Massachusetts line to Canada; an Appalachian Trail from Mount Katahdin in Maine to Georgia; and there are many trails in the Shenandoah National Park and Blue Ridge Parkway.[8]

Since the early thirties the Park Service has been subject to some criticism from a growing number of "purists" and wilderness lovers, who want only the most splendid areas included in the park system, and want them kept more largely as wilderness areas, with few roads or none at all, who object to the attention the Park Service gives to historical and battlefield parks and monuments, recreation areas, state parks, and various "side issues." As we have seen, Albright, Cammerer, and Wirth were sometimes accused of departing from "pure park standards." In the purist and wilderness camp have been the National Parks Association, the Wilderness Society, the Sierra Club, and a number of other conservation organizations, although there has of course been some diversity in the views of members of these organizations. At times the attacks of the purists and wilderness lovers have been fairly vigorous, and have been resented by men in the Park Service.

It is impossible to make a fair appraisal of the merits of this controversy. Many of the critics have been sincere, devoted men and women, some of them distinguished and widely known authorities in their various fields, worthy of a respectful hearing; but the men in the Park Service have also been sincere, and devoted to "national park standards" as they understand them; and they are in a good position to understand them. No one should be categorical in defining "national park standards" or "pure park standards," for there can be different conceptions of these terms. The establishing acts and the National Parks Act of 1916 called for the preservation of the scenic wonders unimpaired for future generations, but they also called for development of tourist facilities, explicitly or by implication. The Park Service has never believed that it was not maintaining national park standards, except when forced by Congress to permit grazing, mining, or other improper activities. Most National Park leaders have thought of themselves as wilderness men.

The difference between some of the Park Service administrators—Albright, Cammerer, Drury, Demaray, and Wirth—and the purists

8 *American Forests*, Sept. 1936, 395; Oct. 1938, 470; July 1940. *A Study of the Park and Recreation Problem of the United States* (Washington: National Park Service, 1941), 126. See also *Living Wilderness*, Summer-Fall 1957, 19.

who have scolded them for too much development of the parks—
for "departing from true park standards"—is to some extent the difference between men who have a practical job to do, in getting new
parks, in making the parks accessible to the public, in making
friends for them, and in protecting them from the invasion of commercial interests, on the one hand, and on the other hand men of
fine idealism who do not have these responsibilities. Too rigid
maintenance of wilderness standards, too few roads and accommodations, might have endangered the parks. The parks are safer when
they have many friends who have seen their wonders. It is quite
possible that some of them might have been abolished or invaded if
they had been kept as inviolate wilderness areas, with no roads.
Dinosaur would have been safer if there had been good roads into
the canyons, and Olympic would be safer today if there were a good
highway from which the mountains and some of the great forests
could be seen. In some of the attacks on Olympic there has been
criticism of the wilderness character of the park and of the conse-
quent small numbers of tourists.

The purists and the wilderness advocates have performed a real
service in stressing the dangers of over-development and the value
of wilderness preservation, for most political forces push the Park
Service in the direction of development, and park Directors have
not always been free of the common bureaucratic ambition for
growth and expansion. The purists and wilderness people have done
a particularly valuable service in stressing the need for wilderness
areas in the national forests and indeed in working hard for conservation generally.

So there can be no definite appraisal of the criticisms the purists
and wilderness lovers level at the Park Service. Here we have simply two opposing views, both honestly held. To the writer, the Park
Service seems to have followed a generally middle-of-the-road policy
in balancing development against wilderness preservation.

The first Wilderness Conference was held in Berkeley, California,
in 1947 and has been held in alternate years since then. A Pacific
Northwest Wilderness Conference, sponsored by the Federation of
Outdoor Clubs and held in Portland April 7 and 8, 1955, was devoted to the various aspects of wilderness preservation; and the 24th
Annual Conference of the Federation of Western Outdoor Clubs
on Labor Day, 1955, was much concerned with wilderness area expansion. The conference urged establishment of the Glacier Peak

Wilderness Area and the Mount Washington and Diamond Peak Wild Areas in Washington, the Three Sisters Wilderness Area in Oregon, and a wilderness area in Alaska. The federation further-more voted to devote its next meeting to the discussion of a proposal for a national wilderness system; and at its 1956 meeting the feder-ation adopted a resolution urging the creation of such a system.[9]

A "NATIONAL WILDERNESS PRESERVATION SYSTEM" In re-sponse to widespread agitation for wilderness preservation, bills to establish a national wilderness preservation system were in-troduced in 1956, in the second session of the 84th Congress, by Representatives Saylor of Pennsylvania, Metcalf of Montana, Reuss of Wisconsin, and Miller of California, and by Senator Humphrey, the fighting conservationist from Minnesota, the Humphrey bill co-sponsored by Neuberger and Morse of Oregon, Mrs. Smith of Maine, Lehman of New York, Duff of Pennsylvania, Douglas of Illinois, Kuchel of California, Mundt of South Dakota and Laird of West Virginia.[10] The Saylor bill in the House and the Humphrey bill in the Senate were identical, and they were drawn with the help of leading conservationists of the wilderness persuasion.

The Saylor and Humphrey bills—and the others were similar—were designed to provide for continued preservation of wilderness areas, eighty in the national forests, covering 14 million acres; twenty-seven in national parks, twenty-one in national monuments, one in a recreational area and one in a memorial park; thirteen in national wildlife refuges and seven in ranges; and fifteen in Indian reservations—subject to the approval of the Indians. These areas were to constitute the wilderness preservation system. Additions to the system might be made by Congress or by the President, but eliminations must have Congressional approval. There was to be no change in the jurisdiction over the areas, but a Council was set up to keep records and manage various details.

The Saylor and Humphrey bills, briefly, were designed to "nail down" the wilderness areas, make it difficult to eliminate them, or to administer them in any way but as wilderness areas. They were supported by the National Parks Association, but encountered

9 *Living Wilderness*, Fall and Winter 1956-57, 30.
10 H. R. 11703, H. R. 11751, H. R. 11791, H. R. 11806, S. 4013, 84 Cong. 2 Sess.

immediate opposition from the American Forestry Association,
which wanted flexible control over national forest wilderness areas,
and by the Park Service, which believed that the bill not only would
not provide any better protection for park wilderness areas than
was already provided, but would weaken national park wilderness
protection—"reduce it to the low common denominator of all
wilderness," as one national park leader said. Since the national
parks were already mostly wilderness areas, unchangeable except
by Congressional decree, the wilderness bills did not have much
pertinence with respect to them; they had greater significance with
respect to the national forests and other federal areas.[11] These bills
were introduced too late in the 84th Congress to stand any chance
of passing, but several bills were brought up again in the next
Congress, early in 1957, by Saylor, Humphrey, Metcalf of Montana,
O'Hara of Illinois, Baldwin of Illinois, and Ruess of Wisconsin.[12]

A few days after Humphrey introduced his second wilderness
bill, on February 11, 1957, Acting Secretary of Agriculture True D.
Morse proceeded to demonstrate the need of a wilderness law for
the national forest wilderness areas by cutting 53,000 acres from
the Three Sisters Wilderness Area in Oregon. This beautiful area
of 246,728 acres had been designated as wilderness in 1937, but
early in 1957 Morse turned over 53,000 acres to the lumbermen in
spite of protests from many conservation organizations and from
Senator Morse of Oregon.[13] At the same time, he announced the
establishment of the Diamond Peak and Mount Washington wild
areas, two small areas not far away; but the wilderness advocates
were very unhappy to lose so much of Three Sisters.

The wilderness proposals met stubborn opposition in the hearings again; and in the next session Humphrey and Saylor brought
up a new bill, toned down in some respects to meet the objections
that had been raised.[14]

This bill covered national forests, national parks, wildlife
refuges, and Indian reservations. In the national forests the Secretary of Agriculture might designate wilderness areas after not less

11 *American Forests*, Aug. 1956, 11.
12 H. R. 500, S. 1176, H. R. 361, H. R. 540, H. R. 906, H. R. 1960, 85 Cong.
1 Sess.
13 *Living Wilderness*, Fall and Winter 1956-57, 32; Spring 1957, 24
14 S. 4028, H. R. 13013, 85 Cong. 2 Sess.

than ninety days' public notice. In the national parks the Secretary
of the Interior was given ten years in which to designate wilderness
areas, but after ninety days' public notice. For the wildlife refuges
and game ranges the Secretary was to designate wilderness areas
within five years. For the Indian reservations no time was specified,
but no wilderness reservation was to be made without consultation
with the Indian tribal councils. There could be no addition to,
modification of, or elimination of any wilderness area except after
ninety days' notice and hearings, and it should take effect only
after 120 days of Congressional session, and if no Congressional
resolution had been passed forbidding such action. Thus, the bill
would have made it difficult to modify or eliminate wilderness
areas. Prospecting, mining, water-conservation works and, under
some conditions, grazing were to be permitted. As in the earlier
bills, a council was to be set up to keep records.

Again there were hearings where twenty-two national conservation organizations and fifty-five state and local organizations testified for the bill, and various organizations registered opposition:
the American Forestry Association; the Farm Bureau—representing business and big farmers; the Engine Boat Manufacturers—
fearing that boats might not be allowed in the wilderness areas;
the American Pulpwood Association; the Navajo Tribal Council;
the Upper Colorado River Commission; the National Cattlemen's
Association; the National Lumber Manufacturers' Association; the
Department of Water Resources of California; the Interstate Stream
Commission of New Mexico; the American Mining Congress; the
Chamber of Commerce of the United States; stockmen and other
business and commercial interests, led by Senators Barrett and Watkins and Representative Bennett. General Counsel Arthur Lazarus,
Jr., of the Indian Association, suggested that the Secretary should
not be authorized to set up wilderness areas in Indian reservations
after merely "consulting" the Indian authorities, but should be required to get permission of the Indians.

The opposition was too strong, and the bill made no progress;
but early in 1959, in the 86th Congress, Humphrey and Saylor
again brought up wilderness bills which, although somewhat
changed again to meet some of the objections urged, encountered
stiff opposition, particularly from western men.[15] This time, Secre-

15 S. 1123, H. R. 1960, 86 Cong. 1 Sess.

tary Seaton expressed approval. The present outlook for a wilderness system is not bright.[16]

WILDERNESS VERSUS DEVELOPMENT   How much of the national park areas should be kept as a wilderness, and how stringent should be the rules against roads, development, and use, is a perennial problem with the Park Service, and it is also a problem with the Forest Service. We have seen how good roads have brought such floods of tourists to the parks, some of whom care little for the scenic wonders, that a few areas have lost about all charm or have indeed become slums. James Truslow Adams once said: "Because twenty people can enjoy a beauty spot, it does not follow that two thousand can. . . . There seems to be a law that although up to a certain point we can increase the number of people who can have, see, and enjoy, if we go beyond a certain point instead of giving everybody everything, nobody has anything."[17] There is some truth in this, but it puts the case against crowds too strongly. The two thousand must have found something, or they would not have come.

It is true, too, that as population increases and more people take to the road, the wilderness area constantly shrinks; and there is something satisfying to the soul—to *some* souls—in the quietness and serenity of the wilderness, in being away from the hurrying crowds and the roar and clangor of ubiquitous machines, away from business and commerce, away from all the works of man, away from the "prostitution of civilization." As Bernard DeVoto once said: "It is imperative to maintain portions of the wilderness untouched, so that a tree will rot where it falls, a waterfall will pour its curves without generating electricty, a trumpeter swan may float on uncontaminated water—and moderns may at least see what their ancestors knew in their nerves and blood."[18]

But wilderness areas have more than recreational values; they offer important opportunities for scientific study. Here in the wilderness nature is in fair natural balance, with little of man's disrupting influence; here scientists can study fauna and flora in as near their natural setting as can be found.

16 *Living Wilderness*, Winter-Spring 1956-57, 1 ff; Summer-Fall 1957, 29, 30.
17 *Harper's Magazine*, Apr. 1930.
18 *Fortune*, June 1944, 120.

There are cogent objections, however, to the withdrawal of too much national forest land in wilderness areas. In the first place, as some foresters point out, a wilderness area, without roads, is difficult to protect from fire, and with dead and fallen trees scattered about it may be an excellent place for fires to start and spread. On the other hand, it will normally have fewer man-made fires than a developed area where there are many smokers and campers, and some proposals would admit a minimum of fire roads and trails. A wilderness area is also somewhat difficult to protect against insect pests and diseases.[19]

Wilderness enthusiasts often stress the "effort" of walking and climbing as essential in wilderness recreation. Let the masses ride effortlessly past the scenery, but the true lover of nature will shoulder his pack and hike into the wilderness, like the heroes of old. Truly such recreation builds men and women of physical stamina, if it doesn't give them coronary thrombosis, and for some people there is solid satisfaction in "roughing it." In discussions of the virtues of wilderness exploration various words and phrases appear often: "freedom of action," "self-reliance," "individualism," "health," "hardihood," "unique social experience," "ego satisfaction," even "patriotism." Yet it would be easy to exaggerate the numbers who enjoy the wilderness values. A few years ago, about 5 per cent of the western park visitors used the trail systems, and in the mountain and canyon parks 0.4 of one per cent made trips of more than one day's duration.

There is a faint scent of snobbery in the attitude of some wilderness men. They would like to restrict wide areas to a small "elite," people who have the cultural depth, the physical strength and hardihood, the time—not everyone has time for leisurely hiking— and the money for expeditions into the wilderness, which may be fairly expensive. Howard Flint has said something like this: "Perhaps if one closely analyzes the arguments of the true 'wilderness' advocate, it will become apparent that it is not roads but people he objects to. Perhaps he wants 'wilderness' to himself and the elect few, and objects to roads because they inevitably bring other people. He seems to say, 'There should be wilderness areas preserved for the use of the great American public,' and in the same breath, 'there

19 For an excellent discussion of these points, see an article by H. H. Chapman in *American Forests*, Feb. 1958, 18.

can't be wilderness areas if more than a few of the people enjoy them.' "[20] This has a grain of truth in it.

The reservation of most wilderness areas could never be justified in terms of *present* demand and supply analysis. The wilderness lovers, the hikers and horseback riders, bidding against tourist, commercial, and other users, would seldom or never pay enough to get these areas. To justify their preservation as wilderness we would have to assume that the wilderness use is a higher use, or that *in the long run* the wilderness use will yield more utility than other uses. The first assumption is probably valid, and the second assumption is valid in comparing wilderness use with commercial use. Wilderness use, the enjoyment of the glories of nature, is a higher use than the enjoyment of the sort of material goods that might be produced through the use of these lands for other purposes: beef and mutton, lumber, aluminum, and other metals. Most material goods are in adequate or excessive supply in America, and a few more pounds of beef, electric toasters, or of the gadgets with which Americans litter up their lives, could add little to the richness of life. We do not need more of these but, living in crowded cities, we do need wilderness.

If all future users of the wilderness areas could be brought into the market, they might well bid these areas away from other uses. In wilderness use they should last for centuries, they are not used up, exploited, destroyed in use, and should yield more total utility than in the commercial uses that would destroy them. It is somewhat like the market situation for such great works of art as, let us say, Schubert's songs. In the market of the time they sold for so little that they afforded Schubert only a miserable existence. If all the demanders of future generations could have been brought into the market, they would have made Schubert a millionaire.[21]

This same market analysis applies to the national parks. Present users would not cheerfully pay admission fees high enough to cover costs of administration, but most of the parks are not wearing out, and all future users would represent a very strong demand for the utilities that the parks afford.

[20] *American Forests and Forest Life*, July 1906, 410.
[21] See a scholarly article by L. Gregory Hines on "Wilderness Areas: An Extra-Market Problem in Resource Allocation," in *Land Economics*, Nov. 1951, 306.

There is fundamental validity in the wilderness idea. We have never reserved enough wilderness area, we have too little now. We have always disposed of our federal domain and exploited all our resources much too fast—forests, grass range, minerals, and the agricultural soil itself. For 300 years Americans have pushed westward too fast, seeking land titles rather than productive employment, wasting land, forests, minerals, and all economic resources, and desecrating scenic and archeological areas in their mad migrations. Land was appropriated and exploited not because there was a general need for the products but because individual men thought they could make private profits in exploiting it. If our country had exploited its resources with less haste and waste, our economic situation would be sounder, and we should be wealthier as well as saner.

This means that we have never had enough wilderness areas, have never had enough land shut off from commercial exploitation. Most of our national parks should have been much larger, with far more in wilderness or primitive areas. If we had reserved much more land, the products of the land—lumber, livestock and minerals—would have been somewhat less plentiful, not so cheap, and therefore would have been better conserved. Incidentally, there would have been fewer bankrupt lumbermen, stockmen, farmers, and mining companies. When the time comes in which we really need more of these products we could open up some of our reserved wilderness areas far more wisely than we did in the land-looting days of the '70's, '80's and '90's when much of the land was bought or stolen.

Even if we had twice as much land in park and wilderness areas there would be no need for releasing any of it to commercial exploitation now, for the park and recreational needs of the people have grown far more rapidly than the need for the products of the land. *There's no hurry* about the development of such lands. There is a wealth of fine timber in Olympic, and Washington lumbermen are moved to grief at the "waste." As a representative of lumber interests recently expressed it: "Locking up these trees in a park is like taking Miss America, with a luscious big bust and a solid flank, and making her a nun. It is a goddam waste of talent." There is some good timber in Great Smoky and Isle Royale and some other parks; there are probably some valuable minerals—uranium, for instance—in the parks and monuments. But such timber and minerals will be more needed, more valuable in fifty years than they are now, and the timber is more valuable now to look at in a park than it would be in lumber. If California could have reserved from cutting all coast redwood trees above five feet in diameter, the state would be wealthier as well as more beautiful than it is. Cut today, some of those trees would be worth ten times the price they sold for years ago; but they never should be cut. *There's no hurry* about the "development" of such resources. "God Bless America," and let's save some of it.

As far as the parks and monuments are concerned there is no reason why we should not have both developed and wilderness areas, somewhat as we have them. In our national parks, even the most crowded, there are enough wilderness or primitive areas and enough trails to wear the feet off the most ardent wilderness hiker. In an hour's walk from the most congested area of Yellowstone, one can lose himself in wild forest where there is little scent of man. The lover of nature who does not like to drive his car over the glorious Going-to-the-Sun Highway in Glacier can walk or ride horseback across the divide—horseback if he can get a horse. He has about every freedom that he had before the road was built. Horseback riding in the park has, however, dwindled to a point where few horses are available—where there were once some 1,600. In Olympic, if a road were built across the park through Hurricane Ridge millions of people would be able to see some of the magnificent scenery in the park, and yet there would be vast areas of wilderness for those who enjoy it. If the "nature man" does not like the crowds in the parks he can hike into the wilderness almost anywhere, or he can find millions of acres of forest wilderness in the national forests, perhaps somewhat desecrated by lumbering and mining, but free of the crowds that infest the roads in the parks. He may even be able to drive on national forest roads, poor roads, and find beautiful wild areas where there are camping places and practically no people. In the Cascades of the Northwest there are wide areas of magnificent mountains and lovely meadows where there are almost no evidences of man and his works. Or, if the adventurer wants to go farther from civilization he will find wild spaces in Canada or Alaska.

As a matter of fact he will not have to go very far. The writer has driven on a poor forest road along the Mogollon Rim from

Camp Verde, in Central Arizona, to Show Low, a day's drive through lovely forests with distant views about as fine as can be found anywhere, meeting *no* tourists, and only two or three logging trucks from a small area where lumbering was being carried on. There was a fine campground which he might have had entirely to himself. There is a road from Bryce Canyon through Escalante to Torrey, Utah, a rough road, part of the way through a national forest, with magnificent scenery much of the way. The writer traveled this road a few years ago, taking a full day for the distance of 100 miles, and met two cars on the way. Here was real wilderness, but if the road should be paved the crowds would soon come in. In the western states there are hundreds of miles of roads through splendid scenery, for those who object to the crowds in the national parks and are willing to drive rough roads.

As a general rule, we cannot condone the making of recreation resorts of any national parks, the operation of tennis courts, swimming pools, moving picture theaters, dance halls, or amusement parlors; but in a few places these may have a place, for the use of park employees who, unlike the tourists, have to live in the area and need some such recreation. With this exception, such activities have no place in the national parks. To the young lady who on landing at a properly conducted national park complained, "What's a person supposed to do at this dump? Sit and look at the scenery?" The appropriate answer was, "You are quite correct, Madam, eminently correct; but you can stand if you see better that way."

CHAPTER XXXI

National Parks in Other Countries

The American national park idea, conceived in 1872, spread over much of the rest of the world in the next fifty or seventy-five years, but only in two countries, Canada and New Zealand, have developments been on anything like the American scale. Significantly these two countries, like the United States, were sparsely populated and wealthy enough to afford the luxury of large national parks, reasonably well administered and protected. In most European and Asiatic countries, and most of those south of the Rio Grande, the needs of dense populations have prevented the withdrawal of large areas of land, and sometimes national poverty has made efficient administration impossible.

Discussion of foreign national parks is difficult for several reasons. First, many of the so-called "national parks" were and are not national parks at all, but small areas, perhaps quite like municipal or local parks, without great scenic value, often largely or entirely unprotected, sometimes open to grazing, hunting, mining, lumbering, or even farming. In the second place there were changes in the numbers and areas of the parks abroad, just as in the United States, and in the kind of administration and protection afforded. In spite of these difficulties it seems worth while to consider national parks in foreign countries briefly.

CANADA   Canada was probably the first country to follow our lead, in a beginning which was somewhat parallel to the establishment of Yellowstone. When the Canadian Pacific Railroad was being pushed through the Canadian Rockies workmen discovered hot mineral springs in what is now Banff National Park. These men filed claims on the area and later assigned their claims to a third party, but in November 1885 the government reserved the springs from sale or settlement, and later bought the claims for $1,000. Two years later, in 1887, the government established this area as the first national park in Canada, Rocky Mountain—later changed to Banff—containing 260 square miles, later enlarged to 2,564 square miles. In 1886 a part of what is now Yoho Park was reserved, later to be established as a national park, and soon afterward a small area was reserved which later became Glacier Park. In 1895 Waterton Lakes was reserved as a "forest park."

The earlier parks were set aside as "parks" or "reserves" by Order in Council under authority of the Dominion Lands Act; but in 1911 the Dominion Forest Reserves and Parks Act was passed authorizing the establishment of a Park Service similar to that established by the United States Act of 1916, and authorizing the proclamation as national parks of the areas already reserved. Soon afterward Glacier, Yoho, Jasper, and Waterton Lakes were proclaimed as national parks. Others followed: St. Lawrence Islands, several wildlife parks, including the Wood Buffalo Park, to preserve the wood buffalo, Mount Revelstoke, Kootenay, Prince Albert, Riding Mountain, and Georgian Bay Islands national parks. In 1930 a National Parks Act was passed by the Parliament, and since that time all new national parks have been established by special acts of Parliament. The Governor in Council may set aside national historic parks. Like the United States, Canada has some parks of little distinction, probably more than we have.[1]

The early acts provided for regulations, and the first regulations were issued in 1889 and amended in 1890 and later. They were not

[1] Like our southern parks, some of the Canadian parks were "established" by more than one step, and the dates reported for some of them differ somewhat. Circulars issued by the National Parks Branch of the Department of Northern Affairs and National Resources give the following dates for most of the Canadian parks: Banff 1885, Glacier 1886, Waterton Lakes 1895, Elk Island 1906, Jasper 1907, Revelstoke 1914, St. Lawrence Islands 1914, Point Pelée 1918, Kootenay 1920, Prince Albert 1927, Riding Mountain 1929, Prince Edward Island 1937.

as strict as those governing most parks in the United States, allowed leases for residential sites, for use of mineral waters, and for town lots in towns built in the parks, but the latter were somewhat like our concessioner leases. There was apparently some lumbering, irrigation, and power development, and railroads ran through a few parks. Even more than the United States, Canada was rather slow in achieving the protection of her parks and wildlife, but her task was very much greater, for with a total area greater than that of the United States, and a larger area in her twenty-eight national parks, Canada has less than one-tenth of our population. The financial burden of developing and protecting her great park areas is more than ten times as great per capita. The cost of road construction through some of the mountain wilderness areas was always heavy and roads have been generally poor.

Canadian parks are still administered less strictly than most of ours, in fact some of them are administered rather like our recreation areas, with much more attention to recreation than our Park Service allows in national parks. In some Canadian parks there are swimming pools, using hot springs or even heated, ski lifts, ski tows, chair lifts and snowmobiles, golf courses, tennis courts, and facilities for baseball, softball, motion pictures, games, dances and theatricals, bowling greens, playgrounds for children, with chutes and swings. Power boats are allowed in several, and there have been animal shows since fairly early. An animal show was reported in Rocky Mountain (later Banff) in 1906, with mountain sheep, goats, antelope, mountain lions, bear, wolves, and foxes on display.

The story of the buffalo in Canadian parks runs closely parallel to that of the Yellowstone buffalo. About 1900 there was scarcely a wild buffalo on the Canadian plains, where once there had been perhaps millions. In 1906 arrangements were made for the purchase of a herd from two Montana ranchers, and between 1907 and 1912, 716 head were brought north. The first shipments were sent to Elk Island Park, but later shipments went direct to the newly established Buffalo National Park at Wainwright, Alberta. Elk Island Park is pretty much a wildlife park, with more than a thousand buffalo. In financing Canada's parks, our northern neighbor follows a policy quite different from ours. We assess a moderate entrance fee and make no charge for camping. (Years ago appropriations were made with a stipulation that no funds should go to any park where there was a charge for camping.) The Canadians levy a nominal license fee of $2.00 for entrance to *all* parks, not to *each* park, $3.00 with trailer, 25 or 50 cents for single trip; but they have a charge of 50 cents a day or $2.00 a week per car for camping, 75 cents a day or $3.00 a week for trailers. The camp grounds are reasonably well equipped and cared for. There are also cabins, chalets, bungalows, motels, and hotels of various grades in most of the parks, but in Glacier and in three of the eastern parks there are no hotels or cabins.

In the establishment of new parks Canada follows the procedure employed in setting up our eastern parks, in requiring the provinces to present approved areas to the Dominion government. The provinces have also their own provisional parks—British Columbia has more than fifty of them—some very magnificent, and one, Tweedsmuir, larger than any of our national parks. Ontario has 103 such parks, most of them established in recent years. The fees for entry are nominal—$1.00 per vehicle for entry to all these parks, and $4.00 a week for camp sites. The Department of Lands and Forests even sells sites.[2]

Canada has a very extensive system of wildlife preserves, to protect various animals: wood buffalo, musk ox, barren-ground caribou, white and colored foxes, polar bear, beaver—three reserves for beaver only. A vast number of migratory birds spend the summer in Canada, and there are about eighty sanctuaries for them, established under the Migratory Birds Convention Act of 1917. Wildlife has presented somewhat the same problems as in the United States. Poaching, particularly by the Indians, was common in the early years, with large areas to protect and boundaries not well marked; and miners and lumbermen trapped and killed animals. In later years a problem of over-population appeared.

Like the United States, Canada has a number of historic parks, many of them old historic forts, but in this movement Canada did not follow us, for her first historical park was established in 1917— eighteen years before the passage of our Historic Sites Act. The Canadian National Parks Act authorizes the Governor in Council to set aside such parks somewhat as our Antiquities Act authorizes the President to set aside areas of archeological or historic significance as national monuments.

Canada now has a magnificent system of twenty-eight national parks, with an area of more than 18 million acres—compared with

[2] *American Forests*, June 1959, 24.

13 million acres in our own *parks,* and a total of 23 million acres in all our park areas. The most scenic of the Canadian parks are in the West, in Alberta and British Columbia, but there are others in Saskatchewan and Manitoba and several in the eastern provinces. More and more visitors from the United States and other countries go to see these parks, and some will concede that the mountain scenery of western Canada is more beautiful than that of our mountain parks, there being more snow and glaciers, as in Switzerland. On the other hand, some of the eastern parks are not impressive. In a few parks, particularly Banff, as in our parks, railroads have built excellent concession facilities.[3]

NEW ZEALAND AND AUSTRALIA   In New Zealand, a country with magnificent scenery, the initial interest in national parks appears to have arisen from the establishment of Yellowstone in 1872. About this time leaders in this radical, semi-socialist island, in drawing plans for the development of mountainous areas, set aside large areas for forest, watershed, and scenery preservation, some of which were later established as national parks. The first national park was established in 1894—Tongariro National Park, covering 161,000 acres. Four others were established in the years following; and in 1953 the National Parks Act was passed, setting up a National Parks Authority and other administrative machinery and outlining the principles that should govern park administration. Three more splendid parks were set up, including one wilderness area, rounding out a system of eight fine parks covering 3.8 million acres—nearly 6 per cent of the area of the country. Among the national parks are the Arthur's Pass, Mount Egmont, and Fiordland. The principles of administration are much like those of our own park system, but the Authority has been handicapped by lack of funds.[4]

If sparseness of population, or plenty of land, is the main requirement for the establishment of national parks, Australia should have a splendid system; but there seem not to be enough mag-

3 See Devereux Butcher, *Exploring the National Parks of Canada* (Thomas Allen Ltd. in Canada, and National Parks Association, in United States, 1951); and W. F. Lothian, *A Brief History of National Parks Administration in Canada,* issued by the Canadian National Parks Service.

4 *Living Wilderness,* Summer 1956, 21.

nificent scenic areas to make much of a park system. Yet a park was reported to have been established in New South Wales in 1920, and there is a park, Kuringai National Park, a few miles from Sydney—a lovely park, but hardly magnificent. There are several "nature reserves" for the protection of wildlife. Perhaps no other country has suffered so much from the introduction of exotics— the European fox, the domestic cat, rabbit, rat, mouse, and wild dog (Dingo); and eleven of the native marsupial species were reported exterminated about ten years ago, with others hanging on precariously. The country is awakening to the seriousness of her wildlife situation.

EUROPEAN COUNTRIES   Some of the European countries evinced an interest in national parks fairly early, but real national parks of the American sort have seldom been established because with their dense populations most of these countries could ill spare large areas for park purposes—with forests, water resources, minerals and the soil itself completely withdrawn from commercial use— and because in some European countries forest administration had been developed to a point where forests provided many of the values afforded by our national parks. In the United States we had five national parks before any forest reserves were established.[5] Another reason for the lack of real national parks in some countries is that, as in Denmark for instance, they may have no really spectacular scenery worthy of that name. Perhaps, on the other hand, such countries as Switzerland and Norway have so much splendid scenery that it would scarcely be worthwhile to mark out a part of it for national parks; yet Switzerland has one national park, well managed but subject to frequent attacks by commercial interests that would like to develop the power in it.

In 1920 Secretary Payne reported that when the King of Belgium had visited Yosemite and Grand Canyon he said that he would establish a national park, the Herzogenwald or Duke's Forest near Malmedij, on the Belgian-German frontier. Payne reported further that Spain, which in 1917 was studying our park system, had been considering the establishment of national parks, and had passed a law providing for it; that Italy was preparing to set up a wild game reserve; that France already had a number of excellent national

[5] *American Forests and Forest Life*, July 1927, 100, 101.

parks; that Switzerland had one, and Sweden ten. The Swiss national park had been set up in the Engadine Alps in 1910, but part of the land that should have been included was in Italy, and the Swiss government petitioned the Italian government to cede the right to extend the park over into Italy. This was refused, but the Italian government was interested in parks, and after much talk and study established the Abruzzi National Park in 1922 and the Grand Paradiso National Park—really a wildlife reserve to protect the fast-disappearing bighorn sheep—on land belonging to the King. These were not really national parks, as we use that term. The same may be said of the parks of the Netherlands, which are very small, and those of England.

There was some agitation for national parks in Greece as early as 1913, but the national parks law was not passed until 1937. Mount Olympus and Mount Parnassus national parks were established the next year, of only 10,000 acres each. During the Second World War and the revolutionary period following there was no protection and the forests and wildlife suffered greatly. The mountain goats were nearly exterminated for food.

A few years ago Italy reported two national parks—Grand Paradiso and Stelvio—but they were not protected well; Sweden had fifteen, established between 1909 and 1942, small but well protected like our own. Poland reported eight, also small, not really our conception of national parks. In 1938 Finland set aside ten really scenic "natural and national parks," but after the war with Russia ceded all but two natural parks and two national parks to Russia; Denmark reported a few Jutland heath areas and a few large game reserves; The Netherlands has two small areas called national parks. Russia has many small parks called "national"; Iceland calls an old meeting place of parliament a national park.

Interest in national parks in Great Britain dates from the late twenties when Lord Bledisloe began to campaign for them after seeing the parks of Canada and the United States, pushing particularly the Forest of Dean for park status. The idea did not catch on with the public, but in 1931 the government suggested an appropriation of £500,000 for a system of parks, which was not granted because of financial stringency. After the Second World War there was much interest in the preservation of old castles and particularly beautiful scenery, and in 1949 the National Parks and Access to the Countryside Act was passed to conserve as an inviolate national resource the areas of wild and beautiful countryside. A National Parks Commission was created and later ten national parks were set up.

The National Parks Act also established the Nature Conservancy, to set up "nature reserves" for the protection of wildlife and plant life, and provided measures to safeguard public access to beaches, mountains, moors, cliffs, and heath. England also has "national forest parks." There are now in England and Scotland about eighty-seven nature reserves, managed in various ways, often somewhat like our wildlife sanctuaries. The British national parks are not like ours, owned and managed by the government, but are primarily areas where new development is controlled. Farming may be permitted, quarrying and some mining, but buildings built must be appropriate to the surroundings.[6]

SOUTH AND CENTRAL AMERICAN COUNTRIES   In the South and Central American countries south of us there has been much interest in parks, and some of them have established what they call national parks and monuments, but most of these do not correspond to our definition of the name. A report published in 1940 credited Mexico with thirty-one national parks and a number of national forests and national monuments covering archeological sites. In 1946 forty-six national parks were reported, but they were not administered as national parks; wildlife was scarce, hunting, although illegal, was carried on, forests were cut and the land was being badly eroded.[7]

Influenced by our national park policy, Argentina has established several national parks of scenic importance. Iguassú National Park covers a magnificent waterfall, perhaps the greatest in the world, part of which is in Brazil, and is set aside as a reservation there; Nahuel Hualpi, in western Patagonia, much of it donated by a scientist, Dr. Moreno, was set aside in 1952. Brazil has set aside several reservations, said to approach national park beauty. Chile has two historic and scientific parks, Ecuador has set aside the Galapagos Islands as a wildlife reservation, Peru and Colombia have archeological reservations in the high Andes, Venezuela has

6 *Nineteenth Century*, June 1931, 712. *National Parks Magazine*, Oct. 1959, 5. *Living Wilderness*, Winter 1959-60, 22.
7 *National Parks Magazine*, No. 84, Apr.-June 1946.

a scenic park or so. In Central America, only Nicaragua has done much about parks. In 1941 President Somoza signed a law providing that all archeological, historic, or artistic areas not in private hands should belong to the state as national monuments. Central and South American countries should do much more to protect monuments of Aztec and Mayan civilizations. Dictator Trujillo of the Dominican Republic has done something in nature preservation.

ASIATIC COUNTRIES   Japan has shown spurts of interest in national parks since soon after Yellowstone was set up, when several Japanese tourists visited Yellowstone and went home fired with an ambition to set up similar parks at home; but not until 1921 was anything done. In 1930 a National Parks Investigating Committee was set up, and between 1934 and 1936 twelve national parks were designated as acceptable; but the government was not much interested in the project and granted little money for it. In 1948 Charles H. Richey, Assistant Chief of Land and Recreational Planning, spent three months in Japan studying the national park system and the laws governing it and making recommendations regarding the parks already established and proposed additions. In 1951 the Director of National Parks in Japan spent part of the summer studying the American parks.[8] Today there are nineteen Japanese national parks, covering more than 4 million acres, including a number of historic temples, shrines, and mountains. There are also fourteen "quasi-national" parks located near centers of population, somewhat like our city parks. Annual visitor attendance of 40 millions indicates the heavy pressure on recreational areas, just as in this country. With land as scarce as it is in Japan, the parks cannot be strictly protected from commercial use, farming is permitted, but it must be done properly. The parks are not well protected and cared for anyhow. There are many poor roads and poor accommodations, and litterbugs have rather free range.[9]

Among other Asiatic countries the Philippines has shown some interest in the establishment of national parks. In 1940 President

8 *National Parks Magazine*, No. 97, Apr.-June 1949.
9 Kokuritsu Kōen Kyōkai (National Parks Association of Japan), *National Parks of Japan* (Tokyo: Tokyo News Service, 1957).

Quezon requested that the Park Service send a man over there to study park possibilities; and the Service sent Louis Craft over. China has made a park of the "Dawn sequoia" in the Valley of the Tiger, discovered in 1944. India, with her magnificent scenery, has a system of national parks, but some of them are zoological or botanical.

AFRICA   In Africa there are several great national parks or wildlife refuges, sometimes said to be the first parks in the world to be established for purely scientific purposes, the best of them set up as the result of American influence. The idea of establishing national parks in the Belgian Congo was said to have come to King Albert on a trip through some of the parks in the United States in 1919. In 1921 and 1922 Carl Akeley went to the gorilla country in the Belgian Congo for the American Museum of Natural History and killed five gorillas for the museum. He noticed that the gorillas on the forested slopes of three extinct volcanoes, where they had once been common, had been almost exterminated by hunters and, assisted by John C. Merriam, he persuaded the Belgian King to set aside a preserve, the Albert National Park, in 1925, especially for the preservation of the gorilla. Later additions to the park brought the area up to 500,000 acres, included lower lands, and covered other wildlife; and a zone was established around the park where only the natives, using primitive weapons, were permitted to hunt. The park itself is supposed to be strictly protected, with no hunting allowed or cutting of trees. Part of the park area has been protected from human intrusion. Only scientists are allowed in the park, and even they are barred from about one-fourth of it. Thus it is a wilderness park of the purest type, or perhaps it should be called a wildlife sanctuary.[10] There is also an Addo Elephant National Park, and several others in various parts of Africa for the protection of various animals.

Krueger National Park, in the Eastern Transvaal, another wildlife preserve, planned as early as 1898 by Paul Krueger, was finally set up in 1926, largely as a result of the efforts of Lieutenant Colonel Stevenson Hamilton of London who, like many other Europeans interested in Africa, feared the extermination of some of the South African wildlife. The park is sometimes referred to as the largest natural zoo in the world, and it is open to visitors.

10 *Science*, n. s., July 17, 1931; Dec. 11, 1931.

In 1957 the New York Zoological Society and The Conservation Foundation sent a biogeographer, George Treichel, to Africa to study reported excessive destruction of wildlife, and Treichel mentions several other national parks and wildlife reserves in Africa. Umfalozi White Rhino Reserve in Natal; Serengeti National Park in Northwest Tanganyika; Tsavo, or Royal Tsavo, National Park in Kenya; Etosha Pan Game Reserve in Southwest Africa, near the Angola border; and Garamba National Park in Belgian Congo. Whether called "national parks" or game reserves, these areas are apparently set up largely for wildlife protection.[11]

In the administration of the park many problems are similar to those of our Park Service. The farmers and cattlemen around the park accuse the park authorities of harboring predators—lions, leopards, cheetahs, hyenas, and wild dogs—which get out of the park and kill livestock; the elephants trample and pull up growing crops; diseases sometimes spread from the wildlife to the domestic life. The farmers objected to the withdrawing of lands; and the park animals sometimes suffer from scarcity of forage. There was always difficulty in getting enough funds for protection.[12] The worst problem in park administration, according to Treichel, is the vast, "inconceivable" amount of poaching, largely by natives. He estimated that not less than 3,000 elephants were slaughtered with poisoned arrows in and around Tsavo National Park, and not less than 150,000 large wild animals were killed every year in and around Serengeti National Park. Treichel feared that some animals were in danger of extinction.[13]

A recent article in *Holiday*, for tourist guidance, mentions still other national parks and game reserves: Nairobi National Parks, for animals; Amboseli National Reserve; Mount Kenya National Park; Murchison Falls National Park, for animals; Queen Elizabeth National Park, for animals; Maputo Elephant Reserve; and Hluhluwe Game Reserve, for white and black rhinoceros.[14]

A real park, the Drakensberg National Park was established in the Drakensberg Mountains, Union of South Africa, where there is fishing, and harmless wild animals roam freely somewhat as in

11 *The Atlantic,* Apr. 1959, 85 ff.
12 See an article by Newton Drury in *National Parks Magazine,* No. 93, Apr.-June 1948.
13 *The Atlantic,* Apr. 1959, 85 ff. See also *National Geographic,* Sept. 1960.
14 *Holiday,* Apr. 1959, 143 ff.

our national parks. Some of the African territories have maintained a keen interest in their national parks. In 1951, at the request of the National Parks Board of Trustees of South Africa, Victor Cahalane, Chief Biologist of the Park Service, spent four months in the study of some of the African parks. He was also invited to visit the parks of the Belgian Congo, and at the invitation of the Portuguese government spent ten days in Mozambique, advising officials on park possibilities and nature protection.[15]

MONUMENTS AND "ETHNOLOGICAL" PARKS   National monuments do not usually take as much land as national parks, and foreign countries have set aside a great many to preserve archeological and historic sites, or even scenic sites. In fact, many of the so-called "national parks" abroad are what we would call national monuments.

Years ago an odd sort of "national park" or "life preserve" was suggested by Paul S. Taylor for American Samoa, an *ethnological* national park to preserve for mankind the human society which the natives had built up there.[16] Albright turned the proposal down because the society was no longer primitive enough. Samoa had been "invaded" by the United States Navy, by missionaries; the natives had begun to wear clothes, live in wood houses, and there had been some intermarriage with whites.

15 *Report, Secretary of the Interior, 1951,* 337.
16 *Survey,* Nov. 1, 1930, 159.

Index

Abbe, Dr. Robert, gift to Acadia Park, 240

Acadia National Park, 238 ff; Mount Desert Island 238; Isle des Monts Deserts, 239; Cadillac Mountain, 239; Little Cranberry Island, 239; Schoodic Point, 239; summer homes, 239; no commercial interests, 240; museum, 240; appropriations, 240; no hotels or cabins, 240; additions to, 336; destructive fire, 445

Acker, W. B., wages creation of Park Service, 188

Ackia Battleground National Monument, 410

Adams, Senator, of Colorado, 207, 365, 434, 440

Adirondacks Forest Reserve, 480

Administration, Act to Facilitate, 345, 346

Admiralty Island, considered as wilderness park, 526

Advisory Board, recommendations for reservation, 520; for elimination of park areas, 522, 523; on salvaging lumber in parks, 555

Airplanes in the parks, 428, 429, 486, 487

Alaska, Battle of, 158; game laws, 227; highway, 449; Indians, 158; Dall sheep in, 226, 453; railroad, 226, 230; resources, threat to, 315; attempt to abolish reservations, 476

Albertson, A. W., survey of Grassland National Monument, 526

Albright, Horace: on Yellowstone guides, 29; and South Calaveras sequoia grove, 115, 531; on difference between parks and monuments, 155; enters park work, 187, 188; Assistant

Director, 193; organizes Park Service, 196, 197; and Zion Park, 242, 245, 246, 247; as director of Park Service, 259; and Jackson Hole, 272, 491 ff; 272, 273, 274, 285, 295; and Yellowstone boundary revision, 276, 289; and coast redwoods, 295; fighting Yellowstone dams, 307, 310, 311, 313, 314; additions to parks, 330; study of Everglades, 336, 373; interest in historical parks, 344; 345, 347, 352; on reorganization of government services, 352; retires, 352, 354; 363, 370, 373; criticized by purists, 438; on concession policy, 461; orders wildlife survey, 596

Alpine Lake Limited Area, 526

American Bison Society, 738

American Civic Association, 88, 185, 294, 311

American Forestry Association, 88, 251, 650, 651

American Game Protective Association, 311

American Museum of Natural History, 161

American Ornithological Union, 592

American Scenic and Historical Society, 88

Anderson, George S., Acting Superintendent of Yellowstone Park, 25

Andrew Johnson National Monument authorized, 410

Antelope, 279, 320

Anthony, Senator, of Rhode Island, 21

Antietam Battlefield Site, 161

Antiquities Act, 143-162, 152, 153, 154, 499 ff

Apostle Islands national park authorized, 343

671

674

Park," 328, 339, 340; and Badlands National Monument, 411

Nordenskiold, Baron, and Pueblo Bonito, 164

Norman, Representative, of Washington, 392

Norris, P. W., Superintendent of Yellowstone Park, 21-29

Norris, Senator, of Nebraska, and Tennessee Valley Authority, 362

North Calaveras Grove of sequoias, 97, 98, 531

Northern Pacific Railroad in Mount Rainier Park, 121, 122, 483; and Lewis and Clark Caverns, 159; in Yellowstone Park, 39, 43, 197

Nugent, Senator, of Idaho, 272, 307, 308, 309, 311

Nusbaum, Dr. Jesse, authority on archeological ruins, and Superintendent of Mesa Verde Park, 144-46, 154, 166-68, 170, 481

Nye, Chauncey, 129

Nye, Senator, of South Dakota, on Yellowstone Park boundary revision, 278, 328; bill to transfer national monuments to Park Service, 352; on Yosemite sugar pines, 406

Oastler, Frank R., educational work of Park Service, 199

Ocean Strip, Olympic Park, 390, 393, 489

Ocmulgee National Monument, 408

O'Connor, Representative, of Montana, hostile to parks, 401, 433, 440, 500

Office of Indian Affairs, interest in archeological ruins, 147

Office of National Parks, Buildings and Reservations, 353

Oglethorpe National Trail and Parkway proposed, 420

Oil discovery near Everglades Park, 508

Oil reservations in Everglades, 508

Old Dominion Foundation, gift to Cape Hatteras National Seashore Recreation Area, 519

Old Faithful Camp Company, 210

Old Kasaan National Monument, 289, 523

Olmstead, Frederick Law, landscape architect, 52, 54, 88, 188, 295, 298, 468

Olympic National Park: 382; bills to create, 383; Mount Olympus National Monument proclaimed by Theodore Roosevelt, 383, 384; Roosevelt elk, 383; hunting, 384; Emergency Conservation Committee, 384; Rosalie Edge and Irving Brant work for a park, 384, 385; minerals sought, 384; tourist business vs. lumber business, 386, 387; Forest Service opposition, 387 ff; Franklin D. Roosevelt promotes, 388; establishing act, 389; Lake Quinault, 390; acquiring Queets Corridor and Ocean Strip, 390, 489; state taxation in, 390, 391; tourist facilities, 391; mining threats, 391; war and threats of exploitation, 391 ff; Secretary Krug fights the spoilers, 392; President Truman proclaims addition, 393, 518; exchanging wind-blown timber for private lands, 394, 554, 555; arguments for and against the park, 394; a wilderness park, 395; Hurricane Ridge, developments at, 395; road into, 395; mining in World War II, 451; lumbermen reach for forests, 474, 561

O'Mahoney, Senator, of Wyoming, 499; O'Mahoney and Carey, bill to add Jackson Hole to Grand Teton Park, 495, 497, 505n, 506, 507, 508

O'Malley, Representative, of Wisconsin, 406

Oregon Caves National Monument, 158

Oregon, Columbia River scenic road, 421

Oregon Dunes coast, reservation proposal, 520

Organ Pipe Cactus National Monument, 408, 409, 436; opened to mining, 474

Ouachita national park proposal, 298, 343

Outboard motors in the parks, 487

Outdoor Recreation Resources Review Commission, 546

Outland, Representative, of California, defense of Jackson Hole National Monument, 501

Overman, Representative, of Texas, 219

Owens, Ruth Bryan, Representative, of Florida, 373

Date Due

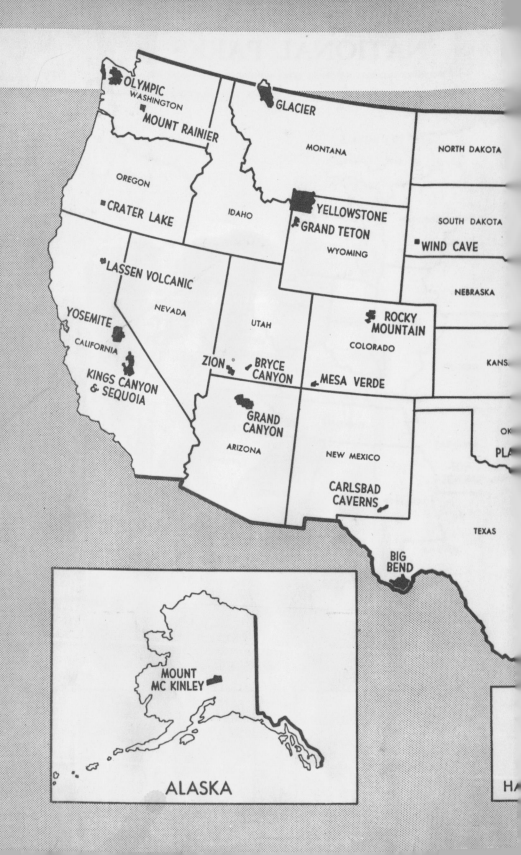